John W. Hogg

**Compilation of Laws Relating to the Navy, Marine Corps, Etc.**

From the Revised Statutes and Subsequent Acts to March 3, 1883

John W. Hogg

**Compilation of Laws Relating to the Navy, Marine Corps, Etc.**
*From the Revised Statutes and Subsequent Acts to March 3, 1883*

ISBN/EAN: 9783743393349

Manufactured in Europe, USA, Canada, Australia, Japa

Cover: Foto ©Suzi / pixelio.de

Manufactured and distributed by brebook publishing software (www.brebook.com)

John W. Hogg

**Compilation of Laws Relating to the Navy, Marine Corps, Etc.**

# COMPILATION OF LAWS

RELATING TO

# THE NAVY, MARINE CORPS, ETC.,

FROM THE

# REVISED STATUTES

AND

# SUBSEQUENT ACTS

TO

MARCH 3, 1883.

PREPARED BY

JOHN W. HOGG,

AND

PUBLISHED BY AUTHORITY OF THE NAVY DEPARTMENT.

WASHINGTON:
GOVERNMENT PRINTING OFFICE.
1883.

# PREFACE.

This compilation, it is hoped, will prove to the Navy a convenient hand-book; and the fact that it was prepared under many difficulties and during unofficial hours, may excuse any omissions.

The arrangement of the work is not so complete as it would be by further dissection of the subject-matter, with more numerous headings; but by its division into parts and an alphabetical grouping of subjects, with a full index at the end, it is believed little difficulty will be experienced, especially after some familiarity with its arrangement, in finding any portion of its contents sought.

Many of the sections are repeated in the compilation, with the view of placing matter under appropriate heads. The citation of the acts, from the Statutes at Large, on which the sections are based, which was omitted in the compilation of 1875, and some references to opinions and decisions, have been introduced—the latter not, however, as authority for action or decision on any case, but rather as information.

The words in *italics*, in certain sections, are intended to make such sections conform to existing law; legislation subsequent to the revision of the Statutes rendering it necessary. Headings are in some instances supplied.

Much that was in the compilation of 1875, although possessing value to many seeking information, has been omitted from this, as not essentially necessary for those for whom the work is designed. Portions of Part IV may be seldom referred to, but it was thought advisable to retain such matter, as it may be brought into use occasionally.

JNO. W. HOGG,
*Chief Clerk, Navy Department.*

Digitized by the Internet Archive
in 2007 with funding from
Microsoft Corporation

http://www.archive.org/details/compilationoflaw00unitrich

# GENERAL ARRANGEMENT.

## PART I.

### RELATING TO THE NAVY, PRINCIPALLY.

Articles governing the Navy, and other miscellaneous provisions.
Chaplains.
Civil engineers.
Contracts and supplies.
Deserters and desertion.
Dismissal and resignation of officers.
Engineer Corps.
Hospitals, asylums, artificial limbs, and cemeteries.
Hydrographic Office.
Line officers.
Mates.
Medical Corps.
Nautical Almanac.
Naval Academy—Naval cadets.
Naval constructors.
Naval Observatory.
Naval storekeepers.
Navy-yards.
Pay Corps.
Pay and allowances.
Professors of mathematics.
Promotion and advancement.
Rank and precedence.
Retirement.
Rations.
Secretaries and clerks.
Seamen and petty officers.
Vessels of the Navy.
Volunteer service.
Warrant officers.

## PART II.

### THE MARINE CORPS.

## PART III.

### ACCOUNTS, ACCOUNTING AND DISBURSING OFFICERS, PUBLIC MONEY AND PROPERTY, NAVY DEPARTMENT AND BUREAUS, CIVIL SERVICE, ETC.

Appropriations and estimates.
Accounting officers and accounts.
Advertising.
Attorney-General and Department of Justice.
Civil service—Department employés and regulations.
Claims and claim agents.
Court of Claims.
Contingent funds.
Debts due by and to the United States.
Distress warrants.
Disbursing officers and agents—Checks, drafts, coins, and currency.
Navy Department and Bureaus.
Public documents, public printing and binding.
Public or Department records.
Public property and public buildings.
Statutes.

## PART IV.

### MISCELLANEOUS.

Bribes, presents, and contributions.
Bounty and bounty land.
Coast Survey.
Collisions—Rules of the sea.
Diplomatic and consular officers.
Expatriation.
Extradition.
Fish Commission.
Flags and standards.
Fraud, forgery, and theft.
Guano Islands.
Habeas corpus.
Homesteads.
Importation.
Life-Saving Service.
Lights and buoys.
Merchant vessels and service, and yachts.
Murder, mutiny, &c.
Neutrality.
Patents.
Pensions.
Pension funds.
Perjury.
Piracy.
Pilotage.
Postal laws, &c.
Prize and salvage.
Quarantine and Board of Health.
Railroads and telegraphs.
Reserved timber lands.
Revenue-Cutter Service.
Slave and cooly trade; kidnapping.
Treason, conspiracy, insurrection, and rebellion.

# LAWS.

## PART I.

## ARTICLES FOR THE GOVERNMENT OF THE NAVY.

Sec.
1624. Articles established.

Art.
1. Commander's duties of supervision and correction.
2. Divine service.
3. Irreverent behavior.
4. Offenses punishable by death:
    1. Mutiny.
    2. Disobedience of orders.
    3. Striking superior officer.
    4. Intercourse with an enemy.
    5. Messages from an enemy.
    6. Desertion in time of war.
    7. Deserting trust.
    8. Sleeping on watch.
    9. Leaving station.
    10. Willful stranding or injury of vessel.
    11. Unlawful destruction of public property.
    12. Striking flag or treacherously yielding.
    13. Cowardice in battle.
    14. Deserting duty in battle.
    15. Neglecting orders to prepare for battle.
    16. Neglecting to clear for action.
    17. Neglecting to join on signal for battle.
    18. Failing to encourage the men to fight.
    19. Failing to seek encounter.
    20. Failing to afford relief in battle.
5. Spies.
6. Murder.
7. Imprisonment in penitentiary.
8. Offenses punishable at discretion of court-martial:
    1. Profanity, falsehood, &c.
    2. Cruelty.
    3. Quarreling.
    4. Fomenting quarrels.
    5. Duels.
    6. Contempt of superior officer.
    7. Combinations against superior officer.
    8. Mutinous words.
    9. Neglect of orders.
    10. Not preventing destruction of public property.
    11. Negligent stranding.
    12. Negligence in convoy service.
    13. Receiving articles for freight.
    14. False muster.
    15. Waste of public property, &c.
    16. Plundering on shore.
    17. Refusing to apprehend offenders.
    18. Refusing to receive prisoners.
    19. Absence from duty without leave.
    20. Violating general orders or regulations.
    21. Desertion in time of peace.
    22. Harboring deserters.
9. Officers absent without leave may be reduced.
10. Desertion by resignation.
11. Dealing in supplies on private account.
12. Importing dutiable goods in public vessels.
13. Distilled spirits only as medical stores.
14. Certain crimes of fraud against the United States.

Art.
15. Transmission of prize-lists.
16. Removing property from captured vessels before condemned as prize.
17. Maltreating persons taken on a prize.
18. Returning fugitives from service.
19. Enlisting deserters, minors, &c.
20. Duties of commanding officers:
    1. Men received on board.
    2. List of officers, men, and passengers.
    3. Deaths and desertions.
    4. Property of deceased persons.
    5. Accounts of men received.
    6. Accounts of men sent from the ship.
    7. Inspection of provisions.
    8. Health of the crew.
    9. Attendance at final payment of the crew.
    10. Articles to be hung up and read. Punishment for offending against this article.
21. Authority of officers after loss of vessel.
22. Offenses not specified.
23. Offenses committed on shore.
24. Punishments by order of commander.
25. Punishment by officer temporarily commanding.
26. **Summary courts-martial.**
27. Constitution of summary courts-martial.
28. Oath of members and recorder.
29. Testimony.
30. Punishments by summary courts.
31. Disrating for incompetency.
32. Execution of sentence of summary court.
33. Remission of sentence.
34. Manner of conducting proceedings.
35. Same punishments by general court-martial.
36. Dismissal of officers.
37. Officers dismissed by President may demand trial.
38. **General courts-martial,** by whom convened.
39. Constitution of.
40. Oaths of members and judge-advocate.
41. Oath of witness.
42. Contempts of court.
43. Charges.
44. Duty of officer arrested.
45. Suspension of proceedings.
46. Absence of members.
47. Witnesses examined in absence of a member.
48. Suspension of pay.
49. Flogging, branding, &c.
50. Sentences, how determined.
51. Adequate punishment; recommendation to mercy.
52. Authentication of judgment.
53. Confirmation of sentence.
54. Remission and mitigation of sentence.
55. **Courts of Inquiry,** by whom ordered.
56. Constitution of.
57. Powers of.
58. Oath of members and judge-advocate.
59. Rights of party inquired of.
60. Proceedings, how authenticated and used as evidence.

SEC. 1624. The Navy of the United States shall be governed by the following articles:

17 July, 1862, s. 1, v. 12, p. 600.

Title 13, Chap. 10.
Articles established.

## COMMANDING OFFICERS TO SHOW GOOD EXAMPLE, ETC.

*Commander's duty of supervision and correction.*

ARTICLE 1. The commanders of all fleets, squadrons, naval stations, and vessels belonging to the Navy, are required to show in themselves a good example of virtue, honor, patriotism, and subordination; to be vigilant in inspecting the conduct of all persons who are placed under their command; to guard against and suppress all dissolute and immoral practices, and to correct, according to the laws and regulations of the Navy, all persons who are guilty of them; and any such commander who offends against this article shall be punished as a court-martial may direct.

*Ibid.*, art. 1.

## DIVINE SERVICE—IRREVERENT BEHAVIOR.

*Divine service.*

ART. 2. The commanders of vessels and naval stations to which chaplains are attached shall cause divine service to be performed on Sunday, whenever the weather and other circumstances allow it to be done; and it is earnestly recommended to all officers, seamen, and others in the naval service diligently to attend at every performance of the worship of Almighty God.

*Irreverent behavior.*

ART. 3. Any irreverent or unbecoming behavior during divine service shall be punished as a general or summary court-martial may direct.

*Ibid.*, art. 2.

## OFFENSES PUNISHABLE BY DEATH OR OTHER PUNISHMENT.

ART. 4. The punishment of death, or such other punishment as a court-martial may adjudge, may be inflicted on any person in the naval service—

*Mutiny.*

First. Who makes, or attempts to make, or unites with any mutiny or mutinous assembly, or, being witness to or present at any mutiny, does not do his utmost to suppress it; or, knowing of any mutinous assembly or of any intended mutiny, does not immediately communicate his knowledge to his superior or commanding officer;

*Disobedience of orders.*

Second. Or disobeys the lawful orders of his superior officer;

*Striking superior officer.*

Third. Or strikes or assaults, or attempts or threatens to strike or assault, his superior officer while in the execution of the duties of his office;

*Intercourse with an enemy.*

Fourth. Or gives any intelligence to, or holds or entertains any intercourse with, an enemy or rebel, without leave from the President, the Secretary of the Navy, the commander-in-chief of the fleet, the commander of the squadron, or, in case of a vessel acting singly, from his commanding officer;

*Messages from an enemy.*

Fifth. Or receives any message or letter from an enemy or rebel, or, being aware of the unlawful reception of such message or letter, fails to take the earliest opportunity to inform his superior or commanding officer thereof;

*Desertion in time of war.*

Sixth. Or, in time of war, deserts or entices others to desert; [See §§ 1996-1998, DESERTION.]

*Deserting trust.*

Seventh. Or, in time of war, deserts or betrays his trust, or entices or aids others to desert or betray their trust;

*Sleeping on watch.*

Eighth. Or sleeps upon his watch;

*Leaving station.*

Ninth. Or leaves his station before being regularly relieved;

*Willful stranding or injury of vessel.*

Tenth. Or intentionally or willfully suffers any vessel of the Navy to be stranded, or run upon rocks or shoals, or improperly hazarded; or maliciously or willfully injures any vessel of the Navy, or any part of her tackle, armament, or equipment, whereby the safety of the vessel is hazarded or the lives of the crew exposed to danger;

*Unlawful destruction of public property.*

Eleventh. Or unlawfully sets on fire, or otherwise unlawfully destroys, any public property not at the time in possession of an enemy, pirate, or rebel;

*Striking flag or treacherously yielding.*

Twelfth. Or strikes or attempts to strike the flag to an enemy or rebel, without proper authority, or, when engaged in battle, treacherously yields or pusillanimously cries for quarters;

*Cowardice in battle.*

Thirteenth. Or, in time of battle, displays cowardice, negligence, or disaffection, or withdraws from or keeps out of danger to which he should expose himself;

Fourteenth. Or, in time of battle, deserts his duty or station, or entices others to do so; *Deserting duty in battle.*

Fifteenth. Or does not properly observe the orders of his commanding officer, and use his utmost exertions to carry them into execution, when ordered to prepare for or join in, or when actually engaged in, battle, or while in sight of an enemy; *Neglecting orders to prepare for battle.*

Sixteenth. Or, being in command of a fleet, squadron, or vessel acting singly, neglects, when an engagement is probable, or when an armed vessel of an enemy or rebel is in sight, to prepare and clear his ship or ships for action; *Neglecting to clear for action.*

Seventeenth. Or does not, upon signal for battle, use his utmost exertions to join in battle; *Neglecting to join on signal for battle.*

Eighteenth. Or fails to encourage, in his own person, his inferior officers and men to fight courageously; *Failing to encourage the men to fight.*

Nineteenth. Or does not do his utmost to overtake and capture or destroy any vessel which it is his duty to encounter; *Failing to seek encounter.*

Twentieth. Or does not afford all practicable relief and assistance to vessels belonging to the United States or their allies when engaged in battle. *Failing to afford relief in battle.*

23 April, 1800, v. 2, p. 47.
17 July, 1862, v. 12, p. 601.

ART. 5. All persons who, in time of war, or of rebellion against the supreme authority of the United States, come or are found in the capacity of spies, or who bring or deliver any seducing letter or message from an enemy or rebel, or endeavor to corrupt any person in the Navy to betray his trust, shall suffer death, or such other punishment as a court-martial may adjudge.* *Spies.*

17 July, 1862, s. 1, v. 12, p. 602, art. 4.
13 Feb., 1862, s. 4, v. 12, p. 340.
3 Mar., 1863, s. 38, v. 12, p. 737.

ART. 6. If any person belonging to any public vessel of the United States commits the crime of murder without the territorial jurisdiction thereof, he may be tried by court-martial and punished with death. [See PIRACY, &c., Part IV.] *Murder.*

17 July, 1862, s. 1, v. 12, p. 602, art. 5.

## IMPRISONMENT FOR LIFE, ETC.

ART. 7. A naval court-martial may adjudge the punishment of imprisonment for life, or for a stated term, at hard labor, in any case where it is authorized to adjudge the punishment of death; and such sentences of imprisonment and hard labor may be carried into execution in any prison or penitentiary under the control of the United States, or which the United States may be allowed, by the legislature of any State, to use; and persons so imprisoned in the prison or penitentiary of any State or Territory shall be subject, in all respects, to the same discipline and treatment as convicts sentenced by the courts of the State or Territory in which the same may be situated. *Imprisonment in a penitentiary.*

17 July, 1862, s. 1, v. 12, p. 602, art. 6.

NOTE—A naval or marine court-martial, upon conviction for an offence not capital, under articles 7 and 8, may sentence to imprisonment at hard labor.—Ops. 12, p. 510, Evarts, Oct. 9, 1868; 10, p. 158, Bates, Nov. 1, 1861; 9, p. 80, Black, Sept. 5, 1857. It is held in Army practice that a sentence of penitentiary confinement in a case of a purely military offense is wholly unauthorized and should be disapproved. Larceny, embezzlement, violent crime, or other offenses made punishable with penitentiary confinement by the law of the State, &c., may be legally visited with this punishment.—Winthrop's Digest, p. 80. The same principles are now applied by the Navy Department.

### OFFENSES PUNISHABLE AT DISCRETION OF COURT.

ART. 8. Such punishment as a court-martial may adjudge may be inflicted on any person in the Navy—

First. Who is guilty of profane swearing, falsehood, drunkenness, gambling, fraud, theft, or any other scandalous conduct tending to the destruction of good morals; *Profanity, falsehood, &c.*

---

* Such other punishment is limited only to that kind of punishment which has become usual.—Op. X, 159. Sentence of incapacity or disability not within that range. Can only be awarded when specially authorized by law.—Naval contractor's case, Op. XII, 528. To be limited to the customs of the service. Cruel and unusual punishments are forbidden by the law-martial and the Constitution.—Op. X, 169.

| | |
|---|---|
| Cruelty. | Second. Or is guilty of cruelty toward, or oppression or maltreatment of, any person subject to his orders; |
| Quarreling. | Third. Or quarrels with, strikes, or assaults, or uses provoking or reproachful words, gestures, or menaces toward, any person in the Navy; |
| Fomenting quarrels. | Fourth. Or endeavors to foment quarrels between other persons in the Navy; |
| Duels. | Fifth. Or sends or accepts a challenge to fight a duel or acts as a second in a duel; |
| Contempt of superior officer. | Sixth. Or treats his superior officer with contempt, or is disrespectful to him in language or deportment, while in the execution of his office; |
| Combinations against superior officer. | Seventh. Or joins in or abets any combination to weaken the lawful authority of, or lessen the respect due to, his commanding officer; |

17 July, 1862, s. 1, v. 12, p. 602, art. 7.

| | |
|---|---|
| Mutinous words. | Eighth. Or utters any seditious or mutinous words; |

23 April, 1800, art. 13, v. 2, p. 47.

| | |
|---|---|
| Neglect of orders. | Ninth. Or is negligent or careless in obeying orders, or culpably inefficient in the performance of duty; |
| Preventing destruction of public property. | Tenth. Or does not use his best exertions to prevent the unlawful destruction of public property by others; |
| Negligent stranding. | Eleventh. Or, through inattention or negligence, suffers any vessel of the Navy to be stranded, or run upon a rock or shoal, or hazarded; |
| Negligence in convoy service. | Twelfth. Or, when attached to any vessel appointed as convoy to any merchant or other vessels, fails diligently to perform his duty, or demands or exacts any compensation for his services, or maltreats the officers or crews of such merchant or other vessels; |
| Receiving articles for freight. | Thirteenth. Or takes, receives, or permits to be received, on board the vessel to which he is attached, any goods or merchandise, for freight, sale, or traffic, except gold, silver, or jewels, for freight or safe-keeping; or demands or receives any compensation for the receipt or transportation of any other article than gold, silver, or jewels, without authority from the President or Secretary of the Navy; |
| False muster. | Fourteenth. Or knowingly makes or signs, or aids, abets, directs, or procures the making or signing of, any false muster; |
| Waste of public property, &c. | Fifteenth. Or wastes any ammunition, provisions, or other public property, or, having power to prevent it, knowingly permits such waste; |
| Plundering on shore. | Sixteenth. Or, when on shore, plunders, abuses, or maltreats any inhabitant, or injures his property in any way; |
| Refusing to apprehend offenders. | Seventeenth. Or refuses, or fails to use, his utmost exertions to detect, apprehend, and bring to punishment all offenders, or to aid all persons appointed for that purpose; |
| Refusing to receive prisoners. | Eighteenth. Or, when rated or acting as master-at-arms, refuses to receive such prisoners as may be committed to his charge, or, having received them, suffers them to escape, or dismisses them without orders from the proper authority; |
| Absence from duty without leave. | Nineteenth. Or is absent from his station or duty without leave, or after his leave has expired; |
| Violating general orders or regulations. | Twentieth. Or violates or refuses obedience to any lawful general order or regulation issued by the Secretary of the Navy; |
| Desertion in time of peace. | Twenty-first. Or, in time of peace, deserts or attempts to desert, or aids and entices others to desert; |
| Harboring deserters. | Twenty-second. Or receives or entertains any deserter from any other vessel of the Navy, knowing him to be such, and does not, with all convenient speed, give notice of such deserter to the commander of the vessel to which he belongs, or to the commander-in-chief, or to the commander of the squadron. |

23 April, 1800, v. 2, p. 47.    17 July, 1862, v. 12, p. 602.

### REDUCTION OF OFFICERS, AND DESERTION.

| | |
|---|---|
| Officer absent without leave may be reduced. | ART. 9. Any officer who absents himself from his command without leave, may, by the sentence of a court-martial, be reduced to the rating of an ordinary seaman. |

16 May, 1864, s. 2, v. 13, p. 75.

| | |
|---|---|
| Desertion by resignation. | ART. 10. Any commissioned officer of the Navy or Marine Corps who, having tendered his resignation, quits his post or proper duties without leave, and with intent to remain permanently absent therefrom, prior |

to due notice of the acceptance of such resignation, shall be deemed and punished as a deserter. [See DISMISSAL; also DESERTION.]

5 Aug. 1861, s. 2, v. 12, p. 316.

#### DEALING IN SUPPLIES—IMPORTATIONS—DISTILLED SPIRITS.

ART. 11. No person in the naval service shall procure stores or other articles or supplies for, and dispose thereof to, the officers or enlisted men on vessels of the Navy, or at navy-yards or naval stations, for his own account or benefit. Dealing in supplies on private account.

26 Aug , 1842, s. 1, v. 5, p. 535.

ART. 12. No person connected with the Navy shall, under any pretense, import in a public vessel any article which is liable to the payment of duty. Importing dutiable goods in public vessels.

30 July, 1846, s. 10, v. 9, p. 44.

ART. 13. Distilled spirits shall be admitted on board of vessels of war only upon the order and under the control of the medical officers of such vessels, and to be used only for medical purposes. Distilled spirits only as medical stores.

14 July, 1862, s. 4, v. 12, p. 565.

#### FRAUD, FORGERY, THEFT, ETC.

ART. 14. Fine and imprisonment, or such other punishment* as a court-martial may adjudge, shall be inflicted upon any person in the naval service of the United States— Certain crimes of fraud against the United States.

Who presents or causes to be presented to any person in the civil, military, or naval service thereof, for approval or payment, any claim against the United States or any officer thereof, knowing such claim to be false or fraudulent; or Presenting false claims.

Who enters into any agreement or conspiracy to defraud the United States by obtaining, or aiding others to obtain, the allowance or payment of any false or fraudulent claim; or Agreement to obtain payment of false claims.

Who, for the purpose of obtaining, or aiding others to obtain, the approval, allowance, or payment of any claim against the United States or against any officer thereof, makes or uses, or procures or advises the making or use of, any writing, or other paper, knowing the same to contain any false or fraudulent statement; or False papers.

Who, for the purpose of obtaining, or aiding others to obtain, the approval, allowance, or payment of any claim against the United States or any officer thereof, makes, or procures or advises the making of, any oath to any fact or to any writing or other paper, knowing such oath to be false; or Perjury.

Who, for the purpose of obtaining, or aiding others to obtain, the approval, allowance, or payment of any claim against the United States or any officer thereof, forges or counterfeits, or procures or advises the forging or counterfeiting of, any signature upon any writing or other paper, or uses, or procures or advises the use of, any such signature, knowing the same to be forged or counterfeited; or Forgery.

Who, having charge, possession, custody, or control of any money or other property of the United States, furnished or intended for the naval service thereof, knowingly delivers, or causes to be delivered, to any person having authority to receive the same, any amount thereof less than that for which he receives a certificate or receipt; or Delivering less property than receipt calls for.

Who, being authorized to make or deliver any paper certifying the receipt of any money or other property of the United States, furnished or intended for the naval service thereof, makes, or delivers to any person, such writing, without having full knowledge of the truth of the statements therein contained, and with intent to defraud the United States; or Giving receipts without knowing truth of.

Who steals, embezzles, knowingly and willfully misappropriates, applies to his own use or benefit, or wrongfully and knowingly sells or disposes of any ordnance, arms, equipments, ammunition, clothing, subsistence stores, money or other property of the United States, furnished or intended for the military or naval service thereof; or Stealing, wrongfully selling, &c.

Who knowingly purchases, or receives in pledge for any obligation or indebtedness, from any other person who is a part of or employed in said service, any ordnance, arms, equipments, ammunition, clothing, Buying public military property.

---

*Such other punishment is limited only to that kind of punishment which has become usual.—Op. X, 159. Sentence of incapacity or disability not within that range. Can only be awarded when specially authorized by law.—Naval contractor's case, Op. XII, 528. To be limited to the customs of the service. Cruel and unusual punishments are forbidden by the law—martial and the Constitution.—Op. X, 160.

subsistence stores, or other property of the United States, such other person not having lawful right to sell or pledge the same; or

2 March, 1863, s. 1, v. 12, p. 696.

*Other frauds.* Who executes, attempts, or countenances any other fraud against the United States.

17 July, 1862, art. 7, v. 12, p. 602.

*Liable to arrest and trial after discharge and dismissal.* And if any person, being guilty of any of the offenses described in this article while in the naval service, receives his discharge, or is dismissed from the service, he shall continue to be liable to be arrested and held for trial and sentence by a court-martial, in the same manner and to the same extent as if he had not received such discharge nor been dismissed.

2 March, 1863, s. 2, v. 12, p. 697.

## DUTY AS TO PRIZES AND THEIR CREWS.

*List of persons claiming prize-money.* ART. 15. The commanding officer of every vessel in the Navy entitled to or claiming an award of prize-money shall, as soon as it may be practicable after the capture, transmit to the Navy Department a complete list of the officers and men of his vessel entitled to share, stating therein the quality of each person rating; and every commanding officer who offends against this article shall be punished as a court-martial may direct. [See § 4615, PRIZE.]

17 July, 1862, s. 5, v. 12, p. 607.

*Removing property from a prize.* ART. 16. No person in the Navy shall take out of a prize, or vessel seized as a prize, any money, plate, goods, or any part of her equipment, unless it be for the better preservation thereof, or unless such articles are absolutely needed for the use of any of the vessels or armed forces of the United States, before the same are adjudged lawful prize by a competent court; but the whole, without fraud, concealment, or embezzlement, shall be brought in, in order that judgment may be passed thereon; and every person who offends against this article shall be punished as a court-martial may direct.

Id., s. 7.

*Maltreating persons taken on a prize.* ART. 17. If any person in the Navy strips off the clothes of, or pillages, or in any manner maltreats, any person taken on board a prize, he shall suffer such punishment as a court-martial may adjudge.

Id., s. 8.

## FUGITIVES FROM SERVICE.

*Returning fugitives from service.* ART. 18. If any officer or person in the naval service employs any of the forces under his command for the purpose of returning any fugitive from service or labor, he shall be dismissed from the service.

13 March, 1862, s. 1, v. 12, p. 354.

## ENLISTING DESERTERS, MINORS, ETC.

*Enlisting deserters, minors, &c.* ART. 19. Any officer who knowingly enlists into the naval service any deserter from the naval or military service of the United States, or any insane or intoxicated person, or any minor between the ages of *fifteen\** and eighteen years, without the consent of his parents or guardian, or any minor under the age of *fifteen\** years, shall be punished as a court-martial may direct. [See §§ 1418, 1419, 1420, SEAMEN, NAVY.]

3 March, 1865, s. 18, v. 13, p. 490.    12 May, 1879, v. 21, p. 3.

## RULES FOR COMMANDING OFFICERS.

ART. 20. Every commanding officer of a vessel in the Navy shall obey the following rules:

*Men received on board.* First. Whenever a man enters on board, the commanding officer shall cause an accurate entry to be made in the ship's books, showing his name, the date, place, and term of his enlistment, the place or vessel from which he was received on board, his rating, his descriptive list, his age, place of birth, and citizenship, with such remarks as may be necessary.

---

*Sections 1418, 1419, and 1420 Revised Statutes have been amended forbidding the enlistment of minors under *fourteen* instead of fifteen years of age.

Second. He shall, before sailing, transmit to the Secretary of the Navy a complete list of the rated men under his command, showing the particulars set forth in rule one, and a list of officers and passengers, showing the date of their entering. And he shall cause similar lists to be made out on the first day of every third month and transmitted to the Secretary of the Navy as opportunities occur, accounting therein for any casualty which may have happened since the last list. *(List of officers' men, and passengers. Deaths and desertions.)*

Third. He shall cause to be accurately minuted on the ship's books the names of any persons dying or deserting, and the times at which such death or desertion occurs. *(Property of deceased persons.)*

Fourth. In case of the death of any officer, man, or passenger on said vessel, he shall take care that the paymaster secures all the property of the deceased, for the benefit of his legal representatives. *(Accounts of men received.)*

Fifth. He shall not receive on board any man transferred from any other vessel or station to him, unless such man is furnished with an account, signed by the captain and paymaster of the vessel or station from which he came, specifying the date of his entry on said vessel or at said station, the period and term of his service, the sums paid him, the balance due him, the quality in which he was rated, and his descriptive list.

Sixth. He shall, whenever officers or men are sent from his ship, for whatever cause, take care that each man is furnished with a complete statement of his account, specifying the date of his enlistment, the period and term of his service, and his descriptive list. Said account shall be signed by the commanding officer and paymaster. *(Accounts of men sent from the ship.)*

Seventh. He shall cause frequent inspections to be made into the condition of the provisions on his ship, and use every precaution for their preservation. *(Inspection of provisions.)*

Eighth. He shall frequently consult with the surgeon in regard to the sanitary condition of his crew, and shall use all proper means to preserve their health. And he shall cause a convenient place to be set apart for sick or disabled men, to which he shall have them removed, with their hammocks and bedding, when the surgeon so advises, and shall direct that some of the crew attend them and keep the place clean. *(Health of crew.)*

Ninth. He shall attend in person, or appoint a proper officer to attend, when his crew is finally paid off, to see that justice is done to the men and to the United States in the settlement of the accounts. *(Attendance at final payment of crew.)*

Tenth. He shall cause the articles for the government of the Navy to be hung up in some public part of the ship and read once a month to his ship's company. *(Articles to be hung up and read.)*

Every commanding officer who offends against the provisions of this article shall be punished as a court-martial may direct. *(Punishment for offending against this article.)*

17 July, 1862, s. 16, v. 12, p. 609.

## AUTHORITY OVER CREW AFTER LOSS OF VESSEL.

ART. 21. When the crew of any vessel of the United States are separated from their vessel by means of her wreck, loss, or destruction, all the command and authority given to the officers of such vessel shall remain in full force until such ship's company shall be regularly discharged from or ordered again into service, or until a court-martial or court of inquiry shall be held to inquire into the loss of said vessel. And if any officer or man, after such wreck, loss, or destruction, acts contrary to the discipline of the Navy, he shall be punished as a court-martial may direct. *(Authority of officers after loss of vessel.)*

17 July, 1862, s. 14, v. 12, p. 609.

## OFFENSES NOT SPECIFIED AND ON SHORE.

ART. 22. All offenses committed by persons belonging to the Navy which are not specified in the foregoing articles shall be punished as a court-martial may direct. *(Offenses not specified.)*

NOTE.—On board a United States vessel of war on the Thames River, under way, opposite New London, a fatal assault was committed upon a member of the crew by another. *Held,* That a naval court-martial could, under article 22, section 1624 Revised Statutes, take jurisdiction of the offense as manslaughter. The state authorities could have tried the case, but it would not have ousted the court-martial of jurisdiction over the same offense so far as it affected the order and discipline of the ship.—Op. XVI, 578, published in General Order Navy Department 259, January 25, 1881.

14 ARTICLES GOVERNING THE NAVY.

Offenses committed on shore.
ART. 23. All offenses committed by persons belonging to the Navy while on shore shall be punished in the same manner as if they had been committed at sea.

17 July, 1862, s. 1, v. 12, p. 602, arts. 8 and 9.

## PUNISHMENT BY ORDER OF COMMANDER.

Punishment by order of commander.
ART. 24. No commander of a vessel shall inflict upon a commissioned or warrant officer any other punishment than private reprimand, suspension from duty, arrest, or confinement, and such suspension, arrest, or confinement shall not continue longer than ten days, unless a further period is necessary to bring the offender to trial by a court-martial; nor shall he inflict, or cause to be inflicted, upon any petty officer, or person of inferior rating, or marine, for a single offense, or at any one time, any other than one of the following punishments, namely:

First, Reduction of any rating established by himself.

Second. Confinement, with or without irons, single or double, not exceeding ten days, unless further confinement be necessary, in the case of a prisoner to be tried by court-martial.

Third. Solitary confinement, on bread and water, not exceeding five days.

Fourth. Solitary confinement not exceeding seven days.

Fifth. Deprivation of liberty on shore.

Sixth. Extra duties.

No other punishment shall be permitted on board of vessels belonging to the Navy, except by sentence of a general or summary court-martial. All punishments inflicted by the commander, or by his order, except reprimands, shall be fully entered upon the ship's log.

17 July, 1862, s. 1, v. 12, p. 603, art. 10.

Punishment by officers temporarily commanding.
ART. 25. No officer who may command by accident, or in the absence of the commanding officer, except when such commanding officer is absent for a time by leave, shall inflict any other punishment than confinement.

23 April, 1800, s. 1, v. 2, p. 49, art. 30.

## SUMMARY COURTS-MARTIAL.

Summary courts-martial.
ART. 26. Summary courts-martial may be ordered upon petty officers and persons of inferior ratings, by the commander of any vessel, or by the commandant of any navy-yard, naval station, or marine barracks to which they belong, for the trial of offenses which such officer may deem deserving of greater punishment than such commander or commandant is authorized to inflict, but not sufficient to require trial by a general court-martial.

2 March, 1855, s. 4, v. p. 627. 10.
15 July, 1870, s. 14, v. 16, p. 334.

Constitution of summary courts-martial.
ART. 27. A summary court-martial shall consist of three officers not below the rank of ensign, as members, and of a recorder. The commander of a ship may order any officer under his command to act as such recorder.

2 March, 1855, ss. 5, 6, v. 10, p. 628.

Oath of members and recorder.
ART. 28. Before proceeding to trial the members of a summary court-martial shall take the following oath or affirmation, which shall be administered by the recorder: "I, A B, do swear (or affirm) that I will well and truly try, without prejudice or partiality, the case now depending, according to the evidence which shall be adduced, the laws for the government of the Navy, and my own conscience." After which the recorder of the court shall take the following oath or affirmation, which shall be administered by the senior member of the court: "I, A B, do swear (or affirm) that I will keep a true record of the evidence which shall be given before this court and of the proceedings thereof."

Id., s. 5.

Testimony.
ART. 29. All testimony before a summary court-martial shall be given orally, upon oath or affirmation, administered by the senior member of the court.

Punishments by summary courts.
ART. 30. Summary courts-martial may sentence petty officers and persons of inferior ratings to any one of the following punishments, namely:

First. Discharge from the service with bad conduct discharge; but the sentence shall not be carried into effect in a foreign country.
Second. Solitary confinement, not exceeding thirty days, in irons, single or double, on bread and water, or on diminished rations.
Third. Solitary confinement in irons, single or double, not exceeding thirty days.
Fourth. Solitary confinement not exceeding thirty days.
Fifth. Confinement not exceeding two months.
Sixth. Reduction to next inferior rating.
Seventh. Deprivation of liberty on shore on foreign station.
Eighth. Extra police duties, and loss of pay, not to exceed three months, may be added to any of the above-mentioned punishments.

*Ibid.*, s. 7.

ART. 31. A summary court-martial may disrate any rated person for incompetency. — *Disrating for incompetency.*

17 July, 1862, s. 1, art. 10, v. 12, p. 603.

ART. 32. No sentence of a summary court-martial shall be carried into execution until the proceedings and sentence have been approved by the officer ordering the court and by the commander-in-chief, or, in his absence, by the senior officer present. And no sentence of such court which involves loss of pay shall be carried into execution until the proceedings and sentence have been approved by the Secretary of the Navy. — *Execution of sentence of summary court.*

2 March, 1855, s. 8, v. 10, p. 628.
2 March, 1867, s. 5, v. 14, p. 516.

ART. 33. The officer ordering a summary court-martial shall have power to remit, in part or altogether, but not to commute, the sentence of the court. And it shall be his duty either to remit any part or the whole of any sentence, the execution of which would, in the opinion of the surgeon or senior medical officer on board, given in writing, produce serious injury to the health of the person sentenced; or to submit the case again, without delay, to the same or to another summary court-martial, which shall have power, upon the testimony already taken, to remit the former punishment and to assign some other of the authorized punishments in the place thereof. — *Remission of sentence.*

2 March, 1855, s. 8, v. 10, p. 628.

ART. 34. The proceedings of summary courts-martial shall be conducted with as much conciseness and precision as may be consistent with the ends of justice, and under such forms and rules as may be prescribed by the Secretary of the Navy, with the approval of the President; and all such proceedings shall be transmitted, in the usual mode, to the Navy Department. — *Manner of conducting proceedings.*

*Id.*, s. 9.

ART. 35. Any punishment which a summary court-martial is authorized to inflict may be inflicted by a general court-martial. — *Same punishments by general court-martial.*

*Id.*, s. 10.

### DISMISSAL OF OFFICERS.

ART. 36. No officer shall be dismissed from the naval service except by the order of the President or by sentence of a general court-martial; and in time of peace no officer shall be dismissed except in pursuance of the sentence of a general court-martial or in mitigation thereof. — *Dismissal of officers.*

13 July, 1866, s. 5, v. 14, p. 92.

ART. 37. When any officer, dismissed by order of the President since 3d March, 1865, makes, in writing, an application for trial, setting forth, under oath that he has been wrongly dismissed, the President shall, as soon as the necessities of the service may permit, convene a court-martial to try such officer on the charges on which he shall have been dismissed. And if such court-martial shall not be convened within six months from the presentation of such application for trial, or if such court, being convened, shall not award dismissal or death as the punishment of such officer, the order of dismissal by the President shall be void. [See under head of DISMISSAL.] — *Officer dismissed by the President may demand trial.*

3 March, 1865, s. 12, v. 13, p. 489.

## GENERAL COURTS-MARTIAL.*

*General courts-martial, by whom convened.*

ART. 38. General courts-martial may be convened by the President, the Secretary of the Navy, or the commander-in-chief of a fleet or squadron; but no commander of a fleet or squadron in the waters of the United States shall convene such court without express authority from the President.

17 July, 1862, s. 1, art. 11 v. 12, p. 603.

*Constitution of.*

ART. 39. A general court-martial shall consist of not more than thirteen nor less than five commissioned officers as members; and as many officers, not exceeding thirteen, as can be convened without injury to the service, shall be summoned on every such court. But in no case, where it can be avoided without injury to the service, shall more than one-half, exclusive of the president, be junior to the officer to be tried. The senior officer shall always preside and the others shall take place according to their rank.

Id., art. 11.

NOTE.—The *minority* of some of the members of a court-martial is not available as an objection to the validity of the proceedings.—Op. XVI, 550.

*Oaths of members and judge-advocate.*

ART. 40. The president of the general court-martial shall administer the following oath or affirmation to the judge-advocate or person officiating as such:

"I, A B, do swear (or affirm) that I will keep a true record of the evidence given to and the proceedings of this court; that I will not divulge or by any means disclose the sentence of the court until it shall have been approved by the proper authority; and that I will not at any time divulge or disclose the vote or opinion of any particular member of the court, unless required so to do before a court of justice in due course of law."

This oath or affirmation being duly administered, each member of the court, before proceeding to trial, shall take the following oath or affirmation, which shall be administered by the judge-advocate or person officiating as such:

"I, A B, do swear (or affirm) that I will truly try without prejudice or partiality, the case now depending, according to the evidence which shall come before the court, the rules for the government of the Navy, and my own conscience; that I will not by any means divulge or disclose the sentence of the court until it shall have been approved by the proper authority; and that I will not at any time divulge or disclose the vote or opinion of any particular member of the court, unless required so to do before a court of justice in due course of law."

Id., art. 12.

*Oath of witness.*

ART. 41. An oath or affirmation in the following form, shall be administered to all witnesses, before any court-martial, by the president thereof:

"You do solemnly swear (or affirm) that the evidence you shall give in the case now before this court shall be the truth, the whole truth, and nothing but the truth, and that you will state everything within your knowledge in relation to the charges. So help you God; (or 'this you do under the pains and penalties of perjury.')"

Id., art. 14.

*Contempts of court.*

ART. 42. Whenever any person refuses to give his evidence or to give it in the manner provided by these articles, or prevaricates, or behaves with contempt to the court, it shall be lawful for the court to imprison him for any time not exceeding two months.

Id., art. 13.

*Charges.*

ART. 43. The person accused shall be furnished with a true copy of the charges, with the specifications, at the time he is put under arrest; and no other charges than those so furnished shall be urged against him at the trial, unless it shall appear to the court that intelligence of such other charge had not reached the officer ordering the court when the accused was put under arrest, or that some witness material to the support of such charge was at that time absent and can be produced at

---

*The proceedings of all general and summary courts-martial and courts of inquiry, after action thereon by the reviewing officer, will be forwarded direct to the Judge-Advocate-General of the Navy, accompanied by a communication addressed to him. All communications pertaining to questions of law before such courts, requiring the action of the Department, must also be addressed to him.—General Order 250, June 20, 1880.

the trial; in which case reasonable time shall be given to the accused to make his defense against such new charge. *The person so charged shall, at his own request but not otherwise, be a competent witness. And his failure to make such request shall not create any presumption against him.*

*Id.*, art. 15.
16 March, 1878. v. 20, p. 30.

ART. 44. Every officer who is arrested for trial shall deliver up his sword to his commanding officer and confine himself to the limits assigned him, on pain of dismissal from the service. — Duty of officer arrested.

17 July, 1862, art. 15, v. 12, p. 604.

ART. 45. When the proceedings of any general court-martial have commenced, they shall not be suspended or delayed on account of the absence of any of the members, provided five or more are assembled; but the court is enjoined to sit from day to day, Sundays excepted, until sentence is given, unless temporarily adjourned by the authority which convened it. — Suspension of proceedings.

*Id.*, art. 16.

ART. 46. No member of a general court-martial shall, after the proceedings are begun, absent himself therefrom, except in case of sickness, or of an order to go on duty from a superior officer, on pain of being cashiered. — Absence of members.

*Id.*, art. 16.

ART. 47. Whenever any member of a court-martial, from any legal cause, is absent from the court after the commencement of a case, all the witnesses who have been examined during his absence must, when he is ready to resume his seat, be recalled by the court, and the recorded testimony of each witness so examined must be read over to him, and such witness must acknowledge the same to be correct and be subject to such further examination as the said member may require. Without a compliance with this rule, and an entry thereof upon the record, a member who shall have been absent during the examination of a witness shall not be allowed to sit again in that particular case. — Witnesses examined in absence of a member.

*Id.*, art. 17.

ART. 48. Whenever a court-martial sentences an officer to be suspended, it may suspend his pay and emoluments for the whole or any part of the time of his suspension. — Suspension of pay.

*Id.*, art. 18.

ART. 49. In no case shall punishment by flogging, or by branding, marking, or tattooing on the body be adjudged by any court-martial or be inflicted upon any person in the Navy. — Flogging, branding, &c.

*Id.*, art. 8.
6 June, 1872, s. 2, v. 17. p. 261.

ART. 50. No person shall be sentenced by a court-martial to suffer death, except by the concurrence of two-thirds of the members present, and in the cases where such punishment is expressly provided in these articles. All other sentences may be determined by a majority of votes. — Sentences, how determined.

17 July, 1862, s. 1, v. 12, p. 605, art. 19.

ART. 51. It shall be the duty of a court-martial, in all cases of conviction, to adjudge a punishment adequate to the nature of the offense; but the members thereof may recommend the person convicted as deserving of clemency, and state, on the record, their reasons for so doing. [See Art. 35, SUMMARY COURTS-MARTIAL.] — Adequate punishment; recommendation to mercy.

*Id.*, art. 21.

ART. 52. The judgment of every court-martial shall be authenticated by the signature of the president, and of every member who may be present when said judgment is pronounced, and also of the judge-advocate. — Authentication of judgment.

*Id.*, art. 22.

ART. 53. No sentence of a court-martial, extending to the loss of life, or to the dismissal of a commissioned or warrant officer, shall be carried into execution until confirmed by the President. All other sentences of a general court-martial may be carried into execution on confirmation of the commander of the fleet or officer ordering the court. — Confirmation of sentence.

*Id.*, art. 19.

**Remission and mitigation of sentence.**

ART. 54. Every officer who is authorized to convene a general court-martial shall have power, on revision of its proceedings, to remit or mitigate, but not to commute, the sentence of any such court which he is authorized to approve and confirm.

*Id.*, art. 20.

NOTES.—A milder punishment may be substituted by the President for dismissal. In mitigating, may substitute suspension without pay, which is an inferior degree of the same punishment. Mitigation must be of the punishment adjudged by reducing and modifying its severity, except in case of death, where there is no inferior degree. The Executive cannot add to the punishment; cannot suspend pay or emoluments where they were not suspended by the court. Sentence of suspension merely does not deprive the party of pay or emoluments. Where forfeiture or loss of pay is made part of the sentence, in addition to confinement or suspension from duty, the former may be remitted by the proper authority, in whole or in part, without also remitting the latter.—Op. IV, 432, 444; V 45; VI, 200; XV, 175.

It is well settled that it is beyond the power of the President to annul or revoke the sentence of a court-martial which has been approved and executed under a former President. The rule is not confined to cases in which the sentence is required to be approved by the President.—Op. X p., 64. Refers to Op. I, 486; IV, 170, 274; VI, 514, 360; VII, 98.

Forfeiture or loss of pay, by confinement or suspension from duty, under a sentence of a court-martial, is not incurred unless the forfeiture or loss be imposed by the sentence.—Op. XV, 175

The action of an officer who ordered the court, on forwarding the proceedings with the indorsement "that the finding of the court is not sustained by the evidence," cannot be deemed to be a disapproval of the sentence of the court. Such disapproval should be distinctly expressed.—Op. XVI, 312.

Notice by the Secretary of the Navy of the approval by the President of the sentence of a court-martial is sufficient evidence of approval and promulgation.—Op. XVI, 550; see also XV, 290. Sign-manual of the President not necessary.

A disapproval of a sentence by the proper reviewing officer, release from confinement, and restoration to duty is tantamount to an acquittal by the court.—Op. XIII, 459.

When the sentence of a court-martial, lawfully confirmed, has been executed, the proceedings in the case are no longer subject to review by the President.—Op. XV, 290. In a note to this opinion, observations are submitted upon the authority of the President to appoint general courts-martial in cases other than those in which he is expressly authorized to do so by Congress, and the conclusion reached that such authority is well established.

A midshipman was nominated and confirmed as an ensign, subject to examination, but subsequently tried, never having been examined, and sentenced to be dismissed. Under the circumstances, was properly tried as a midshipman. Op. XVI, 550.

Any person having an interest in the record of a naval court-martial is entitled to have an exemplified copy of it, after the proceedings are consummated by the proper authority.—Op. XI, 137.

## COURTS OF INQUIRY.†

**Courts of inquiry, by whom ordered.**

ART. 55. Courts of inquiry may be ordered by the President, the Secretary of the Navy, or the commander of a fleet or squadron.

17 July, 1862, s. 1, v. 12, p. 605, art. 23.

**Constitution of.**

ART. 56. A court of inquiry shall consist of not more than three commissioned officers as members, and of a judge-advocate, or person officiating as such.

*Id.*, art. 23.

**Powers of.**

ART. 57. Courts of inquiry shall have power to summon witnesses, administer oaths, and punish contempts, in the same manner as courts-martial; but they shall only state facts, and shall not give their opinion, unless expressly required so to do in the order for convening.

*Id.*, art. 23.

**Oath of members and judge-advocate.**

ART. 58. The judge-advocate, or person officiating as such, shall administer to the members the following oath or affirmation: "You do swear (or affirm) well and truly to examine and inquire, according to the evidence, into the matter now before you, without partiality." After which the president shall administer to the judge-advocate, or person officiating as such, the following oath or affirmation: "You do swear (or affirm) truly to record the proceedings of this court and the evidence to be given in the case in hearing."

*Id.*, art. 25.

**¶Rights of party inquired of.**

ART. 59. The party whose conduct shall be the subject of inquiry, or his attorney, shall have the right to cross-examine all the witnesses.*

*Id.*, art. 23.

---

* See act of March 16, 1878, as noted under general courts-martials, article 43.
† See note, page 15.

MISCELLANEOUS PROVISIONS GOVERNING THE NAVY. 19

ART. 60. The proceedings of courts of inquiry shall be authenticated by the signature of the president of the court and of the judge-advocate, and shall, in all cases not capital, nor extending to the dismissal of a commissioned or warrant officer, be evidence before a court-martial, provided oral testimony cannot be obtained. *Proceedings, how authenticated, and used as evidence.*

*Id.*, art. 24.

NOTE.—Courts of inquiry are open or close, as the authority ordering it may determine.—De Hart, 276. Action of courts not decision, but advice, only for information of Executive. Scope not limited to a prescription of time. May be ordered at any subsequent date.—Op. VIII, 335; VI, 239. A court of inquiry cannot be ordered on a civilian. A body of officers convened to inquire into and report on the facts of the case of an officer who has been legally dismissed is a mere board of investigation, and can exercise none of the special powers of a court-martial or court of inquiry.—Winthrop's Digest, 125; see same as to powers of boards of investigation.
A copy of the record of a court of inquiry is not to be furnished to parties, or their agents, as a matter of *right*, as is the copy of the record of a court-martial.—Holt's Digest, 43.

## MISCELLANEOUS PROVISIONS.

| Sec. | Sec. |
|---|---|
| 1433. Exercise of consular powers. | 2003. Interference in elections. |
| 1440. Appointments in diplomatic service. | 5510. Depriving citizens of civil rights. |
| 1442. Furloughing officers. | 5528. Troops at elections. |
| 1547. Regulations and general orders. | 5529. Intimidating voters. |
| 1548. Officers to be furnished general orders. | 5530. Prescribing voters' qualifications. |
| 1571. Sea service defined. | 5531. Interfering in elections. |
| 1586. Medicines and medical expenses. | 5532. Disqualification to hold office. |
| 1587. Funeral expenses. | —— Credit for volunteer service. |
| 1860. Voting and holding office in Territories. | —— Acceptance of decorations. |
| 2002. Bringing troops to places of election. | —— Employment on shore duty. |

SEC. 1433. The commanding officer of any fleet, squadron, or vessel acting singly, when upon the high seas or in any foreign port where there is no resident consul of the United States, shall be authorized to exercise all the powers of a consul in relation to mariners of the United States. *Title 15, Chap. 2. Consular powers.*

20 Feb., 1845, s. 2, v. 5, p. 725.

SEC. 1440. If any officer of the Navy accepts or holds an appointment in the diplomatic or consular service of the Government, he shall be considered as having resigned his place in the Navy, and it shall be filled as a vacancy. *Accepting appointments in diplomatic service.*

30 March, 1868, s. 2, v. 15, p. 58.

SEC. 1442. The Secretary of the Navy shall have authority to place on furlough any officer on the active list of the Navy. *Furloughing officers.*

3 March, 1835, s. 1, v. 4, p. 756.  3 March, 1845, s. 6, v. 5, p. 794.
28 Feb., 1855, s. 3, v. 10, p. 617.  1 June, 1860, s. 4, v. 12, p. 27.

NOTE.—*Furloughed*, in ordinary sense of the administration of the Department, is a question of duty and pay, not of rank or place on the roll of the Navy. The officer may be restored by the same power, retains his place in the line of promotion, and it cannot be occupied by another.—Op. VIII, 223, Dec. 10, 1856.

SEC. 1547. The orders, regulations, and instructions issued by the Secretary of the Navy prior to July 14, 1862, with such alterations as he may since have adopted, with the approval of the President, shall be recognized as the regulations of the Navy, subject to alterations adopted in the same manner. *Title 15, Chap. 7. Regulations.*

14 July, 1862, s. 5, v. 12, p. 565.

NOTES.—Congress is empowered by the Constitution to make Navy Regulations. Those made by the President, or subordinates, must be in execution of and supplemental to the statutes and statute regulations.—Op. VI, p. 10 (see also X, p. 413); XIII, p. 9.
A regulation of the Department (Treasury) made in pursuance of an act of Congress becomes a part of the law, and is of the same force as if incorporated in the body of the act itself.—U. S. v. Barrows, 1 Abbott, U.S. R., 351.
A regulation of a Department is a rule made by the head of such Department for its action, under a statute conferring such power, and has the force of law; a mere order of the President, or the Secretary of the Department, is not a regulation.—Court of Claims, III, p. 39.
The Navy Regulations on the subject of payments to administrators and under wills are to be construed as binding only upon the officers and seamen of the Navy; they are not applicable to nor binding upon the accounting officers of the Treasury Department in the settlement of naval accounts, and it was not intended that they should control these officers.—Op. XVI, p. 494, Devens, May 21, 1880. The general tenor of this opinion is that the Navy Regulations are not intended to affect any persons except those subject to the orders of the Secretary of the Navy.

## MISCELLANEOUS PROVISIONS GOVERNING THE NAVY.

**Copy to be furnished to officers.**

SEC. 1548. The Secretary of the Navy shall cause each commissioned or warrant officer of the Navy, on his entry into the service, to be furnished with a copy of the regulations and general orders of the Navy Department then in force, and thereafter with a copy of all such as may be issued.

17 July, 1862, s. 19, v. 12, p. 610.

**Title 15, chap. 8.**
**Sea service.**

SEC. 1571. No service shall be regarded as sea service except such as shall be performed at sea, under the orders of a Department and in vessels employed by authority of law.

1 June, 1860, s. 3, v. 12, p. 27.

NOTE.—The service which entitles an officer to the pay allowed for "duty at sea," begins when, having been ordered to a particular duty, he reports himself, in obedience to the orders, at the place designated, and enters upon that duty.— Op. X, p. 191, Feb. 19, 1862, and p. 97, Aug. 13, 1861, Bates.

**Medicines and medical attendance.**

SEC. 1586. Expenses incurred by any officer of the Navy for medicines and medical attendance shall not be allowed unless they were incurred when he was on duty, and the medicines could not have been obtained from naval supplies, or the attendance of a naval medical officer could not have been had.

15 July, 1870, s. 17, v. 16, p. 334.

**Funeral expenses.**

SEC. 1587. No funeral expense of a naval officer who dies in the United States, nor expenses for travel to attend the funeral of an officer who dies there, shall be allowed. But when an officer on duty dies in a foreign country the expenses of his funeral, not exceeding his sea-pay for one month, shall be defrayed by the Government, and paid by the paymaster upon whose books the name of such officer was borne for pay.

15 July, 1870, s. 17, v. 16, p. 334.

NOTE.—Section 1581 prohibits the allowance of the funeral expenses of an officer who dies in the United States. The fact that an officer who had started on foreign service, but died in a port of the United States, at which his vessel had touched, does not relieve the case from the prohibition in the statute.—Op. XIII, p. 341, Nov. 17, 1870, case of Captain Harrison. Not held by the Navy Department as prohibiting an allowance of an officer's funeral expenses, to the limit in the statute, who dies *at sea* on the way home from a foreign station.—Case of Captain Lewis, 1880.

**Title 23, Chap. 1.**
**Voting and holding office in Territories.**

SEC. 1860. * * * Third. No officer, soldier, seaman, mariner, or other person in the Army or Navy, or attached to troops in the service of the United States, shall be allowed to vote in any Territory, by reason of being on service therein, unless such Territory is, and has been for the period of six months, his permanent domicile.

Fourth. No person belonging to the Army or Navy shall be elected to or hold any civil office or appointment in any Territory, *except officers of the Army on the retired list.*

2 March, 1853, s. 5, v. 10. p. 174.   3 March, 1883, P. E., 567.
8 Feb., 1861, s. 8. v. 12, p. 174.

**Title 26.**
**Bringing armed troops to places of election.**

SEC. 2002. No military or naval officer, or other person engaged in the civil, military, or naval service of the United States, shall order, bring, keep, or have under his authority or control, any troops or armed men at the place where any general or special election is held in any State, unless it be necessary to repel the armed enemies of the United States, or to keep the peace at the polls. [See §§ 5528, 5529, 5530, 5532.]

**Interference with freedom of elections.**

SEC. 2003. No officer of the Army or Navy of the United States shall prescribe or fix, or attempt to prescribe or fix, by proclamation, order, or otherwise, the qualifications of voters in any State, or in any manner interfere with the freedom of any election in any State, or with the exercise of the free right of suffrage in any State. [See §§ 5530, 5530.]

25 Feb., 1865, s. 1, v. 13, p. 437.

**Title 70, Chap. 7.**
**Depriving citizens of civil rights.**

SEC. 5510. Every person who, under color of any law, statute, ordinance, regulation, or custom, subjects, or causes to be subjected, any inhabitant of any State or Territory to the deprivation of any rights, privileges, or immunities, secured or protected by the Constitution and laws of the United States, or to different punishments, pains, or penalties, on account of such inhabitant being an alien, or by reason of his color or race, than are prescribed for the punishment of citizens, shall be punished by a fine of not more than one thousand dollars, or by imprisonment not more than one year, or by both.

31 May, 1870, s. 17, v. 16, p. 144.

SEC. 5528. Every officer of the Army or Navy, or other person in the civil, military, or naval service of the United States, who orders, brings, keeps, or has under his authority or control, any troops or armed men at any place where a general or special election is held in any State, unless such force be necessary to repel armed enemies of the United States or to keep the peace at the polls, shall be fined not more than five thousand dollars, and suffer imprisonment at hard labor not less than three months nor more than five years. [See § 2002, 5531, 5532.] *Unlawful presence of troops at elections.*

25 Feb., 1865, s. 1, v. 13, p. 437.

SEC. 5529. Every officer or other person in the military or naval service who, by force, threat, intimidation, order, advice, or otherwise, prevents, or attempts to prevent, any qualified voter of any State from freely exercising the right of suffrage at any general or special election in such State, shall be fined not more than five thousand dollars, and imprisoned at hard labor not more than five years. [See § 2003.] *Intimidation of voters.*

*Ibid.*, s. 2.

SEC. 5530. Every officer of the Army or Navy who prescribes or fixes, or attempts to prescribe or fix, whether by proclamation, order, or otherwise, the qualifications of voters at any election in any State, shall be punished as provided in the preceding section. [See § 2003.] *Officers of Army or Navy prescribing qualifications of voters.*

*Ibid.*, s. 1.

SEC. 5531. Every officer or other person in the military or naval service who, by force, threat, intimidation, order, or otherwise, compels, or attempts to compel, any officer holding an election in any State to receive a vote from a person not legally qualified to vote, or who imposes, or attempts to impose, any regulations for conducting any general or special election in a State different from those prescribed by law, or who interferes in any manner with any officer of an election in the discharge of his duty, shall be punished as provided in section fifty-five hundred and twenty-nine. *Officers, &c., of Army or Navy interfering with officer of election, &c.*

*Ibid.*, s. 2..

SEC. 5532. Every person convicted of any of the offenses specified in the five preceding sections, shall, in addition to the punishments therein severally prescribed, be disqualified from holding any office of honor, profit, or trust under the United States; but nothing in those sections shall be construed to prevent any officer, soldier, sailor, or marine from exercising the right of suffrage in any election district to which he may belong, if otherwise qualified according to the laws of the State in which he offers to vote. *Disqualification for holding office.*

*Ibid.*, s. s. 1, 2.

And all officers of the Navy shall be credited with the actual time they may have served as officers or enlisted men in the regular or volunteer Army or Navy, or both, and shall receive all the benefits of such actual service in all respects in the same manner as if all said service had been continuous and in the regular Navy in the lowest grade having graduated pay held by such officer since last entering the service: *Provided*, That nothing in this clause shall be so construed as to authorize any change in the dates of commission or in the relative rank of such officers: *Provided further*, That nothing herein contained shall be so construed as to give any additional pay to any such officer during the time of his service in the volunteer army or navy. *3 March, 1883. Credit for regular and volunteer service.*

March 3, 1883, P. E., p. 473. [Naval appropriation act.]
5 Aug., 1882, P. E. L., p. 287.

No decoration, or other thing, the acceptance of which is authorized by this act, and no decoration heretofore accepted, or which may hereafter be accepted, by consent of Congress, by any officer of the United States, from any foreign government, shall be publicly shown or exposed upon the person of the officer so receiving the same. *31 Jan., 1881. Acceptance of decorations.*

31 Jan., 1881, s. 2, chap. 32, P. E., p. 80.

Hereafter any present, decoration, or other thing, which shall be conferred or presented by any foreign government to any officer of the United States, civil, naval, or military, shall be tendered through the Department of State, and not to the individual in person, but such present, decoration, or other thing shall not be delivered by the Department of State unless so authorized by act of Congress.

*Ibid.*, s. 3.

22 CHAPLAINS.

3 March, 1883.
Employment on shore duty.

Hereafter no officer of the Navy shall be employed on any shore duty, except in cases specially provided by law, unless the Secretary of the Navy shall determine that the employment of an officer on such duty is required by the public interests, and he shall so state in the order of employment, and also the duration of such service, beyond which time it shall not continue.

3 March, 1883, s. 2, P. E., p. 481. [Naval appropriation act.]
5 Aug., 1882, s. 3. [Naval appropriation act.]

NOTE.—A naval officer cannot lawfully serve as a master of a private steam vessel in the merchant service without having previously obtained the license required by Sec. 4438 R. S., although he may be eligible by virtue of his commission to take command of a steam vessel of the United States in the naval service.—Op. XV, 61, Pierrepont, Oct. 26, 1875, Commander Philips' case.

(See also BRIBES, PRESENTS, ETC.—PART IV.)

## CHAPLAINS.

Sec.
1395. Number and appointment of.
1396. Qualifications of.
1397. Form of worship.
3198. Annual report.

Sec. 47.
1479. Rank.
1481. Rank when retired from age, &c.
1556. Pay.

Title 15, Chap. 1.
Number and appointment of.

SEC. 1395. There shall be in the Navy, for the public armed vessels of the United States in actual service not exceeding twenty-four chaplains, who shall be appointed by the President with the advice and consent of the Senate.

21 Apr., 1806, s. 3, v. 2, p. 390.
16 Apr., 1814, s. 5, v. 3, p. 125.
4 Aug., 1842. s. 1, v. 5, p. 500.

Qualifications of.

SEC. 1396. A chaplain shall not be less than twenty-one nor more than thirty-five years of age at the time of his appointment.

14 July, 1862. s. 7, v. 12, p. 565.

NOTE.—Under this act the President cannot appoint a chaplain above the age of thirty-five, although before its passage he had instructed the Secretary of the Navy to prepare the nomination of the person to the Senate.—Op. X, p. 324, Bates, Aug. 28, 1862.

Form of worship.

SEC. 1397. Every chaplain shall be permitted to conduct public worship according to the manner and forms of the church of which he may be a member.

1 June, 1860, s. 1, v. 12, p. 24.

Annual report.

SEC. 1398. Chaplains shall report annually to the Secretary of the Navy the official services performed by them.

1 June, 1860, s. 1, v. 12, p. 24.

Title 15, Chap. 4.
Rank.

SEC. 1479. Chaplains shall have relative rank as follows: Four, the relative rank of captain; seven, that of commander; and not more than seven, that of lieutenant-commander or lieutenant.

3 March, 1871, s. 9, v. 16, p. 536.

Rank when retired for age or length of service.

SEC. 1481. * * * Chaplains, * * * who shall have served faithfully for forty-five years, shall, when retired, have the relative rank of commodore; and * * * who have been or shall be retired at the age of sixty-two years, before having served for forty-five years, but who shall have served faithfully until retired, shall, on the completion of forty years from their entry into the service, have the relative rank of commodore.

3 March, 1871, s. 11, v. 16, p. 337.

Title 15, Chap. 8.
Pay.

SEC. 1556. Chaplains, during the first five years after date of commission, when at sea, two thousand five hundred dollars; on shore duty, two thousand dollars; on leave, or waiting orders, one thousand six hundred dollars; after five years from such date, when at sea, two thousand eight hundred dollars; on shore duty, two thousand three hundred dollars; on leave, or waiting orders, one thousand nine hundred dollars.

15 July, 1870, s. 3, v. 16, p. 331.

## CIVIL ENGINEERS.

Sec.
416. In Bureau Yards and Docks.
1413. Appointment of civil engineers.

Sec.
1478. Rank. General order.
1556. Pay.

SEC. 416. There shall be in the * * * Bureau of Yards and Docks: one civil engineer. * * *

5 July, 1862, v. 12, p. 510.

*Title 10.*
*Yards and Docks.*

SEC. 1413. The President, by and with the advice and consent of the Senate, may appoint a civil engineer * * * at each of the navy-yards where such officers may be necessary.

2 March, 1867, s. 1, v. 14, p. 490.
17 June, 1868, s. 1, v. 15, p. 69.

*Title 15, Chap. 1.*
*Appointment at navy-yards.*

SEC. 1478. Civil engineers shall have such relative rank as the President may fix.

3 March, 1871, s. 9, v. 16, p. 536.

*Title 15, Chap. 4.*
*Rank.*

The President of the United States has this day, under the provision[1] of section 1478 of the Revised Statutes, conferred relative rank on civil engineers of the Navy, and fixed the same as follows:
One with the relative rank of captain.
Two with the relative rank of commander.
Three with the relative rank of lieutenant-commander.
Four with the relative rank of lieutenant.
Civil engineers will take precedence in their corps, and with other officers with whom they hold relative rank, in accordance with the law regulating precedence of officers of the Navy.

General Order 263. 24 February, 1881.

NOTE.—See Ops. XV, p. 165 and 597; XVI, p. 203, and June 17, 1881.

SEC. 1556. * * * Civil engineers, during the first five years after date of appointment, when on duty, two thousand four hundred dollars; on leave, or waiting orders, one thousand five hundred dollars; during the second five years after such date, when on duty, two thousand seven hundred dollars; on leave, or waiting orders, one thousand eight hundred dollars; during the third five years after such date, when on duty, three thousand dollars; on leave, or waiting orders, two thousand one hundred dollars; after fifteen years from such date, when on duty, three thousand five hundred dollars; on leave, or waiting orders, two thousand six hundred dollars.

15 July, 1870, s. 3, v. 16, p. 331.

*Title 15, Chap. 8.*
*Pay.*

## CONTRACTS, SUPPLIES, ETC.

Sec.
1549. Regulations of supplies.
3648. Advances of public money on contracts.
3709. Advertisements for proposals.
3710. Opening bids.
3714. Contracts for the military or naval service, how controlled.
3718. Naval supplies to be furnished by contract.
3719. Guarantee.
3720. Record of bid and report to Congress.
3721. Purchase without advertisements.
3722. What bids may be rejected, &c.; opening bids.
3723. Contracts for foreign supplies for the Navy.
3724. Rejection of excessive bids.
3725. Hemp.
3726. Preserved meats, &c.
3727. Flour and bread.
3728. Home manufactures to be preferred; fuel.
3729. Bunting.
3730. Relinquishment of reservations on deliveries.
3731. Name of contractor to appear on supplies.
3732. Unauthorized contracts prohibited.
3733. No contract to exceed appropriation.
3734. Restrictions on commencement of new buildings.
3735. Contracts limited to one year.
3736. Restriction on purchases of land.
3737. No transfer of contract.
3738. Eight hours to be a day's work.

Sec.
3739. Members of Congress not to be interested in contracts.
3740. What interest members of Congress may have.
3741. Stipulation that no member of Congress has an interest.
3742. Penalty against officer for making contract with a member of Congress.
3743. Deposit of contracts.
3744. Contracts to be in writing.
3745. Oath to contract.
3746. Penalty for omitting returns.
3747. Instructions.
[512–515. Returns office.]
5503. Contracting beyond appropriations.
Rent of buildings.
Materials for steam-boilers.
Tobacco for the Navy.
Cotton cordage for the Navy.
Life-saving dress.
Torpedoes for the Navy.
Small stores fund.
3711. Inspection of fuel in District of Columbia; appointment of inspectors, &c.
3712. Appointment of inspectors, &c., to be notified to accounting officers.
3713. No payment without certificates.

24             CONTRACTS AND SUPPLIES.

**Title 15, Chap. 7.**
*Regulations of supplies.*

SEC. 1549. It shall be the duty of the President to make, subject to the provisions of law concerning supplies, such regulations for the purchase, preservation, and disposition of all articles, stores, and supplies for persons in the Navy, as may be necessary for the safe and economical administration of that branch of the public service.

26 Aug., 1842, s. 2, v. 5, p. 535.      3 March, 1847, s. 1, v. 9, p. 171.

NOTES.—Authority given by Congress to make a contract implies none to change it after it is made.—Op. IX, 80 and 104. [See *post*, Supreme Court Decisions.]

Where a contract is made, after advertisement, with the lowest bidder, the head of a Department has no authority to modify its terms inregard to time of delivery, or any other of its material elements.—Op. IV, Sept. 24, 1844, p. 334.

Cannot be renewed and extended at the pleasure of a head of a Department. No extension, unless for a period fixed as an alternative in the proposals, is authorized or sanctioned by law.—Op. XIII, 175, Dec. 4, 1869.

An act directing the Secretary of the Navy to enter into a contract is not a contract *per se*. The Secretary makes the contract and may vary the details.—Wallace, VIII, p. 358; C. C. I, 28.

Where the Secretary of the Navy may enter into a contract for the construction of a vessel, he may suspend the work contracted for and agree with the contractors as to the compensation to be paid for the partial completion of the same.—C. C., vol. II, p. 126; Otto, V, 91, p. 321.

When a contract is closed the general rule is that it must be executed without change of terms, which are not subject, in general. to change at the will of either party or of both parties.—Op. X, 480. Later authorities appear to favor the exercise, by the head of a Department, of a discretion to consent to modifications of detail, in the course of the execution of public contracts, when such modifications (not being in contravention of law) are found to be for the public interest, and are not of such a character as to operate to the pecuniary disadvantage of the United States.—Winthrop's Digest cites Otto 91, p. 321, and Op. XV, 481.

Where Congress authorized the examination of a claim and appropriated a sum not exceeding a fixed amount to pay it, and a less sum was found due, *held* that the appropriation was exhausted when latter amount was paid.—Op. IX, 451. See Op. IX, 449, as to principles governing payment of money to a citizen under a special act of Congress.

In breach of contract the law contemplates two elements of damage: 1, losses sustained; 2, gains prevented.—C. C. VII, 543. Affirmed by S. C.

A military board of survey is an *ex parte* tribunal; decision not binding on a contractor, its proceedings not evidence against him, &c.—C. C. VIII, p. 213. The award by a commission on a contract, can be refused to be received, or the contractor can accompany his receipt of it with a proper protest.—*Idem*. See also C. C.II, 95.

The sureties of a contractor are not responsible for fulfillment, after his death, on what are called personal contracts, where skill or taste is required.—Op. VI, p. 410.

A claim for damages was adjusted by the appropriate Department on a basis to which the contractor agreed. His acceptance and receipt, in full, for the sum allowed is a bar to his suit for a further sum.—S. C. Otto, 104, 464. See also Wallace, XIV, 535.

*Rescinding or renouncing contracts.* See C. C. I, 61, 336; III, 38; V, 406; VII, 331; VIII, 67, 319. Op. X, 416. *Government delaying or preventing performance by contractor.* See C. C., IV, 258. 271; IX, p. 244. Op. XI, 265. *Government requesting alterations.* C. C., IX, 50; Wallace, XVII, p. 502. *Willingness and efforts to perform.* C. C., VII, 93, V, 490; Wallace, VIII, 77. *Fraudulent contracts.* Wallace, VII, 463. *Set offs.* Op. IV, 380, XI, 120. C. C. XVII. 39, 236, 322. *Fines and penalties.* Op. IX, 32. *Erasures and substitution of items.* C. C. II, 366; Wallace, VIII, 489. Op. XV, 226. C. C. V, 215.

**Title 40.**
*Advances of public money on contracts.*

SEC. 3648. No advance of public money shall be made in any case whatever. And in all cases of contracts for the performance of any service, or the delivery of articles of any description, for the use of the United States, payment shall not exceed the value of the service rendered, or of the articles delivered previously to such payment. * * *

31 Jan., 1823, s. 1, v. 3, p. 723.

**Title 43.**
*Advertisements for proposals.*

SEC. 3709. All purchases and contracts for supplies or services, in any of the Departments of the Government, except for personal services, shall be made by advertising a sufficient time previously for proposals respecting the same, when the public exigencies do not require the immediate delivery of the articles, or performance of the service. When immediate delivery or performance is required by the public exigency, the articles or service required may be procured by open purchase or contract, at the places and in the manner in which such articles are usually bought and sold, or such services engaged, between individuals. [See § 3718.]

2 March, 1861, s. 10, v. 12, p. 220.     22 June, 1874, v. 18, p. 177.

NOTE.—This section invests the officer charged with the duty of contracting for supplies, or services, with discretion to dispense with advertising if the exigencies of the service require immediate delivery or performance.—C. C. VII, 93; S. C. Wallace, VIII, 77. See, also, Op. III, 437; C. C. I, 48; VII, 84; II, 96; IX, 291.

A navy paymaster purchasing under instructions from commanding officer, entitled to credit for sum expended, although purchased without advertising.—C. C. XV, 247.

SEC. 3710. Whenever proposals for supplies have been solicited, the parties responding to such solicitation shall be duly notified of the time and place of opening the bids, and be permitted to be present either in person or by attorney, and a record of each bid shall then and there be made.

*Opening bids.*

31 Jan., 1868, 8, Res., v. 16, p. 246.

### NAVAL SUPPLIES GENERALLY.

SEC. 3714. All purchases and contracts for supplies or services for the military and naval service shall be made by or under the direction of the chief officers of the Departments of War and of the Navy, respectively. And all agents or contractors for supplies or service as aforesaid shall render their accounts for settlement to the accountant of the proper Department for which such supplies or services are required, subject, nevertheless, to the inspection and revision of the officers of the Treasury in the manner before prescribed.

*Contracts for the military or naval service, how controlled.*

16 July, 1798, s. 3, v. 1, p. 610.     27 Feb., 1877, v. 19, p. 249.

SEC. 3718. All provisions, clothing, hemp, and other materials of every name and nature, for the use of the Navy [*excepting ordnance, gunpowder, or medicines, or the supplies which it may be necessary to purchase out of the United States for vessels on foreign stations; bunting, cheese, things contraband of war, preserved meats, pickles, butter, and desiccated vegetables, flour, fuel, and materials for boilers. Sections 3721, 3726, 3727, 3728, 3729, and acts of June 14, 1878, and March 3, 1881*], and the transportation thereof, when time will permit, shall be furnished by contract, by the lowest bidder, as follows: In the case of provisions, clothing, hemp, and other materials, the Secretary of the Navy shall advertise, once a week, for at least four weeks, in one or more of the principal papers published in the place where such articles are to be furnished, for sealed proposals for furnishing the same, or the whole of any particular class thereof, specifying the classes of materials and referring bidders to the several chiefs of Bureaus, who will furnish them with printed schedules, giving a full description of each and every article, with dates of delivery, and so forth. In the case of transportation of such articles, he shall advertise for a period of not less than five days. All such proposals shall be kept sealed until the day specified in such advertisement for opening the same, when they shall be opened by or under the direction of the officer making such advertisement, in the presence of at least two persons. The person offering to furnish any class of such articles, and giving satisfactory security for the performance thereof, under a forfeiture not exceeding twice the contract price in case of failure, shall receive a contract for furnishing the same. [See § 3709.]

*Naval supplies to be furnished by contract.*

3 March, 1843, v. 5, p. 617.     28 Sept., 1850, s. 1, v. 9, p. 513.
5 Aug., 1854, s. 1, v. 10, p. 585.     17 Apr., 1866, s. 4, v. 14, p. 38.

NOTES.—The acceptance of the proposition of a bidder creates a contract of the same force and effect as if a formal contract had been written out and signed by the parties.—Otto, 93. 242. C. C., XVII, 92. See Op. XV, 648, as to time in which bids may be withdrawn.

When a party furnishes sureties and binds himself for the performance of his bid, if accepted, the contract becomes mutual and binding from the moment of its acceptance, although a formal written contract is to be subsequently executed.—C. C., vol. I, 192.

A formal notice to a bidder of the acceptance of his bid and of the award of the contract to him, is beyond recall, and binding on the United States as a completed obligation. An award thus made is in the nature of a preliminary contract.—Op. XV, 226.

Head of Department has power in advertising for proposals to reserve "the right to reject any and all bids if, in his judgment, the interests of the Government require it." Right of lowest bidder perfect against others, but does not exclude the counter right of the head of the Department of considering, in the interest of the Government, the whole subject, and deciding whether it be fit that any bid should be accepted.—Op. XIV, 682.

The statutory advertisement for proposals does not enlarge, control, or change the express terms of the contract, and is to be considered as merged therein.—C. C., V, p. 416.

The advertisement and the proposals in response thereto do not form a part of the subsequent contract, and cannot be admitted to contradict or vary the terms thereof.—C. C. VIII, 501.

Under a contract for a certain quantity of an article, or more if required, a Department is not precluded from advertising for new proposals and awarding a contract for a superior article. Not obliged to receive more than the specified quantity.—Op. XVI, 183. See also Op. X, 93.

26 CONTRACTS AND SUPPLIES.

**Guarantee of bid.**

SEC. 3719. Every proposal for naval supplies invited by the Secretary of the Navy, under the preceding section, shall be accompanied by a written guarantee, signed by one or more responsible persons, to the effect that he or they undertake that the bidder, if his bid is accepted, will, at such time as may be prescribed by the Secretary of the Navy, give bond, with good and sufficient sureties, to furnish the supplies proposed; and no proposal shall be considered, unless accompanied by such guarantee. If, after the acceptance of a proposal, and a notification thereof to the bidder, he fails to give such bond within the time prescribed by the Secretary of the Navy, the Secretary shall proceed to contract with some other person for furnishing the supplies; and shall forthwith cause the difference between the amount contained in the proposal so guaranteed and the amount for which he may have contracted for furnishing the supplies, for the whole period of the proposal, to be charged up against the bidder and his guarantor; and the same may be immediately recovered by the United States, for the use of the Navy Department, in an action of debt against either or all of such persons.

10 Aug., 1846, s. 6, v. 9, p. 101.

**Record of bid and report to Congress.**

SEC. 3720. All such proposals for naval supplies shall be preserved and recorded, and reported by the Secretary of the Navy to Congress at the commencement of every regular session. The report shall contain a schedule embracing the offers by classes, indicating such as have been accepted. In case of a failure to supply the articles or to perform the work by the person entering into such contract, he and his sureties shall be liable for the forfeiture specified in such contract, as liquidated damages, to be sued for in the name of the United States.

3 March, 1843, v. 5, p. 617.

**Purchases that may be made without advertising.**

SEC. 3721. The provisions which require that supplies shall be purchased by the Secretary of the Navy from the lowest bidder, after advertisement, shall not apply to ordnance, gunpowder, or medicines, or the supplies which it may be necessary to purchase out of the United States for vessels on foreign stations, or bunting delivered for the use of the Navy, or tabacco,* or butter or cheese destined for the use of the Navy, or things contraband of war. Contracts for butter and cheese for the use of the Navy may be made for periods longer than one year, if, in the opinion of the Secretary of the Navy, economy and the quality of the ration will be promoted thereby. The Secretary of the Navy may enter into contracts for tobacco,* from time to time, as the service requires, for a period not exceeding four years; and in making such contracts he shall not be restricted to the lowest bidder, unless, in his opinion, economy and the best interests of the service will be thereby promoted. [See § 3718.]

3 March, 1845, s. 3, v. 5, p. 794. 3 March, 1847, s. 2, v. 9, p. 173.
3 Aug., 1848, s. 11, v. 9, p. 272. 2 March, 1865, s. 7, v. 13, p. 467

**What bids may be rejected.**

SEC. 3722. The chief of any Bureau of the Navy Department, in contracting for naval supplies, shall be at liberty to reject the offer of any person who, as principal or surety, has been a defaulter in any previous contract with the Navy Department. Parties who have made default as principals or sureties in any former contract shall not be received as sureties on other contracts; nor shall the copartners of any firm be received as sureties for such firm or for each other; nor, in contracts with the same Bureau, shall one contractor be received as surety for another. Every contract shall require the delivery of a specified quantity, and no bids having nominal or fictitious prices shall be considered. If more than one bid be offered by any one party, by or in the name of his or their clerk, partner, or other person, all such bids may be rejected: and no person shall be received as a contractor who is not a manufacturer of, or regular dealer in, the articles which he offers to supply. All persons offering bids shall have the right to be present when the bids are opened and inspect the same.

**Opening bids.**

3 March, 1863, s. 2, v. 12, p. 828.

**Contracts for foreign supplies for the Navy.**

SEC. 3723. No chief of a Bureau shall make any contract for supplies for the Navy, to be executed in a foreign country, except it be on first advertising for at least thirty days in two daily newspapers of the city of New York, inviting sealed bids for furnishing the supplies desired;

---

* Tobacco to be procured after advertisement. See act of March 3, 1881, *post.*

which bids shall be opened in the presence of the Secretary of the Navy and the heads of two Bureaus; and contracts shall in all cases be awarded to the lowest bidder; and paymasters for the Navy on foreign stations shall render, when practicable, with their accounts, an official certificate from the resident consul, or commercial or consular agent of the United States, if there be one, to be furnished gratuitously, vouching that all purchases and expenditures made by the paymasters were made at the ruling market-prices of the place at the time of purchase or expenditure.

3 March, 1871, s. 3, v. 16, p. 535.

SEC. 3724. Where articles are advertised and bid for in classes, and in the judgment of the Secretary of the Navy any one or more articles appear to be bid for at excessive or unreasonable prices, exceeding ten per centum above their fair market-value, he shall be authorized to reject such bid. *Rejection of excessive bids.*

4 July, 1864, s. 7, v. 13, p. 394.

SEC. 3725. All hemp, or preparations of hemp, used for naval purposes by the Government of the United States, shall be of American growth or manufacture, when the same can be obtained of as good quality and at as low a price as foreign hemp. *Hemp.*

14 July, 1862, s. 11, v. 12, p. 554.

SEC. 3726. The Secretary of the Navy is authorized to procure the preserved meats, pickles, butter, and desiccated vegetables, in such manner and under such restrictions and guarantees as in his opinion will best insure the good quality of said articles. *Preserved meats, &c.*

18 July, 1861, s. 7. v. 12, p. 265.

SEC. 3727. The Secretary of the Navy is authorized to purchase, in such manner as he shall deem most advantageous to the Government, the flour required for naval use; and to have the bread for the Navy baked from this flour by special contract under naval inspection. *Flour and bread.*

3 March, 1863, s. 4, v. 12, p. 818.

SEC. 3728. The Secretary of the Navy, in making contracts and purchases of articles for naval purposes, shall give the preference, all other things, including price and quality, being equal, to articles of the growth, production, and manufacture of the United States. In purchasing fuel for the Navy, or for naval stations and yards, the Secretary of the Navy shall have power to discriminate and purchase, in such manner as he may deem proper, that kind of fuel which is best adapted to the purpose for which it is to be used. *Home manufactures to be preferred.* *Fuel.*

28 Sept., 1850, s. 1, v. 9, pp. 513, 515.

SEC. 3729. The Secretary of War, the Secretary of the Navy, and the Secretary of the Treasury may enter into contract, in open market, for bunting of American manufacture, as their respective services require, for a period not exceeding one year, and at a price not exceeding that at which an article of equal quality can be imported. *Bunting.*

2 March, 1865, s. 7, v. 13, p. 467.

SEC. 3730. The Secretary of the Navy may relinquish and pay all reservations of the ten per centum upon deliveries made under contracts with the Navy Department, where these reservations have arisen and the contracts have been afterward extended, or where the contracts have been completed after the time of delivery, by and with the consent of the Department, or where the contracts have been dissolved by the like consent, or have been terminated, or an extension thereof has been prevented by operation of law, where no injury has been sustained by the public service. *Relinquishment of reservations on deliveries.*

17 June, 1844, s. 5, v. 5, p. 703.

NOTES.—Where a contractor failed to complete, and other parties did it on much less terms, *held* that the United States having sustained no loss, the original contractor was entitled to the 10 per cent. reservation, but not to the profits he would have made, nor to the difference between the contract price and that which others were paid. [Some special provisions were in this contract.]—Otto, 99, p. 30.

In a failure to fulfill, neither the head of the Department nor the accounting officers can pay the reservations. They have no authority to adjust claims for damages under contracts. Congress alone can afford relief.—Op. II, 481; IV, 327; VI, 516. Claim for unliquidated damages, breach of contract, cannot be entertained by the accounting officers.—Op. XIV, p. 24.

Contract fully performed and no damage whatever sustained by Government, *per diem* forfeiture not warranted.—Op. XV, p. 420.

The head of a Department may waive a forfeiture in a case of good faith where the forfeiture occurred through misfortune. "The officers of the Government are not bound, from the nature of our institutions, to perpetuate an act of injustice in the name of the United States. Op. II, p. 485."—Op. XII, p. 112.

Name of contractor to appear on supplies.

SEC. 3731. Every person who shall furnish supplies of any kind to the Army or Navy shall be required to mark and distinguish the same with the name of the contractor furnishing such supplies, in such manner as the Secretary of War and the Secretary of the Navy may, respectively, direct; and no supplies of any kind shall be received, unless so marked and distinguished.

17 July, 1862, s. 15, v. 12, p. 596.

Unauthorized contracts prohibited.

SEC. 3732. No contract or purchase on behalf of the United States shall be made, unless the same is authorized by law or is under an appropriation adequate to its fulfillment, except in the War and Navy Departments, for clothing, subsistence, forage, fuel, quarters, or transportation, which, however, shall not exceed the necessities of the current year.

2 March, 1861, s. 10, v. 12, p. 220.

NOTE.—Contracts for clothing, subsistence, forage, fuel, quarters, and transportation may be made, though there is no appropriation adequate to the fulfillment of the contract or purchase, not to exceed the necessities of the current year.—Op. XV, 124 and 209. See also Op. VI, 27.

No contract to exceed appropriation.

SEC. 3733. No contract shall be entered into for the erection, repair, or furnishing of any public building, or for any public improvement which shall bind the government to pay a larger sum of money than the amount in the Treasury appropriated for the specific purpose. [See § 5503.]

25 July, 1868, s. 3, v. 15, p. 177.

Restrictions on commencement of new buildings.

SEC. 3734. Before any new buildings for the use of the United States are commenced, the plans and full estimates therefor shall be prepared and approved by the Secretary of the Treasury, the Postmaster-General, and the Secretary of the Interior; and the cost of each building shall not exceed the amount of such estimate. [See § 3663, APPROPRIATIONS, Part III.]

15 July, 1870, v. 16, p. 296.

Contracts limited to one year.

SEC. 3735. It shall not be lawful for any of the Executive Departments to make contracts for stationery or other supplies for a longer term than one year from the time the contract is made.

31 Jan., 1868, Res., v. 15, p. 246.
24 *March*, 1874, Res., v. 18, p. 286. [Modifying as to certain articles under Post-Office Department.]

NOTE.—The head of a department is the competent judge of the matters of fact involved in the aceptance or rejection of any of the proposals for stationary.—Op. VI, p. 226.

Restriction on purchases of land.

SEC. 3736. No land shall be purchased on account of the United States, except under a law authorizing such purchase. (See PUBLIC PROPERTY and BUILDINGS, Part III.)

1 May, 1820, s. 7, v. 3, p. 568.

No transfer of contracts.

SEC. 3737. No contract or order, or any interest therein, shall be transferred by the party to whom such contract or order is given to any other party, and any such transfer shall cause the annulment of the contract or order transferred, so far as the United States are concerned. All rights of action, however, for any breach of such contract by the contracting parties, are reserved to the United States.

17 July, 1862, s. 14, v. 12, p. 596.

NOTES.—This section (3737) is intended simply for the benefit of the United States, which is not compelled to avail itself of a transfer by the contractor, but may recognize the same and accept and pay the assignee.—Ops. XVI, p. 278; XV, p. 236.

Contracts of a personal nature, importing high trust and confidence in contractors, cannot be assigned or transferred without the consent of the Department.—Op. X, p. 5.

An assignment of contract, under act of July 17, 1862, is void, and passes no title, legal or equitable. An assignment of a claim for money due under a contract passes title to the money due, as though it were the sale of a chattel.—C. C., IX, p. 156. See also C. C., V, 504.

SEC. 3738. Eight hours shall constitute a day's work for all laborers, workmen, and mechanics who may be employed by or on behalf of the Government of the United States. [See § 3689, under APPROPRIATIONS.] — Eight hours to be a day's work.

25 June, 1868, v. 15, p. 77.

See S. C. 94, 400. Op. XII, 530; XIII, 29, 424; XIV, 37, 45, 128; XVI, 58. 1882.

CONGRESSMEN AND PUBLIC OFFICERS NOT TO BE INTERESTED IN CONTRACTS.

SEC. 3739. No member of or delegate to Congress shall directly or indirectly, himself, or by any other person in trust for him, or for his use or benefit, or on his account, undertake, execute, hold, or enjoy, in whole or in part, any contract or agreement made or entered into in behalf of the United States, by any officer or person authorized to make contracts on behalf of the United States. Every person who violates this section shall be deemed guilty of a misdemeanor, and shall be fined three thousand dollars. All contracts or agreements made in violation of this section shall be void; and whenever any sum of money is advanced on the part of the United States, in consideration of any such contract or agreement, it shall be forthwith repaid; and in case of refusal or delay to repay the same, when demanded, by the proper officer of the Department under whose authority such contract or agreement shall have been made or entered into, every person so refusing or delaying, together with his surety or sureties, shall be forthwith prosecuted at law for the recovery of any such sum of money so advanced. — Title 43. Members of Congress not to be interested in contracts.

21 April, 1808, s. 1, v. 2, p. 484.

NOTE.—There is no law preventing government officers, Executive branch, contracting with the Government in matters separate from their offices and in no way connected with the performance of their official duties, nor against their acquiring an interest in contracts after they are procured.—Op. XIV, 483.

SEC. 3740. Nothing contained in the preceding section shall extend or be construed to extend, to any contract or agreement, made or entered into, or accepted, by any incorporated company, where such contract or agreement is made for the general benefit of such incorporation or company; nor to the purchase or sale of bills of exchange or other property by any member of or delegate to Congress, where the same are ready for delivery, and payment therefor is made, at the time of making or entering into the contract or agreement. — What interest members of Congress may have.

21 April, 1808, s. 2, v. 2, p. 484.    27 Feb., 1877, v. 19, p. 249.

SEC. 3741. In every such contract or agreement to be made or entered into, or accepted by or on behalf of the United States, there shall be inserted an express condition that no member of or delegate to Congress shall be admitted to any share or part of such contract or agreement, or to any benefit to arise thereupon. — Stipulation that no member of Congress has an interest.

21 April, 1808, s. 3, v. 2, p. 484.    27 Feb., 1877, v. 19, p. 240.

SEC. 3742. Every officer who, on behalf of the United States, directly or indirectly makes or enters into any contract, bargain, or agreement in writing or otherwise, other than such as are hereinbefore excepted, with any member of or delegate to Congress, shall be deemed guilty of a misdemeanor, and shall be fined three thousand dollars. — Penalty against officer for making contract with a member of Congress.

21 April, 1808, s. 4, v. 2, p. 484.    27 Feb., 1877, v. 19, p. 249.

MAKING AND DISPOSITION OF CONTRACTS.

SEC. 3743. All contracts to be made, by virtue of any law, and requiring the advance of money, or in any manner connected with the settlement of public accounts, shall be deposited in the office of the First Comptroller of the Treasury of the United States, the Second Comptroller of the Treasury of the United States, or the Commissioner of Customs, respectively, according to the nature thereof, within ninety days after their respective dates. — Title 43. Deposit of contracts.

16 July, 1798, s. 6, v. 1, p. 610.    27 Feb., 1877, v. 19, p. 249.

SEC. 3744. It shall be the duty of the Secretary of War, of the Secretary of the Navy, and of the Secretary of the Interior, to cause and require every contract made by them severally on behalf of the Government, or by their officers under them appointed to make such contracts, to be reduced to writing, and signed by the contracting parties with their names at the end thereof; a copy of which shall be filled by the — Contracts to be in writing.

officer making and signing the contract in the Returns Office of the Department of the Interior, as soon after the contract is made as possible, and within thirty days, together with all bids, offers, and proposals to him made by persons to obtain the same, and with a copy of any advertisement he may have published inviting bids, offers, or proposals for the same. All the copies and papers in relation to each contract shall be attached together by a ribbon and seal, and marked by numbers in regular order, according to the number of papers composing the whole return. [See §§ 512-515, *post.*]

2 June, 1862, s. 1, v. 12, p. 411.

NOTES.—The requirement in section 3744, "to be reduced to writing and signed by the contracting parties," is mandatory and obligatory on contractors and officers. Oral agreement void as an executory contract.—C. C., IV, p. 75, and V, p. 65, 338.

This section is not infringed by the proper officer having charge of such matter accepting delivery of supplies after the day stipulated, nor is a verbal agreement to extend the time of performance invalid.—Wallace, XIX, p. 17; C. C., IX, 54. When an "emergency" is declared, need not be in writing.—C. C., IX, 187 and 291.

Oath to contract.
SEC. 3745. It shall be the further duty of the officer, before making his return, according to the preceding section, to affix to the same his affidavit in the following form, sworn to before some magistrate having authority to administer oaths: "I do solemnly swear (or affirm) that the copy of contract hereto annexed is an exact copy of a contract made by me personally with ———; that I made the same fairly without any benefit or advantage to myself, or allowing any such benefit or advantage corruptly to the said ———, or any other person; and that the papers accompanying include all those relating to the said contract, as required by the statute in such case made and provided."

*Ibid.*, s. 2.

Penalty for omitting returns.
SEC. 3746. Every officer who makes any contract, and fails or neglects to make return of the same, according to the provisions of the two preceding sections, unless from unavoidable accident or causes not within his control, shall be deemed guilty of a misdemeanor, and shall be fined not less than one hundred dollars nor more than five hundred, and imprisoned not more than six months.

*Ibid.*, s. 3.

Instructions.
SEC. 3747. It shall be the duty of the Secretary of War, of the Secretary of the Navy, and of the Secretary of the Interior to furnish every officer appointed by them with authority to make contracts on behalf of the Government with a printed letter of instructions, setting forth the duties of such officer, under the two preceding sections, and also to furnish therewith forms, printed in blank, of contracts to be made, and the affidavit of returns required to be affixed thereto, so that all the instruments may be as nearly uniform as possible.

*Ibid.*, s. 5.

Title 11, Chap. 8.
Returns Office.
SEC. 512. The Secretary of the Interior shall from time to time provide a proper apartment, to be called the Returns Office, in which he shall cause to be filed the returns of contracts made by the Secretary of War, the Secretary of the Navy, and the Secretary of the Interior, and shall appoint a clerk of the first class to attend to the same.

Clerk to file returns.
SEC. 513. The clerk of the Returns Office shall file all returns made to the Office, so that the same may be of easy access, keeping all returns made by the same officer in the same place, and numbering them in the order in which they are made.

Index book.
SEC. 514. The clerk of the Returns Office shall provide and keep an index-book, with the names of the contracting parties, and the number of each contract opposite to the names; and shall submit the index-book and returns to any person desiring to inspect it.

Copies of returns.
SEC. 515. The clerk of the Returns Office shall furnish copies of such returns to any person paying therefor at the rate of five cents for every one hundred words, to which copies certificates shall be appended in every case by the clerk making the same, attesting their correctness, and that each copy so certified is a full and complete copy of the return.

2 June, 1862, ss. 2, 4, v. 12, p. 412.

CONTRACTS AND SUPPLIES. 31

### ERECTION, REPAIR, AND RENT OF BUILDINGS.

SEC. 5503. Every officer of the Government who knowingly contracts for the erection, repair, or furnishing of any public building, or for any public improvement, to pay a larger amount than the specific sum appropriated for such purpose, shall be punished by imprisonment not less than six months nor more than two years, and shall pay a fine of two thousand dollars. [See §§ 3733, 3734.] — *Title 70, Chap. 6. Contracting beyond specific appropriation.*

25 July, 1868, s. 3, v. 15, p. 177.

Hereafter no contract shall be made for the rent of any building, or part of any building, to be used for the purposes of the Government in the District of Columbia, until an appropriation therefor shall have been made in terms by Congress, and that this clause be regarded as notice to all contractors or lessors of any such building or any part of building. — *3 March, 1877. Contract for rent of buildings in the District of Columbia.*

22 June, 1874, v. 18, p. 133.   3 March, 1877, v. 19, p. 370.\*

And where buildings are rented for public use in the District of Columbia, the Executive Departments are authorized, whenever it shall be advantageous to the public interest, to rent others in their stead: *Provided*, That no increase in the number of buildings now in use, nor in the amounts paid for rents, shall result therefrom.\* — *15 June, 1880. Rent of buildings.*

15 June, 1880, v. 21, p. 228.   5 Aug., 1882, P. E. L., 241, ch. 389.

### BOILER MATERIALS.

That the Secretary of the Navy be, and he is hereby, authorized to purchase, at the lowest market price, such plate iron and other material as may enter into the construction of steam boilers for the Navy without advertising for bids to furnish the same: *Provided*, That he shall cause to be sent to the principal dealers and manufacturers of iron and such other materials as may be required, specifications of the quality, description, and character of such iron and materials so required: *And provided further*, That such plate iron and materials shall be subjected to the same tests and inspection as now provided for, and which inspection and tests shall be made publicly and in presence of such bidders or their authorized agents as may choose to attend at the making thereof. — *14 June, 1878. Materials for steam boilers. Notice to dealers. Tests.*

14 June, 1878, v. 20, p. 253.

### TOBACCO.

That the Secretary of the Navy be, and he is hereby, directed to cause all purchases of tobacco for the use of the Navy to be made in the city of Washington, and as follows: — *3 March, 1881. Tobacco, how purchased.*

In the month of February or March of each year the Secretary of the Navy shall cause proposals for bids for supplying the Navy with tobacco during the next year to be advertised thirty days in one daily newspaper in each of the cities of New York, Harrisburg, Pennsylvania, Baltimore, Richmond, Raleigh, North Carolina, Saint Louis, Louisville, Nashville, Hartford, Connecticut, Detroit, Cairo, Illinois, and Chicago; said tobacco to be manufactured during the months of June, July, August, and September; the bids to be accompanied by samples of the tobacco which each bidder may propose to furnish. The lowest bid for furnishing tobacco equal to the United States Navy standard now in use shall be accepted.

3 March, 1881, v. 21, p. 509.

### COTTON CORDAGE.

That the Secretary of the Navy be authorized and directed to introduce into the naval service rope and cordage manufactured of cotton according to the recent methods to such an extent as will furnish a fair test of the value and efficiency thereof as compared with the kinds now in use: *Provided, however*, That no person shall have any claim whatever against the United States or any department thereof or receive any compensation therefor. — *10 June, 1880. Cotton cordage for the Navy.*

10 June, 1880, v. 21, p. 172.

---

\*The act of August 5, 1882, required the heads of the Departments to submit a statement of buildings rented, and estimates for the year ending 30 June, 1884, for rental.

## LIFE-SAVING DRESS.

3 March, 1883.
Life-saving dress.

The Secretary of the Navy is authorized and empowered, within his discretion, to constitute and introduce, as a portion of the equipment of the Navy, the life-saving dress adopted and approved by the Life-Saving Service of the United States.

3 March, 1883, ch. 97, P. E. L., p. 475. [Naval appropriation act.]

## TORPEDOES.

Torpedoes.

For the purchase and manufacture, after full investigation and test in the United States under the direction of the Secretary of the Navy, of torpedoes adapted to naval warfare, or of the right to manufacture the same and for the fixtures and machinery necessary for operating the same, one hundred thousand dollars: *Provided*, That no part of said money shall be expended for the purchase or manufacture of any torpedo or of the right to manufacture the same until the same shall have been approved by the Secretary of the Navy, after a favorable report to be made to him by a board of naval officers to be created by him to examine and test said torpedoes and inventions.

*Idem.*

## SMALL STORES FUND.

14 Feb., 1879.
Small stores fund.

From and after the first day of April, eighteen hundred and seventy-nine, the value of issues of small stores shall be credited to a fund to be designated as the "small stores fund", in the same manner as the value of the issues of clothing is now credited to the "clothing fund"; the resources of the fund to be used hereafter in the purchase of supplies of small stores for issue. * * *

14 Feb., 1879, v. 20, p. 284.

## INSPECTION OF FUEL.—DISTRICT OF COLUMBIA.

Title 43.

Inspection of fuel in District of Columbia.

Appointment of inspectors, &c.

SEC. 3711. It shall not be lawful for any officer or person in the civil, military, or naval service of the United States in the District of Columbia to purchase anthracite or bituminous coal or wood for the public service except on condition that the same shall, before delivery, be inspected and weighed or measured by some competent person to be appointed by the head of the Department or chief of the branch of the service for which the purchase is made. The person so appointed shall, before entering upon the duty of inspector, weigher, and measurer, and to the satisfaction of the appointing officer, give bond, with not less than two sureties, in the penal sum of five thousand dollars, and with condition that each ton of coal weighed by him shall consist of two thousand two hundred and forty pounds, and that each cord of wood to be so measured shall be of the standard measure of one hundred and twenty-eight cubic feet. The inspector, weigher, and measurer so appointed shall be entitled to receive from the venders of fuel weighed and measured by him twenty cents for each ton of coal weighed, and nine cents for each cord of wood measured by him. Each load or parcel of wood or coal weighed and measured by him shall be accompanied by his certificate of the number of tons or pounds of coal and the number of cords or parts of cords of wood in each load or parcel.

11 July, 1870, s. 1, v. 16, p. 229.

Accounting officer to be notified.

SEC. 3712. The proper accounting officer of the Treasury shall be furnished with a copy of the appointment of each inspector, weigher, and measurer appointed under the preceding section.

*Ibid.*, s. 2.

No payment without certificate.

SEC. 3713. It shall not be lawful for any accounting officer to pass or allow to the credit of any disbursing officer in the District of Columbia any money paid by him for purchase of anthracite or bituminous coal or for wood, unless the voucher therefor is accompanied by a certificate of the proper inspector, weigher, and measurer that the quantity paid for has been determined by such officer.

*Ibid.*

# DESERTERS AND DESERTION.

Sec.
1420. Deserters not to be enlisted.
1553. Enticing persons to desert.
1624. Punishment for desertion, enlisting deserters, &c.
1996. Citizenship forfeited.

Sec.
1997. When not to be held as a deserter.
1998. Avoiding draft.
4749. Certain soldiers and sailors not to be deemed deserters.
5455. Enticing desertion, harboring deserters.

SEC. 1420. No * * * deserter from the naval or military service of the United States shall be enlisted in the naval service. *Title 15, Chap. 1. Deserters not to be enlisted.*

3 March, 1865, s. 18, v. 13, p. 490.

SEC. 1553. Any person who shall entice or procure, or attempt to entice or procure, any seaman or other person in the naval service of the United States, or who has been recruited for such service, to desert therefrom, or who shall in anywise aid or assist any such seaman or other person in deserting, or in attempting to desert from such service, or who shall harbor, conceal, protect, or in anywise assist any such seaman or other person who may have deserted from said service, knowing him to have deserted therefrom, or who shall refuse to give up and deliver such person on the demand of an officer authorized to receive him, shall be punished by imprisonment for not less than six months nor more than three years, and by fine of not more than two thousand dollars, to be enforced in any court of the United States having jurisdiction. *Title 15, Chap. 7. Enticing persons to desert.*

1 July, 1864, v. 13, p. 343.

SEC. 1624. * * * * * * * *Title 15, Chap.10.*

ART. 4. The punishment of death, or such other punishment as a court-martial may adjudge, may be inflicted on any person in the naval service— *Offenses punishable by death.*

who * * * * * *

Sixth. * * , in time of war, deserts or entices others to desert; *Desertion in time of war.*

Seventh. * * , in time of war, deserts or betrays his trust, or entices or aids others to desert or betray their trust; *Deserting trust.*

17 July, 1862, s. 1, v. 12, p. 600.   23 April, 1800, art. 17, v. 2, p. 47.

ART. 8. Such punishment as a court-martial may adjudge may be inflicted on any person in the Navy—

who * * * * * *

Twenty-first. * * in time of peace, deserts or attempts to desert, or aids and entices others to desert; *Desertion in time of peace.*

Twenty-second. Or receives or entertains any deserter from any other vessel of the Navy, knowing him to be such, and does not, with all convenient speed, give notice of such deserter to the commander of the vessel to which he belongs, or to the commander-in-chief, or to the commander of the squadron. *Harboring deserters.*

17 July, 1862, s. 1, v. 12, p. 600.   23 April, 1800, v. 2, p. 47.

ART. 9. Any officer who absents himself from his command without leave, may, by the sentence of a court-martial, be reduced to the rating of an ordinary seaman. *Officers absent without leave.*

16 May, 1864, s. 2, v. 13, p. 75.

ART. 10. Any commissioned officer of the Navy or Marine Corps who, having tendered his resignation, quits his post or proper duties without leave, and with intent to remain permanently absent therefrom, prior to due notice of the acceptance of such resignation, shall be deemed and punished as a deserter. *Desertion by resignation.*

5 Aug., 1861, s. 2, v. 12, p. 316.

ART. 19. Any officer who knowingly enlists into the naval service any deserter from the naval or military service of the United States * * shall be punished as a court-martial may direct. *Enlisting deserters.*

3 March, 1865, s. 18, v. 13, p. 490.   12 May, 1879, v. 21, p. 3.

SEC. 1996. All persons who deserted the military or naval service of the United States and did not return thereto or report themselves to a provost-marshal within sixty days after the issuance of the proclamation by the President, dated the 11th day of March, 1865, are deemed to have *Title 25. Rights as citizens forfeited for desertion, &c.*

11181——3

DESERTERS AND DESERTION.

voluntarily relinquished and forfeited their rights of citizenship, as well as their right to become citizens; and such deserters shall be forever incapable of holding any office of trust or profit under the United States, or of exercising any rights of citizens thereof.

3 March, 1865, s. 21, v. 13, p. 490.

**Certain soldiers and sailors not to incur the forfeitures of the last section.**

SEC. 1997. No soldier or sailor, however, who faithfully served according to his enlistment until the 19th day of April, 1865, and who, without proper authority or leave first obtained, quit his command or refused to serve after that date, shall be held to be a deserter from the Army or Navy; but this section shall be construed solely as a removal of any disability such soldier or sailor may have incurred, under the preceding section, by the loss of citizenship and of the right to hold office, in consequence of his desertion. [See § 4749.]

19 July, 1867, v. 15, p. 14.

**Avoiding the draft.**

SEC. 1998. Every person who hereafter deserts the military or naval service of the United States, or who, being duly enrolled, departs the jurisdiction of the district in which he is enrolled, or goes beyond the limits of the United States, with intent to avoid any draft into the military or naval service, lawfully ordered, shall be liable to all the penalties and forfeitures of section nineteen hundred and ninety-six.

3 March, 1865, s. 21, v. 13, p. 490.

**Title 57.**

**Certain soldiers and sailors not to be deemed deserters, &c.**

SEC. 4749. No soldier or sailor shall be taken or held to be a deserter from the Army or Navy who faithfully served according to his enlistment until the nineteenth day of April, eighteen hundred and sixty-five, and who, without proper authority or leave first obtained, quit his command or refused to serve after that date; but nothing herein contained shall operate as a remission of any forfeiture incurred by any such soldier or sailor of his pension; but this section shall be construed solely as a removal of any disability such soldier or sailor may have incurred by the loss of his citizenship in consequence of his desertion. [See § 2438, BOUNTY LAND, Part IV.]

19 July, 1867, v. 15, p. 14.

**Title 70, Chap. 5.**

**Enticing desertions from the military or naval service.**

SEC. 5455. Every person who entices or procures, or attempts or endeavors to entice or procure, any soldier in the military service of the United States, or who has been recruited for such service, to desert therefrom, or who aids any such soldier in deserting or attempting to desert from such service, or who harbors, conceals, protects, or assists any such soldier who may have deserted from such service, knowing him to have deserted therefrom, or who refuses to give up and deliver such soldier on the demand of any officer authorized to receive him, shall be punished by imprisonment not less than six months nor more than two years, and by a fine not exceeding five hundred dollars; and every person who entices or procures, or attempts or endeavors to entice or procure, any seaman or other person in the naval service of the United States, or who has been recruited for such service, to desert therefrom, or who aids any such seamen or other person in deserting or in attempting to desert from such service, or who harbors, conceals, protects, or assists any such seaman or other person who may have deserted from such service, knowing him to have deserted therefrom, or who refuses to give up and deliver such sailor or other person on the demand of any officer authorized to receive him, shall be punished by imprisonment not less than six months nor more than three years, and by a fine of not more than two thousand dollars, to be enforced in any court of the United States having jurisdiction.

3 March, 1863, s. 24, v. 12, p. 735.
1 July, 1864, v. 13, p. 343.
27 February, 1877, v. 19, p. 253.

NOTES.—The President may grant conditional pardon for desertion; may remit a part of the penalty or punishment without remitting the whole; may reenfranchise without giving right to forfeited pay.—Op. XIV, 124.
If pay forfeited or a fine has passed into the Treasury, by a covering warrant or otherwise, neither can be released without authority of Congress.—Op. VIII, 281; XIV, 599; and XVI, 1.
Desertion is a *continuing* offense. Limitation to trial begins to run from commencement of the offense, except where, by reason of "manifest impediment," the accused is not amenable to justice within two years from that time. In such a case it runs from the removal of the impediment. Continuing commission limited by the obligation to serve under engagement. When that ceases the commission terminates in cases not excepted. "Amenable" signifies within

the reach and power of the military authorities to bring to trial.—Op. XV, p. 152, Taft, Sept. 1, 1876.

Where forfeiture or loss of pay is made part of a sentence, in addition to confinement or suspension from duty, the former may be remitted by the proper authority, in whole or in part, without also remitting the latter.—Op. XV, p. 175. Taft, Nov. 9, 1876.

Forfeiture by desertion does not include money of the deserter found in possession of or deposited with paymaster.—Op. XIII, p. 210, Hoar, Feb. 8, 1870.

The honorable discharge of a soldier is a formal, final judgment passed by the Government on his entire military record, and an authoritative declaration that he left the service in a *status of honor*. As such it relieves him from a charge of desertion appearing on the rolls. Does not restore pay and allowances forfeited by sentence of a military court-martial for desertion.—Court of Claims, VIII, 110; IX, 190; Wallace, XV, 34.

A seaman charged before a court-martial with desertion may be found guilty of attempting to desert.—Howard, 20, p. 65.

In a trial for theft and desertion, sentence and conviction disapproved and prisoner restored to duty. Action of reviewing officer in effect an acquittal by the court. No authority to withhold pay on account of alleged desertion.—Op. XIII, p. 459, Bristow, June 21, 1871.

## DISMISSAL AND RESIGNATION OF OFFICERS.

APPOINTMENTS, ETC.   See Addenda, PART I.

Sec.
1229. Dismissal in time of peace.
1441. Officers dismissed or resigning to escape dismissal.
1624. Dismissal of officers.  Art. 36.

Sec.
1624. Officers dismissed by President may demand trial.  Art. 37.
—— Act amending article 37.
—— Failing in examination.

SEC. 1229. * * * No * * * * officer in the military, or naval service shall in time of peace be dismissed from service except upon and in pursuance of the sentence of a court-martial to that effect, or in commutation thereof.

*Title 14, Chap. 1.*

15 July, 1870, s. 17, v. 16, p. 319.   13 July, 1866, s. 5, v. 14, p. 92.

[Section 1230 of the Revised Statutes is almost the same as art. 37, sec. 1624, except the words "since 3d March, 1865," are omitted.]

SEC. 1441. No officer of the Navy who has been dismissed by the sentence of a court-martial, or suffered to resign in order to escape such dismissal, shall ever again become an officer of the Navy.

*Title 15, Chap. 2.*
Officers dismissed, or resigning to escape dismissal.

16 July, 1862, s. 11, v. 12, p. 585.

NOTE.—Congress did not intend by this clause to preclude the President from reappointing officers dismissed by sentence of court-martial to whom he has extended a pardon. Pardon purges the offense, but does not of itself restore lost position.—Op. XI, p. 19, March 12, 1864.

SEC. 1624, ART. 36. No officer shall be dismissed from the naval service except by the order of the President or by sentence of a general court-martial; and in time of peace no officer shall be dismissed except in pursuance of the sentence of a general court-martial or in mitigation thereof.

*Title 15, Chap. 10.*
Dismissal of officers.

13 July, 1866, s. 5, v. 14, p. 92.

SEC. 1624, ART. 37. When any officer, dismissed by order of the President since 3d March, 1865, makes, in writing, an application for trial, setting forth, under oath that he has been wrongfully dismissed, the President shall, as soon as the necessities of the service may permit, convene a court-martial to try such officer on the charges on which he shall have been dismissed. And if such court-martial shall not be convened within six months from the presentation of such application for trial, or if such court, being convened, shall not award dismissal or death as the punishment of such officer, the order of dismissal by the President shall be void. [See act of June 22, 1874, and notes *infra*.]

Officer dismissed by the President may demand trial.

3 March, 1865, s. 12, v. 13, p. 489.

That the accounting officers of the Treasury be, and are hereby, prohibited from making any allowance to any officer of the Navy who has been, or may hereafter be, dismissed from the service and restored to the same under the provisions of the twelfth section of the act of March third, eighteen hundred and sixty-five, entitled, "An act to amend the several acts heretofore passed to provide for the enrolling and calling out the national forces, and for other purposes," [sec. 1624, R. S.] to exceed more than pay as on leave for six months from the date of dismissal, unless it shall appear that the officer demanded in

June 22, 1874.
Pay on restoration.

**36**  DISMISSAL AND RESIGNATION OF OFFICERS.

writing, addressed to the Secretary of the Navy, and continued to demand as often as once in six months, a trial as provided for in said act.

22 June, 1874, s. 2, v. 18, p. 191.

NOTE.—An officer, between date of dismissal and restoration, not demanding, in writing, as often as six months, a trial, when restored is not entitled to more than "pay as on leave for six months", from date of dismissal.—Op. XV, 569, Taft, July 21, 1876.

**Aug. 5, 1882.**
**Officers failing in examination.**

Whenever on an inquiry had pursuant to law, concerning the fitness of an officer of the Navy for promotion, it shall appear that such officer is unfit to perform at sea the duties of the place to which it is proposed to promote him, by reason of drunkenness, or from any cause arising from his own misconduct, and having been informed of and heard upon the charges against him, he shall not be placed on the retired-list of the Navy, and if the finding of the board be approved by the President, he shall be discharged with not more than one year's pay. [One year's *leave* pay, as decided by the accounting officers in 1882.]

5 Aug., 1882, P. E., p. 286. [Naval appropriation act.]

NOTES.—After a sentence of dismissal from the service has been approved and carried into execution, the President cannot reconsider his approval and revoke the sentence.—Op. IV, p. 274, Nov. 3, 1843; Op. VII, p. 99, April 11, 1855; Op. X, p. 64, June 13, 1861; Op. XI, pp. 19 and 251, March 12, 1864, and June 20, 1865, respectively; Op. XV, p. 291 and Feb. 24, 1881.
The President by and with the advice and consent of the Senate, can supersede a military or naval officer by the nomination of a successor. The confirmation and appointment of the latter vacates the office of the former.—Blake's case, Supreme Court, Otto, 103, p. 227; also see Otto, 97, p. 426, Mimmack's case, and Otto, 102, 426, McElrath's case.
So much of this section (1624) as relates to dismissal in time of peace did not take effect before August 20, 1866, on which day, in contemplation of law, the rebellion against the national authority was suppressed.—S. C., Otto, 102, p. 426.
Not the effect of this act (sec. 1624) to withdraw the power of the President to supersede an officer by appointment, by and with the advice and consent of the Senate, of another.—Otto, 103, p. 226.
Article 37, section 1624 (12 of act of March 3, 1865, 13 Statutes, 489), is constitutional and imperative. It provides, in certain contingencies, for the restoration of the officer to the service, and leaves the dismissal in full force if those contingencies do not happen.—Op. XII, p. 4, Stanbery, August 6, 1866.
The President in 1861 had the power to dismiss an officer from the Marine Corps.—Tyler's case, Op. 15, p. 421, Jan. 8, 1878.
Dismissal of an acting master, March, 1862, by the Secretary of the Navy, lawful. In the absence of legislation, the Secretary had a right to determine at what time an acting appointment should cease.—A. M. Smith's case, Op. XV, p. 560, April 25, 1876.
The Secretary of the Navy had the power to dismiss an "acting gunner on temporary service" in the volunteer Navy. The power to appoint gunners to an undefined extent does not preclude the appointment of acting gunners also.—Soper's case, Op. XV, p. 564, June 10, 1876.
The 17th section of the act of July 12, 1862, chap. 200, v. 12, p. 594, authorized and requested the President to dismiss and discharge from the military service, either in the Army, Navy, Marine Corps, or volunteer force in the United States service, any officer for any cause which, in his judgment, either rendered such officer unsuitable for, or whose dismission would promote, the public service. This section was repealed by section 5 of an act approved July 13, 1866, chap. 176, v. 14, p. 90.
In a case where an officer was dismissed by the President, and the dismissal revoked in due form, no unreasonable time having elapsed, the vacancy not having been filled, and the rights of other parties not having intervened, the revocation presents only a case of Executive authority, which has repeatedly been exercised; but in view of late decisions the court gave judgment for the claimant in order that the case might go to the Supreme Court.—C. C., XVII, p. 344, *Corson's* case, Dec., 1881, term.

**Title 15, Chap. 10.**
**Desertion by resignation.**

SEC. 1624, ART. 10. Any commissioned officer of the Navy or Marine Corps who, having tendered his resignation, quits his post or proper duties without leave, and with intent to remain permanently absent therefrom, prior to due notice of the acceptance of such resignation, shall be deemed and punished as a deserter.

5 Aug., 1861, s. 2, v. 12, p. 316.

NOTES.—An offer to resign is revokable by the officer prior to its acceptance. After acceptance and before it has taken effect it may be modified or withdrawn entirely by the consent of both parties. Control over it, in point of duration, extends no further.—Op. XIV, p. 260, June 17, 1873; Op. XII, p. 555, Feb. 10, 1869.
A resignation tendered to take effect on a future day, and placed in the hands of a party to be delivered to the President, can be recalled before delivery. Its subsequent delivery is not binding.—Op, XIII, p. 77, June 2, 1869.
A valid resignation of a military officer, followed by an unconditional acceptance of it, operates to remove the incumbent, and a new appointment is required to restore him to the office.—Op. XII, p. 555, Feb. 10, 1869. But in cases where the officer was insane at time of resignation, his action was held to be a nullity and capable of being rectified.—Ops. III, p. 641, VI, p. 456, and X,

p. 229. If the vacancy has been properly filled, the acceptance cannot be legally revoked.—Op. XV, p. 469, March 22, 1878; Otto, 103, p. 227.

A civil officer has a right to resign at his own pleasure, and it is only necessary that it should be received by the Executive. Its acceptance or rejection by him is unimportant.—U. S. vs. Wright, 1 McLean, 509.

A resignation does not become operative until the officer is officially notified of the acceptance of the same. Mere acceptance, without notice, does not give effect to the resignation. It is not until due notice of the same is received that the officer is legally separated from the Army and made a civilian, and up to the date of such notice he is entitled to pay.—Winthrop's Digest, p. 430.

## ENGINEER CORPS. [SEE ALSO NAVAL ACADEMY.]

Sec.
424. Chief of Bureau.
1390. Engineer Corps, number and rank.
—— Restriction on promotions.
1391 Appointment of.
1392. Qualifications of.
1393. Engineer of the fleet.
1471. Rank and title of Chief of Bureau.

Sec.
1476. Rank, active list.
1481. Rank, retired, &c.
1484. Engineer officers graduated at the Academy.
1488. No authority to exercise military command.
1556. Pay of engineers.
—— Assignment to colleges.

SEC. 424. The Chief of the Bureau of Steam Engineering shall be appointed from the chief engineers of the Navy, and shall be a skillful engineer.

Title 10.
Chief of Bureau.

5 July, 1862, s. 1, v. 12, p. 510.

SEC. 1390. The active list of the Engineer Corps of the Navy shall consist of seventy chief engineers, who shall be divided into three grades, by relative rank, as provided in Chapter Four of this Title; [See § 1476.]

Title 15, Chap. 1,
Engineer Corps, number and rank.

Ten chief engineers;
Fifteen chief engineers; and
Forty-five chief engineers, who shall have the relative rank of lieutenant-commander or lieutenant.

And each and all of the above-named officers of the Engineer Corps shall have the pay of chief engineers of the Navy, as now provided.

*Sixty* passed assistant engineers, who shall have the relative rank of lieutenant or master†; and

*Forty* assistant engineers, who shall have the relative rank of master or ensign; and the said assistant engineers shall have the pay of *passed* and *assistant* engineers of the Navy, respectively, as now provided.*

3 March, 1871, s. 7, v. 16, p. 536.
24 Feb., 1874, v. 18, p. 17.
5 Aug., 1882, P. E. L., 286.

Hereafter only one-half of the vacancies shall be filled by promotion until the number is reduced as required by act of August 5, 1882. [Sec. 1390.]

March 3, 1883.
Restriction on promotion.

3 March, 1883. [Naval appropriation act.]

SEC. 1391. Engineers shall be appointed by the President, by and with the advice and consent of the Senate.

Title 15, Chap. 1.
Appointment.

31 Aug., 1842, s. 6, v. 5, p. 577.
3 March, 1845, s. 7, v. 5, p. 794.
25 July, 1866, s. 7, v. 14, p. 223.

SEC. 1392. No person under nineteen or over twenty-six years of age shall be appointed an *assistant* engineer in the Navy; nor shall any person be appointed or promoted in the Engineer Corps until after he has been found qualified by a board of competent engineers and medical officers designated by the Secretary of the Navy, and has complied with existing regulations.

Qualifications.

3 March, 1871, s. 8, v. 16, p. 536.
24 Feb., 1874, v. 18, p. 17.
25 July, 1866, s. 7, v. 14, p. 223.

NOTE.—The naval appropriation act approved August 5, 1882, requires that thereafter all appointments to the Engineer Corps shall be made from naval cadets, graduates of the year in which the vacancies which they are appointed to fill shall occur. See NAVAL ACADEMY.

SEC. 1393. The President may designate among the chief engineers in the service, and appoint to every fleet or squadron, an engineer, who shall be denominated "engineer of the fleet."

Engineer of the fleet.

21 April, 1864, s. 7, v. 13, p. 54.

* The titles of first and second assistant engineers were changed to passed and assistant engineers, respectively, Feb. 24, 1874. The grade of third assistant was abolished July 15, 1870.
† Lieutenant of the junior grade. (March 3, 1883.)

38                        ENGINEER CORPS.

**Title 15, Chap. 4.**   SEC. 1471. The Chief * * * of the Bureau of Steam Engineering
Rank of Chief   shall have the relative rank of commodore while holding said position,
of Bureau.      * * * and the title of engineer-in-chief.
                               3 March, 1871, s. 12, v. 16, p. 537.

Rank.            SEC. 1476. Officers of the Engineer Corps on the active list shall have
                relative rank as follows:
                 Of the chief engineers, ten shall have the relative rank of captain,
On the active   fifteen that of commander, and forty-five that of lieutenant-commander
list.           or lieutenant.
                 *Passed* assistant engineers shall have the relative rank of lieutenant
                or master*, and *assistant* engineers that of master* or ensign.
                               3 March, 1871, s. 7, v. 16, p. 536.
                               24 Feb., 1874, v. 18, p. 17.

When retired    SEC. 1481. Officers of the * * * Engineer Corps * * * who
from age or     shall have served faithfully for forty-five years, shall, when retired,
length of service. have the relative rank of commodore; and * * * who have been
                or shall be retired at the age of sixty-two years, before having served
                for forty-five years, but who shall have served faithfully until retired,
                shall, on the completion of forty years from their entry into the service,
                have the relative rank of commodore.
                               3 March, 1871, s. 11, v. 16, p. 537.

Engineers       SEC. 1484. Engineer officers graduated at the Naval Academy shall
graduated at the take precedence with all other officers with whom they have relative
Academy.        rank, according to the actual length of service in the Navy.
                               3 March, 1873, s. 1, v. 17, p. 555.

>  NOTE.—Engineer officers, graduates of the Naval Academy, are not entitled
>  to the six years' constructive service allowed to other staff officers of the Navy
>  in estimating length of service. Engineer officers not graduated at the Academy,
>  stand on the same footing with other staff officers, and are entitled to the
>  constructive service.—Op. XV, p. 336, Devens, July 11, 1877.

Military com-   SEC. 1488. The relative rank given by the provisions of this chapter
mand.           to officers of the * * * Engineer Corps shall confer no authority to
                exercise military command.
                               5 Aug., 1854, s. 4, v. 10, p. 587.
                               G. O., 31 Aug., 1846, and 27 May, 1847.
                               3 March, 1859, s. 2, v. 11, p. 407.

**Title 15, Chap. 8.**   SEC. 1556. * * * Fleet engineers, four thousand four hundred dol-
Pay of fleet en- lars. * * * Chief engineer having the same rank as pay director
gineers.        and pay inspector, when on duty at sea, four thousand four hundred
                dollars. When not at sea, the same as surgeons and paymasters, respect-
Chief engineers. ively. * * Chief engineers, who have the same rank with paymasters,
                during the first five years after date of commission, when at sea, two
                thousand eight hundred dollars; on shore duty, two thousand four
                hundred dollars; on leave, or waiting orders, two thousand dollars;
                during the second five years after such date, when at sea, three thousand
                two hundred dollars; on shore duty, two thousand eight hundred dol-
                lars; on leave, or waiting orders, two thousand four hundred dollars;
                during the third five years after such date, when at sea, three thousand
                five hundred dollars; on shore duty, three thousand two hundred dol-
                lars; on leave, or waiting orders, two thousand six hundred dollars;
                during the fourth five years after such date, when at sea, three thousand
                seven hundred dollars; on shore duty, three thousand six hundred dol-
                lars; on leave, or waiting orders, two thousand eight hundred dollars;
                after twenty years from such date, when at sea, four thousand four hun-
                dred dollars; on shore duty, four thousand dollars; on leave, or waiting
                orders, three thousand dollars. * * *

Passed assistant  *Passed* assistant engineers, during the first five years after date of
engineers.      appointment, when at sea, two thousand dollars; on shore duty, one
                thousand eight hundred dollars; on leave, or waiting orders, one thou-
                sand five hundred dollars; after five years from such date, when at sea,
                two thousand two hundred dollars; on shore duty, two thousand dol-
                lars; on leave, or waiting orders, one thousand seven hundred dollars.

Assistant en-   *Assistant* engineers, during the first five years after date of appoint-
gineers.        ment, when at sea, one thousand seven hundred dollars; on shore duty,
                one thousand four hundred dollars; on leave, or waiting orders, one
                thousand dollars; after five years from such date, when at sea, one
                thousand nine hundred dollars; on shore duty, one thousand six hun-

---

*Lieutenant of the junior grade. (March 3, 1883.)

dred dollars; on leave, or waiting orders, one thousand two hundred dollars.

15 July, 1870, s. 3, v. 16, p. 331.
24 Feb., 1874, v. 18, p. 17.
3 March, 1871, ss. 5, 6, v. 16, p. 535.
3 March, 1873, s. 1, v. 17, p. 555.

For the purpose of promoting a knowledge of steam-engineering and iron-ship building among the young men of the United States, the President may, upon the application of an established scientific school or college within the United States, detail an officer from the Engineer Corps of the Navy as professor in such school or college: *Provided*, That the number of officers so detailed shall not at any time exceed twenty-five, and such details shall be governed by rules to be prescribed from time to time by the President: *And provided further*, That such details may be withheld or withdrawn whenever, in the judgment of the President, the interests of the public service shall so require.

26 Feb., 1879, v. 20, p. 322.

26 Feb., 1879.
Detail of engineers for colleges.

## HOSPITALS, ASYLUMS, ETC.

Sec.
1614. Deduction from pay of marines.
4807. Superintendence of Navy hospitals.
4808. Deductions from pay of seamen, &c., for Navy-hospital fund.
4809. Appropriation of fines.
4810. Purchase and erection of Navy hospitals.

Sec.
4811. Government of Naval Asylum.
4812. Allowance of rations to Navy hospitals.
4813. Allowance from pensions.
—— Hospital at Hot Springs, Ark.
—— Closing of hospitals.

SEC. 1614. The Secretary of the Navy shall deduct from the pay due each of the officers and enlisted men of the Marine Corps at the rate of twenty cents per month for every officer and marine, to be applied to the fund for Navy hospitals.

2 March, 1799, s. 2, v. 1, p. 729.
26 Feb., 1811, s. 1, v. 2, p. 650.

Title 15, Chap. 9.
Deduction for hospitals.

SEC. 4807. The Secretary of the Navy shall have the general charge and superintendence of Navy hospitals.

26 Feb., 1811, s. 1, v. 2, p. 650.
10 July, 1832, s. 5, v. 4, p. 573.

Title 59, Chap. 1.
Superintendence of Navy hospitals.

SEC. 4808. The Secretary of the Navy shall deduct from the pay due each officer, seaman and marine, in the Navy, at the rate of twenty cents per month for each person, to be applied to the fund for Navy hospitals.

2 March, 1799, s. 2, v. 1, p. 729.
26 Feb., 1811, s. 1, v. 2, p. 650.

Deduction from pay of seamen, &c., for Navy-hospital fund.

SEC. 4809. All fines imposed on Navy officers, seamen, and marines shall be paid to the Secretary of the Navy, for the maintenance of Navy hospitals.

26 Feb., 1811, s. 2, v. 2, p. 650.
10 July, 1832, s. 5, v. 4, p. 573.

Appropriation of fines.

SEC. 4810. The Secretary of the Navy shall procure at suitable places proper sites for Navy hospitals, and if the necessary buildings are not procured with the site, shall cause such to be erected, having due regard to economy, and giving preference to such plans as with most convenience and least cost will admit of subsequent additions, when the funds permit and circumstances require; and shall provide, at one of the establishments, a permanent asylum for disabled and decrepit Navy officers, seaman, and marines. [Naval Asylum now located at Philadelphia.]

26 Feb., 1811, s. 3, v. 2, p. 650.
10 July, 1832, s. 5, v. 4, p. 573.

Purchase and erection of Navy hospitals.

SEC. 4811. The asylum for disabled and decrepit Navy officers, seamen, and marines shall be governed in accordance with the rules and regulations prescribed by the Secretary of the Navy. [See section 5757, naval pension fund, as to provision for those preferring pension to the asylum.]

26 Feb., 1811, s. 4, v. 2, p. 650.

Government of Naval Asylum.

SEC. 4812. For every Navy officer, seaman, or marine admitted into a Navy hospital, the institution shall be allowed one ration per day during his continuance therein, to be deducted from the account of the United States with such officer, seaman, or marine.

*Ibid.*, s. 5.

Allowance of rations to Navy hospitals.

40 INSANE OF THE NAVY—GOVERNMENT HOSPITAL.

Allowance from pension.

Sec. 4813. Whenever any Navy officer, seaman, or marine, entitled to a pension, is admitted to a Navy hospital, the pension, during his continuance in the hospital, shall be paid to the Secretary of the Navy and deducted from the account of such pensioner.

*Ibid.*

30 June, 1882.

Army and Navy hospital at Hot Springs, Ark.

*Provided,* That one hundred thousand dollars be, and hereby is, appropriated for the erection of an Army and Navy hospital at Hot Springs, Arkansas, which shall be erected by and under the direction of the Secretary of War, in accordance with plans and specifications to be prepared and submitted to the Secretary of War by the Surgeons-General of the Army and Navy; which hospital, when in a condition to receive patients, shall be subject to such rules, regulations, and restrictions as shall be provided by the President of the United States: *Provided further,* That such hospital shall be erected on the government reservation at or near Hot Springs, Arkansas.

30 June, 1882, P. E. L., p. 121. [Army appropriation act.]

3 March, 1883.

Closing of hospitals.

And if the Secretary of the Navy shall not be able to maintain properly the whole number of naval hospitals now kept open on the amounts hereby appropriated for the maintenance of and civil establishment at naval hospitals, he shall close those which are least necessary to the service, and provide for the patients now cared for therein ch other naval hospitals as may be most convenient.

5 Aug., 1882, and 3 March, 1883. [Naval appropriation acts.]

## INSANE OF THE NAVY—GOVERNMENT HOSPITAL.

Sec.
1551. Authority of the Secretary of the Navy, &c.
4838. Establishment of the Government Hospital for the Insane.
4843. Admission of insane persons of the Army Navy, &c.

Sec.
—— Limit to admission.
—— Transfer of insane convicts, &c.
—— Admission of insane inmates of National Home for Disabled Volunteers.

Title 15, Chap. 7.

Insane of the Navy.

Sec. 1551. The Secretary of the Navy may cause persons in the naval service or Marine Corps, who become insane while in the service, to be placed in such hospital for the insane as, in his opinion, will be most convenient and best calculated to promise a restoration of reason. And he may pay to any such hospital, other than the Government Hospital for the Insane in the District of Columbia, the pay which may from time to time be due to such insane person, and he may, in addition thereto, pay to such institution, from the annual appropriation for the naval service, under the head of contingent enumerated, any deficiency of a reasonable expense, not exceeding one hundred dollars per annum.

3 Aug., 1848, s. 13, v. 9, p. 272.
2 July, 1864, s. 2, v. 13, p. 348.

Title 59, Chap. 4.

Government Hospital for the Insane.

Sec. 4838. There shall be in the District of Columbia a Government Hospital for the insane, and its objects shall be the most humane care and enlightened curative treatment of the insane of the Army and Navy of the United States and of the District of Columbia.

3 March, 1855, s. 1, v. 10, p. 682.

Admission of insane persons of the Army, Navy, Marine Corps, &c.

Sec. 4843. The superintendent, upon the order of the Secretary of War, of the Secretary of the Navy, and of the Secretary of the Treasury, respectively, shall receive, and keep in custody until they are cured, or removed by the same authority which ordered their reception, insane persons of the following descriptions:

First. Insane persons belonging to the Army, Navy, Marine Corps, and revenue-cutter service.

Second. Civilians employed in the Quartermaster's and Subsistence Departments of the Army who may be, or may hereafter become, insane while in such employment.

Third. Men who, while in the service of the United States, in the Army, Navy, or Marine Corps, have been admitted to the hospital, and have been thereafter discharged from it on the supposition that they have recovered their reason, and have, within three years after such discharge, become again insane from causes existing at the time of such discharge, and have no adequate means of support.

Fourth. Indigent insane persons who have been in either of the said services and been discharged therefrom on account of disability arising from such insanity.

Fifth. Indigent insane persons who have become insane within three years after their discharge from such service, from causes which arose during and were produced by said service.

15 June, 1860, s. 1, v. 12, p. 23.
13 July, 1866, ss. 1, 2, v. 14, pp. 93, 94.

Hereafter the admission to the hospital shall be limited to such persons as are entitled to treatment therein under the provisions of title 59, chap. 4, of the Revised Statutes of the United States, and under the act approved March 3, 1875, chap. 156. [See notes.] 16 June, 1880.<br>Limit to admission.

16 June, 1880, v. 21, p. 259.

That upon the application of the Attorney-General the Secretary of the Interior be, and he is hereby, authorized and directed to transfer to the Government Hospital for the Insane in the District of Columbia all persons who, having been charged with offenses against the United States, are in the actual custody of its officers, and all persons who have been or shall be convicted of any offense in a court of the United States and are imprisoned in any State prison or penitentiary of any State or Territory, and who during the term of their imprisonment have or shall become and be insane. Aug. 7, 1882.<br>Transfer of insane convicts, &c., to Government Hospital.

23 June, 1874, s. 1, v. 18, p. 251.
Aug. 7, 1882, P. E., p. 330.

In addition to the persons now entitled to admission to said hospital, any inmate of the National Home for Disabled Volunteer Soldiers, who is now or may hereafter become insane shall, upon an order of the president of the board of managers of the said National Home, be admitted to said hospital and treated therein; and if any inmate so admitted from said National Home is or thereafter becomes a pensioner, and has neither wife, minor child, nor parent dependent on him, in whole or in part, for support, his arrears of pension and his pension money accruing during the period he shall remain in said hospital shall be applied to his support in said hospital, and be paid over to the proper officer of said institution for the general uses thereof. Admission of insane from National Home for Disabled Volunteers.

7 Aug., 1882, P. E. L., p. 330.

NOTES.—Volunteer soldiers who have become insane within a period of *more* than three years after their discharge from service may be admitted to the Government Asylum for the Insane in the District of Columbia, whether at the time they became insane they were inmates of any volunteer soldiers asylum or not.— Op. XIV, p. 225, Williams, April 23, 1873. But see act of 16 June, 1880, *ante*.

An act approved March 3, 1875, v. 18, p. 485, chap. 156, sec. 5, provides that insane patients of the Marine Hospital Service may be admitted to the Government Hospital for the Insane upon the order of the Secretary of the Treasury, at a charge not exceeding four dollars and fifty cents a week.

An act approved June 23, 1874, 18 Stat., 251, provides for the admission of insane convicts to the insane asylum in the District of Columbia.

## NATIONAL HOME FOR VOLUNTEER SOLDIERS AND SAILORS.

Sec.
4832. Persons entitled to admission

Sec.
——— Disposition of pensions.

SEC. 4832. The following persons only shall be entitled to the benefits of the National Home for disabled volunteer soldiers, and may be admitted thereto, upon the recommendation of three of the board of managers, namely: All officers and soldiers who served in the late war for the suppression of the rebellion, and the volunteer soldiers and sailors of the war of eighteen hundred and twelve and of the Mexican war, and not provided for by existing laws, who have been or may be disabled by wounds received or sickness contracted in the line of their duty; and such of these as have neither wife, child, nor parent dependent upon them, on becoming inmates of this home, or receiving relief therefrom, shall assign thereto their pensions when required by the board of managers, during the time they shall remain therein or receive its benefits. [These homes are at Augusta, Me., Milwaukee, Wis., Dayton, Ohio, Knightstown, Ind., and Hampton, Va.] Title 59, Chap. 3.<br>What persons entitled to admission, &c.

21 March, 1866, s. 7, v. 14, p. 11.
28 Feb., 1871, Res. 45, v. 16, p. 599.
23 Jan., 1873, s. 1, v. 17, p. 417.

42    ARTIFICIAL LIMBS, TRUSSES, AND APPLIANCES.

Aug. 7, 1882.

Pensions of inmates of homes to be paid to treasurers of such institutions.

That all pensions and arrears of pensions payable or to be paid to pensioners who are or may become inmates of the National Home for Disabled Volunteer Soldiers shall be paid to the treasurers of said home, to be applied by such treasurers as provided by law, under the rules and regulations of said home. Said payments shall be made by the pension agent upon a certificate of the proper officer of the home that the pensioner is an inmate thereof on the day to which said pension is drawn. The treasurers of said home, respectively, shall give security, to the satisfaction of the managers of said home, for the payment and application by them of all arrears of pension and pension-moneys they may receive under the aforesaid provision. And section two of the act entitled "An act making appropriations for the payment of invalid and other pensions of the United States for the fiscal year ending June thirtieth, eighteen hundred and eighty-two, and for deficiencies, and for other purposes," approved February twenty-sixth, eighteen hundred and eighty-one, is hereby revived and continued in force."

Aug. 7, 1882, P. E., p. 322. [Sundry civil act].

## ARTIFICIAL LIMBS, TRUSSES, AND APPLIANCES.

Sec.
1176. Trusses, to whom furnished.
1177. Applications for trusses.
1178. Purchase of trusses.
4787. Artificial limbs to be furnished every five years.
4788. Commutation rates in money value for limb, &c.

Sec.
4789. Money commutation, how paid.
4790. Commutation to persons who cannot use artificial limbs.
4791. Transportation for persons to whom artificial limbs are furnished.
——  Surgical appliances.

Title 14, Chap. 1.

Trusses, to whom furnished.

SEC. 1176. That every soldier of the Union Army, or petty-officer, seaman, or marine in the naval service, who was ruptured while in the line of duty during the late war for the suppression of the rebellion, or who shall be so ruptured thereafter in any war, shall be entitled to receive a single or double truss of such style as may be designated by the Surgeon-General of the United States Army as best suited for such disability; and whenever the said truss or trusses so furnished shall become useless from wear, destruction, or loss, such soldier, petty-officer, seaman, or marine shall be supplied with another truss on making a like application as provided for in section two of the original act of which this is an amendment: *Provided*, That such application shall not be made more than once in two years and six months: *And provided further*, That sections two and three [secs. 1177 and 1178 R. S.] of the said act of May twenty-eighth, eighteen hundred and seventy-two, shall be construed so as to apply to petty-officers, seamen, and marines of the naval service, as well as to soldiers of the Army. [Amended section.]

28 May, 1872, s. 1, v. 17, p. 164.    3 March, 1879, v. 20, p. 353.

NOTE.—It is left with the Surgeon-General of the Army to adopt one style, or different styles, keeping in view the selection of that which in his judgment is best adapted to the purpose for which intended.—Op. XIV, 72. July 30, 1872.

Application for trusses.

SEC. 1177. Application for such truss shall be made by the ruptured soldier, to an examining surgeon for pensions, whose duty it shall be to examine the applicant, and when found to have a rupture or hernia, to prepare and forward to the Surgeon-General an application for such truss without charge to the soldier. [See § 4787.]

28 May, 1872, s. 2, v. 17, p. 164.

Trusses, purchase of.

SEC. 1178. The Surgeon-General is authorized and directed to purchase the trusses required for such soldiers, at wholesale prices, and the cost of the same shall be paid upon the requisition of the Surgeon-General out of any moneys in the Treasury not otherwise appropriated.

28 May, 1872, s. 3, v. 17, p. 164.

Title 57.

Artificial limbs, &c., to be furnished every five years.

SEC. 4787. Every officer, soldier, seaman, and marine, who was disabled, during the war for the suppression of the rebellion, in the military or naval service, and in the line of duty, or in consequence of wounds received or disease contracted therein, and who was furnished by the War Department, since the seventeenth day of June, eighteen hundred and seventy, with an artificial limb or apparatus for resection,

---

* Under the act of Feb. 26, 1881, the pensions are to be paid over to the treasurer, without deduction for fines or penalties. Any balance on discharge of inmate is to be paid over to him; in case of death to his widow, children, or legal representatives.

or who was entitled to receive such limb or apparatus since said date, shall be entitled to receive a new limb or apparatus at the expiration of every five years thereafter, under such regulations as have been or may be prescribed by the Surgeon-General of the Army.

The provisions of this section shall apply to all officers, non-commissioned officers, enlisted and hired men of the land and naval forces of the United States, who, in the line of their duty as such, shall have lost limbs or sustained bodily injuries depriving them of the use of any of their limbs, to be determined by the Surgeon-General of the Army; and the term of five years herein specified shall be held to commence in each case with the filing of the application for the benefits of this section. Persons entitled.

27 July, 1868, s. 14, v. 15, p. 237.    23 March, 1876, v. 19, p. 8.<br>
17 June, 1870, s. 1, v. 16, p. 153.    27 Feb., 1877, v. 19, p. 252.<br>
30 June, 1870, v. 16, p. 174.

NOTE.—Held by the War Department that desertion does not affect the rights of a person disabled, as this section indicates, to artificial limbs or apparatus, and that it might be properly construed to include the mechanics and laborers employed at the arsenals under Title XVII, R. S.—Winthrop's Digest, 122.

The act of Aug. 15, 1876, v. 19, page 203, allows *commutation* for an artificial limb or appliances every five years.

SEC. 4788. Every person entitled to the benefits of the preceding section may, if he so elects, receive, instead of such limb or apparatus, the money value thereof, at the following rates, namely: For artificial legs, seventy-five dollars; for arms, fifty dollars; for feet, fifty dollars; for apparatus for resection, fifty dollars. Commutation rates in money value for limb.

17 June, 1870, s. 1, v. 16, p. 153.    15 Aug., 1876, v. 19, p. 203.

SEC. 4789. The Surgeon-General shall certify to the Commissioner of Pensions a list of all soldiers who elect to receive money commutation instead of limbs or apparatus, with the amount due to each, and the Commissioner of Pensions shall cause the same to be paid to such soldiers in the same manner as pensions are paid. Money commutation, how to be paid.

17 June, 1870, s. 2, v. 16, p. 153.

SEC. 4790. Every person in the military or naval service who lost a limb during the war of the rebellion, or is entitled to the benefits of section forty-seven hundred and eighty-seven, but from the nature of his injury is not able to use an artificial limb, shall be entitled to the benefits of section forty-seven hundred and eighty-eight, and shall receive money commutation as therein provided. Money commutation to those who cannot use artificial limb.

17 June, 1870, s. 2, v. 16, p. 153.    27 Feb., 1877, v. 19, p. 252.

SEC. 4791. The Secretary of War is authorized and directed to furnish to the persons embraced by the provisions of section forty-seven hundred and eighty-seven, transportation to and from their homes and the place where they may be required to go to obtain artificial limbs provided for them under authority of law. The transportation allowed for having artificial limbs fitted shall be furnished by the Quartermaster-General of the Army, the cost of which shall be refunded from the appropriations for invalid pensions. Transportation for persons to whom artificial limbs are furnished.

28 July, 1866, v. 14, p. 342.<br>
23 March, 1876, v. 19, p. 8.<br>
15 Aug., 1876, s. 2, v. 19, p. 204.<br>
27 Feb., 1877, v. 19, p. 252.

The sundry civil act, approved March 3, 1883, appropriates two thousand dollars, to be expended under the direction of the Secretary of War, "for providing surgical appliances for persons disabled in the military or naval service of the United States, and not entitled to artificial limbs." Surgical appliances.

## CEMETERIES—NATIONAL.

| Sec. | Sec. |
|---|---|
| 4877. Inclosures, headstones, &c. | 4878. Who may be buried in national cemeteries. |

SEC. 4877. In the arrangement of the national cemeteries established for the burial of deceased soldiers and sailors, the Secretary of War is hereby directed to have the same inclosed with a good and substantial stone or iron fence; and to cause each grave to be marked with a small headstone or block, which shall be of durable stone, and of such design and weight as shall keep it in place when set, and shall bear the name of the soldier and the name of his State inscribed thereon, when the Title 59, Chap. 6. Inclosures, headstones, and registers.

same are known, and also with the number of the grave inscribed thereon, corresponding with the number opposite to the name of the party in a register of burials to be kept at each cemetery and at the office of the Quartermaster-General, which shall set forth the name, rank, company, regiment, and date of death of the officer or soldier; or if these are unknown, it shall be so recorded.*

22 Feb., 1867, s. 1, v. 14, p. 399.
8 June, 1872, v. 17, p. 345.
3 March, 1873, v. 17, p. 545.

Who may be buried in national cemeteries. SEC. 4878. All soldiers, sailors, or marines, dying in the service of the United States, or dying in a destitute condition, after having been honorably discharged from the service, or who served during the late war, either in the regular or volunteer forces, may be buried in any national cemetery free of cost. The production of the honorable discharge of a deceased man shall be sufficient authority for the superintendent of any cemetery to permit the interment.

17 July, 1862, s. 18, v. 12, p. 596.
1 June, 1872, v. 17, p. 202.
3 March, 1873, v. 17, p. 603.

## HYDROGRAPHIC OFFICE.

Sec.
431. Establishment of office.
432. Maps, charts, &c.
433. Money received from sale.
686. Foreign hydrographic surveys.

Sec.
3692. Proceeds of sales of stores.
——— to surveying expeditions.
——— Charts, how sold.
——— Civil employees.

**Title 10.**

Hydrographic Office. SEC. 431. There shall be a Hydrographic Office attached to the Bureau of Navigation in the Navy Department, for the improvement of the means for navigating safely the vessels of the Navy and of the mercantile marine, by providing, under the authority of the Secretary of the Navy, accurate and cheap nautical charts, sailing directions, navigators, and manuals of instructions for the use of all vessels of the United States, and for the benefit and use of navigators generally.

21 June, 1866, s. 1, v. 14, p. 69.

Maps, charts, &c. SEC. 432. The Secretary of the Navy is authorized to cause to be prepared, at the Hydrographic Office attached to the Bureau of Navigation in the Navy Department, maps, charts, and nautical books relating to and required in navigation, and to publish and furnish them to navigators at the cost of printing and paper, and to purchase the plates and copyrights of such existing maps, charts, navigators, sailing directions and instructions, as he may consider necessary, and when he may deem it expedient to do so, and under such regulations and instructions as he may prescribe.

*Ibid., s. 2.*

Money received from sales of maps, charts, &c. SEC. 433. All moneys which may be received from the sale of maps, charts, and nautical books shall be returned by the Secretary of the Navy into the Treasury of the United States, to be used in the further preparation and publication of maps, charts, navigators, sailing directions, and instructions for the use of seamen, to be sold at the rates as set forth in the preceding section.

*Ibid., s. 3.*

**Title 41.**

Foreign hydrographic surveys. SEC. 3686. All appropriations made for the preparation or publication of foreign hydrographic surveys shall only be applicable to their object, upon the approval by the Secretary of the Navy, after a report from three competent naval officers, to the effect that the original data for proposed charts are such as to justify their publication; and it is hereby made the duty of the Secretary of the Navy to order a board of three naval officers to examine and report upon the data, before he shall approve of any application of money to the preparation or publication of such charts or hydrographic surveys.

21 Feb., 1861, s. 7, v. 12, p. 150.

Proceeds of certain sales, &c., of material. SEC. 3692. All moneys received from * * * * sale of materials, stores, or supplies to any exploring or surveying expedition authorized by law, shall respectively revert to that appropriation out of which

---

* An act approved Feb. 3, 1879, chap. 44, provides for headstones for soldiers graves in private cemeteries. V. 20, p. 281.

they were originally expended, and shall be applied to the purposes for which they are appropriated by law.

8 May, 1872, s. 5, v. 17, p. 83.
3 March, 1847, s. 1, v. 9, p. 171.
20 April, 1866, ss. 1, 2, v. 14, p. 40.
28 July, 1866, s. 25, v. 14, p. 336.
8 June, 1872, v. 17, p. 337.

All charts hereafter furnished to mariners or others not in the Government service shall be paid for at the cost price of paper and printing paid by the Government.

<small>14, Feb. 1879.</small>
<small>Cost price for charts.</small>

14 Feb., 1879, v. 20, p. 284.
4 May, 1878, v. 20, p. 50.

Hydrographic Office: For chief of engraving and draughting, two thousand four hundred dollars; two clerks of class two; one assistant messenger; and one office attendant, four hundred and twenty dollars; in all, six thousand three hundred and forty dollars.

For draughtsmen, engravers, copyists, copper-plate printers, printers' apprentices, and laborers in the Hydrographic Office, thirty-two thousand six hundred and sixty dollars.

<small>3 March, 1883.</small>
<small>Civil employees</small>

3 March, 1883. [Legislative appropriation act.]

## LINE OFFICERS OF THE NAVY.

Sec.
1362. Grades of line officers.
— Change of titles.
1363. Number on the active list.
— Restriction.
1364. When exceeded.
1365. Selection of rear-admirals during war.
1366. Promotion of rear-admirals during peace.
1367. Secretaries to Admiral, &c.
— Officers as secretaries and clerks afloat.

Sec.
1434. Command of squadrons, flag-officer.
1435. Assignment of lieutenant-commanders.
1467. Rank of line officers.
1468. Precedence of commanding officers.
1469. Aid or executive.
1470. Rights of staff officers, senior to aid.
1472. Line officer as chief of a bureau.
1490. Ensigns as steerage officers.

SEC. 1362. The active list of the line officers of the Navy of the United States shall be divided into eleven grades, as follows, namely:
 First. Admiral.
 Second. Vice-Admiral.
 Third. Rear-admirals.
 Fourth. Commodores.
 Fifth. Captains.
 Sixth. Commanders.
 Seventh. Lieutenant-commanders.
 Eighth. Lieutenants.
 Ninth. Masters. [See act March 3, 1883.]
 Tenth. Ensigns.
 Eleventh. Midshipmen. [See act March 3, 1883.]

<small>Title 15, Chap. 1.</small>
<small>Grades of line officers.</small>

*Provided*, That vacancies occurring in the grades of Admiral and Vice-Admiral shall not be filled by promotion, or in any other manner; and that when the offices of said grades shall become vacant, the grade itself shall cease to exist.

<small>Admiral and Vice-Admiral to cease.</small>

16 July, 1862, s. 1, v. 12, p. 583.
21 Dec., 1864, s. 1, v. 13, p. 420.
25 July, 1866, s. 1, v. 14, p. 222.
2 March, 1867, s. 1, v. 14, p. 516.
24 Jan., 1873, v. 17, p. 418.

The title *of master* is hereby changed to that of lieutenants, and the masters now on the list shall constitute a junior grade of, and be commissioned as, lieutenants, having the same rank and pay as now provided by law for masters, but promotion to and from said grade shall be by examination as provided by law for promotion to and from the grade of master, and nothing herein contained shall be so construed as to increase the pay now allowed by law to any officer in the line or staff; * * the title of *midshipman* is hereby changed to that of ensign, and the midshipmen now on the list shall constitute a junior grade of, and be commissioned as, ensigns, having the same rank and pay as now provided by law for midshipmen, but promotions to and from said grade shall be under the same regulations and requirements as now provided by law for promotion to and from the grade of midshipmen, and nothing herein contained shall be so construed as to increase the

<small>3 March, 1883.</small>
<small>Titles of master and midshipman changed.</small>

**Title 15, Chap. 1.**
Number on the active list.

pay now allowed by law to any officer of said grade or of any officer or relative rank.

3 March, 1883, P. E. L., p. 97. [Navy appropriation act.]

SEC. 1363. There shall be allowed on the active list of the line officers of the Navy one Admiral, one Vice-Admiral, *six* rear-admirals, *ten* commodores, *forty-five* captains, *eighty-five* commanders, *seventy-four* lieutenant-commanders, *two hundred and fifty* lieutenants, *seventy-five* masters, and *seventy-five* ensigns.

25 July, 1866, s. 1, v. 14, p. 222.
15 July, 1870, ss. 9, 10, v. 16, p. 333.
5 Aug., 1882, P. E., p. 286.

**5 Aug., 1882.**
Rule of promotion in the line.

Hereafter only one-half of the vacancies in the various grades in the line of the Navy shall be filled by promotion until such grades shall be reduced to the following numbers [as in sec. 1363], and thereafter promotions to all vacancies shall be made but not to increase either of said grades above the the number aforesaid.

5 Aug., 1882, P. E., p. 286.

**Title 15, Chap. 1.**
When exceeded.

SEC. 1364. The provisions of the foregoing section [1363 and August 5, 1882] shall not have the effect to vacate the commission of any lieutenant-commander, lieutenant, master, or ensign appointed according to law, in excess of the respective number therein fixed; nor to preclude the advancement of any officer to a higher grade, for distinguished conduct in battle, or for extraordinary heroism, under the provisions of sections fifteen hundred and six and fifteen hundred and eight. [PROMOTION.]

25 July, 1866, ss. 1, 2, v. 14, p. 222.
16 July, 1862, s. 9, v. 12, p. 584.

Selection of rear-admirals during war.

SEC. 1365. During war rear-admirals shall be selected from those officers on the active list, not below the grade of commanders, who shall have eminently distinguished themselves by courage, skill, and genius in their profession; but no officer shall be so promoted, under this provision, unless, upon recommendation of the President by name, he has received the thanks of Congress for distinguished service.

16 July, 1862, s. 7, v. 12, p. 584.

Promotion of rear-admirals during peace.

SEC. 1366. During peace, vacancies in the grade of rear-admiral shall be filled by regular promotion from the list of commodores, subject to examination according to law. [See PROMOTION; also act Aug. 5, 1882, *ante*.]

16 July, 1862, s. 7, v. 12, p. 584.

Secretaries to Admiral and Vice-Admiral.

SEC. 1367. The Admiral and Vice-Admiral shall each be allowed a secretary, who shall be entitled to the rank and allowances of a lieutenant in the Navy. [See *post*.]

21 Dec., 1864, s. 2, v. 13, p. 420.
16 May, 1866, v. 14, p. 48.
25 July, 1866, s. 6, v. 14, p. 223.
2 March, 1867, s. 1, v. 14, p. 516.

**4 May, 1878.**
Secretaries to Admiral and Vice-Admiral on sea service.

On and after the first day of July, eighteen hundred and seventy-eight, there shall be no appointments made from civil life of secretaries or clerks to the Admiral or Vice-Admiral, when on sea service, commanders of squadrons, or of clerks to commanders of vessels; and an officer not above the grade of lieutenant shall be detailed to perform the duties of secretary to the Admiral or Vice-Admiral, when on sea service, and one not above the grade of master* to perform the duties of clerk to a rear-admiral or commander, and one not above the grade of ensign to perform the duties of clerk to a captain, commander, or lieutenant-commander when afloat. * * *

4 May, 1878, v. 20, p. 50.

**Title 15, Chap. 2.**
Command of squadrons.

SEC. 1434. The President may select any officer not below the grade of commander on the active list of the Navy, and assign him to the command of a squadron, with the rank and title of "flag-officer;" and any officer so assigned shall have the same authority and receive the same obedience from the commanders of ships in his squadron, holding commissions of an older date than his, that he would be entitled to receive if his commission were the oldest.

21 Dec., 1861, s. 4, v. 12, p. 329.

---

* Lieutenant of the junior grade. (March 3, 1883.)

Sec. 1435. Lieutenant-commanders may be assigned to duty as first lieutenants of naval stations, as navigation and watch officers on board of vessels of war, and as first lieutenants of vessels not commanded by lieutenant-commanders. Lieutenant-commanders, how assignable.

16 July, 1862, s. 3, v. 12, p. 584.
25 July, 1866, s. 5, v. 14, p. 223.

Sec. 1467. Line officers shall take rank in each grade according to the dates of their commissions. Title 15, Chap. 4. Rank.

16 July, 1862, s. 1, v. 12, p. 583.
21 April, 1864, s. 7, v. 13, p. 54.
24 Jan., 1865, s. 1, v. 13, p. 424.

Sec. 1468. Commanding officers of vessels of war and of naval stations shall take precedence over all officers placed under their command. Commanding officers of vessels and stations.

3 March, 1871, s. 12, v. 16, p. 537.

Sec. 1469. The Secretary of the Navy may, in his discretion, detail a line officer to act as the aid or executive of the commanding officer of a vessel of war or naval station, which officer shall, when not impracticable, be next in rank to said commanding officer. Such aid or executive shall, while executing the orders of the commanding officer on board the vessel or at the station, take precedence over all officers attached to the vessel or station. All orders of such aid or executive shall be regarded as proceeding from the commanding officer, and the aid or executive shall have no independent authority in consequence of such detail. Aid or executive officer.

3 March, 1871, s. 12, v. 16, p. 537.

Sec. 1470. Staff officers, senior to the officers so detailed, shall have the right to communicate directly with the commanding officer. Rights of staff-officers.

3 March, 1871, s. 12, v. 16, p. 537.

Sec. 1472. When the office of Chief of Bureau is filled by a line officer below the rank of commodore, said officer shall have the relative rank of commodore during the time he holds said office. Relative rank as chief of bureau.

3 March, 1871, s. 12, v. 16, p. 537.

Sec. 1490. Ensigns shall be steerage officers, unless assigned to duty as watch and division officers. Ensigns as steerage officers.

15 July, 1870, s. 10, v. 16, p. 334.

PAY OF LINE OFFICERS. [See under PAY OF THE NAVY.]

PROMOTION. [See under that head.]

RETIREMENT. [See under that head.]

## MATES.

Sec.
1408. Seamen may be rated as mates.
1409. Rating shall not discharge from enlistment.

Sec.
1556. Pay of mates.

Sec. 1408. Mates may be rated, under authority of the Secretary of the Navy, from seamen and ordinary seamen who have enlisted in the naval service for not less than two years. Title 15, Chap. 1. Seamen may be rated as mates.

17 May, 1864, s. 3, v. 13, p. 79.
3 March, 1865, s. 3, v. 13, p. 539.

Sec. 1409. The rating of an enlisted man as a mate, or his appointment as a warrant officer, shall not discharge him from his enlistment. Rating shall not discharge from enlistment.

Idem.

Sec. 1556. * * * Mates, when at sea, nine hundred dollars; on shore duty, seven hundred dollars; on leave, or waiting orders, five hundred dollars. Title 15, Chap. 8. Pay of mates.

15 July, 1870, s. 3, v. 16, p. 330.

NOTE.—See Op. XI, p. 251, June 20, 1865, defining the status of mates and setting master's mates. Not warranted officers.

## MEDICAL CORPS.

| Sec. | Sec. |
|---|---|
| 426. Chief of Bureau. | 1375. Details of medical officers to Bureau of Medicine and Surgery. |
| 1368. Medical Corps, number of. | 1411. Acting assistant surgeons. |
| 1369. Appointments in, how made. | 1471. Rank and title of chief of Bureau. |
| 1370. Appointment of assistant surgeons. | 1473. Rank when retired. |
| 1371. Appointment of surgeons. | 1474. Rank of medical officers. |
| 1372. Rank of assistant surgeon in case of delayed examination. | 1481. Retired from age or length of service, rank. |
| 1373. Surgeon of the fleet. | 1556. Pay. |
| 1374. Duties of surgeon of the fleet. | |

**Title 10.**
Chief of Bureau.

SEC. 426. The chief of the Bureau of Medicine and Surgery shall be appointed from the list of the surgeons of the Navy.

5 July, 1862, s. 1, v. 12, p. 510.

**Title 15, Chap. 1.**
Medical Corps; number of.

SEC. 1368. The active list of the Medical Corps of the Navy shall consist of fifteen medical directors, fifteen medical inspectors, fifty surgeons, and *ninety* assistant and *passed* assistant surgeons.

3 March, 1871, s. 5, v. 16, p. 535.
5 Aug., 1882, P. E. L., p. 285.

Appointments in, how made.

SEC. 1369. All appointments in the Medical Corps shall be made by the President, by and with the advice and consent of the Senate.

21 April, 1806, s. 3, v. 2, p. 390.
16 April, 1814, s. 5, v. 3, p. 125.
24 May, 1828, s. 3, v. 4, p. 313.

Appointment of assistant surgeons.

SEC. 1370. No person shall be appointed assistant surgeon until he has been examined and approved by a board of naval surgeons, designated by the Secretary of the Navy; nor who is under twenty-one or over twenty-six years of age.

24 May, 1828, s. 1, v. 4, p. 313.
3 March, 1871, s. 5, v. 16, p. 536.

Appointment of surgeons.

SEC. 1371. No person shall be appointed surgeon until he has served as an assistant surgeon at least two years, on board a public vessel of the United States at sea, nor until he has been examined and approved for such appointment, by a board of naval surgeons, designated by the Secretary of the Navy.

24 May, 1828, s. 1, v. 4, p. 313.

NOTE.—The custom and practice of the Navy Department requiring competitive examination of assistant surgeons and assigning them positions on the Navy Register, in the order of relative merit as ascertained and reported by the board of examiners authorized by existing law and regulations, is not, under the present law, correct.
Having passed the necessary examination for promotion, the claim of * * * to be promoted according to seniority is, in my opinion, well founded.—Op. Feb. 25, 1881, Ames case; Gen. order 282.

Rank of assistant surgeons in case of delayed examination.

SEC. 1372. When any assistant surgeon was absent from the United States, on duty, at the time when others of his date were examined, he shall, if not rejected at a subsequent examination, be entitled to the same rank with them; and if, from any cause, his relative rank cannot be assigned to him, he shall retain his original position on the register.

3 March, 1835, s. 1, v. 4, p. 757.

Surgeon of the fleet.

SEC. 1373. The President may designate among the surgeons in the service, and appoint to every fleet or squadron an experienced and intelligent surgeon, who shall be denominated "surgeon of the fleet," and shall be surgeon of the flag-ship.

24 May, 1828, s. 2, v. 4, p. 313.

Duties of surgeon of the fleet.

SEC. 1374. The surgeon of the fleet shall, in addition to his duties as surgeon of the flag-ship, examine and approve all requisitions for medical and hospital stores for the squadron or fleet, and inspect their quality. He shall, in difficult cases, consult with the surgeons of the several ships, and he shall make, and transmit to the Navy Department, records of the character and treatment of diseases in the squadron or fleet.

24 May, 1828, s. 2, v. 4, p. 313.

SEC. 1375. A surgeon, assistant surgeon, or passed assistant surgeon, may be detailed as assistant to the Bureau of Medicine and Surgery, *who shall receive the highest shore-pay of his grade.* {Detail of medical officer to Bureau as assistant.}

16 July, 1862, s. 18, v. 12, p. 587.   27 Feb., 1877, v. 19, p. 244.

NOTE.—By the act of 27 Feb., 1877, section 1375 was to have the same effect as though the amendment (in *italics*) had been enacted therein.

SEC. 1411. The Secretary of the Navy may appoint, for temporary service, such acting assistant surgeons as the exigencies of the service may require, *in case of war only,* who shall receive the compensation of assistant surgeons. {Acting assistant surgeons.}

15 July, 1870, s. 13, v. 16, p. 334.   3 March, 1865, s. 6, v. 13, p. 539.
13 Feb., 1879, s. 2, v. 20, p. 295.

SEC. 1471. The chief of the Bureau of Medicine and Surgery * * * shall have the relative rank of commodore while holding said position, and shall have * * * the title of Surgeon-General. * * * {Title 15, Chap. 4. Rank and title of chief of Bureau.}

3 March, 1871, s. 12, v. 16, p. 537.

SEC. 1473. Officers who have been or who shall be retired from the position of chief of the Bureau of Medicine and Surgery, * * * by reason of age or length of service, shall have the relative rank of commodore. {Retired from position of chief of Bureau.}

*Idem.*

SEC. 1474. Officers of the Medical Corps on the active list of the Navy shall have relative rank as follows: {Relative rank of medical officers.}
Medical directors, the relative rank of captain.
Medical inspectors, the relative rank of commander.
Surgeons, the relative rank of lieutenant-commander or lieutenant.
Passed assistant surgeons, the relative rank of lieutenant or master.*
Assistant surgeons, the relative rank of master* or ensign.

3 March, 1871, s. 5, v. 16, p. 535.

SEC. 1481. Officers of the Medical * * * Corps * * * who shall have served faithfully for forty-five years, shall, when retired, have the relative rank of commodore; and * * * who have been or shall be retired at the age of sixty-two years, before having served for forty-five years, but who shall have served faithfully until retired, shall, on the completion of forty years from their entry into the service, have the relative rank of commodore. {Retired for age or length of service.}

3 March, 1871, s. 11, v. 16, p. 537.

{Title 15, Chap. 8.}

SEC. 1556. Fleet-surgeons, * * * *, four thousand four hundred dollars. {Pay of fleet surgeons.}
Medical directors, medical inspectors, * * *, when on duty at sea, four thousand four hundred dollars. {Medical directors and inspectors.}
When not at sea, the same as surgeons and paymasters, respectively. {Surgeons.}
Surgeons, * * *, during the first five years after date of commission, when at sea, two thousand eight hundred dollars; on shore duty, two thousand four hundred dollars; on leave, or waiting orders, two thousand dollars; during the second five years after such date, when at sea, three thousand two hundred dollars; on shore duty, two thousand eight hundred dollars; on leave, or waiting orders, two thousand four hundred dollars; during the third five years after such date, when at sea, three thousand five hundred dollars; on shore duty, three thousand two hundred dollars; on leave, or waiting orders, two thousand six hundred dollars; during the fourth five years after such date, when at sea, three thousand seven hundred dollars; on shore duty, three thousand six hundred dollars; on leave, or waiting orders, two thousand eight hundred dollars; after twenty years from such date, when at sea, four thousand two hundred dollars; on shore duty, four thousand dollars; on leave, or waiting orders, three thousand dollars.
Passed assistant surgeons, * * *, during the first five years after date of appointment, when at sea, two thousand dollars; on shore duty, one thousand eight hundred dollars; on leave, or waiting orders, one thousand five hundred dollars; after five years from such date, when at sea, two thousand two hundred dollars; on shore duty, two thousand dollars; on leave, or waiting orders, one thousand seven hundred dollars. {Passed assistant surgeons.}

NOTE.—The words "after date of appointment," and "from such date," sec. 1556, fixing the annual pay of passed assistant surgeons of the Navy, refer not to the original entry of the officer into the service as an assistant surgeon, but to

---

* Lieutenant of the junior grade. (Act of March 3, 1883.)

| | the notification by the Secretary of the Navy that he has passed his examination for promotion to the grade of surgeon, and will thereafter, until such promotion, be considered as a passed assistant surgeon. A passed assistant surgeoncy is an office, and the notification of the Secretary of the Navy is a valid appointment to it.—United States v. Moore, Otto, 95, 760. |
|---|---|
| Assistant surgeons. | Assistant surgeons, * * * , during the first five years after date of appointment, when at sea, one thousand seven hundred dollars; on shore duty, one thousand four hundred dollars; on leave, or waiting orders, one thousand dollars; after five years from such date, when at sea, one thousand nine hundred dollars; on shore duty, one thousand six hundred dollars; on leave, or waiting orders, one thousand two hundred dollars. |
| Assistant surgeons qualified for promotion. | Assistant surgeons of three years' service, who have been found qualified for promotion by a medical board of examiners, the pay of passed assistant surgeons. |
| | 15 July, 1870, s. 3, v. 16, pp. 330, 331. |
| | 3 March, 1871, ss. 5, 6, v. 16, pp. 535, 536. |
| | 3 March, 1873, s. 1, v. 17, p. 555. |

## NAUTICAL ALMANAC.

Sec.
436. Superintendent, pay of.
—— Printing and sale.

Sec.
—— Civil employés.

| Title 10. Superindendent, pay of. | Sec. 436. The Secretary of the Navy may place the supervision of the Nautical Almanac in charge of any officer or professor of mathematics in the Navy who is competent for that service. Such officer or professor, when so employed, shall be entitled to receive the shore-duty pay of his grade, and no other. |
|---|---|
| | 3 March, 1857, 3, v. 11, p. 246. |
| 11 Feb., 1880. Printing and sale of. | That there shall be printed annually at the Government Printing Office fifteen hundred copies of the American Ephemeris and Nautical Almanac and of the papers supplementary thereto, of which one hundred shall be for the use of the Senate, four hundred for the House of Representatives, and one thousand for the public service, to be distributed by the Navy Department. |
| | Sec. 2. That additional copies of the Ephemeris and of the Nautical Almanac extracted therefrom may be ordered by the Secretary of the Navy for sale: *Provided*, That all moneys received from such sale shall be deposited in the Treasury to the credit of the appropriation for public printing. |
| | 11 Feb., 1880, v. 21, p. 301. |
| 3 March, 1883. Civil employés. | Nautical Almanac Office: For the following assistants, namely: Three at one thousand six hundred dollars each; two at one thousand four hundred dollars each; three at one thousand two hundred dollars each; two at one thousand dollars each; one assistant messenger; and one copyist, at four hundred and eighty dollars; in all, fourteen thousand four hundred dollars. |
| | For pay of computers on piece-work in preparing for publication the American Ephemeris and Nautical Almanac, and improving the Tables of the Planets, eight thousand six hundred dollars. |
| | 3 March, 1883, P. E., L., p. 534. [Legislative act.] |

## NAVAL ACADEMY—NAVAL CADETS.

Sec.
1483. Rank of graduates of the Academy.
1511. Where established.
1512. Title of students.
1513. Number of naval cadets.
1514. Nomination of candidates.
1515. Examination of candidates.
1516. Second recommendation.
1517. Qualifications.
—— Traveling expenses.
1518. Appropriations, how applied.
1519. Naval cadets found deficient.
1520. Academic course.

Sec.
1521. Promotion to midshipmen.
1522. Naval constructors and steam engineers.
—— Special course.
1526. Studies not to be pursued on Sunday.
1527. Store-keeper at the Academy.
1528. Professors of ethics, Spanish, and drawing.
1556. Pay of cadets, &c.
1577. Rations.
—— Prevention of hazing.
—— Board of Visitors.
—— Pay of civil officers.

NAVAL ACADEMY—NAVAL CADETS. 51

SEC. 1483. Graduates of the Naval Academy shall take rank according to their proficiency as shown by their order of merit at the date of graduation.

*Title 15, Chap. 4.*
*Rank of graduates of Naval Academy.*

23 May, 1872, s. 1, v. 17, p. 153.

NOTE.—The positions given the midshipmen on their final examination (sections 1483 and 1521) cannot be disturbed. See Ops. XI, p. 158; XV, p. 637; XVI, p. 296; Court of Claims, X, p. 474; Op. Aug. 12, 1881.

SEC. 1511. The Naval Academy shall be established at Annapolis, in the State of Maryland.

*Title 15, Chap. 5.*
*Where established.*

21 May, 1864, s. 4, v. 13, p. 85.

SEC. 1512. [Superseded by act of August 5, 1882, as follows:] *Provided,* That hereafter there shall be no appointments of cadet-midshipmen or cadet-engineers at the Naval Academy, but in lieu thereof naval cadets shall be appointed from each Congressional district and at large, as now provided by law for cadet-midshipmen, and all the undergraduates at the Naval Academy shall hereafter be designated and called "naval cadets;" and from those who successfully complete the six years' course appointments shall hereafter be made as it is necessary to fill vacancies in the lower grades of the line and Engineer Corps of the Navy and of the Marine Corps: *And provided further,* That no greater number of appointments into these grades shall be made each year than shall equal the number of vacancies which has occurred in the same grades during the preceding year; such appointments to be made from the graduates of the year, at the conclusion of their six years' course, in the order of merit, as determined by the academic board of the Naval Academy; the assignment to the various corps to be made by the Secretary of the Navy upon the recommendation of the academic board. But nothing herein contained shall reduce the number of appointments from such graduates below ten in each year, nor deprive of such appointment any graduate who may complete the six years' course during the year eighteen hundred and eighty-two. And if there be a surplus of graduates, those who do not receive such appointment shall be given a certificate of graduation, an honorable discharge, and one year's sea-pay, as now provided by law for cadet-midshipmen; and so much of section fifteen hundred and twenty-one of the Revised Statutes as is inconsistent herewith is hereby repealed.

*Title of students.*

That any cadet whose position in his class entitles him to be retained in the service may, upon his own application, be honorably discharged at the end of four years' course at the Naval Academy, with a proper certificate of graduation.

5 Aug., 1882, P. E. L., p. 285.

SEC. 1513. There shall be allowed at said Academy one *naval cadet* for every Member or Delegate of the House of Representatives, one for the District of Columbia, and ten appointed annually at large: *Provided, however,* That there shall not be at any time more in said Academy appointed at large than ten.

*Number of naval cadets.*

2 March, 1867, s. 8, v. 14, p. 517.   17 June, 1878, v. 20, p. 143.
15 July, 1870, s. 12, v. 16, p. 334.   5 Aug., 1882, P. E., p. 285.

NOTE.—A joint resolution, approved July 25, 1868, v. 15, p. 261, authorizes the Secretary of the Navy to receive for instruction at the Naval Academy, not exceeding six persons, to be designated by the government of the empire of Japan, *provided* that no expense shall thereby accrue to the United States; and that the Secretary of the Navy may, in the case of the said persons, modify or dispense with any provisions of the rules and regulations of the said Academy which circumstances may, in his opinion, render necessary or desirable.

SEC. 1514. The Secretary of the Navy shall, as soon after the 5th of March in each year as possible, notify, in writing, each Member and Delegate of the House of Representatives of any vacancy that may exist in his district. The nomination of a candidate to fill said vacancy shall be made upon the recommendation of the Member or Delegate, if such recommendation is made by the first day of July of that year; but if it is not made by that time, the Secretary of the Navy shall fill the vacancy. The candidate allowed for the District of Columbia and all the candidates appointed at large shall be selected by the President.

*Nomination of candidates.*

16 July, 1862, s. 11, v. 12, p. 585.

SEC. 1515. All candidates for admission into the Academy shall be examined according to such regulations and at such stated times as the Secretary of the Navy may prescribe. Candidates rejected at such examination shall not have the privilege of another examination for

*Examination of candidates.*

admission to the same class, unless recommended by the board of examiners.

16 July, 1862, s. 11, v. 12, p. 585.  17 April, 1866, s. 5, v. 14, p. 38.

NOTE.—Section 1515 is to be read as if the dates fixed by the regulations of the Academy for the examination of candidates for admission were inserted therein; and hence by the existing law the season for recommendations and nominations of naval cadets begins after the 5th of March and expires on the 22d of September in each year.—Op. XVI, p. 621. This opinion was given in the case of a member whose candidates, sent down in June, and September failed, and he wished to send another in January following. It was held that no nomination could be made until after the 5th of March.

Second recommendation.

SEC. 1516. When any candidate who has been nominated upon the recommendation of a Member or Delegate of the House of Representatives is found, upon examination, to be physically or mentally disqualified for admission, the Member or Delegate shall be notified to recommend another candidate, who shall be examined according to the provisions of the preceding section.

16 July, 1862, s. 11, v. 12, p. 585.  17 July, 1866, s. 5, v. 14, p. 38.

Qualifications.

SEC. 1517. Candidates allowed for congressional districts, for Territories, and for the District of Columbia must be actual residents of the districts or Territories, respectively, from which they are nominated. And all candidates must, at the time of their examination for admission, be between the ages of fourteen and eighteen years, and physically sound, well formed, and of robust constitution.

14 July, 1862, s. 9. v. 12, p. 565.  16 July, 1862, s. 11, v. 12, p. 585.
1 April, 1864, s. 2, v. 13, p. 39.

NOTE.—A candidate under fourteen or over eighteen years of age is not *between* the two ages, and cannot be appointed.—Op. 10, p. 315, July 29, 1862. For further discussion of the subject of appointments see Op. 10, pp. 46, 495. Op. 16, p. 621.

[The naval appropriation act of March 3, 1883, provides for the actual and necessary traveling expenses of naval cadets while proceeding from their homes to the Naval Academy for examination and *appointment* as naval cadets. Such expenses are not allowed to those not appointed.]

Appropriations, how applied.

SEC. 1518. No money appropriated for the support of the Naval Academy shall be applied to the support of any *naval cadet* appointed otherwise than in strict conformance with the provisions of this chapter.

21 May, 1864, s. 1, v. 13, p. 84.  5 Aug., 1882, P. E. L., p. 285.

Cadet-midshipmen found deficient.

SEC. 1519. *Naval cadets* found deficient at any examination shall not be continued at the Academy or in the service unless upon the recommendation of the academic board.

16 July, 1862, s. 11, v. 12, p. 585.  5 Aug., 1882, P. E. L., p. 285.

NOTES.—Under section 1519 the Secretary of the Navy has no right to continue at the Academy cadets found at any examination deficient in their *studies*, without the recommendation of the Academic Board.—Op. XV, p. 634.

By statutory definition, cadets are not to be included, in general, in legislation confined to "officers" of the Navy.—*Idem*.

Cadets, after the four years' course, are not entirely emancipated from probationary study; they are students at sea.—Op. XVI, p. 296.

Academic course.

SEC. 1520. The academic course of *naval cadets* shall be six years.

3 March, 1873, s. 1, v. 17, p. 555.  5 Aug., 1882, P. E. L., p. 285.

NOTE.—Under the act of July 4, 1864, s. 5, v. 13, p. 393, the academic course of cadet engineers was two years, and by the act of 3 March, 1873, s. 1, v. 17, p. 555, the course of instruction was made four years, including "two years of service in naval steamers, in addition to the period at the Naval Academy now provided by law." An act approved Feb. 24, 1874, s. 2, v. 18, p. 17, provided that after the 30th of June, 1874, the course of instruction at the Naval Academy for cadet engineers should be four years, instead of two, the provision to first apply to the class of cadet engineers entering the Academy in the year 1874, and to all subsequent classes.

Promotion to midshipmen.

SEC. 1521. When cadet midshipmen shall have passed successfully the graduating examination at the Academy, they shall receive appointments as midshipmen and shall take rank according to their proficiency as shown by the order of their merit at date of graduation. [See sec. 1512, and note under sec. 1483.]

15 July, 1870, s. 12, v. 16, p 334.

NOTE.—This section has been entirely altered by the act of August 5, 1882, as given in section 1512, above, and the act of March 3, 1883, under LINE OFFICERS, changing the title of midshipman to that of ensign.

Constructors and steam engineers.

SEC. 1522. The Secretary of the Navy is authorized to make provision, by regulations issued by him, for educating at the Naval Academy, as naval constructors or steam engineers, such midshipmen and others as may show a peculiar aptitude therefor. He may, for this purpose, form a separate class at the Academy, to be styled cadet engineers, or otherwise afford to such persons all proper facilities for such a scientific mechanical education as will fit them for said professions.

4 July, 1864, s. 1, v. 13, p. 393.

NOTE.—While so much of this section as authorized the formation of a class to be styled *cadet engineers* is, in effect, repealed by the act of August 5, 1882, sec. 1512, *ante.*, there still seems to be authority left to educate at the Academy persons for constructors, at least.—See, in this connection, next paragraph.

That the Secretary of the Navy may prescribe a special course of study and training at home or abroad for any naval cadet.  5 Aug., 1882.
Special course.

5 Aug., 1882, P. E. L., p. 285.

NOTE.—The deficiency act approved March 3, 1883, appropriates nine hundred dollars for tuition of two naval cadets at the Royal Naval College, Greenwich, and the naval appropriation act approved March 3, 1883, contains an item under Contingent Navy "for cost of special instruction abroad."

SEC. 1526. The Secretary of the Navy shall arrange the course of Title 15, Chap.44. studies and the order of recitations at the Naval Academy so that the students in said institution shall not be required to pursue their studies on Sunday.  Studies not to be pursued on Sunday.

15 July, 1870, s. 21, v. 16, p. 319.

SEC. 1527. The store-keeper at the Naval Academy shall be detailed Store-keeper at from the Paymaster's Corps, and shall have authority, with the approval of the Secretary of the Navy, to procure clothing and other necessaries for the *naval cadets* in the same manner as supplies are furnished to the Navy, to be issued under such regulations as may be prescribed by the Secretary of the Navy.  the Academy.

2 March, 1867, s. 4, v. 14, p. 516.  5 Aug., 1882, P. E. L., p. 285.

SEC. 1528. Three professors of mathematics shall be assigned to duty Professors of at the Naval Academy, one as professor of ethics and English studies, ethics, Spanish, one as professor of the Spanish language, and one as professor of drawing.  and drawing.

21 May, 1864, s. 3, v. 13, p. 85.

NOTE.—The three professors of mathematics for duty at the Naval Academy (ethics and English, Spanish, and drawing), should be commissioned as professors of mathematics under this section, after passing the examination required by act of January 21, 1881.—Op. May 18, 1881, McVeagh.

SEC. 1556. * * Cadet midsipmen, five hundred dollars. *During such* Title 15, Chap. 8. *period of their course of instruction as they shall be at sea in other than practice-ships, not exceeding nine hundred and fifty dollars.*  Pay of cadet-midshipmen.

15 July, 1870, s. 3, v. 16, p. 330.  3 March, 1877, v. 19, p. 390.
16 July, 1862, s. 15, v. 12, p. 586.

That the pay of naval cadets shall be that now allowed by law to 5, Aug., 1882. cadet midshipmen.  Pay of naval cadets.

5 Aug., 1882, P. E. L., p. 285.

NOTE.—Cadet engineers who complete the six years' course, pass successfully, and are subsequently commissioned assistant engineers, to fill vacancies, are entitled to the pay of the latter grade from the date they take rank therein, when subsequent to the vacancies they are appointed to fill. The words "any officer of the Navy," act June 22, 1874, chap. 392, sec. 1, comprehend cadet engineers. They are officers within the meaning of sections 1557 and 1558, and of a class subject to examination, sec. 1562. The signification of the word "officer," art. 36, sec. 1624, as given in Op. 15, p. 635, has reference to the sense in which that word is used in said article, between which and the statutory provisions herein cited there is no connection.—Op. April 10, 1882, Brewster.

SEC. 1577. Midshipmen and *naval cadets* in the Navy shall be entitled Title 15, Chap.8. to one ration, or to commutation therefor.  Rations.

28 July, 1866, s. 8, v. 14, p. 322.  28 Feb., 1867, s. 2, v. 14, p. 416.
5 Aug., 1882, P. E., p. 285,

NOTE.—Although the title of midshipman has been abolished or merged in that of ensign, constituting a junior grade thereof, the latter continue entitled to a ration.

In all cases when it shall come to the knowledge of the superintend- 23 June, 1874. ent of the Naval Academy, at Annapolis, that any *naval cadet* has been guilty of the offense commonly known as hazing, it shall be the duty of said superintendent to order a court-martial, composed of not less than three commissioned officers, who shall minutely examine into all the facts and circumstances of the case and make a finding thereon; and any *naval cadet* found guilty of said offense by said court shall, upon recom-  Hazing at Naval Academy.

Offenders to be court-martialed.

54    NAVAL CONSTRUCTORS.

Cadet found guilty to be dismissed. To be forever ineligible to reappointment.
mendation of said court be dismissed; and such finding, when approved by said superintendent, shall be final; and the cadet so dismissed from said Naval Academy shall be forever ineligible to reappointment to said Naval Academy.

23 June, 1874, v. 18, p. 203.
5 Aug., 1882, s. 1, P. E. L., p. 285.

NOTES.—Finding approved by the superintendent final. Secretary of the Navy no power to review it—he can only proceed to execute the sentence. Taft, Beale's case, Nov. 20, 1876 [not printed]. Designed to cut off a cadet found guilty of the offense, and sentence approved by superintendent, from all chance of reinstatement or reappointment. Must seek relief from Congress. Advises against pardon.—Op. 15, March 15 1876, p. 80.
When found guilty of hazing, the court must *recommend* dismissal, instead of sentencing to be dismissed.—Cases of Garrett and others, sentences set aside by Secretary of the Navy, June 9, 1877, O. L. B., p. 8.
Art. 36, sec. 1624, does not extend to cadets at the Naval Academy. They may be dismissed for misconduct without trial by court-martial. For hazing they must be tried.—Op. 15, p. 634, July 10, 1877.

14 Feb., 1879.
Board of Visitors.

There shall be appointed every year, in the following manner, a Board of Visitors, to attend the annual examination of the Academy: Seven persons shall be appointed by the President, and two Senators and three Members of the House of Representatives shall be designated as visitors by the Vice-President or President pro tempore of the Senate and the Speaker of the House of Representatives, respectively, at the session of Congress next preceding such examination. Each member of said board shall receive not exceeding eight cents per mile traveled by the most direct route from his residence to Annapolis, and eight cents per mile for each mile from said place to his residence on returning.

14 Feb., 1879, v. 20, p. 284. [Act of March 3, 1883, appropriated $1,500 for the expenses of the board.]

3 March, 1883.
Civil employés and their pay.

For pay of professors and others: For two professors, namely, one of mathematics and one of chemistry, at two thousand five hundred dollars each; three professors (assistants), namely, one of physics, one of Spanish, and one of English studies, history, and law, at two thousand two hundred dollars each; six assistant professors, namely, four of French, one of English studies, history, and laws, and one of drawing, at one thousand eight hundred dollars each; swordmaster, at one thousand five hundred dollars, and two assistants, at one thousand dollars each; boxing-master and gymnast, at one thousand two hundred dollars; assistant librarian, at one thousand four hundred dollars; secretary of the Naval Academy, one thousand eight hundred dollars; three clerks to superintendent, at one thousand two hundred dollars, one thousand dollars, and eight hundred dollars, respectively; one clerk to commandant of cadets, one thousand two hundred dollars; one clerk to paymaster, one thousand dollars; one dentist, one thousand six hundred dollars. * * *

3 March, 1883, P. E. L., p. 478. [Naval appropriation act.]

## NAVAL CONSTRUCTORS.

Sec.
425. Chief of Bureau.
1402. Number and appointment.
1404. Duty.
1471. Chief Constructor.

Sec.
1477. Rank.
1481. Rank on retirement.
1522. Education of, at Academy.
1556. Pay.

Title 10.
Chief of Bureau.

SEC. 425. The Chief of the Bureau of Construction and Repair shall be appointed from the list of officers of the Navy, not below the grade of commander, and shall be a skillful naval constructor. [Sec. 1471.]

5 July, 1862, s. 1, v. 12, p. 510.

NOTE.—See sec. 1481, as to the rank of constructors when retired from age or length of service.

Title 15, Chap. 1.
Number, appointment of, &c.

SEC. 1402. The President, by and with the advice and consent of the Senate, may appoint naval constructors, who shall have rank and pay as officers of the Navy.

25 July, 1866, s. 7, v. 14, p. 223.
3 March, 1871, s. 9, v. 16, p. 536.

Duty.

SEC. 1404. Naval constructors may be required to perform duty at any navy-yard or other station.

3 March, 1845, s. 2, v. 5, p. 724.

## ASSISTANT NAVAL CONSTRUCTORS.

SEC. 1471. The Chief of the Bureau of * * * Construction and Repair shall have the relative rank of commodore while holding said position, and shall have the title * * of Chief Constructor.

Title 15, Chap. 4.
Chief Constructor.

3 March, 1871, s. 12, v. 16, p. 537.

SEC. 1477. Of the naval constructors, two shall have the relative rank of captain, three of commander, and all others that of lieutenant-commander or lieutenant. * * *

Rank.

3 March, 1871, s. 9, v. 16, p. 536.

SEC. 1481. * * * Constructors who shall have served faithfully for forty-five years, shall, when retired, have the relative rank of commodore; and * * * who have been or shall be retired at the age of sixty-two years, before having served for forty-five years, but who shall have served faithfully until retired, shall, on the completion of forty years from their entry into the service, have the relative rank of commodore.

Rank on retirement.

3 March, 1871, s. 11, v. 16, p. 537.

SEC. 1522. The Secretary of the Navy is authorized to make provision, by regulations issued by him, for educating at the Naval Academy, as naval constructors * * * such *naval cadets* and others as may show a peculiar aptitude therefor. He may, for this purpose, form a separate class at the academy, * . * or otherwise afford to such persons all proper facilities for such a scientific mechanical education as will fit them for said profession. [See notes under sec. 1522, p. 53.]

Title 15, Chap. 5.
Education at Naval Academy

4 July, 1864, s. 1, v. 13, p. 303.    5 Aug., 1882, P. E. L., p. 285.

SEC. 1556. * * * Naval constructors, during the first five years after date of appointment, when on duty, three thousand two hundred dollars; on leave, or waiting orders, two thousand two hundred dollars; during the second five years after such date, when on duty, three thousand four hundred dollars; on leave, or waiting orders, two thousand four hundred dollars; during the third five years after such date, when on duty, three thousand seven hundred dollars; on leave, or waiting orders, two thousand seven hundred dollars; during the fourth five years after such date, when on duty, four thousand dollars; on leave, or waiting orders, three thousand dollars; after twenty years from such date, when on duty, four thousand two hundred dollars; on leave, or waiting orders, three thousand two hundred dollars.

Title 15, Chap. 8.
Pay.

15 July, 1870, s. 3, v. 16, p. 331.

## ASSISTANT NAVAL CONSTRUCTORS.

Sec.
1403. Appointment of.
1477. Rank.

Sec.
1556. Pay.

SEC. 1403. Cadet-engineers who are graduated with credit in the scientific and mechanical class of the Naval Academy may, upon the recommendation of the academic board, be immediately appointed as assistant naval constructors. [See § 1522, NAVAL CONSTRUCTORS.]

Title 15, Chap. 4.
Assistant naval constructors.

4 July, 1864, s. 2, v. 13, p. 393.

SEC. 1477. * * * Assistant naval constructors shall have the relative rank of lieutenant or master.*

Rank.

3 March, 1871, s. 9, v. 16, p. 536.

SEC. 1556. * * * Assistant naval constructors, during the first four years after date of appointment, when on duty, two thousand dollars; on leave, or waiting orders, one thousand five hundred dollars; during the second four years after such date, when on duty, two thousand two hundred dollars; on leave, or waiting orders, one thousand seven hundred dollars; after eight years from such date, when on duty, two thousand six hundred dollars; on leave, or waiting orders, one thousand nine hundred dollars.

Title 15, Chap. 8.
Pay.

15 July, 1870, s. 3, v. 16, p. 331.

---

*Lieutenant of the junior grade.

## NAVAL OBSERVATORY.

Sec.
434. Pay of superintendent.
435. Meridians adopted.
1401. Professors' duties.

Sec.
——. Assistant astronomers and clerk.
——. Purchase of new site.

Title 10.  
Pay of superintendent.

SEC. 434. The officer of the Navy employed as superintendent of the Naval Observatory at Washington shall be entitled to receive the shore duty pay of his grade, and no other.

3 March, 1865, v. 13, p. 533.

Meridians.

SEC. 435. The meridian of the Observatory at Washington shall be adopted and used as the American meridian for all astronomical purposes, and the meridian of Greenwich shall be adopted for all nautical purposes.

28 Sept., 1850, s. 1, v. 9, p. 515.

Title 15, Chap. 1  
Duties of professors.

SEC. 1401. Professors of mathematics shall perform such duties as may be assigned them by order of the Secretary of the Navy, at the * * * Naval Observatory. * * *

3 Aug., 1848, s. 12, v. 9, p. 272.

Assistant astronomers and clerk.

Naval Observatory: For pay of three assistant astronomers, four thousand nine hundred dollars; one clerk of class four; one instrument-maker, fifteen hundred dollars; four watchmen, including one for new Naval Observatory grounds; two skilled laborers, one at one thousand dollars, and one at seven hundred and twenty dollars; and seven laborers; in all, seventeen thousand four hundred and twenty dollars.

3 March, 1883, P. E. L., p. 554.

[Under an act approved Febuary 14, 1880, v. 21, p. 65, a commission was appointed by whom a site was selected and purchased for a new Observatory. The sum of $75,000 was appropriated.]

## NAVAL STORE-KEEPERS.

Sec.
1413. Store-keepers at navy-yards.
1414. Store-keepers on foreign stations.
1415. Store-keeper's bond.
1438. Officers to act as store-keepers on foreign stations.

Sec.
1439. Bonds of.
1527. Store-keeper at the Academy.
1567. Officers serving as store-keepers on foreign stations.
1568. Civilians, store-keepers on foreign stations.

Title 15, Chap. 1.  
Store-keepers at navy-yards.

SEC. 1413. The President, by and with the advice and consent of the Senate, may appoint * * * a naval store-keeper at each of the navy-yards where such officers may be necessary.

2 March, 1867, s. 1, v. 14, p. 490.
17 June, 1868, s. 1, v. 15 p. 69.

Store-keepers on foreign stations.

SEC. 1414. The Secretary of the Navy may appoint citizens who are not officers of the Navy to be store-keepers on foreign stations, when suitable officers of the Navy cannot be ordered on such service, or when, in his opinion, the public interest will be thereby promoted. [Sec. 1568.]

17 June, 1844, s. 1, v. 5, p. 700.
3 March, 1847, s. 3, v. 9. p. 172.

Store-keeper's bond.

SEC. 1415. Every person who is appointed store-keeper under the provisions of the preceding section shall be required to give a bond, in such amount as may be fixed by the Secretary of the Navy, for the faithful performance of his duty.

*Idem.*

Title 15, Chap. 2.  
Officers to act as store-keepers on foreign stations.

SEC. 1438. The Secretary of the Navy shall order a suitable commissioned or warrant officer of the Navy, except in the case provided in section fourteen hundred and fourteen, to take charge of the naval stores for foreign squadrons at each of the foreign stations where such stores may be deposited, and where a store-keeper may be necessary [See § 1567.]

*Idem.*

NAVY-YARDS AND STATIONS. 57

Sec. 1439. Every officer so acting as store-keeper on a foreign station shall be required to give a bond, in such amount as may be fixed by the Secretary of the Navy, for the faithful performance of his duty.  **Bonds of.**

17 June, 1844, s. 1, v. 5, p. 700.

Sec. 1527. The store-keeper at the Naval Academy shall be detailed from the Paymasters' Corps, and shall have authority, with the approval of the Secretary of the Navy, to procure clothing and other necessaries for the *naval cadets* in the same manner as supplies are furnished to the Navy, to be issued under such regulations as may be prescribed by the Secretary of the Navy.  **Title 15, Chap. 5. Store-keeper at the Academy.**

2 March, 1867, s. 4, v. 14, p. 516.    5 Aug., 1882, P. E. L., p. 285.

Sec. 1567. Officers who are ordered to take charge of naval stores for foreign squadrons, in the place of naval store-keepers, shall be entitled to receive, while so employed, the shore-duty pay of their grades; and when the same is less than fifteen hundred dollars a year, they may be allowed compensation, including such shore-duty pay, at a rate not exceeding fifteen hundred dollars a year.  **Title 15, Chap. 8. Pay of officers serving as store-keepers on foreign stations.**

17 June, 1844, s. 1, v. 5, p. 700.

Sec. 1568. Civilians appointed as store-keepers on foreign stations shall receive compensation for such services, at a rate not exceeding fifteen hundred dollars a year.  **Pay of civilians, store-keepers on foreign stations.**

17 June, 1844, s. 1, v. 5, p. 700.    3 March, 1847, s. 3, v. 9, p. 172.

## NAVY-YARDS AND STATIONS.

| Sec. | | Sec. | |
|---|---|---|---|
| 355. | Title to land to be purchased. | 3738. | Eight hours a day's labor. |
| 1413. | Civil engineers and storekeepers. | —— | Rates of wages. |
| 1416. | Civil officers at yards may be discontinued. | 5385. | Arson in navy-yards, &c. |
| 1542. | Commandants of navy-yards. | 5386. | Same. |
| 1543. | Master workmen. | 5387. | Arson of vessels of war. |
| 1544. | Laborers, how selected. | —— | Prohibition on increasing force. |
| 1545. | Salaries; per diem compensation. | —— | Wet dock at Norfolk. |
| 1546. | Requiring contributions for political purposes at navy-yards. | —— | Navy-yard commission. |
| 1638. | Land purchased for yards. | —— | Coaling station, Port Royal. |
| 3728. | Fuel for navy-yards. | —— | Establishment of Government foundry. |
| 3730. | No land to be purchased without authority of law. | —— | Training station, Coaster's Harbor Island. |
| | | —— | Closing the yards. |

Sec. 355. No public money shall be expended upon any site or land purchased by the United States for the purposes of erecting thereon any armory, arsenal, fort, fortification, navy-yard, custom-house, light-house, or other public building, of any kind whatever, until the written opinion of the Attorney-General shall be had in favor of the validity of the title, nor until the consent of the legislature of the State in which the land or site may be, to such purchase, has been given. The district attorneys of the United States, upon the application of the Attorney-General, shall furnish any assistance or information in their power in relation to the titles of the public lying within their respective districts. And the Secretaries of the Departments, upon the application of the Attorney-General, shall procure any additional evidence of title which he may deem necessary, and which may not be in the possession of the officers of the Government, and the expense of procuring it shall be paid out of the appropriations made for the contingencies of the Departments respectively. [See sec. 1838.]  **Title 8. Title to land to be purchased by the United States.**

11 Sept., 1841, v. 5, p. 468.

Sec. 1413. The President, by and with the advice and consent of the Senate, may appoint a civil engineer and a naval store-keeper at each of the navy-yards where such officers may be necessary. [See 1415, NAVAL STORE-KEEPERS.]  **Title 15, Chap. 1. Civil engineers and store-keepers at navy-yards**

2 March, 1867, s. 1, v. 14, p. 490.    17 June, 1868, s. 1, v. 15, p. 69.

Sec. 1416. The Secretary of the Navy is authorized, when in his opinion the public interest will permit it, to discontinue the office or employment of any measurer and inspector of timber, clerk of the yard, clerk of the commandant, clerk of the store-keeper, clerk of the naval constructor, and the keeper of the magazine employed at any navy-yard, and to require the duties of the keeper of the magazine to be performed by gunners.  **Discontinuation of civil officers.**

10 Aug., 1846, s. 1, v. 9, p. 98.

**Title 15, Chap. 6.**

*Selection of commandants.*

SEC. 1542. The President may select the commandants of the several navy-yards from officers not below the grade of commander.

2 Aug., 1861, v. 12, p. 285.
5 July, 1862, s. 2, v. 12, p. 510.

*Selection of master workmen.*

SEC. 1543. The persons employed at the several navy-yards to superintend the mechanical departments, and heretofore known as master mechanics, master carpenters, master joiners, master blacksmiths, master boiler-makers, master sail-makers, master plumbers, master painters, master calkers, master masons, master boat-builders, master spar-makers, master block-makers, master laborers, and the superintendents of rope-walks shall be men skilled in their several duties and appointed from civil life, and shall not be appointed from the officers of the Navy.

17 June, 1868, s. 1, v. 15, p. 69.

*Selection of laborers.*

SEC. 1544. Laborers shall be employed in the several navy-yards by the proper officers in charge with reference to skill and efficiency, and without regard to other considerations.

23 May, 1872, s. 1, v. 17, p. 146.

*Salaries; per diem compensation.*

SEC. 1545. Salaries shall not be paid to any employés in any of the navy-yards, except those who are designated in the estimates. All other persons shall receive a per diem compensation for the time during which they may be actually employed.

14 July, 1862, s. 1, v. 12, p. 564.

NOTE.—By the acts of July 28, 1870, R. S. D. C., s. 902, and January 31, 1879, v. 20, p. 277, the first day of January, the twenty-second day of February, the fourth day of July, the twentyfifth day of December, and any day appointed or recommended by the President of the United States as a day of fast or thanksgiving, shall be holidays in the District of Columbia.

*Political contributions.*

SEC. 1546. No officer or employé of the Government shall require or request any working man in any navy-yard to contribute or pay any money for political purposes, nor shall any working man be removed or discharged for political opinion; and any officer or employé of the Government who shall offend against the provisions of this section shall be dismissed from the service of the United States. [See under Ex. Departments, act Jan. 16, 1883, Part III.]

2 March, 1867, s. 3, v. 14, p. 492.

**Title 22.**

*Assent of States to purchase of lands for forts, &c.*

SEC. 1838. The President of the United States is authorized to procure the assent of the legislature of any State, within which any purchase of land has been made for the erection of forts, magazines, arsenals, dock-yards, and other needful buildings, without such consent having been obtained.

28 April, 1828, s. 2, v. 4, p. 264.

**Title 43.**

*Fuel.*

SEC. 3728. " * * In purchasing fuel for the Navy, or for naval stations and yards, the Secretary of the Navy shall have power to discriminate and purchase, in such manner as he may deem proper, that kind of fuel which is best adapted to the purpose for which it is to be used.

28 Sept., 1850, s. 1, v. 9, p. 513.

*Restriction on purchase of land.*

SEC. 3736. No land shall be purchased on account of the United States, except under a law authorizing such purchase.

1 May, 1820, s. 7, v. 3, p. 568.

*Eight hours a day's labor.*

SEC. 3738. Eight hours shall constitute a day's work for all laborers, workmen, and mechanics who may be employed by or on behalf of the Government of the United States. [See this section under CONTRACTS, Part I, and § 3689, under APPROPRIATIONS, Part III.]

25 June, 1868, v. 15, p. 77.

*16 July, 1862. Rate of wages and hours of labor.*

That the hours of labor and the rate of wages of the employés in the navy-yards shall conform, as nearly as is consistent with the public interest, with those of private establishments in the immediate vicinity of the respective yards, to be determined by the commandants of the navy-yards, subject to the approval and revision of the Secretary of the Navy.

12 Dec., 1861, s. 8, v. 12, p. 330. 8 July, 1862, v. 12, p. 587.

NOTE.—This act is omitted from the Revised Statutes, but has been always recognized as governing the rates of wages, also the hours of labor until the passage of the eight-hour law.

# NAVY-YARDS AND STATIONS. 59

SEC. 5385. Every person who, within any fort, dock-yard, navy-yard, arsenal, armory, or magazine, the site whereof is under the jurisdiction of the United States, or on the site of any light-house, or other needful building belonging to the United States, the site whereof is under their jurisdiction, willfully and maliciously burns any dwelling-house, or mansion-house, or any store, barn, stable, or other building, parcel of any dwelling or mansion-house, shall suffer death.

*Title 70, Chap. 3.*
*Arson of dwelling-house within a fort, &c.*

3 March, 1825, s. 1, v. 4, p. 115.

SEC. 5386. Every person who, in any of the places mentioned in the preceding section, maliciously sets fire to, or burns, any arsenal, armory, magazine, rope-walk, ship-house, warehouse, block-house, or barrack, or any store-house, barn, or stable, not parcel of a dwelling-house, or any other building not mentioned in such section, or any vessel built, or begun to be built, or repairing, or any light-house, or beacon, or any timber, cables, rigging, or other materials for building, repairing, or fitting out vessels, or any pile of wood, boards, or other lumber, or any military, naval, or victualing stores, arms, or other munitions of war, shall be punished by a fine of not more than five thousand dollars, and by imprisonment at hard labor not more than ten years.

*Arson of armory, arsenal, &c.*

*Idem*, s. 2.

SEC. 5387. Every person who maliciously sets on fire, or burns, or otherwise destroys, any vessel of war of the United States, afloat on the high seas, or in any arm of the sea, or in any river, haven, creek, basin, or bay within the admiralty jurisdiction of the United States, and out of the jurisdiction of any particular State, shall suffer death.

*Arson of vessel of war.*

*Idem*, s. 11, p. 117.

No increase of the force at any navy-yard shall be made at any time within sixty days next before any election to take place for President of the United States, or member of Congress, except when the Secretary of the Navy shall certify that the needs of the public service make such increase necessary at that time, which certificate shall be immediately published when made.

*30 June, 1876.*
*Prohibition on increase of force.*

30 June, 1876, v. 19, p. 65.

(See also under SECRETARIES and CLERKS.)

That the Secretary of the Navy be, and he is hereby, authorized and directed to ascertain on what terms can be had such additional lands and water front contiguous to the Norfolk navy-yard as are deemed necessary for the construction of a wet-dock, and such other works as are demanded for the sufficient capacity and efficiency of that yard; and that he report the result of such negotiations to the next session of Congress.

*5 Aug., 1882.*
*Wet-dock at Norfolk.*

5 Aug., 1882, P. E. L., p. 289. [Naval appropriation act.]

That the Secretary of the Navy shall appoint a commission, to consist of three persons, one of whom shall be appointed from the line officers and one from the staff officers of the Navy, and one from civil life, which commission shall consider and report to the next session of Congress upon the question whether it is advisable to sell any of the navy-yards, and, if so, which; and as to each of said yards said commission shall report as to its cost, its area, its present value, including in separate items the value of the land, structures, machinery, and other personal property; the depth of water at the yard, and whether it remains and will remain at such depth, or will require expense to keep open its water communication; its condition as to being in working order or otherwise; the condition and value of its "plant" in the different departments; its advantages and disadvantages as a naval station, and for the construction of vessels; its probable value for other purposes, in case the yard is discontinued; whether there is any demand for the yard for mercantile or other purposes; whether it can probably be sold, and at what price, in case of discontinuance; the annual cost during each of the past fifteen years of maintaining it; the value of what it has produced during each of said years, so far as it can be ascertained; its value or necessity for purposes of defense on that part of the coast where it is situated, or in general, and also as regards any city in its vicinity;

*Navy-yard commission.*

## NAVY-YARDS AND STATIONS.

and any other facts which such commission may deem useful or advisable to report in regard to this question.

*Idem.*

NOTE.—The sundry civil act of March 3, 1883, appropriated $1,500 for the expenses and services of the civil commissioner and the incidental expenses of the commission.

7 Aug., 1882.
Coaling-dock, Port Royal.

For establishing and completing a coaling-dock and naval storehouse at Port Royal Harbor, South Carolina, twenty thousand dollars, the site for said coaling-dock and naval storehouse to be located by a board of naval officers appointed by the Secretary of the Navy for that purpose.

7 Aug., 1882. P. E. L., p. 324. [Sundry civil act.]

3 March, 1883.
Coaling station at Port Royal.

That the Secretary of the Navy be, and he is hereby, authorized to purchase a site for a coaling dock and naval storehouse at Port Royal, South Carolina, located by the board of naval officers in pursuance of the provisions of an act entitled "An act making appropriations for sundry civil expenses of the government for the fiscal year ending June thirtieth, eighteen hundred and eighty-three, and for other purposes," approved August seventh, eighteen hundred and eighty three, and the sum of five thousand dollars, or so much thereof as may be necessary, is hereby appropriated for that purpose, out of any money in the Treasury not otherwise appropriated.

3 March, 1883, P. E. L., p. 627. [Sundry civil act.]

3 March, 1883.
Establishment of a Government foundry.

That the President of the United States is hereby authorized and requested to select from the Army and Navy six officers, who shall constitute a board for the purpose of examining and reporting to Congress which of the navy-yards or arsenals owned by the Government has the best location and is best adapted for the establishment of a government foundry, or what other method, if any, should be adopted for the manufacture of heavy ordnance adapted to modern warfare, for the use of the Army and Navy of the United States, the cost of all buildings, tools, and implements necessary to be used in the manufacture thereof, including the cost of a steam-hammer or apparatus of sufficient size for the manufacture of the heaviest guns; and that the President is further requested to report to Congress the finding of said board at as early a date as possible; *Provided,* That no extra compensation shall be paid the officers serving on the board hereby created.

3 March, 1883, P. E. L., p. 474. [Naval appropriation act.]

7 Aug., 1882.
Training station, Coasters' Harbor Island.

For repairing and extending wharf and the erection of boat-houses on Coasters' Harbor Island, five thousand dollars. And the cession by the State of Rhode Island to the United States of said Island for use as a Naval Training Station is hereby accepted.

7 Aug., 1882. Sundry civil act. P. E. L., p. 324.

For continuation of the wharf and for a rigging and sail loft and drill-hall on Coasters' Harbor Island, forty-five thousand dollars.

3 March, 1883, P. E. L., p. 620. [Sundry civil act.]

### CLOSING OF YARDS.

5 Aug., 1882.
Suspension of work.

Closing of yards.

Exceptions.

For the civil establishment at navy-yards and stations, eighteen thousand nine hundred and fifty-three dollars and twelve cents: *Provided,* That if the Secretary of the Navy shall find that work at all the navy-yards now maintained cannot be carried on during the current fiscal year with advantage to the service and economy to the Government for the amounts in this act appropriated for the maintenance of and civil establishment at the navy-yards, he shall not make any deficiency for these purposes, but he shall suspend work at those yards where he finds it can best be dispensed with, and shall close such yards and transfer all perishable property and stores therefrom to other yards for use therein, and report the facts and the reasons governing his action to the next session of Congress; and at the yards so closed only such officers and employés shall be retained as are necessary to preserve and take care of the property of the Government, and all other persons shall be transferred or discharged: *Provided further,* That the navy-yard at Washington, District of Columbia, may, at the discretion of the Secretary of the Navy, be maintained as a manufacturing yard for the Bureaus of Equipment and Recruiting and Ordnance, and that work may be continued in the rope-walk in the Boston navy-yard: *And provided further,* That nothing herein shall be held to interfere with the permanent improvement of any navy-yard as now authorized by law, or the expenditure for such purpose of any money appropriated by Congress therefor.

5 Aug., 1882, P. E. L., p. 289.

(See also PUBLIC PROPERTY, Part III, as to inventories and sale of old materials.)

## PAY CORPS.*

(See also ACCOUNTS and DISBURSING OFFICERS, Part III.)

Sec.
- 425. Paymaster-General.
- 1376. Pay Corps, number of.
- 1378. Appointments, how made.
- 1379. Qualifications of assistant paymasters.
- 1380. Order of promotion.
- 1381. Acting appointments on ships at sea.
- 1382. Paymaster of the fleet.
- 1383. Bonds.
- 1384. New bonds.
- 1385. Bond not affected by new commission.
- 1386. Clerks, when allowed.
- 1387. Clerks, when not allowed.

Sec.
- 1388. Clerks of passed assistant and assistant paymasters.
- 1389. Loans to officers by paymasters.
- 1432. Commanding officers not required to act as paymasters.
- 1471. Rank Paymaster-General.
- 1475. Rank generally.
- 1481. Rank of retired officers.
- 1527. Storekeeper at Naval Academy.
- 1556. Pay.
- 1564. Vacancies occurring at sea.

SEC. 425. The Chief of the Bureau of Provisions and Clothing shall be appointed from the list of paymasters of the Navy of not less than ten years' standing. [See 1471 and 1481.]   *Title 10.*

5 July, 1862, s. 1, v. 12, p. 510.

SEC. 1376. The active list of the Pay Corps of the Navy shall consist of thirteen pay directors, thirteen pay inspectors, *forty* paymasters, *twenty* passed assistant paymasters, and *ten* assistant paymasters.   *Title 15, Chap. 1. Pay Corps, number of.*

15 July, 1870, s. 11, v. 16, p. 334.   3 March, 1871, s. 6, v. 16, p. 536.
5 Aug., 1882, P. E. L., p. 284.

[The naval appropriation act, approved March 3, 1883, provides that thereafter only one-half of the vacancies in the Pay Corps shall be filled by promotion until the number in each grade is reduced to that fixed by the act of August 5, 1882, § 1376.]

---

*Pay does not include rations or subsistence.—Op. II, 420, 593. The word "pay" in acts of Congress concerning compensation of officers of the Army, Navy, and Marine Corps does not embrace the emoluments or allowances which are given by law in the absence of a clearly expressed intention to that effect.—"Levant," case, Op. X, 284. The word "emolument," in military statutes, includes every allowance or perquisite annexed to an office for the benefit of the officer, and by way of compensation for services. Quarters are so given, and whether in money or in kind, are none the less an emolument. Pay and emoluments include quarters.—Op. IX, 281. "Compensation" is equivalent to the words "pay" or "salary;" does not include rations nor extra expenses.—Op. II, 593; III, 152.

It is within the authority of Congress to *reduce* the pay or allowances of officers and soldiers at any time during their period of service or enlistment. It cannot be done by executive authority or military authority; nor can a soldier's pay be *withheld* except in pursuance of law or sentence.—Winthrop, 366.

Where an act of Congress fixes the compensation of an officer of the Government it can neither be enlarged nor diminished by any regulation or order of the President or of a Department, unless the power to make the same is given by act of Congress.—Goldsborough *v.* United States, Taney, 80.

An officer or soldier cannot be dismissed, discharged, or mustered out as of a prior date with the effect of depriving him of pay accrued between that date and the date of the actual discharge, &c.—Winthrop's Digest, 362.

It is not within the power of the executive department, or any branch of it, to reduce the pay of an officer of the Army.—Winthrop, p. 366; quotes 23 Wallace, 416.

So long as a person is in the Army or the Navy he is entitled to receive the pay belonging to the position, unless he has forfeited it in accordance with the provisions of law.—Op. XIII. 104, June 16, 1869.—Op. XV, 175, Nov. 9, 1876.

An officer is entitled to the salary allowed by law, and is not limited to the amount appropriated by Congress.—C. C., I, 380.

An officer's "pay account" is not commercial paper, but in its legal aspect a mere receipt. If assigned, and payment made to the assignee, the name of the latter on the back does not make him responsible to the paymaster as an *indorser*, on ascertaining that the officer had already drawn his pay for the month.—Winthrop's Digest, 361.

A paymaster on shore duty at a navy-yard is not entitled to pay for sea duty, though required by the Secretary of the Navy, in addition to his regular duties, to take charge of the accounts of certain iron-clads temporarily at anchor off the yard and in commission for sea service.—Carpenter's case, C. C., XV, 247.

*Graduated pay of officers:* See Op. X, p. 97, Aug. 13; p. 101, Aug. 19, 1861; and p. 326, Aug. 28, 1862.

## PAY CORPS.

**Appointments, how made.**

SEC. 1378. All appointments in the Pay Corps shall be made by the President, by and with the advice and consent of the Senate.

30 March, 1812, s. 6, v. 2, p. 699.    22 June, 1860, s. 3, v. 12, p. 83.
17 July, 1861, s. 1, v. 12, p. 258.    3 May, 1866, s. 1, v. 14, p. 43.

**Qualifications of assistant paymasters**

SEC. 1379. No person shall be appointed assistant paymaster who is, at the time of such appointment, less than twenty-one or more than twenty-six years of age; nor until his physical, mental, and moral qualifications have been examined and approved by a board of paymasters appointed by the Secretary of the Navy, and according to such regulations as he may prescribe.

17 July, 1861, s. 2, v. 12, p. 258.

**Order of promotion.**

SEC. 1380. Passed assistant paymasters shall be regularly promoted and commissioned from assistant paymasters, and paymasters from passed assistant paymasters; subject to such examinations as may be prescribed by the Secretary of the Navy. [See March 3, 1883, under PROMOTION.]

17 July, 1861, s. 5, v. 12, p. 258.    3 May, 1866, s. 1, v. 14, p. 43.

**Acting appointments on ships at sea.**

SEC. 1381. When the office of paymaster or assistant paymaster becomes vacant, by death or otherwise, in ships at sea, or on foreign stations, or on the Pacific coast of the United States, the senior officer present may make an acting appointment of any fit person, who shall perform the duties thereof until another paymaster or assistant paymaster shall report for duty, and shall be entitled to receive the pay of such grade while so acting. [See § 1564.]

17 July, 1861, s. 4, v. 12, p. 258.

**Paymasters of the fleet.**

SEC. 1382. The President may designate among the paymasters in the service, and appoint to every fleet or squadron a paymaster, who shall be denominated "paymaster of the fleet."

24 May, 1828, s. 2, v. 4, p. 313.    21 April, 1864, s. 7, v. 13, p. 54.

**Bonds.**

SEC. 1383. Every paymaster, passed assistant paymaster, and assistant paymaster shall, before entering on the duties of his office, give bond, with two or more sufficient sureties, to be approved by the Secretary of the Navy, for the faithful performance thereof. Paymasters shall give bonds in the sum of twenty-five thousand dollars, passed assistant paymasters in the sum of fifteen thousand dollars, and assistant paymasters in the sum of ten thousand dollars.

30 March, 1812, s. 6, v. 2, p. 699.    17 July, 1861, s. 5, v. 12, p. 258.
1 March, 1817, s. 1, v. 3, p. 350.    14 July, 1862, s. 1, v. 12, s. 575.
22 June, 1860, s. 3, v. 12, p. 83.    3 May, 1866, s. 2, v. 14, p. 43.

**New bonds.**

SEC. 1384. Officers of the Pay Corps shall give new bonds with sufficient sureties, whenever required to do so by the Secretary of the Navy.

26 Aug., 1842, s. 4, v. 5, p. 535.

**Bond not affected by a new commission.**

SEC. 1385. The issuing of a new appointment and commission to any officer of the Pay Corps shall not affect or annul any existing bond, but the same shall remain in force, and apply to such new appointment and commission.

3 March, 1871, s. 6, v. 16, p. 536.

NOTES.—An appointment, by the President, to the end of the next session of Congress, is not continued by a new appointment and commission by and with the advice and consent of the Senate. The latter is a distinct appointment, and requires a new bond. Sureties on the first not released on account of failure of the Senate to confirm the second.—*United States v. Kilpatrick*, 9 Wheaton, 720; *United States v. Spencer*, 2d McLean, 265; Op. IV, p. 30, May 20, 1842.

A bond is confined, in its obligatory force, to acts done whilst a commission has a legal continuance.—Op. XV, p. 214, cites 9 Wheaton, 734.

A bond, to be accepted by the Government, ought to be executed by the obligees and not by their attorneys.—Op. IX, p. 128, Nov. 5, 1857.

The Supreme Court has repeatedly decided that the sureties of a bonded officer are only responsible for the faithful performance of his duties for the legal term of his appointment.—Op. XI, p. 286, July 11, 1865.

Bonds cover not merely duties imposed by existing law, but duties belonging to and naturally connected with the office, imposed by subsequent law, provided that the new duties have relation to such office.—*United States v. Sanger*, 15 Wallace, p. 112.

A paymaster's bond takes effect from the date of its approval by the Secretary of the Navy. See Op. XIV, p. 7, and 19 Howard, p. 73, as to when bonds go into effect. Under sec. 1560, R. S., the pay of a bonded officer of the Navy commences on the day of the approval, by the proper authority, of his bond.

Duties imposed on an officer different in their nature from those which he was required to perform at the time his official bond was given do not render it void as an undertaking for the faithful performance of those which he at first assumed.—Otto 97, p. 584.

## PAY CORPS. 63

Judgment cannot be rendered beyond the penalty, to be discharged on the payment of the sum actually due. Cannot exceed the penalty with interest from the breach.—United States v. Picketts, 2 Cranch C. C., 553; Farrar v. United States, 5 Peters, 373.

*Memoranda of Instructions.* (*Approved by the Navy Department.*)

A bond should bear even date with or prior to the affidavits of sureties and certificates of their sufficiency.

Two or more witnesses are required to the signing and sealing of the bond.

Seals of wafer or wax must be attached where indicated on the bond, opposite the places for the signatures of the principal and each surety.

Two or more sureties are required, but pay officers are advised not to divide the penalty among many sureties in small amounts. This is cumbersome and unnecessary, as each surety is bound for the full penalty of the bond.

The sureties are to be certified to by a United States judge or attorney of the district in which the sureties reside.

In case females are offered as sureties, an additional certificate will be required (from the United States judge or attorney, whose certificate is required to the sufficiency of all the sureties) to the effect that such surety is unmarried, and that she holds her property in her own right.

Pay officers will be careful to avoid erasures or alterations in any portion of the bond. The form should be neatly filled, and signatures legibly written.

A married woman may be accepted as surety on a bond if her contract is executed in a State, &c., where by statute a woman, though married, is authorized to enter into contracts and hold property in her own right precisely as if she were single. A statement should be properly added in the affidavit that the affiant is worth the sum specified *in her own right.*—Winthrop's Digest, p. 127.

SEC. 1386. Paymasters of the fleet, paymasters on vessels having complements of more than one hundred and seventy-five persons, on supply-steamers, store-vessels, and receiving-ships, paymasters at stations and at the Naval Academy, and paymasters detailed at stations as inspectors of provisions and clothing, shall each be allowed a clerk. — Clerks, when allowed.

14 July, 1862, s. 3, v. 12, p. 565.   26 May, 1864, v. 13. p. 92.

SEC. 1387. No paymaster shall be allowed a clerk in a vessel having the complement of one hundred and seventy-five persons or less, excepting in supply-steamers and store-vessels. — Clerks, when not allowed.

26 May, 1864, v. 13, p. 92.

SEC. 1388. Passed assistant paymasters and assistant paymasters attached to vessels of war shall be allowed clerks, if clerks would be allowed by law to paymasters so attached. — Clerks of passed assistant and assistant paymasters.

3 March, 1863, s. 5, v. 12, p. 818.

SEC. 1389. It shall not be lawful for any paymaster, passed assistant paymaster, or assistant paymaster, to advance or loan, under any pretense whatever, to any officer in the naval service, any sum of money, public or private, or any credit, or any article or commodity whatever. — Loans to officers by paymasters.

26 Aug., 1842, s. 6, v. 5, p. 536.   22 June, 1860, s. 3, v. 12, p. 83.

SEC. 1432. No commanding officer of any vessel of the Navy shall be required to perform the duties of a paymaster, passed assistant paymaster, or assistant paymaster. — Title 15, Chap. 2. Commanding officers not to act as paymasters.

17 July, 1861, s. 4, v. 12, p. 256.

SEC. 1471. The Chief of the Bureau of * * Provisions and Clothing * * shall have the relative rank of commodore while holding said position, and shall have the title of * * paymaster-general. — Title 15, Chap. 4. Rank.

3 March, 1871, s. 12, v. 16, p. 537.

SEC. 1475. Officers of the Pay Corps on the active list of the Navy shall have relative rank as follows:

Pay directors, the relative rank of captain.
Pay inspectors, the relative rank of commander.
Paymasters, the relative rank of lieutenant-commander or lieutenant.
Passed assistant paymasters, the relative rank of lieutenant or master.*
Assistant paymasters, the relative rank of master* or ensign.

3 March, 1871, s. 6, v. 16, p. 536.

SEC. 1481. Officers of the * * Pay Corps * * who shall have served faithfully for forty-five years, shall, when retired, have the relative rank of Commodore; * * and who have been or who shall be retired at the age of sixty-two years before having served for forty-five years, but who shall have served faithfully until retired, shall, on the completion of forty years from their entry into the service, have the relative rank of Commodore.

3 March, 1871, s. 11, v. 16, p. 256.

---

* *Lieutenant of the junior grade.*

## PAY CORPS.

**Title 15, Chap. 5.**

*Store-keeper at the academy.*

SEC. 1527. The store-keeper at the Naval Academy shall be detailed from the Paymaster's Corps, and shall have authority, with the approval of the Secretary of the Navy, to procure clothing and other necessaries for the *naval cadets* in the same manner as supplies are furnished to the Navy, to be issued under such regulation as may be prescribed by the Secretary of the Navy.

2 March, 1867, s. 4, v. 14, p. 516.
5 Aug., 1882, P. E. L., p. 285.

**Title 15, Chap. 8.**

*Pay of fleet paymasters.*

SEC. 1556. * * * Fleet paymasters, * * * four thousand four hundred dollars.

15 July, 1870, s. 3, v. 16, p. 330.

*Pay directors and inspectors.*

* * * Pay directors and pay inspectors, * * * when on duty at sea, four thousand four hundred dollars. When not at sea, the same as * * paymasters.

15 July, 1870, s. 3, v. 16, p. 331.
3 March, 1871, ss. 5, 6, v. 16, pp. 535, 536.
3 March, 1873, s. 1, v. 17, p. 535.

*Paymasters.*

* * * Paymasters, during the first five years after date of commission, when at sea, two thousand eight hundred dollars; on shore duty, two thousand four hundred dollars; on leave, or waiting orders, two thousand dollars; during the second five years after such date, when at sea, three thousand two hundred dollars; on shore duty, two thousand eight hundred dollars; on leave, or waiting orders, two thousand four hundred dollars; during the third five years after such date, when at sea, three thousand five hundred dollars; on shore duty, three thousand two hundred dollars; on leave, or waiting orders, two thousand six hundred dollars; during the fourth five years after such date, when at sea, three thousand seven hundred dollars; on shore duty, three thousand six hundred dollars; on leave, or waiting orders, two thousand eight hundred dollars; after twenty years from such date, when at sea, four thousand two hundred dollars; on shore duty, four thousand dollars; on leave, or waiting orders, three thousand dollars.

*Passed assistant paymasters.*

* * * Passed assistant paymasters, * * * during the first five years after date of appointment, when at sea, two thousand dollars; on shore duty, one thousand eight hundred dollars; on leave, or waiting orders, one thousand five hundred dollars; after five years from such date, when at sea, two thousand two hundred dollars; on shore duty, two thousand dollars; on leave, or waiting orders, one thousand seven hundred dollars.

*Assistant paymasters.*

* * * Assistant paymasters, * * * during the first five years after date of appointment, when at sea, one thousand seven hundred dollars; on shore duty, one thousand four hundred dollars; on leave, or waiting orders, one thousand dollars; after five years from such date, when at sea, one thousand nine hundred dollars; on shore duty, one thousand six hundred dollars; on leave, or waiting orders, one thousand two hundred dollars.

15 July, 1870, s. 3, v. 16, p. 330.

*Person acting as paymaster when office vacant in ship at sea.*

SEC. 1564. Any person performing the duties of paymaster, acting assistant paymaster, or assistant paymaster, in a ship at sea, or on a foreign station, or on the Pacific coast of the United States, by appointment of the senior officer present, in case of vacancy of such office, in accordance with the provisions of section thirteen hundred and eighty-one, and not otherwise, shall be entitled to receive the pay of such grade while so acting.

17 July, 1861, s. 4, v. 12, p. 258.

## PAY AND ALLOWANCES.

PAY (*active, retired, and furlough*); EXTRA PAY; ALLOWANCES; TRAVELING EXPENSES.

### PAY, ACTIVE AND RETIRED.

Sec.
1556. Pay of officers on active list.
1557. Furlough pay.
1558. No additional allowances except as herein specified.
1559. Volunteer service.
1560. Commencement of pay, original entry.
1561. Commencement of pay of promoted officers.
1562. In cases of delayed examination.
—— Commencement of.
1564. Acting as paymaster.
1565. Chiefs of Bureaus.
1567. Officers serving as store-keepers on foreign stations.
1568. Civilians store-keepers on foreign stations.

Sec.
1569. Of enlisted men.
1570. Additional to firemen, &c.
1572. Additional for detention.
1573. Bounty pay for re-enlisting.
1574. When vessels are wrecked.
1575. When taken by an enemy.
1576. Assignment of pay.
1588. Of retired officers.
1589. Of certain rear-admirals, retired.
1590. Third assistant engineers, retired.
1591. Retired pay not increased by promotion.
1592. Retired officers on active duty.
1593. Retired officers on furlough.
4688. Allowances on Coast Survey.

SEC. 1556. The commissioned officers and warrant officers on the active list of the Navy of the United States, and the petty-officers, seamen, ordinary seamen, firemen, coal-heavers, and employés in the Navy, shall be entitled to receive annual pay at the rates herein stated after their respective designations: — Title 15, Chap. 8. General rule.

The Admiral, thirteen thousand dollars. — The Admiral.

The Vice-Admiral, when at sea, nine thousand dollars; on shore duty, eight thousand dollars; on leave, or waiting orders, six thousand dollars. — Vice-Admiral.

Rear-admirals, when at sea, six thousand dollars; on shore duty, five thousand dollars; on leave, or waiting orders, four thousand dollars. — Rear-admirals.

Commodores, when at sea, five thousand dollars; on shore duty, four thousand dollars; on leave, or waiting orders, three thousand dollars. — Commodores.

Captains, when at sea, four thousand five hundred dollars; on shore duty, three thousand five hundred dollars; on leave, or waiting orders, two thousand eight hundred dollars. — Captains.

Commanders, when at sea, three thousand five hundred dollars; on shore duty, three thousand dollars; on leave, or waiting orders, two thousand three hundred dollars. — Commanders.

Lieutenant-commanders, during the first four years after date of commission, when at sea, two thousand eight hundred dollars; on shore duty, two thousand four hundred dollars; on leave, or waiting orders, two thousand dollars; after four years from such date, when at sea, three thousand dollars; on shore duty, two thousand six hundred dollars; on leave, or waiting orders, two thousand two hundred dollars. — Lieutenant-commanders.

Lieutenants, during the first five years after date of commission, when at sea, two thousand four hundred dollars; on shore duty, two thousand dollars; on leave, or waiting orders, one thousand six hundred dollars; after five years from such date, when at sea, two thousand six hundred dollars; on shore duty, two thousand two hundred dollars; on leave, or waiting orders, one thousand eight hundred dollars. *Lieutenants, junior grade, the pay of masters.* — Lieutenants.

Masters, during the first five years after date of commission, when at sea, one thousand eight hundred dollars; on shore duty, one thousand five hundred dollars; on leave, or waiting orders, one thousand two hundred dollars; after five years from such date, when at sea, two thousand dollars; on shore duty, one thousand seven hundred dollars; on leave, or waiting orders, one thousand four hundred dollars. — Masters. [Grade abolished.]

Ensigns, during the first five years after date of commission, when at sea, one thousand two hundred dollars; on shore duty, one thousand dollars; on leave, or waiting orders, eight hundred dollars; after five years from such date, when at sea, one thousand four hundred dollars; on shore duty, one thousand two hundred dollars; on leave, or waiting orders, one thousand dollars. *Ensigns, junior grade, the pay of midshipmen.* — Ensigns.

Midshipmen, after graduation, when at sea, one thousand dollars; on shore duty, eight hundred dollars; on leave, or waiting orders, six hundred dollars. [Grade abolished.] — Midshipmen.

15 July, 1870, s. 3, v. 16, p. 330.   20 Feb., 1874, v. 18, p. 17.
3 March, 1883, P. E. L., p. 472.

66                     PAY AND ALLOWANCES.

Cadet-midshipmen.  Cadet midshipmen [naval cadets], five hundred dollars; *during such period of their course of instruction as they shall be at sea in other than practice ships, shall each receive as annual pay not exceeding nine hundred and fifty dollars.*
15 July, 1870, s. 3, v. 16, p. 330.   3 March, 1877, v. 19, p. 390.
5 Aug., 1882, P. E. L., p. 284.

Cadet-engineers.  Cadet engineers, before final academic examination, five hundred dollars; after final academic examination, and until warranted as assistant engineers, when on duty at sea, one thousand dollars; on shore duty, eight hundred dollars; on leave, or waiting orders, six hundred dollars. [Now styled Naval Cadets.]
4 July, 1864, s. 5, v. 13, p. 393.   3 March, 1865, s. 1, v. 13, p. 539.
15 July, 1870, s. 3, v. 16, p. 330–332.

NOTE.—The act of 5 Aug., 1882, P. E. L., p. 284, changing the title of all students at the Academy to naval cadets, gives them the pay cadet midshipmen were then receiving.

Mates.  Mates, when at sea, nine hundred dollars; on shore duty, seven hundred dollars; on leave, or waiting orders, five hundred dollars.
15 July, 1870, s. 3, v. 16, p. 330.

Fleet officers.  Fleet-surgeons, fleet-paymasters, and fleet-engineers, four thousand four hundred dollars.
15 July, 1870, s. 3, v. 16, p. 330.

Medical directors and inspectors, pay directors and inspectors, and chief engineer, of same rank, &c.  Medical directors, medical inspectors, pay directors, and pay inspectors, and chief engineer, having the same rank as pay director and pay inspector, when on duty at sea, four thousand four hundred dollars. When not at sea, the same as surgeons and paymasters, respectively.
15 July, 1870, s. 3, v. 16, p. 331.   3 March, 1871, ss. 5, 6, v. 16, p. 535.
3 March, 1873, s. 1, v. 17, p. 555.

Surgeons, paymasters, and chief engineers.  Surgeons, paymasters, and chief engineers who have the same rank with paymasters, during the first five years after date of commission, when at sea, two thousand eight hundred dollars; on shore duty, two thousand four hundred dollars; on leave, or waiting orders, two thousand dollars; during the second five years after such date, when at sea, three thousand two hundred dollars; on shore duty, two thousand eight hundred dollars; on leave, or waiting orders, two thousand four hundred dollars; during the third five years after such date, when at sea, three thousand five hundred dollars; on shore duty, three thousand two hundred dollars; on leave, or waiting orders, two thousand six hundred dollars; during the fourth five years after such date, when at sea, three thousand seven hundred dollars; on shore duty, three thousand six hundred dollars; on leave, or waiting orders, two thousand eight hundred dollars; after twenty years from such date, when at sea, four thousand two hundred dollars; on shore duty, four thousand dollars; on leave, or waiting orders, three thousand dollars.

Passed assistant surgeons, paymasters, and engineers.  Passed assistant surgeons, passed assistant paymasters, and *passed* assistant engineers, during the first five years after date of appointment, when at sea, two thousand dollars; on shore duty, one thousand eight hundred dollars; on leave, or waiting orders, one thousand five hundred dollars; after five years from such date, when at sea, two thousand two hundred dollars; on shore duty, two thousand dollars; on leave or waiting orders, one thousand seven hundred dollars.
15 July, 1870, s. 3, v. 16, p. 330.   24 Feb., 1874, s. 1, v. 18, p. 17.

Assistant surgeons, paymasters, and engineers.  Assistant surgeons, assistant paymasters, and *assistant* engineers, during the first five years after date of appointment, when at sea, one thousand seven hundred dollars; on shore duty, one thousand four hundred dollars; on leave, or waiting orders, one thousand dollars; after five years from such date, when at sea, one thousand nine hundred dollars; on shore duty, one thousand six hundred dollars; on leave, or waiting orders, one thousand two hundred dollars.
15 July, 1870, s. 3, v. 16, p. 330.   24 Feb., 1874, s. 1, v. 18, p. 17.

Assistant surgeons qualified for promotion.  Assistant surgeons of three years' service, who have been found qualified for promotion by a medical board of examiners, the pay of passed assistant surgeons.
3 March, 1871, s. 5, v. 16, p. 535.

Naval constructors.  Naval constructors, during the first five years after date of appointment, when on duty, three thousand two hundred dollars; on leave, or

# PAY AND ALLOWANCES.

waiting orders, two thousand two hundred dollars; during the second five years after such date, when on duty, three thousand four hundred dollars; on leave, or waiting orders, two thousand four hundred dollars; during the third five years after such date, when on duty, three thousand seven hundred dollars; on leave, or waiting orders, two thousand seven hundred dollars; during the fourth five years after such date, when on duty, four thousand dollars; on leave, or waiting orders, three thousand dollars; after twenty years from such date, when on duty, four thousand two hundred dollars; on leave, or waiting orders, three thousand two hundred dollars.

Assistant naval constructors, during the first four years after date of appointment, when on duty, two thousand dollars; on leave, or waiting orders, one thousand five hundred dollars; during the second four years after such date, when on duty, two thousand two hundred dollars; on leave, or waiting orders, one thousand seven hundred dollars; after eight years from such date, when on duty, two thousand six hundred dollars; on leave, or waiting orders, one thousand nine hundred dollars. {margin: Assistant naval constructors.}

15 July, 1870, s. 3, v. 16, p. 331.

Chaplains, during the first five years after date of commission, when at sea, two thousand five hundred dollars; on shore duty, two thousand dollars; on leave, or waiting orders, one thousand six hundred dollars; after five years from such date, when at sea, two thousand eight hundred dollars; on shore duty, two thousand three hundred dollars; on leave, or waiting orders, one thousand nine hundred dollars. {margin: Chaplains.}

15 July, 1870, s. 3, v. 16, p. 331.

Professors of mathematics and civil engineers, during the first five years after date of appointment, when on duty, two thousand four hundred dollars; on leave, or waiting orders, one thousand five hundred dollars; during the second five years after such date, when on duty, two thousand seven hundred dollars; on leave, or waiting orders, one thousand eight hundred dollars; during the third five years after such date, when on duty, three thousand dollars; on leave, or waiting orders, two thousand one hundred dollars; after fifteen years from such date, when on duty, three thousand five hundred dollars; on leave, or waiting orders, two thousand six hundred dollars. {margin: Professors of mathematics and civil engineers.}

15 July, 1870, s. 3, v. 16, p. 331.

Boatswains, gunners, carpenters, and sail-makers, during the first three years after date of appointment, when at sea, one thousand two hundred dollars; on shore duty, nine hundred dollars; on leave, or waiting orders, seven hundred dollars; during the second three years after such date, when at sea, one thousand three hundred dollars; on shore duty, one thousand dollars; on leave, or waiting orders, eight hundred dollars; during the third three years after such date, when at sea, one thousand four hundred dollars; on shore duty, one thousand three hundred dollars; on leave, or waiting orders, nine hundred dollars; during the fourth three years after such date, when at sea, one thousand six hundred dollars; on shore duty, one thousand three hundred dollars; on leave, or waiting orders, one thousand dollars; after twelve years from such date, when at sea, one thousand eight hundred dollars; on shore duty, one thousand six hundred dollars; on leave, or waiting orders, one thousand two hundred dollars. {margin: Warrant officers. Boatswains, gunners, carpenters, sail-makers.}

15 July, 1870, s. 3, v. 16, p. 332.

Secretaries to the Admiral and the Vice-Admiral, each two thousand five hundred dollars. {margin: Secretaries.}

\* \* \* \* \* \* \*

Secretary of the Naval Academy, one thousand eight hundred dollars.

15 July, 1870, s. 3, v. 16, p. 332.

First clerks to commandants of navy-yards, one thousand five hundred dollars.
Second clerks to commandants of navy-yards, one thousand two hundred dollars.
Clerk to commandant of navy-yard at Mare Island, one thousand eight hundred dollars.
Clerks to commandants of naval stations, one thousand five hundred dollars. {margin: Clerks to commandants of yards and stations.}

# 68  PAY AND ALLOWANCES.

**Clerks to paymasters.** Clerks to paymasters at navy-yards, Boston, New York, Philadelphia, and Washington, one thousand six hundred dollars; Kittery, Norfolk, and Pensacola, one thousand four hundred dollars; Mare Island, one thousand eight hundred dollars.

Clerks to paymasters, at other stations, one thousand three hundred dollars.

Clerks to paymasters of receiving-ships at Boston, New York, and Philadelphia, one thousand six hundred dollars; at Mare Island, one thousand eight hundred dollars; of other receiving-ships, one thousand three hundred dollars.

Clerks to paymasters on vessels of the first rate, one thousand three hundred dollars; on vessels of the second rate, one thousand one hundred dollars; on vessels of the third rate, and supply-vessels and store-ships, one thousand dollars.

Clerks to fleet paymasters, one thousand one hundred dollars.

Clerks to paymasters at the Naval Academy and Naval Asylum, one thousand three hundred dollars.

**Clerks to inspectors.** Clerks to inspectors in charge of provisions and clothing, at navy-yards, Boston, New York, Philadelphia, and Washington, one thousand six hundred dollars; to inspectors in like charge at other inspections, one thousand three hundred dollars.

15 July, 1870, s. 3, v. 16, p. 332.

**Furlough pay.** SEC. 1557. Officers on furlough shall receive only one-half of the pay to which they would have been entitled if on leave of absence. [See § 1593.]

3 March, 1835, s. 1, v. 4, p. 756.   3 March, 1845, s. 6, v. 5, p. 794.
1 June, 1860, s. 4, v. 12, p. 27.

**No additional allowances, except as herein specified.** SEC. 1558. The pay prescribed in the two preceding sections shall be the full and entire compensation of the several officers therein named, and no additional allowance shall be made in favor of any of said officers on any account whatever, except as hereinafter provided. [See § 4688.]

15 July, 1870, s. 4, v. 16, p. 332.

**Volunteer service.** SEC. 1559. When a volunteer naval service is authorized by law, the officers therein shall be entitled to receive the same pay as officers of the same grades, respectively, in the Regular Navy.

16 July, 1862, s. 20, v. 12, p. 587.

**Commencement of pay, original entry.** SEC. 1560. The pay of an officer of the Navy, upon his original entry into the service, except where he is required to give an official bond, shall commence upon the date of his acceptance of his appointment; but where he is required to give such bond his pay shall commence upon the date of the approval of his bond by the proper authority.

15 July, 1870, s. 7, v. 16, p. 333.

**Commencement of pay of promoted officers.** SEC. 1561. When an officer is promoted in course to fill a vacancy, and is in the performance of the duties of the higher grade from the date he is to take rank, he may be allowed the increased pay from such date. [See *post*, June 22, 1874.]

15 July, 1870, s. 7, v. 16, p. 333.   5 June, 1872, s. 1, v. 17, p. 226.

**In case of delayed examination.** SEC. 1562. If an officer of a class subject to examination before promotion shall be absent on duty, and by reason of such absence, or of other cause not involving fault on his part, shall not be examined at the time required by law or regulation, and shall afterward be examined and found qualified, the increased rate of pay to which his promotion would entitle him shall commence from the date when he would have been entitled to it had he been examined and found qualified at the time so required by law or regulation; and this rule shall apply to any cases of this description which may have heretofore occurred. And in every such case the period of service of the party, in the grade to which he was promoted, shall, in reference to the rate of his pay, be considered to have commenced from the date when he was so entitled to take rank. [See 22 June, 1874, *post*.]

15 July, 1870, s. 7, v. 16, p. 333.

**22 June, 1874.**

**Commencement of pay on promotion.** That on and after the passage of this act, any officer of the Navy who may be promoted in course to fill a vacancy in the next higher grade shall be entitled to the pay of the grade to which promoted from the date he takes rank therein, if it be subsequent to the vacancy he is appointed to fill. * * * [See notes under PROMOTION.]

22 June, 1874, v. 18, p. 191.

## PAY AND ALLOWANCES. 69

SEC. 1564. Any person performing the duties of paymaster, acting assistant paymaster, or assistant paymaster, in a ship at sea, or on a foreign station, or on the Pacific coast of the United States, by appointment of the senior officer present, in case of vacancy of such office, in accordance with the provisions of section thirteen hundred and eighty-one, and not otherwise, shall be entitled to receive the pay of such grade while so acting. [See § 1381, under PAY CORPS.] *Title 15, Chap. 8. Person acting as paymaster, when office vacant in ship at sea.*

17 July, 1861, s. 4, v. 12, p. 258.

SEC. 1565. The pay of chiefs of Bureaus in the Navy Department shall be the highest pay of the grade to which they belong, but not below that of commodore. *Chiefs of Bureaus.*

3 March, 1871, s. 12, v. 16, p. 537.

SEC. 1567. Officers who are ordered to take charge of naval stores for foreign squadrons, in the place of naval storekeepers, shall be entitled to receive, while so employed, the shore-duty pay of their grades; and when the same is less than fifteen hundred dollars a year, they may be allowed compensation, including such shore-duty pay, at a rate not exceeding fifteen hundred dollars a year, *Officers serving as store-keepers on foreign stations.*

17 June, 1844, s. 1, v. 5, p. 700.

SEC. 1568. Civilians appointed as storekeepers on foreign stations shall receive compensation for such services, at a rate not exceeding fifteen hundred dollars a year. *Civilians storekeepers on foreign stations.*

17 June, 1844, s. 1, v. 5, p. 700. 3 March, 1847, s. 3, v. 9, p. 172.

SEC. 1569. The pay to be allowed to petty officers, excepting mates and the pay and bounty upon enlistment of seamen, ordinary seamen, firemen, and coal-heavers, in the naval service, shall be fixed by the President: *Provided*, That the whole sum to be given for the whole pay aforesaid, and for the pay of officers, and for the said bounties upon enlistments shall not exceed, for any one year, the amount which may, in such year, be appropriated for such purposes. *Pay of enlisted men.*

18 April, 1814, s. 1, v. 3, p. 136. 3 March, 1847, s. 4, v. 9, p. 173.
1 July, 1864, s. 4, v. 13, p. 342. 3 March, 1865, s. 2, v. 13, p. 539.

SEC. 1570. Every seaman, ordinary seaman, or landsman who performs the duty of a fireman or coal-heaver on board of any vessel of war shall be entitled to receive, in addition to his compensation as seaman, ordinary seaman, or landsman, a compensation at the rate of thirty-three cents a day for the time he is employed as fireman or coal-heaver. *Additional pay for serving as firemen and coal-heavers.*

1 March, 1869, s. 2, v. 15, p. 280.

SEC. 1572. All petty officers and persons of inferior ratings who are detained beyond the terms of service, according to the provisions of section fourteen hundred and twenty-two, or who, after the termination of their service, voluntarily re-enter, to serve until the return to an Atlantic port of the vessel to which they belong, and until their regular discharge therefrom, shall, for the time during which they are so detained or so serve beyond their original terms of service, receive an addition of one-fourth of their former pay. [See § 1422, under SEAMEN.] *Detention beyond term of enlistment.*

17 July, 1862, s. 17, v. 12, p. 610.

SEC. 1573. If any seaman, ordinary seaman, landsman, fireman, coal-heaver, or boy, being honorably discharged, shall re-enlist for three years, within three months thereafter, he shall, on presenting his honorable discharge, or on accounting in a satisfactory manner for its loss, be entitled to pay, during the said three months, equal to that to which he would have been entitled if he had been employed in actual service. *Bounty-pay for re-enlisting.*

2 March, 1855, s. 2, v. 10, p. 627. 2 June, 1864, v. 13, p. 120.

SEC. 1574. When the crew of any vessel of the United States are separated from such vessel, by means of her wreck, loss, or destruction, the pay and emoluments of such of the officers and men as shall appear to the Secretary of the Navy, by the sentence of a court-martial or court of inquiry, or by other satisfactory evidence, to have done their utmost to preserve her, and, after said wreck, loss, or destruction, to have behaved themselves agreeably to the discipline of the Navy, shall go on and be paid them until their discharge or death. *Crews of wrecked or lost vessels.*

17 July, 1862, s. 14, v. 12, p. 608.

SEC. 1575. The pay and emoluments of the officers and men of any vessel of the United States taken by an enemy who shall appear, by the sentence of a court-martial or otherwise, to have done their utmost *Crews of vessels taken by an enemy.*

**Assignments of wages.**

SEC. 1576. Every assignment of wages due to persons enlisted in the naval service, and all powers of attorney, or other authority to draw, receipt for, or transfer the same, shall be void, unless attested by the commanding officer and paymaster. The assignment of wages must specify the precise time when they commence.

30 June, 1864, s. 12, v. 13, p. 310.

**Pay of retired officers.**

SEC. 1588. The pay of all officers of the Navy who have been retired after forty-five years' service after reaching the age of sixteen years, or who have been or may be retired after forty years' service, upon their own application to the President, or on attaining the age of sixty-two years, or on account of incapacity resulting from long and faithful service, from wounds or injuries received in the line of duty, or from sickness or exposure therein, shall, when not on active duty, be equal to seventy-five per centum of the sea-pay provided by this chapter for the grade or rank which they held, respectively, at the time of their retirement. The pay of all other officers on the retired list shall, when not on active duty, be equal to one-half the sea-pay provided by this chapter for the grade or rank held by them, respectively, at the time or their retirement. [See note 1588, RETIREMENT.]

15 July, 1870, s. 5, v. 16, p. 333.    3 March, 1873, s. 1, v. 17, p. 555.

**Rear-admirals, retired.**

SEC. 1589. Rear-admirals on the retired list of the Navy, who were retired as captains when the highest grade in the Navy was captain, at the age of sixty-two years, or after forty-five years' service, and who, after their retirement, were promoted to the grade of rear-admiral, and performed the duties of that grade in time of war, shall be considered as having been retired as rear-admirals.

5 June, 1872, s. 1, v. 17, p. 226.    3 March, 1873, s. 1, v. 17, p. 555.

**Third assistant engineers, retired.**

SEC. 1590. Officers who have been retired as third assistant engineers shall continue to receive pay at the rate of four hundred dollars a year.

3 March, 1859, s. 2, v. 11, p. 407.    12 April, 1864, s. 7, v. 13. p. 54.
3 Aug., 1861. s. 22, v. 12, p. 290.    15 July, 1870, s. 5, v. 16. p. 333.
16 July, 1862, s. 20, v. 12, p. 587.

**Pay not increased by promotion.**

SEC. 1591. No officer, heretofore or hereafter promoted upon the retired list, shall, in consequence of such promotion, be entitled to any increase of pay.

15 July, 1870, s. 5, v. 16, p. 333.    2 March, 1867, s. 9, v. 14, p. 517.

**Pay on active duty.**

SEC. 1592. Officers on the retired list, when on active duty, shall receive the full pay of their respective grades.

2 March, 1867, s. 9, v. 14, p. 517.    1 June, 1860, s. 5, v. 12, p. 27.

**Officers retired on furlough-pay.**

SEC. 1593. Officers placed on the retired list, on furlough pay, shall receive only one-half of the pay to which they would have been entitled if on leave of absence on the active list. [See § 1594, FURLOUGH.]

3 March, 1835, s. 1, v. 4, p. 756.    3 Aug., 1861, s. 23, v.12, p. 291.
28 Feb., 1855, s. 2, v. 10, p. 616.    28 July, 1866, s. 2, v. 14, p. 345.
16 Jan., 1857, s. 1, v. 11, p. 154.    30 Jan., 1875, v. 18, p. 504.

**Title 56.**

**Allowance for subsistence.**

SEC. 4688. The Secretary of the Treasury may make such allowances to the officers and men of the Army and Navy, while employed on Coast Survey service, for subsistence, in addition to their compensation, as he may deem necessary, not exceeding the sum authorized by the Treasury regulation of the eleventh day of May, eighteen hundred and forty-four.

12 June, 1858, s. 1, v. 11, p. 319.

NOTE.—Additional allowances for subsistence may be legally made to officers of the Army or Navy while employed on coast survey service. The word pay in section 4684, Coast Survey, Part III, refers to the pay proper of an officer.—Op. XV, p. 283, Devens. May 23, 1877.

EXTRA PAY, EXTRA SALARIES, ETC. 71

## FURLOUGH AND FURLOUGH-PAY.

Sec.
1442. Placing on furlough.
1557. Furlough-pay.

Sec.
1594. Transfer from furlough to retired pay.

SEC. 1442. The Secretary of the Navy shall have authority to place on furlough any officer on the active list of the Navy. [See note, p. 19.] *Title 15, Chap. 2.* Placing on furlough.
3 March, 1835, s. 1, v. 4. p. 756.   3 March, 1845, s. 6, v. 5, p. 794.
28 Feb., 1855, s. 3, v. 10, p. 617.   1 June, 1860, s. 4, v. 12, p. 27.

SEC. 1557. Officers on furlough shall receive only one-half of the pay to which they would have been entitled if on leave of absence. *Title 15, Chap. 8.* Furlough-pay.
1 June, 1860, s. 4, v. 12, p. 27.   3 March, 1845, s. 6, v. 5, p. 794.
3 March 1835, s. 1, v. 4, p. 756.

SEC. 1594. The President, by and with the advice and consent of the Senate, may transfer any officer on the retired list from the furlough to the retired-pay list. *Transfer from furlough to retired pay.*
16 Jan., 1857, s. 3, v. 11, p. 154.
16 July, 1862, s. 20, v. 12, p. 587.

NOTE.—When an officer is transferred, as authorized by this section, the causes for his retirement determine the rate of his pay under section 1588. An officer retired on furlough pay from causes not incident to the service cannot be transferred to the 75 per cent. pay list. If so transferred by nomination and confirmation, it would not be the duty of the accounting officer to pay him 75 per cent. of sea pay.—Op. XVI, p. 23, Devens, May 29, 1878.

[An act approved January 30, 1875, v. 18, p. 304, allows difference of pay to certain officers, or their heirs, who were furloughed under the act of February 28, 1855, and subsequently restored to the active list.]

## EXTRA PAY, EXTRA SALARIES, ETC.

Sec.
170. To clerks prohibited.
1763. Double salaries.
1764. Extra services.
1765. Extra allowances.

Sec.
2687. Apportionment of salaries.
3654. Extra compensation for disbursements.
—— Extra compensation forbidden.

SEC. 170. No money shall be paid to any clerk employed in either Department at an annual salary, as compensation for extra services, unless expressly authorized by law. *Title 4.* Extra compensation to clerks prohibited.
17 June, 1844, s. 1, v. 5, pp. 681, 687.
3 March, 1863, s. 3, v. 10, pp. 209, 211.
28 Feb., 1867, res. 30, s. 2, v. 14, p. 569.

SEC. 1763. No person who holds an office, the salary or annual compensation attached to which amounts to the sum of two thousand five hundred dollars, shall receive compensation for discharging the duties of any other office, unless expressly authorized by law. [See 20 June, 1874, *post.*] *Title 19.* Double salaries.
31 Aug., 1852, s. 18, v. 10, p. 100.

SEC. 1764. No allowance or compensation shall be made to any officer or clerk, by reason of the discharge of duties which belong to any other officer or clerk in the same or any other Department; and no allowance or compensation shall be made for any extra services whatever, which any officer or clerk may be required to perform, unless expressly authorized by law. *Extra services.*
26 Aug., 1842, s. 12, v. 5, p. 525.

SEC. 1765. No officer in any branch of the public service, or any other person whose salary, pay, or emoluments are fixed by law or regulations, shall receive any additional pay, extra allowance, or compensation, in any form whatever, for the disbursement of public money, or for any other service or duty whatever, unless the same is authorized by law, and the appropriation therefor explicitly states that it is for such additional pay, extra allowance, or compensation. *Extra allowances.*
3 March, 1839, s. 3, v. 5, p. 349.
23 Aug., 1842, s. 2, v. 5, p. 510.

An officer who has been appointed to and is fully invested with two distinct offices may receive the compensation appropriated for each. Sections 1763, 1764, 1765 do not apply to such a case. It is for the appointing power to determine whether the party can properly and fully perform the duties of the two offices.—Op. XVI, 7, May 9, 1878. See also Op. XII, 459, on this subject. Also under EXECUTIVE DEPARTMENT, Part III.

## TRAVELING EXPENSES.

**Title 34, Chap 2.**
Apportionment of compensation for part of a year's service.

SEC. 2687. Collectors and all other officers of the customs, serving for a less period than a year, shall not be paid for the entire year, but shall be allowed in no case a greater than a pro rata of the maximum compensation of such officers respectively for the time only which they actually serve as such collectors or officers, whether the same be under one or more appointments, or before or after confirmation. And no collector or other officer shall, in any case, receive for his services, either as fees, salary, fines, penalties, forfeitures, or otherwise, for the time he may be in service, beyond the maximum pro rata rate provided by law. And this section shall be applied and enforced in regard to all officers, agents, and employés of the United States whomsoever, as well those whose compensation is determined by a commission on disbursements, not to exceed an annual maximum, as those paid by salary or otherwise.

11 Feb., 1846, s. 1, v. 9, p. 3.   18 July, 1866, s. 34, v. 14, p. 186.

**Title 40.**
Extra compensation for disbursements.

SEC. 3654. No extra compensation exceeding one-eighth of one per centum shall in any case be allowed or paid to any officer, person, or corporation for disbursing moneys appropriated to the construction of any public building. See 3 March, 1875, *post*.

3 March, 1869, v. 15, p. 312.

**3 March, 1875.**

The provisions of the act of March 3, 1869 [sec. 3654] were intended and shall be deemed and held to limit the compensation to be allowed to any disbursing officer who disburses moneys appropriated for and expended in the construction of any public building as aforesaid to three-eighths of one per centum for said services.

3 March, 1875, v. 18, p. 415.

**June 20, 1874.**
Extra compensation to civil officers prohibited.

That no civil officer of the Government shall hereafter receive any compensation or perquisites, directly or indirectly, from the treasury or property of the United States beyond his salary or compensation allowed by law: *Provided*, That this shall not be construed to prevent the employment and payment by the Department of Justice of district attorneys as now allowed by law for the performance of services not covered by their salaries or fees. [See C. C., XVI, Warden's case, and XV, p. 22.]

20 June, 1874, s. 3, v. 18, p. 85.

[EXTRA PAY TO ENLISTED PERSONS. See under SEAMEN.]

## TRAVELING EXPENSES.

Sec.
—— Actual expenses.
—— Mileage.
1566. Allowance in foreign countries.

Sec.
—— Approval of Secretary required.
850. Clerks, &c., sent off as witnesses.
—— Traveling expenses of naval cadets.

**16 June, 1874.**
Traveling expenses.

Only actual traveling expenses shall be allowed to any person holding employment or appointment under the United States, and all allowances for mileages and transportation in excess of the amount actually paid are hereby declared illegal; and no credit shall be allowed to any of the disbursing officers of the United States for payment or allowances in violation of this provision.*

16 June, 1874, s. 1, v. 18, p. 72.  [See June 30, 1876.]

**30 June, 1876.**
Mileage to officers of the Navy.

So much of the act of June 16, 1874 [*supra*] "as is applicable to officers of the Navy so engaged, is hereby repealed:

"And the sum of eight cents per mile shall be allowed such officers, while so engaged, in lieu of their actual expenses." [See Aug. 5, 1862.]

30 June, 1876, v. 19, p. 65.

NOTE.—Mileage is allowed to officers of the Navy in lieu of actual expenses by the act of June 30, 1876 (19 Stat. L., 65). Congress knew that naval officers were required to travel across oceans and through foreign countries when they passed the above act. The statute establishes one rule—mileage for all travel by naval officers.—C. C., XIV, 377. Affirmed on same grounds by Supreme Court, Otto. 97150. See also Op. XVI, 147, XV, 311, XIV, 590, 681, 683 ; 1 X, 261, 411, 417 ; XIII, 526, as to traveling expenses, residence, &c.

**Title 15, Chap. 8.**
Allowance to officers traveling in foreign countries.

SEC. 1566. * * *  And an allowance may be made to officers traveling in foreign countries under orders, for expenses of transportation of baggage necessarily incurred. And no officer shall be paid mileage, except for travel actually performed at his own expense and in obedience to orders. [See Aug. 5, 1882, *post*.]

3 March, 1835, s. 2, v. 4, p. 757.   17 July, 1862, s. 7, v. 12. p. 595.
15 July, 1870, s. 4, v. 16, p. 332.

---

* An act of Feb. 22, 1875, exempted attorneys, marshals, and clerks of the U. S. courts; the clause of June 16, 1874, was repealed March 3, 1875, with like exemption.

\* \* \* No allowance shall be made in the settlement of any account for traveling expenses unless the same be incurred on the order of the Secretary of the Navy, or the allowance be approved by him.

18 Jan., 1875.

Allowance to be approved by Secretary of Navy.

18 Jan., 1875, v. 18, p. 297. [Naval appropriation act.]

Officers of the Navy traveling abroad under orders hereafter issued shall travel by the most direct route, the occasion and necessity for such order to be certified by the officer issuing the same; and shall receive, in lieu of the mileage now allowed by law, only their actual and reasonable expenses, certified under their own signatures and approved by the Secretary of the Navy.

5 Aug., 1882.

Travel abroad.

5 Aug., 1882. P. E. L. p. 285.

SEC. 850. When any clerk or other officer of the United States is sent away from his place of business as a witness for the Government, his necessary expenses, stated in items and sworn to, in going, returning, and attendance on the court, shall be audited and paid; but no mileage, or other compensation in addition to his salary, shall in any case be allowed.

Clerks, &c., sent away as witnesses.

26 Feb., 1863, s. 3, v. 10, p. 167.

NOTE.—The necessary expenses incurred by soldiers as witnesses for the Government allowable under section 850 may be paid by marshals upon proper proof thereof.—XVI, Op. 147. Army officers and soldiers are entitled to receive their *necessary expenses* in going, returning, and attendance on the court, which must be stated in items and sworn to. They are not in such cases entitled to *mileage* or *witness fees*. The section embraces any person who is an employé of the United States, in however humble a capacity.—Op. XVI, 113.

[The naval appropriation act of March 3, 1883, provides for the actual and necessary traveling expenses of naval cadets while proceeding from their homes to the Naval Academy for examination and *appointment* as naval cadets.]

[TRAVELING EXPENSES OF MARINE OFFICERS. See Part II.]

## PROFESSORS OF MATHEMATICS.

Sec.
436. In charge of Nautical Almanac.
1399. Number allowed.
1400. How appointed.
1401. Duties.
1480. Rank on active list.

Sec.
1481. Rank when retired.
1528. Duty at Naval Academy.
1556. Pay.
—— Qualifications.

SEC. 436. The Secretary of the Navy may place the supervision of the Nautical Almanac in charge of any officer or professor of mathematics in the Navy who is competent for that service. Such officer or professor, when so employed, shall be entitled to receive the shore-duty pay of his grade, and no other.

Title 10.

May be placed in charge of Nautical Almanac. Pay.

3 March, 1857, s. 3, v. 11, p. 246.

SEC. 1399. The number of professors of mathematics in the Navy shall not exceed twelve.

Title 15, Chap 1.

Number.

3 Aug., 1848, s. 12, v. 9, p. 272. 31 May, 1872, s. 1, v. 17, p. 192.

SEC. 1400. Professors of mathematics shall be appointed and commissioned by the President of the United States, by and with the advice and consent of the Senate. [See Jan. 20, 1881, *post*.]

Appointment.

3 Aug., 1848, s. 12, v. 9, p. 272.

SEC. 1401. Professors of mathematics shall perform such duties as may be assigned them by order of the Secretary of the Navy, at the Naval Academy, the Naval Observatory, and on board ships of war, in instructing the midshipmen of the Navy, or otherwise.

Duties.

3 Aug., 1848, s. 12, v. 9, p. 272.

SEC. 1480. Professors of mathematics shall have relative rank as follows: Three, the relative rank of captain; four, that of commander; and five, that of lieutenant-commander or lieutenant.

Title 15, Chap. 4.

Rank.

31 May, 1872, s. 1, v. 17, p. 192.

SEC. 1481. \* \* Professors of mathematics \* \* who shall have served faithfully for forty-five years, shall, when retired, have the relative rank of commodore; and \* \* who have been or shall be retired at the age of sixty-two years, before having served for forty-five years, but who shall have served faithfully until retired, shall, on the completion of forty years from their entry into the service, have the relative rank of commodore.

Relative rank when retired from age or length of service.

March, 1871, s. 11, v. 16, p. 537.

74  PROMOTION OR ADVANCEMENT IN THE NAVY.

**Title 15, Chap. 5.**
Professors of ethics, Spanish, and drawing.

SEC. 1528. Three professors of mathematics shall be assigned to duty at the Naval Academy, one as professor of ethics and English studies, one as professor of the Spanish language, and one as professor of drawing. [See note, same section, Naval Academy.]

21 May, 1864, s. 3, v. 13, p. 85.

**Title 15, Chap. 8.**
Pay.

SEC. 1556. * * Professors of mathematics * * * during the first five years after date of appointment, when on duty, two thousand four hundred dollars; on leave, or waiting orders, one thousand five hundred dollars; during the second five years after such date, when on duty, two thousand seven hundred dollars; on leave, or waiting orders, one thousand eight hundred dollars; during the third five years after such date, when on duty, three thousand dollars; on leave, or waiting orders, two thousand one hundred dollars; after fifteen years from such date, when on duty, three thousand five hundred dollars; on leave, or waiting orders, two thousand six hundred dollars.

15 July, 1870, s. 3, v. 16, p. 331.

**20 Jan., 1881.**
Qualifications.

Hereafter no person shall be appointed a professor of mathematics in the Navy until he shall have passed a physical examination before a board of naval surgeons, and a professional examination before a board of professors of mathematics in the Navy, to be convened for that purpose by the Secretary of the Navy, and received a favorable report from said boards.

20 Jan., 1881, v. 21, p. 317.

## PROMOTION OR ADVANCEMENT IN THE NAVY.

### GENERAL PROVISIONS.

Sec.
1407. Promotion of seamen.
1447. Retirement on not passing both boards.
1458. Promotion to vacancies by retirement.
—— Rule of promotion, line and staff.
1493. Physical examination.
1494. Physical disqualification by wounds.
1495. Examinations, when, and effect of.
1496. Examination of professional fitness.
1497. Promotion to rear-admiral in time of peace.
1498. Examining board.
1499. Powers of.
—— Restriction on examination.
1500. Officer may be present, &c.
1501. Record.
1502. Revision by the President.

Sec.
1503. No officer to be rejected without examination.
1504. Report of recommendation.
1505. Failing in examination.
—— Failing in moral examination.
1506. Advancement in number.
1507. Promotion when grade is full.
1508. Officers receiving thanks of Congress.
1509. Effect of vote of thanks.
1510. Vacancies occasioned by death, &c., of officers thanked.
1560. Commencement of pay, original entry.
1561. Commencement of pay of promoted officers.
—— Commencement of pay on promotion.
1562. Pay in delayed examinations.

**Title 15, Chap. 1.**
Promotion of seamen to warrant officers.

SEC. 1407. Seamen distinguishing themselves in battle, or by extraordinary heroism in the line of their profession, may be promoted to forward warrant officers, upon the recommendation of their commanding officer, approved by the flag-officer and Secretary of the Navy. And upon such recommendation they shall receive a gratuity of one hundred dollars and a medal of honor, to be prepared under the direction of the Navy Department.

17 May, 1864, s. 3, v. 13, p. 79.

**Title 15, Chap. 3.**
Officers rejected from promotion.

SEC. 1447. When the case of any officer has been acted upon by a board of naval surgeons and an examining board for promotion, as provided in Chapter Four of this Title, and he shall not have been recommended for promotion by both of the said boards, he shall be placed upon the retired list. [See § 1505; also act Aug. 5, 1882.]

21 April, 1864, s. 4, v. 13, p. 53.

NOTE.—The President has power to review the action and finding of a board of naval surgeons constituted under the fourth section of the act of April 21, 1864. Both examinations must precede a promotion, and the finding as to both must be approved by the President.—Op. XII, 347, Dec. 30, 1867, Stanbery.

Promotion to vacancies caused by retirement.

SEC. 1458. The next officer in rank shall be promoted to the place of a retired officer, according to the established rules of the service, and the same rule of promotion shall be applied successively to the vacancies consequent upon the retirement of an officer. [See act following.]

3 Aug., 1861, s. 22, v. 12, p. 291.   21 Dec., 1862, s. 6, v. 12, p. 330.

**5 Aug., 1882.**
Rule of promotion in the line.

Hereafter only one-half of the vacancies in the various grades in the line of the Navy shall be filled by promotion until such grades shall be reduced to the following numbers, namely: rear admirals, six; commodores, ten; captains, forty-five; commanders, eighty-five; lieutenant commanders, seventy-four; lieutenants, two hundred and fifty; *lieutenant of the junior grade*, seventy-five; ensigns, seventy-five; and thereafter promotions to all vacancies shall be made but not to increase either of said grades above the numbers aforesaid.

5 Aug., 1882, P. E. L., p. 286. [Naval appropriation act.]<br>3 March, 1883, P. E. L., p. 472.

Hereafter only one-half of the vacancies in the various grades in the staff corps of the Navy shall be filled by promotion until such grades shall be reduced to the numbers fixed for the several grades of the staff corps of the Navy by the act of August fifth, eighteen hundred and eighty two, making appropriations for the naval service for the fiscal year ending June thirtieth, eighteen hundred and eighty three, and for other purposes. [See under PAY CORPS and ENGINEER CORPS.] — *3 March, 1883. Rule of promotion in the staff.*

3 March, 1883, P. E. L. p. 472. [Naval appropriation act.]

SEC. 1493. No officer shall be promoted to a higher grade on the active list of the Navy, except in the case provided in the next section, until he has been examined by a board of naval surgeons and pronounced physically qualified to perform all his duties at sea. — *Title 15, Chap. 4. Physical examination.*

21 April, 1864, s. 4, v. 13, p. 53.    28 July, 1866, s. 1, v. 14, p. 344.

NOTE.—The acceptance of a promotion in the Navy is not necessary to consummate the appointment of an officer to a higher grade. [Case of an officer who died before the appointment promoting him was received, and the accounting officers objected to crediting him with the pay of a higher grade.]—Op. XII, 229, Stanberry, Aug. 1, 1867.

SEC. 1494. The provisions of the preceding section shall not exclude from the promotion to which he would otherwise be regularly entitled any officer in whose case such medical board may report that his physical disqualification was occasioned by wounds received in the line of his duty, and that such wounds do not incapacitate him for other duties in the grade to which he shall be promoted. — *Physical disqualification by wounds.*

*Idem.*

SEC. 1495. Officers subject to examination before promotion to a grade limited in number by law shall not be entitled to examination in such a sense as to give increase of pay until designated by the Secretary of the Navy to fill vacancies in the higher grade; and officers eligible for promotion to a grade not limited in number shall not be entitled to examination until ordered to present themselves for examination or until a class, in which they are included, has been so ordered by the Secretary of the Navy. [See §§ 1561 and 1562.] — *Examinations, when, and effect of.*

3 March, 1873, s. 1, v. 17, p. 555.

SEC. 1496. No line officer below the grade of commodore, and no officer not of the line, shall be promoted to a higher grade on the active list of the Navy until his mental, moral, and professional fitness to perform all his duties at sea have been established to the satisfaction of a board of examining officers appointed by the President. — *Examination of professional fitness.*

21 April, 1864, s. 1, v. 13, p. 53.

SEC. 1497. In time of peace no person shall be promoted from the list of commodores to the grade of rear-admiral, on the active list, until his mental, moral, and professional fitness to perform all his duties at sea has been established as provided in the preceding section. — *Promotion to rear-admiral in time of peace.*

16 July, 1862, s. 7, v. 12, p. 584.    21 April, 1864, v. 13, p. 53.

SEC. 1498. Such examining board shall consist of not less than three officers, senior in rank to the officer to be examined. — *Examining board.*

21 April, 1864, s. 2, v. 13, p. 53.

SEC. 1499. Said board shall have power to take testimony and to examine all matter on the files and records of the Navy Department relating to any officer whose case may be considered by them. The witnesses, when present, shall be sworn by the president of the board. — *Powers of.*

*Idem*, s. 1. [See *post*, June 18, 1878.]

Hereafter in the examination of officers in the Navy for promotion, no fact which occurred prior to the last examination of the candidate whereby he was promoted, which has been inquired into and decided upon, shall be again inquired into, but such previous examination, if approved, shall be conclusive, unless such fact continuing shows the unfitness of the officer to perform all his duties at sea. — *20 June, 1878. Matters once inquired into not to be again brought up.*

## PROMOTION OR ADVANCEMENT IN THE NAVY.

SEC. 2. The President of the United States may, in any cases wherein the rule herein prescribed has been violated, order and direct the re-examination of the same.

18 June, 1878, v. 20, 265.

**Title 15, Chap. 4.**
*Officer may be present and make statement.*

SEC. 1500. Any officer whose case is to be acted upon by such examining board shall have the right to be present, if he so desires, and to submit a statement of his case on oath.

21 April, 1864, s. 3, v. 13, p. 53.

*Record.*

SEC. 1501. The statement of such officer, if made, and the testimony of the witnesses and his examination shall be recorded.

Idem,

*Revision by the President.*

SEC. 1502. Any matter on the files and records of the Navy Department, touching each case, which may, in the opinion of the board, be necessary to assist them in making up their judgment, shall, together with the whole record and finding, be presented to the President for his approval or disapproval of the finding.

Idem.

*No officer to be rejected without examination.*

SEC. 1503. No officer shall be rejected until after such public examination of himself and of the records of the Navy Department in his case, unless he fails, after having been duly notified, to appear before said board.

Idem.

NOTE.—An officer was under an examination for promotion (sections 1493 to 1505), and the examination was temporarily suspended and the officer granted permission to go home and be absent until notified to appear. He failed to receive the notice; the examination was resumed and concluded, the proceedings approved, and the officer retired. The vacancy not having been filled, and the rights of no other person having intervened: *Held*, That the action of the President could be revoked and the officer allowed a rehearing.—Op. XVI, 20, May 29, 1878, Tracy's case.

*Report of recommendation.*

SEC. 1504. Such examining board shall report their recommendation of any officer for promotion in the following form: "We hereby certify that ——————— has the mental, moral, and professional qualifications to perform efficiently all the duties, both at sea and on shore, of the grade to which he is to be promoted, and recommend him for promotion."

16 July, 1862, s. 4, v. 12, p. 584.   28 July, 1866, s. 1, v. 14, p. 344.
21 April, 1864, s. 4, v. 13, p. 53.

*Failing in examination.*

SEC. 1505. Any officer of the Navy on the active list below the grade of commander, who, upon examination for promotion, is not found professionally qualified, shall be suspended from promotion for one year, with corresponding loss of date when he shall be re-examined, and in case of his failure upon such re-examination he shall be dropped from the service. [See § 1447 and act Aug. 5, 1882, *post.*]

15 July, 1870, s. 8, v. 16, p. 333.

NOTE.—"Shall be suspended from promotion for one year, with corresponding loss of date," does not mean that the loss of date is to be *contemporaneous* with the term of suspension, but only that it shall agree therewith in point of duration. When an officer is so suspended, the loss of a year is to be reckoned from the occurrence of the vacancy, the date from which he would have taken rank had he been qualified; and the year of suspension from the approval of the President of the finding of the Examining Boards. While under suspension is ineligible to promotion, and no vacancy is to be kept open for him. The officers eligible during that period are entitled to fill the vacancies. The loss of *date* being one year, if found qualified, on a second examination, to fill a vacancy occurring after the period of suspension, he will be entitled, on promotion thereto, to take rank one year from the date of the vacancy which he would have originally filled. Will not be entitled to the pay of the higher grade from the ranking date in his commission.—Op. XVI, 587, Dec. 10, 1880. Published in Gen. Order 262.

*5 Aug., 1882.*
*Failure for misconduct.*

Whenever on an inquiry had pursuant to law, concerning the fitness of an officer of the Navy for promotion, it shall appear that such officer is unfit to perform at sea the duties of the place to which it is proposed to promote him, by reason of drunkenness, or from any cause arising from his own misconduct, and having been informed of and heard upon the charges against him, he shall not be placed on the retired-list of the Navy, and if the finding of the board be approved by the President, he shall be discharged with not more than one year's pay.

5 Aug., 1882, P. E. L., p. 286.

NOTE.—In the only case so far coming under this act, "one year's pay" was held by the accounting officers to mean one year's "leave" pay.

SEC. 1506. Any officer of the Navy may, by and with the advice and consent of the Senate, be advanced, not exceeding thirty numbers in rank, for eminent and conspicuous conduct in battle or extraordinary heroism; *and the rank of officers shall not be changed except in accordance with the provisions of existing law, and by and with the advice and consent of the Senate.* — Title 15, Chap. 4. Advancement in number.

21 April, 1864, v. s. 6, 13, p. 54.   24 Jan., 1865 s. 1, v. 13, p. 424.
17 June, 1878, v. 20, p. 143.

NOTES.—Congress leaves to the discretion of the President the determination of what acts of heroism should be recommended to the Senate for reward, and in providing that the Senate must advise and consent to the advancement has indicated the only forum which may inquire into the wisdom with which that discretion has been exercised. It is not within the power of a Secretary of the Navy to inquire into the acts of heroism which induced his predecessor and the President to make an advancement. Their action is conclusive on the executive department.—Op. April 23, 1881, MacVeagh. Stevenson's case.

By advancement under section 1506 an ensign was promoted to master March 3, 1879, to take rank from November 27, 1877. Not having been "promoted in course to fill a vacancy," not entitled to the pay of the higher grade, under section 1561 of the Revised Statutes, from the date he takes rank, but from the date of his appointment.—Op. March 29, 1882, Brewster. Young's case.

The advancement of an officer under section 1506, when the advancement is confined to the same grade in which he already holds a commission, confers upon him no right to an increase of compensation over that which he is in receipt of in virtue of that commission.—Op. XIV, 547, March 18, 1875. Billing's case.

SEC. 1507. Any officer who is nominated to a higher grade by the provisions of the preceding section, shall be promoted, notwithstanding the number of said grade may be full; but no further promotions shall take place in that grade, except for like cause, until the number is reduced to that provided by law. — Promotion when grade is full.

24 Jan., 1865, s. 2, v. 13, p. 424.

SEC. 1508. Any line officer, whether of volunteers or of the regular Navy, may be advanced one grade, if, upon recommendation of the President by name, he receives the thanks of Congress for highly distinguished conduct in conflict with the enemy or for extraordinary heroism in the line of his profession. — Officers receiving thanks of Congress.

16 July, 1862, s. 9, v. 12, p. 584.   24 Jan., 1865, s. 2, v. 13, p. 424.
25 July, 1866, s. 1, v. 14, p. 222.

SEC. 1509. A vote of thanks by Congress to any officer of the Navy shall be held to affect such officer only; and whenever, as an incident thereof, an officer who would otherwise be retired is retained on the active list, such retention shall not interfere with the regular promotion of others who would otherwise have been entitled by law to promotion. — Effect of vote of thanks.

1 July, 1870, res., s. 1, v. 16, p. 384.

SEC. 1510. No promotion shall be made to fill a vacancy occasioned by the final retirement, death, resignation, or dismissal of an officer who has received a vote of thanks, unless the number of officers left in the grade where the vacancy occurs shall be less than the number authorized by law. — Vacancies occasioned by death, &c., of officers thanked.

*Idem.*

SEC. 1560. The pay of an officer of the Navy, upon his original entry into the service, except where he is required to give an official bond, shall commence upon the date of his acceptance of his appointment; but where he is required to give such bond his pay shall commence upon the date of the approval of his bond by the proper authority. — Title XV, Chap. 8. Commencement of pay, original entry.

15 July, 1870, s. 7, v. 16, p. 333.

SEC. 1561. When an officer is promoted in course to fill a vacancy, and is in the performance of the duties of the higher grade from the date he is to take rank, he may be allowed the increased pay from such date. [See following act and note.] — Commencement of pay of promoted officers.

15 July, 1870, s. 7, v. 16, p. 333.   5 June, 1872, s. 1, v. 17, p. 226.

That on and after the passage of this act, any officer of the Navy who may be promoted in course to fill a vacancy in the next higher grade shall be entitled to the pay of the grade to which promoted from the date he takes rank therein, if it be subsequent to the vacancy he is appointed to fill. — 22 June, 1874. Commencement of pay on promotion.

22 June, 1874. s. 1, v. 18, p. 91.

NOTE.—Previous to the act of July 15, 1870, chapter 205, the increased pay of a promoted officer commenced from the date of the signing of his appointment.

to perform the duties of the higher grade, if before the date of his commission, or from the date of his commission if no appointment was previously given. The seventh section of that act provided that it should commence from the date of rank as stated in his commission. The act of June 5, 1872, substantially section 1561, provided that the promotion must have been in course to fill a vacancy, and the officer must have been in the performance of the duties of the higher grade from the date he takes rank. Under the act of June 22, 1874, which now regulates it, the promotion must have been in "course to fill a vacancy" to entitle an officer to the pay of the higher grade from the date he takes rank therein, which date must be subsequent to the vacancy he is appointed to fill.

**Title XV, Chap. 8.**
In cases of delayed examinations.

SEC. 1562. If an officer of a class subject to examination before promotion shall be absent on duty, and by reason of such absence, or of other cause not involving fault on his part, shall not be examined at the time required by law or regulation, and shall afterward be examined and found qualified, the increased rate of pay to which his promotion would entitle him shall commence from the date when he would have been entitled to it had he been examined and found qualified at the time so required by law or regulation; and this rule shall apply to any cases of this description which may have heretofore occurred. And in every such case the period of service of the party, in the grade to which he was promoted, shall, in reference to the rate of his pay, be considered to have commenced from the date when he was so entitled to take rank. [See *ante*, July 22, 1874, and note, and § 1495.]

15 July, 1870, s. 7, v. 16, p. 333.

## RANK AND PRECEDENCE.

Sec.
1367. Rank of secretaries to Admiral and Vice-Admiral.
1372. Of assistant surgeons delayed in examination.
1466. Relative rank of Navy and Army officers.
1467. Rank according to date.
1468. Commanding officers of vessels and stations.
1469. Aid or executive officer.
1470. Staff officers, when to communicate directly with commanding officers.
1471. Chiefs of Bureaus.
1472. Chief of Bureau, below rank of commodore.
1473. Chief of Bureau, retired.
1474. Medical Corps.
1475. Pay Corps.
1476. Engineer Corps.
1477. Naval constructors.
1478. Civil engineers.
1479. Chaplains.
1480. Professors of mathematics and staff generally.

Sec.
1481. Staff officers retired, length of service.
1482. Staff officers retired, incident to service.
1483. Graduates at Naval Academy.
1484. Engineer graduates.
1485. Precedence by length of service.
1486. Length of service, how estimated.
1487. Quarters.
1488. Military command.
1489. Processions, boards, &c.
1490. Ensigns.
1491. Warrant officers.
1492. Officers of revenue marine.
1506. Advanced in rank; rank not to be changed, except, &c.
1521. Cadet midshipmen promoted.
1601. Commandant Marine Corps.
1602. Staff officers Marine Corps.
1603. Marine Corps with the Army.
—— Judge-Advocate-General of the Navy.

**Title 15, Chap. 1.**
Secretaries to Admiral and Vice-Admiral.

SEC. 1367. The Admiral and Vice-Admiral shall each be allowed a secretary, who shall be entitled to the rank and allowances of a lieutenant in the Navy.

21 Dec., 1864, s. 2, v. 13, p. 420.
16 May, 1866, v. 14, p. 48.
25 July, 1866, s. 6, v. 14, p. 223.
2 March, 1867, s. 1, v. 14, p. 516.

Rank of assistant surgeons in case of delayed examination.

SEC. 1372. When any assistant surgeon was absent from the United States, on duty, at the time when others of his date were examined, he shall, if not rejected at a subsequent examination, be entitled to the same rank with them; and if, from any cause, his relative rank cannot be assigned to him, he shall retain his original position on the register.

3 March, 1835, s. 1, v. 4, p. 757.

**Title 15, Chap. 4.**
Relative rank of Navy and Army officers.

SEC. 1466. The relative rank between officers of the Navy, whether on the active or retired list, and officers of the Army, shall be as follows, lineal rank only being considered:
The Vice-Admiral shall rank with the Lieutenant-General.
Rear-admirals with major-generals.
Commodores with brigadier-generals.
Captains with colonels.
Commanders with lieutenant-colonels.
Lieutenant commanders with majors.

RANK AND PRECEDENCE. 79

Lieutenants with captains.
Masters (*lieutenants of the junior grade*) with first lieutenants.
Ensigns with second lieutenants.

16 July, 1862, s. 13, v. 12, p. 585.   21 Dec., 1864, s. 1, v. 13, p. 420.
25 July, 1866, s. 1, v. 14, p. 222.   2 March, 1867, s. 1, v. 14, p. 515.
3 March, 1883, P. E. L., p. 485.

SEC. 1467. Line officers shall take rank in each grade according to the dates of their commissions. — Rank according to date.

16 July, 1862, s. 1, v. 12, p. 583.
21 April, 1864, s. 7, v. 13, p. 54.
24 Jan., 1865, s. 1, v. 13, p. 424.

SEC. 1468. Commanding officers of vessels of war and of naval stations shall take precedence over all officers placed under their command. — Commanding officers of vessels and stations.

3 March, 1871, s. 12, v. 16, p. 537.

SEC. 1469. The Secretary of the Navy may, in his discretion, detail a line officer to act as the aid or executive of the commanding officer of a vessel of war or naval station, which officer shall, when not impracticable, be next in rank to said commanding officer. Such aid or executive shall, while executing the orders of the commanding officer on board the vessel or at the station, take precedence over all officers attached to the vessel or station. All orders of such aid or executive shall be regarded as proceeding from the commanding officer, and the aid or executive shall have no independent authority in consequence of such detail. — Aid or executive officer.

*Idem.*

SEC. 1470. Staff officers, senior to the officers so detailed, shall have the right to communicate directly with the commanding officer. — Rights of staff officers.

*Idem.*

SEC. 1471. The chiefs of the Bureau of Medicine and Surgery, Provisions and Clothing, Steam Engineering, and Construction and Repair shall have the relative rank of commodore while holding said position, and shall have, respectively, the title of Surgeon-General, Paymaster-General, Engineer-in-Chief, and Chief Constructor. [See § 1481.] — Chiefs of Bureaus.

*Idem.*

SEC. 1472. When the office of chief of Bureau is filled by a line officer below the rank of commodore, said officer shall have the relative rank of commodore during the time he holds said office. — Chief of Bureau, when below rank of commander.

*Idem.*

SEC. 1473. Officers who have been or who shall be retired from the position of chiefs of the Bureau of Medicine and Surgery, of Provisions and Clothing, of Steam Engineering, or of Construction and Repair, by reason of age or length of service, shall have the relative rank of commodore. — Retired from position of chief of Bureau.

*Idem.*

SEC. 1474. Officers of the Medical Corps on the active list of the Navy shall have relative rank as follows: — Medical Corps.
Medical directors, the relative rank of captain.
Medical inspectors, the relative rank of commander.
Surgeons, the relative rank of lieutenant-commander or lieutenant.
Passed assistant surgeons, the relative rank of lieutenant or master*.
Assistant surgeons, the relative rank of master* or ensign.

*Idem*, s. 5, p. 535.

SEC. 1475. Officers of the Pay Corps on the active list of the Navy shall have relative rank as follows: — Pay Corps.
Pay directors, the relative rank of captain.
Pay inspectors, the relative rank of commander.
Paymasters, the relative rank of lieutenant-commander or lieutenant.
Passed assistant paymasters, the relative rank of lieutenant or master.*
Assistant paymasters, the relative rank of master* or ensign.

*Ibid.*, s. 6, p. 536.

SEC. 1476. Officers of the Engineer Corps on the active list shall have relative rank as follows: — Engineer Corps.

---

*\* Lieutenant of the junior grade* (3 March, 1883).

Of the chief engineers, ten shall have the relative rank of captain, fifteen that of commander, and forty-five that of lieutenant-commander or lieutenant.

*Passed* assistant engineers shall have the relative rank of lieutenant or master, and *assistant* engineers that of *lieutenant of the junior grade* or ensign. [See 1390, ENGINEER CORPS.]

*Ibid.*, s. 7, p. 536.
24 Feb., 1874, v. 18, p. 17.
3 March, 1883, P. E. L., p. 472.

Naval constructor.

SEC. 1477. Of the naval constructors, two shall have the relative rank of captain, three of commander, and all others that of lieutenant-commander or lieutenant. Assistant naval constructors shall have the relative rank of lieutenant or master.

3 March, 1871, s. 9, v. 16, p. 536.

Civil engineers.

SEC. 1478. Civil engineers shall have such relative rank as the President may fix.

3 March, 1871, s. 9, v. 16, p. 536.

The President of the United States has this day, under the provisions of section 1478 of the Revised Statutes, conferred relative rank on Civil Engineers of the Navy, and fixed the same as follows:
One with the relative rank of captain.
Two with the relative rank of commander.
Three with the relative rank of lieutenant commander.
Four with the relative rank of lieutenant.
Civil engineers will take precedence in their corps, and with other officers with whom they hold relative rank, in accordance with the law regulating precedence of officers of the Navy.

General Order 263, 24 Feb., 1881.

Chaplains.

SEC. 1479. Chaplains shall have relative rank as follows: Four, the relative rank of captain; seven, that of commander; and not more than seven, that of lieutenant-commander or lieutenant.

3 March, 1871, s. 9, v. 16, p. 536.

Professors of mathematics.

SEC. 1480. Professors of mathematics shall have relative rank as follows: Three, the relative rank of captain; four, that of commander; and five, that of lieutenant-commander or lieutenant.

The grades established in the six preceding sections for the staff corps of the Navy shall be filled by appointment from the highest members in each corps, according to seniority; and new commissions shall be issued to the officers so appointed, in which the titles and grades established in said sections shall be inserted; and no existing commission shall be vacated in the said several staff corps, except by the issue of the new commissions required by the provisions of this section; and no officer shall be reduced in rank or lose seniority in his own corps by any change which may be required under the provisions of the said six preceding sections: *Provided*, That the issuing of a new appointment and commission to any officer of the Pay Corps under the provisions of this section shall not affect or annul any existing bond, but the same shall remain in force, and apply to such new appointment and commission.

31 May, 1872, s. 1, v. 17, p. 192.
27 Feb., 1877, v. 19, p. 244.

NOTE.—Section 1475 does not give to a pay inspector in the Navy the *grade* of commander. It confers upon him the *rank* of commander *by relation* (only) to the rank of a line officer of that grade. The designation "pay inspector" expresses both title and grade in the Pay Corps. The commission of an officer as "pay inspector," "with the relative rank of commander," gives the appropriate title and grade of the officer named therein, and fully satisfies the requirement of section 1480. R. S.—Op. XVI, 414, Jan. 8, 1880, Devens. [For a definition of the words "title," "grade," and "rank," see this opinion and C. C., XV, 151. The latter defines the rank of staff officers of the Navy as usually operative only in determing the relation of the different officers of the service to each other in matters of precedence, privilege, and the like, and is generally called relative rank. *Grade* is a step or degree in either office or rank, and has reference to the divisions of the one or the other, or both, according to the connection in which the word is employed.]

When retired for age or length of service.

SEC. 1481. Officers of the Medical, Pay, and Engineer Corps, chaplains, professors of mathematics, and constructors, who shall have served faithfully for forty-five years, shall, when retired, have the relative rank of commodore; and officers of these several corps who have been or shall be retired at the age of sixty-two years, before having served for forty-five years, but who shall have served faithfully until retired, shall, on the completion of forty years from their entry into the service, have the relative rank of commodore.

3 March, 1871, s. 11, v. 16, p. 537.

SEC. 1482. Staff-officers, who have been or shall be retired for causes incident to the service before arriving at sixty-two years of age, shall have the same rank on the retired list as pertained to their position on the active list. {Retired for causes incident to service.}

*Ibid.*

SEC. 1483. Graduates of the Naval Academy shall take rank according to their proficiency as shown by their order of merit at the date of graduation. {Graduates of Naval Academy.}

23 May, 1872. s. 1, v. 17, p. 153.

SEC. 1484. Engineer officers graduated at the Naval Academy shall take precedence with all other officers with whom they have relative rank, according to the actual length of service in the Navy. [See § 1394, ENGINEER CORPS.] {Engineers graduated at Naval Academy.}

3 March, 1873, s. 1, v. 17, p. 555.

SEC. 1485. The officers of the staff corps of the Navy shall take precedence in their several corps, and in their several grades, and with officers of the line with whom they hold relative rank according to length of service in the Navy. {Precedence by length of service.}

3 March, 1871, s. 10, v. 16, p. 537.

SEC. 1486. In estimating the length of service for such purpose, the several officers of the staff corps shall, respectively, take precedence in their several grades and with those officers of the line of the Navy with whom they hold relative rank who have been in the naval service six years longer than such officers of said staff corps have been in said service; and officers who have been advanced or lost numbers on the Navy Register shall be considered as having gained or lost length of service accordingly: *Provided, That nothing in this section shall be so construed as to give to any officer of the staff corps precedence by, or a higher relative rank than that of, another staff officer in the same grade and corps, and whose commission in such grade and corps antedates that of such officer.* {Length of service, how estimated.}

3 March, 1871, s. 10, v. 16, p. 537.    3 March, 1881, v. 21, p. 510.
See Op. Feb. 25, 1881.  Gen. Order 264.

SEC. 1487. No staff officer shall, in virtue of his relative rank or precedence, have any additional right to quarters. {Quarters.}

3 March, 1871, s. 10, v. 16, p. 537.

SEC. 1488. The relative rank given by the provisions of this chapter to officers of the Medical, Pay, and Engineer Corps shall confer no authority to exercise military command. {Military command.}

General Orders, 31 Aug., 1846, and 27 May, 1847.    5 Aug., 1854, s. 4, v. 10, p. 587.
3 March, 1859, s. 2, v. 11, p. 407.

SEC. 1489. In processions on shore, or courts-martial, summary courts, courts of inquiry, boards of survey, and all other boards, line and staff officers shall take precedence according to rank. {Processions, boards, &c.}

3 March, 1871, s. 12, v. 16, p. 537.

SEC. 1490. Ensigns shall be steerage officers, unless assigned to duty as watch and division officers. {Ensigns as steerage officers.}

15 July, 1870, s. 10, v. 16, p. 334.

SEC. 1491. The President may, if he shall deem it conducive to the interests of the service, give assimilated rank to boatswains, gunners, carpenters, and sail-makers, as follows: After five years' service, to rank with ensigns, and after ten years' service, to rank with *junior lieutenants.* {Warrant officers.}

2 July, 1864, s. 1, v. 13, p. 373.    3 March, 1883, P. E. L., p. 472.

SEC. 1492. The officers of the revenue-cutter service when serving, in accordance with law, as a part of the Navy, shall be entitled to relative rank, as follows: Captains, with and next after lieutenants commanding in the Navy; first lieutenants, with and next after lieutenants in the Navy; second lieutenants, with and next after *junior lieutenants* {Revenue-cutter officers serving as part of the Navy.}

in the Navy; third lieutenants, with and next after ensigns in the Navy.

2 Feb., 1863, s. 4, v. 12, p. 640.
2 March, 1799, s. 98, v. 1, p. 699.
16 July, 1862, ss. 1, 11, v. 12, pp. 583–585.
3 March, 1883, P. E. L., p 472.

**Officers advanced in rank.**
**Rank not to be changed, except, &c.**

SEC. 1506. Any officer of the Navy may, by and with the advice and consent of the Senate, be advanced, not exceeding thirty numbers in rank, for eminent and conspicuous conduct in battle or extraordinary heroism; *and the rank of officers shall not be changed except in accordance with the provisions of existing law, and by and with the advice and consent of the Senate.* [See 1508, PROMOTION.]

21 April, 1864, s. 6, v. 13, p. 54.
24 Jan., 1865, s. 1, v. 13, p. 424.
17 June, 1878, v. 20, p. 143.

**Title 15, Chap. 5.**
**Promotion to midshipmen; rank.**

SEC. 1521. When cadet midshipmen shall have passed successfully the graduating examination at the Academy, they shall receive appointments as midshipmen and shall take rank according to their proficiency as shown by the order of their merit at date of graduation.

NOTE.—Section 1521 is changed by the acts of Aug. 5, 1882, and March 3, 1883. Cadet midshipmen are now styled naval cadets until they complete the six years course, and, under certain contingencies, are mustered out or appointed to other places. There are no midshipmen or cadet midshipmen. See NAVAL ACADEMY.

15 July, 1870, s. 12, v. 16, p. 334.

**Title 15, Chap. 9.**
**Rank of commandant Marine Corps.**

SEC. 1601. The commandant of the Marine Corps shall have the rank and pay of a colonel in the Army, and shall be appointed by selection by the President from the officers of said corps.

2 March, 1867, s. 7, v. 14, p. 517.
6 June, 1874, v. 18, p. 58.

**Staff rank, Marine Corps.**

SEC. 1602. The adjutant and inspector, the paymaster, and the quartermaster shall have the rank of major; *each* assistant quartermaster shall have the rank of captain.

2 March, 1847, s. 3, v. 9, p. 154.
27 Feb., 1877, v. 19, p. 244.

**Relative rank of Marine Corps with the Army.**

SEC. 1603. The officers of the Marine Corps shall be, in relation to rank, on the same footing as officers of similar grades in the Army.

30 June, 1834, s. 4, v. 4, p. 713.

**8 June, 1880.**
**Rank of Judge-Advocate-General.**

That the President of the United States be, and he is hereby, authorized to appoint, for the term of four years, by and with the advice and consent of the Senate, from the officers of the Navy or the Marine Corps, a Judge-Advocate-General of the Navy, with the rank pay, and allowances of a captain in the Navy or a colonel in the Marine Corps, as the case may be. * * *

8 March, 1880, v. 21, p. 164.

## RATIONS.

Sec.
1143. Detachments with the Army.
1577. Rations to naval cadet.
1578. Rations of other officers.
1579. When rations not allowed.
1580. Navy ration, constituents of.
1581. Substitutions in.
1582. Short allowance.
1583. Rations stopped for the sick.
1584. Additional ration.

Sec.
1585. Commutation price of ration.
1595. None to retired officers.
1615. To enlisted marines.
3721. Purchases of butter and cheese.
3726. Preserved meats.
3727. Flour and bread.
4812. Allowance to Navy hospitals.
—— Desiccated tomatoes.

**Title 14, Chap. 1.**
**Naval detachments co-operating with the Army.**

SEC. 1143. The officers of the subsistence department shall, upon the requisition of the naval or marine officer commanding any detachment of seamen or marines under orders to act on shore, in co-operation with the land troops, and during the time such detachment is so acting or proceeding to act, furnish rations to the officers, seamen, and marines of the same.

15 Dec., 1814, s. 1, v. 3, p. 151.

**Title 15, Chap. 8.**
**Rations to naval cadets.**

SEC. 1577. Midshipmen and *Naval cadets* in the Navy shall be entitled to one ration, or to commutation therefor.

28 July, 1866, s. 8, v. 14, p. 322.
28 Feb., 1867, s. 2, v. 14, p. 416.
5 Aug., 1882, P. E. L., p. 285.

## RATIONS. 83

SEC. 1578. All officers shall be entitled to one ration, or to commutation therefor, while at sea or attached to a sea-going vessel. — *Rations of other officers.*

16 July, 1862, s. 10, v. 12, p. 587.　　3 March, 1851, s. 1, v. 9, p. 631.
Op. X, 52, July 10, 1861.

SEC. 1579. No person not actually attached to and doing duty on board a sea-going vessel, except the petty officers, seamen, and ordinary seamen attached to receiving-ships or to the ordinary of a navy-yard, and *ensigns of the junior grade and naval cadets*, shall be allowed a ration. — *When rations not allowed.*

3 March, 1851, s. 1. v. 9, p. 621.　　5 Aug., 1882, P. E. L., p. 285.
28 Feb., 1867, s. 2, v. 14, p. 416.　　3 March, 1883, P. E. L., p. 472.
28 July, 1866, s. 8, v. 14, p. 322.

SEC. 1580. The Navy ration shall consist of the following daily allowance of provisions to each person: One pound of salt pork, with half a pint of beans or pease; or one pound of salt beef, with half a pound of flour, and two ounces of dried apples, or other dried fruit; or three-quarters of a pound of preserved meat, with a half pound of rice, two ounces of butter, and one ounce of desiccated "mixed vegetables;" or three-quarters of a pound of preserved meat, two ounces of butter, and two ounces of desiccated potatoes; together with fourteen ounces of biscuit, one-quarter of an ounce of tea, or one ounce of coffee or cocoa, and two ounces of sugar; and a weekly allowance of half a pint of pickles, half a pint of molasses, and half a pint of vinegar. [See May 3, 1880, *post*.] — *Navy ration, constituents of.*

18 July, 1861, s. 1, v. 12, p. 264.　　14 July, 1862, s. 4, v. 12, p. 565.

SEC. 1581. The following substitution for the components of the ration may be made when it is deemed necessary by the senior officer present in command: For one pound of salt beef or pork, one pound and a quarter of fresh meat or three-quarters of a pound of preserved meat; for any or all of the articles usually issued with the salted meats, vegetables equal to the same in value; for fourteen ounces of biscuit, one pound of soft bread, or one pound of flour, or half a pound of rice; for half a pint of beans or pease, half a pound of rice, and for half a pound of rice, half a pint of beans or pease. And the Secretary of the Navy may substitute for the ration of coffee and sugar the extract of coffee combined with milk and sugar, if he shall believe such substitution to be conducive to the health and comfort of the Navy, and not to be more expensive to the Government than the present ration: *Provided*, That the same shall be acceptable to the men. [See *post*, May 3, 1880.] — *Substitutions in.*

18 July, 1861, ss. 2, 3, 4, v. 12, p. 265.　　17 April, 1862, s. 4, v. 12, p. 381.

SEC. 1582. In case of necessity the daily allowance of provisions may be diminished at the discretion of the senior officer present in command; but payment shall be made to the persons whose allowance is thus diminished, according to the scale of prices for the same established at the time of such diminution. And every commander who makes any diminution or variation shall give to the paymaster written orders therefor, specifying particularly the diminution or variation which is to be made, and shall report to his commanding officer, or to the Navy Department, the necessity for the same. — *Short allowance.*

18 July, 1861, s. 4, v. 12, p. 265.

SEC. 1583. Rations stopped for the sick on board vessels shall remain and be accounted for by the paymaster as a part of the provisions of the vessels. — *Rations stopped for the sick.*

3 March, 1851, s. 1, v. 9, p. 621.　　22 June, 1860, s. 3, v. 12, p. 83.

SEC. 1584. An additional ration of tea or coffee and sugar shall be hereafter allowed to each seaman, to be provided at his first "turning out." — *Additional ration.*

23 May, 1872, s. 1, v. 17, p. 151.

SEC. 1585. Thirty cents shall in all cases be deemed the commutation price of the Navy ration. — *Commutation price of ration.*

15 July, 1870, s. 4, v. 16, p. 333.

SEC. 1595. Rations shall not be allowed to officers on the retired list. — *Retired officers.*

16 July, 1862, s. 20, v. 12, p. 587.

SEC. 1615. The non-commissioned officers, privates, and musicians of the Marine Corps shall, each, be entitled to receive one Navy ration daily. — *Title 15, Chap. 9. Rations to enlisted men, Marine Corps.*

1 July, 1797, s. 6, v. 1, p. 524.
11 July, 1798, s. 2, v. 1, p. 595.

84 RETIREMENT.

**Title 13.**

**Purchases without advertisements.**

SEC. 3721. The provisions which require that supplies shall be purchased by the Secretary of the Navy from the lowest bidder, after advertisement, shall not apply to * * * the supplies which it may be necessary to purchase out of the United States for vessels on foreign stations, * * * or butter * * destined for the use of the Navy.

**Butter.**

* * * Contracts for butter * * * for the use of the Navy may be made for periods longer than one year, if, in the opinion of the Secretary of the Navy, economy and the quality of the ration will be promoted thereby. * * *

3 March, 1845, s. 3, v. 5, p. 794.     3 March, 1847, s. 2, v. 9, p. 172.
3 Aug., 1848, s. 11, v. 9, p. 272.     2 March, 1865, s. 7, v. 13, p. 467.

**Preserved meats, &c.**

SEC. 3726. The Secretary of the Navy is authorized to procure the preserved meats, pickles, butter, and desiccated vegetables, in such manner and under such restrictions and guarantees as in his opinion will best insure the good quality of said articles.

18 July, 1861, s. 7, v. 12, p. 265.

**Flour and bread.**

SEC. 3727. The Secretary of the Navy is authorized to purchase, in such manner as he shall deem most advantageous to the Government, the flour required for naval use; and to have the bread for the Navy baked from this flour by special contract under naval inspection.

3 March, 1863, s. 4, v. 12, p. 818.

**Title 59, Chap. 1.**

**Allowance of rations to Navy hospitals.**

SEC. 4812. For every Navy officer, seaman, or marine admitted into a Navy hospital, the institution shall be allowed one ration per day during his continuance therein, to be deducted from the account of the United States with such officer, seaman, or marine.

26 Feb., 1811, s. 4, v. 2, p. 650.

**May 3, 1880.**

**Desiccated tomatoes as a substitute.**

The Secretary of the Navy may substitute for the ration of "two ounces of desiccated potatoes" six ounces of desiccated tomatoes if he shall believe such substitution to be conducive to the health and comfort of the Navy, and not to be more expensive to the Government than the present ration, provided the same shall be acceptable to the men. In the event the Secretary of the Navy orders such substitution he is authorized to have sold at public auction any desiccated potatoes on hand, the proceeds of which sale shall be used in the purchase of desiccated tomatoes for the use of the Navy.

3 May, 1880, v. 21, p. 86.

## RETIREMENT.

Sec.
1443. After forty years' service.
1444. After sixty-two years of age, or forty-five years of service.
1445. Officers of certain ranks to be retired only for disability.
1446. Officers who have received a vote of thanks.
1447. Officers rejected for promotion.
— Officers rejected for misconduct.
1448. Retiring-board.
1449. Powers and duties of.
1450. Oath of members.
1451. Findings.
1452. Revision by the President.
1453. Disability by an incident of the service.
1454. Disability by other causes.
1455. Not to be retired without a hearing.
1456. Not to be retired for misconduct.
1457. Privileges and liabilities.
1458. Vacancies by retirement.

Sec.
1459. Withdrawn from command.
— Act Aug. 5, 1882, prohibiting promotion.
1462. Active duty.
1463. Assigned to command of squadrons and ships.
1464. Commanders of squadrons, from what grades selected.
1465. When restored to active list.
1473. Retired Chiefs of Bureaus.
1481. When retired for age or length of service.
1482. Retired for causes incident to service staff.
1588. Pay.
1589. Pay of certain rear-admirals.
1590. Pay of third assistant engineers.
1591. Pay not increased by promotion.
1592. Pay on active duty.
1593. Pay of officers retired on furlough.
1594. Transfer from furlough to retired pay.
1595. Not entitled to rations.

**Title 15, Chap. 3.**

**After 40 years' service.**

SEC. 1443. When any officer of the Navy has been forty years in the service of the United States he may be retired from active service by the President upon his own application.

3 Aug., 1861, s. 21, v. 12, p. 290.

**After 62 years of age or 45 years' service.**

SEC. 1444. When any officer below the rank of Vice-Admiral is sixty-two years old, he shall, except in the case provided in the next section, be retired by the President from active service.

21 Dec., 1861, s. 1, v. 12, p. 329.
25 June, 1864, s. 1, v. 13, p. 183.
21 Dec., 1864, s. 3, v. 13, p. 420.
16 July, 1862, s. 8, v. 12, p. 584.
3 March, 1873, v. 17, p. 556.

# RETIREMENT.   85

SEC. 1445. The two preceding sections shall not apply to any lieutenant-commander, lieutenant, *lieutenant of the junior grade*, ensign, passed assistant surgeon, passed assistant paymaster, *passed* assistant engineer, assistant surgeon, assistant paymaster, or *assistant* engineer; and such officers shall not be placed upon the retired list, except on account of physical or mental disability. Officers of certain ranks to be retired only for disability.

15 July, 1870, s. 6, v. 16, p. 333.   24 Feb., 1874, v. 18, p. 17.
3 March, 1883, P. E. L., p. 472.

SEC. 1446. Officers on the active list, not below the grade of commander, who have, upon the recommendation of the President, received by name, during the war for the suppression of the rebellion, a vote of thanks of Congress for distinguished service, shall not be retired, except for cause, until they have been fifty-five years in the service of the United States. Officers who have received a vote of thanks.

16 July, 1862, s. 8, v. 12, p. 584.

SEC. 1447. When the case of any officer has been acted upon by a board of naval surgeons and an examining board for promotion, as provided in Chapter Four of this Title, and he shall not have been recommended for promotion by both of the said boards, he shall be placed upon the retired list. [See § 1456, and act of Aug. 5, 1882.] Officers rejected for promotion.

21 April 1864, s. 4, v. 13, p. 53.

Whenever on an inquiry had pursuant to law, concerning the fitness of an officer of the Navy for promotion, it shall appear that such officer is unfit to perform at sea the duties of the place to which it is proposed to promote him, by reason of drunkenness, or from any cause arising from his own misconduct, and having been informed of and heard upon the charges against him, he shall not be placed on the retired-list of the Navy, and if the finding of the board be approved by the President, he shall be discharged with not more than one year's pay. [See § 1456.] 5 Aug. 1882.<br>Not to be retired for misconduct.

5 Aug., 1882, P. E. L., p. 286.

SEC. 1448. Whenever any officer, on being ordered to perform the duties appropriate to his commission, reports himself unable to comply with such order, or whenever, in the judgment of the President, an officer is incapacitated to perform the duties of his office, the President, at his discretion, may direct the Secretary of the Navy to refer the case of such officer to a board of not more than nine nor less than five commissioned officers, two-fifths of whom shall be members of the Medical Corps of the Navy. Said board, except the officers taken from the Medical Corps, shall be composed, as far as may be, of seniors in rank to the officer whose disability is inquired of. Title 15, Chap. 3.<br>Retiring board.

3 Aug., 1861, s. 23, v. 12, p. 291.

SEC. 1449. Said retiring-board shall be authorized to inquire into and determine the facts touching the nature and occasion of the disability of any such officer, and shall have such powers of a court-martial and of a court of inquiry as may be necessary. Powers and duties of.

3 Aug., 1861, s. 17, v. 12, p. 290.

SEC. 1450. The members of said board shall be sworn in each case to discharge their duties honestly and impartially. Oath of members.

3 Aug., 1861, s. 23, v. 12, p. 291.

SEC. 1451. When said retiring-board finds an officer incapacitated for active service, it shall also find and report the cause which, in its judgment, produced his incapacity, and whether such cause is an incident of the service. Findings.

*Idem.*

SEC. 1452. A record of the proceedings and decision of the board in each case shall be transmitted to the Secretary of the Navy, and shall be laid by him before the President for his approval or disapproval, or orders in the case. Revision by the President.

*Idem.*

NOTES.—No power of review over the proceedings of a retiring board exists by law where its finding has been once approved by the President and his "orders in the case" executed.—Op. XV, p. 446. Devens, Feb. 8, 1878. Rodney's case.

Where a naval retiring board, convened to inquire into the nature and cause of the disability of an officer, has once finished its work, rendered a complete judgment in the case, and adjourned, a subsequent reconsideration of its judgment by the board, unless authorized or directed by proper authority, can have no legal effect.—Op. XVI, p. 104. Devens, July 25, 1878. Rodney's case.

## RETIREMENT.

**Disability by an incident of the service.**
SEC. 1453. When a retiring-board finds that an officer is incapacitated for active service, and that his incapacity is the result of an incident of the service, such officer shall, if said decision is approved by the President, be retired from active service with retired pay, as allowed by Chapter Eight of this Title.

3 Aug., 1861, s. 23, v. 12, p. 291.

**Disability by other causes.**
SEC. 1454. When said board finds that an officer is incapacitated for active service and that his incapacity is not the result of any incident of the service, such officer shall, if said decision is approved by the President, be retired from active service on furlough-pay, or wholly retired from service with one year's pay, as the President may determine. [See Aug. 5, 1882, *ante.*]

*Idem.*

**Not to be retired without a hearing.**
SEC. 1455. No officer of the Navy shall be retired from active service, or wholly retired from the service, without a full and fair hearing before such Navy retiring-board, if he shall demand it, except in cases where he may be retired by the President at his own request, or on account of age or length of service, or on account of his failure to be recommended by an examining board for promotion.

*Idem.*

**Not to be retired for misconduct.**
SEC. 1456. No officer of the Navy shall be placed on the retired list because of misconduct; but he shall be brought to trial by court-martial for such misconduct. [See § 1447 and act Aug. 5, 1882.]

15 July, 1870, s. 6, v. 16, p. 333.

**Privileges and liabilities.**
SEC. 1457. Officers retired from active service shall be placed on the retired list of officers of the grades to which they belonged respectively at the time of their retirement, and continue to be borne on the Navy Register. They shall be entitled to wear the uniform of their respective grades, and shall be subject to the rules and articles for the government of the Navy and to trial by general court-martial. The names of officers wholly retired from the service shall be omitted from the Navy Register.*

3 Aug., 1861, ss. 22, 23, 24, v. 12, pp. 290, 291.
16 Jan., 1857, s. 4, v. 11, p. 154.

NOTE.—The appointment of a line officer of the Navy to be the chief of a bureau is an investiture of him with an additional office. While holding that office he has the relative rank of commodore, but remains in his lineal position in the Navy. The grade to which he belongs for the purposes of section 1457 is that which he holds in the Navy, and not that of the relative rank incidental to his temporary occupation of another and distinct office.—Op. —, July 8, 1881, Mac-Veigh, Whiting's case. See also Op. X, p. 378.

**Vacancies by retirement.**
SEC. 1458. The next officer in rank shall be promoted to the place of a retired officer, according to the established rules of the service; and the same rule of promotion shall be applied successively to the vacancies consequent upon the retirement of an officer. [Act of Aug. 5, 1882, establishes a different rule as to LINE officers. See under that head.]

3 Aug., 1861, s. 22, v. 12, p. 291.   21 Dec., 1861, s. 6, v. 12, p. 330.

**Withdrawn from command.**
SEC. 1459. Officers on the retired list shall be withdrawn from command, except in the case provided in sections fourteen hundred and sixty-three and fourteen hundred and sixty-four, and from the line of promotion on the active list. [See Aug. 5, 1882, *post.*]

3 Aug., 1861, s. 22, v. 12, p. 290.   21 Dec., 1861, ss. 3, 4, v. 12, p. 329.

[Sections 1460 and 1461, from the acts of 16 July, 1862, s. 14, v. 12, p. 585; 15 Aug., 1876, v. 19, p. 204; 25 July, 1866, s. 1, v. 14, p. 222; 16 Jan., 1857, s. 4 and 11, p. 154; 30 Jan., 1875, v. 18, p. 304, and 2 March, 1867, s. 9, v. 14, p. 517, contained provisions for the promotion of officers on the retired list, under certain conditions. They were repealed or annulled by the act of Aug. 5, 1882, page 88, *post*, forbidding such promotion.]

**Active duty.**
SEC. 1462. No officer on the retired list of the Navy shall be employed on active duty except in time of war.

3 March, 1873, v. 17, p. 547.

**Assigned to command squadrons and ships.**
SEC. 1463. In time of war the President, by and with the advice and consent of the Senate, may detail officers on the retired list for the command of squadrons and single ships, when he believes that the good of the service requires that they shall be so placed in command.

21 Dec., 1861, s. 3, v. 12, p. 329.   3 March, 1873, s. 1, v. 17, p. 547.

---

*An act of January 30, 1875, v. 18, p. 304, provided for difference of pay for certain officers dropped, retired, &c., under the act of February 28, 1855.

SEC. 1464. In making said details the President may select any officer not below the grade of commander and assign him to the command of a squadron, with the rank and title of "flag-officer;" and any officer so assigned shall have the same authority and receive the same obedience from the commanders of ships in his squadron holding commissions of an older date than his that he would be entitled to receive if his commission were the oldest.

<small>21 Dec., 1861, s. 4, v. 12, p. 329.</small>

*Commanders of squadrons, from what grades selected.*

SEC. 1465. Retired officers so detailed for the command of squadrons and single ships may be restored to the active list, if, upon the recommendation of the President, they shall receive a vote of thanks of Congress for their services and gallantry in action against the enemy, and not otherwise.

<small>*Idem*, s. 3.</small>

*When restored to active list.*

SEC. 1473. Officers who shall have been, or who shall be, retired from the positions of chiefs of the Bureaus of Medicine and Surgery, of Provisions and Clothing, of Steam Engineering, or of Construction and Repair, by reason of age or length of service, shall have the relative rank of commodore.

<small>3 March, 1871, s. 5, v. 16, p. 535.</small>

*Title 15, Chap. 4.*
*Retired from position of Chief of Bureau.*

SEC. 1481. Officers of the Medical, Pay, and Engineer Corps, chaplains, professors of mathematics, and constructors, who shall have served faithfully for forty-five years, shall, when retired, have the relative rank of commodore; and officers of these several corps who have been or shall be retired at the age of sixty-two years, before having served for forty-five years, but who shall have served faithfully until retired, shall, on the completion of forty years from their entry into the service, have the relative rank of commodore.

<small>3 March, 1871, s. 11, v. 16, p. 537.</small>

*Relative rank of staff officers when retired for age or length of service.*

SEC. 1482. Staff-officers, who have been or shall be retired for causes incident to the service before arriving at sixty-two years of age, shall have the same rank on the retired list as pertained to their position on the active list.

<small>*Idem.*</small>

*When retired for causes incident to service.*

SEC. 1588. The pay of all officers of the Navy who have been retired after forty-five years' service after reaching the age of sixteen years, or who have been or may be retired after forty years' service, upon their own application to the President, or on attaining the age of sixty-two years, or on account of incapacity resulting from long and faithful service, from wounds or injuries received in the line of duty, or from sickness or exposure therein, shall, when not on active duty, be equal to seventy-five per centum of the sea pay provided by this chapter for the grade or rank which they held, respectively, at the time of their retirement. The pay of all other officers on the retired list shall, when not on active duty, be equal to one-half the sea-pay provided by this chapter for the grade or rank held by them, respectively, at the time of their retirement.

<small>15 July, 1870, s. 3, v. 16, p. 333.   3 March, 1873, s. 1, v. 17, p. 555.</small>

*Title 15, Chap. 8.*
*Pay of retired officers.*

<small>NOTE.—Sections 1588, 1590, and 1593, which contain provisions both of a general and special character prescribing the compensation of naval retired officers, and embracing within their scope all such officers, whether of the line or staff, superseded all provisions in force at the adoption of the Revised Statutes by which that compensation was previously regulated, and those sections thereafter furnished the only law upon the subject.—Op. XV, p. 316, Devens, June 18, 1877.</small>

SEC. 1589. Rear-admirals on the retired list of the Navy, who were retired as captains when the highest grade in the Navy was captain, at the age of sixty-two years, or after forty-five years' service, and who, after their retirement, were promoted to the grade of rear-admiral, and performed the duties of that grade in time of war, shall be considered as having been retired as rear-admirals.

<small>5 June, 1872, s. 1, v. 17, p. 226.   3 March, 1873, s. 1, v. 17, p. 555.</small>

*Rear-admirals.*

SEC. 1590. Officers who have been retired as third assistant engineers shall continue to receive pay at the rate of four hundred dollars a year.

*Third assistant engineers.*

<small>3 March, 1859, s. 2, v. 11, p. 407.      21 April, 1864, s. 7, v. 13, p. 54.
3 Aug., 1861, s. 22, v. 12, p. 290.    15 July, 1870, s. 5, v. 16, p. 333.
July, 1862, s. 20, v. 12, p. 587.</small>

88 SECRETARIES AND CLERKS.

Pay not increased by promotion.
SEC. 1591. No officer, heretofore or hereafter promoted upon the retired list, shall, in consequence of such promotion, be entitled to any increase of pay. [See Aug. 5, 1882, *post*.]

2 March, 1867, s. 9, v. 14, p. 517. 15 July, 1870, s. 5, v. 16, p. 333.

5 Aug., 1882.
No promotion, &c., of retired officers.
Hereafter there shall be no promotion or increase of pay in the retired list of the Navy but the rank and pay of officers on the retired list shall be the same that they are when such officers shall be retired.

5 Aug., 1882. P. E. L., p. 285.

Title 15, Chap. 8.
Pay on active duty.
SEC. 1592. Officers on the retired list, when on active duty, shall receive the full pay of their respective grades.

1 June, 1860, s. 5, v. 12, p. 27. 2 March, 1867, s. 9, v. 14, p. 517.

Officers retired on furlough pay.
SEC. 1593. Officers placed on the retired list, on furlough pay, shall receive only one-half of the pay to which they would have been entitled if on leave of absence on the active list.

3 March, 1835, s. 1, v. 4, p. 756. 3 Aug., 1861, s. 23, v. 12, p. 291.
28 Feb., 1855, s. 2, v. 10, p. 616. 28 July, 1866, s. 2, v. 14, p. 345.
16 Jan., 1857, s. 1, v. 11, p. 154. 30 Jan., 1875, v. 18, p. 304.

Transfer from furlough to retired pay.
SEC. 1594. The President, by and with the advice and consent of the Senate, may transfer any officer on the retired list from the furlough to the retired-pay list. [See notes under PAY, FURLOUGH.]

16 Jan., 1857, s. 3, v. 11, p. 154. 16 July, 1862, s. 20, v. 12, p. 537.
30 Jan., 1875, v. 18, p. 304.

Rations.
SEC. 1595. Rations shall not be allowed to officers on the retired list.

16 July, 1862, s. 20, v. 12, p. 587.

RETIREMENT in MARINE CORPS (*see* MARINE CORPS, Part II).

## SECRETARIES AND CLERKS.

Sec.
1367. Rank of secretaries to Admiral and Vice-Admiral.
1556. Pay of same.
1556. Secretary at Naval Academy.
—— Clerks at Naval Academy.
1386. Clerks to paymasters.
1387. When not allowed to paymasters.

Sec.
1388. Clerks to passed assistant and assistant paymasters.
1556. Pay of same.
1556. Clerks to commandants.
1416. Discontinuance of, at yards.
—— No more appointments afloat.
—— Officers as secretaries and clerks.

### TO ADMIRAL AND VICE-ADMIRAL.

Title 15, Chap. 1.
Number and rank.
SEC. 1367. The Admiral and Vice-Admiral shall each be allowed a secretary, who shall be entitled to the rank and allowances of a lieutenant in the Navy. [See May 4, 1878, *post*.]

21 Dec., 1864, s. 2, v. 13, h. 420.
16 May, 1866, y. 14, p. 48.
25 July, 1866, s. 6, v. 14, p. 223.
2 March, 1867, s. 1, v. 14, h. 516.

Title 15, Chap. 8.
Pay.
SEC. 1556. Secretaries to the Admiral and the Vice-Admiral, each two thousand five hundred dollars. [See § 1367]

15 July, 1870, s. 3, v. 16, p. 332.

### AT NAVAL ACADEMY.

Secretary of the Naval Academy, one thousand eight hundred dollars.

15 July, 1870, s. 3, v. 16, p. 332.

23 Feb., 1881.
Clerks and their pay.
Three clerks to superintendent, at one thousand two hundred dollars, one thousand dollars, and eight hundred dollars respectively; one clerk to commandant of cadets, one thousand two hundred dollars; one clerk to paymaster, one thousand dollars.

3 March, 1883, pamphlet edition, p. 478.

### TO PAY OFFICERS.

Title 15, Chap. 1.
Clerks to paymasters of the fleet and others.
SEC. 1386. Paymasters of the fleet, paymasters on vessels having complements of more than one hundred and seventy-five persons, on supply-steamers, store-vessels, and receiving ships, paymasters at stations and at the Naval Academy, and paymasters detailed at stations as inspectors of provisions and clothing, shall each be allowed a clerk.

14 July, 1862, s. 3, v. 12, p. 565. 26 May, 1864, v. 13, p. 92.

## SECRETARIES AND CLERKS. 89

SEC. 1387. No paymaster shall be allowed a clerk in a vessel having the complement of one hundred and seventy-five persons or less, excepting in supply steamers and store-vessels. *When not allowed.*

20 May, 1864, v. 13, p. 92.

SEC. 1388. Passed assistant paymasters and assistant paymasters attached to vessels of war shall be allowed clerks, if clerks would be allowed by law to paymasters so attached. *Clerks of passed assistant and assistant paymasters.*

3 March, 1863, s. 5, v. 12, p. 818.

SEC. 1556. * * * Clerks to paymasters at navy-yards, Boston, New York, Philadelphia, and Washington, one thousand six hundred dollars; Kittery, Norfolk, and Pensacola, one thousand four hundred dollars; Mare Island, one thousand eight hundred dollars. *Title 15, Chap. 8. Clerks to paymasters of yards and stations.*

Clerks to paymasters, at other stations, one thousand three hundred dollars.

Clerks to paymasters of receiving-ships at Boston, New York, and Philadelphia, one thousand six hundred dollars; at Mare Island, one thousand eight hundred dollars; of other receiving-ships, one thousand three hundred dollars. *Clerks to paymasters of receiving-ships, &c.*

Clerks to paymasters on vessels of the first rate, one thousand three hundred dollars; on vessels of the second rate, one thousand one hundred dollars; on vessels of the third rate, and supply-vessels and store-ships, one thousand dollars. *Clerks to paymasters of vessels.*

Clerks to fleet paymasters, one thousand one hundred dollars. *Clerks to fleet paymasters.*

Clerks to paymasters at the Naval Academy and Naval Asylum, one thousand three hundred dollars. *Clerks to paymasters at Asylum and Academy.*

Clerks to inspectors in charge of provisions and clothing, at navy-yards, Boston, New York, Philadelphia, and Washington, one thousand six hundred dollars; to inspectors in like charge at other inspections, one thousand three hundred dollars. *Clerks to inspectors.*

15 July, 1870, s. 3, v. 16, p. 332.

NOTES.—The clerk of a paymaster in the Navy is subject to the jurisdiction of a court-martial, and may be arrested and tried for an offense committed while in the service, even after his connection with it has been legally severed.—*Ex parte Bogart*, 17 Int. Rev. Rec., 155.

Under the act of March 2, 1863, a paymaster's clerk is a person in the military service, and liable to trial by court-martial.—*United States v. Bogart*, 3 Benedict R., 257.

A regularly appointed clerk of a paymaster in the Navy is a "person in the naval service of the United States" within the meaning of article 14, sec. 1624 of the Revised Statutes, and for a violation of its provisions is subject to be tried, convicted, and sentenced by a naval general court-martial. Otto, S. C., 100, p. 13, Oct., 1879. See same, case of Reed, paymaster's clerk, tried by court-martial where, on *habeas corpus*, the Supreme Court decided that the court-martial had jurisdiction, and was competent to pass the sentence of which he complained.

### AT YARDS AND STATIONS.

SEC. 1556. * * * First clerks to commandants of navy-yards, one thousand five hundred dollars. *Pay.*

Second clerks to commandants of navy-yards, one thousand two hundred dollars.

Clerk to commandant of navy-yard at Mare Island, one thousand eight hundred dollars.

Clerks to commandants of naval stations, one thousand five hundred dollars.

15 July, 1870, s. 3, v. 16, p. 332.

SEC. 1416. The Secretary of the Navy is authorized, when in his opinion the public interest will permit it, to discontinue the office or employment of * * * any clerk of the yard, clerk of the commandant, clerk of the store-keeper, clerk of the naval constructor. * * * *Title 15, Chap. 1. Clerks at yards may be discontinued.*

10 Aug., 1846, s. 1, v. 9, p. 98.

### OFFICERS AS SECRETARIES AND CLERKS.

On and after the first day of July, eighteen hundred and seventy-eight, there shall be no appointments made from civil life of secretaries or clerks to the Admiral, or Vice-Admiral, when on sea service, commanders of squadrons, or of clerks to commanders of vessels; and an officer *4 May, 1878. Secretaries and clerks from civil life not to be appointed afloat.*

Detail of officers to perform the duties.
not above the grade of lieutenant shall be detailed to perform the duties of secretary to the Admiral or Vice-Admiral, when on sea service, and one not above a *lieutenant of the junior* grade to perform the duties of clerk to a rear-admiral or commander, and one not above the grade of ensign to perform the duties of clerk to a captain, commander, or lieutenant-commander when afloat. * * *

4 May, 1878, v. 20, p. 30.
3 March, 1883, P. E. L., p. 472.

## SEAMEN IN THE NAVY.

Sec.
1407. Promotion of seamen.
1408. Seamen rated as mates.
1409. Not discharged from enlistment by being rated mates.
1410. Petty officers.
1417. Enlisted men, number of.
1418. Term of enlistment.
1419. Consent of parents and guardians.
1420. Persons not to be enlisted.
1421. Transfer from military to naval service.
1422. Men sent home at expiration of term.
1423. Subject to regulations, &c.
1424. Limit of detention.
1425. What to be contained in shipping-articles.

Sec.
1426. Honorable discharge, to whom granted.
1427. Form of honorable discharge.
1429. Men entitled to honorable discharge.
1430. Sale of wages and prize-money.
1431. Duty as to granting leave and liberty.
1569. Pay of enlisted men.
1570. Additional pay for serving as firemen, &c.
1572. Detention beyond term of enlistment.
1573. Bounty-pay for re-enlisting.
1574. Crews of lost or wrecked vessels.
1575. Crews taken by an enemy.
1576. Assignment of wages.
4878. Burial of seamen in national cemeteries.
—— Machinists in the Navy.

Title 15, Chap. 1.

Promotion of seamen to warrant officers.

SEC. 1407. Seamen distinguishing themselves in battle, or by extraordinary heroism in the line of their profession, may be promoted to forward warrant officers, upon the recommendation of their commanding officer, approved by the flag-officer and Secretary of the Navy. And upon such recommendation they shall receive a gratuity of one hundred dollars and a medal of honor, to be prepared under the direction of the Navy Department.

17 May, 1864, s. 3, v. 13, p. 79.

NOTE.—The 7th section of the act of December 21, 1861, vol. 12, p. 329, authorized the Secretary of the Navy to prepare medals of honor, with suitable emblematic devices, to be bestowed upon such petty officers, seamen, landsmen, and marines as should most distinguish themselves by their gallantry in action, and other seaman-like qualities during the war of the rebellion. Appropriations have since been made for such medals, which are bestowed in meritorious cases, although no promotion takes place.

Seamen may be rated as mates.

SEC. 1408. Mates may be rated, under authority of the Secretary of the Navy, from seamen and ordinary seamen who have enlisted in the naval service for not less than two years.

17 May, 1864, s. 3, v. 13, p. 79.
3 March, 1865, s. 3, v. 13, p. 539.

Rating shall not discharge from enlistment.

SEC. 1409. The rating of an enlisted man as a mate, or his appointment as a warrant officer, shall not discharge him from his enlistment.

*Idem.*

Petty officers.

SEC. 1410. All officers not holding commissions or warrants, or who are not entitled to them, except such as are temporarily appointed to the duties of a commissioned or warrant officer, and except secretaries and clerks, shall be deemed petty officers, and shall be entitled to obedience, in the execution of their offices, from persons of inferior ratings.

17 July, 1862, s. 18, v. 12, p. 610.

Enlisted men, number of.

SEC. 1417. *The number of persons who may at one time be enlisted into the Navy of the United States, including seamen, ordinary seamen, landsmen, mechanics, firemen, and coal-heavers, and including seven hundred and fifty apprentices and boys, hereby authorized to be enlisted annually, shall not exceed eight thousand two hundred and fifty: Provided, That in the appointment of warrant-officers in the naval service of the United States, preference shall be given to men who have been honorably discharged upon the expiration of an enlistment as an apprentice or boy, to serve during minority, and re-enlisted within three months after such discharge, to serve during a term of three or more years: Provided further, That nothing in this act [section] shall be held to abrogate the provisions of section fourteen hundred and seven of the Revised Statutes of the United States.*

7 June, 1864, v. 13, p. 120.
17 June, 1868, s. 2, v. 15, p. 72.
12 May, 1879, v. 21, p. 3.
30 June, 1876, v. 19, p. 66.

SEAMEN IN THE NAVY.     91

SEC. 1418. Boys between the ages of *fourteen* and eighteen years may be enlisted to serve in the Navy until they shall arrive at the age of twenty-one years; other persons may be enlisted to serve for a period not exceeding five years, unless sooner discharged by direction of the President.   *Term of enlistment.*

2 March, 1837, s. 1, v. 5, p. 153.<br>
12 May, 1879, v. 21, p. 3.<br>
23 Feb., 1881, v. 21, p. 331.

SEC. 1419. Minors between the ages of *fourteen* and eighteen years shall not be enlisted for the naval service without the consent of their parents or guardians.   *Consent of parents and guardians.*

2 March, 1837, s. 1, v. 5, p. 153.<br>
3 March, 1865, s. 18, v. 13, p. 490.<br>
12 May, 1879, v. 21, p. 3.<br>
23 Feb., 1881, v. 21, p. 331.

SEC. 1420. No minor under the age of *fourteen* years, no insane or intoxicated person, and no deserter from the naval or military service of the United States, shall be enlisted in the naval service.   *Persons not to be enlisted.*

3 March, 1865, s. 18, v. 13, p. 490.<br>
12 May, 1879, v. 21, p. 3.<br>
23 Feb., 1881, v. 21, p. 331.

NOTES.—United States courts can inquire into the validity of enlistments on *habeas corpus,* and thereupon discharge enlisted persons in proper cases. This power cannot legally be exercised by State courts. Winthrop's Digest, p. 250 and 280, with authorities given. Subject discussed.—Also Op. XII, 259.

It has generally been held that the enlistment of minors in the Navy, over 18, was legal. The circuit court of the United States district of Massachusetts, however, January 30, 1883, ordered the discharge of a minor, basing its action on a decision of Judge Lowell in 1870, which was that Congress had the right to pass a law making legal the enlistment of a minor, but not having done so by explicit statute the common law of the State must rule—the services of a minor belonging to its legal guardian.

The Executive Department has discretionary authority to discharge before the term of service has expired, but has no power to vary the contract of enlistment.—Op. IV, 538; XV, 362.

Enlistment *"for three years* or *during the war,"* means three years from date of muster, if war should last so long, and if it should not, then until it should end. Reference to *duration,* a restriction, not an extension. Cannot be legally retained over three years, although the war may extend beyond that period. Winthrop, p. 252. Refers to decision of supreme court of Pennsylvania, and other authorities.

An alien can be enlisted in the naval service or the Marine Corps, and is bound the same as a citizen to serve for his term of enlistment.—Op. III, 671; IV, 350; VI, 474, 607. A minor is not bound by his contract, although entered into with the consent of his guardian, after he becomes of age.—Op. IV, 350.

SEC. 1421. Any person enlisted in the military service of the United States may, on application to the Navy Department, approved by the President, be transferred to the Navy or Marine Corps, to serve therein the residue of his term of enlistment, subject to the laws and regulations for the government of the Navy. But such transfer shall not release him from any indebtedness to the Government, nor, without the consent of the President, from any penalty incurred for a breach of military law.   *Transfer from military to naval service.*

1 July, 1864, s. 1, v. 13, p. 342.

SEC. 1422. That it shall be the duty of the commanding officer of any fleet, squadron, or vessel acting singly, when on service, to send to an Atlantic or to a Pacific port of the United States, as their enlistment may have occurred on either the Atlantic or Pacific coast of the United States, in some public or other vessel, all petty-officers and persons of inferior ratings desiring to go there at the expiration of their terms of enlistment, or as soon thereafter as may be, unless, in his opinion, the detention of such persons for a longer period should be essential to the public interests, in which case he may detain them, or any of them, until the vessel to which they belong shall return to such Atlantic or Pacific port. All persons enlisted without the limits of the United States may be discharged, on the expiration of their enlistment, either in a foreign port or in a port of the United States, or they may be detained as above provided beyond the term of their enlistment; and that all persons sent home, or detained by a commanding officer, according to the provisions of this act, shall be subject in all respect to the laws and regulations for the government of the Navy until their return to an Atlantic or Pacific port and their regular discharge; and all persons so detained by such officer, or re-entering to serve until the return to an   *Men to be sent home at expiration of term of enlistment.*  *Detention beyond term.*  *Persons enlisted without limits of United States.*  *Men subject to regulations until return or discharge.*

92                       SEAMEN IN THE NAVY.

**How long held in service after arrival.**
Atlantic or Pacific port of the vessel to which they belong, shall in no case be held in service more than thirty days after their arrival in said port; and that all persons who shall be so detained beyond their terms of enlistment or who shall, after the termination of their enlistment, voluntarily re-enter to serve until the return to an Atlantic or Pacific port of the vessel to which they belong, and their regular discharge therefrom, shall receive for the time during which they are so detained, or shall so serve beyond their original terms of enlistment, an addition of one-fourth of their former pay: *Provided*, That the shipping-articles shall hereafter contain the substance of this section. [See § 1572, *infra*.]

**Additional pay for detention.**

**This section to be contained in shipping-articles.**

17 July, 1862, s. 17, v. 12, p. 610.
3 March, 1875, v. 18, p. 484.

**Subject to regulations while sent home or detained.**
SEC. 1423. All persons sent home, or detained by a commanding officer, according to the provisions of the preceding section, shall be subject in all respects to the laws and regulations for the government of the Navy, until their return to an Atlantic port and their regular discharge.

17 July, 1862, s. 17, v. 12, p. 610.

**Limit of detention.**
SEC. 1424. Persons so detained by a commanding officer, or re-entering to serve until the return to an Atlantic port of the vessel to which they belong, shall in no case be held in service more than thirty days after their arrival in said port.

*Idem.*

**What to be contained in shipping-articles.**
SEC. 1425. The shipping articles shall contain the substance of the three sections next preceding and of section fifteen hundred and seventy-two.

*Idem.*

**Honorable discharge, to whom granted.**
SEC. 1426. Honorable discharges may be granted to seamen, ordinary seamen, landsmen, firemen, coal-heavers, and boys who have enlisted for three years.

2 March, 1855, s. 1, v. 10, p. 627.
7 June, 1864, v. 13, p. 120.

**Form of honorable discharge.**
SEC. 1427. Honorable discharges shall be granted according to a form prescribed by the Secretary of the Navy.

*Idem.*

**Titlel 5, Chap. 2.**

**Report of men entitled to honorable discharge.**
SEC. 1429. It shall be the duty of every commanding officer of a vessel, on returning from a cruise, and immediately on his arrival in port, to forward to the Secretary of the Navy a list of the names of such of the crew who enlisted for three years as, in his opinion, on being discharged, are entitled to an "honorable discharge" as a testimonial of fidelity and obedience; and he shall grant the same to the persons so designated.

2 March, 1855, s. 1, v. 10, p. 627.

**To discourage sale of prize-money or wages.**
SEC. 1430. Every commanding officer of a vessel is required to discourage his crew from selling any part of their prize-money, bounty-money, or wages, and never to attest any power of attorney for the transfer thereof until he is satisfied that the same is not granted in consideration of money given for the purchase of prize-money, bounty-money, or wages. [See § 4643, PRIZE. Part IV.]

30 June, 1864, s. 12, v. 13, p. 310.

**Duty as to granting leave and liberty.**
SEC. 1431. It shall be the duty of commanding officers of vessels, in granting temporary leave of absence and liberty on shore, to exercise carefully a discrimination in favor of the faithful and obedient.

2 March, 1855, s. 3, v. 10, p. 627.

**Title 15, Chap. 8.**

**Pay of enlisted men.**
SEC. 1569. The pay to be allowed to petty officers, excepting mates, and the pay and bounty upon enlistment of seamen, ordinary seamen, firemen, and coal-heavers, in the naval service, shall be fixed by the President: *Provided*, That the whole sum to be given for the whole pay aforesaid, and for the pay of officers, and for the said bounties upon enlistments shall not exceed, for any one year, the amount which may, in such year, be appropriated for such purposes.

18 April, 1814, s. 1, v. 3, p. 136.
3 March, 1847, s. 4, v. 9, p. 173.
1 July, 1864, s. 4, v. 13, p. 342.
3 March, 1865, s. 2, v. 13, p. 539.

SEC. 1570. Every seaman, ordinary seaman, or landsman who performs the duty of a fireman or coal-heaver on board of any vessel of war shall be entitled to receive, in addition to his compensation as seaman, ordinary seaman, or landsman, a compensation at the rate of thirty-three cents a day for the time he is employed as fireman or coal-heaver.

*Additional pay for serving as firemen and coal-heavers.*

1 March, 1869, s. 2, v. 15, p. 280.

SEC. 1572. All petty officers and persons of inferior ratings who are detained beyond the terms of service, according to the provisions of section fourteen hundred and twenty-two, or who, after the termination of their service, voluntarily re-enter, to serve until the return to an Atlantic port of the vessel to which they belong, and until their regular discharge therefrom, shall, for the time during which they are so detained or so serve beyond their original terms of service, receive an addition of one-fourth of their former pay.

*Detention beyond term of enlistment.*

17 July, 1862, s. 17, v. 12, p. 610.

SEC. 1573. If any seaman, ordinary seaman, landsman, fireman, coal-heaver, or boy, being honorably discharged, shall re-enlist for three years, within three months thereafter, he shall, on presenting his honorable discharge, or on accounting in a satisfactory manner for its loss, be entitled to pay, during the said three months, equal to that to which he would have been entitled if he had been employed in actual service.

*Bounty-pay for re-enlisting.*

7 June, 1864, v. 13, p. 120.
2 March, 1865, s. 2, v. 10, p. 627.

SEC. 1574. When the crew of any vessel of the United States are separated from such vessel, by means of her wreck, loss, or destruction, the pay and emoluments of such of the officers and men as shall appear to the Secretary of the Navy, by the sentence of a court-martial or court of inquiry, or by other satisfactory evidence, to have done their utmost to preserve her, and, after said wreck, loss, or destruction, to have behaved themselves agreeably to the discipline of the Navy, shall go on and be paid them until their discharge or death.

*Crews of wrecked or lost vessels.*

17 July, 1862, s. 14, v. 12, p. 608.

SEC. 1575. The pay and emoluments of the officers and men of any vessel of the United States taken by an enemy who shall appear, by the sentence of a court-martial or otherwise, to have done their utmost to preserve and defend their vessel, and, after the taking thereof, to have behaved themselves agreeably to the discipline of the Navy, shall go on and be paid to them until their exchange, discharge, or death.

*Crews of vessels taken by an enemy.*

*Idem*, s. 15, p. 609.

SEC. 1576. Every assignment of wages due to persons enlisted in the naval service, and all powers of attorney, or other authority to draw, receipt for, or transfer the same, shall be void, unless attested by the commanding officer and paymaster. The assignment of wages must specify the precise time when they commence.

*Assignments of wages.*

30 June, 1864, s. 12, v. 13, p. 310.

SEC. 4878. All soldiers, sailors, or marines, dying in the service of the United States, or dying in a destitute condition, after having been honorably discharged from the service, or who served during the late war, either in the regular or volunteer forces, may be buried in any national cemetery free of cost. The production of the honorable discharge of a deceased man shall be sufficient authority for the superintendent of any cemetery to permit the interment.

*Title 59, Chap. 6.*

*Who may be buried in national cemeteries.*

17 July, 1862, s. 18, v. 12, p. 596.
1 June, 1872, v. 17, p. 202.
3 March, 1873, v. 17, p. 605.

All men now serving in the Navy who may be discharged as machinists, with continuous-service certificates entitling them to honorable discharge, and those discharged in the said rating with such certificates since the twentieth day of November, eighteen hundred and seventy-nine, shall receive one-third of one year's pay as a machinist for each good-conduct badge they have received, or may receive, not exceeding three in number under the said certificates, the said gratuity to be received in lieu of re-enlistment as a machinist under such certificate, and to be in full and in lieu of all claims against the United States in connection therewith, for extra pay for re-enlisting, or for continuous service, or for enlistment as a petty officer; and the amount nec-

*June 16, 1880.*

*Machinists' in the Navy, discharge of, &c.*

essary to carry out the provisions of this act is hereby appropriated, out of any money in the Treasury not otherwise appropriated: *Provided*, That nothing herein contained shall be so construed as to prevent the re-enlistment of machinists in the Navy.

June 16, 1880, v. 21, p. 290.

# VESSELS OF THE NAVY.

| Sec. | | Sec. | |
|---|---|---|---|
| 1428. | Officers of vessels to be citizens of the United States. | 1539. | Repairs on sails and rigging. |
| 1437. | Officers to inspect vessels under War Department. | 1540. | Sale of vessels unfit to be repaired. |
| | | 1541. | Sale of unserviceable vessels and materials. |
| 1529. | Four classes; their commanders. | — | Unfit for service; removal from Register. |
| 1530. | How rated. | — | Sale of vessels stricken from Register. |
| 1531. | Rule for naming. | — | Restriction on repairs. |
| 1532. | Two vessels not to bear the same name. | 1552. | Coal depots for vessels. |
| 1533. | Names of purchased vessels. | 4293. | Suppression of piracy. |
| 1534. | Vessels kept in service in time of peace. | 4686. | Employment on coast survey. |
| 1535. | How officered and manned. | — | Marine schools. |
| 1536. | Cruising to assist distressed navigators. | — | Hulks for quarantine purposes. |
| 1537. | Patented articles connected with marine engines. | — | Steam cruisers for the Navy. |
| | | — | Double-turreted monitors. |
| 1538. | Repairs on hull and spars. | — | Accidents to vessels. |

**Title 15, Chap. 2.**

*Officers to be citizens of United States.*

SEC. 1428. The officers of vessels of the United States shall in all cases be citizens of the United States.

28 June, 1864, s. 1, v. 13, p. 201.

*Officers for service of War Department.*

SEC. 1437. The President may detail, temporarily, three competent naval officers for the service of the War Department in the inspection of transport vessels, and for such other services as may be designated by the Secretary of War.

12 Feb., 1862, v. 12, p. 338.

**Title 15, Chap. 6.**

*Four classes; their commanders.*

SEC. 1529. The vessels of the Navy of the United States shall be divided into four classes, and shall be commanded as nearly as may be as follows:

First rates, by commodores; second rates, by captains; third rates, by commanders; fourth rates, by lieutenant-commanders.

16 July, 1862, s. 3, v. 12, p. 583.

*How rated.*

SEC. 1530. Steamships of forty guns or more shall be classed as first rates, those of twenty guns and under forty as second rates, and all those of less than twenty guns as third rates.

12 June, 1858, s. 5, v. 11, p. 319.

*Rule for naming.*

SEC. 1531. The vessels of the Navy shall be named by the Secretary of the Navy, under the direction of the President, according to the following rule:

Sailing-vessels of the first class shall be named after the States of the Union, those of the second class after the rivers, those of the third class after the principal cities and towns, and those of the fourth class as the President may direct.

Steamships of the first class shall be named after the States of the Union, those of the second class after the rivers and principal cities and towns, and those of the third class as the President may direct.

3 March, 1819, s. 1, v. 3, p. 538.
12 June, 1858, s. 5, v. 11, p. 319.

*Two vessels not to bear the same name.*

SEC. 1532. Care shall be taken that not more than one vessel in the Navy shall bear the same name.

Idem.

*Names of purchased vessels.*

SEC. 1533. The Secretary of the Navy may change the names of any vessels purchased for the Navy by authority of law.

5 Aug., 1861, s. 2, v. 12, p. 316.

*Vessels kept in service in time of peace.*

SEC. 1534. The President is authorized to keep in actual service in time of peace, such of the public armed vessels as, in his opinion, may be required by the nature of the service, and to cause the residue thereof to be laid up in ordinary in convenient ports.

21 April, 1806, s. 2, v. 2, p. 390.

*How officered and manned.*

SEC. 1535. Vessels in actual service, in time of peace, shall be officered and manned as the President may direct, subject to the provisions of section fifteen hundred and twenty-nine.

*Idem.*, s. 3.

Sec. 1536. The President may, when the necessities of the service permit it, cause any suitable number of public vessels adapted to the purpose to cruise upon the coast in the season of severe weather and to afford such aid to distressed navigators as their circumstances may require; and such public vessels shall go to sea fully prepared to render such assistance. *Cruising to assist distressed navigators.*

22 Dec., 1837, v. 5, p. 208.

Sec. 1537. No patented article connected with marine engines shall hereafter be purchased or used in connection with any steam-vessels of war until the same shall have been submitted to a competent board of naval engineers, and recommended by such board, in writing, for purchase and use. *Patented articles connected with marine engines.*

18 July, 1861, s. 3, v. 12, p. 268.

### REPAIR, APPRAISEMENT, AND SALE OF VESSELS.

Sec. 1538. Not more than three thousand dollars shall be expended at any navy-yard in repairing the hull and spars of any vessel, until the necessity and expediency of such repairs and the probable cost thereof are ascertained and reported to the Navy Department by an examining board, which shall be composed of one captain or commander in the Navy, designated by the Secretary of the Navy, the naval constructor of the yard where such vessel may be ordered for repairs, and two master workmen of said yard, or one master workman and an engineer of the Navy, according to the nature of the repairs to be made. Said master workmen and engineer shall be designated by the head of the Bureau of Construction and Repair. [See Aug. 5, 1882, and March 3, 1883, *post.*] *Repairs on hull and spars.*

21 Feb., 1861, s. 1, v. 12, p. 147.

Sec. 1539. Not more than one thousand dollars shall be expended in repairs on the sails and rigging of any vessel, until the necessity and expediency of such repairs and the estimated cost thereof have been ascertained and reported to the Navy Department by an examining board, which shall be composed of one naval officer, designated by the Secretary of the Navy, and the master rigger and the master sail-maker of the yard where such vessel may be ordered. [See Aug. 5, 1882, and March 3, 1883, *post.*] *Repairs on sails and rigging.*

Idem.

Sec. 1540. The President may direct any armed vessel of the United States to be sold when, in his opinion, such vessel is so much out of repair that it will not be for the interest of the United States to repair her. [See Aug. 5, 1882, and March 3, 1883, *post.*] *Sale of vessels unfit to be repaired.*

21 April, 1806, s. 3, v. 2, p. 402.

NOTE.—A vessel condemned for naval purposes cannot be exchanged for another, notwithstanding the change might be of advantage to the public service.—Op. XIV, 369.

Sec. 1541. The Secretary of the Navy is authorized and directed to sell, at public sale, such vessels and materials of the United States Navy as, in his judgment, cannot be advantageously used, repaired, or fitted out; and he shall, at the opening of each session of Congress, make a full report to Congress of all vessels and materials sold, the parties buying the same, and the amount realized therefrom, together with such other facts as may be necessary to a full understanding of his acts. [See Aug. 5, 1882, and March 3, 1883, *post.*] *Sale of unserviceable vessels and materials.*

23 March, 1872, s. 2, v. 17, p. 154.

It shall also be the duty of the Secretary of the Navy, as soon as may be after the passage of this act, to cause to be examined by competent boards of officers of the Navy, to be designated by him for that duty, all vessels belonging to the Navy not in actual service at sea, and vessels at sea as soon as practicable after they shall return to the United States, and hereafter all vessels on their return from foreign stations, and all vessels in the United States as often as once in three years, when practicable; and said boards shall ascertain and report to the Secretary of the Navy, in writing, which of said vessels are unfit for further service, or, if the same are unfinished in any navy-yard, those which cannot be finished without great and disproportionate expense, and shall in such report state fully the grounds and reasons for their *5 Aug., 1882. Examination of naval vessels.*

opinion. And it shall be the duty of the Secretary of the Navy, if he shall concur in opinion with said report, to strike the name of such vessel or vessels from the Navy Register and report the same to Congress.

5 Aug., 1882, P. E. L., p. 296. [Naval appropriation act.] [See *post.*]

3 March, 1883.

Appraisement of vessels stricken from Register.

Sale of such vessels.

Requirements from bidders.

When to be delivered to purchaser.

Removal of condemned vessels.

It shall be the duty of the Secretary of the Navy to cause to be appraised, in such manner as may seem best, all vessels of the Navy which have been stricken from the Navy Register under the provisions of the act making appropriations for the naval service for the fiscal year ending June thirtieth, eighteen hundred and eighty-three, and for other purposes, approved August fifth, eighteen hundred and eighty-two. And if the said Secretary shall deem it for the best interest of the United States to sell any such vessel or vessels, he shall, after such appraisal, advertise for sealed proposals for the purchase of the same, for a period not less than three months, in such newspapers as other naval advertisements are published, setting forth the name and location and the appraised value of such vessel, and that the same will be sold, for cash, to the person or persons or corporation or corporations offering the highest price therefor above the appraised value thereof; and such proposals shall be opened on a day and hour and at a place named in said advertisement, and record thereof shall be made. The Secretary of the Navy shall require to accompany each bid or proposal a deposit in cash of not less than ten per centum of the amount of the offer or proposal, and also a bond, with two or more sureties to be approved by him, conditioned for the payment of the remaining ninety per centum of the amount of such offer or proposal within the time fixed in the advertisement. And in case default is made in the payment of the remaining ninety per centum, or any part thereof, the Secretary, within the prescribed time thereof, shall advertise and resell said vessel under the provisions of this act. And in that event said cash deposit of ten per centum shall be considered as forfeited to the government, and shall be applied, first, to the payment of all costs and expenditures attending the advertisement and resale of said vessel; second, to the payment of the difference, if any, between the first and last sale of said vessel; and the balance, if any, shall be covered into the Treasury: *Provided, however,* That nothing herein contained shall be construed to prevent a suit upon said bond for breach of any of its conditions. Any vessel sold under the foregoing provisions shall be delivered to the purchaser upon the full payment to the Secretary of the Navy of the amount of such proposal or offer; and the net proceeds of such sale shall be covered into the Treasury. But no vessel of the Navy shall hereafter be sold in any other manner than herein provided, or for less than such appraised value, unless the President of the United States shall otherwise direct in writing. In case any vessel now in process of construction in any navy yard has been or shall be found to be unworthy of being completed, and has been and shall be condemned under the provisions of said act, and cannot properly be sold, and it becomes necessary to remove the same, the cost of such removal shall be paid out of the net proceeds derived from the sale of other vessels hereby authorized to be sold.

3 March, 1883, s. 5, P. E. L., p. 599. [Deficiency act.]

3 March, 1883.

Restriction on repair of wooden vessels.

That no part of this sum [appropriation for preservation of vessels, &c.] shall be applied to the repairs of any wooden ship when the estimated cost of such repairs, to be appraised by a competent board of naval officers, shall exceed twenty per centum of the estimated cost, appraised in like manner, of a new ship of the same size and like material: *Provided further,* That nothing herein contained shall deprive the Secretary of the Navy of the authority to order repairs of ships damaged in foreign waters or on the high seas, so far as may be necessary to bring them home.

3 March, 1883, P. E. L., p. 476. [Naval appropriation act.]

3 March, 1883.

Restriction on repairs of engines, &c.

That no part of said sum [appropriation for repairs of machinery, &c.] shall be applied to the repair of engines and machinery of wooden ships where the estimated costs of such repair shall exceed twenty per centum of the estimated cost of new engines and machinery of the same character and power, but nothing herein contained shall prevent the repair or building of boilers for wooden ships, the hulls of which can be fully repaired for twenty per centum of the estimated cost of a new ship of the same size and material.

3 March, 1883, P. E. L., p. 477.

# VESSELS OF THE NAVY.

SEC. 1552. The Secretary of the Navy may establish, at such places as he may deem necessary, suitable depots of coal, and other fuel, for the supply of steamships of war.

*Title 15, Chap. 7.*
*Coal-depots.*

31 Aug., 1842, s. 7, v. 5, p. 577.

SEC. 4293. The President is authorized to employ so many of the public armed vessels as in his judgment the service may require, with suitable instructions to the commanders thereof, in protecting the merchant-vessels of the United States and their crews from piratical aggressions and depredations. [See PIRACY, SLAVE TRADE, &c., Part IV.]

*Title 48, Chap. 8.*
*Public vessels to suppress piracy.*

3 March, 1819, s. 1, v. 3, p. 510.   30 Jan., 1823, v. 3, p. 721.

SEC. 4686. The President is authorized, for any of the purposes of surveying the coast of the United States, to cause to be employed such of the public vessels in actual service as he deems it expedient to employ, and to give such instructions for regulating their conduct as he deems proper, according to the tenor of this Title. [Coast Survey.]

*Title 56.*
*Power to employ vessels.*

10 Feby., 1807, s. 3, v. 2, p. 414.   14 April, 1818, s. 1, v. 3, p. 425.

NOTES.—In naval "parlance," "cruise" means the whole period between the time when a vessel goes to sea and when she returns to the place where her crew is paid off and she is put out of commission.—Op. IX, 375, July 27, 1859, Black.

Government vessels are not required to employ and pay branch pilots upon entering the ports and harbors of the United States. The exemption extends to all public vessels whether armed or not.—Op. IV, 532, Sept. 9, 1846, Mason.

The penalties imposed by State laws for piloting vessels without due license from the State, have no application to persons employed as pilots on board public vessels of the United States, the latter vessels being within the exclusive jurisdiction of the United States.—Op. XVI, 647, Oct. 22, 1879.

The term "public vessels" does not apply to vessels of the Navy alone. Within the meaning of the inspection and navigation laws public vessels are those owned by the United States, and those used by them for public purposes. Those laws warrant no distinction between public vessels under the control of the Navy Department and public vessels under the control of any other department of the Government. Unlicensed pilots and engineers can be lawfully employed on them —Op. XIII, p. 249, Hoar, June 1, 1870.

## MARINE SCHOOLS.

The Secretary of the Navy, to promote nautical education, is hereby authorized and empowered to furnish, upon the application in writing of the Governor of the State, a suitable vessel of the Navy, with all her apparel, charts, books, and instruments of navigation, provided the same can be spared without detriment to the naval service, to be used for the benefit of any nautical school, or school or college having a nautical branch, established at each or any of the ports of New York, Boston, Philadelphia, Baltimore, Norfolk, San Francisco, *Wilmington, Charleston, Savannah, Mobile, New Orleans, Baton Rouge, Galveston, and in Narragansett Bay*, upon the condition that there shall be maintained, at such port, a school or branch of a school for the instruction of youths in navigation, seamanship, marine enginery and all matters pertaining to the proper construction, equipment and sailing of vessels or any particular branch thereof: And the President of the United States is hereby authorized, when in his opinion the same can be done without detriment to the public service, to detail proper officers of the Navy as superintendents of, or instructors in, such schools: *Provided*, That if any such school shall be discontinued, or the good of the naval service shall require, such vessels shall be immediately restored to the Secretary of the Navy, and the officers so detailed recalled: *And provided further*, That no person shall be sentenced to, or received at, such schools as a punishment or commutation of punishment for crime.

*20 June, 1874.*
*Secretary of the Navy may furnish vessels for marine schools.*

*Condition.*

*Detail of officers.*

*Restoration of vessels.*
*Schools not for penal purposes.*

20 June, 1874, v. 18, p. 121.
3 March, 1881, v. 21, p. 505.

## QUARANTINE HULKS.

That the Secretary of the Navy be, and he is hereby, authorized, in his discretion, at the request of the National Board of Health, to place gratuitously, at the disposal of the commissioners of quarantine, or the proper authorities at any of the ports of the United States, to be used by them temporarily for quarantine purposes, such vessels or hulks belonging to the United States as are not required for other uses of the national government, subject to such restrictions and regulations as the said Secretary may deem necessary to impose for the preservation thereof.

*14 June, 1879.*
*Vessels or hulks for quarantine purposes.*

14 June, 1879, v. 21, p. 50.

11181——7

## STEAM CRUISERS—INCREASE OF NAVY.

5 Aug., 1882.

*Two steam cruisers, of steel.*

Any portion of said sum not required for the purposes aforesaid may be applied toward the construction of two steam cruising vessels of war, which are hereby authorized, at a total cost, when fully completed, not to exceed the amount estimated by the late Naval Advisory Board for such vessels, the same to be constructed of steel, of domestic manufacture, having as near as may be a tensile strength of not less than sixty thousand pounds to the square inch, and a ductility in eight inches of not less than twenty-five per centum; said vessels to be provided with full sail-power and full steam-power. One of said vessels shall be

*Tonnage, speed, armament.*

of not less than five thousand nor more than six thousand tons displacement, and shall have the highest attainable speed, and shall be adapted to be armed with not more than four breech-loading rifled cannon, of high power, of not less than eight-inch caliber, or two of ten-inch caliber, and not more than twenty-one breech-loading rifled cannon, of high power, of not less than six-inch caliber; one of said vessels shall be of not less than four thousand three hundred nor more than four thousand seven hundred tons displacement, and shall have the highest attainable speed, and shall be adapted to be armed with four breech-loading rifled cannon, of high power, of not less than eight-inch caliber, or two of ten-inch caliber, and not more than fifteen breech-loading rifled cannon, of high power, of not less than six-inch caliber. The Secretary of the Navy is hereby empowered and directed to organize a board of naval officers and experts for his advice and assistance, to be

*Naval Advisory Board.*

called the "Naval Advisory Board," to serve during the period required for the construction, armament, and trial of the vessels hereby authorized to be constructed, and no longer. Said board shall consist of five officers on the active list of the Navy in the line and the staff, to be detailed by the Secretary of the Navy, without reference to rank and with reference only to character, experience, knowledge, and skill, and two persons of established reputation and standing, as experts in naval or marine construction, to be selected from civil life, and employed for this sole duty by the Secretary of the Navy, and to be paid such sum,

*Compensation. Proviso.*

out of the appropriation hereby made, not exceeding eleven thousand dollars, as he may direct: *Provided however,* That no person shall be a member of said board who has any interest, direct or indirect, in any invention, device, or process, patented or otherwise, to be used in the construction of said vessels, their engines, boilers, or armament, nor in

*Duties and powers of board.*

any contract for the same. It shall be the duty of said board to advise and assist the Secretary of the Navy, in his office or elsewhere, in all matters referred to them by him relative to the designs, models, plans, specifications, and contracts for said vessels in all their parts, and relative to the materials to be used therein and to the construction thereof, and especially relative to the harmonious adjustment, respectively, of their hulls, machinery, and armament; and they shall examine all materials to be used in said vessels, and inspect the work on the same as it progresses, and have general supervision thereof, under the direction of said Secretary. But said board shall have no power to make or enter into any contract, nor to direct or control any officer of the Navy, the chief of any bureau of the Navy, or any contractor. Neither of the vessels hereby authorized to be built shall be contracted for or com-

*Drawings, specifications, &c.*

menced until full and complete detail drawings and specifications thereof, in all its parts, including the hull, engines, and boilers, shall have been provided or adopted by the Navy Department, and shall have been approved, in writing, by said board, or by a majority of the members thereof, and by the Secretary of the Navy; and after said drawings and specifications have been provided, adopted, and approved as aforesaid, and the work has been commenced or a contract made for it, they

*Changes or alterations.*

shall not be changed in any respect, when the cost of such change shall in the construction exceed five hundred dollars, except upon the approval of said board, or a majority of the members thereof, in writing, and upon the written order of the Secretary of the Navy; and, if changes are thus made, the actual cost thereof and the damage caused thereby shall be ascertained, estimated, and determined by said board; and in any contract made pursuant to this act it shall be provided in the terms thereof that the contractor shall be bound by the determination of said board, or a majority thereof, as to the amount of the increased or diminished compensation said contractor shall be entitled to receive, if any, in consequence of such change or changes. The Secretary of the Navy is hereby authorized to cause the said cruising vessels of war aforesaid to be provided with interior deflective steel armor, if the same, upon full investigation, shall seem to be practicable and desirable, and if the same shall be approved by said board, or a majority thereof, in writing. Before any of the vessels hereby authorized shall be contracted for or commenced the Secretary of the Navy shall, by proper public advertisement and notice, invite all engineers and mechanics of established reputation, and all reputable manufacturers of vessels, steam-engines, boilers, and ordnance, having or controlling regular establishments, and being engaged in the business, all officers of the Navy, and especially all naval constructors, steam-engineers, and ordnance officers of the Navy, having plans, models, or designs of any vessels of the classes hereby authorized, or of any part thereof, within any given period, not less than sixty days, to submit the same to said board; and it shall be the duty of said board to carefully and fully examine the same and to hear any proper explanation thereof, and to report to the Secretary of the Navy, in writing, whether, in their opinion, any such plan, model, or design, or any suggestion therein, is worthy of adoption in the construction of said vessels, their engines, boilers, or armament; and if in such construction any such plan, model, design, or suggestion shall be adopted, for the use of which any citizen not an officer of the Navy would have a just claim for compensation, the contractor shall bind himself to discharge the Government from all liability on account of such adoption and use: *Provided*, That said Naval Advisory Board, herein provided for shall, under the direction of the Secretary of the Navy, prepare plans, drawings, and specifications for vessels, their machinery, and armament, recommended by the late Naval Advisory Board not herein authorized to be built.

<small>Deflective steel armor.</small>

<small>Advertisement for plans, &c.</small>

<small>Board to report on plans, &c.</small>

<small>*Proviso.*
Further duties of board.</small>

5 Aug., 1882, P. E. L., p. 291.

3 March, 1883.

For the construction of the steel cruiser of not less than four thousand three hundred tons displacement now specially authorized by law, two steel cruisers of not more than three thousand nor less than two thousand five hundred tons displacement each, and one dispatch boat, as recommended by the Naval Advisory Board in its report of December twentieth, eighteen hundred and eighty-two, one million three hundred thousand dollars; and for the construction of all which vessels, except their armament, the Secretary of the Navy shall invite proposals from all American ship-builders whose ship-yards are fully equipped for building or repairing iron or steel steamships, and constructors of marine engines, machinery, and boilers; and the Secretary of the Navy is authorized to construct said vessels and procure their armament at a total cost for each not exceeding the amounts estimated by the Naval Advisory Board in said report, and in the event that such vessels or any of them shall be built by contract, such building shall be under contracts with the lowest and best responsible bidder or bidders, made after at least sixty days' advertisement, published in five of the leading newspapers of the United States, inviting proposals for constructing said vessels, subject to all such rules, regulations, superintendence, and provisions as to bonds and security for the due completion of the work as the Secretary of the Navy shall prescribe; and no such vessel shall be accepted unless completed in strict conformity with the contract, with the advice and assistance of the Naval Advisory Board, and in all respects in accordance with the provisions of the act of August fifth, eighteen hundred and eighty-two, except as they are hereby modified; and the authority to construct the same shall take effect at once; and the Secretary of the Navy may, in addition to the appropriation hereby made, apply to the constructing and finishing of the vessels in this clause referred to any balance of the appropriation made to the Bureaus of Construction and Repair and Steam-Engineering for the current fiscal year or in the present act which may remain available for that purpose: *Provided*, That he shall utilize the national navy-yards, with the machinery, tools, and appliances belonging to the government there in use in the building of said ships, or any parts thereof, as fully and to as great an extent as the same can be done with advantage to the government.

The services and expenses of the two civilian expert members of the Naval Advisory Board may be paid from the appropriations for the increase of the Navy, not exceeding eleven thousand dollars.

For investigating and testing the practicability of deflective turrets designed by Passed Assistant Engineer N. B. Clark, twenty thousand

<small>Steel cruisers and dispatch boat.</small>

<small>Proposals to be invited.</small>

<small>Cost.</small>

<small>Contracts.</small>

<small>Assistance of Naval Advisory Board.</small>

<small>Yards to be utilized.</small>

<small>Civilian experts.</small>

<small>Deflective turrets.</small>

dollars, to be available immediately, the investigation and test to be made by the Naval Advisory Board.

3 March, 1883, P. E. L., p. 477.

### DOUBLE-TURRETED MONITORS.

Aug., 1882.
Turrets for Miantonomoh.

That four hundred thousand dollars of the above amount [Repairs, &c., machinery, &c.], or so much thereof as may be necessary, shall be applied by the Secretary of the Navy to the following objects, namely: Under the Bureau of Construction and Repair: To building and fitting the turrets and pilot-house of the iron-clad steamer Miantonomoh; and

Launching of double-turreted monitors.

to the launching to the best advantage, with such necessary attachments and appliances as will render redocking of the ships unnecessary, of the iron-clad steamers Monadnock, Puritan, Amphitrite, and Terror; and that no further steps shall be taken or contracts entered into or approved for the repairs or completion of any of the four iron-clads aforesaid until the further order of Congress; and the Naval Advisory Board, created by this act, is directed to report to the Secretary of the Navy in detail by the first day of December, eighteen hundred and eighty-two, as to the wisdom and expediency of undertaking and completing the engines, armor, and armaments of said iron-clads, and whether any changes in the original plan or plans should be made, together with the cost of the completion of each according to the plans recommended, if the completion of any of them is recommended; and the said Secretary shall trans-

Report to Congress.

mit said report to Congress at its next session with his recommendation thereon, and that any part of the appropriation for said Bureau not used as above specified may be applied toward the construction of engines and machinery of the two new cruising vessels provided for in this act.

5 Aug., 1882, P. E. L., p. 293.

3 March, 1883.
Appropriation.

To be applied by the Secretary of the Navy under the appropriate Bureaus: For engines and machinery for the double-turreted iron-clads, in accordance with the recommendations of the Naval Advisory Board, one million dollars.

Contracts, &c.

The execution of no contract shall be entered upon for the completion of the engines and machinery of either of these vessels until the terms thereof shall be approved by said Board, who shall approve only contracts which may be to the best advantage of the Government, and fair and reasonable, according to the lowest market price for similar work. And the Secretary of the Navy shall take possession of the double-turreted iron-clads, and if he thinks best, remove the same to the Government navy-yards; and he shall ascertain the amounts which ought to be paid to the contractors severally for the use and occupation of their yards with said ships, and for the care thereof, and report the same, with all the facts connected therewith, to Congress.

3 March, 1883, P. E. L., p. 477.

### REPORT OF ACCIDENTS, ETC.

20 June, 1874.
Report of accidents, &c., to vessels.

* * * "whenever any vessel of the United States has sustained or caused any accident involving the loss of life, the material loss of property, or any serious injury to any person, or has received any material damage affecting her seaworthiness or her efficiency, the managing owner, agent, or master of such vessel, shall within five days after the happening of such accident or damage, or as soon thereafter as possible, send, by letter to the collector of customs of the district wherein such vessel belongs or of that within which such accident or damage occurred, a report thereof, signed by such owner, agent, or master, stating the name and official number (if any) of the vessel, the port to which she belongs, the place where she was, the nature and probable occasion of the casualty, the number and names of those lost, and the estimated amount of loss or damage to the vessel or cargo; and shall furnish, upon the request of either of such collectors of customs, such other information concerning the vessel, her cargo, and the casualty as may be called for; and if he neglect or refuse to comply with the foregoing requirements after a reasonable time, he shall incur a penalty of one hundred dollars." * * *

20 June, 1874, s. 10, v. 18, p. 128.

NOTE.—The above act is regarded as applying to vessels of the Navy, and a report should be made as indicated, in case of loss or accident, to the collector, from whom the necessary blanks can be procured.

## VOLUNTEER SERVICE.

Sec.
1411. Acting assistant surgeons.
1412. Credit for volunteer service.
1559. Pay of volunteer service.
1600. Credit to marine officers for volunteer service.

Sec.
—— Acting assistant surgeons allowed only in case of war
—— Credit for continuous service.

SEC. 1411. The Secretary of the Navy may appoint, for temporary service, such acting assistant surgeons as the exigencies of the service may require, who shall receive the compensation of assistant surgeons. [See *post*, 15 Feb., 1879.]     *Title 15, Chap. 1.*   *Acting assistant surgeons.*

15 July, 1870, s. 13, v. 16, p. 334.     3 March, 1865, s. 6, v. 13, p. 539.

SEC. 1412. Officers who have been, or may be, transferred from the volunteer service to the Regular Navy shall be credited with the sea service performed by them as volunteer officers, and shall receive all the benefits of such duty in the same manner as if they had been, during such service, in the Regular Navy. [See Aug. 5, 1882 and March 3, 1883, *post*.]     *Credit for volunteer sea-service.*

2 March, 1867, s. 3, v. 14, p. 516.

SEC. 1559. When a volunteer naval service is authorized by law, the officers therein shall be entitled to receive the same pay as officers of the same grades, respectively, in the Regular Navy.     *Title 15, Chap. 8.*   *Pay volunteer service.*

16 July, 1862, s. 20, v. 12, p. 587.

SEC. 1600. All marine officers shall be credited with the length of time they may have been employed as officers or enlisted men in the volunteer service of the United States.     *Title 15, Chap. 9.*   *Credit to marine officers.*

2 March, 1867, s. 3, v. 14, p. 516.

That from and after the passage of this act, the Secretary of the Navy shall not appoint acting assistant surgeons for temporary service, as authorized by section fourteen hundred and eleven, Revised Statutes, except in case of war.     *15 Feb., 1879.*   *Acting assistant surgeons only in time of war.*

15 Feb., 1879, s. 2, v. 20, p. 292.

[An act approved 15 Feb., 1879, v. 20, p. 294, abolished the volunteer Navy of the United States; providing for the transfer of some of them to the Regular Navy. Mates were not considered as coming within its provisions.]

And all officers of the Navy shall be credited with the actual time they may have served as officers or enlisted men in the regular or volunteer Army or Navy, or both, and shall receive all the benefits of such actual service in all respects in the same manner as if all said service had been continuous and in the Regular Navy in the lowest grade having graduated pay held by such officer since last entering the service: *Provided*, That nothing in this clause shall be so construed as to authorize any change in the dates of commission or in the relative rank of such officers: *Provided further*, That nothing herein contained shall be so construed as to give any additional pay to any such officer during the time of his service in the volunteer army or navy.     *3 March, 1883.*   *Credit for service in volunteer Army or Navy.*

5 Aug., 1882, P. E. L., p. 287.     3 March, 1883, P. E. L., p. 473.

NOTES.—Credit for volunteer service under section 1412 of the Revised Statutes "as an acting third assistant engineer, is of no benefit to the officer, so far as regards promotion to, or pay in, the grade of passed assistant engineer in the regular Navy;" cannot be used to make up the period of sea service required for promotion from the grade of second or assistant engineer to that of first or passed assistant.—Op., June, 1882. Webster's case.

This provision (Sec. 1412) was designed to give the transferred officers the free benefit of their former sea service, in so far as it might go to complete the period of such service required in their respective grades previous to examination for promotion, and in so far as it ought properly to be taken into account in the matter of assignment to duty, and it confers no advantages beyond these. A volunteer officer transferred to the regular Navy is not entitled to hold a commission dated as of the date of his volunteer commission, but he must take his place upon the register according to the rank given him by his commission as an officer of the regular Navy.—Op. XIV, 191, 358, and August 11, 1881.—Gen. order, 275.

To entitle an officer to credit for sea service, under the act of March 2, 1867, he must have been in the volunteer Navy at the time of his appointment to the regular Navy. Where he ceased to be an officer in the volunteer Navy prior to such appointment, however brief the interval, he does not come within the provisions referred to.—Op. XIV, 142, November 20, 1872. *Gray's* case.

The act of 3 March, 1883, *supra*, may have changed the effect of some of the foregoing opinions.

## WARRANT OFFICERS.

Sec.
1405. Number and appointment of.
1406. Title.
1407. Promotion of seamen to warrant officers.
1409. Not to discharge from enlistment.
1416. Gunners as keepers of magazines.

Sec.
1417. Preference to enlisted boys.
1438. As naval store-keepers.
1439. Bonds as store-keepers.
1491. Rank.
1556. Pay.

**Title 15, Chap. 1.**

*Number and appointment of.*

SEC. 1405. The President may appoint for the vessels in actual service, as many boatswains, gunners, sailmakers, and carpenters as may, in his opinion, be necessary and proper.

21 April, 1806, s. 3, v. 2, p. 390.
4 Aug., 1842, s. 1, v. 5, p. 500.
3 March, 1847, s. 1, v. 9, p. 172.

*Title.*

SEC. 1406. Boatswains, gunners, carpenters, and sailmakers shall be known and shall be entered upon the Naval Register as "warrant officers in the naval service of the United States."

2 July, 1864, s. 2, v. 13, p. 373.

*Promotion of seamen to warrant officers.*

SEC. 1407. Seamen distinguishing themselves in battle, or by extraordinary heroism in the line of their profession, may be promoted to forward warrant officers, upon the recommendation of their commanding officer, approved by the flag-officer and Secretary of the Navy. And upon such recommendation they shall receive a gratuity of one hundred dollars and a medal of honor, to be prepared under the direction of the Navy Department.

17 May, 1864, s. 3, v. 13, p. 79.

*Rating not to discharge.*

SEC. 1409. The rating of an enlisted man as a mate, or his appointment as a warrant officer, shall not discharge him from his enlistment.

17 May, 1864, s. 3, v. 13, p. 79.
3 March, 1865, s. 3, v. 13, p. 539.

*Gunners as keepers of magazines.*

SEC. 1416. The Secretary of the Navy is authorized, when in his opinion the public interest will permit it, to discontinue the office or employment of * * * the keeper of the magazine employed at any navy-yard, and to require the duties of the keeper of the magazine to be performed by gunners.

10 Aug., 1846, s. 1, v. 9, p. 98.

*Preference in appointment to be given to apprentices, &c.*

SEC. 1417. * * * In the appointment of warrant officers in the naval service of the United States, preference shall be given to men who have been honorably discharged upon the expiration of an enlistment as an apprentice or boy, to serve during minority, and re-enlisted within three months after such discharge, to serve during a term of three or more years: *Provided further,* That nothing in this act shall be held to abrogate the provisions of section fourteen hundred and seven of the Revised Statutes of the United States.

12 May, 1879, v. 21, p. 3.

**Title 15, Chap. 2.**

*Acting as store-keepers.*

SEC. 1438. The Secretary of the Navy shall order a suitable commissioned or warrant officer of the Navy, except in the case provided in section fourteen hundred and fourteen, to take charge of the naval stores for foreign squadrons at each of the foreign stations where such stores may be deposited, and where a store-keeper may be necessary. [See § 1414, under NAVAL STORE-KEEPERS.]

17 June, 1844, s. 1, v. 5, p. 700.
3 March, 1847, s. 3, v. 9, p. 172.

*Bonds of.*

SEC. 1439. Every officer so acting as store-keeper on a foreign station shall be required to give a bond, in such amount as may be fixed by the Secretary of the Navy, for the faithful performance of his duty.

17 June, 1844, s. 1, v. 5, p. 700.

**Title 15, Chap. 4.**

*Rank.*

SEC. 1491. The President may, if he shall deem it conducive to the interests of the service, give assimilated rank to boatswains, gunners, carpenters, and sailmakers, as follows: After five years' service, to rank with ensigns, and after ten years' service to rank with *lieutenants of the junior grade.*

2 July, 1864, s. 1, v. 13, p. 373.
3 March, 1883, P. E. L., p. 472.

SEC. 1556. * * * Boatswains, gunners, carpenters, and sail-makers, during the first three years after date of appointment, when at sea, one thousand two hundred dollars; on shore duty, nine hundred dollars; on leave, or waiting orders, seven hundred dollars; during the second three years after such date, when at sea, one thousand three hundred dollars; on shore duty, one thousand dollars; on leave, or waiting orders, eight hundred dollars; during the third three years after such date, when at sea, one thousand four hundred dollars; on shore duty, one thousand three hundred dollars; on leave, or waiting orders, nine hundred dollars; during the fourth three years after such date, when at sea, one thousand six hundred dollars; on shore duty, one thousand three hundred dollars; on leave, or waiting orders, one thousand dollars; after twelve years from such date, when at sea, one thousand eight hundred dollars; on shore duty, one thousand six hundred dollars; on leave, or waiting orders, one thousand two hundred dollars.

Title 15, Chap. 8.

Pay.

15 July, 1870, s. 3, v. 16, p. 332.

# ADDENDA.

## APPOINTMENTS, REINSTATEMENT, ETC.

NOTES.—Appointments to office can be made only by the Executive branch of the Government in the manner provided by the Constitution (Art. II, §2), and not by Congressional enactment.—C. C., XV, 151, Wood's case.

It is necessary that the President should nominate, the Senate advise and consent, and that, in pursuance of such nomination and confirmation the appointment should actually be made. The nomination and confirmation do not divest the President of the power to withhold the appointment.—Op. IV, 31, 218. The appointment of a commissioned officer is not perfected, and is entirely within the power of the President until the commission is issued.—Op. IX, 297; XIII. 44; XIV, 344, C. C. V., 97.

When a commission has been signed by the President the appointment is complete, and the commission is complete when the seal of the United States has been affixed.—1 Cranch, Curtis' edition 377, Marbury's case.

The Senate cannot originate an appointment; its constitutional action is confined to a simple affirmation or rejection of the nomination, and it fails when they disagree. May suggest limitations or conditions, but cannot vary the nomination. No appointment can be made except on the President's nomination agreed to without qualification or alteration.—Op. III, 189.

When a person appointed to an office refuses to accept the same, the successor is nominated in the place of the person who has declined, and not in place of the person who had been previously in office.—1 Cranch, Curtis' edition, 377.

The President, by and with the advice and consent of the Senate, may, by reappointment and commission, restore lost rank, including seniority, to an officer of the Army or Navy. Cases cited.—Op. VIII, 223 Cushing, Dec. 10, 1856.

In the same way he can correct the date of a military appointment, or an error in the date of appointment, or an inadvertence to nominate an officer entitled to promotion by ten years' service.—Op. III, 307; VIII, 223.

The right of a reinstated officer to pay during the time he was out of the service must depend upon the will of Congress, as expressed in the act authorizing his reinstatement, and not upon the date of his commission.—C. C., XV, 41, Kilburn's case.

Commissions signed by his predecessor should be regarded by the President as conclusive evidence of the officers' right to the rank and authority given thereby. While their commissions stand the President should respect them, and in making promotions by seniority have regard for them. If wrong has been sustained, Congress can remedy it by a special relief act empowering the President.—Op. XVI, 583, Devens, Dec. 9, 1880.

Where an act directed the Secretary of War to amend the record of an officer dismissed by court-martial, so that he should appear on the rolls and records as if he had been continuously in the service: *Held*, That it conferred on the President the power to appoint in the usual way. If so appointed the commission should refer to the act, in a proper manner, under which the appointment was made, by nomination and confirmation of the Senate.—Op. XIV, 448, Williams, Aug. 13, 1874; but see Court of Claims, XIV, 573; XV, 22.

Congress as a general rule, has authorized the President to restore officers to the retired list without requiring the advice and consent of the Senate. Where they have been reinstated to form a part of the *active force* of the Army, a different phraseology has been employed—requiring the advice and consent of the Senate. An officer dismissed by sentence of a court-martial cannot, under section 1228 R. S., be reinstated except by reappointment, confirmed by the Senate. This is a clear recognition that restoration of officers separated from the service under other circumstances, can be accomplished without confirmation of the Senate. The words "inferior officers" used in the Constitution, mean subordinate or inferior officers in whom, respectively, the power of appointment may be invested by Congress in the President, the courts of law, and the heads of Departments.—C. C., XIV, 573, Collin's case.

When the President is authorized by law to reinstate a discharged Army officer, he may do so without the advice and consent of the Senate. When he exercises the discretion vested in him by an act of Congress, of reinstating an officer, and expresses his will by an order to that effect, the officer acquires a vested right to the office. By antedating an appointment or commission, he cannot create a liability on the part of the Government, but the legislative branch of the Government can.—C. C., XV, 22, Collin's case.

Where an officer was of lawful age when nominated but was over age when confirmed, his commission can be issued to him. The Senate could have arrested it.—Op. X, 308, Bates, July 1, 1862.

[See also under CIVIL SERVICE, Part III.]

# PART II.

## THE MARINE CORPS.

ORGANIZATION, ETC., RETIREMENT, PAY AND RATIONS, MILEAGE AND TRANSPORTATION, FORAGE, FUEL, AND QUARTERS.

# MARINE CORPS

## ORGANIZATION, &C.

Sec.
1135. Camp equipage of detachments serving with the Army.
1143. Rations to detachments serving with Army.
1342. Association with Army on courts-martial.
1342. Command when different corps join.
1421. Transfer of enlisted men from Army.
1596. Number of.
1597. What commissions and promotions not affected by number fixed.
1598. Staff.
1599. Qualifications for appointment.
1600. Credit for volunteer service.
1601. Rank of commandant.
1602. Staff rank.
1603. Relative rank with the Army.
—— Judge-Advocate-General.
1604. Brevets. [1209-11-12-64, Army.]

Sec.
1605. Advancement in number.
1606. Promotion when grade is full.
1607. Promotion for gallantry.
1608. Enlistments.
1609. Oath.
1610. Exemption from arrest.
1611. Companies and detachments.
1616. Services on armed vessels.
1617. Marine officers not to command navy-yards or vessels.
1618. Marines substituted for landsmen.
1619. Duty on shore.
1620. Regulations.
1621. Subject to laws governing the Navy, except when serving with the Army.
—— Post-traders.
1624. Desertion by resignation.

SEC. 1135. The officers of the Quartermaster's Department shall, upon the requisition of the naval or marine officer commanding any detachment of seamen or marines under orders to act on shore, in co-operation with land troops, and during the time such detachment is so acting or proceeding to act, furnish the officers and seamen with camp equipage, together with transportation for said officers, seamen, and marines, their baggage, provisions, and cannon, and shall furnish the naval officer commanding any such detachment, and his necessary aids, with horses, accouterments, and forage. *Title 14, Chap. 1. Supplies to naval and marine detachments.*

15 Dec., 1814, ss. 1, 2, v. 3, p. 151.

SEC. 1143. The officers of the Subsistence Department shall, upon the requisition of the naval or marine officer commanding any detachment of seamen or marines under orders to act on shore, in co-operation with the land troops, and during the time such detachment is so acting or proceeding to act, furnish rations to the officers, seamen, and marines of the same. *Rations to detachments with the Army.*

15 Dec., 1814, s. 1, v. 3, p. 151.

SEC. 1342. ART. of WAR 78. Officers of the Marine Corps, detached for service with the Army by order of the President, may be associated with officers of the Regular Army on courts-martial for the trial of offenders belonging to the Regular Army, or to forces of the Marine Corps so detached; and in such cases the orders of the senior officer of either corps, who may be present and duly authorized, shall be obeyed. *Title 14, Chap. 5. Marine and Regular Army officers associated on courts.*

30 June, 1834, s. 2, v. 4, p. 713.

SEC. 1342. ART. of WAR 122. If, upon marches, guards, or in quarters, different corps of the Army happen to join or do duty together, the officer highest in rank of the line of the Army, Marine Corps, or Militia, by commission, there on duty or in quarters, shall command the whole, and give orders for what is needful to the service, unless otherwise specially directed by the President, according to the nature of the case. *Command when different corps happen to join.*

3 March, 1863, s. 27, v. 12, p. 736.
3 March, 1863, s. 25, v. 12, p. 754.

SEC. 1421. Any person enlisted in the military service of the United States may, on application to the Navy Department, approved by the President, be transferred to the Navy or Marine Corps, to serve therein the residue of his term of enlistment, subject to the laws and regulations for the government of the Navy. But such transfer shall not release him from any indebtedness to the Government, nor, without the consent of the President, from any penalty incurred for a breach of military law. *Title 15, Chap. 1. Transfer, from military to naval service.*

1 July, 1864, s. 1, v. 13, p. 342.

107

108  ORGANIZATION, ETC.

**Title 15, Chap. 9.**
**Number of.**

SEC. 1596. The Marine Corps of the United States shall consist of one commandant, *with the rank and pay of a colonel*, one colonel, two lieutenant-colonels, four majors, one adjutant and inspector, one paymaster, one quartermaster, two assistant quartermasters, twenty captains, thirty first lieutenants, thirty second lieutenants, one sergeant-major, one quartermaster-sergeant, one drum-major, one principal musician, two hundred sergeants, two hundred and twenty corporals, thirty musicians for a band, sixty drummers, sixty fifers, and twenty-five hundred privates.

25 July, 1861, s. 7, v. 12, p. 275.
2 Mar., 1867, s. 7, v. 14, p. 517.
6 June, 1874, v. 18, p. 58.

The commandant is stationed at the headquarters of the Marine Corps, Washington, D. C.; is responsible to the Secretary of the Navy for the general efficiency and discipline of the corps, and under his direction issues, through the office of the adjutant and inspector of the corps, orders for the movement of officers and troops, and such general orders and instructions for their guidance as may be necessary. In the absence of the commandant on duty, the business of his office is conducted by the adjutant and inspector, as "by order of the commandant"; in case of his absence on leave, disability, retirement, or death, his duties are performed by the adjutant and inspector, as "by direction of the Secretary of the Navy".

**When number may be increased by promotion.**

SEC. 1597. The provisions of the preceding section shall not preclude the advancement of any officer to a higher grade for distinguished conduct in conflict with the enemy, or for extraordinary heroism in the line of his profession, as authorized by sections sixteen hundred and five and sixteen hundred and seven.

25 July, 1861, s. 2, v. 12, p. 275.
16 July, 1862, s. 9, v. 12, p. 584.
24 Jan., 1865, s. 2, v. 13, p. 424.

**Staff.**

SEC. 1598. The staff of the Marine Corps shall be separate from the line.

2 Mar., 1847, s. 3, v. 9, p. 154.
30 June, 1834, s. 6, v. 4, p. 713.

**Appointments.**

SEC. 1599. Superseded by act of August 5, 1882, as follows: All the undergraduates at the Naval Academy shall hereafter be designated and called "naval cadets"; and from those who successfully complete the six years' course appointments shall hereafter be made as it is necessary to fill vacancies in the lower grades of the line and engineer corps of the Navy and of the Marine Corps: *And provided further*, That no greater number of appointments into these grades shall be made each year than shall equal the number of vacancies which has occurred in the same grades during the preceding year; such appointments to be made from the graduates of the year at the conclusion of their six years' course, in the order of merit, as determined by the academic board of the Naval Academy; the assignment to the various corps to be made by the Secretary of the Navy upon the recommendation of the academic board.

5 Aug., 1882, s. 1, P. E. L., p. 285.

**Credit for volunteer service.**

SEC. 1600. All marine officers shall be credited with the length of time they may have been employed as officers or enlisted men in the volunteer service of the United States. [See Aug. 5, 1882, Part I, under Volunteer Service.]

2 Mar., 1867, s. 3, v. 14, p. 516.

**Rank and pay of commandant.**

SEC. 1601. The commandant of the Marine Corps shall have the rank and pay of a *colonel, and shall be appointed by selection by the President from the officers of said corps.*

2 Mar., 1867, s. 7, v. 14, p. 517.
6 June, 1874, v. 18, p. 58.

**Staff rank.**

SEC. 1602. The adjutant and inspector, the paymaster, and the quartermaster shall have the rank of major; each assistant quartermaster shall have the rank of captain.

2 Mar., 1847, s. 3, v. 9, p. 154.
27 Feb. 1877, v. 19, p. 244.

ORGANIZATION, ETC. 109

Sec. 1603. The officers of the Marine Corps shall be, in relation to rank, on the same footing as officers of similar grades in the Army. [See 1406, RANK AND PRECEDENCE, Part I.] — Relative rank with the Army.

30 June, 1834, s. 4, v. 4, p. 713.

That the President of the United States be, and he is hereby, authorized to appoint, for the term of four years, by and with the advice and consent of the Senate, from the officers of the Navy or the Marine Corps, a judge-advocate-general of the Navy, with the rank, pay, and allowances of a captain in the Navy or a colonel in the Marine Corps, as the case may be. And the office of the said judge-advocate-general shall be in the Navy Department, where he shall, under the direction of the Secretary of the Navy, receive, revise, and have recorded the proceedings of all courts-martial, courts of inquiry, and boards for the examination of officers for retirement and promotion in the naval service, and perform such other duties as have heretofore been performed by the solicitor and naval judge-advocate-general. [See note, page 15, Part I.] — June 8, 1880. Judge-advocate-general. Office in the Navy Departm't.

8 June, 1880, v. 21, p. 164, ch. 129.

Sec. 1604. Commissions by brevet may be conferred upon commissioned officers of the Marine Corps in the same cases, upon the same conditions, and in the same manner as are or may be provided by law for officers of the Army. — Title 15, Chap. 9. Brevets.

16 Apr., 1814, s. 3, v. 3, p. 124.  16 Apr., 1818, s. 2, v. 3, p. 427.
30 June, 1834, s. 9, v. 4, p. 713.  6 July, 1812, s. 4, v. 2, p. 785.
1 Mar., 1869, s. 2, v. 15, p. 281.  3 Mar., 1869, s. 7, v. 15, p. 318.
15 July, 1870, s. 16, v. 16, p. 319.

The following are the sections relating to the conferring of brevets in the Army: — Title 14, Chap. 1. Brevets.

Sec. 1209. The President, by and with the advice and consent of the Senate, may, in time of war, confer commissions by brevet upon commissioned officers of the Army, for distinguished conduct and public service in presence of the enemy.

6 July, 1812, s. 4, v. 2, p. 785.
16 April, 1818, s. 2, v. 3, p. 427.
1 March, 1869, s. 2, v. 15, p. 281.

Sec. 1210. Brevet commissions shall bear date from the particular action or service for which the officers were brevetted.

1 March, 1869, s. 2, v. 15, p. 281.

Sec. 1211. Officers may be assigned to duty or command according to their brevet rank by special assignment of the President; and brevet rank shall not entitle an officer to precedence or command except when so assigned.

16 April, 1818, s. 1, v. 3, p. 427.
3 March, 1869, s. 7, v. 15, p. 318.

Sec. 1212. No officer shall be entitled, on account of having been brevetted, to wear, while on duty, any uniform other than that of his actual rank; and no officer shall be addressed in orders or official communications by any title other than that of his actual rank.

15 July, 1870, s. 16, v. 16, p. 319.

Sec. 1264. Brevets conferred on commissioned officers shall not entitle them to any increase of pay. — Title 16, Chap. 3.

3 March, 1863, v. 12, p. 758.
3 March, 1865, s. 9, v. 13, p. 488.

Officers of the Army shall only be assigned to duty or command according to their brevet rank when actually engaged in hostilities. — 3 March, 1883.

3 March, 1883, s. 1, P. E. L., p. 457.

Sec. 1605. Any officer of the Marine Corps may, by and with the advice and consent of the Senate, be advanced not exceeding thirty numbers in rank, for eminent and conspicuous conduct in battle or extraordinary heroism. — Title 15, Chap. 9. Advancement in number.

24 Jan., 1865, s. 1, v. 13, p. 424.
21 Apr., 1864, s. 6, v. 13, p. 54.

Sec. 1606. Any officer who is nominated to a higher grade by the provisions of the preceding section shall be promoted, notwithstanding the number of said grade may be full, but no further promotion — Promotion when grade is full.

110 ORGANIZATION, ETC.

shall take place in that grade, except for like cause, until the number is reduced to that provided by law.

24 Jan., 1865, s. 2, v. 13, p. 424.

Promotion for gallantry.
SEC. 1607. Any officer of the Marine Corps may, by and with the advice and consent of the Senate, be advanced one grade, if, upon recommendation of the President by name, he receives the thanks of Congress for highly distinguished conduct in conflict with the enemy, or for extraordinary heroism in the line of his profession.

16 July, 1862, s. 9, v. 12, p. 584.
24 Jan., 1865, s. 2, v. 13, p. 424.

Enlistments.
SEC. 1608. Enlistments into the Marine Corps shall be for a period not less than five years.

11 July, 1870. Res. 106, v. 16, p. 387.

NOTE.—It is not in the power of the Secretary [of War] to suspend the enlistment of a soldier, retaining the right to resume his proper control over him as an enlisted man at any definite or indefinite period. He may discharge him from the service according to the contract which is made by enlistment, but the right to suspend the contract does not exist upon the part of the Secretary, even with the consent of the soldier. To use the language of Attorney-General Clifford (Op. 4, 538), "The Executive Department has discretionary authority to discharge before the term of service has expired, but has no power to vary the contract of enlistment."

Op. XV, 362, Devens, Sept. 4, 1877.

NOTES.—Enlisted men serving within the United States can be discharged by order of the commandant on expiration of enlistment, in pursuance of the sentence of a general or summary court-martial, or by reason of unfitness for service from causes properly ascertained. Special discharges are not issued by the commandant except in cases of urgent necessity, and when, in his opinion, such discharge will not be prejudicial to the interests of the service.

The regulations for the recruiting service of the Army are applied, as far as practicable, to the recruiting service of the Marine Corps. No person is enlisted or re-enlisted other than as private, drummer, fifer, or apprentice. Marines will not be enlisted nor discharged on foreign stations.

Oath.
SEC. 1609. The officers and enlisted men of the Marine Corps shall take the same oaths, respectively, which are provided by law for the officers and enlisted men of the Army.

11 July, 1798, s. 4, v. 1, p. 595.

## Oath for enlisted men.

Title 14, Chap. 5.
Oath.
SEC. 1342, ART. 2. "I, A B, do solemnly swear (or affirm) that I will bear true faith and allegiance to the United States of America; that I will serve them honestly and faithfully against all their enemies whomsoever; and that I will obey the orders of the President of the United States, and the orders of the officers appointed over me, according to the rules and articles of war." This oath may be taken before any commissioned officer of the Army.

29 January, 1813, s. 13, v. 2, p. 796.
3 Aug., 1861, s. 11, v. 12, p. 289.

Title 15, Chap. 9.
Exemption from arrest.
SEC. 1610. Marines shall be exempt, while enlisted in said service, from all personal arrest for debt or contract.

30 June, 1834, s. 3, v. 4, p. 713.
11 July, 1798, s. 5, v. 1, p. 595.

Companies and detachments.
SEC. 1611. The Marine Corps may be formed into as many companies or detachments as the President may direct, with a proper distribution of the commissioned and non-commissioned officers and musicians to each company or detachment.

11 July, 1798, s. 1, v. 1, p. 594.

Title 15, Chap. 9
Service on armed vessels.
SEC. 1616. Marines may be detached for service on board the armed vessels of the United States, and the President may detach and appoint, for service on said vessels, such of the officers of said corps as he may deem necessary.

11 July, 1798, ss. 1, 3, v. 1, p. 595.
1 July, 1797, s. 4, v. 1, p. 523.

Not to command yards or vessels.
SEC. 1617. No officer of the Marine Corps shall exercise command over any navy-yard or vessel of the United States.

30 June, 1834, s. 4, v. 4, p. 713.

Marines as landsmen.
SEC. 1618. The President may substitute marines for landsmen in the Navy, as far as he may deem it for the good of the service.

3 March, 1849, s. 1, v. 9, p. 377.

RETIREMENT. 111

Sec. 1619. The Marine Corps shall be liable to do duty in the forts and garrisons of the United States, on the sea-coast, or any other duty on shore, as the President, at his discretion, may direct. *Duty on shore.*
11 July, 1798, s. 6, v. 1, p. 596.

Sec. 1620. The President is authorized to prescribe such military regulations for the discipline of the Marine Corps as he may deem expedient. *Regulations for discipline.*
30 June, 1834, s. 8, v. 4, p. 713.

Sec. 1621. The Marine Corps shall, at all times, be subject to the laws and regulations established for the government of the Navy, except when detached for service with the Army by order of the President; and when so detached they shall be subject to the rules and articles of war prescribed for the government of the Army. *Laws and regulations to which subject.*
30 June, 1834, s. 2, v. 4, p. 713.
11 July, 1798, s. 4, v. 1, p. 595.

Every military post may have one trader, to be appointed by the Secretary of War, on the recommendation of the council of administration, approved by the commanding officer, who shall be subject in all respects to the rules and regulations for the government of the Army. *24 July, 1876.*
*Post traders.*
24 July, 1876, v. 19, p. 97.

Notes.—The Secretary of the Navy determines at what marine posts traders shall be allowed, and appoints them on the recommendation of the council of administration, formed under Army regulations, approved by the commanding officers of the post and the commandant of the station.
Post traders are governed by the Army regulations, and such orders as the commandant of the Marine Corps may issue. They cannot keep, have, or sell spirituous liquors.—Order of the Secretary of the Navy, March 16, 1883.
Post traders are subject to the regulations of the Army applicable to the occupation or business carried on by them, in like manner, and to the same extent, that sutlers were.—Op. XVI, 658, Feb. 2, 1880. Phillips.

Sec. 1624, Art. 10. Any commissioned officer of the Navy or Marine Corps who, having tendered his resignation, quits his post or proper duties without leave, and with intent to remain permanently absent therefrom, prior to due notice of the acceptance of such resignation, shall be deemed and punished as a deserter. *Title 15, Chap. 10.*
*Sec. 1624. Desertion by resignation.*
5 Aug., 1861, s. 2, v. 12, p. 316.


## RETIREMENT—*Marine Corps.*

| Sec. | Sec. |
|---|---|
| 1622. Retirement, as in the Army. | 1623. Composition of board. |

### *Retirement in the Army.*

| Sec. | Sec. |
|---|---|
| 1243. Retirement upon officer's own application. | 1252. Disability not by an incident of service. |
| 1244. After forty-five years, or at the age of sixty-two. | 1253. Officers entitled to a hearing. |
| | 1254. Retired rank. |
| ——. Amendments. | 1255. Status of retired officers. |
| 1245. For disability. | 1256. Rights and liabilities. |
| 1247. Oath of members. | 1257. Vacancies by retirement. |
| 1248. Powers and duties. | 1574. Pay. |
| 1249. Findings. | 1575. Wholly retired. |
| 1250. Revision by the President. | ——. Rank and pay. |
| 1251. Finding of disability by incident of service. | |

Sec. 1622. The commissioned officers of the Marine Corps shall be retired in like cases, in the same manner, and with the same relative conditions, in all respects, as are provided for officers of the Army, except as is otherwise provided in the next section. *Title 15, Chap. 9.*
*Retirement.*
3 Aug., 1861, ss. 15, 16, 17, v. 12, p. 289.   15 July, 1870, s. 4, v. 16, p. 317.
17 July, 1862, s. 12, v. 12, p. 596.   10 June, 1872, s. 1, v. 17, p. 378.
21 Jan., 1870, s. 1, v. 16, p. 62.

Sec. 1623. In case of an officer of the Marine Corps, the retiring board shall be selected by the Secretary of the Navy, under the direction of the President. Two-fifths of the board shall be selected from the Medical Corps of the Navy, and the remainder shall be selected *Retiring board, how composed.*

112  RETIREMENT.

from officers of the Marine Corps, senior in rank, so far as may be, to the officer whose disability is to be inquired of.

3 Aug., 1861, s. 17, v. 12, p. 289.

> NOTE.—Retirement in the Marine Corps is governed by secs. 1622, 1623, R. S.; *i. e.*, officers are to be retired in like cases and in the same manner and "with the same relative conditions in all respects" as officers of the Army. Wholly retired, to receive one year's pay and emoluments; otherwise retired, 75 per cent. of the pay of the "actual rank" held by them at the time of retirement.— Op. XV, p. 442, Devens, Jan. 31, 1878, Welles case.
> An officer of the Marine Corps is not subject to the requirements of sec. 1493 (relating to the promotion of officers of the Navy) on coming up for promotion.—Op. June 16, 1881, MacVeagh, Major Houston's case.

**Title 14, Chap. 2.** The following sections relate to retirement in the Army:

*Retirement on own application.* SEC. 1243. When an officer has served forty consecutive years as a commissioned officer, he shall, if he makes application therefor to the President, be retired from active service and placed upon the retired list. When an officer has been thirty years in service, he may, upon his own application, in the discretion of the President, be so retired, and placed on the retired list. [See 30 June, 1882, and 3 March, 1883, *post.*]

3 Aug., 1861, s. 15, v. 12, p. 289.
15 July, 1870, ss. 4, 5, v. 16, p. 317.

*After 45 years, or when 62.* SEC. 1244. When any officer has served forty-five years as a commissioned officer, or is sixty-two years old, he may be retired from active service at the discretion of the President. [See 30 June, 1882, and 3 March, 1883, *post.*]

17 July, 1862, s. 12, v. 12, p. 596.

*30 June, 1882.*
*Retirement after 40 years service on own application.*
*Retirement compulsory at 64 years of age.*
On and after the passage of this act when an officer has served forty years either as an officer or soldier in the regular or volunteer service, or both, he shall, if he make application therefor to the President, be retired from active service and placed on the retired list, and when an officer is sixty-four years of age, he shall be retired from active service and placed on the retired list.

30 June, 1882, chap. 254, s. 1, P. E. L., p. 118.

*3 March, 1883.* Nothing contained in the above "shall be so construed as to prevent, limit or restrict retirements from active service in the Army, as authorized by law in force at the date of the approval of said act," retirement under the provisions thereof "being in addition to those theretofore authorized by law."

3 March, 1883, chap. 93, s. 1, P. E. L., p. 457.

*For disability.* SEC. 1245. When any officer has become incapable of performing the duties of his office, he shall be either retired from active service, or wholly retired from the service, by the President, as hereinafter provided.

3 Aug., 1861, s. 16, v. 12, p. 289.

*Board, and powers and duties of.* SEC. 1247. The members of said board shall be sworn in every case to discharge their duties honestly and impartially.

SEC. 1248. A retiring board may inquire into and determine the facts touching the nature and occasion of the disability of any officer who appears to be incapable of performing the duties of his office, and shall have such powers of a court-martial and of a court of inquiry as may be necessary for that purpose.

SEC. 1249. When the board finds an officer incapacitated for active service, it shall also find and report the cause which, in its judgment, has produced his incapacity, and whether such cause is an incident of service.

SEC. 1250. The proceedings and decision of the board shall be transmitted to the Secretary of War, and shall be laid by him before the President for his approval or disapproval and orders in the case.

SEC. 1251. When a retiring board finds that an officer is incapacitated for active service, and that his incapacity is the result of an incident of service, and such decision is approved by the President, said officer shall be retired from active service and placed on the list of retired officers.

SEC. 1252. When the board finds that an officer is incapacitated for active service, and that his incapacity is not the result of any incident of service, and its decision is approved by the President, the officer shall be retired from active service, or wholly retired from the service, as the President may determine. The names of officers wholly retired from the service shall be omitted from the Army Register.

SEC. 1253. Except in cases where an officer may be retired by the President upon his own application, or by reason of his having served forty-five years, or of his being sixty-two years old, no officer shall be retired from active service, nor shall an officer, in any case, be wholly retired from the service, without a full and fair hearing before an Army retiring board, if, upon due summons, he demands it. — *Officers entitled to a hearing.*

3 Aug., 1861, s. 17, v. 12, p. 290.

SEC. 1254. Officers hereafter retired from active service shall be retired upon the actual rank held by them at the date of retirement. [See March 3, 1875.] — *Rank.*

10 June, 1872, v. 17, p. 378.
3 March, 1875, v. 18, p. 512.

SEC. 1255. Officers retired from active service shall be withdrawn from command and from the line of promotion. — *Status.*

3 Aug., 1861, s. 16, v. 12, p. 289.
17 July, 1862, s. 12, v. 12, p. 596.

SEC. 1256. Officers retired from active service shall be entitled to wear the uniform of the rank on which they may be retired. They shall continue to be borne on the Army Register, and shall be subject to the rules and articles of war, and to trial by general court-martial for any breach thereof. — *Rights and liabilities.*

3 Aug., 1861, s. 18, v. 12, p. 290.

SEC. 1257. When any officer in the line of promotion is retired from active service, the next officer in rank shall be promoted to his place, according to the established rules of the service; and the same rule of promotion shall be applied, successively, to the vacancies consequent upon such retirement. — *Vacancies.*

Ibid., s. 16.

SEC. 1274. Officers retired from active service shall receive seventy-five per centum of the pay of the rank upon which they are retired. [See *post*, March 3, 1875.] — *Title 14, Chap. 3.* *Pay.*

15 July, 1870, s. 24, v. 16, p. 320.
3 March, 1875, v. 18, p. 512.

NOTE.—An officer of the Army who is "retired from active service" is still in the military service of the United States, and, in addition to the percentage of pay of the rank on which he was retired, is entitled to the ten per cent. allowed by R. S. 1262, 1263 for each term of five years service.—Otto 105, 244, Tyler v. U. S. C. C. XVI, 223. See note under 1267, p. 116.

SEC. 1275. Officers wholly retired from the service shall be entitled to receive, upon their retirement, one year's pay and allowances of the highest rank held by them, whether by staff or regimental commission, at the time of their retirement. — *Wholly retired.*

3 Aug., 1861, s. 17, v. 12, p. 290.

That all officers of the Army who have been heretofore retired by reason of disability arising from wounds received in action shall be considered as retired upon the actual rank held by them, whether in the regular or volunteer service, at the time when such wound was received, and shall be borne on the retired list and receive pay hereafter accordingly; and this section shall be taken and construed to include those now borne on the retired list placed upon it on account of wounds received in action: *Provided*, That no part of the foregoing act shall apply to those officers who had been in service as commissioned officers twenty-five years at the date of their retirement; nor to those retired officers who had lost an arm or leg, or has an arm or leg permanently disabled by reason of resection, on account of wounds, or both eyes by reason of wounds received in battle; and every such officer now borne on the retired list shall be continued thereon notwithstanding the provisions of section two [one], chapter thirty-eight, act of March thirty, eighteen hundred and sixty-eight [§ 1223]: *And be it also provided*, That no retired officer shall be affected by this act, who has been retired or may hereafter be retired on the rank held by him at the time of his retirement; and that all acts or parts of acts inconsistent herewith be, and are hereby, repealed. — *March 3, 1875.* *Rank and pay under certain conditions.* *See OP. XV, 83, 199, and 407.*

3 March, 1875, s. 2, v. 18, p. 512.

NOTES.—Under section 1253 an officer is entitled to appear before the board (with counsel, if desired), and to introduce testimony of his own, and cross-examine the witnesses examined by the board, including the medical members of the board who may have taken part in the medical examination and have stated or reported to the board the result of the same. If the officer does not elect to appear before the board when summoned he waives the right to a hearing, and cannot properly take exception to a conclusion arrived at in his absence.—Winthrop's Digest, p. 432.

A retired officer in the Army may draw his pay as such, and may also draw the salary of a civil office which he may hold under the Government (not diplomatic or consular), assuming always that the duties of the civil office are performed under and by virtue of a commission appointing him to that office which he holds in addition to his rank as a retired officer.—Op. XV, p. 306, June 11, 1877, Devens. See Op. XV, p. 407, Dec. 11, 1877, on the subject of retired officers accepting positions in the diplomatic or consular service.

An officer, on being wholly retired, becomes a civilian, and can be readmitted to the service only by a new appointment. He cannot be reappointed to the retired list, but must first be appointed on the active list to a certain rank. None but a commissioned officer on the active list of the Army can be placed on the retired list. A civilian cannot.—Winthrop's Digest, p. 433. Op. XIV, 506.

The finding of a retiring board under sec. 1521, is in the nature of a recommendation, and until it is "approved by the President" no retirement can be ordered thereupon.—Winthrop, 431. It does not affect the authority to retire, that the incapacity of the officer may have resulted from a wound received by him while in the *volunteer* service before entering the regular army.—*Idem.*

Under section 1252 an officer may, in the discretion of the President, legally be retired by reason of incapacity resulting from habitual drunkenness.—Winthrop's Digest, p. 432.

Under section 1275 an officer wholly retired is entitled to receive a sum equal to the total of one year's pay, and all the pecuniary allowances of an officer of his rank. The fact of being under a sentence of suspension from rank and pay does not affect his right to receive such full sum upon the retirement.—Winthrop's Digest, 432.

*Held,* that a retired officer of the Army, though not *actively* employed, was an "officer in the employment of the Government," in the sense of this statute. Sec. 1782. Receiving compensation for services in matters in which the government is interested.—Winthrop's Digest, p. 434.

*Held,* that retired officers of the Army, though relieved in general from active military service, were nevertheless, as a part of the Army, properly exempt from the public obligations peculiar to civilians, and were, therefore, no more liable than officers on the active list to be required to serve on juries. The question, however, of exemption is one for the determination of the courts. *Advised,* in such a case, that the officer appear before the court, in compliance with the summons, and there urge to the judge the objection arising from his military status to his serving on a civil jury.—Winthrop's Digest, 433.

## PAY, RATIONS, AND MILEAGE OF THE MARINE CORPS.

Sec.
1612. Pay of officers and enlisted men.
1613. Pay of the band.

Sec.
1614. Deduction for hospitals.
1615. Rations.

**Title 15, Chap. 9.**

*Pay of Marine Corps.*

SEC. 1612. The officers of the Marine Corps shall be entitled to receive the same pay and allowances, and the enlisted men shall be entitled to receive the same pay and bounty for re-enlisting, as are or may be provided by or in pursuance of law for the officers and enlisted men of like grades in the infantry of the Army. [See tables, *post.*]

30 June, 1834, s. 5, v. 4, p. 713.
5 Aug., 1854, s. 1, v. 10, p. 586.

*Marine band.*

SEC. 1613. The marines who compose the corps of musicians known as the "Marine band" shall be entitled to receive at the rate of four dollars a month, each, in addition to their pay as non-commissioned officers, musicians, or privates of the Marine Corps, so long as they shall perform, by order of the Secretary of the Navy, or other superior officer, on the Capitol grounds or the President's grounds.

18 Aug., 1856, s. 5, v. 11, p. 118.
5 Aug., 1854, s. 1, v. 10, p. 586.

*Deduction for hospitals.*

SEC. 1614. The Secretary of the Navy shall deduct from the pay due each of the officers and enlisted men of the Marine Corps at the rate of twenty cents per month for every officer and marine, to be applied to the fund for Navy hospitals.

2 March, 1790, s. 2, v. 1, p. 729.
26 Feb., 1811, s. 1, v. 2, p. 650.

*Rations of enlisted men.*

SEC. 1615. The non-commissioned officers, privates, and musicians of the Marine Corps shall, each, be entitled to receive one Navy ration daily.

11 July, 1798, s. 2, v. 1, p. 595.
1 July, 1797, s. 6, v. 1, p. 524.

PAY, RATIONS, AND MILEAGE OF MARINE CORPS.   115

*Pay-table of officers as per sections following.*

| Grades. | Pay per annum. |
|---|---|
| Colonel commandant | $3,500 |
| Colonel | 3,500 |
| Lieutenant-colonel | 3,000 |
| Major (staff and line) | 2,500 |
| Captain and assistant quartermaster | 2,000 |
| Captain | 1,800 |
| First lieutenant | 1,500 |
| Second lieutenant | 1,400 |

NOTE.—All officers below the rank of brigadier-general are entitled to ten per centum in addition to their current yearly pay as given above, for each and every period of five years' service: *Provided*, The total amount of such increase shall not exceed forty per centum of their current yearly pay: *And provided further*, That the pay of a colonel shall not exceed $4,500 per annum, and that of a lieutenant-colonel $4,000 per annum. [Sec. 1267, R. S.] Officers on the retired list are entitled to seventy-five per centum of pay (salary and increase) of their rank, but no increase accrues for time subsequent to date of retirement. [Sec. 1254, RETIREMENT.]

## Statutes relating to the Army which apply to the Marine Corps.

### PAY OF OFFICERS.

Sec.
1261. Rates of pay.
1262. Service pay.
1263. Not to exceed forty per centum on yearly pay.
—— Longevity pay and retirement.
1264. Brevets.

Sec.
1265. Pay during absence.
1267. Maximum of colonel's and lieutenant-colonel's pay.
1268. To be paid monthly.
1269. Allowances.

SEC. 1261. The officers of the Army shall be entitled to the pay herein stated after their respective designations: **Title 14, Chap. 3.**

* * * * * *

Colonel, three thousand five hundred dollars a year. [See § 1267.] **Rates of pay.**
Lieutenant-colonel, three thousand dollars a year. [See § 1267.]
Major, two thousand five hundred dollars a year.

* * * * * *

Captain, mounted, two thousand dollars a year.
Captain, not mounted, eighteen hundred dollars a year.
First lieutenant, mounted, sixteen hundred dollars a year.
First lieutenant, not mounted, fifteen hundred dollars a year.
Second lieutenant, mounted, fifteen hundred dollars a year.
Second lieutenant, not mounted, fourteen hundred dollars a year.

2 March, 1867, s. 7, v. 14, p. 423.
15 June, 1870, s. 24, v. 16, p. 320.
24 July, 1876, v. 19, p. 97.

NOTE.—Officers are not "mounted," so as to entitle them to the "pay, emoluments, and allowances of cavalry officers of the same grade," when they are furnished by the Government with horses and equipments.—C. C. XVII, 132.

SEC. 1262. There shall be allowed and paid to each commissioned officer below the rank of brigadier-general, including chaplains and others having assimilated rank or pay, ten per centum of their current yearly pay for each term of five years of service. [See June 18, 1878, and June 30, 1882.] **Service pay.**

15 July, 1870, s. 24, v. 16, p. 320.

NOTE.—An officer's longevity pay is to be computed, not from the time of his entering West Point, but from the time when he was commissioned second lieutenant.—C. C. XVI, 262. *Babbitt's* case.

SEC. 1263. The total amount of such increase for length of service shall in no case exceed forty per centum on the yearly pay of the grade as provided by-law. [See June 18, 1878, and June 30, 1882.]

*Idem.*

On and after the passage of this act, all officers of the Army of the United States who have served as officers in the volunteer forces during the war of the rebellion, or as enlisted men in the armies of the United States, regular or volunteer, shall be, and are hereby, credited with the **June 18, 1878. Longevity pay, and retirement.**

**116**  PAY, RATIONS, AND MILEAGE OF MARINE CORPS.

full time they may have served as such officers and as such enlisted men in computing their service for longevity pay and retirement.

18 June, 1878, s. 7, v. 20, p. 145.

**June 30, 1882.**
*Computing of longevity pay.*

The actual time of service in the Army or Navy, or both, shall be allowed all officers in computing their pay: *Provided*, That from and after the first day of July, eighteen hundred and eighty-two, the ten per centum increase for length of service allowed to certain officers by section twelve hundred and sixty-two of the Revised Statutes shall be computed on the yearly pay of the grade fixed by sections twelve hundred and sixty-one and twelve hundred and seventy-four of the Revised Statutes. [Sec. 1274, RETIREMENT.]

30 June, 1882, chap. 254, s. 1, P. E. L., p. 118.

**Title 14, Chap. 3.**
*Brevets.*

SEC. 1264. Brevets conferred upon commissioned officers shall not entitle them to any increase of pay.

3 March, 1863, v. 12, p. 758.
3 March, 1865, s. 9, v. 13, p. 488.

**Pay during absence.**

SEC. 1265. Officers when absent on account of sickness or wounds, or lawfully absent from duty and waiting orders, shall receive full pay; when absent with leave, for other causes, full pay during such absence not exceeding in the aggregate thirty days in one year, and half-pay during such absence exceeding thirty days in one year. When absent without leave, they shall forfeit all pay during such absence, unless the absence is excused as unavoidable. [See 29 July, 1876, *post*.]

3 Aug., 1861, s. 20, v. 12, p. 290.   15 July, 1870, s. 24, v. 16, p. 320.
3 March, 1863, s. 31, v. 12, p. 736.   8 May, 1874, v. 18, p. 43.
20 June, 1864, s. 11, v. 13, p. 145.   29 July, 1876, v. 19, p. 102.

**29 July, 1876.**
*Pay when absent.*

All officers on duty shall be allowed, in the discretion of the Secretary of War, sixty days' leave of absence without deduction of pay or allowance: *Provided*, That the same be taken once in two years: *And provided further*, That the leave of absence may be extended to three months, if taken once only in three years, or four months if taken only once in four years.

29 July, 1876, v. 19, p. 202.
8 May, 1874, v. 18, p. 43.

NOTES.—This act, taken in connection with section 24 of the act of July 15, 1870, continued to Army officers on leave of absence (during the period for which such leave may be granted them thereunder "without deduction of pay or allowances") *quarters in kind*, but it did not authorize an allowance of commutation therefor. [See next note.]—Op. XVI, p. 619, Jan. 16. 1879.  Phillips.

Where an officer, to whom leave of absence "without deduction of pay or allowances" has been granted, is at the time he takes his leave entitled to the allowance of commutation for quarters, this allowance must be deemed to be continued to him, by force of that provision, whilst he is on leave of absence, though for a period not exceeding that for which the leave was granted thereunder.—Op. XVI, p. 577; Nov. 15, 1880.  Devens.

Where a military officer is ordered to the headquarters of a department to await further orders, and pursuant to the order remains there for a long period performing no duty, he is nevertheless entitled to quarters or commutation of quarters.—C. C. XIV, p. 148.  Lippitt v. U. S.

**Title 14, Chap. 3.**
*Maximum of colonel's and lieutenant-colonel's pay.*

SEC. 1267. In no case shall the pay of a colonel exceed four thousand five hundred dollars a year, or the pay of a lieutenant-colonel exceed four thousand dollars a year.

15 July, 1870, s. 24, v. 16, p. 320.

NOTE.—A lieutenant-colonel retired is entitled to three-fourths of what he was entitled to receive when retired, and not three-fourths of allowances which he was debarred from receiving under this section.—C. C. X, p. 283.  *Robert's case.*

**To be paid monthly.**

SEC. 1268. The sums hereinbefore allowed shall be paid in monthly payments by the paymaster.

*Ibid.*

**Allowances.**

SEC. 1269. No allowances shall be made to officers in addition to their pay except as hereinafter provided. [See MILEAGE, QUARTERS, &C.]

*Ibid.*

## PAY, RATIONS, AND MILEAGE OF MARINE CORPS.

PAY-TABLE OF NON-COMMISSIONED OFFICERS, &C., AS PER SECTIONS FOLLOWING.

| Grades. | First period of 5 years' service. | Second period of 5 years. | Third period of 5 years. | Fourth period of 5 years. | Fifth period of 5 years. |
|---|---|---|---|---|---|
| | Per mo. | Per mo. | Per mo. | Per mo. | Per mo. |
| Sergeant-major | $26 | $27 | $28 | $29 | $30 |
| Quartermaster-sergeant | 23 | 27 | 28 | 29 | 30 |
| Drum-major | 22 | 26 | 27 | 28 | 29 |
| First sergeant | 22 | 26 | 27 | 28 | 29 |
| Sergeant | 17 | 21 | 22 | 23 | 24 |
| Corporal | 15 | 19 | 20 | 21 | 22 |
| Drummers and fifers | 13 | 17 | 18 | 19 | 20 |
| Privates | 13 | 17 | 18 | 19 | 20 |
| Leader of the band | 79 | 81 | 82 | 83 | 84 |
| Musician, first class | 38 | 40 | 41 | 42 | 43 |
| Musician, second class | 24 | 26 | 27 | 28 | 29 |
| Musician, third class | 21 | 23 | 24 | 25 | 26 |

All enlisted men, except musicians of the band, serving on a first period of five years' service, are entitled to one dollar per month for the third year, two dollars per month for the fourth year, and three dollars per month for the fifth year's service, in addition to the sums given in the first column above, which additional amounts are retained until expiration of service and paid only upon final settlement and *honorable* discharge.

One dollar per month is retained from all enlisted men (except the Marine Band) serving under a re-enlistment. This retained pay is not included in the above table, and is to be credited and paid only upon final settlement and *honorable* discharge from service. [As per sections below.]

### Statutes relating to the Army which apply to the Marine Corps.

Sec.
1273. Mileage.
1280. Pay of enlisted men.
1281. Additional pay.
1282. Re-enlistment pay.
1283. Service-pay of men already in service.
1284. Re-enlistment.
1285. Certificate of merit.

Sec.
1286. Non-commissioned officers of Mexican war.
1287. Extra duty.
1288. During captivity.
1289. Travel-pay to officers.
1290. Travel-pay to soldiers.
1291. Soldiers' pay not assignable.

### MILEAGE.

SEC. 1273. When any officer travels under orders, and is not furnished transportation by the Quartermaster's Department, or on a conveyance belonging to or chartered by the United States, or on any railroad on which troops and supplies are entitled to be transported free of charge, he shall be allowed eight cents a mile, and no more, for each mile actually traveled under such order, distances to be calculated by the shortest usually traveled route; and no payment shall be made to any officer except by a paymaster of the Army. [See 3 March, 1883, *post.*]

*Title 14, Chap. 3.*
*Mileage*

    15 July, 1870, s. 24, v. 16, p. 320.
    16 June, 1874, v. 18, p. 72.
    3 March, 1875, v. 18, p. 452.
    24 July, 1876, v. 19, p. 100.

From and after the passage of this act mileage of officers of the Army shall be computed over the shortest usually traveled routes between the points named in the order, and the necessity for such travel in the military service shall be certified to by the officer issuing the order and stated in said order.

*March 3, 1883.*
*Computation of mileage, &c.*

    3 March, 1883, s. 1, P. E. L., p. 456.

> NOTES.—If an officer on leave of absence be ordered to temporary duty at a place where he happens to be, so that the order involves no traveling to the place of temporary duty, and he be kept there until after his leave of absence expires and then ordered to his proper station, he is not entitled to mileage under General Orders 97 of 1876.—C. C. XIV, 272, Barr *v.* U. S.

Where an officer has received but not yet accepted leave of absence from the War Department, is ordered by his commanding officer to convey prisoners to another post, his leave of absence is to that extent suspended, and he is entitled to mileage from his post to the place of performance and back.—C. C. XV, 264, Andrew v. U. S.

An officer's "station" means his permanent station, the place of performance of his military duties, and not a place to which he was temporarily ordered for a special duty and at which he accepted his leave of absence. An officer's station cannot be changed by his being ordered to perform a temporary duty while on leave of absence.—*Idem.*

## PAY, ETC., OF ENLISTED MEN.

**Pay of enlisted men.**  SEC. 1280. The monthly pay of the following enlisted men of the Army shall, during their first term of enlistment, be as follows, with the contingent additions thereto, hereinafter provided:

Sergeant-majors of * * * infantry, twenty-three dollars.
Quartermaster-sergeants * * * infantry, twenty-three dollars.
Principal musicians of * * infantry, twenty-two dollars.
Sergeants of * * * infantry, seventeen dollars.
Corporals of * * infantry, fifteen dollars.
Musicians, drummers and fifers, * * infantry, thirteen dollars.
Privates of * * * infantry, thirteen dollars.

15 May, 1872, s. 1, v. 17, p. 116.
27 Feb., 1877, chap. 69, v. 19, p. 243.

**Additional pay.**  SEC. 1281. To the rates of pay stated in the preceding section one dollar per month shall be added for the third year of enlistment, one dollar more per month for the fourth year, and one dollar more per month for the fifth year, making in all three dollars' increase per month for the last year of the first enlistment of each enlisted man named in said section. But this increase shall be considered as retained pay, and shall not be paid to the soldier until his discharge from the service, and shall be forfeited unless he serves honestly and faithfully to the date of discharge.

15 May, 1872, s. 2, v. 17, p. 116.

**Re-enlistment pay.**  SEC. 1282. All enlisted men mentioned in section twelve hundred and eighty, who, having been honorably discharged, have re-enlisted or shall re-enlist within one month thereafter, shall, after five years' service, including their first enlistment, be paid at the rate allowed in said section to those serving in the fifth year of their first enlistment: *Provided*, That one dollar per month shall be retained from the pay of the re-enlisted men, of whatever grade, named in section twelve hundred and eighty-one during the whole period of their re-enlistment, to be paid to the soldier on his discharge, but to be forfeited unless he shall have served honestly and faithfully to the date of discharge

4 Aug., 1854, s. 2, v. 10, p. 575.
15 May, 1872, s. 3, v. 17, p. 116.
3 March, 1875, s. 10, v. 18, p. 419.

**Service pay of men already in service.**  SEC. 1283. Enlisted men, now in the service, shall receive the rates of pay established in this chapter according to the length of their service. [See act of June 18, 1878, p. 115.]

15 May, 1872, s. 4, v. 17, p. 117.

NOTE.—The 10th section of the act of March 3, 1875, ch. 131, v. 18, p. 402, provides that the enlisted musicians of the band shall have the benefits as to pay, arising from re-enlistments and length of service, applicable to other enlisted men of the Army.

**Re-enlistment.**  SEC. 1284. Every soldier who, having been honorably discharged, re-enlists within one month thereafter, shall be further entitled, after five years' service, including his first enlistment, to receive, for the period of five years next thereafter, two dollars per month in addition to the ordinary pay of his grade; and for each successive period of five years of service, so long as he shall remain continuously in the Army, a further sum of one dollar per month. The past continuous service, of soldiers now in the Army, shall be taken into account, and shall entitle such soldier to additional pay according to this rule; but services rendered prior to August fourth, eighteen hundred and fifty-four, shall in no case be accounted as more than one enlistment.

4 Aug., 1854, s. 2, v. 10, p. 575.
15 May, 1872, s. 4, v. 17, p. 117.

**Certificate of merit.**  SEC. 1285. A certificate of merit granted to a private soldier by the President for distinguished services shall entitle him to additional pay, at the rate of two dollars per month, while he remains continuously in the service; and such certificate of merit granted to a private soldier who served in the war with Mexico shall entitle him to such additional pay, although he may not have remained continuously in the service.

3 March, 1847, s. 17, v. 9, p. 186.
4 Aug., 1854, s. 3, v. 10, p. 575.

SEC. 1286. Non-commissioned officers who served in the war with Mexico, and have been recommended by the commanding officers of their regiments for promotion by brevet to the lowest grade of commissioned officer, but have not received such recommended promotion, shall be entitled to additional pay at the rate of two dollars per month, although they may not have remained continuously in the service.  *Non-commissioned officers of Mexican war.*

*Ibid.*

SEC. 1287. When soldiers are detailed for employment as artificers or laborers in the construction of permanent military works, public roads, or other constant labor of not less than ten days' duration, they shall receive, in addition to their regular pay, the following compensation: Privates working as artificers, and non-commissioned officers employed as overseers of such work, not exceeding one overseer for twenty men, thirty-five cents per day, and privates employed as laborers, twenty cents per day. This allowance of extra pay shall not apply to the troops of the Ordnance Department.  *Extra duty.*

13 July, 1866, s. 7, v. 14, p. 93.
1 Feb., 1873, v. 17, p. 422.
See Ops. II, 706; III, 116; IV, 325; and X, 472.

SEC. 1288. Every non-commissioned officer and private of the Regular Army, and every officer, non-commissioned officer, and private of any militia or volunteer corps in the service of the United States who is captured by the enemy, shall be entitled to receive during his captivity, notwithstanding the expiration of his term of service, the same pay, subsistence, and allowance to which he may be entitled while in the actual service of the United States; but this provision shall not be construed to entitle any prisoner of war of such militia corps to any pay or compensation after the date of his parole, except the traveling expenses allowed by law.  *During captivity.*

30 March, 1814, s. 14, v. 3, p. 115.

NOTES.—This section does not extend to one who was not in the discharge of his duties at the time of his capture, and who contributed to the disaster culpably.—C. C. IV, p. 209. *Phelps' case.*
The sentence of a court-martial, including a forfeiture of all pay due at the time of trial, or to become due thereafter, precludes an officer from a right to receive pay after trial and during his captivity, under the act of March 30, 1814, Sec. 1288, Revised Statutes.

SEC. 1289. When an officer is discharged from the service, except by way of punishment for an offense, he shall be allowed transportation and subsistence from the place of his discharge to the place of his residence at the time of his appointment, or to the place of his original muster into the service. The Government may furnish the same in kind, but in case it shall not do so, he shall be allowed travel-pay and commutation of subsistence, according to his rank, for such time as may be sufficient for him to travel from the place of discharge to the place of his residence, or original muster into service, computed at the rate of one day for every twenty miles.  *Travel-pay to officers.*

11 Jan., 1812, s. 22, v. 2, p. 674.
29 Jan., 1813, s. 15, v. 2, p. 796.
20 June, 1864, s. 8, v. 13, p. 145.
27 Feb., 1877, v. 19, p. 244.

SEC. 1290. When a soldier is discharged from the service, except by way of punishment for an offense, he shall be allowed transportation and subsistence from the place of his discharge to the place of his enlistment, enrollment, or original muster into the service. The Government may furnish the same in kind, but in case it shall not do so, he shall be allowed travel-pay and commutation of subsistence for such time as may be sufficient for him to travel from the place of discharge to the place of his enlistment, enrollment, or original muster into the service, computed at the rate of one day for every twenty miles.  *Travel-pay to soldiers.*

*Ibid.*

**Soldiers' pay not assignable.**

SEC. 1291. No assignment of pay by a non-commissioned officer or private, previous to his discharge, shall be valid.

8 May, 1792, s. 4, v. 1, p. 280.

*Held,* That the provision in section 1291, that "no assignment of pay by a non-commissioned officer or private previous to his discharge shall be valid," does not preclude a soldier so situated as to be unable to receive his pay in person from giving an order to another person to receive and receipt for the same *for* him, and that a soldier in the custody of the civil authorities under a criminal charge might legally be paid the amount of pay due him upon an order given by him for the same to the attorney employed to defend him; also, that the pay due an insane officer or soldier might legally be rendered to a person duly appointed as his guardian under the State laws.—Winthrop's Digest, 369.

## FORAGE, FUEL, QUARTERS.

Sec.
1269. Allowances limited.
1270. Fuel, forage, &c., in kind.
—. Commutation for forage not to be paid.
1271. Forage, allowance in kind.
1272. Forage, to whom furnished.
—. Allowance of forage specified.

Sec.
—. No discrimination east of the Mississippi.
—. Fuel, allowance, &c.
—. Quarters for officers.
—. Commutation for quarters.
—. No allowance of claims for servants' quarters.

Title 14, Chap. 3.
**Allowances limited.**

SEC. 1269. No allowances shall be made to officers in addition to their pay except as hereinafter provided.

15 July, 1870, s. 24, v. 16, p. 320.

**Fuel, quarters, and forage.**

SEC. 1270. Fuel, quarters, and forage may be furnished in kind to officers by the Quartermaster's Department according to law and regulations. *Provided however,* That when forage in kind cannot be furnished by the proper departments, then and in all such cases, officers entitled to forage may commute the same according to existing regulations: *Provided further,* That officers of the Army and of volunteers assigned to duty which requires them to be mounted shall, during the time they are employed on such duty, receive the pay, emoluments, and allowances of cavalry officers of the same grade respectively. [See acts of June 18, 1878.]

15 July, 1870, s. 24, v. 16, p. 320.
27 Feb., 1877, v. 19, p. 243.

**Commutation for forage not to be paid.**

It is provided in the naval appropriation acts, approved August 5, 1882, and March 3, 1883, which make appropriations for the purchase of forage for the Marine Corps, "That no commutation for forage shall be paid."

**Forage in kind.**

SEC. 1271. Forage in kind may be furnished to officers by the Quartermaster's Department as follows: [See 18 June, 1878.]

17 July, 1862, s. 2, v. 12, p. 594.
9 April, 1864, s. 1, v. 13, p. 46.
15 July, 1870, s. 24, v. 16, p. 320.

**Forage. To whom furnished.**

SEC. 1272. Forage shall be allowed to officers only for horses authorized by law, and actually kept by them in service when on duty and at the place where they are on duty. [See 18 June, 1878.]

24 Ap., 1816, s. 12, v. 3, p. 299.
17 July, 1862, s. 1, v. 12, p. 594.

18 June, 1878.
**Allowance of forage.**

And forage in kind may be furnished to the officers of the Army, by the Quartermaster's Department, only for horses owned and actually kept by such officers in the performance of their official military duties when on duty with troops in the field or at such military posts west of the Mississippi River [See post] as may be from time to time designated by the Secretary of War, and not otherwise, as follows:

To a colonel, two horses.
To a lieutenant-colonel, two horses.
To a major, two horses.
To a captain (mounted), two horses.
To a lieutenant (mounted), two horses.

\* \* \*

18 June, 1878, s. 8, v. 20, p. 150.

May 4, 1880.
**No discrimination east of the Mississippi.**

*Provided,* That there shall be no discrimination in the issue of forage against officers serving east of the Mississippi River, provided they are required by law to be mounted, and actually keep and own their animals.

24 Feb., 1881, v. 21, p. 346.
4 May, 1880, v. 21, p. 111.

## FORAGE, FUEL, QUARTERS. 121

Allowance of or commutation for fuel to commissioned officers is hereby prohibited; but fuel may be furnished to the officers of the Army by the Quartermaster's Department, for the actual use of such officers only, at the rate of three dollars per cord for standard oak wood, or at an equivalent rate for other kinds of fuel, according to the regulations now in existence: * * *

18 June, 1878.

Fuel.

18 June, 1878, s. 8, v. 20, p. 150.

NOTE.—The provisions of sec. 8, act June 18, 1878, giving to Army officers the privilege of purchasing fuel at the rate of $3 per cord for standard oak wood, do not extend to retired officers. A cord of hard wood is made, under the regulations, the standard by which other grades of fuel are tested. This section authorizes the sale only of the quantity of other fuel for $3, which is made the equivalent of a cord of standard wood.—Op. XVI, 92, Devens, July 18, 1878.

That at all posts and stations where there are public quarters belonging to the United States, officers may be furnished with quarters in kind in such public quarters, and not elsewhere, by the Quartermaster's Department, assigning to the officers of each grade, respectively, such number of rooms as is now allowed to such grade by the rules and regulations of the Army; *Provided*, That at places where there are no public quarters, commutation therefor may be paid by the Pay Department to the officer entitled to the same at a rate not exceeding *twelve* dollars per room per month. * * * [See notes, p. 116.]

18 June, 1878.

Quarters for officers.

Rate of commutation.

18 June, 1878, s. 9, v. 20, p. 151.
23 June, 1879, v. 21, p. 31.

NOTE.—A military post or station where there are public quarters for officers, but insufficient for the accommodation of all the officers, is, in regard to those officers who are necessarily excluded from the public quarters, a place where there are "no public quarters," within the meaning of the *proviso* in sec. 9, act of June 18, 1878, and the officers thus excluded may be allowed commutation for quarters.—Op. XVI, 611, Aug 7, 1878.

That no allowance shall be made for claims for quarters for servants heretofore or hereafter. * * *

23 June, 1879.

No allowance for claims for servants' quarters.

23 June, 1879, s. 1, v. 21, p. 30.

# PART III.

## ACCOUNTS, ACCOUNTING AND DISBURSING OFFICERS, PUBLIC MONEY AND PROPERTY, NAVY DEPARTMENT AND BUREAUS, CIVIL SERVICE, ETC.

Accounting officers and accounts.
Advertising.
Appropriations and estimates.
Attorney-General and Department of Justice.
Attorneys and agents of the government.
Civil service—Department employés and regulations.
Claims and claim agents.
Court of Claims.
Contingent funds.

Debts due by and to the United States.
Disbursing officers and agents—Checks, drafts coins, and currency.
Distress warrants.
Navy Department and Bureaus.
Public documents, public printing and binding.
Public or Department records.
Public property and public buildings.
Statutes.

# ACCOUNTING OFFICERS AND ACCOUNTS.

See also DISBURSING OFFICERS and AGENTS.

| Sec. | Sec. |
|---|---|
| 191. Certified balances. | 274. Power of Second Comptroller as to arrears of pay. |
| 236. Public accounts to be settled in the Department of the Treasury. | 277. Duties of the Fourth Auditor. |
| 237. Commencement of the fiscal year. | 283. Manner of keeping accounts of Departments of War and the Navy. |
| 250. Settlement of accounts within fiscal year. | 297. Auditors may administer oaths. |
| 260. Reports upon appropriations for Departments of War and Navy. | 3673. Warrants, drawing and countersigning. |
| 273. Duties of the Second Comptroller. | 3675. Warrants, form of drawing and how charged |

SEC. 191. The balances which may from time to time be stated by the Auditor and certified to the heads of Departments by the Commissioner of Customs, or the Comptrollers of the Treasury, upon the settlement of public accounts, shall not be changed or modified by the heads of Departments, but shall be conclusive upon the executive branch of the Government, and be subject to revision only by Congress or the proper courts. The head of the proper Department, before signing a warrant for any balance certified to him by a Comptroller, may, however, submit to such Comptroller any facts in his judgment affecting the correctness of such balance, but the decision of the Comptroller thereon shall be final and conclusive, as hereinbefore provided.

Title 4.

Certified balances.

30 March, 1868, s. 1, v. 15, p. 54.

NOTES.—If the Auditor and Comptroller certify a balance due from a public officer or contractor, the latter may refuse payment, and when the United States bring suit to recover, the defense may be interposed and the matter undergo judicial investigation and scrutiny. So if an officer or creditor claim a larger amount than the accounting officers allow, he may refuse it and sue in the Court of Claims or apply to Congress for relief.—C. C., V, 61.

The balances, as certified to, are subject to revision by Congress or the proper courts. The Court of Claims is a proper court.—C. C., V, p. 5.

The head of a Department, before signing a warrant for any balance certified by a Comptroller, may submit to the latter any facts which in his judgment affect the correctness of such balance; but the decision of the Comptroller thereon is final and conclusive upon the executive branch of the Government, and subject to revision by Congress or the proper courts only.—Op. XIV, 65, Williams, July 22, 1872. See also Op. XII, 43; XIII, 6.

SEC. 236. All claims and demands whatever by the United States or against them, and all accounts whatever in which the United States are concerned, either as debtors or as creditors, shall be settled and adjusted in the Department of the Treasury.

Title 7, Chap. 1.

Public accounts. Where to be adjusted.

3 March, 1817, s. 2, v. 3, p. 366.

NOTES.—Settlements made of the accounts of individuals by the accounting officers, appointed by law, are final and conclusive so far as the Executive Departments are concerned. Aggrieved parties can apply to Congress.—Op. I, 624; II, 302; V, 176.

Adjusted accounts should not, as a rule, be re-opened without authority of law.—Op. II, 625, 640; III, 148, 461, 521; IV, 378; X, 231; XI, 129.

If duly settled, adjusted, and closed by the proper officers, upon a full knowledge of all the facts, and no errors in calculation have been made, an account cannot be re-opened without express authority of law.—Op. XII, 386; Browning, Ap. 26, 1868. See also Op. IX, 505.

According to the general practice of the Treasury, accounts are never closed; and in neither the legal nor mercantile sense of the term is an officer's account with the Treasury ever "finally adjusted."—C. C., XIV, 114.

The accounting officers in settling accounts and claims have a right to adopt the report of a committee in Congress as establishing the principles which are to govern them in the examination thereof. A bill is considered part of a report, and its passage a virtual adoption thereof. The report is in the light of a preamble to the law.—Op. I, 596.

There is a difference between the construction placed upon an act by *individual* members in debate and the opinion of the committee having the matter in charge. Proper to look into the report of the committee in giving construction to ambiguous language in an act.—Op. XIV, 624, Williams, February 21, 1874.

The rejection of a claim, in whole or in part, by the accounting officers leaves

125

126 ACCOUNTING OFFICERS AND ACCOUNTS.

the party free to pursue his remedy at law, viz, an action in the Court of Claims although he may have accepted the portion allowed.—C. C., XVII, 288.

A pure matter of account belongs to the Department; does not belong to the Court of Claims until it is within the range of judicial cognizance. Accounting Bureaus were organized to settle accounts; the Court of Claims was established to adjudicate claims. Unless a case becomes such as to "involve disputed facts or controverted questions of law," it is an account; when it does it is a claim.—C. C., V. 5, p. 293.

**Commencement of the fiscal year.**
SEC. 237. The fiscal year of the Treasury of the United States in all matters of accounts, receipts, expenditures, estimates, and appropriations, * * shall commence on the first day of July in each year; and all accounts of receipts and expenditures required by law to be published annually shall be prepared and published for the fiscal year as thus established. * *

26 Aug., 1842, ss. 1, 2, v. 5, p. 536.
8 May, 1872, s. 1, v. 17, p. 61.
3 March, 1873, s. 1, v. 17, p. 486.

**[Title 7, Chap. 2.**
**Settlement of accounts within fiscal year.**
SEC. 250. The Secretary of the Treasury shall cause all accounts or the expenditure of public money to be settled within each fiscal year, except where the distance of the places where such expenditure occurs may be such as to make further time necessary; and in respect to expenditures at such places, the Secretary of the Treasury, with the assent of the President, shall establish fixed periods at which a settlement shall be required.

3 March, 1817, s. 13, v. 3, p. 368.

NOTES.—Fractions of a day are not noticed for legal purposes. If the law authorizes a certain thing to be done within a certain number of days, the *first* day is excluded from the calculation. Divisions of a day excluded in public proceedings.—Op. IX, 132, Black, March 10, 1858.
Whole quarter of a year means a whole fiscal quarter in accordance with the division of a year used in the Treasury Department from its organization.—Op. III, p. 156, Butler, Oct. 27, 1836.
Two years from and after the 4th of March, 1836, includes the 4th of March, 1838.—Op. III, p. 157, Butler, Nov. 3, 1836.
"From and after," "On and after," are equivalents of each other.—Op. XIV, p. 542, Williams, March 10, 1875.

**Reports upon appropriations for Departments of War and Navy.**
SEC. 260. The Secretary of the Treasury shall lay before Congress at the commencement of each regular session, accompanying his annual statement of the public expenditure, the reports which may be made to him by the Auditors charged with the examination of the accounts of the Department of War and the Department of the Navy, respectively, showing the application of the money appropriated for those Departments for the preceding year.

3 March, 1817, s. 6, v. 3, p. 367.

**Title 7, Chap. 3.**
**Duties of the Second Comptroller.**
SEC. 273. It shall be the duty of the Second Comptroller:
First. To examine all accounts settled by the Second, Third, and Fourth Auditors, and certify the balances arising thereon to the Secretary of the Department in which the expenditure has been incurred.
Second. To countersign all warrants drawn by the Secretaries of War and of the Navy, which shall be warranted by law. [See § 3673, APPROPRIATIONS.]
Third. To report to the Secretaries of War and of the Navy the official forms to be issued in the different offices for disbursing the public money in those Departments, and the manner and form of keeping and stating the accounts of the persons employed therein.
Fourth. To superintend the preservation of the public accounts subject to his revision.

3 March, 1817, s. 9, v. 3, p. 367.
7 May, 1822, s. 3, v. 3, p. 689.

**Power of Second Comptroller as to arrears of pay.**
SEC. 274. The Second Comptroller may prescribe rules to govern the payment of arrears of pay due to any petty officer, seaman, or other person not an officer, on board any vessel in the employ of the United States, which has been sunk or destroyed, in case of the death of such petty officer, seaman, or person, to the person designated by law to receive the same.

4 July, 1864, s. 3, v. 13, p. 390.

ACCOUNTING OFFICERS AND ACCOUNTS. 127

SEC. 277. The duties of the Auditors shall be: **Title 7, Chap. 4.**

\* \* \* \* \* \* \*

Fifth. The Fourth Auditor shall receive and examine all accounts accruing in the Navy Department or relative thereto, and all accounts relating to Navy pensions ; and, after examination of such accounts, he shall certify the balances, and shall transmit such accounts, with the vouchers and certificate, to the Second Comptroller for his decision thereon. *Duties of the Auditors.*

3 March, 1817, s. 4, v. 3, p. 366.  8 June, 1872, s. 22, v. 17, p. 28.
20 July, 1868, s. 1, v. 15, p. 106.  3 March, 1849, s. 3, v. 9, p. 395, 415.
28 July, 1866, s. 8, v. 14, p. 327.  30 June, 1864, s. 2, v. 13, p. 223.

NOTES.—Every account falling within the scope of sec. 277 R. S. must undergo, successively, an examination by the Auditor and the Comptroller; the action of the former is primary altogether and indefinite ; that of the latter wholly revisory and final. "Settled," equivalent in meaning to "finally acted on." A certificate to the Department must be accompanied by the auditor's action; need not be incorporated in the certificate.—Op. XV, 139, Taft, Aug. 2, 1876. See also 192.

The President cannot interpose in the settlement of accounts by the accounting officers and direct credits to be allowed ; cannot interfere legally with the duties belonging to the accounting officers ; an appeal does not lie to him from the determination of the accounting officers acting in the sphere of their duties; he cannot interfere in their decisions ; he does not possess the power to examine into the correctness of their settlements for the purpose of correcting any errors they may have committed.—Op. I, 624, 636, 678, 706, Wirt; II, 507, 544, Taney; v. 630, Crittenden.

SEC. 283. The Auditors charged with the examination of the accounts of the Departments of War and of the Navy, shall keep all accounts of the receipts and expenditures of the public money in regard to those Departments, and of all debts due to the United States on moneys advanced relative to those Departments; shall receive from the Second Comptroller the accounts which shall have been finally adjusted, and shall preserve such accounts, with their vouchers and certificates, and record all requisitions drawn by the Secretaries of those Departments, the examination of the accounts of which has been assigned to them. They shall annually, on the first Monday in November, severally report to the Secretary of the Treasury the application of the money appropriated for the Department of War and the Department of the Navy, and they shall make such reports on the business assigned to them as the Secretaries of those Departments may deem necessary and require. *Manner of keeping accounts of Departments of War and the Navy.*

3 March, 1817, ss. 5, 6, v. 3, p. 367.

[EXAMINATION OF ACCOUNTS UNDER EXHAUSTED APPROPRIATIONS. *See* APPROPRIATIONS.]

[ADJUSTMENT OF LIABILITIES WITH "GENERAL ACCOUNT AT ADVANCES." *See* APPROPRIATIONS.]

SEC. 297. The several Auditors are empowered to administer oaths to witnesses in any case in which they may deem it necessary for the due examination of the accounts with which they shall be charged. *Auditors may administer oaths.*

3 March, 1817, s. 12, v. 3, p. 368.
8 June, 1872, s. 24, v. 17, p. 288.

SEC. 3673. All moneys appropriated for the use of the War and Navy Departments shall be drawn from the Treasury, by warrants of the Secretary of the Treasury, upon the requisitions of the Secretaries of those Departments, respectively, countersigned by the Second Comptroller of the Treasury, and registered by the proper Auditor. [March 4, 1874, v. 18, p. 19, modifies as to War Department.] *Title 41. Drafts for War and Navy Departments.*

7 May, 1822, s. 3, v. 3, p. 689.
3 March, 1817, ss. 5, 9, v. 3, p. 367.

SEC. 3675. All warrants drawn by the Secretary of the Treasury, upon the Treasurer of the United States, shall specify the particular appropriation to which the same should be charged ; and the moneys paid by virtue of such warrants shall, in conformity therewith, be charged to such appropriation in the books of the Secretary, First Comptroller, and Register. *Form of drawing and charging warrants.*

3 March, 1809, s. 1, v. 2, p. 535.
2 Sept., 1789, s. 6, v. 1, p. 67.

## ACCOUNTS OF LOST VESSELS AND CLOTHING.

Sec.
274. Payments to representatives of person lost.
284. Settlement of accounts of paymaster of lost or captured public vessels.
286. Fixing date of loss of missing vessels.
287. Accounts of petty officers, seamen, &c., on lost vessel.

Sec.
288. Compensation for personal effects lost.
289. Payment of accounts of deceased petty officers, seamen, &c., of lost vessel.
290. Allowance for effects of officer of lost vessel.

**Title 7, Chap. 3.**
*Arrears of pay to deceased persons.*

SEC. 274. The Second Comptroller may prescribe rules to govern the payment of arrears of pay due to any petty officer, seaman, or other person not an officer, on board any vessel in the employ of the United States, which has been sunk or destroyed, in case of the death of such petty officer, seaman, or person, to the person designated by law to receive the same.

4 July, 1864, s. 3, v. 13, p. 390.

**Title 7, Chap. 4.**
*Settlement of accounts of paymaster of lost or captured public vessels.*

SEC. 284. In every case of the loss or capture of a vessel belonging to the Navy of the United States, the proper accounting officers of the Treasury, under the direction of the Secretary of the Navy, are authorized, in the settlement of the accounts of the paymaster of such vessel, to credit him with such portion of the amount of the provisions, clothing, small stores, and money, with which he stands charged on the books of the Fourth Auditor of the Treasury, as they shall be satisfied was inevitably lost by such capture or loss of a public vessel; and such paymaster shall be fully exonerated by such credit from all liability on account of the provisions, clothing, small stores, and money so proved to have been captured or lost.

3 March, 1847, s. 6, v. 9, p. 173.
22 June, 1860, s. 3, v. 12, p. 83.

*Fixing date of loss of missing vessels.*

SEC. 286. The proper accounting officers of the Treasury are authorized, under the direction of the Secretary of the Navy, in settling the accounts of seamen, and others, not officers, borne on the books of any vessel in the Navy which shall have been wrecked, or which shall have been unheard from so long that her wreck may be presumed, or which shall have been destroyed or lost with such rolls and papers necessary to a regular and exact settlement of such accounts, to fix a day when such wreck, destruction, or loss shall be deemed to have occurred.

4 July, 1864, s. 1, v. 13, p. 389.

*Accounts of petty officers, seamen, &c., on lost vessel.*

SEC. 287. The proper accounting officers of the Treasury are authorized, in settling the accounts of the petty officers, seamen, and others, not officers, on board of any vessel in the employ of the United States, which by any casualty, or in action with the enemy, has been or may be sunk or otherwise destroyed, together with the rolls and papers necessary to the exact ascertainment of the several accounts of the same at the date of such loss, to assume the last quarterly return of the paymaster of any such vessel as the basis for the computation of the subsequent credits to those on board, to the date of such loss, if there be no official evidence to the contrary. Where such quarterly return has, from any cause, not been made, the accounting officers are authorized to adjust and settle such accounts on principles of equity and justice. [See § 274.]

*Idem, s. 2.*

*Compensation for personal effects lost.*

SEC. 288. The proper accounting officers of the Treasury Department are authorized, in settling the accounts of the petty officers, seamen, and others, not officers, on board of any vessel in the employ of the United States, which, by any casualty, or in action with the enemy, has been or may be sunk or otherwise destroyed, to allow and pay to each person, not an officer, employed on the vessel so sunk or destroyed, and whose personal effects have been lost, a sum not exceeding sixty dollars, as compensation for the loss of his personal effects.

*Idem, s. 2.*

*Payment of accounts of deceased petty officers, seamen, &c., of lost vessel.*

SEC. 289. In case of the death of any such petty officer, seaman, or other person, not an officer, such payment shall be made to the widow, child or children, father, mother, or brothers and sisters jointly, following that order of preference; such credits and gratuity to be paid out of any money in the Treasury not otherwise appropriated.

*Idem, s. 3.*

The "legal representatives" of deceased persons are generally their executors or their administrators, but may mean their heirs or next of kin.—Op. III, 29; VII, 60; XIV, 515; C. C., IV, 456; Wallace, XIII, 351.

To insert "marines" and to construe orphans to mean father or mother or brother or sister, would be legislation, not interpretation.—Op. VIII, 28, Aug. 8, 1856, Cushing, on the construction of relief acts.

Where money is due to the heirs of a deceased person and there is a dispute as to the legal descent, the latter question should be decided by the court rather than by the executive officers.—Op. V, 670, Jan. 28, 1853.

SEC. 290. In case any officer of the Navy or Marine Corps on board a vessel in the employ of the United States which, by any casualty, or in action with the enemy, at any time since the nineteenth day of April, eighteen hundred and sixty-one, has been or may be sunk or destroyed, shall thereby have lost his personal effects, without negligence or want of skill or foresight on his part, the proper accounting officers are authorized, with the approval of the Secretary of the Navy, to allow to such officer a sum not exceeding the amount of his sea-pay for one month as compensation for such loss. But the accounting officers shall in all cases require a schedule and certificate from the officer making the claim for effects so lost. *Allowance for effects of officer of lost vessel.*

6 April, 1866, s. 1, v. 14, p. 14.

[For continuation of pay to officers and crews of lost vessels, see §§ 1574 and 1575, Part I, page 69.]

## ADVERTISING.

Sec.
3828. Written authority required.
—— Restriction on advertising in the District of Columbia.
—— Prices to be paid.

Sec.
—— Papers to be used in the District of Columbia.
3709. Advertisement for supplies and services.
3718. Advertisement for provisions, &c., and transportation.

SEC. 3828. No advertisement, notice, or proposal for any Executive Department of the Government, or for any Bureau thereof, or for any office therewith connected, shall be published in any newspaper whatever, except in pursuance of a written authority for such publication from the head of such Department; and no bill for any such advertising, or publication, shall be paid, unless there be presented, with such bill, a copy of such written authority. *Title 45. No advertisement without authority.*

15 July, 1870, s. 2, v. 16, p. 308.

NOTE.—The provisions of section 3828, forbidding the publication of advertisements for any Executive Department of the Government, or for any Bureau thereof, or for any office therewith connected, except "under written authority from the head of the Department," extend to offices connected as aforesaid, no matter where located.—Op. XVI, 616, Phillips, Dec. 16, 1878.

In no case of advertisement for contracts for the public service shall the same be published in any newspaper published and printed in the District of Columbia unless the supplies or labor covered by such advertisement are to be furnished or performed in said District of Columbia. [See *post.*] *July 31, 1876. Restriction on advertising in the District of Columbia.*

July 31, 1876, ch. 246, v. 19, p. 102.

Hereafter all advertisements, notices, proposals for contracts, and all forms of advertising required by law for the several Departments of the Government may be paid for at a price not to exceed the commercial rates charged to private individuals, with the usual discounts; such rates to be ascertained from sworn statements to be furnished by the proprietors or publishers of the newspapers proposing so to advertise. * * * But the heads of the several Departments may secure lower terms at special rates whenever the public interest requires it. *June 20, 1878. Prices to be paid.*

June 20, 1878, ch. 359, v. 20, p. 306.

All advertising required by existing laws to be done in the District of Columbia by any of the Departments of the Government shall be given to one daily and one weekly newspaper of each of the two principal political parties, and to one daily and one weekly neutral newspaper: *Provided,* That the rates of compensation for such service shall in no case exceed the regular commercial rate of the newspapers selected; nor shall any advertisement be paid for unless published in accordance with section thirty-eight hundred and twenty-eight of the Revised Statutes. *January 21, 1881. Advertisements in the District of Columbia.*

11181——9

130 APPROPRIATIONS—ESTIMATES.

SEC. 2. All laws or parts of laws inconsistent herewith are hereby repealed.

January 21, 1881, ch. 25, v. 21, p. 317.

**Title 43.**
Advertisements for proposals.

SEC. 3709. All purchases and contracts for supplies or services, in any of the Departments of the Government, except for personal services, shall be made by advertising a sufficient time previously for proposals respecting the same, when the public exigencies do not require the immediate delivery of the articles, or performance of the service. * * *

2 March, 1861, s. 10, v. 12, p. 220.

Advertisements for clothing, hemp, &c.

SEC. 3718. * * In the case of provisions, clothing, hemp, and other materials, the Secretary of the Navy shall advertise, once a week, for at least four weeks, in one or more of the principal papers published in the place where such articles are to be furnished, for sealed proposals for furnishing the same. * * * In the case of transportation of such articles, he shall advertise for a period of not less than five days. * * [See 21 Jan., 1881, *ante*.]

3 March, 1843, v. 5, p. 617.

SEE NOTES, P. 25, PART I.

## APPROPRIATIONS—ESTIMATES.

Sec.
430. Estimates for expenses.
3660. Manner of communicating estimates.
3661. Estimates for printing and binding.
3662. Estimates for salaries.
3663. Requisites of estimates for appropriations for public works.
3664. What additional explanations are required.
3665. Amount of outstanding appropriation to be designated.
3666. Items of expenditure to be specified in estimates and accounts.
—— Estimates for pay of Navy.
3667. Estimates of claims, &c., on Navy pension-fund.
3669. Estimates to be submitted to Congress.
3670. What statements shall accompany estimates.
3672. Sales of public property to be included in book of estimates.
—— Estimates to be furnished by 1st October.

Sec.
3673. Drafts of War and Navy Departments.
3675. Form of drawing and charging warrants.
3676. Appropriations for Navy controlled by Secretary; for each Bureau to be kept separately.
3678. Application of moneys appropriated.
3679. No expenditures beyond appropriations.
3681. Expenses of commissions and inquiries.
3682. Contingent, &c., expenses.
3685. Special appropriations available only for two years, except, &c.
3686. Foreign hydrographic surveys.
3689. Permanent indefinite appropriations.
3690. Expenditure of balances of appropriations.
3691. Disposals of balances after two years.
—— Unexpended balances of appropriations.
3692. Proceeds of certain sales of material.
—— "General account of advances."
—— Statement of receipts, expenditures, and balances.

ESTIMATES.

**Title 10.**
Estimates for expenses.

SEC. 430. All estimates for specific, general, and contingent expenses of the Department, and of the several Bureaus, shall be furnished to the Secretary of the Navy by the chiefs of the respective Bureaus. [See § 3666, *post.*]

5 July, 1862, s. 5, v. 12, p. 511.

**Title 41.**
Manner of communicating estimates.

SEC. 3660. The heads of Departments, in communicating estimates of expenditures and appropriations to Congress, or to any of the committees thereof, shall specify, as nearly as may be convenient, the sources from which such estimates are derived, and the calculations upon which they are founded, and shall discriminate between such estimates as are conjectural in their character and such as are framed upon actual information and applications from disbursing officers. They shall also give references to any law or treaty by which the proposed expenditures are, respectively, authorized, specifying the date of each, and the volume and page of the Statutes at Large, or of the Revised Statutes, as the case may be, and the section of the act in which the authority is to be found. [See 3 March, 1875, p. 132.]

26 Aug., 1842, s. 14, v. 5, p. 525.

Estimates for printing and binding.

SEC. 3661. The head of each of the Executive Departments, and every other public officer who is authorized to have printing and binding done at the Congressional Printing-Office for the use of his Department or public office, shall include in his annual estimate for appropriations for the next fiscal year such sum or sums as may to him seem nec-

essary "for printing and binding, to be executed under the direction of the Congressional Printer." [See § 3802, PUBLIC DOCUMENTS.]
8 May, 1872, s. 2, v. 17, p. 82.

SEC. 3662. All estimates for the compensation of officers authorized by law to be employed shall be founded upon the express provisions of law, and not upon the authority of executive distribution. {Estimates for salaries.}
3 March, 1855, s. 8, v. 10, p. 670.

SEC. 3663. Whenever any estimate submitted to Congress by the head of a Department asks an appropriation for any new specific expenditure, such as the erection of a public building, or the construction of any public work, requiring a plan before the building or work can be properly completed, such estimate shall be accompanied by full plans and detailed estimates of the cost of the whole work. All subsequent estimates for any such work shall state the original estimated cost, the aggregate amount theretofore appropriated for the same, and the amount actually expended thereupon, as well as the amount asked for the current year for which such estimate is made. And if the amount asked is in excess of the original estimate, the full reasons for the excess, and the extent of the anticipated excess, shall be also stated. [See § 3734, CONTRACTS, PART I, p. 28.] {Requisites for estimates for appropriation for public works.}
17 June, 1844, s. 2, v. 5, p. 693.
3 March, 1855, s. 8, v. 10, p. 670.
27 Feb., 1877, v. 19, p. 249.

SEC. 3664. Whenever the head of a Department, being about to submit to Congress the annual estimates of expenditures required for the coming year, finds that the usual items of such estimates vary materially in amount from the appropriation ordinarily asked for the object named, and especially from the appropriation granted for the same objects for the preceding year, and whenever new items not theretofore usual are introduced into such estimates for any year, he shall accompany the estimates by minute and full explanations of all such variations and new items, showing the reasons and grounds upon which the amounts are required, and the different items added. [See March 3, 1875, *post.*] {What additional explanations are required.}
*Ibid.*

SEC. 3665. The head of each Department, in submitting to Congress his estimates of expenditures required in his Department during the year then approaching, shall designate not only the amount required to be appropriated for the next fiscal year, but also the amount of the outstanding appropriation, if there be any, which will probably be required for each particular item of expenditure. [See § 429, NAVY DEPARTMENT.—Reports to be made by the Secretary of the Navy.] {Amount of outstanding appropriations to be designated.}
2 June, 1858, s. 2, v. 11, p. 308.

SEC. 3666. The estimates for expenditures required by the Department of the Navy for the following purposes shall be given in detail, and the expenditures made under appropriations therefor shall be accounted for so as to show the disbursements of each Bureau under each respective appropriation: {Items of expenditure to be specified in estimates and accounts.}
  First. Freight and transportation.
  Second. Printing and stationery.
  Third. Advertising in newspapers.
  Fourth. Books, maps, models, and drawings.
  Fifth. Purchase and repair of fire-engines and machinery.
  Sixth. Repairs of and attending to steam-engines in navy-yards.
  Seventh. Purchase and maintenance of horses and oxen, and driving teams.
  Eighth. Carts, timber-wheels, and the purchase and repair of workmen's tools.
  Ninth. Postage of public letters.
  Tenth. Fuel, oil, and candles for navy-yards and shore-stations.
  Eleventh. Pay of watchmen and incidental labor not chargeable to any other appropriation.
  Twelfth. Transportation to, and labor attending the delivery of provisions and stores on foreign stations.
  Thirteenth. Wharfage, dockage, and rent.
  Fourteenth. Traveling expenses of officers and others under orders.
  Fifteenth. Funeral expenses.

## APPROPRIATIONS—ESTIMATES.

Sixteenth. Store and office rent, fuel, commissions, and pay of clerks to navy-agents and store-keepers.
Seventeenth. Flags, awnings, and packing-boxes.
Eighteenth. Premiums and other expenses of recruiting.
Nineteenth. Apprehending deserters.
Twentieth. Per-diem pay to persons attending courts-martial, courts of inquiry, and other services authorized by law.
Twenty-first. Pilotage and towage of vessels, and assistance to vessels in distress.
Twenty-second. Bills of health and quarantine expenses of vessels of the United States Navy in foreign ports. [See § 430, *ante*.]

22 June, 1860, s. 1, v. 12, p. 81.

23 Feb., 1881.
Estimates for pay of the Navy.

Hereafter the estimates for pay of the Navy shall be submitted in the book of estimates in detailed classifications and paragraphs, after the manner above set forth.

23 Feb., 1881, v. 21, p. 331.

[Paragraph I. Pay of Active List; II. Pay of Retired List; III. Pay of petty officers and seamen; IV. Pay of clerks, secretaries, mileage, &c., giving classification and number in each case, when possible.]

Title 41.
Estimates for Navy pension-fund.

SEC. 3667. The Secretary of the Navy shall annually submit to Congress estimates of the claims and demands chargeable upon and payable out of the naval pension fund.

11 July, 1870, v. 16, p. 222.

Estimates to be submitted to Congress.

SEC. 3669. All annual estimates for the public service shall be submitted to Congress through the Secretary of the Treasury, and shall be included in the book of estimates prepared under his direction.

2 Sept., 1789, s. 2, v. 1, p. 65.
10 March, 1800, v. 2, p. 79.
7 Jan., 1846, Res., v. 9, p. 108.
4 Aug., 1854, s. 15, v. 10, p. 573.
18 May, 1865, s. 4, v. 14, p. 49.

What statements shall accompany estimates.

SEC. 3670. The Secretary of the Treasury shall annex to the annual estimates of the appropriations required for the public service, a statement of the appropriations for the service of the year, which may have been made by former acts.

1 May, 1820, s. 8, v. 3, p. 568.

Statement of proceeds of sales of old material.

SEC. 3672. A detailed statement of the proceeds of all sales of old material, condemned stores, supplies, or other public property of any kind, except materials, stores, or supplies sold to officers and soldiers of the Army, or to exploring or surveying expeditions authorized by law, shall be included in the appendix to the book of estimates.

8 May, 1872, s. 5, v. 17, p. 83.
27 Feb., 1877, v. 19, p. 249.

March 3, 1875.
Estimates, when to be furnished.

Extracts from reports to be included in appendix to estimates.

That it shall be the duty of the heads of the several Executive Departments, and of other officers authorized or required to make estimates, to furnish to the Secretary of the Treasury, on or before the first day of October of each year, their annual estimates for the public service, to be included in the book of estimates prepared by law under his direction; and the Secretary of the Treasury shall submit, as a part of the appendix to the book of estimates, such extracts from the annual reports of the several heads of Departments and Bureaus as relate to estimates for appropriations, and the necessities therefor.

3 March, 1875, s. 3, v. 18, p. 340.

### APPROPRIATIONS.

Title 41.
Drafts for War and Navy Departments.

SEC. 3673. All moneys appropriated for the use of the War and Navy Departments shall be drawn from the Treasury, by warrants of the Secretary of the Treasury, upon the requisitions of the Secretaries of those Departments, respectively, countersigned by the Second Comptroller of the Treasury, and registered by the proper Auditor. [See §§ 273, 277, under ACCOUNTS.]

7 May, 1822, s. 3, v. 3, p. 689.
3 March, 1817, s. 5, 9, v. 3, p. 367.

NOTE.—The different subdivisions ordinarily employed in an appropriation act, viz, Legislative, Executive, Judicial, are intended to classify the appropriations and not to designate the Department to which they belong.—C. C., XI, 152; 91 U. S. R., 817.

APPROPRIATIONS—ESTIMATES. 133

*Appropriations:* Permanent, those for an indefinite period; indefinite, those in which no amount is named. *Unexpended balances* may be applied to expenses properly incurred within the year, and upon contracts made within the year, but not performed until later. Appropriations which in terms are for one year cannot be used for payment of expenses not incurred in the year. Money cannot be taken by counter requisition to settle old accounts.—Op., XIII, 289, July 27, 1870, Akerman.

SEC. 3675. All warrants drawn by the Secretary of the Treasury, upon the Treasurer of the United States, shall specify the particular appropriation to which the same should be charged; and the moneys paid by virtue of such warrants shall, in conformity therewith, be charged to such appropriation in the books of the Secretary, First Comptroller, and Register. — *Form of drawing and charging warrants.*

3 March, 1809, s. 1, v. 2, p. 535.
2 Sept., 1789, s. 6, v. 1, p. 67.

SEC. 3676. All appropriations for specific, general, and contingent expenses of the Navy Department shall be under the control and expended by the direction of the Secretary of the Navy, and the appropriation for each Bureau shall be kept separate in the Treasury. — *Appropriation for Navy controlled by Secretary; for each Bureau to be kept separately.*

5 July, 1862, s. 5, v. 12, p. 511.

NOTES.—The Secretary of the Navy can draw on the contingent fund for purposes of a contingent character—that is, such as might or might not happen, and which Congress could not easily foresee, and therefore could not provide for definitely.—Op. I, 302, Wirt.

The words "Contingent expenses," as used in the appropriation acts, mean such incidental, casual expenses as are necessary, or at least appropriate and convenient, in order to the performance of the duties *required by law* of the Department or the office for which the appropriation is made.—Op. XVI, 412, Devens, Dec. 19, 1879.

The appropriations for Contingent of the Bureaus (Civil) are merged with that for the Secretary's Office by Legislative Act approved March 3, 1883.

SEC. 3678. All sums appropriated for the various branches of expenditure in the public service shall be applied solely to the objects for which they are respectively made, and for no others. — *Applications of moneys appropriated.*

3 March, 1809, s. 1, v. 2, p. 535.
12 Feb., 1868, s. 2, v. 15, p. 36.

NOTES.—Section 3678 extends only to such cases as relate to "proceeds of sales"—receipts which are in the nature of revenue belonging to no appropriation, and not available for expenditure without authority from Congress. It does not prohibit one Department from supplying articles to another, and the transfer of appropriations to make reimbursements.—Op., Dec. 20, 1882, Brewster.

Section 3678 makes unlawful the diversion of funds appropriated for one object of expenditure to another object of expenditure, and forbids an appropriation for any purpose to be thus *enlarged* beyond the amount thereof, as fixed by Congress. The furnishing of articles by one Department to another, and subsequent reimbursements by transfer of appropriation, not a diversion or an enlargement contemplated by this section.—Op., Dec. 20, 1882, Brewster.

SEC. 3679. No Department of the Government shall expend, in any one fiscal year, any sum in excess of appropriations made by Congress for that fiscal year, or involve the Government in any contract for the future payment of money in excess of such appropriations. [See §§ 3732, 3733, 5503, CONTRACTS, PART I, p. 28.] — *No expenditures beyond appropriations.*

12 July, 1870, s. 7, v. 16, p. 251.

NOTE.—No contract can be made for rent of buildings until appropriations are made therefor. See Part I, p. 31.

SEC. 3681. No accounting or disbursing officer of the Government shall allow or pay any account or charge whatever, growing out of, or in any way connected with, any commission of inquiry, except courts-martial or courts of inquiry in the military or naval service of the United States, until special appropriations shall have been made by law to pay such accounts and charges * * *.

26 Aug., 1842, s. 25, v. 5, p. 533.
See Op. IV, p. 106, Oct. 25, 1842.

SEC. 3682. No moneys appropriated for contingent, incidental, or miscellaneous purposes shall be expended or paid for official or clerical compensation. [See under CONTINGENT FUNDS.] — *Restrictions on contingent, &c., appropriations.*

*Idem*, s. 3, p. 250.

SEC. 3685. * * * In no case shall any special appropriation be available for more than two years without further provision of law. [Exception for establishing light-houses.] — *Special appropriation available for two years.*

10 June, 1872, s. 1, v. 17, p. 355.

**Foreign hydrographic surveys.**

SEC. 3686. All appropriations made for the preparation or publication of foreign hydrographic surveys shall only be applicable to their object, upon the approval by the Secretary of the Navy, after a report from three competent naval officers, to the effect that the original data for proposed charts are such as to justify their publication; and it is hereby made the duty of the Secretary of the Navy to order a board of three naval officers to examine and report upon the data, before he shall approve of any application of money to the preparation or publication of such charts or hydrographic surveys.

21 Feb., 1861, s. 7, v. 12, p. 150.

**Permanent indefinite appropriations.**

SEC. 3689. There are appropriated, out of any moneys in the Treasury not otherwise appropriated, for the purposes hereinafter specified, such sums as may be necessary for the same respectively; and such appropriations shall be deemed permanent annual appropriations. * * *

Allowance for reduction of wages under eight-hour law:

Of such sum as may be required in the settlement of all accounts for the services of laborers, workmen, and mechanics employed by or on behalf of the Government, between the twenty-fifth day of June, eighteen hundred and sixty-eight, the date of the act constituting eight hours a day's work for all such laborers, workmen, and mechanics, and the nineteenth day of May, eighteen hundred and sixty-nine, the date of the proclamation of the President concerning such pay, to settle and pay for the same without reduction on account of reduction of hours of labor by said act, when it shall be made to appear that such was the sole cause of the reduction of wages. [See § 3738, CONTRACTS, PART I, p. 29.]

18 May, 1872, s. 2, v. 17, p. 134.

Indemnity to seamen and marines for lost clothing:

To allow and pay to each person, not an officer, employed on a vessel of the United States, sunk or otherwise destroyed, and whose personal effects have been lost, a sum not exceeding sixty dollars. In the event of the death of the person, this sum is to be paid to his proper legal representatives.

4 July, 1864, ss. 2, 3, v. 13, p. 390.

Prize money to captors:

For one moiety of the proceeds of prizes captured by vessels of the United States, to be distributed to the officers and crews thereof, in conformity to the provisions of Title "PRIZE;" also, the proceeds of derelict and salvage cases adjudged by the courts of the United States to salvors.

30 June, 1864, s. 16, v. 13, p. 311.

**Expenditure of balances of appropriations.**

SEC. 3690. All balances of appropriations contained in the annual appropriation bills and made specifically for the service of any fiscal year, and remaining unexpended at the expiration of such fiscal year, shall only be applied to the payment of expenses properly incurred during that year, or to the fulfillment of contracts properly made within that year; and balances not needed for such purposes shall be carried to the surplus fund. This section, however, shall not apply to appropriations known as permanent or indefinite appropriations. [See § 3689.]

12 July, 1870, s. 5, v. 16, p. 251.

**Disposal of balances after two years.**

SEC. 3691. All balances of appropriations which shall have remained on the books of the Treasury, without being drawn against in the settlement of accounts, for two years from the date of the last appropriation made by law, shall be reported by the Secretary of the Treasury to the Auditor of the Treasury, whose duty it is to settle accounts thereunder, and the Auditor shall examine the books of his Office, and certify to the Secretary whether such balances will be required in the settlement of any accounts pending in his Office; and if it appears that such balances will not be required for this purpose, then the Secretary may include such balances in his surplus-fund warrant, whether the head of the proper Department shall have certified that it may be carried into the general Treasury or not. But no appropriation for the payment of the interest or principal of the public debt, or to which a longer duration is given by law, shall be thus treated. [See June 20, 1874, *post*.]

12 July, 1870, s. 6, v. 16, p. 251.

That from and after the first day of July, eighteen hundred and seventy-four, and of each year thereafter, the Secretary of the Treasury shall cause all unexpended balances of appropriations which shall have remained upon the books of the Treasury for two fiscal years to be carried to the surplus fund and covered into the Treasury: *Provided*, That this provision shall not apply to permanent specific appropriations, appropriations for rivers and harbors, light-houses, fortifications, public buildings, or the pay of the Navy and Marine Corps; but the appropriations named in this proviso shall continue available until otherwise ordered by Congress \* \* \* *And provided further*, That this section shall not operate to prevent the fulfillment of contracts existing at the date of the passage of this act.

*June 20, 1874.*

Unexpended balances to be covered into the Treasury.

Exceptions, to continue available.

Existing contracts not affected.

20 June, 1874, s. 5, v. 18, p. 85.
14 June, 1878, s. 4, v. 20, p. 130.

NOTE.—This section was adopted, after the fullest consideration by Congress, expressly to cut off the payment of accrued claims by covering into the Treasury, after two years, the balance of the appropriation from which they might have been paid. The plain purpose of this act was to confine the officers of the Government to the allowance and payment of liabilities within three fiscal years. Decision of the Secretary of the Treasury, April 20, 1877. The use of appropriations is discussed in this decision.

SEC. 3692. All moneys received from the leasing or sale of marine hospitals, or the sale of revenue cutters, or from the sale of commissary stores to the officers and enlisted men of the Army, or from the sale of materials, stores, or supplies sold to officers and soldiers of the Army, or from sales of condemned clothing of the Navy, or from sales of materials, stores, or supplies to any exploring or surveying expedition authorized by law, shall respectively revert to that appropriation out of which they were originally expended, and shall be applied to the purposes for which they are appropriated by law.

Title 41.

Proceeds of certain sales, &c., of material.

8 May, 1872, s. 5, v. 17, p. 83.
3 March, 1847, s. 1, v. 9, p. 171.
20 Ap., 1866, ss. 1, 2, v. 14, p. 40.
28 July, 1866, s. 25, v. 14, p. 336.

8 June, 1872, v. 17, p. 337.
3 March, 1875, v. 18, p. 388, 410.
27 Feb., 1877, v. 19, p. 249.

## GENERAL ACCOUNT OF ADVANCES.

That the Secretary of the Navy be, and he is hereby, authorized to issue his requisitions for advances to disbursing officers and agents of the Navy under a "General account of advances," not to exceed the total appropriation for the Navy, the amount so advanced to be exclusively used to pay current obligations upon proper vouchers, and that "Pay of the Navy" shall hereafter be used only for its legitimate purpose as provided by law.

*June 19, 1878.*

Requisitions of Secretary Navy for advances.

19 June, 1878, chap. 311, s. 1, v. 20, p. 167.

That the amount so advanced be charged to the proper appropriations, and returned to " General account of advances " by pay and counter warrant; the said charge, however, to particular appropriations shall be limited to the amount appropriated to each.

Advances, how charged.

*Idem*, s. 2.

That the Fourth Auditor shall declare the sums due from the several special appropriations upon complete vouchers, as heretofore, according to law; and he shall adjust the said liabilities with the "General account of advances."

Settlements by Fourth Auditor.

*Idem*, s. 3.

## RECEIPTS, EXPENDITURES AND BALANCES.

From and after the passage of this act, it shall be the duty of the Secretary of the Treasury to transmit to Congress, annually, a tabular statement showing in detail the receipts and expenditures in the naval service under each appropriation, as made up and determined by the proper officers of the Treasury Department, upon the accounts of disbursing officers rendered for settlement.

There shall be appended to this statement an account of balances in the hands of disbursing agents at the close of each fiscal year, and a report of any amounts lost or unaccounted for by voucher.

*June 19, 1878.*

Tabular statement of Navy appropriations and expenditures.

Statement of balances in hands of the disbursing officers, and amounts lost.

19 June, 1878, chap. 312, ss. 1, 2, v. 20, p. 167.

# ATTORNEY-GENERAL—DEPARTMENT OF JUSTICE.

| Sec. | | Sec. | |
|---|---|---|---|
| 354. | Duties of Attorney-General. | 361. | Officers of, to perform services for other Departments. |
| 356. | Opinion of Attorney-General upon questions of law. | 363. | Retaining counsel to aid district attorneys. |
| 357. | Legal advice to Departments of War and Navy. | 364. | Attendance of counsel. |
| | | 365. | Counsel fees restricted. |
| 358. | Reference of questions by Attorney-General to subordinates. | 366. | Appointment of special counsel. |
| | | 367. | Detail of officers to attend suits. |
| 359. | Conduct and argument of cases. | 370. | Traveling expenses of officers so detailed. |
| 360. | Duties of officers of Department of Justice. | 383. | Publication of opinions. |

**Title 8.**

**Duties of Attorney-General.**

SEC. 354. The Attorney-General shall give his advice and opinion upon questions of law, whenever required by the President.
24 Sep., 1789, s. 35, v. 1, p. 92.
27 Feb., 1877, v. 19, p. 241.

**Opinion of Attorney-General upon questions of law.**

SEC. 356. The head of any Executive Department may require the opinion of the Attorney-General on any questions of law arising in the administration of his Department.
22 June, 1870, s. 6, v. 16, p. 163.

NOTES.—The law does not declare the effect of advice; practice of the Departments to heed it.—Op. V, 97, Johnson.
Not the duty of the Attorney-General to give opinions on questions of fact, nor to review the proceedings of a court-martial in search of questions of law.—Op. V, 626, Crittenden.
Does not reply to speculative points or supposed cases. Gives advice on actual cases where the special facts are set forth by the Department.—Op. IX, 82, Black. XIII, 531-568, Akerman, XII, 433, Browning.
The opinion of the Attorney-General for the time being is in terms advisory to the Secretary who calls for it; but it is obligatory as the law of the case unless, on appeal by such Secretary to the common superior of himself and the Attorney-General, namely, the President of the United States, it is by the latter overruled.—Op. VII, 602, Cushing.
Will not review the opinion of a former Attorney-General unless a proper case is presented therefor and submitted by a head of a Department.—Op. XI, 189, Speed.
Cannot act as *arbitrator* between the Government and an individual, and can therefore render no *award* in the sense in which the phrase is generally understood.—Op. I, 209, Wirt. Declines to give an opinion upon a question involving the estimation of the weight and credibility of testimony.—Op. XIV, p. 54, Bristow.
Not required to give an opinion to the Senate.—Op. X, 165, Bates. Not his duty to give opinion on matters pending in Congress on request of either house or any committee.—Op. XII, 544. Evarts. XIV, 17, 177, Williams. Not authorized to give an opinion (official) in response to a call of the head of a Department, although made at the request of a committee of Congress, where the question proposed does not arise in the administration of such Department.—Op. XV, 138, Taft.
Subordinate officers who desire an official opinion must seek it through the head of the Department to which said subordinate is accountable.—Op. X, 458. No right to give an official opinion except where it his duty to do so, that is, to the President and heads of Departments.—Op. I, 335, VI, 21, 147. See Op. XIV, 21, declining to approve or disapprove of an opinion of an assistant attorney-general of an Executive Department—not having been called for by the President or the head of a Department.

**Legal advice to Departments of War and Navy.**

SEC. 357. Whenever a question of law arises in the administration of the Department of War or the Department of the Navy, the cognizance of which is not given by statute to some other officer from whom the head of the Department may require advice, it shall be sent to the Attorney-General, to be by him referred to the proper officer in his Department, or otherwise disposed of as he may deem proper.

*Idem.*

**Reference of questions by Attorney-General to subordinates.**

SEC. 358. Any question of law submitted to the Attorney-General for his opinion, except questions involving a construction of the Constitution of the United States, may be by him referred to such of his subordinates as he may deem appropriate, and he may require the written opinion thereon of the officer to whom the same may be referred. If the opinion given by such officer is approved by the Attorney-General, such approval indorsed thereon shall give the opinion the same force and effect as belong to the opinions of the Attorney-General.

*Idem, s. 4.*

**Conduct and argument of cases.**

SEC. 359. Except when the Attorney-General in particular cases otherwise directs, the Attorney-General and Solicitor-General shall conduct and argue suits and writs of error and appeals in the Supreme Court

ATTORNEY-GENERAL—DEPARTMENT OF JUSTICE. 137

and suits in the Court of Claims in which the United States is interested, and the Attorney-General may, whenever he deems it for the interest of the United States, either in person conduct and argue any case in any court of the United States in which the United States is interested, or may direct the Solicitor-General or any officer of the Department of Justice to do so.

24 Sept., 1789, s. 35, v. 1, p. 92.
25 June, 1868, s. 5, v. 15, p. 75.
22 June, 1870, s. 5, v. 16, p. 162.

SEC. 360. The Attorney-General may require any solicitor or officer of the Department of Justice to perform any duty required of the Department or any officer thereof. *Performance of duty by officers of Department of Justice.*

22 June, 1870, s. 14, v. 16, p. 164.

SEC. 361. The officers of the Department of Justice, under the direction of the Attorney-General, shall give all opinions and render all services requiring the skill of persons learned in the law necessary to enable the President and heads of Departments, and the heads of Bureaus and other officers in the Departments, to discharge their respective duties; and shall, on behalf of the United States, procure the proper evidence for, and conduct, prosecute, or defend all suits and proceedings in the Supreme Court and in the Court of Claims, in which the United States, or any officer thereof, as such officer, is a party or may be interested; and no fees shall be allowed or paid to any other attorney or counselor at law for any service herein required of the officers of the Department of Justice, except in the cases provided by section three hundred and sixty-three. *Officers of the Department to perform all legal services required for other Departments.*

*Idem*, s. 14.

SEC. 363. The Attorney-General shall, whenever in his opinion the public interest requires it, employ and retain, in the name of the United States, such attorneys and counselors at law as he may think necessary to assist the district attorneys in the discharge of their duties, and shall stipulate with such assistant attorneys and counsel the amount of compensation, and shall have supervision of their conduct and proceedings. *Retaining counsel to aid district attorneys.*

2 Aug., 1861, s. 2, v. 12, p. 285.
3 March, 1869, s. 1, v. 15, p. 294.
10 Ap., 1869, v. 16, p. 46.
22 June, 1870, s. 16, v. 16, p. 164.

SEC. 364. Whenever the head of a Department or Bureau gives the Attorney-General due notice that the interests of the United States require the service of counsel upon the examination of witnesses touching any claim, or upon the legal investigation of any claim, pending in such Department or Bureau, the Attorney-General shall provide for such service. [See § 187, CLAIMS, p. 152.] *Attendance of counsel.*

14 Feb., 1871, s. 3, v. 16, p. 412.

SEC. 365. No compensation shall hereafter be allowed to any person, besides the respective district attorneys and assistant district attorneys, for services as an attorney or counselor to the United States, or to any branch or Department of the Government thereof, except in cases specially authorized by law, and then only on the certificate of the Attorney-General that such services were actually rendered, and that the same could not be performed by the Attorney-General, or Solicitor-General, or the officers of the Department of Justice, or by the district attorneys. *Counsel fees restricted.*

22 June, 1870, s. 17, v. 16, p. 164.

SEC. 366. Every attorney or counselor who is specially retained, under the authority of the Department of Justice, to assist in the trial of any case in which the Government is interested, shall receive a commission from the head of such Department, as a special assistant to the Attorney-General, or to some one of the district attorneys, as the nature of the appointment may require; and shall take the oath required by law to be taken by the district attorneys, and shall be subject to all the liabilities imposed upon them by law. *Appointment and oath of special attorneys or counsel.*

*Idem*, s 17.

SEC. 367. The Solicitor-General, or any officer of the Department of Justice, may be sent by the Attorney-General to any State or District in the United States to attend to the interests of the United States in any suit pending in any of the courts of the United States, or in the courts of any State, or to attend to any other interest of the United States. *Interest of United States in pending suits, who may attend to.*

*Idem*, s. 5.

Traveling expenses of officers of the Department.

SEC. 370. Whenever the Solicitor-General, or any officer of the Department of Justice, is sent by the Attorney-General to any State, District, or Territory, to attend to any interest of the United States, the person so sent shall receive, in addition to his salary, his actual and necessary expenses while absent from the seat of Government; the account thereof to be verified by affidavit.

*Idem*, s. 5.

Publication of opinions.

SEC. 383. The Attorney-General shall from time to time cause to be edited, and printed at the Government Printing-Office, an edition of one thousand copies of such of the opinions of the law-officers herein authorized to be given as he may deem valuable for preservation in volumes. * * * Each volume shall contain proper head-notes, a complete and full index, and such foot-notes as the Attorney-General may approve. Such volumes shall be distributed in such manner as the Attorney-General may from time to time prescribe.

*Idem*, s. 18.

## ATTORNEYS AND AGENTS OF GOVERNMENT.

| Sec. | | Sec. | |
|---|---|---|---|
| 187. | Professional assistance. | 1783. | Persons interested not to act as agents of the Government. |
| 189. | Employment of attorneys or counsel. | 3614. | Bond of special agents. |
| 1550. | Agents to disburse money abroad. | | |

Title 4.

Professional assistance; how obtained.

SEC. 187. Whenever any head of a Department or Bureau having made application pursuant to section one hundred and eighty-four, for a subpœna to procure the attendance of a witness to be examined, is of opinion that the interests of the United States require the attendance of counsel at the examination, or require legal investigation of any claim pending in his Department or Bureau, he shall give notice thereof to the Attorney-General, and of all facts necessary to enable the Attorney-General to furnish proper professional service in attending such examination, or making such investigation, and it shall be the duty of the Attorney-General to provide for such service. [See 184 CLAIMS.]

14 Feb., 1871, s. 3, v. 16, p. 412.

Employment of attorneys or counsel.

SEC. 189. No head of a Department shall employ attorneys or counsel at the expense of the United States; but when in need of counsel or advice, shall call upon the Department of Justice, the officers of which shall attend to the same. [See §§ 364, 365, ATTORNEY-GENERAL.]

22 June, 1870, s. 17, v. 16, p. 164.

Title 15, Chap. 7.

Appointment of persons to disburse money on foreign stations.

SEC. 1550. No person shall be employed or continued abroad, to receive and pay money for the use of the naval service on foreign stations, whether under contract or otherwise, who has not been, or shall not be, appointed by and with the advice and consent of the Senate.

17 June, 1844, s. 4, v. 5, p. 703.

Title 19.

Persons interested not to act as agents of the Government.

SEC. 1783. No officer or agent of any banking or other commercial corporation, and no member of any mercantile or trading firm, or person directly or indirectly interested in the pecuniary profits or contracts of such corporation or firm, shall be employed or shall act as an officer or agent of the United States for the transaction of business with such corporation or firm; and every such officer, agent, or member, or person, so interested, who so acts, shall be imprisoned not more than two years, and fined not more than two thousand dollars nor less than five hundred dollars.

2 March, 1863, s. 8, v. 12, p. 698.

Title 40.

Bond of special agents.

SEC. 3614. Whenever it becomes necessary for the head of any Department or office to employ special agents, other than officers of the Army or Navy, who may be charged with the disbursement of public moneys, such agents shall, before entering upon duty, give bond in such form and with such security as the head of the Department or office employing them may approve.

4 Aug., 1854, s. 14, v. 10, p. 573.

NOTES.—No allowance can be made for any commission or inquiry, except military or naval, until special appropriations are made by Congress for the purpose.—Op. IV, 106, Oct. 25, 1842, Legaré.

An Executive Department being charged with the duty of seeing that the laws are faithfully executed, has authority to appoint commissioners or agents to make investigations required by acts or resolutions of Congress, but it cannot pay them except from an appropriation for that purpose.—Op. IV, 248, Nelson, Sept. 21, 1843.

An authority of a special agent appointed to do a particular act must be limited to that act and to such acts as are necessary to the performance of it.—Op. XI, 521.

The Government is not bound by the act or declaration of its agent unless it manifestly appears that he acted within the scope of his authority, or was employed in his capacity as a public agent to do the act or make the declaration for it.—Otto, 93, p. 247. See C. C. II, 599, IV, 401, and VII, 65, and Wallace, VII, 666, as to the power of agents.

*Held* by the First Comptroller, that a chief engineer of the Navy, appointed superintendent of the State, War, and Navy Department building, under the legislative appropriation act approved March 3, 1883, should give a bond, as his duties as such were in no way connected with the Navy and his disbursements would be of civil appropriations.

## CIVIL SERVICE—THE EXECUTIVE DEPARTMENTS.

Sec.
163. Classification of Department clerks.
165. Clerkships open to women.
166. Distribution of clerks.
167. Salaries of persons employed in the Departments.
168. Temporary clerks.
169. Authority to employ clerks and other employes.
— Restriction.
170. Extra compensation to clerks prohibited.
— Restriction on employing extra clerks and their pay.
— Employés not to be paid from contingent fund.
— Unauthorized rates of pay forbidden.
— Lapsed salaries, disposition of.
1753. Admissions to the civil service.
— Civil Service Commissioners.

Sec.
— Duties of.
— Rules for civil service act.
— Places of meeting; boards of examiners.
— Corruptly defeating objects of the commission.
— Revision and classification of clerks.
— Persons subject to, and exempt from the rules.
— Habitual use of intoxicating beverages a bar against appointment to civil office.
— Recommendations of Congressmen not to be received except, &c.
1754. Preference to disabled soldiers, &c.
1755. Honorably discharged soldiers, &c., commended to bankers, &c.
— In reducing force, preference to honorably discharged soldiers, &c., for.

SEC. 163. The clerks in the Departments shall be arranged in four classes, distinguished as the first, second, third, and fourth classes.

Title 4.
Classification of Department clerks.

3 March, 1853, s. 3, v. 10, p. 209.
3 March, 1855, s. 4, v. 10, p. 669.

SEC. 165. Women may, in the discretion of the head of any Department, be appointed to any of the clerkships therein authorized by law, upon the same requisites and conditions, and with the same compensations, as are prescribed for men.

Clerkships open to women.

12 July, 1870, s. 2, v. 16, pp. 230-250.

SEC. 166. Each head of a Department may from time to time alter the distribution among the various Bureaus and offices of his Department, of the clerks allowed by law, as he may find it necessary and proper to do. [See Aug. 5, 1882, p. 140.]

Distribution of clerks.

3 March, 1853, s. 3, v. 10, p. 211.

SEC. 167. The annual salaries of clerks and employés in the Departments, whose compensation is not otherwise prescribed, shall be as follows:

Salaries of persons employed in the Departments.

First. To clerks of the fourth class, eighteen hundred dollars.
Second. To clerks of the third class, sixteen hundred dollars.
Third. To clerks of the second class, fourteen hundred dollars.
Fourth. To clerks of the first class, twelve hundred dollars.
Fifth. To the women employed in duties of a clerical character, subordinate to those assigned to clerks of the first class, including copyists and counters, or temporarily employed to perform the duties of a clerk, nine hundred dollars.
Sixth. To messengers, eight hundred and forty dollars.
Seventh. To assistant messengers, seven hundred and twenty dollars.
Eighth. To laborers, seven hundred and twenty dollars. [$660, by legislative act March 3, 1883, except otherwise specially appropriated for.]
Ninth. To watchmen, seven hundred and twenty dollars.

3 March, 1853, s. 3, v. 10, pp. 209, 210.
22 April, 1854, s. 1, v. 10, p. 276.
18 Aug., 1856, Res. 18, v. 11, p. 145.
23 July, 1866, s. 6, v. 14, p. 207.
12 July, 1870, s. 3, v. 16, pp. 230, 250.

140  CIVIL SERVICE—THE EXECUTIVE DEPARTMENTS, ETC.

Temporary clerks.  SEC. 168. Except when a different compensation is expressly prescribed by law, any clerk temporarily employed to perform the same or similar duties with those belonging to clerks of either class, is entitled to the same salary as is allowed to clerks of that class.

22 April, 1854, s. 1, v. 10, p. 276.

NOTE.—A clerk with a fixed salary is bound to perform the duties of the office for the salary. If the work of the office be increased, requiring his services beyond the established or customary hours, he cannot, if the increased labor pertains to the business of the office, receive additional compensation.—C. C., XVII, 383.

Authority to employ clerks and other employés.  SEC. 169. Each head of a Department is authorized to employ in his Department such number of clerks of the several classes recognized by law, and such messengers, assistant messengers, copyists, watchmen, laborers, and other employés, and at such rates of compensation, respectively, as may be appropriated for by Congress from year to year. [See act Aug. 5, 1882, *post*.]

15 Aug., 1876.
Restriction.  That the executive officers of the Government are hereby prohibited from employing any clerk, agent, engineer, draughtsman, messenger, watchman, laborer, or other employé, in any of the Executive Departments in the city of Washington, or elsewhere, beyond provision made by law. [See Aug. 5, 1882, *post*.]

15 Aug., 1876, s. 5, v. 19, p. 196.

NOTE.—In the absence of constitutional restriction, the future compensation of a public officer may be altered at pleasure by the legislature during his incumbency, without violating any legal right vested in him by virtue of his appointment.—Op. XV, 317, Devens, June 18, 1877.

Title 4.
Extra compensation to clerks prohibited.  SEC. 170. No money shall be paid to any clerk employed in either Department at an annual salary, as compensation for extra services, unless expressly authorized by law. [See EXTRA PAY, &c., Part I, p. 71.]

3 March, 1863, s. 3, v. 10, pp. 209, 211.
17 June, 1844, s. 1, v. 5, pp. 681, 687.
28 Feb., 1867, Res. 30, s. 2, v. 14, p. 569.

NOTE.—Where the service is one required by law and compensation is fixed by competent authority and is appropriated, an officer who under due authorization performs the service is entitled to the compensation.—Op. XV, 608.

5 Aug., 1882.
Restriction on number and pay of clerks, &c.  That no civil officer, clerk, draughtsman, copyist, messenger, assistant messenger, mechanic, watchman, laborer, or other employé shall after the first day of October next be employed in any of the Executive Departments, or subordinate Bureaus or offices thereof at the seat of Government, except only at such rates and in such numbers, respectively, as may be specifically appropriated for by Congress for such clerical and other personal services for each fiscal year.

5 Aug., 1882, s. 4, P. E, L., p. 255.

Civil employés not to be paid from contingent appropriations.  No civil officer, clerk, draughtsman, copyist, messenger, assistant messenger, mechanic, watchman, laborer, or other employé shall hereafter be employed at the seat of Government in any Executive Department or subordinate Bureau or office thereof or be paid from any appropriation made for contingent expenses, or for any specific or general purpose, unless such employment is authorized and payment therefor specifically provided in the law granting the appropriation, and then only for services actually rendered in connection with and for the purposes of the appropriation from which payment is made, and at the rate of compensation usual and proper for such services.

*Ibid.*

Unauthorized rates of pay forbidden.  After the first day of October next section one hundred and seventy-two of the Revised Statutes, and all other laws and parts of laws inconsistent with the provisions of this act, and all laws and parts of laws authorizing the employment of officers, clerks, draughtsmen, copyists, messengers, assistant messengers, mechanics, watchmen, laborers, or other employés at a different rate of pay or in excess of the numbers authorized by appropriations made by Congress, be, and they are hereby, repealed; and thereafter all details of civil officers, clerks, or other subordinate employés from places outside of the District of Columbia for duty within the District of Columbia, except temporary details for duty connected with their respective offices, be, and are hereby, pro-

Details not to be made from outside District of Columbia for duty therein.

hibited; and thereafter all moneys accruing from lapsed salaries, or from unused appropriations for salaries, shall be covered into the Treasury. *Lapsed salaries.*
*Ibid.*

NOTES.—Civil officers are usually divided into three classes: political, judicial, and ministerial. But persons actually and properly employed in the Executive Departments or in Bureaus or Divisions thereof, by an officer charged with that duty and authorized by law to fix their compensation, are persons in the civil service.—Wallace, XIII, 568. C. C., VII, 290.

Laborers, mechanics, machinists, &c., in navy-yards, paid by the day, are civil employés within the meaning of the 20 per cent. acts. Printers paid by the *em*, or note engravers by the *piece*, are not.—Wallace, XX, 179. C. C., IX, 104.

## THE CIVIL SERVICE.

SEC. 1753. The President is authorized to prescribe such regulations for the admission of persons into the civil service of the United States as may best promote the efficiency thereof, and ascertain the fitness of each candidate in respect to age, health, character, knowledge, and ability for the branch of service into which he seeks to enter; and for this purpose he may employ suitable persons to conduct such inquiries, and may prescribe their duties, and establish regulations for the conduct of persons who may receive appointments in the civil service. *Title 19. President to regulate admissions to the civil service.*

3 March, 1871, s. 9, v. 16, p. 514.

The President is authorized to appoint, by and with the advice and consent of the Senate, three persons, not more than two of whom shall be adherents of the same party, as Civil Service Commissioners, and said three commissioners shall constitute the United States Civil Service Commission. Said commissioners shall hold no other official place under the United States. *16 Jan., 1883. Appointment of Civil Service Commissioners.*

The President may remove any commissioner; and any vacancy in the position of commissioner shall be so filled by the President, by and with the advice and consent of the Senate, as to conform to said conditions for the first selection of commissioners.

The commissioners shall each receive a salary of three thousand five hundred dollars a year. And each of said commissioners shall be paid his necessary traveling expenses incurred in the discharge of his duty as a commissioner. *Salary and expenses.*

SEC. 2. That it shall be the duty of said commissioners: *Duty of the commissioners.*

FIRST. To aid the President, as he may request, in preparing suitable rules for carrying this act into effect, and when said rules shall have been promulgated it shall be the duty of all officers of the United States in the Departments and offices to which any such rules may relate to aid, in all proper ways, in carrying said rules, and any modifications thereof, into effect.

SECOND. And, among other things, said rules shall provide and declare, as nearly as the conditions of good administration will warrant, as follows: *Rules for civil service act.*

First, for open, competitive examinations for testing the fitness of applicants for the public service now classified or to be classified hereunder. Such examinations shall be practical in their character, and so far as may be shall relate to those matters which will fairly test the relative capacity and fitness of the persons examined to discharge the duties of the service into which they seek to be appointed.

Second, that all the offices, places, and employments so arranged or to be arranged in classes shall be filled by selections according to grade from among those graded highest as the results of such competitive examinations.

Third, appointments to the public service aforesaid in the Departments at Washington shall be apportioned among the several States and Territories and the District of Columbia upon the basis of population as ascertained at the last preceding census. Every application for an examination shall contain, among other things, a statement, under oath, setting forth his or her actual bona fide residence at the time of making the application, as well as how long he or she has been a resident of such place.

Fourth, that there shall be a period of probation before any absolute appointment or employment aforesaid.

Fifth, that no person in the public service is for that reason under any obligations to contribute to any political fund, or to render any political service, and that he will not be removed or otherwise prejudiced for refusing to do so.

Sixth, that no person in said service has any right to use his official authority or influence to coerce the political action of any person or body.

Seventh, there shall be non-competitive examinations in all proper cases before the commission, when competent persons do not compete, after notice has been given of the existence of the vacancy, under such rules as may be prescribed by the commissioners as to the manner of giving notice.

Eighth, that notice shall be given in writing by the appointing power to said commission of the persons selected for appointment or employment from among those who have been examined, of the place of residence of such persons, of the rejection of any such persons after probation, of transfers, resignations, and removals, and of the date thereof, and a record of the same shall be kept by said commission. And any necessary exceptions from said eight fundamental provisions of the rules shall be set forth in connection with such rules, and the reasons therefor shall be stated in the annual reports of the commission.

THIRD: Said commission shall, subject to the rules that may be made by the President, make regulations for, and have control of, such examinations, and, through its members or the examiners, it shall supervise and preserve the records of the same; and said commission shall keep minutes of its own proceedings.

FOURTH. Said commission may make investigations concerning the facts, and may report upon all matters touching the enforcement and effects of said rules and regulations, and concerning the action of any examiner or board of examiners hereinafter provided for, and its own subordinates, and those in the public service, in respect to the execution of this act.

FIFTH. Said commission shall make an annual report to the President for transmission to Congress, showing its own action, the rules and regulations and the exceptions thereto in force, the practical effects thereof, and any suggestions it may approve for the more effectual accomplishment of the purposes of this act.

*Places of meeting and boards of examiners.*

SEC. 3. * * * The commission shall, at Washington, and in one or more places in each State and Territory where examinations are to take place, designate and select a suitable number of persons, not less than three, in the official service of the United States, residing in said State or Territory, after consulting the head of the Department or office in which such persons serve, to be members of boards of examiners, and may at any time substitute any other person in said service living in such State or Territory in the place of any one so selected. Such boards of examiners shall be so located as to make it reasonably convenient and inexpensive for applicants to attend before them; and where there are persons to be examined in any State or Territory, examinations shall be held therein at least twice in each year. It shall be the duty of the collector, postmaster, and other officers of the United States, at any place outside of the District of Columbia where examinations are directed by the President or by said board to be held, to allow the reasonable use of the public buildings for holding such examinations, and in all proper ways to facilitate the same.

\* \* \* \* \* \*

*Penalty for corruptly defeating the objects of the commission.*

SEC. 5. That any said commissioner, examiner, copyist, or messenger, or any person in the public service who shall willfully and corruptly, by himself or in co-operation with one or more other persons, defeat, deceive, or obstruct any person in respect of his or her right of examination according to any such rules or regulations, or who shall willfully, corruptly, and falsely mark, grade, estimate, or report upon the examination or proper standing of any person examined hereunder, or aid in so doing, or who shall willfully and corruptly make any false representations concerning the same or concerning the person examined, or who shall willfully and corruptly furnish to any person any special or secret information for the purpose of either improving or injuring the prospects or chances of any person so examined, or to be examined, being appointed, employed, or promoted, shall for each such offense be deemed guilty of a misdemeanor, and upon conviction thereof, shall be punished by a fine of not less than one hundred dollars, nor more than one thousand dollars, or by imprisonment not less than ten days, nor more than one year, or by both such fine and imprisonment.

CIVIL SERVICE—THE EXECUTIVE DEPARTMENTS, ETC. 143

SEC. 6. * * * Third. That from time to time * * * each of the heads of Departments mentioned in the one hundred and fifty-eighth section of the Revised Statutes [*the 7 principal Departments*] and each head of an office, shall, on the direction of the President, and for facilitating the execution of this act, respectively revise any then existing classification or arrangement of those in their respective Departments and offices, and shall, for the purposes of the examination herein provided for, include in one or more of such classes, so far as practicable, subordinate places, clerks, and officers in the public service pertaining to their respective Departments not before classified for examination. Revision, classification, and arrangement of clerks by the heads of Departments.

SEC. 7. That after the expiration of six months from the passage of this act no officer or clerk shall be appointed, and no person shall be employed to enter or be promoted in either of the said classes now existing, or that may be arranged hereunder pursuant to said rules, until he has passed an examination, or is shown to be specially exempted from such examination in conformity herewith. But nothing herein contained shall be construed to take from those honorably discharged from the military or naval service any preference conferred by the seventeen hundred and fifty-fourth section of the Revised Statutes, nor to take from the President any authority not inconsistent with this act conferred by the seventeen hundred and fifty-third section of said statutes; nor shall any officer not in the executive branch of the Government, or any person merely employed as a laborer or workman, be required to be classified hereunder; nor, unless by direction of the Senate, shall any person who has been nominated for confirmation by the Senate, be required to be classified or to pass an examination. Persons subject to, and exempt from the rules.

SEC. 8. That no person habitually using intoxicating beverages to excess shall be appointed to, or retained in, any office, appointment, or employment to which the provisions of this act are applicable. Habitual use of intoxicating beverages a bar against appointment.

SEC. 9. That whenever there are already two or more members of a family in the public service in the grades covered by this act, no other member of such family shall be eligible to appointment to any of said grades. Not more than two of a family eligible.

SEC. 10. That no recommendation of any person who shall apply for office or place under the provisions of this act which may be given by any Senator or member of the House of Representatives, except as to the character or residence of the applicant, shall be received or considered by any person concerned in making any examination or appointment under this act. Recommendations of Congressmen not to be received, except, &c.

*       *       *       *       *

16 Jan., 1883, P. E. L., p. 406.

NOTE.—There are three branches of service classified under the civil service act. Those in the Departments at Washington are designated "The classified Departmental service." The general board of examiners for this service consists of two persons from the Treasury Department, two from the Post-Office Department, two from the Interior Department, and one from each of the other Departments.

SEC. 1754. Persons honorably discharged from the military or naval service by reason of disability resulting from wounds or sickness incurred in the line of duty, shall be preferred for appointments to civil offices, provided they are found to possess the business capacity necessary for the proper discharge of the duties of such offices. Title 19.<br>Preference of persons disabled in military or naval service.

3 March, 1865, Res. No. 27, s. 1, v. 13, p. 571.

SEC. 1755. In grateful recognition of the services, sacrifices, and sufferings of persons honorably discharged from the military and naval service of the country, by reason of wounds, disease, or the expiration of terms of enlistment, it is respectfully recommended to bankers, merchants, manufacturers, mechanics, farmers, and persons engaged in industrial pursuits, to give them the preference for appointments to remunerative situations and employments. Recommendation for employment of such persons.

*Idem*, sec. 2.

*Provided*, That in making any reduction of force in any of the Executive Departments, the head of such Department shall retain those persons who may be equally qualified, who have been honorably discharged from the military or naval service of the United States, and the widows and orphans of deceased soldiers and sailors. 15 Aug., 1876.<br>Preference to discharged soldiers and sailors in matter of reductions.

15 Aug., 1876, s. 3, v. 19, p. 143.

# 144 CIVIL SERVICE—THE EXECUTIVE DEPARTMENTS, ETC.

## OATH OF OFFICE, &C.

Sec.
1756. Form of oath of office.
1757. Oath for certain persons.
1758. Who may administer oath.

Sec.
1759. Custody of oath.
1778. Other persons before whom oath may be taken.

**Title 19.**

**Form of oath of office.**

SEC. 1756. Every person elected or appointed to any office of honor or profit, either in the civil, military, or naval service, excepting the President and the persons embraced by the section following, shall, before entering upon the duties of such office, and before being entitled to any part of the salary or other emoluments thereof, take and subscribe the following oath: "I, A B, do solemnly swear (or affirm) that I have never voluntarily borne arms against the United States since I have been a citizen thereof; that I have voluntarily given no aid, countenance, counsel, or encouragement to persons engaged in armed hostility thereto; that I have neither sought, nor accepted, nor attempted to exercise the functions of any office whatever, under any authority, or pretended authority, in hostility to the United States; that I have not yielded a voluntary support to any pretended government, authority, power, or constitution within the United States, hostile or inimical thereto. And I do further swear (or affirm) that, to the best of my knowledge and ability, I will support and defend the Constitution of the United States against all enemies, foreign and domestic; that I will bear true faith and allegiance to the same; that I take this obligation freely, without any mental reservation or purpose of evasion, and that I will well and faithfully discharge the duties of the office on which I am about to enter, so help me God."

2 July, 1862, chap. 128, v. 12, p. 502.

NOTE.—See Op. 13, p. 390, as to whom this oath is applicable.

**Oath for certain persons.**

SEC. 1757. Whenever any person who is not rendered ineligible to office by the provisions of the fourteenth amendment to the Constitution is elected or appointed to any office of honor or trust under the Government of the United States, and is not able, on account of his participation in the late rebellion, to take the oath prescribed in the preceding section, he shall, before entering upon the duties of his office, take and subscribe in lieu of that oath the following oath: "I, A B, do solemnly swear (or affirm) that I will support and defend the Constitution of the United States against all enemies, foreign and domestic; that I will bear true faith and allegiance to the same; that I take this obligation freely without any mental reservation or purpose of evasion; and that I will well and faithfully discharge the duties of the office on which I am about to enter. So help me God."

11 July, 1868, chap. 139, v. 15, p. 85.
15 Feb., 1871, chap 53, v. 16, p. 412.

**Who may administer oath.**

SEC. 1758. The oath of office required by either of the two preceding sections may be taken before any officer who is authorized either by the laws of the United States, or by the local municipal law, to administer oaths, in the State, Territory, or District where such oath may be administered.

6 Aug., 1861, s. 2, v. 12, p. 326.
18 April 1876, ch. 66, v. 19, p. 34, as to administrating oaths in the Senate.

**Custody of oath.**

SEC. 1759. The oath of office taken by any person pursuant to the requirements of section seventeen hundred and fifty-six, or of section seventeen hundred and fifty-seven, shall be delivered in by him to be preserved among the files of the House of Congress, Department, or court to which the office in respect to which the oath is made may appertain.

2 July, 1862, chap. 128, v. 12, p. 502.

**Taking oaths or acknowledgments.**

SEC. 1778. In all cases in which, under the laws of the United States, oaths or acknowledgments may now be taken or made before any justice of the peace of any State or Territory, or in the District of Columbia, they may hereafter be also taken or made by or before any notary public duly appointed in any State, District, or Territory, or any of the commissioners of the circuit courts, and, when certified under the hand and official seal of such notary or commissioner, shall have the same force and effect as if taken or made by or before such justice of the peace.

16 Sept., 1850, v. 9, p. 458.
29 July, 1854, s. 1, v. 10, p. 315.

## CIVIL SERVICE—THE EXECUTIVE DEPARTMENTS, ETC.   145

### DEPARTMENT REGULATIONS.

Sec.
161. Departmental regulations.
—— Hours of business.
—— Holidays.
173. Chief clerks to supervise subordinate clerks.
174. Chief clerks to distribute duties, &c.

Sec.
175. Duty of chief on receipt of report.
176. Disbursing clerks.
194. Report of clerks employed.
195. Time of submitting annual reports.
198. Biennial list of employés.

SEC. 161. The head of each Department is authorized to prescribe regulations, not inconsistent with law, for the government of his Department, the conduct of its officers and clerks, the distribution and performance of its business, and the custody, use, and preservation of the records, papers, and property appertaining to it. **Title 4.** Departmental regulations.

27 July, 1789, v. 1, p. 28.   8 June, 1872, v. 17, p. 283.
15 Sept., 1789, v. 1, p. 68.   30 April, 1798, v. 1, p. 553.
7 Aug., 1849, p. 49.   22 June, 1870, s. 8, v. 16, p. 163.
2 Sept., 1789, v. 1, p. 65.   3 March, 1849, v. 9, p. 395.

SEC. 4. That hereafter it shall be the duty of the heads of the several Executive Departments, in the interest of the public service, to require of all clerks and other employés, of whatever grade or class, in their respective Departments not less than seven hours of labor each day, except Sundays and days declared public holidays by law, or executive order: *Provided,* That the heads of the Departments may by special order, stating the reason, further extend or limit the hours of service of any clerk or employé in their Departments respectively, but in case of an extension it shall be without additional compensation, and all absence from the Departments on the part of said clerks or other employés, in excess of such leave of absence as may be granted by the heads thereof, which shall not exceed thirty days in any one year, except in case of sickness, shall be without pay. **3 March, 1883.** Hours of labor of employés in the Executive Departments.

SEC. 5. That all acts or parts of acts inconsistent or in conflict with the provisions of this act are hereby repealed.

March 3, 1883, chap. 128, P. E. L., p. 563.

The following days, to wit: The first day of January, commonly called New Year's day, the twenty-second day of February, the fourth day of July, the twenty-fifth day of December, commonly called Christmas day, and any day appointed or recommended by the President of the United States as a day of public fast or thanksgiving, shall be holidays within the District of Columbia, and shall, for all purposes of presenting for payment or acceptance for the maturity and protest, and giving notice of the dishonor of bills of exchange, bank checks, and promissory notes or other negotiable or commercial paper, be treated and considered as is the first day of the week, commonly called Sunday, and all notes, drafts, checks, or other commercial or negotiable paper falling due or maturing on either of said holidays shall be deemed as having matured on the day previous. **June 28, 1870.** Holidays in the District of Columbia.

28 June, 1870, v. 16, p. 168.
31 Jan., 1879, v. 20, p. 277.

NOTE.—A joint resolution, approved April 16, 1880, v. 21, p. 304, allows pay to the employés in the Government Printing Office on these holidays.

SEC. 173. Each chief clerk in the several Departments, and Bureaus, and other offices connected with the Departments, shall supervise, under the direction of his immediate superior, the duties of the other clerks therein, and see that they are faithfully performed. **Title 4.** Chief clerks to supervise subordinate clerks.

26 Aug., 1842, s. 13, p. 525.

SEC. 174. Each chief clerk shall take care, from time to time, that the duties of the other clerks are distributed with equality and uniformity, according to the nature of the case. He shall revise such distribution from time to time, for the purpose of correcting any tendency to undue accumulation or reduction of duties, whether arising from individual negligence or incapacity, or from increase or diminution of particular kinds of business. And he shall report monthly to his superior officer any existing defect that he may be aware of in the arrangement or dispatch of business. Chief clerks to distribute duties, &c.

*Idem.*

SEC. 175. Each head of a Department, chief of a Bureau, or other superior officer, shall, upon receiving each monthly report of his chief clerk, rendered pursuant to the preceding section, examine the facts Duty of chief on receipt of report.

146  CIVIL SERVICE—THE EXECUTIVE DEPARTMENTS, ETC.

stated therein, and take such measures, in the exercise of the powers conferred upon him by law, as may be necessary and proper to amend any existing defects in the arrangement or dispatch of business disclosed by such report.

*Idem.*

Disbursing clerks.
SEC. 176. The disbursing clerks authorized by law in the several Departments shall be appointed by the heads of the respective Departments, from clerks of the fourth class; and shall each give a bond to the United States for the faithful discharge of the duties of his office according to law in such amount as shall be directed by the Secretary of the Treasury, and with sureties to the satisfaction of the Solicitor of the Treasury; and shall from time to time renew, strengthen, and increase his official bond, as the Secretary of the Treasury may direct. Each disbursing clerk, except the disbursing clerk of the Treasury Department, must, when directed so to do by the head of the Department, superintend the building occupied by his Department.* Each disbursing clerk is entitled to receive, in compensation for his services in disbursing, such sum in addition to his salary as a clerk of the fourth class as shall make his whole annual compensation two thousand dollars a year.

3 March, 1853, s. 3, v. 10, p. 209-211.   3 March, 1873, s. 1, v. 17, p. 485.
3 March, 1855, s. 4, v. 10, p. 669.

Report of clerks employed.
SEC. 194. The head of each Department shall make an annual report to Congress of the names of the clerks and other persons that have been employed in his Department and the offices thereof; stating the time that each clerk or other person was actually employed, and the sums paid to each; also, whether they have been usefully employed; whether the services of any of them can be dispensed with without detriment to the public service, and whether the removal of any individuals, and the appointment of others in their stead, is required for the better dispatch of business.

26 Aug., 1842, s. 11, v. 5, p. 525.

Time of submitting annual reports.
SEC. 195. Except where a different time is expressly prescribed by law, the various annual reports required to be submitted to Congress by the heads of Departments shall be made at the commencement of each regular session and shall embrace the transactions of the preceding year.
[Various acts of Congress.]

Biennial lists of employés to be filed in Interior Department.
SEC. 198. The head of each Department shall, as soon as practicable after the *first* day in *July* in each year in which a new Congress is to assemble, cause to be filed in the Department of the Interior a full and complete list of all officers, agents, clerks, and employés employed in his Department, or in any of the offices or Bureaus connected therewith. He shall include in such list all the statistics peculiar to his Department required to enable the Secretary of the Interior to prepare the Biennial Register. [See PUBLIC DOCUMENTS.]

27 April, 1816, s. 1, v. 3, p. 342.   |   15 Dec., 1877, s. 2, v. 20, p. 13.
3 March, 1851, s. 1, v. 9, p. 600.   |   16 June, 1880, v. 21, p. 259.
14 July, 1832, v. 4, p. 608.

TEMPORARY VACANCIES.

Sec.
177. Vacancies, how temporarily filled.
178. Vacancies in subordinate offices.
179. Discretionary authority of the President.

Sec.
180. Temporary appointments limited to ten days.
181. Restriction on temporary appointments.
182. Extra compensation disallowed.

Title 4.
Vacancies, how temporarily filled.
SEC. 177. In case of the death, resignation, absence, or sickness of the head of any Department, the first or sole assistant thereof shall, unless otherwise directed by the President, as provided by section one hundred and seventy-nine, perform the duties of such head until a successor is appointed, or such absence or sickness shall cease.

23 July, 1868, s. 1, v. 15, p. 168.

NOTE.—Under sections 177 to 180, a vacancy occasioned by the death or resignation of the head of a Department, or of a chief of a Bureau therein, can be filled by appointment *ad interim* for a period of ten days only. The power is then exhausted.—Op. XVI, 596, Devens, Dec. 31, 1880. The ten days is to be computed from the date of the President's action.—*Ibid,* 457.

Vacancies in subordinate offices.
SEC. 178. In case of the death, resignation, absence, or sickness of the chief of any Bureau, or of any officer thereof, whose appointment is not vested in the head of the Department, the assistant or deputy of such

---

*See act March 3, 1883, providing for a Superintendent of State, War, and Navy Department building, under NAVY DEPARTMENT.

CIVIL SERVICE—THE EXECUTIVE DEPARTMENTS, ETC. 147

chief or of such officer, or if there be none, then the chief clerk of such Bureau, shall, unless otherwise directed by the President, as provided by section one hundred and seventy-nine, perform the duties of such chief or of such officer until a successor is appointed or such absence or sickness shall cease.

*Idem*, s. 2.

SEC. 179. In any of the cases mentioned in the two preceding sections, except the death, resignation, absence, or sickness, of the Attorney-General, the President may, in his discretion, authorize and direct the head of any other Department or any other officer in either Department, whose appointment is vested in the President, by and with the advice and consent of the Senate, to perform the duties of the vacant office until a successor is appointed, or the sickness or absence of the incumbent shall cease. {Discretionary authority of the President.}

23 July, 1868, s. 3, v. 15, p. 168.
22 June, 1870, s. 2, v. 16, p. 162.

SEC. 180. A vacancy occasioned by death or resignation must not be temporarily filled under the three preceding sections for a longer period than ten days. {Temporary appointments limited to ten days.}

23 July, 1868, s. 3, v. 15, p. 168.

SEC. 181. No temporary appointment, designation, or assignment of one officer to perform the duties of another, in the cases covered by sections one hundred and seventy-seven and one hundred and seventy-eight, shall be made otherwise than as provided by those sections, except to fill a vacancy happening during a recess of the Senate. {Restriction on temporary appointments.}

*Idem*, s. 2.

SEC. 182. An officer performing the duties of another office, during a vacancy, as authorized by sections one hundred and seventy-seven, one hundred and seventy-eight, and one hundred and seventy-nine, is not by reason thereof entitled to any other compensation than that attached to his proper office. {Extra compensation disallowed.}

*Idem*, s. 3.

NOTE.—This provision (Section 182) was designed to be general, and applies as well to those vacancies which are supplied by operation of the statute as to those which are filled by designation of the President.—Op. XIII, 7, March 26, 1862, Hoar.

## TENURE OF OFFICE, &C.

Sec.
1760. Unauthorized office, no salary for.
1761. Appointees to fill vacancies during recess of Senate.
1762. Salaries to officers improperly holding over.
1767. Tenure of office.
1768. Suspension and filling vacancies.
1769. Filling vacancies temporarily.
1770. Term of office not to be extended.
1771. Accepting or exercising office contrary to law.
1772. Removing, appointing, or commissioning officer contrary to law.

Sec.
1773. Commissions.
1774. Notification of appointments to Secretary of Treasury.
1775. Notification of nominations, rejections, &c., to Secretary of Treasury.
1786. Proceedings against persons illegally holding office.
1787. Penalty for illegally holding office.

SEC. 1760. No money shall be paid from the Treasury to any person acting or assuming to act as an officer, civil, military, or naval, as salary, in any office when the office is not authorized by some previously existing law, unless such office is subsequently sanctioned by law. {Title 19. Unauthorized office, no salary for.}

9 Feb., 1863, s. 2, v. 12, p. 646.

SEC. 1761. No money shall be paid from the Treasury, as salary, to any person appointed during the recess of the Senate, to fill a vacancy in any existing office, if the vacancy existed while the Senate was in session and was by law required to be filled by and with the advice and consent of the Senate, until such appointee has been confirmed by the Senate. {No salaries to certain appointees to fill vacancies during recess of Senate.}

*Idem.*

SEC. 1762. No money shall be paid or received from the Treasury, or paid or received from or retained out of any public moneys or funds of the United States, whether in the Treasury or not, to or by or for the benefit of any person appointed to or authorized to act in or holding or exercising the duties or functions of any office contrary to sections seventeen hundred and sixty-seven to seventeen hundred and seventy, inclu- {Salaries to officers improperly holding over.}

**148** CIVIL SERVICE—THE EXECUTIVE DEPARTMENTS, ETC.

sive; nor shall any claim, account, voucher, order, certificate, warrant, or other instrument providing for or relating to such payment, receipt, or retention, be presented, passed, allowed, approved, certified, or paid by any officer, or by any person exercising the functions or performing the duties of any office or place of trust under the United States, for or in respect to such office, or the exercising or performing the functions or duties thereof. Every person who violates any of the provisions of this section shall be deemed guilty of a high misdemeanor, and shall be imprisoned not more than ten years, or fined not more than ten thousand dollars, or both.

2 March, 1867, s. 9, v. 14, p. 431.
20 June, 1875, v. 18, p. 109.

**Tenure of office.** SEC. 1767. Every person holding any civil office to which he has been or hereafter may be appointed by and with the advice and consent of the Senate, and who shall have become duly qualified to act therein, shall be entitled to hold such office during the term for which he was appointed, unless sooner removed by and with the advice and consent of the Senate, or by the appointment, with the like advice and consent, of a successor in his place, except as herein otherwise provided.

2 March, 1867, s. 1, v. 14. p. 430.
5 April, 1869, s. 1, v. 16, p. 6.

**Suspension and filling vacancies** SEC. 1768. During any recess of the Senate the President is authorized, in his discretion, to suspend any civil officer appointed by and with the advice and consent of the Senate, except judges of the courts of the United States, until the end of the next session of the Senate, and to designate some suitable person, subject to be removed, in his discretion, by the designation of another, to perform the duties of such suspended officer in the mean time; and the person so designated shall take the oath and give the bond required by law to be taken and given by the suspended officer, and shall, during the time he performs the duties of such officer, be entitled to the salary and emoluments of the office, no part of which shall belong to the officer suspended. The President shall, within thirty days after the commencement of each session of the Senate, except for any office which in his opinion ought not to be filled, nominate persons to fill all vacancies in office which existed at the meeting of the Senate, whether temporarily filled or not, and also in the place of all officers suspended; and if the Senate during such session shall refuse to advise and consent to an appointment in the place of any suspended officer, then, and not otherwise, the President shall nominate another person as soon as practicable to the same session of the Senate for the office.

2 March, 1867, s. 2, v. 14, p. 430.
5 April, 1869, s. 2, v. 16, p. 7.

NOTES.—Section 1768 recognizes the existence of a discretion in the President to not fill an office which has become vacant, where, in his judgment, it is unnecessary in order to execute the laws. The office is not thereby abolished, but is merely left unfilled.—Op. XVI, 266, Devens, Feb. 20, 1879.

An officer suspended under section 1768, Revised Statutes, is not entitled to the salary of the office during the period of suspension, though no person be nominated for the place or appointed to discharge its duties.—C. C., XVII, 149.

Suspension under this section takes effect on due notice thereof to the officer, unless the terms of the order fix a stated time after notice. Receipt of the order is due notice.—Op. XV, 62, Pierrepont, Nov. 20, 1875.

The acts of a suspended officer, performing the duties of the office (no other person having been authorized to perform them) are those of an officer *de facto*, and are valued so far as they concern the interests of the public.—*Idem*.

When no nomination is made, or when one is made and not confirmed, the suspended officer becomes reinstated, but may again be suspended.—Op. XV, 376, Devens, Oct. 4, 1877; also, XIII, 301-308.

Where an officer has been suspended during a recess of the Senate and another person designated to perform his duties, the President may, at any time, revoke the suspension, and thus reinstate the officer.—Op. XV, 380, Devens, Oct. 13, 1877.

The President, in nominating a person to the place of a suspended officer, need not give any reasons for the suspension.—Op. XV, 376, Devens, Oct. 4, 1877.

A suspended officer can under no circumstances be allowed the salary of the office for the period of his suspension.—Op. XIV, 247, Williams, March 31, 1873.

The President may revoke the suspension of an officer and reinstate him in the functions of his office after the rejection by the Senate of a nomination to fill his place.—Op. XIII, 221, Hoar, April 2, 1870.

The "Tenure of Civil Office Act" impresses upon a class of civil officers a tenure at the will of the officeholder, which cannot be terminated except by the concurrence of the President and the Senate in the appointment of a successor and his actual induction in the office.—Op. XII, 307, Stanbery, Nov. 21, 1867.

SEC. 1769. The President is authorized to fill all vacancies which may happen during the recess of the Senate by reason of death or resignation or expiration of term of office, by granting commissions which shall expire at the end of their next session thereafter. And if no appointment, by and with the advice and consent of the Senate, is made to an office so vacant or temporarily filled during such next session of the Senate, the office shall remain in abeyance, without any salary, fees, or emoluments attached thereto, until it is filled by appointment thereto by and with the advice and consent of the Senate; and during such time all the powers and duties belonging to such office shall be exercised by such other officer as may by law exercise such powers and duties in case of a vacancy in such office. *Filling vacancies temporarily.*

2 March, 1867, s. 3, v. 14, p. 430.
5 April, 1869, s. 3, v. 16, p. 7.

NOTES.—The term of office of a chief of a Bureau being for four years from appointment, with the consent of the Senate, it begins from the date of such appointment, and not from the date specified in the nomination.—Op. XVI, 656, Jan. 27, 1880.

Under art. II, sec. 2 of the Constitution, the President has authority to fill, during the recess of the Senate, not only vacancies that have originated in the recess, but also such as originated while the Senate was in session.—Op. XVI, 522, Devens, June 18, 1880.

SEC. 1770. Nothing in sections seventeen hundred and sixty-seven, seventeen hundred and sixty-eight, or seventeen hundred and sixty-nine shall be construed to extend the term of any office the duration of which is limited by law. *Term of office not to be extended.*

2 March, 1867, s. 4, v. 14, p. 431.

SEC. 1771. Every person who, contrary to the four preceding sections, accepts any appointment to or employment in any office, or holds or exercises, or attempts to hold or exercise, any such office or employment, shall be deemed guilty of a high misdemeanor, and shall be imprisoned not more than five years, or fined not more than ten thousand dollars, or both. *Accepting or exercising office contrary to law.*

*Idem,* s. 5.

SEC. 1772. Every removal, appointment, or employment, made, had, or exercised, contrary to sections seventeen hundred and sixty-seven to seventeen hundred and seventy, inclusive, and the making, signing, sealing, countersigning, or issuing of any commission or letter of authority for or in respect to any such appointment or employment, shall be deemed a high misdemeanor, and every person guilty thereof shall be imprisoned not more than five years, or fined not more than ten thousand dollars, or both. *Removing, appointing, or commissioning officer contrary to law.*

*Idem,* s. 6.

SEC. 1773. The President is authorized to make out and deliver, after the adjournment of the Senate, commissions for all officers whose appointments have been advised and consented to by the Senate. *Commissions.*

*Idem.*

SEC. 1774. Whenever the President, without the advice and consent of the Senate, designates, authorizes, or employs any person to perform the duties of any office, he shall forthwith notify the Secretary of the Treasury thereof, and the Secretary of the Treasury shall thereupon communicate such notice to all the proper accounting and disbursing officers of his Department. *Notification of appointments to Secretary of Treasury.*

*Idem,* s. 8.

SEC. 1775. The Secretary of the Senate shall, at the close of each session thereof, deliver to the Secretary of the Treasury, and to each of the Assistant Secretaries of the Treasury, and to each of the Auditors, and to each of the Comptrollers in the Treasury, and to the Treasurer, and to the Register of the Treasury, a full and complete list, duly certified, of all the persons who have been nominated to and rejected by the Senate during such session, and a like list of all the officers to which nominations have been made and not confirmed and filled at such session. *Notification of nominations, rejections, &c., to Secretary of Treasury.*

*Idem,* s. 7.

**Proceedings against persons illegally holding office.**

SEC. 1786. Whenever any person holds office, except as a member of Congress or of some State legislature, contrary to the provisions of the third section* of the fourteenth article of amendment of the Constitution, the district attorney for the district in which such person holds office shall proceed against him by writ of quo warranto, returnable to the circuit or district court of the United States in such district, and prosecute the same to the removal of such person from office.

31 May, 1870, s. 14, v. 16, p. 143.

**Penalty for illegally holding office.**

SEC. 1787. Every person who knowingly accepts or holds any office under the United States, or any State, to which he is ineligible under the third section* of the fourteenth article of amendment of the Constitution, or who attempts to hold or exercise the duties of any such office, shall be deemed guilty of a misdemeanor, and shall be imprisoned not more than one year, or fined not more than one thousand dollars, or both.

*Idem*, s. 15.

NOTES.—Functionaries of the Government in all of its Departments, civil or military, supreme or subordinate, general or provincial, political or municipal, are undoubtedly public officers.—Op. VIII, 107, Cushing, Sept. 30, 1856.

No public officer has authority to enter into a submission on behalf of the United States which will be binding, unless the power be given by statute.—U. S. v. Ames, 1 Woodbury & Minot, p. 76, B. F. D.

The acts of a public officer, on public matters within his jurisdiction and where he has a discretion, are presumed to be legal until the contrary be shown.—Miller v. Dinsman, 7 Howard, p. 89, B. F. D.

Where a particular authority is confided to a public officer, to be exercised in his discretion, upon an examination of facts, of which he is the appropriate judge, his decision thereon, in the absence of any controlling provision, is absolutely final.—Allen v. Blunt, 3 Story's Reports, 742, B. F. D.

The executive officers of the Government are personally liable at law for damages, in the ordinary form of action, for illegal official, ministerial acts or omissions, to the injury of an individual.—Brightley Federal Digest, p. 597. *Cites authorities.*

A public officer, sued for an illegal act, cannot justify under the instructions of the head of an Executive Department.

An officer is responsible in damages for an illegal act done under instructions of a superior, but the Government is bound to indemnify him.

Where a statute imposes a particular duty upon an executive officer and he has acted (performed his duty according to the understanding of the statute), there is no appeal from his action to the President or to any other executive officer, unless such appeal is provided for by law.—Op. XVI, 317, Devens, May 2, 1879.

Usages have been established in every Department of the Government, which have become a kind of common law, and regulate the rights and duties of those who act within their respective limits. And no such change of usage can have a retrospective effect, but must be limited to the future. Usage cannot alter the law, but it is evidence of the construction given to it, and must be considered binding on past transactions.—VII, Peters, 1–14, cited by Cushing.—Op. VIII, 7.

An Executive Department has no right to omit or delay the discharge of the duties imposed upon it by law, at the request of a committee of a House of Congress; it can only pay attention to such a request when it affects a discretionary power.—Op. XIII, 113, Hoar, June 22, 1869.

No process issued under the authority of a State government can obstruct, directly, or indirectly, the operations of the Government of the United States.—Op. XV, 524.

Where an officer of the United States is acting for the Government in any transaction, the benefits of which are to the Government, or where the end is to protect the interests of the Government, there seems to be good ground why the Government should interpose and assume his defense in case he is sued on account of such proceedings.—Op. XIV, 189, Williams, 20 Feb., 1873.

The orders of the head of an Executive Department, in reference to matters within its general supervision and control, are in contemplation of law, those of the President, and have the same binding effect.—Otto, 101, p. 755; Wolsey v. Chapman, see 13 Peters, 498; Wilcox v. Jackson; also Op. IX, 463, and XI, 400.

It is a settled rule of administrative practice that the official acts of a previous administration are to be considered by its successors as final so far as the Executive is concerned.—Op. XV, 208. The Secretary of the Interior should not review the decision of his predecessor, no new facts having been presented. Principal of *res adjudicata* applies.—Op. XV, 315, Devens. See also Op. VIII, 214, and V, 29. The well considered decision of the head of a Department ought only to be reversed upon clear evidence of mistake or wrong.—Op. X, 63.

Congress, in case of appointments, may provide that certain acts shall be done by the appointee before he shall enter on the possession of his office under his appointment. These acts then become conditions precedent to the complete investure of the office.—U. S. v. LeBaron, 19 Howard, 78.

---

* No person * * shall hold any office, civil or military, under the United States, who, having previously taken an oath * * as an officer of the United States * * to support the Constitution of the United States, shall have engaged in insurrection or rebellion against the same, or given aid or comfort to the enemies thereof. But Congress may, by a vote of two-thirds of each house, remove such disability.
3d sec. 14th art. amendment to Constitution.

In a matter which the law confides to the pure discretion of the Executive, the decision by the President or the proper head of the Department, of any question of fact involved, is conclusive and is not subject to revision by any authority in the United States.—Op. VI, 226, Cushing, Nov. 23, 1853.

The lawful will of the President may be announced and an act in the authority of the President be performed, not only by a head of a Department, but in the second or other degree of delegation by some officer subordinate to such head.—Op. VII, 453, Cushing, Aug. 31, 1855. See this opinion for a full discussion of the relation of the President to the Executive Departments.

A public officer is not liable to an action for an honest mistake made in a matter where he was obliged to exercise his judgment, though an individual may thereby suffer.—*Kendall* v. *Stokes*, 3 Howard, 87. B. F. D.

## PARDONING POWER.

The power of pardon, conferred by the Constitution on the President, is unlimited except in case of impeachment. It extends to every offense known to the law, and may be exercised at any time after its commission, either before legal proceedings are taken or during their pendency, or after conviction and judgment. The power is not subject to legislative control. A pardon reaches the punishment prescribed for the offense and the guilt of the offender. If granted before conviction it prevents any of the penalties and disabilities consequent upon conviction from attaching; if granted after conviction it removes the penalties and disabilities, and restores him to all his civil rights. It gives him a new credit and capacity. There is only this limitation to its operation—it does not restore offices forfeited or property or interests vested in others in consequence of the conviction and judgment.—S. C., Wallace, 4, p. 334, Dec., 1866.

Fines and penalties, where they have not been actually covered into the Treasury, are restorable under a full pardon.—Op. XVI, p. 3, April 29, 1878, Devens. See also Op. XIV, June 28, 1872, Williams; XII, 81, Stanbery; VIII, p. 281, Cushing; Holt's Digest, p. 261.

The pardon of a deceased officer or soldier is impracticable for the reason that it is essential to the validity of a pardon that it should be accepted. A pardon, like a deed, must be delivered to and accepted by the party to whom it is granted in order to be valid.—Holt's Digest, p. 262, cites U. S. *v.* Wilson, 7 Peters, 150.

A remission of the penalty by a pardon by the President will restore an officer whose rank has been reduced by sentence of a court-martial to his former relative rank according to the date of his commission [Case of an officer reduced in rank by having his name placed lower down on the list of officers of the same grade. The officer loses such opportunities for promotion as may in the meantime have occurred.]—Op. XII, p. 547, Jan. 22, 1869, Evarts.

The pardoning power of the President cannot reach an *executed sentence* which has been regularly imposed by a competent court. When a sentence has been executed in part he can remit the remainder.—Holt's Digest, p. 260.

For a statement of the principal grounds on which the Judge-Advocate-General of the Army has favored pardon or remission of the unexpired punishments of *soldiers*, see Winthrop's Digest, pp. 359-360.

An application for a pardon was addressed to the President and referred to the War Department. The latter asked the opinion of the Attorney-General on the subject, who declined to give it, as it would only be advising the Secretary of War what to advise the President.—Op. XIV, p. 20, March 23, 1872, Williams.

The general power of pardoning by the President includes the power of pardoning conditionally, or of commuting to a milder punishment that which has been adjudged against the offender. The commutation of the President is but a conditional pardon, and that the President may grant such a conditional pardon has been always recognized and decided.—Op. V, 368, May 10, 1851, Crittenden, cites *U. S.* vs. *Wilson*, 7 Peters, 158.

# CLAIMS AND CLAIM AGENTS.

| Sec. | |
|---|---|
| 184. | Subpœnas to witnesses on claims pending. |
| 185. | Fees of witnesses. |
| 186. | Compelling testimony. |
| 187. | Professional assistance, how obtained. |
| 190. | Former employés acting as counsel. |
| 236. | Public accounts to be settled in the Treasury. |
| 3469. | Compromise of claims. |
| 3477. | Assignment of claims void, unless, &c. |

| Sec. | |
|---|---|
| 3478. | Oath by persons prosecuting claims. |
| 3479. | Who may administer oath. |
| 3480. | Claims of disloyalists. |
| 5454. | Unlawful taking papers relating to claims. |
| 5498. | Officers, &c., interested in claims. |
| —— | Deductions of debts due United States. |
| —— | Claims against exhausted appropriations. |
| —— | Claims based on fraud. |

SEC. 184. Any head of a Department or Bureau in which a claim against the United States is properly pending may apply to any judge or clerk of any court of the United States, in any State, District, or Territory, to issue a subpœna for a witness being within the jurisdiction of such court, to appear at a time and place in the subpœna stated, before any officer authorized to take depositions to be used in the courts of the United States, there to give full and true answers to such written interrogatories and cross-interrogatories as may be sub-

*Title 4.*
Subpœnas to witnesses.

mitted with the application, or to be orally examined and cross-examined upon the subject of such claim.

14 Feb., 1871, s. 1, v. 16, p. 412.

NOTE.—Where the law imposes on officers the examination and settlement of claims, it gives them the authority to require that the claim shall be established, or supported at least, by oaths of witnesses.—Op. XIV, Williams, July 23, 1874.

**Witnesses' fees.** SEC. 185. Witnesses subpœnaed pursuant to the preceding section shall be allowed the same compensation as is allowed witnesses in the courts of the United States.

14 Feb., 1871, s. 1, v. 16, p. 412.

NOTE.—Under sec. 848, R. S., for each day's attendance in court or before any officer, pursuant to law, a witness is allowed one dollar and fifty cents, and five cents a mile for going from his place of residence to the place of trial or hearing, and five cents a mile for returning. When subpœnaed in more than one cause between the same parties, at the same court, only one travel fee and one per diem compensation for attendance shall be allowed—See sec. 850, page 73, part I.

**Compelling testimony.** SEC. 186. If any witness, after being duly served with such subpœna, neglects or refuses to appear, or, appearing, refuses to testify, the judge of the district in which the subpœna issued may proceed, upon proper process, to enforce obedience to the subpœna, or to punish the disobedience, in like manner as any court of the United States may do in case of process of subpœna ad testificandum issued by such court.

*Idem.*

**Professional assistance; how obtained.** SEC. 187. Whenever any head of a Department or Bureau having made application pursuant to section one hundred and eighty-four, for a subpœna to procure the attendance of a witness to be examined, is of opinion that the interests of the United States require the attendance of counsel at the examination, or require legal investigation of any claim pending in his Department or Bureau, he shall give notice thereof to the Attorney-General, and of all facts necessary to enable the Attorney-General to furnish proper professional service in attending such examination, or making such investigation, and it shall be the duty of the Attorney-General to provide for such service.

*Idem,* s. 3.

**Persons formerly in the Departments not to prosecute claims in them.** SEC. 190. It shall not be lawful for any person appointed after the first day of June, one thousand eight hundred and seventy-two, as an officer, clerk, or employé in any of the Departmen's, to act as counsel, attorney, or agent for prosecuting any claim against the United States which was pending in either of said Departments while he was such officer, clerk, or employé, nor in any manner, nor by any means, to aid in the prosecution of any such claim, within two years next after he shall have ceased to be such officer, clerk, or employé.

1 June, 1872, s. 5, v. 17, p. 202.

NOTE.—By the act of July 11, 1864, a member of Congress elect is, previous to as well as after taking the oath of office, debarred from acting as counsel for parties, and from prosecuting claims against the Government before any Department, court-martial, Bureau, office, or any civil, naval, or military commission, if he have received, or has agreed to receive any compensation whatever, directly or indirectly therefor.—Op. XIV, 133, Williams, Nov, 2, 1872.

**Title 7, Chap. 1.** SEC. 236. All claims and demands whatever by the United States, or against them, and all accounts whatever in which the United States are concerned, either as debtors or as creditors, shall be settled and adjusted in the Department of the Treasury.

3 March, 1817, s. 2, v. 3, p. 366.

NOTES.—Services voluntarily rendered, however valuable, and however strongly they may appeal to the liberality and equity of the Government, cannot be said to give the party who renders them a legal right to compensation. The person must have been duly appointed to some office, or duly employed in some duty recognized by law.—Op. III, 357, Butler, Aug. 13, 1838.

Services voluntarily performed without contract for compensation, create no legal liability.—C. C., XIII.

An agent who received payment on a claim in good faith and paid it over to his principal before informed of a mistake made, is not liable. The principal is liable either at the suit of the rightful claimant or of the United States. The officer of the Treasury who made the mistake is legally chargeable with the amount, to be passed to his credit on recovering the money. The rightful owner does not lose his right to be paid out of any money in the Treasury not otherwise appropriated, as the law authorized.—Op. XVI, 193, Devens, Oct. 23, 1878. See also Op. IV, 298, 307, V. 183.

Claims against the Government which are disputed by the officers authorized to adjust such accounts may be compromised. If the claimant voluntarily enters into such a compromise, accepting a smaller sum than his demand and giving a receipt in full for the whole, he is bound by the adjustment.—C. C., v. 8, p. 134, Sweeney's case.

Where Congress appropriated a certain sum to pay a claimant, and the head of a Department found a less sum due and paid the latter, the appropriation was exhausted when the amount awarded was paid. A succeeding Secretary has no jurisdiction to award claimant an additional sum.—Op. IX, 451, Black, July, 20, 1860. See also Op. X, 238, Bates, Apr. 29, 1862.

If funds to pay a claim are sent at request of claimant, by express, the claim is thereby discharged, whether the funds were received or not. If sent by draft, at his request, claim subsists, unless draft has been paid [to proper party]. A disbursing agent remitting funds due claimant, to his attorney, under instructions from the attorney, given without the knowledge or consent of the claimant, which were not paid over, would be liable to the Government and the Government to the claimant.—Op. XIV, 485, Williams, Oct. 29, 1874.

Where Congress directs the "adjustment and settlement" of a claim "according to the rules and regulations heretofore adopted by the United States in the settlement of like cases," and it appears that Congress has generally given interest in like cases, it will be allowed.—C. C., X, p. 231. Affirmed by Supreme Court.

It is a general rule, founded upon sound principles and uniformly adhered to in the administration of the Government, that the Executive Departments neither allow nor charge interest to parties in account with the United States, excepting by virtue of express agreement or in pursuance of some special provision of law.—Holt's Digest. p. 204.

Interest cannot be allowed except "upon a contract expressly stipulating for the payment of interest."—C. C., I, p. 220.

As to interest, see Op. IV, 14, 79, 136; V, 105, 138.

SEC. 3469. Upon a report by a district attorney, or any special attorney or agent having charge of any claim in favor of the United States, showing in detail the condition of such claim, and the terms upon which the same may be compromised, and recommending that it be compromised upon the terms so offered, and upon the recommendation of the Solicitor of the Treasury, the Secretary of the Treasury is authorized to compromise such claim accordingly. But the provisions of this section shall not apply to any claim arising under the postal laws.

**Title 36.**
**Compromise.**

3 March, 1863, s. 10, v. 12, p. 740.

NOTES.—Under section 3469, the Solicitor of the Treasury may properly recommend the acceptance of a compromise offered in discharge of a claim of the United States before payment, where the district attorney advises acceptance upon the ground that, from want of evidence to establish the facts on which a verdict must depend, he doubts his ability to obtain a judgment, even though the defendant is able to pay the amount of the claim.—Op. XVI, 259, Devens, Jan. 30, 1879.

This section was intended to provide for compromising claims in favor of the United States which are of a personal character; does not extend to claims to real property to which the United States asserts ownership and has a record title.—Op. XVI, 385, Devens, Oct. 1, 1879.

It does not confer upon the Solicitor of the Treasury a discretion to recommend for compromise cases in which the claim is entirely solvent, but where circumstances of hardship, &c., exist.—Op. XVI, 617, Phillips, Jan. 8, 1879.

SEC. 3477. All transfers and assignments made of any claim upon the United States, or of any part or share thereof, or interest therein, whether absolute or conditional, and whatever may be the consideration therefor, and all powers of attorney, orders, or other authorities for receiving payment of any such claim, or of any part or share thereof, shall be absolutely null and void, unless they are freely made and executed in the presence of at least two attesting witnesses, after the allowance of such a claim, the ascertainment of the amount due, and the issuing of a warrant for the payment thereof. Such transfers, assignments, and powers of attorney, must recite the warrant for payment, and must be acknowledged by the person making them, before an officer having authority to take acknowledgments of deeds, and shall be certified by the officer; and it must appear by the certificate that the officer, at the time of the acknowledgment, read and fully explained the transfer, assignment, or warrant of attorney to the person acknowledging the same.

**Title 36.**
**Assignments of claims void, unless, &c.**

26 Feb., 1853, s. 1, v. 10, p. 170.
29 July, 1846, v. 9, p. 41.

NOTES.—Though the assignment of a claim against the Government be void under section 3477, R. S., yet if the Treasury recognizes the assignment and pays the amount found due on an accounting to the assignee, an action will not lie to recover it back.—C. C. XIII, 292.] See in this opinion a statement as to the manner in which accounts and claims against the Government are settled by the accounting officers.]

This section, 3477, not only extends to claims which are to be paid by Treasury warrants, but extends to those which relate to claims otherwise payable.—Op. XVI, 261, Devens, Feb. 7, 1879.

A power of attorney for the collection of a claim against the Government, not executed in the presence of "two attesting witnesses after the allowance of such claim, the ascertainment of the amount due, and the issuing of a warrant for the payment thereof," is void under the act of February 26, 1853.—C. C. V, 362; see also Op. IX, 188.

The revocation of a power of attorney can only be affected by notice to the agent. Notice to a third party, without notice to the agent, leaves the power in force.—C. C. VII, 535.

A power of attorney not given on account of any valuable consideration paid to the principal, may be revoked before the exercise of authority under it.—Op. IX, 128.

Where a letter of attorney forms part of a contract, and is security for money, or for the performance of any act which is deemed valuable, it is generally made irrevocable in terms, or, if not so, it is deemed irrevocable in law. If a power of attorney be coupled with an "*interest*" it survives the person giving it and may be executed after his death. VIII, Wheaton, 203. See Op. VII, 35.

A naked power of attorney is revokable at the will of him who gave it, although the writing should say it was irrevocable.—Op. VII, 38.

See Op. XI, 7, where it was held that, although an agent, under a power to prosecute, demand, recover, and receive a claim, did prosecute it to the award, and another was appointed to collect, the installment could be paid to the latter—the power of the former not having been coupled with an interest.

**Oath by persons prosecuting claims.**

SEC. 3478. Any person prosecuting claims, either as attorney or on his own account, before any of the Departments or Bureaus of the United States, shall be required to take the oath of allegiance, and to support the Constitution of the United States, as required of persons in the civil service.

17 July, 1862, s. 1, v. 12, p. 610.

**Who may administer the oath.**

SEC. 3479. The oath provided for in the preceding section may be taken before any justice of the peace, notary public, or other person who is legally authorized to administer an oath in the State or district where the same may be administered.

*Idem.* s. 2.

NOTE.—It is competent to the head of a Department, as a measure for the protection of the public interests committed to his charge, to decline to recognize, or to suspend, the transaction of business with an agent or attorney for frauds and fraudulent practices attempted or committed by him in the prosecution of claims before the Department, and whose character is such that a reasonable degree of confidence cannot be placed in his integrity and honesty in dealing with the Government.—Op. XIII, 156, Hoar, Oct. 4, 1869.

**Claims of disloyalists.**

SEC. 3480. It shall be unlawful for any officer to pay any account, claim, or demand against the United States which accrued or existed prior to the thirteenth day of April, eighteen hundred and sixty-one, in favor of any person who promoted, encouraged, or in any manner sustained the late rebellion, or in favor of any person who during such rebellion was not known to be opposed thereto, and distinctly in favor of its suppression; and no pardon heretofore granted, or hereafter to be granted, shall authorize the payment of such account, claim, or demand, until this section is modified or repealed. But this section shall not be construed to prohibit the payment of claims founded upon contracts made by any of the Departments, where such claims were assigned or contracted to be assigned prior to the first day of April, eighteen hundred and sixty-one, to the creditors of such contractors, loyal citizens of loyal States, in payment of debts incurred prior to the first day of March, eighteen hundred and sixty-one. [See act of March 3, 1877, chap. 105, p. 362, v. 19, as to payment to mail contractors.]

2 March, 1867, Res. 46, v. 14, p. 571.

NOTES.—This section applies only to claims that accrued or existed prior to April 13, 1861. It does not apply to claims in favor of corporations aggregate.—Op. XIII, 398, March 29, 1871, Akerman.

This section created a personal disability only, which could not operate against the heirs of parties thus disqualified.—Winthrop's Digest, p. 168.

Applicable to claims for bounty land.—Op. XV, p. 450.

**Title 70, Chap. 5.**

**Unlawfully taking or using papers relating to claims.**

SEC. 5454. Every person who takes and carries away, without authority from the United States, from the place where it has been filed, lodged, or deposited, or where it may for the time being actually be kept by authority of the United States, any certificate, affidavit, deposition, written statement of facts, power of attorney, receipt, voucher, assignment, or other document, record, file, or paper, prepared, fitted, or intended to be used or presented in order to procure the payment of money from or by the United States, or any officer or agent thereof, or

# CLAIMS AND CLAIM AGENTS. 155

the allowance or payment of the whole or any part of any claim, account, or demand against the United States, whether the same has or has not already been so used or presented, and whether such claim, account, or demand, or any part thereof, has or has not already been allowed or paid, or who presents or uses or attempts to use any such document, record, file, or paper so taken and carried away in order to procure the payment of any money from or by the United States, or any officer or agent thereof, or the allowance or payment of the whole or any part of any claim, account, or demand against the United States, shall be imprisoned at hard labor not more than ten years, or fined not more than five thousand dollars.

5 Feb., 1867, s. 6, v. 14, p. 384.

SEC. 5498. Every officer of the United States, or person holding any place of trust or profit, or discharging any official function under, or in connection with, any Executive Department of the Government of the United States, or under the Senate or House of Representatives of the United States, who acts as an agent or attorney for prosecuting any claim against the United States, or in any manner, or by any means, otherwise than in discharge of his proper official duties, aids or assists in the prosecution or support of any such claim, or receives any gratuity, or any share of or interest in any claim from any claimant against the United States, with intent to aid or assist, or in consideration of having aided or assisted, in the prosecution of such claim, shall pay a fine of not more than five thousand dollars, or suffer imprisonment not more than one year, or both. [See under BRIBES, &c., Part IV.] *Title 70, Chap. 6* — Officers, &c., interested in claims.

26 Feb., 1853, s. 2, v. 10, p. 170.

That when any final judgment recovered against the United States or other claim duly allowed by legal authority, shall be presented to the Secretary of the Treasury for payment, and the plaintiff or claimant therein shall be indebted to the United States in any manner, whether as principal or surety, it shall be the duty of the Secretary to withhold payment of an amount of such judgment or claim equal to the debt thus due to the United States; and if such plaintiff or claimant assents to such set-off, and discharges his judgment or an amount thereof equal to said debt or claim, the Secretary shall execute a discharge of the debt due from the plaintiff to the United States. But if such plaintiff or claimant, denies his indebtedness to the United States, or refuses to consent to the set-off, then the Secretary shall withhold payment of such further amount of such judgment, or claim, as in his opinion will be sufficient to cover all legal charges and costs in prosecuting the debt of the United States to final judgment. And if such debt is not already in suit, it shall be the duty of the Secretary to cause legal proceedings to be immediately commenced to enforce the same, and to cause the same to be prosecuted to final judgment with all reasonable dispatch. And if in such action judgment shall be rendered against the United States, or the amount recovered for debt and costs shall be less than the amount so withheld as before provided, the balance shall then be paid over to such plaintiff by such Secretary with six per cent. interest thereon for the time it has been withheld from the plaintiff. *March 3, 1875.* — Amount of debt due U. S. to be withheld in paying judgments, &c. Secretary to execute discharge, when. Additional amount to be withheld. Duty of Secretary to sue on debt. Balance, how paid to claimant.

3 March, 1875, v. 18, p. 481.

[Claims where appropriations are exhausted or turned in.—See act of June 14, 1878, chap. 191, s. 5, v. 20, p. 130, which expired by limitation June 14, 1883.]

No claim shall hereafter be allowed by the accounting officers, under the provisions of the act of Congress, approved June 16, 1874, or by the Court of Claims, or by Congress, to any person, where such claimant, or those under whom he claims, shall wilfully, knowingly, and with intent to defraud the United States, have claimed more than was justly due in respect to such claim, or presented any false evidence to Congress, or to any Department or court, in support thereof. *April 30, 1878.* — Certain claims not to be allowed.

30 April, 1878, s. 2, v. 20, p. 524.

## COURT OF CLAIMS.

Sec.
188. Evidence to be furnished by the Departments.
1059. Jurisdiction.
1060. Private claims in Congress, when transmitted to Court of Claims.
1061. Judgment for set-off or counter-claim, how enforced.
1062. Decree on account of paymasters, &c.
1063. Claims referred by Departments.
1064. Procedure in cases transmitted by Departments.
1065. Judgments in cases transmitted by Departments, how paid.
1067. Claims pending in other courts not to be prosecuted in Court of Claims.
1069. Limitation.
1072. Petition.

Sec.
1073. Petition dismissed if issue found against claimant as to allegiance, &c.
1074. Burden of proof and evidence as to loyalty.
1076. Power to call upon Departments for information.
1086. Claims forfeited for fraud.
1087. New trial on motion of claimant.
1088. New trial on motion of United States.
1089. Payment of judgments.
1090. Interest.
1091. Interest on claims.
1092. Payment of judgment a full discharge, &c.
1093. Final judgments a bar.
—— Cost of record taxed against losing party.
—— Fraudulently claiming more than is due.
—— Act to relieve Congress and Departments of investigating claims.

**Title 4.**

*Evidence to be furnished by the Departments in suits pending in the Court of Claims.*

SEC. 188. In all suits brought against the United States in the Court of Claims founded upon any contract, agreement, or transaction with any Department, or any Bureau, officer, or agent of a Department, or where the matter or thing on which the claim is based has been passed upon and decided by any Department, Bureau, or officer authorized to adjust it, the Attorney-General shall transmit to such Department, Bureau, or officer, a printed copy of the petition filed by the claimant, with a request that the Department, Bureau, or officer, shall furnish to the Attorney-General all facts, circumstances, and evidence touching the claim in the possession or knowledge of the Department, Bureau, or officer. Such Department, Bureau, or officer shall, without delay, and within a reasonable time, furnish the Attorney-General with a full statement, in writing, of all such facts, information, and proofs. The statement shall contain a reference to or description of all such official documents or papers, if any, as may furnish proof of facts referred to in it, or may be necessary and proper for the defense of the United States against the claim, mentioning the Department, office, or place where the same is kept or may be procured. If the claim has been passed upon and decided by the Department, Bureau, or officer, the statement shall succinctly state the reasons and principles upon which such decision was based. In all cases where such decision was founded upon any act of Congress, or upon any section or clause of such act, the same shall be cited specifically; and if any previous interpretation or construction has been given to such act, section, or clause by the Department, Bureau, or officer, the same shall be set forth succinctly in the statement, and a copy of the opinion filed, if any, shall be annexed to it. Where any decision in the case has been based upon any regulation of a Department, or where such regulation has, in the opinion of the Department, Bureau, or officer transmitting such statement, any bearing upon the claim in suit, the same shall be distinctly quoted at length in the statement. But where more than one case, or a class of cases, is pending, the defense to which rests upon the same facts, circumstances, and proofs, the Department, Bureau, or officer shall only be required to certify and transmit one statement of the same, and such statement shall be held to apply to all such cases, as if made out, certified, and transmitted in each case respectively.

25 June, 1868, s. 6, v. 15, p. 76.

NOTE.—The head of a Department is not at liberty to furnish to the Court of Claims, on a call from that court, information or papers, when to do so would, in his opinion, be injurious to the public interest. A return setting forth such opinion would in all cases be a sufficient answer to the rule.—Op. XIII, 539, Akerman, Nov. 24, 1871.

**Title 13, Chap. 21.**

*Jurisdiction. Claims founded on statutes or contracts, or referred by Congress.*

SEC. 1059. The Court of Claims shall have jurisdiction to hear and determine the following matters:

First. All claims founded upon any law of Congress, or upon any regulation of an Executive Department, or upon any contract, expressed or implied, with the Government of the United States, and all claims which may be referred to it by either House of Congress.

24 Feb., 1855, s. 1, v. 10, p. 612.
3 March, 1875, v. 18, p. 481.
22 June, 1874, s. 2, v. 18, p. 192.

Second. All set offs, counter-claims, claims for damages, whether liquidated or unliquidated, or other demands whatsoever, on the part of the Government of the United States against any person making claim against the Government in said court.

<small>Set-offs and counter-claims of United States.</small>

3 March, 1863, s. 3, v. 12, p. 765.

Third. The claim of any paymaster, quartermaster, commissary of subsistence, or other disbursing officer of the United States, or of his administrators or executors, for relief from responsibility on account of capture or otherwise, while in the line of his duty, of Government funds, vouchers, records, or papers in his charge, and for which such officer was and is held responsible.

<small>Disbursing officers.</small>

9 May, 1866, s. 1, v. 14, p. 44.

Fourth. Of all claims for the proceeds of captured or abandoned property, as provided by the act of March 12, eighteen hundred and sixty-three, chapter one hundred and twenty, entitled "An act to provide for the collection of abandoned property and for the prevention of frauds in insurrectionary districts within the United States," or by the act of July two, eighteen hundred and sixty-four, chapter two hundred and twenty-five, being an act in addition thereto: *Provided*, That the remedy given in cases of seizure under the said acts, by preferring claim in the Court of Claims, shall be exclusive, precluding the owner of any property taken by agents of the Treasury Department as abandoned or captured property in virtue or under color of said acts from suit at common law, or any other mode of redress whatever, before any court other than |said Court of Claims: *Provided also*, That the jurisdiction of the Court of Claims shall not extend to any claim against the United States growing out of the destruction or appropriation of, or damage to, property by the Army or Navy engaged in the suppression of the rebellion. [See sec. 3, of March 3, 1883, p. 161.]

<small>Claims for captured and abandoned property.</small>

18 Feb., 1875, v. 18, p. 318.
12 March, 1863, s. 3, v. 12, p. 820.
2 July, 1864, ss. 2, 3, v. 13, p. 13.
27 July, 1868, s. 3, v. 15, p. 243.

SEC. 1060. All petitions and bills praying or providing for the satisfaction of private claims against the Government, founded upon any law of Congress, or upon any regulation of an Executive Department, or upon any contract, expressed or implied, with the Government of the United States, shall, unless otherwise ordered by resolution of the House in which they are introduced, be transmitted by the Secretary of the Senate or the Clerk of the House of Representatives, with all the accompanying documents, to the Court of Claims.

<small>Private claims in Congress, when transmitted to Court of Claims.</small>

3 March, 1863, s. 2, v. 12, p. 765.

SEC. 1061. Upon the trial of any cause in which any set-off, counter-claim, claim for damages, or other demand is set up on the part of the Government against any person making claim against the Government in said court, the court shall hear and determine such claim or demand both for and against the Government and claimant; and if upon the whole case it finds that the claimant is indebted to the Government, it shall render judgment to that effect, and such judgment shall be final, with the right of appeal, as in other cases provided for by law. Any transcript of such judgment, filed in the clerk's office of any district or circuit court, shall be entered upon the records thereof, and shall thereby become and be a judgment of such court and be enforced as other judgments in such courts are enforced. [See March 3, 1875, CLAIMS, p. 155, as to set-offs.]

<small>Judgments for set-off or counter-claim, how enforced.</small>

*Idem*, s. 3.

SEC. 1062. Whenever the Court of Claims ascertains the facts of any loss by any paymaster, quartermaster, commissary of subsistence, or other disbursing officer, in the cases hereinbefore provided, to have been without fault or negligence on the part of such officer, it shall make a decree setting forth the amount thereof, and upon such decree the proper accounting officers of the Treasury shall allow to such officer the amount so decreed, as a credit in the settlement of his accounts.

<small>Decree on accounts of paymasters, &c.</small>

9 May, 1866, s. 2, v. 14, p. 44.

SEC. 1063. Whenever any claim is made against any Executive Department, involving disputed facts or controverted questions of law, where the amount in controversy exceeds three thousand dollars, or

<small>Claims referred by Departments.</small>

where the decision will affect a class of cases, or furnish a precedent for the future action of any Executive Department in the adjustment of a class of cases, without regard to the amount involved in the particular case, or where any authority, right, privilege, or exemption is claimed or denied under the Constitution of the United States, the head of such Department may cause such claim, with all the vouchers, papers, proofs, and documents pertaining thereto, to be transmitted to the Court of Claims, and the same shall be there proceeded in as if originally commenced by the voluntary action of the claimant; and the Secretary of the Treasury may, upon the certificate of any Auditor or Comptroller of the Treasury, direct any account, matter, or claim, of the character, amount, or class described in this section, to be transmitted, with all the vouchers, papers, documents, and proofs pertaining thereto, to the said court, for trial and adjudication: *Provided*, That no case shall be referred by any head of a Department unless it belongs to one of the several classes of cases which, by reason of the subject-matter and character, the said court might, under existing laws, take jurisdiction of on such voluntary action of the claimant. [See act 3 March, 1883, p. 161.]

25 June, 1868, s. 7, v. 15, p. 76.

NOTES.—The head of a Department may refer a claim direct to the Court of Claims, and he does not waive his right to send a claim there by allowing it in the first instance to be passed upon by the accounting officers of the Treasury.—C. C., V, p. 64.

The head of a Department may transmit a claim to the Court of Claims under sec. 1063 R. S., after the Auditor and Comptroller of the Treasury have settled it and certified a balance due the claimant.—C. C., XII, 319.

The head of an Executive Department cannot transmit a claim to the Court of Claims under section 1063, on the ground that it involves disputed facts or controverted questions of law, if he is forbidden by law to pay the claim.—C. C., XV, 414.

Procedure in cases transmitted by Departments.

SEC. 1064. All cases transmitted by the head of any Department, or upon the certificate of any Auditor or Comptroller, according to the provisions of the preceding section, shall be proceeded in as other cases pending in the Court of Claims, and shall, in all respects, be subject to the same rules and regulations.

25 June, 1868, s. 7, v. 15, p. 76.

Judgments in cases transmitted by Departments, how paid.

SEC. 1065. The amount of any final judgment or decree rendered in favor of the claimant, in any case transmitted to the Court of Claims under the two preceding sections, shall be paid out of any specific appropriation applicable to the case, if any such there be; and where no such appropriation exists, the judgment or decree shall be paid in the same manner as other judgments of the said court.

*Idem*, and 3 March, 1875, v. 18, p. 481.

Claims pending in other courts not to be prosecuted in Court of Claims.

SEC. 1067. No person shall file or prosecute in the Court of Claims, or in the Supreme Court on appeal therefrom, any claim for or in respect of which he or any assignee of his has pending in any other court any suit or process against any person who, at the time when the cause of action alleged in such suit or process arose, was, in respect thereto, acting or professing to act, mediately or immediately, under the authority of the United States.

25 June, 1868, s. 8, v. 15, p. 677.

Limitation.

SEC. 1069. Every claim against the United States, cognizable by the Court of Claims, shall be forever barred unless the petition setting forth a statement thereof is filed in the court, or transmitted to it by the Secretary of the Senate or the Clerk of the House of Representatives as provided by law, within six years after the claim first accrues: *Provided*, That the claims of married women first accrued during marriage, of persons under the age of twenty-one years first accrued during minority, and of idiots, lunatics, insane persons, and persons beyond the seas at the time the claim accrued, entitled to the claim, shall not be barred if the petition be filed in the court or transmitted, as aforesaid, within three years after the disability has ceased; but no other disability than those enumerated shall prevent any claim from being barred, nor shall any of the said disabilities operate cumulatively.

3 March, 1863, s. 10, v. 12, p. 767.

NOTE.—The statute of limitations prescribed by the amended Court of Claims act (March 13, 1863, 12 Stat. L., 765, § 10) does not extend to claims in the Executive Departments.—C. C., XIV, 149.

SEC. 1072. The claimant shall, in all cases, fully set forth in his petition the claim, the action thereon in Congress, or by any of the Departments, if such action has been had; what persons are owners thereof or interested therein, when and upon what consideration such persons became so interested; that no assignment or transfer of said claim, or of any part thereof or interest therein, has been made, except as stated in the petition; that said claimant is justly entitled to the amount therein claimed from the United States, after allowing all just credits and offsets; that the claimant, and, where the claim has been assigned, the original and every prior owner thereof, if a citizen, has at all times borne true allegiance to the Government of the United States, and, whether a citizen or not, has not in any way voluntarily aided, abetted, or given encouragement to rebellion against the said Government, and that he believes the facts as stated in the said petition to be true. And the said petition shall be verified by the affidavit of the claimant, his agent, or attorney. *Petition.*

24 Feb., 1855, s. 1, v. 10, p. 612.
3 March, 1863, s. 12, v. 12, p. 767.

SEC. 1073. The said allegations as to true allegiance and voluntary aiding, abetting, or giving encouragement to rebellion against the Government may be traversed by the Government, and if on the trial such issues shall be decided against the claimant, his petition shall be dismissed. *Petition dismissed, if issue found against claimant as to allegiance, &c.*

3 March, 1863, s. 12, v. 12, p. 767.

SEC. 1074. Whenever it is material in any claim to ascertain whether any person did or did not give any aid or comfort to the late rebellion, the claimant asserting the loyalty of any such person to the United States during such rebellion shall be required to prove affirmatively that such person did, during said rebellion, consistently adhere to the United States, and did give no aid or comfort to persons engaged in said rebellion; and the voluntary residence of any such person in any place where, at any time during such residence, the rebel force or organization held sway, shall be prima-facie evidence that such person did give aid and comfort to said rebellion and to the persons engaged therein. *Burden of proof and evidence as to loyalty.*

25 June, 1868, s. 3, v. 15, p. 75.

SEC. 1076. The said court shall have power to call upon any of the Departments for any information or papers it may deem necessary, and shall have the use of all recorded and printed reports made by the committees of each House of Congress, when deemed necessary in the prosecution of its business. But the head of any Department may refuse and omit to comply with any call for information or papers when, in his opinion, such compliance would be injurious to the public interest. *Power to call upon Departments for information.*

24 Feb., 1855, s. 11, v. 10, p. 614.

SEC. 1086. Any person who corruptly practices or attempts to practice any fraud against the United States in the proof, statement, establishment, or allowance of any claim, or of any part of any claim against the United States, shall ipso facto forfeit the same to the Government; and it shall be the duty of the Court of Claims, in such cases, to find specifically that such fraud was practiced or attempted to be practiced, and thereupon to give judgment that such claim is forfeited to the Government, and that the claimant be forever barred from prosecuting the same. [See act of April 30, 1878, *post.*] *Claims forfeited for fraud.*

3 March, 1863, s. 11, v. 12, p. 767.

SEC. 1087. When judgment is rendered against any claimant, the court may grant a new trial for any reason which, by the rules of common law or chancery in suits between individuals, would furnish sufficient ground for granting a new trial. *New trial on motion of claimant.*

24 Feb., 1855, s. 9, v. 10, p. 614.

SEC. 1088. The Court of Claims, at any time while any claim is pending before it, or on appeal from it, or within two years next after the final disposition of such claim, may, on motion on behalf of the United States, grant a new trial and stay the payment of any judgment therein, upon such evidence, cumulative or otherwise, as shall satisfy the court that any fraud, wrong, or injustice in the premises has been done to the United States; but until an order is made staying the payment of a judgment, the same shall be payable and paid as now provided by law. *New trial on motion of United States.*

25 June, 1868, s. 2, v. 15, p. 75.

## COURT OF CLAIMS.

**Payment of judgments.**
SEC. 1089. In all cases of final judgments by the Court of Claims, or, on appeal, by the Supreme Court, where the same are affirmed in favor of the claimant, the sum due thereby shall be paid out of any general appropriation made by law for the payment and satisfaction of private claims, on presentation to the Secretary of the Treasury of a copy of said judgment, certified by the clerk of the Court of Claims, and signed by the chief justice, or, in his absence, by the presiding judge of said court. [See March 3, 1875, under CLAIMS.]

3 March, 1863, s. 7, v. 12, p. 766.
3 March, 1875, v. 18, p. 481.

**Interest.**
SEC. 1090. In cases where the judgment appealed from is in favor of the claimant, and the same is affirmed by the Supreme Court, interest thereon at the rate of five per centum shall be allowed from the date of its presentation to the Secretary of the Treasury for payment as aforesaid, but no interest shall be allowed subsequent to the affirmance, unless presented for payment to the Secretary of the Treasury as aforesaid.

3 March, 1863, s. 7, v. 12, p. 766.

**Interest claims.**
SEC. 1091. No interest shall be allowed on any claim up to the time of the rendition of judgment thereon by the Court of Claims, unless upon a contract expressly stipulating for the payment of interest.

*Idem.*

**Payment of judgment a full discharge, &c.**
SEC. 1092. The payment of the amount due by any judgment of the Court of Claims and of any interest thereon allowed by law, as hereinbefore provided, shall be a full discharge to the United States of all claim and demand touching any of the matters involved in the controversy.

*Idem.*

**Final judgments a bar.**
SEC. 1093. Any final judgment against the claimant on any claim prosecuted as provided in this chapter shall forever bar any further claim or demand against the United States arising out of the matters involved in the controversy.

*Idem.*

**3 March, 1877.**

**Cost of printing record to be taxed against losing party.**
There shall be taxed against the losing party in each and every cause pending in the Supreme Court of the United States or in the Court of Claims of the United States, the cost of printing the record in such case, which shall be collected, except when the judgment is against the United States, by the clerks of said courts, respectively, and paid into the Treasury of the United States.

3 March, 1877, ch. 105, s. 1, v. 19, p. 344.

**30 April, 1878.**

**Claims not to be allowed where more is fraudulently claimed than is due.**
No claim shall hereafter be allowed * * * by the Court of Claims * * to any person, where such claimant, or those under whom he claims, shall wilfully, knowingly, and with intent to defraud the United States, have claimed more than was justly due in respect of such claim or presented any false evidence to Congress, or to any Department or court, in support thereof.

30 April, 1878, ch. 77, s. 2, v. 20, p. 524.

AN ACT to afford assistance and relief to Congress and the Executive Departments in the investigation of claims and demands against the Government.

**3 March, 1883.**

**Reference of claims pending before Congress.**
*Be it enacted by the Senate and House of Representatives of the United States of America in Congress assembled,* That whenever a claim or matter is pending before any committee of the Senate or House of Representatives, or before either House of Congress, which involves the investigation and determination of facts, the committee or·house may cause the same, with the vouchers, papers, proofs, and documents pertaining thereto, to be transmitted to the Court of Claims of the United States, and the same shall there be proceeded in under such rules as the court may adopt. When the facts shall have been found, the court shall not enter judgment thereon, but shall report the same to the committee or to the house by which the case was transmitted for its consideration.

**Reference of claims pending with Executive Departments.**
SEC. 2. That when a claim or matter is pending in any of the Executive Departments which may involve controverted questions of fact or law, the head of such Department may transmit the same, with the vouchers, papers, proofs, and documents pertaining thereto, to said court, and the same shall be there proceeded in under such rules as the

court may adopt. When the facts and conclusions of law shall have been found, the court shall not enter judgment thereon, but shall report its findings and opinions to the Department by which it was transmitted for its guidance and action.

SEC. 3. The jurisdiction of said court shall not extend to or include any claim against the United States growing out of the destruction or damage to property by the Army or Navy during the war for the suppression of the rebellion, or for the use and occupation of real estate by any part of the military or naval forces of the United States in the operations of said forces during the said war at the seat of war; nor shall the said court have jurisdiction of any claim against the United States which is now barred by virtue of the provisions of any law of the United States. *Claims not within the jurisdiction of the court.*

SEC. 4. In any case of a claim for supplies or stores taken by or furnished to any part of military or naval forces of the United States for their use during the late war for the suppression of the rebellion, the petition shall aver that the person who furnished such supplies or stores, or from whom such supplies or stores were taken, did not give any aid or comfort to said rebellion, but was throughout that war loyal to the Government of the United States, and the fact of such loyalty shall be a jurisdictional fact; and unless the said court shall, on a preliminary inquiry, find that the person who furnished such supplies or stores, or from whom the same were taken as aforesaid, was loyal to the Government of the United States throughout said war, the court shall not have jurisdiction of such cause, and the same shall, without further proceedings, be dismissed. *Claims for supplies, &c., furnished for the suppression of the rebellion.*

SEC. 5. That the Attorney-General, or his assistants, under his direction, shall appear for the defense and protection of the interests of the United States in all cases which may be transmitted to the Court of Claims under this act, with the same power to interpose counter-claims, offsets, defenses for fraud practiced or attempted to be practiced by claimants, and other defenses, in like manner as he is now required to defend the United States in said court. *Defense, &c., for the United States.*

SEC. 6. That in the trial of such cases no person shall be excluded as a witness because he or she is a party to or interested in the same. *Parties in interest may testify.*

SEC. 7. That reports of the Court of Claims to Congress under this act, if not finally acted upon during the session at which they are reported, shall be continued from session to session and from Congress to Congress until the same shall be finally acted upon. *Continuation of reports.*

3 March, 1883, chap. 116, P. E. L., p. 485.

## CONTINGENT FUNDS.

Sec.
192. Expenditure for newspapers.
193. Annual report of expenditure.
430. Estimates for contingent expenses.
1779. Expenditure for newspapers.
1780. Failure to make report.

Sec.
3676. How controlled, &c.
3682. Restrictions on contingent appropriations.
3683. Purchases from contingent fund restricted.
—— Statement to be made to Congress.
—— Not to be used to pay salaries.

SEC. 192. The amount expended in any one year for newspapers, for any Department, except the Department of State, including all the Bureaus and offices connected therewith, shall not exceed one hundred dollars. And all newspapers purchased with the public money for the use of either of the Departments must be preserved as files for such Department. *Title 4. Expenditure for newspapers.*

26 Aug., 1842, s. 16, v. 5, p. 526.

SEC. 193. The head of each Department shall make an annual report to Congress, giving a detailed statement of the manner in which the contingent fund for his Department, and for the Bureaus and offices therein, has been expended, giving the names of every person to whom any portion thereof has been paid; and if for anything furnished, the quantity and price; and if for any service rendered, the nature of such service, and the time employed, and the particular occasion or cause, in brief, that rendered such service necessary; and the amount of all former appropriations in each case on hand, either in the Treasury or in the hands of any disbursing officer or agent. And he shall require of the disbursing officers, acting under his direction and authority, the return of precise and analytical statements and receipts for all the moneys which may have been from time to time during the next preced- *Annual report of expenditure of contingent funds.*

162 CONTINGENT FUNDS.

ing year expended by them, and shall communicate the results of such returns and the sums total, annually, to Congress. [See 20 June, 1874, *post.*]

26 Aug., 1842, s. 20, v. 5, p. 527.

**Title 10.**
Estimates for expenses.

SEC. 430. All estimates for * * contingent expenses of the Department, and of the several Bureaus, shall be furnished to the Secretary of the Navy by the chiefs of the respective Bureaus. [See § 3666, APPROPRIATIONS.]

5 July, 1862, s. 5, v. 12, p. 511.

**Title 19.**
Expenditure for newspapers.

SEC. 1779. No executive officer, other than the heads of Departments, shall apply more than thirty dollars, annually, out of the contingent fund under his control, to pay for newspapers, pamphlets, periodicals, or other books or prints not necessary for the business of his office.

3 March, 1839, s. 3, v. 5, p. 349.

Failure to make returns or reports.

SEC. 1780. Every officer who neglects or refuses to make any return or report which he is required to make at stated times by any act of Congress or regulation of the Department of the Treasury, other than his accounts, within the time prescribed by such act or regulation, shall be fined not more than one thousand dollars and not less than one hundred.

18 July, 1866, s. 42, v. 14, p. 188.

**Title 41.**
Appropriations controlled by Secretary; each Bureau to be kept separate.

SEC. 3676. All appropriations for * * contingent expenses of the Navy Department shall be under the control and expended by the direction of the Secretary of the Navy, and the appropriation for each Bureau shall be kept separate in the Treasury.

5 July, 1862, s. 5, v. 12, p. 511.

Restrictions on contingent, &c., appropriations.

SEC. 3682. No moneys appropriated for contingent, incidental, or miscellaneous purposes shall be expended or paid for official or clerical compensation. [See Aug. 7, 1882, *post.*]

12 July, 1870, s. 3, v. 16, p. 250.

[The naval appropriation act of August 5, 1882, forbids paying from the contingent fund of the Navy for personal services in the Navy Department or any of its subordinate bureaus or offices in the District of Columbia.]

Purchases from contingent funds restricted.

SEC. 3683. No part of the contingent fund appropriated to any Department, Bureau, or office, shall be applied to the purchase of any articles except such as the head of the Department shall deem necessary and proper to carry on the business of the Department, Bureau, or office, and shall, by written order, direct to be procured.

26 Aug., 1842, s. 19, v. 5, p. 527.

NOTES.—The Secretary of the Navy can draw on the contingent fund for purposes of a contingent character—that is, such as might or might not happen, and which Congress could not easily foresee, and therefore could not provide for definitely.—Op. I, 302, Wirt.

The words "Contingent expenses," as used in the appropriation acts, mean such incidental, casual expenses as are necessary, or at least appropriate and convenient, in order to the performance of the duties *required by law* of the Department or the office for which the appropriation is made.—Op. XVI, 412, Devens, Dec. 19, 1879.

20 June, 1874.
Statement of expenditures to be reported at beginning of session.

Hereafter a detailed statement of the expenditure for the preceding fiscal year of all sums appropriated for contingent expenses in any Department or Bureau of the Government, shall be presented to Congress at the beginning of each regular session.

Appropriation acts, v. 18, p. 355; v. 19, p. 156–306, 20 June, 1874, v. 18, p. 85, and subsequent acts.

Aug. 7, 1882.
Contingent not to be used to pay clerks, &c.

And no civil officer, clerk, draughtsman, copyist, messenger, assistant messenger, mechanic, watchman, laborer, or other employé shall hereafter be employed at the seat of government in any executive department or subordinate bureau or office thereof, or be paid from any appropriation made for contingent expenses, or for any specific or general purpose, unless such employment is authorized and payment therefor specifically provided in the law granting the appropriation, and then only for services actually rendered in connection with and for the purposes of the appropriation from which payment is made, and at the rate of compensation usual and proper for such services.

7 Aug., 1882, P. E. L., p. 255.

# DEBTS DUE BY OR TO THE UNITED STATES.

| Sec. | Sec. |
|---|---|
| 3466. Priority established. | 3471. Discharge of poor debtor by Secretary of the Treasury. |
| 3467. Liability of executors. | 3472. Discharge by the President. |
| 3468. Priority of sureties. | —— Deduction of debts due from judgments. |
| 3469. Compromises. | |
| 3470. Purchase on execution. | |

SEC. 3466. Whenever any person indebted to the United States is insolvent, or whenever the estate of any deceased debtor, in the hands of the executors or administrators, is insufficient to pay all the debts due from the deceased, the debts due to the United States shall be first satisfied; and the priority hereby established shall extend as well to cases in which a debtor, not having sufficient property to pay all his debts, makes a voluntary assignment thereof, or in which the estate and effects of an absconding, concealed, or absent debtor are attached by process of law, as to cases in which an act of bankruptcy is committed.

*Title 36.*
*Priority established.*

3 March, 1797, s. 5, v. 1, p. 515.
2 March, 1799, s. 65, v. 1, p. 676.

SEC. 3467. Every executor, administrator, or assignee, or other person, who pays any debt due by the person or estate from whom or for which he acts, before he satisfies and pays the debts due to the United States from such person or estate, shall become answerable in his own person and estate for the debts so due to the United States, or for so much thereof as may remain due and unpaid.

*Liability of executors, &c.*

2 March, 1799, s. 65, v. 1, p. 676.

SEC. 3468. Whenever the principal in any bond given to the United States is insolvent, or whenever, such principal being deceased, his estate and effects which come to the hands of his executor, administrator, or assignee, are insufficient for the payment of his debts, and, in either of such cases, any surety on the bond, or the executor, administrator, or assignee of such surety pays to the United States the money due upon such bond, such surety, his executor, administrator, or assignee, shall have the like priority for the recovery and receipt of the moneys out of the estate and effects of such insolvent or deceased principal as is secured to the United States; and may bring and maintain a suit upon the bond, in law or equity, in his own name, for the recovery of all moneys paid thereon.

*Priority of sureties.*

Ibid.

SEC. 3469. Upon a report by a district attorney, or any special attorney or agent having charge of any claim in favor of the United States, showing in detail the condition of such claim, and the terms upon which the same may be compromised, and recommending that it be compromised upon the terms so offered, and upon the recommendation of the Solicitor of the Treasury, the Secretary of the Treasury is authorized to compromise such claim accordingly. But the provisions of this section shall not apply to any claim arising under the postal laws.

*Compromise.*

*Op. XIII, 480; XVI, 250, 259.*

3 March, 1863, s. 10, v. 12, p. 740.

SEC. 3470. At every sale, on execution, at the suit of the United States, of lands or tenements of a debtor, the United States may, by such agent as the Solicitor of the Treasury shall appoint, become the purchaser thereof; but in no case shall the agent bid in behalf of the United States a greater amount than that of the judgment for which such estate may be exposed to sale, and the costs. Whenever such purchase is made, the marshal of the district in which the sale is held shall make all needful conveyances, assignments, or transfers to the United States.

*Purchase on execution.*

26 May, 1824, s. 2, v. 4, p. 51.

SEC. 3471. Any person imprisoned upon execution issuing from any court of the United States, for a debt due to the United States, which he is unable to pay, may, at any time after commitment, make application, in writing, to the Secretary of the Treasury, stating the circumstances of his case, and his inability to discharge the debt; and thereupon the

*Discharge of poor debtor by Secretary of the Treasury.*

Secretary may make, or require to be made, an examination and inquiry into the circumstances of the debtor, by the oath of the debtor, which the Secretary, or any other person by him specially appointed, is authorized to administer, or otherwise, as the Secretary shall deem necessary and expedient, to ascertain the truth; and upon proof made to his satisfaction, that the debtor is unable to pay the debt for which he is imprisoned, and that he has not concealed or made any conveyance of his estate, in trust, for himself, or with an intent to defraud the United States, or to deprive them of their legal priority, the Secretary is authorized to receive from such debtor any deed, assignment, or conveyance of his real or personal estate, or any collateral security, to the use of the United States. Upon a compliance by the debtor with such terms and conditions as the Secretary may judge reasonable and proper, the Secretary must issue his order, under his hand, to the keeper of the prison, directing him to discharge the debtor from his imprisonment under such execution. The debtor shall not be liable to be imprisoned again for the debt; but the judgment shall remain in force, and may be satisfied out of any estate which may then, or at any time afterward, belong to the debtor. The benefit of this section shall not be extended to any person imprisoned for any fine, forfeiture, or penalty, incurred by a breach of any law of the United States, or for moneys had and received by any officer, agent, or other person, for their use; nor shall its provisions extend to any claim arising under the postal laws.

6 June, 1798, ss. 1, 3, v. 1, pp. 561-562.

**Discharge by the President.** SEC. 3472. Whenever any person is imprisoned upon execution for a debt due to the United States, which he is unable to pay, and his case is such as does not authorize his discharge by the Secretary of the Treasury, under the preceding section, he may make application to the President, who, upon proof made to his satisfaction that the debtor is unable to pay the debt, and upon a compliance by the debtor with such terms and conditions as the President shall deem proper, may order the discharge of such debtor from his imprisonment. The debtor shall not be liable to be imprisoned again for the same debt; but the judgment shall remain in force, and may be satisfied out of any estate which may then, or at any time afterward, belong to the debtor.

3 March, 1817, v. 3, p. 399.

**March 3, 1875.**

**Amount of debt due U. S. to be withheld by Secretary of Treasury in paying judgments, &c., of debtor against U. S.**

**Secretary to execute discharge, when.**

That when any final judgment recovered against the United States or other claim duly allowed by legal authority, shall be presented to the Secretary of the Treasury for payment, and the plaintiff or claimant therein shall be indebted to the United States in any manner, whether as principal or surety, it shall be the duty of the Secretary to withhold payment of an amount of such judgment or claim equal to the debt thus due to the United States; and if such plaintiff or claimant assents to such set off, and discharges his judgment or an amount thereof equal to said debt or claim, the Secretary shall execute a discharge of the debt due from the plaintiff to the United States.

But if such plaintiff, or claimant, denies his indebtedness to the United States, or refuses to consent to the set-off, then the Secretary shall withhold payment of such further amount of such judgment, or claim, as in his opinion will be sufficient to cover all legal charges and costs in prosecuting the debt of the United States to final judgment.

**Proceedings when claimant denies debt.** And if such debt is not already in suit, it shall be the duty of the Secretary to cause legal proceedings to be immediately commenced to enforce the same, and to cause the same to be prosecuted to final judgment with all reasonable dispatch.

**Balance, how paid when claimant obtains judgment against U. S.** And if in such action judgment shall be rendered against the United States, or the amount recovered for debt and costs shall be less than the amount so withheld as before provided, the balance shall then be paid over to such plaintiff by such Secretary with six per cent. interest thereon for the time it has been withheld from the plaintiff.

3 March, 1875, v. 18, p. 481.

NOTE.—Security for a debt is not payment. The Fourth Auditor is not authorized to consider security offered for a debt due the United States, however ample it may be, a payment of a debt.—Op. 1, p. 503, Wirt, Jan. 24, 1823.

# DISTRESS-WARRANTS.

Sec.
3625. Distress-warrant.
3626. Contents of warrant.
3627. Execution against officer.
3628. Execution against surety.
3629. Levy to be a lien.
3630. Sale of lands, &c., on execution.
3631. Conveyance of lands sold.
3632. Disposal of surplus.
3633. Penalty on disbursing officer failing to account.

Sec.
3634. Extent of application of provisions relating to distress-warrants.
3635. Postponement of proceedings for non-accounting, when allowed.
3636. Injunction to stay distress-warrant.
3637. Proceedings on distress-warrant in circuit court.
3638. Rights of United States reserved.

SEC. 3625. Whenever any collector of the revenue, receiver of public money, or other officer who has received the public money before it is paid into the Treasury of the United States, fails to render his account, or pay over the same in the manner or within the time required by law, it shall be the duty of the First Comptroller of the Treasury or the Commissioner of Customs as the case may be, to cause to be stated the account of such officer, exhibiting truly the amount due to the United States, and to certify the same to the Solicitor of the Treasury, who shall issue a warrant of distress against the delinquent officer and his sureties, directed to the marshal of the district in which such officer and his sureties reside. Where the officer and his sureties reside in different districts, or where they, or either of them, reside in a district other than that in which the estate of either may be, which it is intended to take and sell, then such warrant shall be directed to the marshals of such districts, respectively.

*Title 40. Distress-warrant.*

15 May, 1820, s. 2, v. 3, p. 592.
29 May, 1830, s. 1, v. 4, p. 414.
27 Feb., 1877, v. 19, p. 240.

SEC. 3626. The warrant of distress shall specify the amount with which such deliquent is chargeable, and the sums, if any, which have been paid.

*Contents of warrant.*

*Ibid.*

SEC. 3627. The marshal authorized to execute any warrant of distress shall, by himself or by his deputy, proceed to levy and collect the sum remaining due, by distress and sale of the goods and chattels of such dilinquent officer; having given ten days' previous notice of such intended sale, by affixing an advertisement of the articles to be sold at two or more public places in the town and county where the goods or chattels were taken, or in the town or county where the owner of such goods or chattels may reside. If the goods and chattels be not sufficient to satisfy the warrant, the same may be levied upon the person of such officer, who may be committed to prison, there to remain until discharged by due course of law.

*Execution against officer.*

15 May, 1820, s. 2, v. 3, p. 593.

SEC. 3628. If the delinquent officer absconds, or if goods and chattels belonging to him cannot be found sufficient to satisfy the warrant, the marshal or his deputy shall proceed, notwithstanding the commitment of the delinquent officer, to levy and collect the sum which remains due by such delinquent, by the distress and sale of the goods and chattels of his sureties; having given ten days' previous notice of such intended sale, by affixing an advertisement of the articles to be sold at two or more public places in the town or county where the goods or chattels were taken, or in the town or county where the owner resides.

*Execution against surety.*

*Ibid.*

SEC. 3629. The amount due by any delinquent officer is declared to be a lien upon the lands, tenements, and hereditaments of such officer and his sureties, from the date of a levy in pursuance of the warrant of distress issued against him or them, and a record thereof made in the office of the clerk of the district court of the proper district, until the same is discharged according to law.

*Levy to be lien.*

*Ibid.*

SEC. 3630. For want of goods and chattels of a delinquent officer, or his sureties, sufficient to satisfy any warrant of distress issued pursuant to the foregoing provisions, the lands, tenements, and hereditaments of

*Sale of lands regulated.*

such officer and his sureties, or so much thereof as may be necessary for that purpose, after being advertised for at least three weeks in not less than three public places in the county or district where such real estate is situate, before the time of sale, shall be sold by the marshal of such district or his deputy.

*Ibid.*

**Conveyance of lands.**
SEC. 3631. For all lands, tenements, or hereditaments sold in pursuance of the preceding section, the conveyance of the marshal or his deputy, executed in due form of law, shall give a valid title against all persons claiming under such delinquent officer or his sureties.

*Ibid.*

**Disposal of surplus.**
SEC. 3632. All moneys which may remain of the proceeds of sales, after satisfying the warrant of distress, and paying the reasonable costs and charges of the sale, shall be returned to such delinquent officer or surety, as the case may be.

*Ibid.*

**Failure of disbursing officer to account; penalty.**
SEC. 3633. Whenever any officer employed in the civil, military, or naval service of the Government, to disburse the public money appropriated for those branches of the public service, respectively, fails to render his accounts, or to pay over, in the manner and in the times required by law, or by the regulations of the Department to which he is accountable, any sum of money remaining in his hands, it shall be the duty of the First or Second Comptroller of the Treasury, as the case may be, who shall be charged with the revision of the accounts of such officer, to cause to be stated and certified the account of such delinquent officer to the Solicitor of the Treasury, who is hereby authorized and required immediately to proceed against such delinquent officer, in the manner directed in the six preceding sections.

15 May, 1820, s. 3, v. 3, p. 594.
20 May, 1830, s. 1, v. 4, p. 414.

**Extent of application of provision for distress-warrants.**
SEC. 3634. All the provisions relating to the issuing of a warrant of distress against a delinquent officer shall extend to every officer of the Government charged with the disbursement of the public money, and to their sureties, in the same manner and to the same extent as if they were herein described and enumerated.

15 May, 1820, s. 3, v. 3, p. 594.

**Postponement of proceedings for non-accounting, allowed.**
SEC. 3635. With the approval of the Secretary of the Treasury, the institution of proceedings by a warrant of distress may be postponed, for a reasonable time, in cases where, in his opinion, the public interest will sustain no injury by such postponement.

*Ibid.*

**Injunction to stay distress-warrant.**
SEC. 3636. Any person who considers himself aggrieved by any warrant of distress issued under the foregoing provisions may prefer a bill of complaint to any district judge of the United States, setting forth therein the nature and extent of the injury of which he complains; and thereupon the judge may grant an injunction to stay proceedings on such warrant altogether, or for so much thereof as the nature of the case requires. But no injunction shall issue till the party applying for it gives bond, with sufficient security, in a sum to be prescribed by the judge, for the performance of such judgment as may be awarded against him; nor shall the issuing of such injunction in any manner impair the lien produced by the issuing of the warrant. And the same proceedings shall be had on such injunction as in other cases, except that no answer shall be necessary on the part of the United States; and if, upon dissolving the injunction, it appears to the satisfaction of the judge that the application for the injunction was merely for delay, the judge may add to the lawful interest assessed on all sums found due against the complainant such damages as, with such lawful interest, shall not exceed the rate of ten per centum a year. Such injunction may be granted or dissolved by the district judge either in or out of court.

*Ibid.*, ss. 4, 5.

**Proceedings on distress in circuit court.**
SEC. 3637. When the district judge refuses to grant an injunction to stay proceedings on a distress-warrant, as aforesaid, or dissolves such injunction after it is granted, any person who considers himself aggrieved by the decision in the premises may lay before the circuit justice, or

circuit judge of the circuit within which such district lies, a copy of the proceedings had before the district judge; and thereupon the circuit justice or circuit judge may grant an injunction, or permit an appeal, as the case may be, if, in his opinion, the equity of the case requires it. The same proceedings, subject to the same conditions, shall be had upon such injunction in the circuit court as are prescribed in the district court.

*Ibid.*, ss. 4, 6.
10 April, 1869, s. 2, v. 16, p. 44.

SEC. 3638. Nothing contained in the provisions of this Title relating to distress-warrants shall be construed to take away or impair any right or remedy which the United States might have, by law, for the recovery of taxes, debts, or demands.  *Rights of United States reserved.*

15 May, 1820, s. 9, v. 3, p. 596.

## DISBURSING OFFICERS AND AGENTS.

Sec.
285. Disbursements by order of commanding officer.
957. Suits against delinquents.
1389. Paymasters not to loan.
1550. Disbursing agents on foreign stations.
1563. Advances on distant stations.
1766. Officers in arrears.
1788. Disbursing officers forbidden to trade in public funds or property.
3614. Bonds of special agents.
3620. Duty of disbursing officers.
3621. Penalty for failure to deposit when required.
3622. Accounts, when to be rendered.
3623. Distinct accounts required.
3624. Suits to recover moneys from officers.
3639. Duties of custodian of public money.
3648. Advances prohibited.

Sec.
5481. Officers guilty of extortion.
5483. Requiring receipts for larger sums than paid.
5488. Unlawfully depositing, loaning, &c., public moneys.
5489. Failure of Treasurer, &c., to safely keep public money.
5490. Custodian of public money failing to safely keep, without loaning, &c.
5491. Failure of officers to render accounts, &c.
5492. Failure to deposit as required.
5493. Provisions of the five preceding sections, how applied.
5494. Record evidence of embezzlement.
5495. Prima-facie evidence.
5496. Evidence of conversion.
5497. Unlawfully receiving, &c., to be embezzlement.

SEC. 285. Every disbursement of public moneys, or disposal of public stores, made by a disbursing officer pursuant to an order of any commanding officer of the Navy, shall be allowed by the proper accounting officers of the Treasury, in the settlement of the accounts of the officer, upon satisfactory evidence of the making of such order, and of the payment of money or disposal of stores in conformity with it; and the commanding officer by whose order such disbursement or disposal was made, shall be held accountable for the same. *Title 7, Chap. 4. Disbursements, &c., by order of commanding officer of Navy.*

3 March, 1849, Res. 2, v. 9, p. 419.

SEC. 957. When suit is brought by the United States against any revenue officer or other person accountable for public money, who neglects or refuses to pay into the Treasury the sum or balance reported to be due to the United States, upon the adjustment of his account it shall be the duty of the court to grant judgment at the return term, upon motion, unless the defendant, in open court, (the United States attorney being present,) makes and subscribes an oath that he is equitably entitled to credits which had been, previous to the commencement of the suit, submitted to the accounting officers of the Treasury, and rejected; specifying in the affidavit each particular claim so rejected, and that he cannot then safely come to trial. If the court, when such oath is made, subscribed, and filed, is thereupon satisfied, a continuance until the next succeeding term may be granted. Such continuance may also be granted when the suit is brought upon a bond or other sealed instrument, and the defendant pleads non est factum, or makes a motion to the court, verifying such plea or motion by his oath, and the court thereupon requires the production of the original bond, contract, or other paper certified in the affidavit. And no continuance shall be granted except as herein provided. [See § 3624.] *Title 13, Chap. 18. Delinquents for public money; judgment at return term, unless, &c.*

3 March, 1797, s. 3, v. 1, p. 514.

SEC. 1389. It shall not be lawful for any paymaster, passed assistant paymaster, or assistant paymaster, to advance or loan, under any pretense whatever, to any officer in the naval service, any sum of money, public or private, or any credit, or any article or commodity whatever. *Title 15, Chap. 1. Loans to officers by paymasters.*

26 Aug., 1842, s. 6. v. 5, p. 536.
22 June, 1860, s. 3, v. 12, p. 83.

DISBURSING OFFICERS AND AGENTS.

**Title 15, Chap. 7.**
*Disbursements on foreign stations.*

SEC. 1550. No person shall be employed or continued abroad, to receive and pay money for the use of the naval service on foreign stations, whether under contract or otherwise, who has not been, or shall not be, appointed by and with the advice and consent of the Senate.

17 June, 1844, s. 4, v. 5, p. 703.

**Title 15, Chap. 8.**
*Advances to persons on distant stations.*

SEC. 1563. The President of the United States may direct such advances, as he may deem necessary and proper, to such persons in the naval service as may be employed on distant stations where the discharge of the pay and emoluments to which they are entitled cannot be regularly effected. [See § 3648.]

31 Jan., 1823, s. 1, v. 3, p. 723.

**Title 19.**
*Officers in arrears.*

SEC. 1766. No money shall be paid to any person for his compensation who is in arrears to the United States, until he has accounted for and paid into the Treasury all sums for which he may be liable. In all cases where the pay or salary of any person is withheld in pursuance of this section, the accounting officers of the Treasury, if required to do so by the party, his agent or attorney, shall report forthwith to the Solicitor of the Treasury the balance due; and the Solicitor shall, within sixty days thereafter, order suit to be commenced against such delinquent and his sureties.

25 Jan., 1828, v. 4, p. 246.
20 May, 1836, v. 5, p. 31.

NOTES.—The phrase "who is in arrears to the United States" seems to apply materially and properly only to persons who, having previous transactions of a pecuniary nature with the Government, are found, upon the settlement of those transactions, to be in *arrears* to the Government by holding in their hands *public moneys* which they are to refund. Op. I, 676, Wirt, July 22, 1824, III, 52, Butler, March 21, 1836. Pay of officers, ascertained to be in default, can be withheld where the time for the accounting duly has actually passed—not otherwise.—Op. IV, 33, May 24, 1842, Legare.

"Pay," "salary," or "compensation" are synonymous terms, under the act of 25 January, 1828, authorizing the withholding of the pay of persons in arrears. The authority does not extend to rations.—Op. II, 420. "Extra pay," which is not pay proper, cannot be withheld.—Op. II, 593.

The officers of the Treasury are authorized to withhold the pay of officers of the Government who are ascertained to be defaulters, where the time for accounting has actually passed, but not otherwise. "Forthwith" is equivalent to "without unnecessary delay."—Op. IV, 33, Legare, May 24, 1842.

It is the duty of disbursing officers to repay funds remaining in hand when the time for them to go to the surplus fund arrives. *Certificates issued previous* to that time, upon claims definitely ascertained, may be paid out of those appropriations, even though the time has passed for them to go to the surplus fund, if the disbursing officer has any of the appropriation in his hands. For what period and to what amount such officers should be allowed to retain funds in their hands for that purpose is a matter of administration falling within the province of the Secretary of the Treasury to regulate.—Op. XV, 357, Devens, Aug. 10, 1877.

The words "expenditures incurred" do not mean liabilities incurred. To incur an expenditure is to make a payment—to expend money. To incur liability and to incur an expenditure are two different and distinct things; and while the word incur is not frequently used in connection with expenditure, yet when used it means an expenditure actually made.—Op. XIV, 128, Williams, Sept. 17, 1878.

**Title 19.**
*Disbursing officers forbidden to trade in public funds or property.*

SEC. 1788. Every officer of the United States concerned in the disbursement of the revenues thereof who carries on any trade or business in the funds or debts of the United States, or of any State, or in any public property of either, shall be deemed guilty of a misdemeanor, and punished by a fine of three thousand dollars, and shall, upon conviction, be removed from office, and forever thereafter be incapable of holding any office under the United States.

2 Sept., 1789, s. 8, v. 1, p. 67.
8 May, 1792, s. 12, v. 1, p. 281.
2 March, 1799, s. 87, v. 1, p. 695.

**Title 40.**
*Bond of special agents.*

SEC. 3614. Whenever it becomes necessary for the head of any Department or office to employ special agents, other than officers of the Army or Navy, who may be charged with the disbursement of public moneys, such agent shall, before entering upon duty, give bond in such form and with such security as the head of the Department or office employing them may approve. [See notes to this section under AGENTS.]

4 Aug., 1854, s. 14, v. 10, p. 573.

*Duty of disbursing officers.*

SEC. 3620. It shall be the duty of every disbursing officer having any public money intrusted to him for disbursement, to deposit the same with the Treasurer or some one of the assistant treasurers of the United

States, and to draw for the same only as it may be required for payments to be made by him in pursuance of law and draw for the same only in favor of the persons to whom payment is made; and all tranfers from the Treasurer of the United States to a disbursing officer shall be by draft or warrant on the Treasury or an assistant treasurer of the United States. In places, however, where there is no treasurer or assistant treasurer, the Secretary of the Treasury may, when he deems it essential to the public interest, specially authorize in writing the deposit of such public money in any other public depository, or, in writing, authorize the same to be kept in any other manner, and under such rules and regulations as he may deem most safe and effectual to facilitate the payments to public creditors. [See § 5488.]

14 June, 1866, s. 1, v. 14, p. 64.
27 Feb., 1877, v. 19, p. 249.

NOTE.—If a disbursing officer, in good faith, deposits public money in a designated depository, loss of the moneys through failure of the bank cannot be imputed to the fault or negligence of the officer. So long as the Government holds him responsible and does not bring suit, so long he has the right to petition the Court of Claims for relief.—C. C., XVII, 189.

SEC. 3621. Every person who shall have moneys of the United States in his hands or possession shall pay the same to the Treasurer, an assistant treasurer, or some public depositary of the United States, and take his receipt for the same, in duplicate, and forward one of them forthwith to the Secretary of the Treasury. [See § 5492.] *Penalty for failure to deposit money when required.*

3 March, 1857, s. 3, v. 11, p. 249.

NOTES.—Money in the hands of a disbursing officer of the United States, due and payable by him to a private person, cannot be attached by process out of the State courts. 4 Howard, 20. It is not competent to the State courts to enjoin officers of the executive Departments from executing the lawful orders thereof, whether they concern the payment of money for the performance of contracts with the United States or any other matter.—Op. XVI, 257, Devens, Jan. 29, 1879.

The Supreme Court has repeatedly decided that the courts have no jurisdiction or authority over the moneys of the Government in the hands of its agents, and that such moneys cannot be enjoined or controlled by a mandamus.—Op. VII, 81, Cushing, March 29, 1855. Not subject to attachment at the suit of creditors of the parties to whom such money is due.—Op. XIII, Akerman, Jan. 7, 1872. See also Op. X, 120.

SEC. 3622. Every officer or agent of the United States who receives public money which he is not authorized to retain as salary, pay, or emolument, shall render his accounts monthly. Such accounts, with the vouchers necessary to the correct and prompt settlement thereof, shall be sent by mail, or otherwise, to the Bureau to which they pertain, within ten days after the expiration of each successive month, and, after examination there, shall be passed to the proper accounting officer of the Treasury for settlement. Disbursing officers of the Navy shall, however, render their accounts and vouchers direct to the proper accounting officer of the Treasury. In case of the non-receipt at the Treasury, or proper Bureau, of any accounts within a reasonable and proper time thereafter, the officer whose accounts are in default shall be required to furnish satisfactory evidence of having complied with the provisions of this section. The Secretary of the Treasury may, if in his opinion the circumstances of the case justify and require it, extend the time hereinbefore prescribed for the rendition of accounts. Nothing herein contained shall, however, be construed to restrain the heads of any of the Departments from requiring such other returns or reports from the officer or agent, subject to the control of such heads of Departments, as the public interest may require. [See § 5491.] *Accounts.*

17 July, 1862, s. 1, v. 12, p. 503.
2 March, 1867, res. 48, v. 14, p. 571.
15 July, 1870, s. 15, v. 15, p. 334.
27 Feb., 1877, v. 19, p. 249.

SEC. 3623. All officers, agents, or other persons, receiving public moneys, shall render distinct accounts of the application thereof, according to the appropriation under which the same may have been advanced to them. *Distinct accounts required.*

3 March, 1809, s. 1, v. 2, p. 535.

SEC. 3624. Whenever any person accountable for public money, neglects or refuses to pay into the Treasury the sum or balance reported to be due to the United States, upon the adjustment of his account, the First Comptroller of the Treasury shall institute suit for the recovery of the same, adding to the sum stated to be due on such ac- *Suits to recover money from officers, regulated.*

count, the commissions of the delinquent, which shall be forfeited in every instance where suit is commenced and judgment obtained thereon, and an interest of six per centum per annum, from the time of receiving the money until it shall be repaid into the Treasury.

3 March, 1797, s. 1, v. 1, p. 512.

**Duties of officers as custodians of public moneys.**
SEC. 3639. * * * all public officers of whatsoever character, are required to keep safely, without loaning, using, depositing in banks, or exchanging for other funds than as specially allowed by law, all the public money collected by them, or otherwise at any time placed in their possession and custody, till the same is ordered, by the proper Department or officer of the Government, to be transferred or paid out; and when such orders for transfer or payment are received, faithfully and promptly to make the same as directed, and to do and perform all other duties as fiscal agents of the Government which may be imposed by any law, or by any regulation of the Treasury Department made in conformity to law. * * * [See § 5497.]

6 Aug., 1846, s. 6, v. 9, p. 60.<br>
3 March, 1857, s. 2, v. 11, p. 249.<br>
3 July, 1852, s. 7, v. 10, p. 12.<br>
3 March, 1863, s. 5, v. 12, p. 770.<br>
4 July, 1864, s. 5, v. 13, p. 383.<br>
21 April, 1862, s. 5, v. 12, p. 382.<br>
18 Feb., 1869, s. 4, v. 15, p. 271.

**Advances of public moneys prohibited.**
SEC. 3648. No advance of public money shall be made in any case whatever. And in all cases of contracts for the performance of any service, or the delivery of articles of any description, for the use of the United States, payment shall not exceed the value of the service rendered, or of the articles delivered previously to such payment. It shall, however, be lawful, under the special direction of the President, to make such advances to the disbursing officers of the Government as may be necessary to the faithful and prompt discharge of their respective duties, and to the fulfillment of the public engagements. The President may also direct such advances as he may deem necessary and proper, to persons in the military and naval service employed on distant stations, where the discharge of the pay and emoluments to which they may be entitled cannot be regularly effected. [See § 1563.]

31 Jan., 1823, s. 1, v. 3, p. 723.

**Title 70, Chap. 6.**

**Officer of the United States guilty of extortion.**
SEC. 5481. Every officer of the United States who is guilty of extortion under color of his office shall be punished by a fine of not more than five hundred dollars, or by imprisonment not more than one year, except those officers or agents of the United States otherwise differently and specially provided for in subsequent sections of this chapter

3 March, 1825, s. 12, v. 4, p. 118.

**Receipting for larger sums than are paid.**
SEC. 5483. Every officer charged with the payment of any of the appropriations made by any act of Congress, who pays to any clerk, or other employé of the United States, a sum less than that provided by law, and requires such employé to receipt or give a voucher for an amount greater than that actually paid to and received by him, is guilty of embezzlement, and shall be fined in double the amount so withheld from any employé of the Government, and shall be imprisoned at hard labor for the term of two years.

3 March, 1853, s. 4, v. 10, p. 239.

**Disbursing officers unlawfully depositing, converting, loaning, or transferring public money.**
SEC. 5488. Every disbursing officer of the United States who deposits any public money intrusted to him in any place or in any manner, except as authorized by law, or converts to his own use in any way whatever, or loans with or without interest, or for any purpose not prescribed by law withdraws from the Treasurer or any assistant treasurer, or any authorized depository, or for any purpose not prescribed by law transfers or applies any portion of the public money intrusted to him, is, in every such act, deemed guilty of an embezzlement of the money so deposited, converted, loaned, withdrawn, transferred, or applied; and shall be punished by imprisonment with hard labor, for a term not less than one year nor more than ten years, or by a fine of not more than the amount embezzled or less than one thousand dollars, or by both such fine and imprisonment.

14 June, 1866, s. 2, v. 14, p. 64.

**Failure of Treasurer, &c., to safely keep public moneys.**
SEC. 5489. If the Treasurer of the United States, or any assistant treasurer, or any public depositary, fails safely to keep all moneys deposited by any disbursing officer or disbursing agent, as well as all

moneys deposited by any receiver, collector, or other person having moneys of the United States, he shall be deemed guilty of embezzlement of the moneys not so safely kept, and shall be imprisoned not less than six months nor more than ten years, and fined in a sum equal to the amount of money so embezzled. [See § 3639.]

3 March, 1857, s. 2, v. 11, p. 249.

Sec. 5490. Every officer or other person charged by any act of Congress with the safe-keeping of the public moneys, who fails to safely keep the same, without loaning, using, converting to his own use, depositing in banks, or exchanging for other funds than as specially allowed by law, shall be guilty of embezzlement of the money so loaned, used, converted, deposited, or exchanged; and shall be imprisoned not less than six months nor more than ten years, and fined in a sum equal to the amount of money so embezzled. [See § 3639.] Custodians of public money failing to safely keep, without loaning, &c.

6 Aug., 1846, s. 16, v. 9, p. 63.

Sec. 5491. Every officer or agent of the United States who, having received public money which he is not authorized to retain as salary, pay, or emolument, fails to render his accounts for the same as provided by law, shall be deemed guilty of embezzlement, and shall be fined in a sum equal to the amount of the money embezzled, and shall be imprisoned not less than six months or more than ten years. [See §§ 3622, 3633.] Failure of officer to render accounts, &c.

17 July, 1862, s. 1, v. 12, p. 593.
15 July, 1870, s. 15, v. 16, p. 334.
2 March, 1867, res. 48, v. 14, p. 571.
6 Aug., 1846, s. 16, v. 9, p. 63.

Sec. 5492. Every person who, having moneys of the United States in his hands or possession, fails to make deposit of the same with the Treasurer, or some assistant treasurer, or some public depositary of the United States, when required so to do by the Secretary of the Treasury, or the head of any other proper Department, or by the accounting officers of the Treasury, shall be deemed guilty of embezzlement thereof, and shall be imprisoned not less than six months nor more than ten years, and fined in a sum equal to the amount of money embezzled. Failure to deposit as required.

3 March, 1857, s. 3, v. 11, p. 249.
6 Aug., 1846, s. 16, v. 9, p. 63.

Sec. 5493. The provisions of the five preceding sections shall be construed to apply to all persons charged with the safe-keeping, transfer, or disbursement of the public money, whether such persons be indicted as receivers or depositaries of the same. Provisions of the five preceding sections, how applied.

6 Aug., 1846, s. 16, v. 9, p. 63.

Sec. 5494. Upon the trial of any indictment against any person for embezzling public money under the provisions of the six preceding sections, it shall be sufficient evidence, for the purpose of showing a balance against such person, to produce a transcript from the books and proceedings of the Treasury, as required in civil cases, under the provisions for the settlement of accounts between the United States and receivers of public money. [See §§ 3625, 3633, under Distress Warrants.] Record evidence of embezzlement.

*Ibid.*

Sec. 5495. The refusal of any person, whether in or out of office, charged with the safe-keeping, transfer, or disbursement of the public money, to pay any draft, order, or warrant, drawn upon him by the proper accounting officer of the Treasury, for any public money in his hands belonging to the United States, no matter in what capacity the same may have been received, or may be held, or to transfer or disburse any such money promptly, upon the legal requirement of any authorized officer, shall be deemed, upon the trial of any indictment against such person for embezzlement, as prima-facie evidence of such embezzlement. Prima-facie evidence.

6 Aug., 1846, s. 16, v. 9, p. 63.

Sec. 5496. If any officer charged with the disbursement of the public moneys, accepts, receives, or transmits to the Treasury Department to be allowed in his favor, any receipt or voucher from a creditor of the United States, without having paid to such creditor in such funds as the officer received for disbursement, or in such funds as he may be authorized by law to take in exchange, the full amount specified in such receipt or voucher, every such act is an act of conversion, by such Evidence of conversion.

**Unlawfully receiving, &c., to be embezzlement.**

officer, to his own use, of the amount specified in such receipt or voucher. [See § 3652, under CHECKS.]

*Ibid.*

SEC. 5497. Every banker, broker, or other person not an authorized depositary of public moneys, who knowingly receives from any disbursing officer, or collector of internal revenue, or other agent of the United States, any public money on deposit, or by way of loan or accommodation, with or without interest, or otherwise than in payment of a debt against the United States, or who uses, transfers, converts, appropriates, or applies any portion of the public money for any purpose not prescribed by law, and every president, cashier, teller, director, or other officer of any bank or banking association, who violates any of the provisions of this section, is guilty of an act of embezzlement of the public money so deposited, loaned, transferred, used, converted, appropriated, or applied, and shall be punished as prescribed in section fifty-four hundred and eighty-eight. [See § 3639.]

14 June, 1866, s. 3, v. 14, p. 65.

## CHECKS AND DRAFTS.

| Sec. | Sec. |
|---|---|
| 300. Allowance of lost checks. | 3045. Regulations for presenting drafts. |
| 306. Liabilities outstanding three or more years. | 3646. Duplicates for lost or stolen checks. |
| 307. Vouchers for drafts remaining unpaid. | 3047. Duplicate check when officer who issued is dead. |
| 308. Payment upon presentation of outstanding drafts. | 3651. Exchange of funds restricted. |
| 309. Accounts of disbursing officers unchanged for three years. | 3652. Premium on sales of public money to be accounted for. |
| 310. Reports of disbursing officers, &c. | |

**Title 7, Chap. 4.**

**Allowance of lost checks.**

SEC. 300. Whenever the disbursing officer, or agent by whom was issued any check which has been lost, destroyed, or stolen, is dead, or no longer in the service of the United States, the proper accounting officer shall, under such regulations as the Secretary of the Treasury may prescribe, state an account in favor of the owner of such original check for the amount thereof, and charge such amount to the account of such officer or agent.

2 Feb., 1872, ss. 1, 2, v. 17, p. 29.

**Title 7, Chap. 5.**

**Liabilities outstanding three or more years.**

SEC. 306. At the termination of each fiscal year all amounts of moneys that are represented by certificates, drafts, or checks, issued by the Treasurer, or by any disbursing officer of any Department of the Government, upon the Treasurer or any assistant treasurer, or designated depositary of the United States, or upon any national bank designated as a depositary of the United States, and which shall be represented on the books of either of such offices as standing to the credit of any disbursing officer, and which were issued to facilitate the payment of warrants, or for any other purpose in liquidation of a debt due from the United States, and which have for three years or more remained outstanding, unsatisfied, and unpaid, shall be deposited by the Treasurer, to be covered into the Treasury by warrant, and to be carried to the credit of the parties in whose favor such certificates, drafts, or checks were respectively issued, or to the persons who are entitled to receive pay therefor, and into an appropriation account to be denominated "outstanding liabilities."

2 May, 1866, ss. 1, 4, v. 14, pp. 41, 42.

**Vouchers for drafts remaining unpaid.**

SEC. 307. The certificate of the Register of the Treasury, stating that the amount of any draft issued by the Treasurer, to facilitate the payment of a warrant directed to him for payment, has remained outstanding and unpaid for three years or more, and has been deposited and covered into the Treasury in the manner prescribed by the preceding section, shall be, when attached to any such warrant, a sufficient voucher in satisfaction of any such warrant or part of any warrant, the same as if the drafts correctly indorsed and fully satisfied were attached to such warrant or part of warrant. And all such moneys mentioned in this and in the preceding section shall remain as a permanent appropriation for the redemption and payment of all such outstanding and unpaid certificates, drafts, and checks.

2 May, 1866, s. 2, v. 14, p. 41.

# DISBURSING OFFICERS AND AGENTS. 173

Sec. 308. The payee or the bona-fide holder of any draft or check the amount of which has been deposited and covered into the Treasury pursuant to the preceding sections, shall, on presenting the same to the proper officer of the Treasury, be entitled to have it paid by the settlement of an account and the issuing of a warrant in his favor, according to the practice in other cases of authorized and liquidated claims against the United States. *Payment upon presentation of outstanding drafts.*

*Ibid., s. 3.*

Sec. 309. The amounts, except such as are provided for in section three hundred and six, of the accounts of every kind of disbursing officer, which shall have remained unchanged, or which shall not have been increased by any new deposit thereto, nor decreased by drafts drawn thereon, for the space of three years, shall in like manner be covered into the Treasury, to the proper appropriation to which they belong; and the amounts thereof shall, on the certificate of the Treasurer that such amount has been deposited in the Treasury, be credited by the proper accounting officer of the Department of the Treasury on the books of the Department, to the officer in whose name it had stood on the books of any agency of the Treasury, if it appears that he is entitled to such credit. *Accounts of disbursing officers unchanged for three years.*

*Ibid., s. 5.*

Sec. 310. The Treasurer, each assistant treasurer, and each designated depositary of the United States, and the cashier of each of the national banks designated as such depositaries, shall, at the close of business on every thirtieth day of June, report to the Secretary of the Treasury the condition of every account standing, as in the preceding section specified, on the books of their respective offices, stating the name of each depositor, with his official designation, the total amount remaining on deposit to his credit, and the dates, respectively, of the last credit and the last debit made to each account. And each disbursing officer shall make a like return of all checks issued by him, and which may then have been outstanding and unpaid for three years and more, stating fully in such report the name of the payee, for what purpose each check was given, the office on which drawn, the number of the voucher received therefor, the date, number, and amount for which it was drawn, and, when known, the residence of the payee. *Reports of Treasurer, assistant treasurers, &c., and disbursing officers.*

*Ibid., s. 6.*

Sec. 3645. It shall be the duty of the Secretary of the Treasury to issue and publish regulations to enforce the speedy presentation of all Government drafts, for payment, at the place where payable, and to prescribe the time, according to the different distances of the depositaries from the seat of Government, within which all drafts upon them, respectively, shall be presented for payment; and, in default of such presentation, to direct any other mode and place of payment which he may deem proper; but, in all these regulations and directions, it shall be his duty to guard, as far as may be, against those drafts being used or thrown into circulation as a paper currency or a medium of exchange. [See §§ 5495, 5496. Disbursing Officers.] *Title 40. Regulations for presentment of drafts.*

6 Aug., 1846, s. 31, v. 9, p. 65.

Sec. 3646. Whenever any original check is lost, stolen, or destroyed, disbursing officers and agents of the United States are authorized, after the expiration of six months, and within three years from the date of such check, to issue a duplicate check; and the Treasurer, assistant treasurers, and designated depositaries of the United States are directed to pay such duplicate checks, upon notice and proof of the loss of the original checks, under such regulations in regard to their issue and payment, and upon the execution of such bonds, with sureties, to indemnify the United States, as the Secretary of the Treasury shall prescribe. This section shall not apply to any check exceeding in amount the sum of one thousand dollars. *Duplicates for lost or stolen checks authorized.*

2 Feb., 1872, s. 1, v. 17, p. 29.

Sec. 3647. In case the disbursing officer or agent by whom such lost, destroyed, or stolen original check was issued, is dead, or no longer in the service of the United States, it shall be the duty of the proper accounting officer, under such regulations as the Secretary of the Treasury shall prescribe, to state an account in favor of the owner of such orig- *Duplicate check when officer who issued is dead.*

inal check for the amount thereof, and to charge such amount to the account of such officer or agent.

*Ibid.*, s. 2.

**Exchange of funds restricted.**
SEC. 3651. No exchange of funds shall be made by any disbursing officer or agent of the Government, of any grade or denomination whatsoever, or connected with any branch of the public service, other than an exchange for gold, silver, United States notes, and national-bank notes; and every such disbursing officer, when the means for his disbursements are furnished to him in gold, silver, United States notes, or national-bank notes, shall make his payments in the moneys so furnished; or when they are furnished to him in drafts, shall cause those drafts to be presented at their place of payment, and properly paid according to law, and shall make his payments in the money so received for the drafts furnished, unless, in either case, he can exchange the means in his hands for gold and silver at par. And it shall be the duty of the head of the proper Department immediately to suspend from duty any disbursing officer or agent who violates the provisions of this section, and forthwith to report the name of the officer or agent to the President, with the fact of the violation, and all the circumstances accompanying the same, and within the knowledge of the Secretary, to the end that such officer or agent may be promptly removed from office, or restored to his trust and the performance of his duties, as the President may deem just and proper.

6 Aug., 1846, s. 20, v. 9, p. 64.
11 July, 1862, s. 1, v. 12, p. 532.
22 Feb., 1862, s. 1, v. 12, p. 345.
3 June, 1864, s. 23, v. 13, p. 106.
3 March, 1863, s. 3, v. 12, p. 610.

**Premiums on sales of public moneys to be accounted for.**
SEC. 3652. No officer of the United States shall, either directly or indirectly, sell or dispose of to any person, for a premium, any Treasury note, draft, warrant, or other public security, not his private property, or sell or dispose of the avails or proceeds of such note, draft, warrant, or security, in his hands for disbursement, without making return of such premium, and accounting therefor by charging the same in his accounts to the credit of the United States; and any officer violating this section shall be forthwith dismissed from office.

6 Aug., 1846, s. 21, v. 9, p. 65.

NOTES.—Approved bills or accounts or vouchers are not in any proper sense negotiable paper. The Government would not be required to pay to party to whom they were assigned, if it had itself an equitable claim against the contractor; nor if satisfied that the account had been erroneously approved. Revised Statute 3477 regulates the manner of paying assigned bills, &c. That statute is of universal application. The Department can reissue an approved account in favor of contractor. [Case of bills made out in favor of broker instead of contractors, and assigned by former.]—Op. XVI, 191, Devens, Oct. 23, 1878.

The protection which commercial usage throws around negotiable paper cannot be used to establish the authority of an agent who issued it. Whenever negotiable paper is found in market upon which the Government is apparently a party, the purchaser must, at his peril, see that the officer who indorsed or accepted it had authority to bind the Government.—C. C., VII, 65; Wallace, VII, 666.

Acceptance of payment in one kind of money (Treasury notes) is a waiver of a claim, antecedently asserted for gold. It discharges the debt independently of the question whether paper money is a legal tender.—C. C., VI, 216.

There is no objection in point of law, to the indorsement of a bill of exchange, under authority derived from a power of attorney.—Op. I, 188.

Where an officer is authorized to pay money at a distant point, he may transmit it by drafts.—7 Wallace, p. 466; C. C., VII, p. 65.

Checks given by paymasters are valid obligations of the Government, although dishonored for want of funds to the credit of the officers who issued them.—Op. XI, 216, Speed, April 22, 1865. See, also, XI, p. 156.

It does not follow that because an officer may lawfully issue bills of exchange for some purpose, he can in that mode bind the Government in other cases where he has no such authority.—7 Wallace, 666.

Whenever the United States Government, through their authorized officer, accept a bill of exchange, they are bound for its payment to a *bona fide* holder for value, whatever may have been the equities as between them and the drawer.—U. S. v. Bank Metropolis, XV, Peters, 377.

Whether checks shall be made payable only to the person entitled to the money, or "to bearer" or "to order," is a matter to be regulated entirely by the Treasury Department. The only imperative requisition is that the check shall be drawn only in favor of the person to whom the payment is to be made. Op. XV, 288, June 4, 1877, Devens.

It is competent for the Secretary of the Treasury to permit disbursing officers to draw checks payable to themselves or bearer or order for such amounts as may be necessary to make payments of small amounts, to make payments at a distance from a depository, or to make payments of fixed salaries as now authorized by Department regulations of Aug. 24, 1876, provided, always, that such checks bear indorsed upon them the names of the persons to whom the amounts are to be paid, or the claim upon which they are to be paid, or are accompanied by a list or schedule, made a part of the check, containing the same information.—Op. XV, 303, June 8, 1877, Devens.

## COINS, WEIGHTS, AND MEASURES, LEGAL-TENDER, DIES.

### GOLD AND SILVER COINS OF THE UNITED STATES.

| Sec. | Sec. |
|---|---|
| 3511. Gold coins of the United States and their weight. | 3536. Adjusting weight of silver coins. |
| 3513. Silver coins and their weight. | 3537. Adjusting weight of minor coins. |
| 3514. Standard for gold and silver coins. | 3585. Gold coins, legal tender. |
| 3515. Minor coins; their weight and alloy. | ——. Exchange of silver coins. |
| 3517. Inscriptions upon coins. | ——. Twenty-cent piece. |
| 3535. Deviations allowed in adjusting weights of gold coins. | ——. Trade dollars, &c. |

SEC. 3511. The gold coins of the United States shall be a one-dollar piece, which, at the standard weight of twenty-five and eight-tenths grains, shall be the unit of value; a quarter-eagle, or two and a half dollar piece; a three-dollar piece; a half-eagle, or five-dollar piece; an eagle, or ten-dollar piece; and a double-eagle, or twenty-dollar piece. And the standard weight of the gold dollar shall be twenty-five and eight-tenths grains; of the quarter-eagle, or two and a half dollar piece, sixty-four and a half grains; of the three-dollar piece, seventy-seven and four-tenths grains; of the half-eagle, or five-dollar piece, one hundred and twenty-nine grains; of the eagle, or ten-dollar piece, two hundred and fifty-eight grains; of the double-eagle, or twenty-dollar piece, five hundred and sixteen grains.

*Title 37.*
*Gold coins of the United States and their weight.*

12 Feb., 1873, s. 14, v. 17, p. 426.

SEC. 3513. The silver coins of the United States shall be a trade-dollar, a half-dollar, or fifty-cent piece, a quarter dollar, or twenty-five cent piece, a dime, or ten-cent piece; and the weight of the trade-dollar shall be four hundred and twenty grains troy; the weight of the half-dollar shall be twelve grams and one-half of a gram; the quarter-dollar and the dime shall be, respectively, one-half and one-fifth of the weight of said half-dollar.

*Silver coins and their weight.*

Ibid., s. 15.

SEC. 3514. The standard for both gold and silver coins of the United States shall be such that of one thousand parts by weight nine hundred shall be of pure metal and one hundred of alloy. The alloy of the silver coins shall be of copper. The alloy of the gold coins shall be of copper, or of copper and silver; but the silver shall in no case exceed one-tenth of the whole alloy. [See § 5460.]

*Standard for gold and silver coins.*

12 Feb., 1873, s. 13, v. 17, p. 426.

SEC. 3515. The minor coins of the United States shall be a five-cent piece, a three-cent piece, and a one-cent piece. The alloy for the five and three cent pieces shall be of copper and nickel, to be composed of three-fourths copper and one-fourth nickel. The alloy of the one-cent piece shall be ninety-five per centum of copper and five per centum of tin and zinc, in such proportions as shall be determined by the Director of the Mint. The weight of the piece of five cents shall be seventy-seven and sixteen hundredths grains troy; of the three-cent piece, thirty grains; and of the one-cent piece, forty-eight grains.

*Minor coins; their weight and alloy.*

Ibid., s. 16.

SEC. 3517. Upon the coins there shall be the following devices and legends: Upon one side there shall be an impression emblematic of liberty, with an inscription of the word "Liberty" and the year of the coinage, and upon the reverse shall be the figure or representation of an eagle, with the inscriptions "United States of America" and "E Pluribus Unum," and a designation of the value of the coin; but on the gold dollar and three-dollar piece, the dime, five, three, and one-cent piece, the figure of the eagle shall be omitted; and on the reverse of the silver trade-dollar the weight and the fineness of the coin shall be inscribed.

*Inscriptions upon coins.*

Ibid., s. 18.

Deviations allowed in adjusting weights of gold coins.

SEC. 3535. In adjusting the weights of the gold coins, the following deviation shall not be exceeded in any single piece: In the double-eagle and the eagle, one-half of a grain; in the half-eagle, the three-dollar piece, the quarter-eagle, and the one-dollar piece, one-fourth of a grain. And in weighing a number of pieces together, when delivered by the coiner to the superintendent, and by the superintendent to the depositor, the deviation from the standard weight shall not exceed one hundredth of an ounce in five thousand dollars in double-eagles, eagles, half-eagles, or quarter-eagles, in one thousand three-dollar pieces, and in one thousand one-dollar pieces.

*Ibid.*, s. 36.

Of silver coins.

SEC. 3536. In adjusting the weight of the silver coins the following deviations shall not be exceeded in any single piece: In the dollar, the half and quarter dollar, and in the dime, one and one half grains. And in weighing a large number of pieces together, when delivered by the coiner to the superintendent, and by the superintendent to the depositor, the deviations from the standard weight shall not exceed two-hundredths of an ounce in one thousand dollars, half-dollars, or quarter-dollars, and one-hundredth of an ounce in one thousand dimes.

*Ibid.*, s. 37.

Of minor coins.

SEC. 3537. In adjusting the weight of the minor coins provided by this Title, there shall be no greater deviation allowed than three grains for the five-cent piece and two grains for the three and one cent pieces.

*Ibid.*, s. 38.

Title 39.

Gold coins of the United States.

SEC. 3585. The gold coins of the United States shall be a legal tender in all payments at their nominal value when not below the standard weight and limit of tolerance provided by law for the single piece, and, when reduced in weight below such standard and tolerance, shall be a legal tender at valuation in proportion to their actual weight.

*Ibid.*, s. 14.

9 June 1879.

Exchange of silver coins.

The holder of any of the silver coins of the United States of smaller denomination than one dollar may, on presentation of the same in sums of twenty dollars, or any multiple thereof, at the office of the Treasurer or any assistant treasurer of the United States, receive therefor lawful money of the United States.

9 June, 1879, s. 1, v. 21, p. 7.

The present silver coins of the United States of smaller denominations than one dollar shall hereafter be a legal tender in all sums not exceeding ten dollars in full payment of all dues, public and private.

*Idem*, s. 3.

NOTES.—May 2, 1878.—Coinage of the twenty-cent piece of silver authorized by the act of March 3, 1875, prohibited.
By the act of July 22, 1876, v. 19 p. 215, the trade dollar is not thereafter to be a legal tender.
An act of February 28, 1878, v. 20, p. 25, provides for the coinage at the mints of United States silver dollars of the weight of four hundred and twelve and a half grains troy of standard silver as provided in the act of January 18, 1837, which with the silver dollars of that weight and fineness theretofore coined by the United States shall be a legal tender at their nominal value for all debts and dues, public and private, except where otherwise expressly stipulated in the contract.

### FOREIGN COINS.

| Sec. | Sec. |
|---|---|
| 3564. Value of foreign coins, how ascertained. | 3567. Spanish and Mexican coins. |
| 3565. Value of the sovereign or pounds sterling. | 3584. Not a legal tender, &c. |
| 3566. Recoinage of foreign coins. | —— Estimate of value. |

Title 37.

Value of foreign coins, how ascertained.

SEC. 3564. The value of foreign coin as expressed in the money of account of the United States shall be that of the pure metal of such coin of standard value; and the values of the standard coins in circulation of the various nations of the world shall be estimated annually by the Director of the Mint, and be proclaimed on the first day of January by the Secretary of the Treasury.

3 March, 1873, s. 1, v. 17, p. 602.

SEC. 3565. In all payments by or to the Treasury, whether made here or in foreign countries, where it becomes necessary to compute the value of the sovereign or pound sterling, it shall be deemed equal to four dollars eighty-six cents and six and one-half mills, and the same rule shall be applied in appraising merchandise imported where the value is, by the invoice, in sovereigns or pounds sterling, and in the construction of contracts payable in sovereigns or pounds sterling; and this valuation shall be the par of exchange between Great Britain and the United States; and all contracts made after the first day of January, eighteen hundred and seventy-four, based on an assumed par of exchange with Great Britain of fifty-four pence to the dollar, or four dollars forty-four and four-ninths cents to the sovereign or pound sterling, shall be null and void. — Value of the sovereign or pound sterling.

*Ibid.*, s. 2.

SEC. 3566. All foreign gold and silver coins received in payment for moneys due to the United States shall, before being issued in circulation, be coined anew. — Recoinage of foreign coin.

9 Feb., 1793, s. 3, v. 1, p. 301.
21 Feb., 1857, s. 2, v. 11, p. 163.

SEC. 3567. The pieces commonly known as the quarter, eighth, and sixteenth of the Spanish pillar-dollar, and of the Mexican dollar, shall be receivable at the Treasury of the United States, and its several offices, and at the several post-offices, and land-offices, at the rates of valuation following: the fourth of a dollar, or piece of two reals, at twenty cents; the eighth of a dollar, or piece of one real, at ten cents; and the sixteenth of a dollar, or half-real, at five cents. — Spanish and Mexican coins.

21 Feb., 1857, s. 1, v. 11, p. 163.

SEC. 3584. No foreign gold or silver coins shall be a legal tender in payment of debts. — Title 39. Foreign coins.

21 Feb., 1857, s. 3, v. 11, p. 163.

## CIRCULAR ESTIMATING AND PROCLAIMING, IN THE UNITED STATES MONEY OF ACCOUNT, THE VALUES OF THE STANDARD COINS IN CIRCULATION OF THE VARIOUS NATIONS OF THE WORLD.

1883.
DEPARTMENT NO. 1.
*Secretary's Office.*

TREASURY DEPARTMENT,
BUREAU OF THE MINT,
*Washington, D. C., January 1, 1883.*

SIR: In pursuance of the provisions of section 3564 of the Revised Statutes of the United States, I have estimated the values of the standard coins in circulation of the various nations of the world, and submit the same in the accompanying table.

Very respectfully,

HORATIO C. BURCHARD,
*Director of the Mint.*

Hon. CHAS. J. FOLGER,
*Secretary of the Treasury.*

### ESTIMATE of VALUES of FOREIGN COINS.

| Country. | Monetary unit. | Standard. | Value in United States money. | Standard coin. |
|---|---|---|---|---|
| Argentine Republic | Peso | Gold and silver. | $0 96.5 | $\frac{1}{20}$, $\frac{1}{10}$, $\frac{1}{5}$, $\frac{1}{2}$, and 1 peso, $\frac{1}{2}$ argentine and argentine. |
| Austria | Florin | Silver | 40.1 | |
| Belgium | Franc | Gold and silver. | 19.3 | 5, 10, and 20 francs. |
| Bolivia | Boliviano | Silver | 81.2 | Boliviano. |
| Brazil | Milreis of 1,000 reis. | Gold | 54.6 | |
| British Possessions in North America. | Dollar | ....do...... | 1 00 | |

*Estimate of values of foreign coins*—Continued.

| Country. | Monetary unit. | Standard. | Value in United States money. | Standard coin. |
|---|---|---|---|---|
| Chili | Peso | Gold and silver. | 91.2 | Condor, doubloon, and escudo. |
| Cuba | ...do | ...do | 93.2 | 1/16, 1/4, 1/2, and 1 doubloon. |
| Denmark | Crown | Gold | 26.8 | 10 and 20 crowns. |
| Ecuador | Peso | Silver | 81.2 | Peso. |
| Egypt | Piaster | Gold | 04.9 | 5, 10, 25, 50, and 100 piasters. |
| France | Franc | Gold and silver. | 19.3 | 5, 10, and 20 francs. |
| Great Britain | Pound sterling | Gold | 4 86.6½ | ½ sovereign and sovereign. |
| Greece | Drachma | Gold and silver. | 19.3 | 5, 10, 20, 50, and 100 drachmas. |
| German Empire | Mark | Gold | 23.8 | 5, 10, and 20 marks. |
| Hayti | Gourde | Gold and silver. | 96.5 | 1, 2, 5, and 10 gourdes. |
| India | Rupee of 16 annas. | Silver | 38.6 | |
| Italy | Lira | Gold and silver. | 19.3 | 5, 10, 20, 50, and 100 lire. |
| Japan | Yen | Silver | 87.6 | 1, 2, 5, 10, and 20 yen; gold and silver yen. |
| Liberia | Dollar | Gold | 1 00 | |
| Mexico | ...do | Silver | 88.2 | Peso or dollar 5, 10, 25, and 50 centavo. |
| Netherlands | Florin | Gold and silver. | 40.2 | |
| Norway | Crown | Gold | 26.8 | 10 and 20 crowns. |
| Peru | Sol | Silver | 81.2 | Sol. |
| Portugal | Milreis of 1,000 reis. | Gold | 1 08. | 2, 5, and 10 milreis. |
| Russia | Rouble of 100 copecks. | Silver | 65. | ¼, ½, and 1 rouble. |
| Spain | Peseta of 100 centimos. | Gold and silver. | 19.3 | 5, 10, 20, 50, and 100 pesetas. |
| Sweden | Crown | Gold | 26.8 | 10 and 20 crowns. |
| Switzerland | Franc | Gold and silver. | 19.3 | 5, 10, and 20 francs. |
| Tripoli | Mahbub of 20 piasters. | Silver | 73.3 | |
| Turkey | Piaster | Gold | 04.4 | 25, 50, 100, 250, and 500 piasters. |
| United States of Colombia. | Peso | Silver | 81.2 | Peso. |
| Venezuela | Bolivar | Gold and silver. | 19.3 | 5, 10, 20, 50, and 100 Bolivar. |

TREASURY DEPARTMENT,
*Washington, D. C., January* 1, 1883.

The foregoing estimation, made by the Director of the Mint, of the value of the foreign coins above mentioned, I hereby proclaim to be the values of such coins expressed in the money of account of the United States, and to be taken in estimating the values of all foreign merchandise, made out in any of said currencies, imported on or after January 1, 1883.

CHAS. J. FOLGER,
*Secretary of the Treasury.*

## WEIGHTS AND MEASURES.

Sec.
3569. Use of the metric system authorized.

Sec.
3570. Authorized tables of weights and measures.

**Title 37.**

Use of metric system authorized.

SEC. 3569. It shall be lawful throughout the United States of America to employ the weights and measures of the metric system; and no contract or dealing, or pleading in any court, shall be deemed invalid or liable to objection because the weights or measures expressed or referred to therein are weights or measures of the metric system.

28 July, 1866, s. 1, v. 14, p. 339.

DISBURSING OFFICERS AND AGENTS. 179

SEC. 3570. The tables in the schedule hereto annexed shall be recognized in the construction of contracts, and in all legal proceedings, as establishing, in terms of the weights and measures now in use in the United States, the equivalents of the weights and measures expressed therein in terms of the metric system; and the tables may lawfully be used for computing, determining, and expressing in customary weights and measures the weights and measures of the metric system.

*Ibid.*, s. 2.

Authorized tables of weights and measures.

### MEASURES OF LENGTH.

| Metric denominations and values. | | Equivalents in denominations in use. |
|---|---|---|
| Myriameter.... | 10,000 meters. | 6.2137 miles. |
| Kilometer..... | 1,000 meters. | 0.62137 miles, or 3,280 feet and 10 inches. |
| Hectometer.... | 100 meters. | 328 feet and 1 inch. |
| Dekameter..... | 10 meters. | 393.7 inches. |
| Meter......... | 1 meter. | 39.37 inches. |
| Decimeter..... | $\frac{1}{10}$ of a meter. | 3.937 inches. |
| Centimeter... | $\frac{1}{100}$ of a meter. | 0.3937 inches. |
| Millimeter.... | $\frac{1}{1000}$ of a meter. | 0.0394 inches. |

### MEASURES OF CAPACITY.

| Metric denominations and values. | | Equivalents in denominations in use. | | |
|---|---|---|---|---|
| Names. | No. of liters. | Cubic measure. | Dry measure. | Liquor or wine measure. |
| Kiloliter, or stere. | 1,000 | 1 cubic meter.... | 1.308 cub. yards.. | 264.17 galls. |
| Hectoliter. | 100 | $\frac{1}{10}$ of a cubic meter | 2 bushels and 3.35 pecks. | 26.417 galls. |
| Dekaliter.. | 10 | 10 cub. decimeters | 9.08 quarts...... | 2.6417 galls. |
| Liter...... | 1 | 1 cub. decimeter. | 0.908 quarts..... | 1.0567 q'ts. |
| Deciliter .. | $\frac{1}{10}$ | $\frac{1}{10}$ of a cubic decimeter. | 6.1022 cub. inch.. | 0.845 gills. |
| Centiliter . | $\frac{1}{100}$ | 10 cub. centimeters | 0.6102 cub. inch.. | 0.338 fluid ounces. |
| Milliliter.. | $\frac{1}{1000}$ | 1 cub. centimeter. | 0.061 cub. inch.. | 0.27 fluid drams. |

### MEASURES OF SURFACE.

| Metric denominations and values. | | Equivalents in denominations in use. |
|---|---|---|
| Hectare.... | 10,000 square meters. | 2.471 acres. |
| Are........ | 100 square meters. | 119.6 square yards. |
| Centare.... | 1 square meter. | 1550 square inches. |

## WEIGHTS.

| Metric denominations and values. | | | Equivalents in denominations in use. |
|---|---|---|---|
| Names. | Number of grams. | Weight of what quantity of water at maximum density. | Avoirdupois weight. |
| Millier or tonneau | 1,000,000 | 1 cubic meter | 2204.6 pounds. |
| Quintal | 100,000 | 1 hectoliter | 220.46 pounds. |
| Myriagram | 10,000 | 10 liters | 22.046 pounds. |
| Kilogram or kilo | 1,000 | 1 liter | 2.2046 pounds. |
| Hectogram | 100 | 1 deciliter | 3.5274 ounces. |
| Dekagram | 10 | 10 cubic centimeters | 0.3527 ounces. |
| Gram | 1 | 1 cubic centimeter | 15.432 grains. |
| Decigram | $\frac{1}{10}$ | $\frac{1}{10}$ of a cubic centimeter. | 1.5432 grains. |
| Centigram | $\frac{1}{100}$ | 10 cubic millimeters | 0.1543 grains. |
| Milligram | $\frac{1}{1000}$ | 1 cubic millimeter | 0.0154 grains. |

### DIES.

**Title 37.**

**National and other medals may be struck at Mint at Philadelphia.**

SEC. 3551. Dies of a national character may be executed by the engraver, and national and other medals struck by the coiner of the Mint at Philadelphia, under such regulations as the superintendent, with the approval of the director of the Mint, may prescribe. Such work shall not, however, interfere with the regular coinage operations, and no private medal dies shall be prepared at any mint, or the machinery or apparatus thereof be used for that purpose.

12 Feb., 1873, s. 52, v. 17, p. 432.
16 June, 1874, ch. 288, v. 18, p. 76.

# NAVY DEPARTMENT.

### SECRETARY AND BUREAUS.

Sec.
415. Establishment of the Department of the Navy.
417. Procurement of naval stores and equipment of vessels.
418. Custody of the books and records.
419. Establishment of Bureaus.
420. Custody of books and records of Bureaus.
421. Appointment of chiefs of Bureaus.
422. Chiefs of Bureaus of Yards and Docks, Equipment and Recruiting, Navigation, and Ordnance.
423. Chief of Bureau of Construction and Repair.
424. Chief of Bureau of Steam Engineering.

Sec.
425. Chief of Bureau of Provisions and Clothing.
426. Chief of Bureau of Medicine and Surgery.
429. Reports to be made to Congress by the Secretary.
1375. Assistant to Bureau.
1436. Chiefs of Bureaus, staff-officers exempt from sea-duty.
1471. Title of chiefs of Bureaus.
1472. Relative rank of chief of Bureau of lower title than commodore.
1473. Retired chiefs of Bureaus.
1565. Pay of chiefs of Bureaus.

**Title 10.**

**Establishment of the Department of the Navy.**

SEC. 415. There shall be at the seat of Government an Executive Department, to be known as the Department of the Navy, and a Secretary of the Navy, who shall be the head thereof."

30 April, 1798, s. 1, v. 1, p. 553.

**Procurement of naval stores and equipment of vessels.**

SEC. 417. The Secretary of the Navy shall execute such orders as he shall receive from the President relative to the procurement of naval stores and materials, and the construction, armament, equipment, and employment of vessels of war, as well as all other matters connected with the naval establishment. [See Title CONTRACTS. Also §§ 3660–3667, 3669, APPROPRIATIONS.]

*Ibid.*

**Custody of the books and records.**

SEC. 418. The Secretary of the Navy shall have the custody and charge of all the books, records, and other property now remaining in and appertaining to the Department of the Navy, or hereafter acquired by it.

*Ibid.*, s. 3, p. 554.

## NAVY DEPARTMENT. 181

**Sec. 419.** The business of the Department of the Navy shall be distributed in such manner as the Secretary of the Navy shall judge to be expedient and proper among the following Bureaus: — *Establishment of Bureaus.*
First. A Bureau of Yards and Docks.
Second. A Bureau of Equipment and Recruiting.
Third. A Bureau of Navigation.
Fourth. A Bureau of Ordnance.
Fifth. A Bureau of Construction and Repair.
Sixth. A Bureau of Steam Engineering.
Seventh. A Bureau of Provisions and Clothing.
Eighth. A Bureau of Medicine and Surgery.
31 Aug., 1842, s. 2, v. 5, p. 579.
5 July, 1862, ss. 1, 4, v. 12, p. 510.

**Sec. 420.** The several Bureaus shall retain the charge and custody of the books of records and accounts pertaining to their respective duties; and all of the duties of the Bureaus shall be performed under the authority of the Secretary of the Navy, and their orders shall be considered as emanating from him, and shall have full force and effect as such. — *Custody of books and records of Bureaus.*
31 Aug., 1842, s. 8, v. 5, p. 580.
5 July, 1862, s. 4, v. 12, p. 511.

**Sec. 421.** The chiefs of the several Bureaus in the Department of the Navy shall be appointed by the President, by and with the advice and consent of the Senate, from the classes of officers mentioned in the next five sections respectively, or from officers having the relative rank of captain in the staff corps of the Navy, on the active list, and shall hold their offices for the term of four years. — *Appointment of chiefs of Bureaus.*
5 July, 1862, ss. 1, 2, v. 12, p. 510.
3 March, 1871, s. 10, v. 16, p. 537.

**Sec. 422.** The chiefs of the Bureau of Yards and Docks, of the Bureau of Equipment and Recruiting, of the Bureau of Navigation, and of the Bureau of Ordnance, shall be appointed from the list of officers of the Navy, not below the grade of commander.
5 July, 1862, s. 1, v. 12, p. 510.

**Sec. 423.** The chief of the Bureau of Construction and Repair shall be appointed from the list of officers of the Navy, not below the grade of commander, and shall be a skillful naval constructor.
Ibid.

**Sec. 424.** The chief of the Bureau of Steam Engineering shall be appointed from the chief engineers of the Navy, and shall be a skillful engineer.
Ibid.

**Sec. 425.** The chief of the Bureau of Provisions and Clothing shall be appointed from the list of paymasters of the Navy of not less than ten years' standing.
Ibid.

**Sec. 426.** The chief of the Bureau of Medicine and Surgery shall be appointed from the list of the surgeons of the Navy. [See sec. 1375.]
Ibid.

**Sec. 429.** The Secretary of the Navy shall make annual reports to Congress upon the following subjects: [See §§ 195, 196, CIVIL SERVICE.] — *Reports to Congress by Secretary of the Navy.*
First. A statement of the appropriations of the preceding fiscal year for the Department of the Navy, showing the amount appropriated under each specific head of appropriation, the amount expended under each head, and the balance which, on the thirtieth day of June preceding such report, remained unexpended. Such report shall be accompanied by estimates of the probable demands which may remain on each appropriation.
Second. A statement of all offers for contracts for supplies and services made during the preceding year, by classes, indicating such as have been accepted.
Third. A statement showing the amounts expended during the preceding fiscal year for wages of mechanics and laborers employed in building, repairing, or equipping vessels of the Navy, or in receiving and securing stores and materials for those purposes, and for the purchase of material and stores for the same purpose; and showing the

cost or estimated value of the stores on hand, under this appropriation, in the navy-yards, at the commencement of the next preceding fiscal year; and the cost or estimated value of articles received and expended during the year; and the cost or estimated value of the articles belonging to this appropriation which may be on hand in the navy-yards at the close of the next preceding fiscal year.

Fourth. A statement of all acts done by him in making sale of any vessel or materials of the Navy; specifying all vessels and materials sold, the parties buying the same, and the amount realized therefrom, together with such other facts as may be necessary to a full understanding of his acts. [See § 1780, CONTINGENT FUND.]

1 May, 1820, s. 2, v. 3, p. 567.
3 March, 1843, v. 5, p. 617.
27 July, 1866, s. 3, v. 14, p. 365.

**Title 15, Chap. 1.**
Assistant to Bureau of Medicine and Surgery.

SEC. 1375. A surgeon, assistant surgeon, or passed assistant surgeon may be detailed as assistant to the Bureau of Medicine and Surgery, who shall receive the highest shore pay of his grade. [See p. 49.]

16 July, 1862, s. 18, v. 12, p. 587.
27 Feb., 1877, v. 19, p. 244.

**Title 15, Chap. 2.**
Chiefs of Bureaus exempted from sea duty.

SEC. 1436. Any staff officer of the Navy who has performed the duty of a chief of a Bureau of the Navy Department for a full term shall thereafter be exempt from sea duty, except in time of war.

3 March, 1871, s. 10, v. 10, p. 537.

**Title 15, Chap. 4.**
Rank and title of certain chiefs of Bureau.

SEC. 1471. The chiefs of the Bureau of Medicine and Surgery, Provisions and Clothing, Steam Engineering, and Construction and Repair, shall have the relative rank of commodore while holding said position, and shall have respectively the title of Surgeon-General, Paymaster-General, Engineer-in-Chief, and Chief Constructor.

3 March, 1871, s. 12, v. 16, p. 537.

When below rank of commodore.

SEC. 1472. When the office of chief of Bureau is filled by a line officer below the rank of commodore, said officer shall have the relative rank of commodore during the time he holds said office.

*Ibid.*

Rank of chiefs of Bureaus retired.

SEC. 1473. Officers who have been or who shall be retired from the position of chiefs of the Bureau of Medicine and Surgery, of Provisions and Clothing, of Steam Engineering, or of Construction and Repair, by reason of age or length of service, shall have the relative rank of commodore.

*Ibid.*

**Title 15, Chap. 8.**
Pay of chiefs of Bureaus.

SEC. 1565. The pay of chiefs of Bureaus in the Navy Department shall be the highest pay of the grade to which they belong, but not below that of commodore.

*Ibid.*

**Title 10.**
Clerical force.

CLERKS AND OTHER CIVIL EMPLOYEES IN THE NAVY DEPARTMENT AND BUREAUS.

SEC. 416. There shall be in the Department of the Navy:

One chief clerk, at a salary of two thousand five hundred dollars a year, so long as there is no assistant secretary of the Navy, and at a salary of two thousand two hundred dollars a year when there is an assistant secretary of the Navy.*

One disbursing clerk, two thousand dollars. [See Sec. 176, CIVIL SERVICE.]

5 July, 1862, v. 12, p. 510.
2 July, 1864, s. 4, v. 13, p. 373.
2 July, 1866, s. 8, v. 14, p. 207.
3 March, 1871, s. 3, v. 16, p. 492.
3 March, 1873, s. 1, v. 17, p. 501.

In the Bureau of Yards and Docks:

One civil engineer at a salary of three thousand dollars a year. [Now pay of grade and a member of the corps of Civil Engineers.]

One chief clerk, at a salary of one thousand eight hundred dollars a year.

One draughtsman, at a salary of one thousand eight hundred dollars a year.

---

* The legislative act of August 5, 1882, authorized the appointment of an Assistant Secretary from civil life. No appointment was made, and the provision was repealed March 3, 1883.

In the Bureau of Equipment and Recruiting:
One chief clerk, at a salary of one thousand eight hundred dollars a year.

In the Bureau of Construction and Repair:
One chief clerk, at a salary of one thousand eight hundred dollars a year.
One draughtsman, at a salary of one thousand eight hundred dollars a year.

In the Bureau of Steam Engineering:
One chief clerk, at a salary of one thousand eight hundred dollars a year.
One draughtsman at a salary of one thousand eight hundred dollars a year. [See act March 3, 1883, *post*.]
One assistant draughtsman, at a salary of one thousand two hundred dollars a year. [See act March 3 1883, *post*.]

In the Bureau of Navigation:
One chief clerk, at a salary of one thousand eight hundred dollars a year.

In the Bureau of Ordnance:
One chief clerk, at a salary of one thousand eight hundred dollars a year.
One draughtsman, at a salary of one thousand eight hundred dollars a year.

In the Bureau of Provisions and Clothing:
One chief clerk, at a salary of one thousand eight hundred dollars a year.

In the Bureau of Medicine and Surgery:
One chief clerk, at a salary of one thousand eight hundred dollars a year.

*Ibid.*

*Appropriations for civil force, Secretary's office and Bureaus, Navy Department and Navy Department buildings, act of March 3, 1883.*

For compensation of the Secretary of the Navy, eight thousand dollars; for compensation of chief clerk of the Navy Department, two thousand five hundred dollars; one disbursing clerk, two thousand two hundred and fifty dollars; four clerks of class four; three clerks of class three; one stenographer, at one thousand six hundred dollars; two clerks of class two; six clerks of class one; four clerks, at one thousand dollars each; telegraph operator, at one thousand dollars; one carpenter, one thousand dollars; two messengers; three assistant messengers; one messenger boy, at four hundred and twenty dollars; one messenger boy, at two hundred and forty dollars; three laborers; one clerk of class two, and one laborer (for Inspection Board); one clerk of class two, who shall be a stenographer; one clerk of class one, and one assistant messenger (in care of library). Secretary's office.

For one chief clerk, one thousand eight hundred dollars; one draughtsman, one thousand eight hundred dollars; one clerk of class four; one clerk of class three; one clerk of class two; one clerk of class one; one clerk, at one thousand dollars; one assistant messenger; and one laborer. Bureau of yards and docks.

For chief clerk, one thousand eight hundred dollars; one clerk of class four; one clerk of class three; two clerks of class two; three clerks of class one; two copyists, at nine hundred dollars each; one assistant messenger; and one laborer. Bureau of Equipment and Recruiting.

For chief clerk, one thousand eight hundred dollars; one clerk of class three; two clerks of class two; one clerk of class one; one clerk, at one thousand dollars; one copyist, nine hundred dollars; one assistant messenger; and two laborers. Bureau of Navigation.

For chief clerk, one thousand eight hundred dollars; draughtsman, one thousand eight hundred dollars; one clerk of class three; one clerk of class two; one assistant messenger; and one laborer. Bureau of Ordnance.

For chief clerk, one thousand eight hundred dollars; draughtsman, one thousand eight hundred dollars; one assistant draughtsman, one thousand four hundred dollars; one clerk of class four; one clerk of class three; one clerk of class two; one clerk of class one; one assistant messenger; and one laborer. Bureau of Construction and Repair.

For chief clerk, one thousand eight hundred dollars; one chief draughtsman at two thousand two hundred and fifty dollars; one assistant draughtsman, at one thousand four hundred dollars; one clerk Bureau of Steam-Engineering.

of class two; two clerks of class one; one clerk at one thousand dollars; one assistant messenger; and two laborers.

*Bureau of Provisions and Clothing.* For chief clerk, one thousand eight hundred dollars; one clerk of class four; two clerks of class three; two clerks of class two; four clerks of class one; two copyists, nine hundred dollars; one assistant messenger; and one laborer.

*Bureau of Medicine and Surgery.* For chief clerk, one thousand eight hundred dollars; one clerk of class three; one clerk of class two; one clerk of class one; one clerk, at one thousand dollars; one assistant messenger; and one laborer; one janitor, six hundred dollars; one assistant chemist, four hundred and eighty dollars (for Naval Dispensary).

*Judge-Advocate-General.* For one clerk of class three; two clerks of class one; one clerk, at one thousand dollars; one laborer.

### Navy Department Building.

*State, War, and Navy Department building.* The President is hereby authorized and directed to designate from the Engineer Corps of the Army or the Navy, an officer well qualified for the purpose, who shall be detailed to act as superintendent of the completed portions of the State, War, and Navy Department building, under direction of the Secretaries of State, War, and Navy, who are *Commission for care and supervision of building.* hereby constituted a commission for the purposes of the care and supervision of said building, as hereinafter specified. Said officer shall have charge of said building, and all the engines, machinery, steam and *Superintendent.* water supply, heating, lighting, and ventilating apparatus, elevators, and all other fixtures in said building, and all necessary repairs and alterations thereof, as well as the direction and control of such force of engineers, watchmen, laborers, and others engaged about the building or the apparatus under his supervision; of the cleaning of the corridors and water closets; of the approaches, side-walks, lawns, court-yards, and areas of the building, and of all rooms in the sub-basement which contain the boilers and other machinery, or so much of said rooms as may be indispensable to the proper performance of his duties as herein provided.

*Employés in Superintendent's office.* Office of the superintendent: One clerk class one; one chief engineer, at one thousand two hundred dollars; six assistant engineers, at one thousand dollars each; one captain of the watch, one thousand two hundred dollars; two lieutenants of the watch, at eight hundred and forty dollars each; forty-five watchmen; one machinist, at nine hundred dollars; one skilled laborer, at seven hundred and twenty dollars; seventeen firemen; four conductors of the elevator, at seven hundred and twenty dollars each; two assistant conductors of the elevator, at five hundred dollars each; sixteen laborers; one laborer, at six hundred dollars; and fifty-four charwomen, at one hundred and eighty dollars each; in all, eighty-two thousand three hundred dollars.

### Pay of Assistant Messengers, &c.

*Pay of assistant messengers.* SEC. 3. That the pay of assistant messengers, firemen, watchmen, and laborers provided for in this act, unless otherwise specially stated, shall be as follows: For assistant messengers, firemen, and watchmen, seven hundred and twenty dollars per annum each; for laborers, six hundred and sixty dollars per annum each.

3 March, 1883, P. E. L., p, 554.

# PUBLIC DOCUMENTS—PUBLIC PRINTING AND BINDING.

| Sec. | Sec. |
|---|---|
| 196. Annual reports—when to be furnished. | 3788. Heads of Bureaus not to print reports, except, &c. |
| 383. Printing of opinions of Attorney-General. | 3789. Orders and requisitions for printing. |
| 497. Custody and distribution of public documents. | 3790. Style and form of work for Departments. |
| 500. Manner of delivery. | 3802. Accounts with Departments for printing. |
| 505. Distribution of surplus volumes, &c. | —— Style of binding. |
| 3760. Purchase of materials by Public Printer. | —— Binding for members of Congress. |
| 3778. Purchases in open market. | 3809. Extra copies of any document, how sold. |
| —— Purchases without advertising. | 3810. Printed documents, when to be delivered. |
| 3779. Engraving for Congress. | 3813. Documents to be delivered at Interior Department. |
| 3780. Engraving, when to be advertised. | |
| 3783. Accountability for and issue of material. | 3815. Quarterly account. |
| 3785. Only Government printing and binding allowed. | 3821. Report to Congress. |
| 3786. Printing required to be done at Government co. | —— Impressions and vignettes, Bureau of Engraving and Printing. |

SEC. 196. The head of each Department, except the Department of Justice, shall furnish to the Congressional Printer copies of the documents usually accompanying his annual report on or before the first day of November in each year, and a copy of his annual report on or before the third Monday of November in each year.

*Title 4.*
*Annual reports.*

25 June, 1864, ss. 1, 3., v. 13, p. 184.
25 June, 1870, s. 12, v. 16, p. 164.

SEC. 383. The Attorney-General shall from time to time cause to be edited, and printed at the Government Printing-Office, an edition of one thousand copies of such of the opinions of the law-officer herein authorized to be given as he may deem valuable for preservation in volumes, which shall be, as to size, quality of paper, printing, and binding, of uniform style and appearance.

*Title 8.*
*Opinions of the Attorney - General. Title 8, p. 63.*

\* \* \*

Each volume shall contain proper head-notes, a complete and full index, and such foot-notes as the Attorney-General may approve. Such volumes shall be distributed in such manner as the Attorney-General may from time to time prescribe.

*23 June, 1870.*

22 June, 1870, s. 18, v. 16, p. 165.

SEC. 497. The Secretary of the Interior is charged with receiving, arranging, and safe-keeping for distribution, and of distributing to the persons entitled by law to receive the same, all printed journals of the two Houses of Congress, and all other books and documents of every nature whatever, already or hereafter directed by law to be printed or purchased for the use of the Government, except such as are directed to be printed or purchased for the particular use of Congress, or of either House thereof, or for the particular use of the Executive or of any of the Departments, and any person whose duty it shall be by law to deliver any of the same, shall deliver them at the rooms assigned by the Secretary of the Interior therefor.

*Title 11, Chap. 7.*
*Custody and distribution of public documents.*

5 Feb., 1859, ss. 1, 7, 5, v. 11, p. 379.

SEC. 500. The publications received by the Secretary of the Interior for distribution shall be delivered out only on the written requisition of the heads of Departments, Secretary of the Senate, Clerk of the House of Representatives, Librarian of Congress, and other officers and persons who are by law authorized to receive the same, except where by law the Secretary of the Interior is required, without such requisition, to cause the same to be sent and delivered; and in either of such cases it shall be the duty of the Secretary of the Interior to cause the same to be sent and delivered, the expenses thereof, except when otherwise directed, to be charged on the contingent fund of the Department.

*Manner of delivery.*

5 Feb., 1859, s. 4, v. 11, p. 380.

SEC. 505. Whenever there are in the custody of the Department of the Interior any sets of the documents of any session of Congress, or other documents or odd volumes, not necessary to supply deficiencies or losses that may happen in the Library of Congress, or in that of either of the Executive Departments, or in State or territorial libraries, the Secretary of the Interior shall distribute the same as equally as practicable to the several Senators, Representatives, and Delegates in Congress, for distribution to public libraries and other literary institutions in their respective districts.

*Distribution of surplus volumes, &c.*

17 Feb., 1871, Res., v. 16, p. 507.

SEC. 3768. It shall be the duty of the Congressional Printer to purchase all materials and machinery which may be necessary for the Government Printing Office; to take charge of all matter which is to be printed, engraved, lithographed, or bound; to keep an account thereof in the order in which it is received, and to cause the work to be promptly executed; to superintend all printing and binding done at the Government Printing Office, and to see that the sheets or volumes are promptly delivered to the officer who is authorized to receive them. The receipt of such officer shall be a sufficient voucher of their delivery.

*Title 45.*
*Duties of Congressional Printer.*

23 June, 1860, v. 12, p. 117.
22 Feb., 1867, v. 14, p. 398.
20 June, 1874, v. 18, p. 288.

By an act of July 31, 1876, s. 1, v. 19, p. 105, the Congressional Printer is to be called the "Public Printer."

186   PUBLIC DOCUMENTS—PUBLIC PRINTING AND BINDING.

*Purchases in open market.*
27 July, 1866, ch. 287, § 5, vol. 14, p. 306.

SEC. 3778. The Joint Committee on Public Printing, or, during the recess of Congress, the Secretary of the Interior, may authorize the Congressional Printer to make purchases of paper in open market, whenever they may deem the quantity required so small, or the want so immediate, as not to justify advertisement for proposals.

27 July, 1866, s. 5, v. 14, p. 306.

*Purchase of material for printing without advertising.*

That the Joint Committee on the Public Printing be and hereby is authorized to give permission to the Public Printer to purchase material in open market, whenever in their opinion, it would not promote the public interest to advertize for proposals and to make contracts for the same : *Provided, however,* That the purchases authorized by this act shall not in any term of six months, exceed the sum of fifty dollars for any particular article required.

1 Feb., 1878, v. 20, p.

*Title 45.*
*Engraving for Congress.*

SEC. 3779. Whenever any charts, maps, diagrams, views, or other engravings are required, to illustrate any document ordered to be printed by either House of Congress, such engravings shall be procured by the Congressional Printer, under the direction and supervision of the committee on printing of the House ordering the same. [See June 23, 1874, *post.*]

23 June, 1860, s. 8, v. 12, p. 119.

No expensive maps or illustrations shall be printed without the special order of Congress. June 23, 1874, v. 18, p. 204.

*Engraving when to be advertised.*

SEC. 3780. When the probable total cost of the maps or plates accompanying one work or document exceeds *one thousand two hundred dollars,* the lithographing or engraving thereof shall be awarded to the lowest and best bidder, after advertisement by the Congressional Printer, under the direction of the Joint Committee on Public Printing. But the committee may authorize him to make immediate contracts for lithographing or engraving whenever, in their opinion, the exigencies of the public service do not justify advertisement for proposals.

25 June, 1864, s. 19, v. 13, p. 186.
12 Feb., 1883, P. E. L., p. 414.

*Only public printing and binding allowed.*

SEC. 3785. No printing or binding which is not provided for by law shall be executed at the Government Printing Office.

23 June, 1860, Res., s. 11, v. 12, p. 414.
See June 24, 1878, *post.*

*Printing required to be done at Government Printing Office.*

SEC. 3786. All printing, binding, and blank books for the Senate or House of Representatives, and the Executive and Judicial Departments, shall be done at the Government Printing Office, except in cases otherwise provided by law.

*Idem.* p. 118. 2 March, 1867, s. 10, v. 14, p. 467.
20 July, 1868, s. 1, v. 15, p. 111.

*Heads of Bureaus not to print reports, except, &c.*

SEC. 3788. No officer in charge of any Bureau or office in any Department shall cause to be printed, at the public expense, any report he may make to the President or to the head of the Department, except as provided for in this Title.

31 Aug., 1852, s. 8, v. 10, p. 98.

*Orders and requisitions for printing.*

SEC. 3789. No printing or binding shall be done, or blank-books furnished * * * for any of the Executive Departments, except on a written requisition by the head of such Department, or one of his assistants.

14 March, 1864, s. 1, v. 13, p. 25.
3 June, 1864, s. 1, v. 13, p. 118.
3 March, 1871, v. 16, p. 517.

*Style and form of work for Departments.*

SEC. 3790. The forms and style in which the printing or binding ordered by any of the Departments shall be executed, the materials and size of type to be used, shall be determined by the Congressional Printer, having proper regard to economy, workmanship, and the purposes for which the work is needed.

25 June, 1864, s. 12, v. 13, p. 184.
See 20 June, 1878, *post.*

*Accounts with Departments for printing.*

SEC. 3802. Whenever Congress makes an appropriation for any Department or public office, to be expended "for printing and binding to be executed under the direction of the Congressional Printer," the Congressional Printer shall cause an account to be opened with such Department or public office, on which he shall charge for all printing and

PUBLIC DOCUMENTS—PUBLIC PRINTING AND BINDING. 187

binding ordered by the head thereof, at prices established in pursuance of law; and it shall not be lawful for him to cause to be executed any printing or binding the value of which exceeds the amount appropriated for such purpose. [See § 3661, APPROPRIATIONS.]
8 May, 1872, s. 3, v. 17, p. 83.

And hereafter no binding shall be done for any Department of the Government except in plain sheep or cloth, and no books shall be printed and bound except when the same shall be ordered by Congress or are authorized by law, except record and account books, which may be bound in Russia leather, sheep fleshers, and skivers, when authorized by the head of a Department, and this restriction shall not apply to the Congressional Library, *nor to the library of the Surgeon-General's office, nor to the library of the Patent Office, nor to the library of the Department of State*. And when any Department shall require printing to be done the Public Printer shall furnish to such Department an estimate of the cost by the principal items for said printing so called for; and he shall place to the debit of such Department the cost of the same, on certification of the head of the Department, Supreme Court, Court of Claims, or Library of Congress, that said printing is necessary. * * *

*June 20, 1878.*
Style of binding.

Estimates of cost of printing.

20 June, 1878, v. 20, p. 206.<br>27 Jan., 1879, v. 20, p. 267.<br>26 Feb., 1879, v. 20, p. 323.

NOTE.—This act operates to prohibit the practice which theretofore existed (under *implied* authority of law) of printing and binding reports, &c., made in the course of Department business, and requires that thenceforth, for such binding and printing there must be express statutory authorization.—Op. XVI, 57, Phillips, July 2, 1878. See Op. XVI, 127, giving grounds on which the Nautical Almanac can be printed and bound.

That the Public Printer be authorized to bind at the Government Printing Office any books, maps, charts, or documents published by authority of Congress, upon application of any member of the Senate or House of Representatives, upon payment of the actual cost of such binding.

*10 Dec., 1877.*
Members of Congress may have documents bound.

10 Dec., 1877, v. 20, p. 5.

SEC. 3809. If any person desiring extra copies of any document printed at the Government Printing Office by authority of law shall, previous to its being put to press, notify the Congressional Printer of the number of copies wanted, and shall pay to him, in advance, the estimated cost thereof, and ten per centum thereon, the Congressional Printer may, under the direction of the Joint Committee on Public Printing, furnish the same.

Title 45.
Extra copies of any document, how sold.

25 June, 1864, s. 10, v. 13, p. 185.<br>3 March, 1871, s. 1, v. 16, p. 478.

That the Public Printer be, and he is hereby, directed to furnish to all applicants copies of bills and reports and other public documents hereafter printed by order of Congress and distributed from the document rooms of the Senate and House, on said applicant's paying the cost of such printing, with ten per centum added, and giving the notice required by section thirty-eight hundred and nine of Title forty-five of the Revised Statutes.

*8 May, 1880.*
Public documents to applicants at cost, &c.

8 May, 1880, v. 21, p. 306.

SEC. 3810. The annual reports of the Executive Departments and the accompanying documents shall be delivered by the printer to the proper officers of each House of Congress at the first meeting thereof; and the President's Message, the reports of the Executive Departments, and the abridgment of accompanying documents, shall be so delivered on or before the third Wednesday in December next after the meeting of Congress, or as soon thereafter as may be practicable.

Title 45.
Printed documents, when to be delivered.

25 June, 1864, s. 4, v. 13, p. 185.

SEC. 3815. The Congressional Printer shall render to the Secretary of the Treasury, quarterly, a full account of all purchases made by him, and of all printing and binding done in the Government Printing Office for each House of Congress and for each of the Executive and Judicial Departments.

Quarterly account.

23 June, 1860, Res. 25, v. 12, p. 178.

SEC. 3821. The Congressional Printer shall, on the first day of each session, or as soon thereafter as may be practicable, report to Congress the exact condition, and the amount and cost of the public printing,

Report to Congress.

binding, lithographing, and engraving; the amount and cost of all paper purchased for the same; a detailed statement of proposals made and contracts entered into for the purchase of paper and other materials, and for lithographing and engraving; of all payments made, during the preceding year, under his direction; of the amount of work ordered and done, with a general classification thereof, for each Department, and a detailed statement of each account with the Departments or public officers.

<blockquote>
22 June, 1860, ss. 2, 9, v. 12, p. 117.<br>
20 Feb., 1861, s. 1, v. 12, p. 135.<br>
14 March, 1864, s. 1, v. 13, p. 25.<br>
3 March, 1865, v. 13, p. 572.<br>
27 July, 1866, s. 4, v. 14, p. 305.<br>
9 May, 1872, s. 3, v. 17, p. 83.
</blockquote>

**21 Dec., 1879.**

*Impressions from vignettes, &c., in the Bureau of Engraving and Printing.*

That the Secretary of the Treasury, at the request of a Senator, Representative, or Delegate in Congress, the head of a Department, or Bureau, art association or library, be and he is hereby authorized to furnish impressions from any portrait or vignette which is now, or may hereafter be, a part of the engraved stock of the Bureau of Engraving and Printing, at such rates and under such conditions as he may deem necessary to protect the public interests.

<blockquote>22 Dec., 1879, v. 21, p. 59.</blockquote>

## CONGRESSIONAL DIRECTORY.

**5.**

*Congressional Directory.*

SEC. 77. A congressional directory shall be compiled at each session of Congress under the direction of the Joint Committee on Public Printing, and the first edition for each session shall be ready for distribution within one week after the commencement thereof.

<blockquote>14 Feb., 1865, v. 13, p. 568.</blockquote>

**Title 45.**

SEC. 3801. The first edition of the Congressional Directory for each session shall be printed and ready for distribution within one week after the commencement thereof.

<blockquote>*Ibid.*</blockquote>

## BIENNIAL REGISTER.

Sec.<br>
510. Preparation of.

Sec.<br>
——. Number to be printed, and how distributed.

**Title 11, Chap. 7.**

*Preparation of Biennial Register.*

SEC. 510. As soon as practicable after the *first* day of *July* in each year in which a new Congress is to assemble, a register shall be compiled and printed under the direction of the Secretary of the Interior * * * which shall contain the following lists, made up to such *first* day of *July:*

1. Correct lists of all the officers, clerks, employés, and agents, civil, military, and naval, in the service of the United States, including cadets and midshipmen, which lists shall exhibit the amount of compensation, pay, and emoluments allowed to each, the State or country in which he was born, the State or Territory from which he was appointed to office, and where employed.

2. A list of the names, force, and condition of all the ships and vessels belonging to the United States, and when and where built.

3. Lists of all printers of the laws of the United States, and of all printers employed by Congress or by any Department or officer of the Government, during the two years preceding the *first* day of *July* up to which such list is required to be made, with the compensation allowed to each, and designating the Department or officer causing the printing to be executed.

4. A statement of all allowances made by the Postmaster-General, within the same period of two years, to each contractor on contracts for carrying the mail, discriminating the sum paid as stipulated by the original contract and the sums paid as additional allowance.

<blockquote>
27 April, 1816, ss. 1, 2, v. 3, p. 342.<br>
14 July, 1832, v. 4, p. 608.<br>
3 March, 1851, s. 1, v. 9, p. 600.<br>
2 March, 1861, s. 4, v. 12, p. 245.<br>
23 Jan., 1874, v. 18, p. 5.<br>
15 Dec., 1877, v. 20, p. 13.
</blockquote>

\* \* \* \* \* \* \*

In lieu of the number of copies of the Biennial Register, now authorized by law to be printed, the Secretary of the Interior be, and he is hereby, directed to cause to be printed twenty-five hundred copies of the said work, to be distributed as follows: 15 Dec., 1877.

\* \* \* \* \* \* \*

To the Navy Department twenty copies.

\* \* \* \* \* \* \*

The Biennial Register shall be made up to the *first* day of *July* of each year in which a new Congress is to assemble, and shall be filed as soon thereafter as practicable in the Department of the Interior.

15 Dec., 1877, v. 20, p. 13.

## PUBLIC OR DEPARTMENT RECORDS.

Sec.
213. State Department records.
882. Copies of Department records and papers.
883. Transcripts from books of the Treasury in suits against delinquents.
886. Copies of records, &c., in office of Solicitor of Treasury.
887. Transcripts in indictments for embezzlement.

Sec.
888. Copies of returns in returns-office.
896. Copies of consular records.
908. Little & Brown's edition of statutes.
1778. Oaths, acknowledgements.
512–515. Returns office.
5403. Destroying public records.
5408. Officer in charge destroying records.

SEC. 213. For making out and authenticating copies of records in the Department of State, a fee of ten cents for each sheet containing one hundred words shall be paid by the person requesting such copies, except where they are requested by an officer of the United States in a matter relating to his office. 

Title 5.

Fees for copies of records.

15 Sept., 1789, s. 6, v. 1, p. 69.

SEC. 882. Copies of any books, records, papers, or documents in any of the Executive Departments, authenticated under the seals of such Departments, respectively, shall be admitted in evidence equally with the originals thereof.

Title 13, Chap. 17.

Copies of Department records and papers.

15 Sept., 1789, s. 5, v. 1, p. 69.
22 Feb., 1849, s. 3, v. 9, p. 347.
31 May, 1854, s. 2, v. 10, p. 297.

The heads of the Departments are not bound to produce papers or disclose information communicated to them where, in their judgment, the disclosures would, on public considerations, be inexpedient.—Op. XI, 137, Speed.

In general, only such communications as are made in the course of their official duties by the persons making them come within the rule of privileged communications, and are confidential under all circumstances. Other cases may occur (stated in this opinion) in which a Department would be justified in representing to a court that upon public considerations it declined to furnish such communications.—Op. XV, 415, Devens, Dec. 17, 1877. See, also, XV, 378.

In furnishing copies a distinction will properly be made between documents in the nature of permanent records, such as general or special orders, muster rolls, discharges of soldiers, commissions of officers, &c., and the reports and communications of officers addressed to military superiors or to the Secretary of War in the line of their official duty. The latter are generally regarded as *privileged communications* which even the courts, on grounds of public policy, will in general hold to be incompetent testimony, and of which they will refuse to require the production in evidence.—Winthrop's Digest, p. 350.

An official memorandum indorsed on an account as a direction to his subordinates by the head of a Department is not a matter of record of which the public or persons dealing with the Department must take notice.—C. C., XIII, 72.

All collections of natural history and the like, and all field notes and other like local information, taken or obtained by any public officer, civil or military, *in the line of his duty*, belong to the Government. They may lawfully make collections and take notes for their own use, provided the same be done without neglect of public duty or expense to the Government, and provided also that it be done without violation of superior order in their respective Departments.—Op. VI, 599, Cushing, 24 June, 1854.

The records of an Executive Department need not be produced in evidence in court, but their contents may be shown by authenticated copies.—C. C., II, 451. Nock's case. But see Op.

A party cannot, by replevin, take papers from the public archives on the allegation of their being private property, by a writ against the head of a Department or other public officer. The archives are in the possession of the United States.—Op. VI, 8, Cushing, March 25, 1853.

Recommendations for office are not papers or documents required to be kept by the Departments in which they are deposited—filed for the convenience of applicants who are allowed to withdraw them whenever they desire to do so. Such applicants can properly be permitted to see objections that may have been filed against themselves (subject to the limitation, however, that the permission should only be given where the communication is not in its nature privileged) in order that they may, if possible, answer or remove them. The files of the Departments ought not to be submitted to a search, upon the application of a newspaper, with a view to ascertain what persons have been recommended for office by a certain Senator and Representative in Congress. Copies of such papers should not be furnished unless the applicant appears himself to have been directly affected by the writing of a letter of which he demands a copy.—Op. 342, Devens, July 28, 1877.

*Copies of records, &c., in office of Solicitor of the Treasury.*

SEC. 883. Copies of any documents, records, books, or papers in the office of the Solicitor of the Treasury, certified by him under the seal of his office, or, when his office is vacant, by the officer acting as Solicitor for the time, shall be evidence equally with the originals.

22 Feb., 1849, s. 2, v. 9, p. 347.

*Transcripts from books, &c., of the Treasury, in suits against delinquents.*

SEC. 886. When suit is brought in any case of delinquency of a revenue officer, or other person accountable for public money, a transcript from the books and proceedings of the Treasury Department, certified by the Register and authenticated under the Seal of the Department, or, when the suit involves the accounts of the War or Navy Departments, certified by the Auditors respectively charged with the examination of those accounts, and authenticated under the seal of the Treasury Department, shall be admitted as evidence, and the court trying the cause shall be authorized to grant judgment and award execution accordingly. And all copies of bonds, contracts, or other papers relating to, or connected with, the settlement of any account between the United States and an individual, when certified by the Register, or by such Auditor, as the case may be, to be true copies of the originals on file, and authenticated under the seal of the Department, may be annexed to such transcripts, and shall have equal validity, and be entitled to the same degree of credit which would be due to the original papers if produced and authenticated in court: *Provided*, That where suit is brought upon a bond or other sealed instrument, and the defendant pleads "non est factum," or makes his motion to the court, verifying such plea or motion by his oath, the court may take the same into consideration, and, if it appears to be necessary for the attainment of justice, may require the production of the original bond, contract, or other paper specified in such affidavit.

3 March, 1797, s. 1, v. 1, p. 512.
3 March, 1817, s. 11, v. 3, p. 367.

The account of a delinquent officer, as finally adjusted by the accounting officers, is not admissible as evidence under sec. 886, R. S., unless it be certified and authenticated to be a transcript from the books and proceedings of that Department. A certificate that the transcript annexed is a copy of the original on file is the form used in reference to mere copies of bonds, contracts, or other papers connected with the final adjustment.—Otto, 102, 548.

*Transcripts in indictments for embezzlement of public moneys.*

SEC. 887. Upon the trial of any indictment against any person for embezzling public moneys, it shall be sufficient evidence, for the purpose of showing a balance against such person, to produce a transcript from the books and proceedings of the Treasury Department, as provided by the preceding section. [See § 5494, DISBURSING OFFICERS.]

6 Aug., 1846, s. 16, v. 9, p. 63.
2 March, 1797, s. 1, v. 1, p. 512.

*Copies of returns in returns-office.*

SEC. 888. A copy of any return of a contract returned and filed in the returns-office of the Department of the Interior, as provided by law, when certified by the clerk of the said office to be full and complete, and when authenticated by the seal of the Department, shall be evidence in any prosecution against any officer for falsely and corruptly swearing to the affidavit required by law to be made by such officer in making his return of any contract, as required by law, to said returns-office. [See § 3744, CONTRACTS, page 29.]

2 June, 1862, s. 4, v. 12, p. 412.

*Copies of records, &c., in office of United States consuls, &c.*

SEC. 896. Copies of all official documents and papers in the office of any consul, vice-consul, or commercial agent of the United States, and of all official entries in the books or records of any such office, certified under the hand and seal of such officer, shall be admitted in evidence in the courts of the United States. [See § 1707, DIPLOMATIC AND CONSULAR OFFICERS, Part IV.]

8 Jan., 1869, v. 15, p. 266.

*Little & Brown's edition of the statutes to be evidence.*

SEC. 908. The edition of the laws and treaties of the United States, published by Little & Brown, shall be competent evidence of the several public and private acts of Congress, and of the several treaties therein contained, in all the courts of law and equity and of maritime jurisdiction, and in all the tribunals and public offices of the United

States, and of the several States, without any further proof or authentication thereof.

8 Aug., 1846, s. 2, v. 9, p. 76.

SEC. 1778. In all cases in which, under the laws of the United States, oaths or acknowledgments may now be taken or made before any justice of the peace of any State or Territory, or in the District of Columbia, they may hereafter be also taken or made by or before any notary public duly appointed in any State, district, or Territory, or any of the commissioners of the circuit courts, and when certified under the hand and official seal of such notary or commissioner, shall have the same force and effect as if taken or made by or before such justice of the peace. *Title 19.*

*Taking oaths, acknowledgments, &c.*

10 Sept., 1850, v. 9, p. 458.
29 July, 1854. s. 1, v. 10, p. 315.

### RETURNS OFFICE.

SEC. 512. The Secretary of the Interior shall from time to time provide a proper apartment, to be called the Returns Office, in which he shall cause to be filed the returns of contracts made by the Secretary of War, the Secretary of the Navy, and the Secretary of the Interior, and shall appoint a clerk of the first class to attend to the same. [See §§ 3744–3747, CONTRACTS, page 29.] *Title 11, Chap. 8.*

*Returns Office.*

2 June, 1862, s. 4, v. 2, p. 412.

SEC. 513. The clerk of the Returns Office shall file all returns made to the office, so that the same may be of easy access, keeping all returns made by the same officer in the same place, and numbering them in the order in which they are made. *Clerk to file returns.*

*Idem.*

SEC. 514. The clerk of the Returns Office shall provide and keep an index-book, with the names of the contracting parties, and the number of each contract opposite to the names; and shall submit the index-book and returns to any person desiring to inspect it. *Indexes.*

*Idem.*

SEC. 515. The clerk of the Returns Office shall furnish copies of such returns to any person paying therefor at the rate of five cents for every one hundred words, to which copies certificates shall be appended in every case by the clerk making the same, attesting their correctness, and that each copy so certified is a full and complete copy of the return, *Copies of returns.*

*Idem.*

### DESTROYING RECORDS.

SEC. 5403. Every person who willfully destroys or attempts to destroy, or, with intent to steal or destroy, takes and carries away any record, paper, or proceeding of a court of justice, filed or deposited with any clerk or officer of such court, or any paper, or document, or record filed or deposited in any public office, or with any judicial or public officer, shall, without reference to the value of the record, paper, document, or proceeding so taken, pay a fine of not more than two thousand dollars, or suffer imprisonment, at hard labor, not more than three years, or both. [See § 5408.] *Title 70, Chap. 4.*

*Destroying, &c. public records.*

26 Feb., 1853, s. 4, v. 10, p. 170.

SEC. 5408. Every officer having the custody of any record, document, paper, or proceeding specified in section fifty-four hundred and three, who fraudulently takes away, or withdraws, or destroys any such record, document, paper, or proceeding filed in his office or deposited with him or in his custody, shall pay a fine of not more than two thousand dollars, or suffer imprisonment at hard labor not more than three years, or both; and shall, moreover, forfeit his office and be forever afterward disqualified from holding any office under the Government of the United States. *Destroying records by officer in charge.*

*Idem, s. 5.*

# PUBLIC PROPERTY, BUILDINGS AND GROUNDS.

### PURCHASE AND DISPOSITION.

Sec.
355. Title to be examined.
1838. Assent of legislature.
3733. Contract not to exceed appropriation.
3734. Restriction on commencing buildings.

Sec.
3736. No purchase without appropriation.
5503. Contracting beyond appropriations.
—— Rent of buildings. [See page 31.]

**Title 8.**

*Title to land to be purchased by the United States.*

SEC. 355. No public money shall be expended upon any site or land purchased by the United States for the purposes of erecting thereon any armory, arsenal, fort, fortification, navy-yard, custom-house, light-house, or other public building, of any kind whatever, until the written opinion of the Attorney-General shall be had in favor of the validity of the title, nor until the consent of the legislature of the State in which the land or site may be, to such purchase, has been given. The district attorneys of the United States, upon the application of the Attorney-General, shall furnish any assistance or information in their power in relation to the titles of the public property lying within their respective districts. And the Secretaries of the Departments, upon the application of the Attorney-General, shall procure any additional evidence of title which he may deem necessary, and which may not be in the possession of the officers of the Government, and the expense of procuring it shall be paid out of the appropriations made for the contingencies of the Departments respectively.

11 September, 1841, Res. 6, v. 5, p. 468.

**Title 22.**

*Assent of States to purchase of lands for forts, &c.*

SEC. 1838. The President of the United States is authorized to procure the assent of the legislature of any State, within which any purchase of land has been made for the erection of forts, magazines, arsenals, dock-yards, and other needful buildings, without such consent having been obtained.

2d April, 1828 s. 2, v. 4, p. 264.

**Title 43.**

*No contract to exceed appropriation.*

SEC. 3733. No contract shall be entered into for the erection, repair, or furnishing, of any public building, or for any public improvement which shall bind the Government to pay a larger sum of money than the amount in the Treasury appropriated for the specific purpose. [See § 5503.]

25 July, 1868, s. 3, v. 15, p. 177.

*Restrictions on commencement of new buildings.*

SEC. 3734. Before any new buildings for the use of the United States are commenced, the plans and full estimates therefor shall be prepared and approved by the Secretary of the Treasury, the Postmaster-General, and the Secretary of the Interior; and the cost of each building shall not exceed the amount of such estimate. [See § 3663.]

15 July, 1870, v. 16, p. 296.

*Land not to be purchased except under a law.*

SEC. 3736. No land shall be purchased on account of the United States, except under a law authorizing such purchase.

1 May, 1820, s. 7, v. 3, p. 568.

**Title 70, Chap. 6.**

*Contracting beyond specific appropriation for building.*

SEC. 5503. Every officer of the Government who knowingly contracts for the erection, repair, or furnishing of any public building, or for any public improvement, to pay a larger amount than the specific sum appropriated for such purpose, shall be punished by imprisonment not less than six months nor more than two years, and shall pay a fine of two thousand dollars. [See § 3733.]

25 July, 1868, s. 5, v. 15, p. 177.

The Government can purchase land in a State without the consent of the legislature, but cannot without that consent exercise exclusive jurisdiction. The joint resolutions of September 11, 1841 (sec. —, R. S.), does not forbid the payment of the purchase money of any site for the purpose of erecting buildings before the consent of the legislature is obtained, but prohibit the expenditure of public money upon improvements before such consent. If the legislative act of the State amounts to a consent, any exceptions, reservations, or qualifications contained in the act are void.—Op. X, 35, May 6, 1861, Bates. See also Op. XV, 212, Devens, March 27, 1877.

A purchase of land by the Executive without the authority of law is an illegal act.—Op. XI, 201, Speed, April 20, 1865.

Where a contract is made for the purchase of property for Government purposes, and the head of a Department refuses to take it, the Attorney-General declaring the title defective, the contract is at an end. A succeeding Secretary cannot reconsider except upon new evidence, &c.—Op. IX, 100, Black, September 26, 1857.

Compensation to district attorneys for examining titles proper. The amount may be agreed on in advance or fixed after the work is completed.—Op. XI, 433, Speed, May 8, 1866. See also Op. XIII, 15.

PUBLIC PROPERTY, BUILDINGS AND GROUNDS. 193

The discretion given in an act to acquire by purchase or condemnation a lot of land for a public building does not extend to "acquisition" of adjoining land. Authority to purchase in the act does not include authority to acquire by condemnation. In statutes, generally, the word *purchase* is employed in a sense not technical, only as acquisition by agreement with and conveyance from the owners without Governmental interference.—Op. XVI, 226, Devens, May 14, 1879.

The United States cannot accept a cession of jurisdiction from a State coupled with a condition that crimes committed within the limits of the jurisdiction ceded shall continue to be punished by the courts of the State.—Op. VIII, 419, Cushing.

See Op. IX, 528, and the Regulations of the Department of Justice, published in General Orders, War Department, May 13, 1881, concerning examination and evidence of titles of lands to be conveyed to the United States.

The act of a legislature of a State giving consent to the purchase of site for naval purposes is sufficient authority for the expenditure of money in its purchase, if the title is certified to.—Op. IX, 129, Black, November 23, 1877. It is such a cession of jurisdiction that is contemplated by the joint resolution of September 11, 1848.—Op. IX, p. 263.

The term *purchase* embraces any mode of acquiring property other than by descent. The Secretary of War cannot accept a *gift* of land or interest in land, for any use or purpose, independently of statute authority. Public money cannot be expended for the erection of a public building upon land *donated* to the United States, until the Attorney-General has passed the title and the legislature of the State granted jurisdiction.—Winthrop's Digest, 406. See also this Digest for other important decisions and rulings on the subject of public lands and property; and against the power of the heads of the executive departments to lease, give away, or dispose in any manner of such land or property without authority of Congress. See also Op. IV, 480.

Where land is donated to the United States for a site for a public building, for which an appropriation was made by Congress: *Held*, That the consent of the legislature of the State to the grant is required before any part of the appropriation can be lawfully expended in the erection of the building—Op. XVI, 414, Devens, January 7, 1880.

Lands purchased and reserved by the United States for light-house, barracks, navy-yards, and other like purposes are not included in the designation of "public lands." Lands so purchased or reserved are in law and in fact *severed* from the public domain, and no subsequent law or warrant authorizing the appropriation of "public lands" would be construed to embrace land so purchased or reserved.—Op. V, 578, Aug. 1, 1852, Crittenden.

An act appropriating for a movable dam impliedly authorizes the purchase with the approval of the Secretary of War, of such land as is necessary for the construction of the dam. Payment of the purchase money may be made though the legislature of the State has not consented to the purchase. Expenditures for structures or improvements cannot be made upon land already purchased until the consent of the State is obtained.—Op. XV, p. 212, Devens, March 27, 1877.

## CARE AND DESTRUCTION OF PUBLIC PROPERTY.

Sec.
197. Inventory to be kept.
1624. Willfully stranding vessels.
——. Unlawful destruction of public property.
——. Negligent stranding of vessels.
——. Waste of public property.
——. Stealing or wrongfully selling.
3748. Selling uniforms and equipments.
5385. Arson of dwelling houses.

Sec.
5386. Arson of armories, &c.
5387. Arson of vessels of war.
5438. Canceling, selling, and pledging public property.
5439. Embezzling arms, stores, &c.
5456. Robbery and larceny of personal property of the United States.
——. Use of water in public buildings D. C.

SEC. 197. The Secretary of State, the Secretary of the Treasury, the Secretary of the Interior, the Secretary of War, the Secretary of the Navy, the Postmaster-General, the Attorney-General, and Commissioner of Agriculture shall keep, in proper books, a complete inventory of all the property belonging to the United States in the buildings, rooms, offices, and grounds occupied by them, respectively, and under their charge, adding thereto, from time to time, an account of such property as may be procured subsequently to the taking of such inventory, as well as an account of the sale or other disposition of any of such property.

Title 4.
Inventories of property.

15 July, 1870, s. 1, v. 16, p. 364.

SEC. 1624. ART. 4. The punishment of death, or such other punishment as a court-martial may adjudge, may be inflicted on any person in the naval service—

Title 15, Chap. 16.
Offenses punishable by death.

*   *   *   *   *   *   *

Tenth. Or intentionally or willfully suffers any vessel of the Navy to be stranded, or run upon rocks or shoals, or improperly hazarded; or maliciously or willfully injures any vessel of the Navy, or any part of her tackle, armament, or equipment, whereby the safety of the vessel is hazarded or the lives of the crew exposed to danger;

Willful stranding or injury of vessel.

11181——13

## PUBLIC PROPERTY, BUILDINGS AND GROUNDS.

**Unlawful destruction of public property.**
Eleventh. Or unlawfully sets on fire, or otherwise unlawfully destroys, any public property not at the time in possession of an enemy, pirate, or rebel;

23 April, 1800, Art. 17, v. 3, p. 47.

**Offenses punishable at discretion of court-martial.**
ART. 8. Such punishment as a court-martial may adjudge may be inflicted on any person in the Navy—
\* \* \* \* \*

**Negligent stranding.**
Eleventh. Or, through inattention or negligence, suffers any vessel of the Navy to be stranded, or run upon a rock or shoal, or hazarded;
\* \* \* \* \*

**Waste of public property, &c.**
Fifteenth. Or wastes any ammunition, provisions, or other public property, or, having power to prevent it, knowingly permits such waste;

23 April, 1800, Art. 13, v. 2, p. 47.

**Crimes of fraud.**
ART. 14. Fine and imprisonment, or such other punishment as a court-martial may adjudge, shall be inflicted upon any person in the naval service of the United States—
\* \* \* \* \*

**Stealing, wrongfully selling, &c.**
Who steals, embezzles, knowingly and willfully misappropriates, applies to his own use or benefit, or wrongfully and knowingly sells or disposes of any ordnance, arms, equipments, ammunition, clothing, subsistence stores, money or other property of the United States, furnished or intended for the military or naval service thereof; or

**Buying public military property.**
Who knowingly purchases, or receives in pledge for any obligation or indebtedness, from any other person who is a part of or employed in said service, any ordnance, arms, equipments, ammunition, clothing, subsistence stores, or other property of the United States, such other person not having lawful right to sell or pledge the same;

2 March, 1863, s. 1, v. 12, p. 565.

**March 3, 1875.**

**Embezzling, stealing, &c., from United States deemed felony; penalty.**
That any person who shall embezzle, steal, or purloin any money, property, record, voucher, or valuable thing whatever, of the moneys, goods, chattels, records, or property of the United States, shall be deemed guilty of felony, and on conviction thereof before the district or circuit court of the United States in the district wherein said offense may have been committed, or into which he shall carry or have in possession of said property so embezzled, stolen, or purloined, shall be punished therefor by imprisonment at hard labor in the penitentiary not exceeding five years, or by a fine not exceeding five thousand dollars, or both, at the discretion of the court before which he shall be convicted.

**Knowingly receiving, concealing, &c., stolen, &c., property of the United States; penalty.**
SEC. 2. That if any person shall receive, conceal, or aid in concealing, or have, or retain in his possession with intent to convert to his own use or gain, any money, property, record, voucher, or valuable thing whatever, of the moneys, goods, chattels, records, or property of the United States, which has theretofore been embezzled, stolen, or purloined from the United States by any other person, knowing the same to have been so embezzled, stolen, or purloined, such person shall, on conviction before the circuit or district court of the United States in the district wherein he may have such property, be punished by a fine not exceeding five thousand dollars, or imprisonment at hard labor in the penitentiary not exceeding five years, one or both, at the discretion

**May be tried before or after conviction of principal.**
of the court before which he shall be convicted; and such receiver may be tried either before or after the conviction of the principal felon, but if the party has been convicted, then the judgment against him shall be conclusive evidence in the prosecution against such receiver that the property of the United States therein described has been embezzled, stolen, or purloined.

3 March, 1875, v. 18, p. 479.

**Title 44.**

**Uniforms and equipments.**
SEC. 3748. The clothes, arms, military outfits, and accouterments furnished by the United States to any soldier shall not be sold, bartered, exchanged, pledged, loaned, or given away; and no person not a soldier, or duly authorized officer of the United States, who has possession of any such clothes, arms, military outfits or accouterments, so furnished, and which have been the subjects of any such sale, barter, exchange, pledge, loan, or gift, shall have any right, title, or interest therein; but the same may be seized and taken wherever found by any officer of the United States, civil or military, and shall thereupon be delivered to any quartermaster, or other officer authorized to receive

## PUBLIC PROPERTY, BUILDINGS AND GROUNDS. 195

the same. The possession of any such clothes, arms, military outfits, or accouterments by any person not a soldier or officer of the United States shall be presumptive evidence of such a sale, barter, exchange, pledge, loan, or gift.

*3 March, 1863, s. 23, v. 12, p. 735.*

SEC. 5385. Every person who, within any fort, dock-yard, navy-yard, arsenal, armory, or magazine, the site whereof is under the jurisdiction of the United States, or on the site of any light-house, or other needful building belonging to the United States, the site whereof is under their jurisdiction, willfully and maliciously burns any dwelling-house, or mansion-house, or any store, barn, stable, or other building, parcel of any dwelling or mansion-house, shall suffer death.

*3 March, 1825, s. 1, v. 4, p. 115.*

Title 70, Chap. 3.
Arson of dwelling-house within a fort, &c.

SEC. 5386. Every person who, in any of the places mentioned in the preceding section, maliciously sets fire to, or burns, any arsenal, armory, magazine, rope-walk, ship-house, warehouse, block-house, or barrack, or any store-house, barn, or stable, not parcel of a dwelling-house, or any other building not mentioned in such section, or any vessel built, or begun to be built, or repairing, or any light-house, or beacon, or any timber, cables, rigging, or other materials for building, repairing, or fitting out vessels, or any pile of wood, boards, or other lumber, or any military, naval, or victualing stores, arms, or other munitions of war, shall be punished by a fine of not more than five thousand dollars, and by imprisonment at hard labor not more than ten years.

*Ibid, s. 2.*

Arson of armory, arsenal, &c.

SEC. 5387. Every person who maliciously sets on fire, or burns, or otherwise destroys, any vessel of war of the United States, afloat on the high seas, or in any arm of the sea, or in any river, haven, creek, basin, or bay within the admiralty jurisdiction of the United States, and out of the jurisdiction of any particular State, shall suffer death.

*Ibid, s. 11, p. 117.*

Arson of vessel of war.

SEC. 5438. Every person * * * who, having charge, possession, custody, or control of any money or other public property used, or to be used, in the military or naval service, who, with intent to defraud the United States or willfully to conceal such money or other property, delivers or causes to be delivered, to any other person having authority to receive the same, any amount of such money or other property less than that for which he received a certificate or took a receipt, and every person authorized to make or deliver any certificate, voucher, receipt or other paper certifying the receipt of arms, ammunition, provisions, clothing, or other property so used or to be used, who makes or delivers the same to any other person without a full knowledge of the truth of the facts stated therein, and with intent to defraud the United States, and every person who knowingly purchases or receives in pledge for any obligation or indebtedness from any soldier, officer, sailor, or other person called into or employed in the military or naval service any arms, equipments, ammunition, clothes, military stores, or other public property, such soldier, sailor, officer, or other person not having the lawful right to pledge or sell the same, every person so offending in any of the matters set forth in this section shall be imprisoned at hard labor for not less than one nor more than five years, or fined not less than one thousand nor more than five thousand dollars. [See § § 3490, 3491, under CLAIMS.]

*2 March, 1863, ss. 1-3, v. 12, pp. 696-698.*

Title 70, Chap. 5.
Concealing, selling and pledging public property, &c.

SEC. 5439. Every person who steals or embezzles, or knowingly applies to his own use, or who unlawfully sells, conveys, or disposes of, any ordnance, arms, ammunition, clothing, subsistence, stores, money, or other property of the United States, furnished or to be used for the military or naval service, shall be punished as prescribed in the preceding section.

*Ibid.*

Embezzling arms, stores, &c.

SEC. 5456. Every person who robs another of any kind or description of personal property belonging to the United States, or feloniously takes and carries away the same, shall be punished by a fine of not more than five thousand dollars, or by imprisonment at hard labor not less than one nor more than ten years, or by both such fine and imprisonment.

*2 March, 1867, v. 14, p. 557.*

Robbery or larceny of personal property of the United States.

PUBLIC PROPERTY, BUILDINGS AND GROUNDS.

3 March, 1883.
Flow of water to be shut off.

All officers in charge of public buildings in the District of Columbia shall cause the flow of water in the buildings under their charge to be shut off from five o'clock post meridian to eight o'clock ante meridian: *Provided*, That the water in said public buildings is not necessarily in use for public business.

3 March, 1883. [Sundry civil act.]

3 March, 1875.
Payments, contracts, &c., for public buildings.

And hereafter no money shall be paid nor contracts made for payment for any site for a public building in excess of the amount specifically appropriated therefor; and no money shall be expended upon any public building on which work has not yet been actually begun until after drawings and specifications together with detailed estimates of the cost thereof, shall have been made by the Supervising Architect of the Treasury Department, and said plans and estimates shall have been approved by the Secretary of the Treasury, Secretary of the Interior, and the Postmaster-General; and all appropriations made for the construction of such building shall be expended within the limitations of the act authorizing the same or limiting the cost thereof; and no change of said plan involving an increase of expense exceeding ten per centum of the amount to which said building was limited shall be allowed or paid by any officer of the Government without the special authority of Congress.

3 March, 1875, chap. 130, v. 18, p. 395.

The Secretary of the Navy has no authority to grant permission to a city to extend a sewer through the public grounds so as to confer any legal title or right upon the city to maintain the sewer through the grounds. A mere license for the use of the premises is revocable at all times. A legal right to construct and maintain a sewer would have to be granted by Congress.—Op. XVI, 152, October 1, 1878, Devens.

Territory over which exclusive jurisdiction has been ceded to the United States, is subject only to the laws of Congress. Where land is granted by a State to the General Government, reserving a concurrent jurisdiction in executing process within for offenses committed without such tract, the United States have exclusive jurisdiction of offenses committed within the ceded territory. The purchase of land by the General Government for public purposes within the territorial limits of a State, does not, of itself, oust the State jurisdiction therein. Exclusive jurisdiction is the necessary attendant on exclusive legislation. When, therefore, a State legislature has given its consent to a purchase of land by the General Government for the purposes enumerated in the Constitution, the State jurisdiction is completely ousted.—Brightley's Federal Digest, pp. 147, 148, giving numerous authorities and decisions of the courts.

An officer in command of a military post has the right to protect it by force from occupation or injury at the hands of trespassers. One caution should be observed, however, that in executing this duty there should be no unnecessary or wanton harm done either to persons or property.—Op. IX, 476, Black, September 24, 1860.

Where the Government executes a lease with a full knowledge of the condition of the building leased and with no agreement that the lessor shall make repairs it cannot make them at his expense.—C. C., IV, 526.

Premises occupied by the Government under an implied lease; claim presented, which is *reduced* and paid, owner accepting and receipting without protest. He is excluded from afterward seeking to recover the difference.—C. C., VIII, 521. Where there is an express agreement to repair, tenant is liable for loss by accidental fire. Liability attaches although there be no express covenant as to fire. Otherwise where there is no agreement to keep in repair, C. C., IX, 479. Premises rented at a specific rate per month, after expiration of a year lessee notified lessor that the rent must be reduced. The lessor allows the lessee to continue, receiving monthly rent at the reduced rate and giving receipts therefor in full. He thereby consents to chang ein the original contract.—C. C., V, 508.

Where the President has given permission to a railroad or a telegraph company to run lines through the public property, the license is revocable at his pleasure.—Op. XVI, 205, Devens, Nov. 22, 1878.

Persons who reside on lands purchased by, or ceded to the United States, forts and arsenals, and where there is no other reservation or jurisdiction to the State than that of a right to serve civil and criminal process on such lands, are not entitled to the benefits of common schools for their children in the towns in which the lands are situated; nor are they liable to be assessed for their polls and estates to State, county, and town taxes, in such towns; nor do they gain a settlement in such towns for themselves or their children by a residence for any length of time on such lands; nor do they acquire by residing on such lands any elective franchise as inhabitants of such towns.—Supreme court of Massachusetts, 1 Metcalf, 580, quoted in Op. XVI, 468, Devens, Feb., 7, 1880.

# SALE OF PROPERTY AND MATERIALS.

Sec.
1540. Sale of vessels unfit for repairs.
1541. Sale of unserviceable vessels and materials.
—— Removal of vessels from Register.
—— Appraisal and sale of stores, &c.
3617. Moneys to be deposited without deduction.

Sec.
3618. Proceeds of sales of materials.
3619. Penalty for withholding moneys.
3672. Statement of proceeds of sales.
—— Disposition of useless ordinance material.

SEC. 1540. The President may direct any armed vessel of the United States to be sold when, in his opinion, such vessel is so much out of repair that it will not be for the interest of the United States to repair her. [See Aug. 5, 1882, *post*.] *Title 15, Chap. 6. Sale of vessels unfit to be repaired.*

21 April, 1806, s. 3, v. 2, p. 402.

SEC. 1541. The Secretary of the Navy is authorized and directed to sell, at public sale, such vessels and materials of the United States Navy as, in his judgment, cannot be advantageously used, repaired, or fitted out; and he shall, at the opening of each session of Congress, make a full report to Congress of all vessels and materials sold, the parties buying the same, and the amount realized therefrom, together with such other facts as may be necessary to a full understanding of his acts. [See s. 3618 and Aug. 5, 1882, *post*, sec. 429, NAVY DEPARTMENT, p. 181, Part II, and page 96, Part I.] *Sale of unserviceable vessels and materials.*

23 March, 1872, s. 2, v. 17, p. 154.

It shall also be the duty of the Secretary of the Navy, as soon as may be after the passage of this act, to cause to be examined by competent boards of officers of the Navy, to be designated by him for that duty, all vessels belonging to the Navy not in actual service at sea, and vessels at sea as soon as practicable after they shall return to the United States, and hereafter all vessels on their return from foreign stations, and all vessels in the United States as often as once in three years, when practicable; and said boards shall ascertain and report to the Secretary of the Navy, in writing, which of said vessels are unfit for further service, or, if the same are unfinished in any navy-yard, those which cannot be finished without great and disproportionate expense, and shall in such report state fully the grounds and reasons for their opinion. And it shall be the duty of the Secretary of the Navy, if he shall concur in opinion with said report, to strike the name of such vessel or vessels from the Navy Register and report the same to Congress. [See March 3, 1883, VESSELS OF THE NAVY, Part I, p. 96.] *5 Aug., 1882. Examination of vessels, &c. Vessels not fit for further service to be stricken from register.*

5 August, 1882, P. E. L., p. 296.

SEC. 2. That it shall be the duty of the Secretary of the Navy, as soon as may be after the passage of this act, to cause an account to be taken of the stock of stores and supplies pertaining and belonging to the several bureaus of the Navy Department, in which account shall be stated the original cost of each article and the date of purchase, so far as the same is known, and cause an appraisement of the present value of such stores and supplies to be made and entered in such account; and said appraised value, when so entered, shall hereafter be the price at which they shall be charged in accounting with the several bureaus. Such appraisal shall be made by boards of officers of the Navy to be designated by the Secretary; and all such stores and supplies as shall be found by boards of appraisers to be unserviceable for use in the Navy, shall be condemned and sold in the manner hereinafter provided for the sale of old materials, and the proceeds thereof, after deducting the cost of such appraisal, condemnation, and sale, shall be paid into the Treasury. And no old material of the Navy shall hereafter be sold or exchanged by the Secretary of the Navy, or by any officer of the Navy, which can be profitably used by reworking or otherwise in the construction or repair of vessels, their machinery, armor, armament, or equipment; but the same shall be stored and preserved for future use. And when any such old material cannot be profitably used as aforesaid, the same shall be appraised and sold at public auction after public notice and advertisement shall have been given according to law under such rules and regulations and in such manner as the said Secretary may direct. The net proceeds arising from the sales of such old materials shall be paid into the Treasury. It shall be the duty of *5 Aug., 1882. Account of stores to be taken. Appraises. Sale of unprofitable articles.*

## 198 SALE OF PROPERTY AND MATERIALS.

Report to be made to Congress.
the Secretary of the Navy annually to report in detail to Congress, in his annual report, the proceeds of all sales of materials, stores, and supplies, made under the provisions of this act, and the expenses attending such sales.

5 August, 1882, chap. 391, P. E. L., p. 296.

**Title 40.**

Moneys to be deposited without deduction.

SEC. 3617. The gross amount of all moneys received from whatever source for the use of the United States, except as otherwise provided in the next section, shall be paid by the officer or agent receving the same into the Treasury, at as early a day as practicable, without any abatement or deduction on account of salary, fees, costs, charges, expenses, or claim of any description whatever. But nothing herein shall affect any provision relating to the revenues of the Post-Office Department. [See Aug. 5, 1882, *ante*, and March 3, 1883.]

3 March, 1849, s. 1, v. 9, p. 398.
28 Sept., 1850, s. 3, v. 9, p. 507.

Proceeds of sales of material.

SEC. 3618. All proceeds of sales of old material, condemned stores, supplies, or other public property of any kind, except the proceeds of the sale or leasing of marine hospitals, or of the sales of revenue-cutters, or of the sales of commissary stores to the officers and enlisted men of the Army, or of materials, stores, or supplies sold to officers and soldiers of the Army, or of the sale of condemned Navy clothing, or of sales of materials, stores, or supplies to any exploring or surveying expedition authorized by law, shall be deposited and covered into the Treasury as miscellaneous receipts, on account of "proceeds of Government property," and shall not be withdrawn or applied, except in consequence of a subsequent appropriation made by law. [See § 1541, Aug. 5, 1882, *ante*, and March 3, 1875, *post.*]

3 May, 1872, s. 5, v. 17, p. 83.
3 March, 1847, s. 1, v. 9, p. 171.
20 April, 1866, ss. 1, 2, v. 14, p. 40.
28 July, 1866, s. 25, v. 14, p. 330.
8 June, 1872, v. 17, p, 337.
22 June, 1874, v. 18, p. 200.
7 Feb., 1877, v. 19, p. 249.

Penalty for withholding money.

SEC. 3619. Every officer or agent who neglects or refuses to comply with the provisions of section thirty-six hundred and seventeen shall be subject to be removed from office, and to forfeit to the United States any share or part of the moneys withheld, to which he might otherwise be entitled.

18 July, 1866, s. 40, v. 14, p. 187.

**Title 41.**

Statement of process of sales of old material.

SEC. 3672. A detailed statement of the proceeds of all sales of old material, condemned stores, supplies, or other public property of any kind except materials, stores, or supplies sold to officers and soldiers of the Army, or to exploring or surveying expeditions authorized by law, shall be included in the appendix to the book of estimates. [See § 3692, appropriations.]

8 May, 1872, s. 5, v. 17, p. 83.
27 Feb., 1877, v. 19, p. 249.

March 3, 1875.

Disposition of ordnance material.

That the Secretary of the Navy is authorized to dispose of the useless ordnance material on hand at public sale, according to law, the net proceeds of which shall be turned into the Treasury; and an amount equal to the same is hereby appropriated, to be applied to the purpose of procuring a supply of material adapted in manufacture and calibre to the present wants of the service; but there shall be expended, under this provision, not more than seventy-five thousand dollars in one year.

3 March, 1875, v. 18, p. 343.

NOTES.—The Secretary of the Navy cannot exchange a condemned vessel for another. Disposition of former controlled by act of May 23, 1872.—Op. XIV 369, Feb. 18, 1874, Williams.

For the mode in which sales of condemned property shall be conducted, whether by advertisement at public auction or otherwise, no specific provision is made. In these respects the sales are left to the discretion of the officer having charge of such old material. The proceeds must be covered into the Treasury. The Bureau of Engraving and Printing cannot exchange old presses for new ones.—Op. XV, 320, Williams, June 23, 1877.

Inspection, condemnation and public sale, are necessary to a valid sale of unsuitable military stores under the act of March 3, 1825.—C. C., v. 1, p. 85.

# REVISED STATUTES—STATUTES AT LARGE.

## GENERAL PROVISIONS.

Sec.
1. Definitions.
2. County.
3. Vessel.

Sec.
4. Vehicle.
5. Company, association.
6. Seal.

*Be it enacted by the Senate and House of Representatives of the United States of America in Congress assembled,* In determining the meaning of the Revised Statutes, or of any act or resolution of Congress passed subsequent to February twenty-fifth, eighteen hundred and seventy-one, words importing the singular number may extend and be applied to several persons or things; words importing the plural number may include the singular; words importing the masculine gender may be applied to females; the words "insane person" and "lunatic" shall include every idiot, non-compos, lunatic, and insane person; the word "person" may extend and be applied to partnerships and corporations, and the reference to any officer shall include any person authorized by law to perform the duties of such office, unless the context shows that such words were intended to be used in a more limited sense; and a requirement of an "oath" shall be deemed complied with by making affirmation in judicial form.   *Title 1, Chap. 1.*   *Definitions.*

25 Feb., 1871. s. 2, v. 16, p. 431.
13 July, 1866, s. 44, v. 14, p. 163.
30 June, 1864, ss. 82, 126, v. 13, pp. 256, 287.
20 July, 1868, s. 104, v. 15, p. 166.

SEC. 2. The word "county" includes a parish, or any other equivalent subdivision of a State or Territory of the United States.   *County.*

13 July, 1866, s. 9, v. 14, pp. 98, 110.

SEC. 3. The word "vessel" includes every description of water-craft or other artificial contrivance used, or capable of being used, as a means of transportation on water.   *Vessel.*

18 July, 1866, s. 1, v. 14, p. 178.
29 June, 1870, s. 7, v. 16, p. 170.

SEC. 4. The word "vehicle" includes every description of carriage or other artificial contrivance used, or capable of being used, as a means of transportation on land.   *Vehicle.*

18 July, 1866, s. 1, v. 14, p. 178.

SEC. 5. The word "company" or "association," when used in reference to a corporation, shall be deemed to embrace the words "successors and assigns of such company or association," in like manner as if those last-named words, or words of similar import, were expressed.   *Company, association.*

25 July, 1866, s. 9, v. 14, p. 241.

SEC. 6. In all cases where a seal is necessary by law to any commission, process, or other instrument provided for by the laws of Congress, it shall be lawful to affix the proper seal by making an impression therewith directly on the paper to which such seal is necessary; which shall be as valid as if made on wax or other adhesive substance.   *Seal.*

31 May, 1854, s. 2, v. 10, p. 297.

## FORM OF STATUTES AND EFFECT OF REPEALS.

Sec.
7. Enacting clause.
8. Resolving clause.
9. No enacting words after first section.
10. Numbering and frame of sections.

Sec.
11. Title of appropriation acts.
12. Repeal not to revive former act.
13. Repeals not to affect liabilities, unless, &c.

SEC. 7. The enacting clause of all acts of Congress hereafter enacted shall be in the following form: "Be it enacted by the Senate and House of Representatives of the United States of America in Congress assembled."   *Title 1, Chap. 2.*   *Enacting clause.*

SEC. 8. The resolving clause of all joint resolutions shall be in the following form: "Resolved by the Senate and House of Representatives of the United States of America in Congress assembled."   *Resolving clause.*

200 STATUTES.

No enacting words after first section. SEC. 9. No enacting or resolving words shall be used in any section of an act or resolution of Congress except in the first.

Numbering and frame of sections. SEC. 10. Each section shall be numbered, and shall contain, as nearly as may be, a single proposition of enactment.

25 Feb., 1871, s. 1, v. 16, p. 431.

Title of appropriation acts. SEC. 11. The style and title of all acts making appropriations for the support of Government shall be as follows: "An act making appropriations (here insert the object) for the year ending June thirtieth (here insert the calendar year.)

26 Aug., 1842, s. 2, v. 5, p. 537.

Repeal not to revive former SEC. 12. Whenever an act is repealed, which repealed a former act, such former act shall not thereby be revived, unless it shall be expressly so provided.

25 Feb., 1871, s. 3, v. 16, p. 432.

Repeals not to affect liabilities unless, &c. SEC. 13. The repeal of any statute shall not have the effect to release or extinguish any penalty, forfeiture, or liability incurred under such statute, unless the repealing act shall so expressly provide, and such statute shall be treated as still remaining in force for the purpose of sustaining any proper action or prosecution for the enforcement of such penalty, forfeiture, or liability.

*Ibid*, s. 4.

Title 19. Preservation of copies of Statutes at Large. SEC. 1777. The various officers of the United States, to whom, in virtue of their offices and for the uses thereof, copies of the United States Statutes at Large, published by Little, Brown and Company, have been or may be distributed at the public expense, by authority of law, shall preserve such copies, and deliver them to their successors respectively as a part of the property appertaining to the office. A printed copy of this section shall be inserted in each volume of the Statutes distributed to any such officers.

8 Aug., 1846, s. 1, v. 9, p. 75.

## LIMITATIONS.

Sec.
1043. Capital offenses.
1044. Offenses not capital.
1045. Fleeing from justice.
1046. Crimes under the revenue laws.

Sec.
1047. Penalties and forfeitures under laws of the United States.
1048. Parties beyond reach of process during the rebellion.

Title 13, Chap. 19. Capital offenses. SEC. 1043. No person shall be prosecuted, tried, or punished for treason or other capital offense, willful murder excepted, unless the indictment is found within three years next after such treason or capital offense is done or committed.

30 April, 1790, s. 32, v. 1, p. 119.

Offenses not capital. SEC. 1044. No person shall be prosecuted, tried, or punished for any offense, not capital, except as provided in section one thousand and forty-six, unless the indictment is found, or the information is instituted within three years next after such offense shall have been committed; but this act shall not have the effect to authorize the prosecution, trial, or punishment for any offense, barred by the provisions of existing law.

Fleeing from justice. SEC. 1045. Nothing in the two preceding sections shall extend to any person fleeing from justice.

*Ibid.*
30 April, 1876, v. 19, p. 32.

Crimes under the revenue laws. SEC. 1046. No person shall be prosecuted, tried, or punished for any crime arising under the revenue laws, or the slave-trade laws of the United States, unless the indictment is found or the information is instituted within five years next after the committing of such crime.

26 March, 1804, s. 3, v. 2, p. 290.
20 April, 1818, s. 9, v. 3, p. 452.

Penalties and forfeitures under laws of United States. SEC. 1047. No suit or prosecution for any penalty or forfeiture, pecuniary or otherwise, accruing under the laws of the United States, shall be maintained, except in cases where it is otherwise specially provided, unless the same is commenced within five years from the time when the penalty or forfeiture accrued: *Provided*, That the person of the offender, or the property liable for such penalty or forfeiture, shall, within the

STATUTES.  201

same period, be found within the United States; so that the proper process therefor may be instituted and served against such person or property.

28 Feb., 1839, s. 4, v. 5, p. 322,  20 April, 1818, s. 9, v. 3, p. 452.
2 March, 1799, s. 89, v. 1, p. 695.  3 March, 1863, s. 14, v. 12, p. 741.
26 March, 1804, s. 3, v. 2, p. 290.  25 July, 1868, s. 1, v. 15, p. 183.

SEC. 1048. In all cases where, during the late rebellion, any person could not, by reason of resistance to the execution of the laws of the United States, or of the interruption of the ordinary course of judicial proceedings, be served with process for the commencement of any action, civil or criminal, which had accrued against him, the time during which such person was beyond the reach of legal process shall not be taken as any part of the time limited by law for the commencement of such action. *Parties beyond reach of process during the rebellion.*

11 June, 1864, ch. 118, v. 13, p. 123.

## REPEAL PROVISIONS.

Sec.
5595. What Revised Statutes embrace.
5596. Repeal of acts embraced in revision.
5597. Accrued rights reserved.
5598. Prosecutions and punishments.

Sec.
5599. Acts of limitation.
5600. Arrangement and classification of sections.
5601. Acts passed since December 1, 1873, not affected.

SEC. 5595. The foregoing seventy-three titles embrace the statutes of the United States general and permanent in their nature, in force on the 1st day of December one thousand eight hundred and seventy-three, as revised and consolidated by commissioners appointed under an act of Congress, and the same shall be designated and cited, as The Revised Statutes of the United States. *Title 74. What Revised Statutes embrace.*

SEC. 5596. All acts of Congress passed prior to said first day of December one thousand eight hundred and seventy-three, any portion of which is embraced in any section of said revision, are hereby repealed, and the section applicable thereto shall be in force in lieu thereof; all parts of such acts not contained in such revision, having been repealed or superseded by subsequent acts, or not being general and permanent in their nature: *Provided*, That the incorporation into said revision of any general and permanent provision, taken from an act making appropriations, or from an act containing other provisions of a private, local, or temporary character, shall not repeal, or in any way affect any appropriation, or any provision of a private, local, or temporary character, contained in any of said acts, but the same shall remain in force; and all acts of Congress passed prior to said last-named day no part of which are embraced in said revision, shall not be affected or changed by its enactment. *Repeal of acts embraced in revision.*

SEC. 5597. The repeal of the several acts embraced in said revision, shall not affect any act done, or any right accruing or accrued, or any suit or proceeding had or commenced in any civil cause before the said repeal, but all rights and liabilities under said acts shall continue, and may be enforced in the same manner, as if said repeal had not been made; nor shall said repeal, in any manner affect the right to any office, or change the term or tenure thereof. *Accrued rights reserved.*

SEC. 5598. All offenses committed, and all penalties or forfeitures incurred under any statute embraced in said revision prior to said repeal, may be prosecuted and punished in the same manner and with the same effect, as if said repeal had not been made. *Prosecutions and punishments.*

SEC. 5599. All acts of limitation, whether applicable to civil causes and proceedings, or to the prosecution of offenses, or for the recovery of penalties or forfeitures, embraced in said revision and covered by said repeal, shall not be affected thereby, but all suits, proceedings or prosecutions, whether civil or criminal, for causes arising, or acts done or committed prior to said repeal, may be commenced and prosecuted within the same time as if said repeal had not been made. *Acts of limitation.*

SEC. 5600. The arrangement and classification of the several sections of the revision have been made for the purpose of a more convenient and orderly arrangement of the same, and therefore no inference or presumption of a legislative construction is to be drawn by reason of the Title, under which any particular section is placed. *Arrangement and classification of sections.*

SEC. 5601. The enactment of the said revision is not to affect or repeal any act of Congress passed since the 1st day of December, one thousand eight hundred and seventy-three, and all acts passed since that date are to have full effect as if passed after the enactment of this revision, and *Acts passed since December 1, 1873, not affected.*

so far as such acts vary from, or conflict with any provision contained in said revision, they are to have effect as subsequent statutes, and as repealing any portion of the revision inconsistent therewith.

22 June, 1874.

### PRINTING AND PROMULGATION OF LAWS.

**Title 5.**
*Promulgation of laws.*

SEC. 204. Whenever a bill, order, resolution or vote of the Senate and House of Representatives, having been approved by the President, or not having been returned by him with his objections, becomes a law or takes effect, it shall forthwith be received by the Secretary of State from the President; and whenever a bill, order, resolution, or vote is returned by the President with his objections, and, on being reconsidered, is agreed to be passed, and is approved by two-thirds of both Houses of Congress, and thereby becomes a law or takes effect, it shall be received by the Secretary of State from the President of the Senate, or Speaker of the House of Representatives in whichsoever House it shall last have been so approved, and he shall carefully preserve the originals.

15 Sept, 1789, s. 2, v. 1, p. 68.
7 July, 1838, v. 5, p. 302.
28 Dec., 1874. ch. 9, v. 18, p. 294.

**20 June, 1874.**
*Preparation of Revised Statutes for printing, &c.*

*Certification by Secretary of State; printed copies to be evidence.*
*Title of revision.*

That the Secretary of State is hereby charged with the duty of causing to be prepared for printing, publication and distribution the revised statutes of the United States enacted at this present session of Congress; that he shall cause to be completed the head notes of the several titles and chapters and the marginal notes referring to the statutes from which each section was compiled and repealed by said revision; and references to the decisions of the courts of the United States explaining or expounding the same, and such decisions of State courts as he may deem expedient, with a full and complete index to the same. And when the same shall be completed, the said Secretary shall duly certify the same under the seal of the *Department of State*, and when printed and promulgated as hereinafter provided, the printed volumes shall be legal evidence of the laws and treaties therein contained, in all the courts of the United States, and of the several States and Territories.

20 June, 1874, s. 2, v. 18, p. 113.
28 Dec., 1874, s. 1, v. 18, p. 283.

*Revision relating to the District.*

That the revision of the statutes of a general and permanent nature, with the index thereto, shall be printed in one volume, and shall be entitled and labeled "Revised Statutes of the United States"; and the revision of the statutes relating to the District of Columbia; to post roads, and the public treaties in force on the first day of December, one thousand eight hundred and seventy-three, with a suitable index to each, shall be published in a separate volume, and entitled and labeled "Revised Statutes relating to District of Columbia and Post-Roads. Public Treaties."

20 June. 1874, s. 3, v. 18, p. 113.

*To be stereotyped, &c.*
*Distribution and sale.*

That the Secretary of State shall cause the two volumes to be stereotyped and such number of each volume to be printed and substantially bound at the Government Printing Office as he may deem needful, for public distribution as hereinafter provided, and for sale by his office.

*Idem, s. 4.*

[The statutes of the United States are edited, printed, stereotyped and distributed, in accordance with law, under the direction of the Secretary of State. They are sold at the cost of the paper, press work and binding with ten per cent. added thereto, to any person applying for the same.

Under section 8 of the act of Congress approved June 20, 1874, vol. 18, p. 113, the printed copies of the acts of Congress, as edited and printed and issued under the direction of the Secretary of State, are "legal evidence of the laws and treaties therein contained, in all the courts of the United States and of the several States therein."

The 6th section of the act of Congress approved June 20, 1874, provides for the distribution to the Navy Department, including those for the use of the officers of the Navy, of one hundred copies of the pamphlet edition of the acts and resolves of Congress at the close of each session; and the 7th section of the same act provides for distribution of the bound copies of the Statutes at Large for each Congress as follows: "To the Navy Department, including a copy for the library at the Naval Academy at Annapolis, a copy for the library of each navy-yard in the United States, a copy for the library of the Brooklyn Naval Lyceum, and a copy for the library of the Naval Institute at Charlestown, Mass., sixty-five copies." * * *

Joint Resolution No. 22, approved May 22, 1878, v. 20, p. 251, provided for the distribution of the 2d edition of the Revised Statutes recently printed: To the "Navy Department, including three copies for the library of the Naval Academy at Annapolis, a copy for the library of each navy-yard in the United States, a copy for the Brooklyn Naval Lyceum, and a copy for the library of the Naval Institute at Charlestown, Mass., seventy copies."·

Joint Resolution No. 44, approved June 7, 1880, V. 21, p. 308, provides for the publication, sale, and distribution of a "supplement to the Revised Statutes." This supplement is "to be taken to be prima facie evidence of the laws therein contained in all the courts of the United States and of the several States and Territories therein; but shall not preclude reference to, nor control, in case of any discrepancy, the effect of any original act as passed by Congress; *Provided*, That nothing herein contained shall be construed to change or alter any existing law."

The acts approved March 2, 1877, chap. 82, s. 4, v. 19, p. 268, and March 9, 1878, chap. 26, v. 20, p. 27, provide that after the 2d edition of the Revised Statutes is certified to under the seal of the Secretary of State and when printed and promulgated "shall be legal evidence of the laws therein contained, in all the courts of the United States, and of the several States and Territories, but shall not preclude reference to, nor control, in case of any discrepancy, the effect of any original act as passed by Congress since the first day of December, eighteen hundred and seventy-three."]

NOTES.—Whenever a power is given by a statute everything necessary to the making of it effectual or requisite to attain the end is implied. (1 Kent's Com., 464.)—Quoted in Op. XV, p. 213.

Where power is given by a statute to public officers in permissive language, as they "may if deemed advisable" do a certain thing, the language used will be regarded as peremptory when the public interests or individual rights require that it should be.—Wallace, S. C., IV, p. 709.

Where a statute imposes a particular duty on an executive officer and he has acted (performing the duty to his understanding of the statute) there is no appeal from his action to the President or to any other executive officer, unless such appeal is provided for by law.—Op. XVI, 317, Devens, May 2, 1879.

When the intent and meaning of a statute is expressly declared by a provision therein, to carry out that intent all other parts of the act must yield. A proviso in an act "repugnant to the purview thereof is not void, but stands as the last expression of the legislative will."—Op. XV, p. 74. Quotes *Farmers' Bank* vs. *Hale*, 59, N. Y., 53.

A general repealing clause, such as is often introduced at the close of enactments, may make the legislative intent clearer, but it is not necessary to give effect to the legislation otherwise expressed.—C. C., XX, 323. *Fisher's* case.

A later statute, in the affirmative and general, does not take away a former act which is particular and special. Sundry cases cited.—Op. VI, p. 45, Cushing.

An earlier law is never to be taken as repealed by a later, without words to that effect, unless they be so inconsistent that both cannot stand together.—Op. IX, p. 48, Black. The earlier is never abrogated by the later unless the two are so flatly repugnant that they cannot possibly stand together. Any reasonable interpretation is to be adopted which may be necessary to prevent one from interfering with the other.—*Idem*, p. 122.

No statute, however positive in terms, is to be construed as designed to interfere with existing rights of action or vested rights unless the intention that it should so operate is expressly declared or necessarily implied.—C. C., IX, p. 108, S. C., Wallace, XX, p. 179.

A statute may not be repealed, yet its subject-matter may expire and the act become inoperative.—C. C., III, 152, Wallace, 62.

In all statute law, the *particular* provision, especially whenever subsequent, restrains and modifies the general.—Op. IV, p. 182.

In construing statutes aid may be derived from attention to the state of things as it appeared to the legislature when the statute was enacted.—S. C., Otto, 90, p. 48.

The principle is well settled that statutes are to be construed as operative prospectively only, unless their language clearly and imperatively demands that retrospective effect shall be given them.—Op. XV, p. 222, 259. A retroactive effect, especially when it would be a violation of contracts, is not to be given to the words of a statute unless they are too express to admit of any other interpretation.—Op. IV, p. 141.

No effect can be given by the judiciary to an act of Congress which seeks to declare retrospectively the legal effect to be given to other statutes.—C. C., VII, 109, Wallace, VIII, 330.

Every law is presumed to be prospective in its operation unles the *contrary* clearly appears.—Op. XV, 183.

# PART IV.

## MISCELLANEOUS.

Bribes, presents, and contributions.
Bounty and bounty land.
Coast Survey.
Collisions—Rules of the sea.
Diplomatic and consular officers.
Expatriation.
Extradition.
Fish Commission.
Flags and standards.
Fraud, forgery, and theft.
Guano islands.
Habeas corpus.
Homesteads.
Importation.
Life-Saving Service.
Lights and buoys.
Merchant vessels and service, and yachts.

Murder, mutiny, &c.
Naturalization; citizenship.
Neutrality; alien enemies.
Patents.
Pensions.
Pension funds.
Perjury.
Piracy.
Pilotage.
Postal laws, &c.
Prize and salvage.
Quarantine and Board of Health.
Railroads and telegraphs.
Reserved timber lands.
Revenue-Cutter Service.
Slave and cooly trade; kidnapping.
Treason, conspiracy, insurrection, and rebellion.

# BRIBES, CONTRIBUTIONS, PRESENTS, ETC.

| Sec. | Sec. |
|---|---|
| 1546. Contributions for political purposes. | 5451. Bribery of Government officers. |
| 1781. Prohibition on taking, &c., by Government officers. | 5498. Interest in claims, &c. |
| | 5500. Member of Congress accepting bribe, &c. |
| 1782. Taking compensation in matters to which the United States is a party. | 5501. United States officer accepting bribe, &c. |
| | 5502. Forfeiture of office. |
| 1784. Presents to superiors. | ——. Soliciting and receiving contributions for political purposes. |
| 5450. Bribery of member of Congress. | |

SEC. 1546. No officer or employé of the Government shall require or request any workingman in any navy-yard to contribute or pay any money for political purposes, nor shall any workingman be removed or discharged for political opinion; and any officer or employé of the Government who shall offend against the provisions of this section shall be dismissed from the service of the United States. [See acts Aug. 15, 1876, and Jan. 16, 1883, *post.*]

*Title 15, Chap. 6.*
*Contributions for political purposes.*

2 March, 1867, s. 3, v. 14, p. 492.

SEC. 1781. Every member of Congress or any officer or agent of the Government who, directly or indirectly, takes, receives, or agrees to receive, any money, property, or other valuable consideration whatever, from any person for procuring, or aiding to procure, any contract, office, or place, from the Government, or any Department thereof, or from any officer of the United States, for any person whatever, or for giving any such contract, office, or place to any person whomsoever, and every person who, directly or indirectly, offers or agrees to give, or gives, or bestows any money, property, or other valuable consideration whatever, for the procuring or aiding to procure any such contract, office, or place, and every member of Congress who, directly or indirectly, takes, receives, or agrees to receive any money, property, or other valuable consideration whatever after his election as such member, for his attention to, services, action, vote, or decision on any question, matter, cause, or proceeding which may then be pending, or may by law or under the Constitution be brought before him in his official capacity, or in his place as such member of Congress, shall be deemed guilty of a misdemeanor, and shall be imprisoned not more than two years and fined not more than ten thousand dollars. And any such contract or agreement may, at the option of the President, be declared absolutely null and void; and any member of Congress or officer convicted of a violation of this section, shall, moreover, be disqualified from holding any office of honor, profit, or trust under the Government of the United States.

*Title 19.*
*Prohibition upon taking consideration for procuring contracts, offices, &c.*

16 July, 1862, v. 12, p. 577.
25 Feb., 1863, v. 12, p. 696.

NOTE.—Sections 1781 and 1782 make it illegal for an officer of the United States to have that sort of connection with a Government contract which an agent, attorney, or solicitor assumes when he procures or aids to procure such contract for another, and when he prosecutes for another against the Government any claim founded upon a Government contract. They forbid also, the receiving by officers, for such services, any compensation, including that of an interest in the contract.—Op. XIV, 483, Oct. 29, 1874, Williams.

SEC. 1782. No Senator, Representative, or Delegate, after his election and during his continuance in office, and no head of a Department, or other officer or clerk in the employ of the Government, shall receive or agree to receive any compensation whatever, directly or indirectly, for any services rendered, or to be rendered, to any person, either by himself or another, in relation to any proceeding, contract, claim, controversy, charge, accusation, arrest, or other matter or thing in which the United States is a party, or directly or indirectly interested, before any Department, court-martial, Bureau, officer, or any civil, military, or naval commission whatever. Every person offending against this section shall be deemed guilty of a misdemeanor, and shall be imprisoned not more than two years, and fined not more than ten thousand dollars,

*Upon taking compensation in matters to which United States is a party.*

207

11 June, 1864, v. 13, p. 123.

**Prohibition of contributions, presents, &c., to superiors.**

SEC. 1784. No officer, clerk, or employé in the United States Government employ shall at any time solicit contributions from other officers, clerks, or employés in the Government service for a gift or present to those in a superior official position; nor shall any such officials or clerical superiors receive any gift or present offered or presented to them as a contribution from persons in Government employ receiving a less salary than themselves; nor shall any officer or clerk make any donation as a gift or present to any official superior. Every person who violates this section shall be summarily discharged from the Government employ.

1 Feb., 1870, v. 16, p. 63.

**Title 70, Chap. 5.**

**Bribery of member of Congress.**

SEC. 5450. Every person who promises, offers, gives, or causes or procures to be promised, offered or given, any money or other thing of value, or makes or tenders any contract, undertaking, obligation, gratuity, or security for the payment of money, or for the delivery or conveyance of anything of value, to any member of either House of Congress, either before or after such member has been qualified or has taken his seat, with intent to influence his vote or decision on any question, matter, cause, or proceeding which may be at any time pending in either House of Congress, or before any committee thereof, shall be fined not more than three times the amount of money or value of the thing so offered, promised, given, made or tendered, or caused or procured to be so offered, promised, given, made, or tendered, and shall be, moreover, imprisoned not more than three years.

26 Feb., 1853, s. 6, v. 10, p. 171.

**Bribery of any United States officers.**

SEC. 5451. Every person who promises, offers, or gives, or causes or procures to be promised, offered, or given, any money or other thing of value, or makes or tenders any contract, undertaking, obligation, gratuity, or security for the payment of money, or for the delivery or conveyance of anything of value, to any officer of the United States, or to any person acting for or on behalf of the United States in any official function, under or by authority of any department or office of the Government thereof, or to any officer or person acting for or on behalf of either House of Congress, or of any committee of either House, or both Houses thereof, with intent to influence his decision or action on any question, matter, cause, or proceeding which may at any time be pending, or which may by law be brought before him in his official capacity, or in his place of trust or profit, or with intent to influence him to commit or aid in committing, or to collude in, or allow, any fraud, or make opportunity for the commission of any fraud, on the United States, or to induce him to do or omit to do any act in violation of his lawful duty, shall be punished as prescribed in the preceding section.

13 July, 1866, s. 62, v. 14, p. 168.
18 July, 1866, s. 35, v. 14, p. 186.
3 March, 1863, s. 6, v. 12, p. 740.

**Title 70, Chap. 6.**

**Officers, &c., interested in claims.**

SEC. 5498. Every officer of the United States, or person holding any place of trust or profit, or discharging any official function under, or in connection with, any Executive Department of the Government of the United States, or under the Senate or House of Representatives of the United States, who acts as an agent or attorney for prosecuting any claim against the United States, or in any manner, or by any means, otherwise than in discharge of his proper official duties, aids or assists in the prosecution or support of any such claim, or receives any gratuity, or any share of or interest in any claim from any claimant against the United States, with intent to aid or assist, or in consideration of having aided or assisted, in the prosecution of such claim, shall pay a fine of not more than five thousand dollars, or suffer imprisonment not more than one year, or both.

26 Feb., 1853, s. 2, v. 10, p. 170.

**Member of Congress accepting bribe, &c.**

SEC. 5500. Any member of either House of Congress who asks, accepts, or receives any money, or any promise, contract, undertaking, obligation, gratuity, or security for the payment of money, or for the delivery or conveyance of anything of value, either before or after he has been qualified or has taken his seat as such member, with intent to have his vote or decision on any question, matter, cause, or proceeding which may be at any time pending in either house, or before any committee thereof, influenced thereby, shall be punished by a fine not more than three times the amount asked, accepted, or received, and by imprisonment not more than three years. [See § 5450.]

26 Feb., 1853, s. 6, v. 10, p. 171.

SEC. 5501. Every officer of the United States, and every person acting for or on behalf of the United States, in any official capacity under or by virtue of the authority of any department or office of the Government thereof; and every officer or person acting for or on behalf of either House of Congress, or of any committee of either House, or of both Houses thereof, who asks, accepts, or receives any money, or any contract, promise, undertaking, obligation, gratuity, or security for the payment of money, or for the delivery or conveyance of anything of value, with intent to have his decision or action on any question, matter, cause, or proceeding which may, at any time, be pending, or which may be by law brought before him in his official capacity, or in his place of trust or profit, influenced thereby, shall be punished as prescribed in the preceding section. [See § 5498, under CLAIMS.] *United States officer accepting bribe, &c.*

13 July, 1866, s. 62, v. 14, p. 168.
18 July, 1866, s. 35, v. 14, p. 186.
3 March, 1863, s. 6, v. 12, p. 740.

SEC. 5502. Every member, officer, or person, convicted under the provisions of the two preceding sections, who holds any place of profit or trust, shall forfeit his office or place; and shall thereafter be forever disqualified from holding any office of honor, trust, or profit under the United States. *Forfeiture of.*

26 Feb., 1853, s. 6, v. 10, p. 171.

That all executive officers or employees of the United States not appointed by the President, with the advice and consent of the Senate, are prohibited from requesting, giving to, or receiving from, any other officer or employee of the Government, any money or property or other thing of value for political purposes; and any such officer or employee who shall offend against the provisions of this section shall be at once discharged from the service of the United States; and he shall also be deemed guilty of a misdemeanor, and on conviction thereof shall be fined in a sum not exceeding five hundred dollars. *Aug. 15, 1876. Contributions for political purposes forbidden.*

15 Aug., 1876, chap. 287, s. 6, v. 19, p. 143.

No Senator, or Representative, or Territorial Delegate of the Congress, or Senator, Representative, or Delegate elect, or any officer or employee of either of said houses, and no executive, judicial, military, or naval officer of the United States, and no clerk or employee of any department, branch, or bureau of the executive, judicial, or military or naval service of the United States, shall, directly or indirectly, solicit or receive, or be in any manner concerned in soliciting or receiving, any assessment, subscription, or contribution for any political purpose whatever, from any officer, clerk, or employee of the United States, or any department, branch, or bureau thereof, or from any person receiving any salary or compensation from moneys derived from the Treasury of the United States. *16 Jan., 1883. Assessment, &c., for political purposes forbidden.*

16 Jan., 1883, chap. 27, s. 11, P. E. L., p. 406.

No person shall, in any room or building occupied in the discharge of official duties by any officer or employee of the United States mentioned in this act, or in any navy-yard, fort, or arsenal, solicit in any manner whatever, or receive any contribution of money or any other thing of value for any political purpose whatever.

*Ibid., s. 12.*

No officer or employee of the United States mentioned in this act shall discharge, or promote, or degrade, or in manner change the official rank or compensation of any other officer or employee, or promise or threaten so to do, for giving or withholding or neglecting to make any contribution of money or other valuable thing for any political purpose.

*Ibid., s. 13.*

No officer, clerk, or other person in the service of the United States shall, directly or indirectly, give or hand over to any other officer, clerk, or person in the service of the United States, or to any Senator or Member of the House of Representatives, or Territorial Delegate, any money or other valuable thing on account of or to be applied to the promotion of any political object whatever.

*Ibid.,* s. 14.

Any person who shall be guilty of violating any provision of the four foregoing sections shall be deemed guilty of a misdemeanor, and shall, on conviction thereof, be punished by a fine not exceeding five thousand dollars, or by imprisonment for a term not exceeding three years, or by such fine and imprisonment both, in the discretion of the court.

*Ibid.,* s. 15.

[PRESENTS FROM FOREIGN GOVERNMENTS. SEE PART I, P. 21.]

[See also June 14, 1874. Diplomatic officers.]

## BOUNTY-LANDS—BOUNTY, ETC.

Sec.
2418. Bounty-lands for soldiers in certain wars.
2419. Certain classes of persons in the Mexican war, their widows, &c., entitled to forty acres.
2420. Militia and volunteers in service since 1812.
2421. Persons entitled under preceding sections.
2422. Period of captivity added to actual service.
2423. Warrant and patent, to issue when.
2424. Widows of persons entitled.
2425. Additional bounty-lands, &c.
2426. Classes under last section specified.

Sec.
2427. What classes of persons entitled under section 2425, without regard to length of service.
2428. Widows and children of persons entitled under section 2425.
2433. Allowance of time of service for distance from home to place of muster or discharge.
2438. Deserters not entitled to bounty-land.
4635. Bounty for destruction of vessels.
4723. Bounty to colored soldiers.
—— Bounty to sailors and marines.

### BOUNTY-LANDS.

**Title 32, Chap. 10.**
Bounty-lands for soldiers in certain wars.

SEC. 2418. Each of the surviving, or the widow or minor children of deceased commissioned and non-commissioned officers, musicians, or privates, whether of regulars, volunteers, rangers, or militia, who performed military service in any regiment, company, or detachment, in the service of the United States, in the war with Great Britain, declared on the eighteenth day of June, eighteen hundred and twelve, or in any of the Indian wars since seventeen hundred and ninety, and prior to the third of March, eighteen hundred and fifty, and each of the commissioned officers who was engaged in the military service of the United States in the war with Mexico, shall be entitled to lands as follows: Those who engaged to serve twelve months or during the war, and actually served nine months, shall receive one hundred and sixty acres, and those who engaged to serve six months, and actually served four months, shall receive eighty acres, and those who engaged to serve for any or an indefinite period, and actually served one month, shall receive forty acres; but wherever any officer or soldier was honorably discharged in consequence of disability contracted in the service, before the expiration of his period of service, he shall receive the amount to which he would have been entitled if he had served the full period for which he had engaged to serve. All the persons enumerated in this section who enlisted in the Regular Army, or were mustered in any volunteer company for a period of not less than twelve months, and who served in the war with Mexico and received an honorable discharge, or who were killed or died of wounds received or sickness incurred in the course of such service, or were discharged before the expiration of the term of service in consequence of wounds received or sickness incurred in the course of such service, shall be entitled to receive a certificate or warrant for one hundred and sixty acres of land; or at option Treasury scrip for one hundred dollars bearing interest at six per cent. per annum, payable semi-annually, at the pleasure of the Government. In the event of the death of any one of the persons mentioned in this section during service, or after his discharge, and before the issuing of a certificate or warrant, the warrant or scrip shall be issued in favor of his family or relatives; first, to the widow and his children; second, his father; third, his mother; fourth his brothers and sisters.

11 Feb., 1847, s. 9, v. 9, p. 125.
28 Sept., 1850, s. 1, v. 9, p. 520.

BOUNTY-LANDS—BOUNTY, ETC.   211

Sec. 2419. The persons enumerated in the preceding section received into service after the commencement of the war with Mexico, for less than twelve months, and who served such term, or were honorably discharged are entitled to receive a certificate or warrant for forty acres, or scrip for twenty-five dollars if preferred, and in the event of the death of such person during service, or after honorable discharge before the eleventh of February, eighteen hundred and forty-seven, the warrant or scrip shall issue to the wife, child, or children, if there be any, and if none, to the father, and if no father, to the mother of such soldier.  *Certain classes of persons in the Mexican war, their widows, &c., entitled to forty acres.*

11 Feb., 1847, s. 9, p. 125.

Sec. 2420. Where the militia, or volunteers, or State troops of any State or Territory, subsequent to the eighteenth day of June, eighteen hundred and twelve, and prior to March twenty-second, eighteen hundred and fifty-two, were called into service, the officers and soldiers thereof shall be entitled to all the benefits of section two thousand four hundred and eighteen upon proof of length of service as therein required.  *Militia and volunteers in service since 1812.*

22 March, 1852, s. 4, v. 10, p. 4.

Sec. 2421. No person shall take any benefit under the provisions of the three preceding sections, if he has received, or is entitled to receive, any military land-bounty under any act of Congress passed prior to the twenty-second March, eighteen hundred and fifty-two.  *Persons not entitled under preceding sections.*

28 Sept., 1850, s. 1, v. 9, p. 520.

Sec. 2422. The period during which any officer or soldier remained in captivity with the enemy shall be estimated and added to the period of his actual service, and the person so retained in captivity shall receive land under the provisions of sections twenty-four hundred and eighteen and twenty-four hundred and twenty, in the same manner that he would be entitled in case he had entered the service for the whole term made up by the addition of the time of his captivity, and had served during such term.  *Period of captivity added to actual service.*

*Ibid.*, s. 2.

Sec. 2423. Every person for whom provision is made by sections twenty-four hundred and eighteen and twenty-four hundred and twenty shall receive a warrant from the Department of the Interior for the quantity of land to which he is entitled; and upon the return of such warrant, with evidence of the location thereof having been legally made to the General Land-Office, a patent shall be issued therefor.  *Warrant and patent to issue, when.*

*Ibid.*, s. 3.

Sec. 2424. In the event of the death of any person, for whom provision is made by sections twenty-four hundred and eighteen and twenty-four hundred and twenty, and who did not receive bounty-land for his services, a like warrant shall issue in favor of his widow, who shall be entitled to one hundred and sixty acres of land in case her husband was killed in battle; nor shall a subsequent marriage impair the right of any widow to such warrant, if she be a widow at the time of making her application.  *Widows of persons entitled.*

*Ibid.*

Sec. 2425. Each of the surviving persons specified in the classes enumerated in the following section, who has served for a period of not less than fourteen days, in any of the wars in which the United States have been engaged since the year seventeen hundred and ninety, and prior to the third day of March, eighteen hundred and fifty-five, shall be entitled to receive a warrant from the Department of the Interior, for one hundred and sixty acres of land; and, where any person so entitled has, prior to the third day of March, eighteen hundred and fifty-five, received a warrant for any number of acres less than one hundred and sixty, he shall be allowed a warrant for such quantity of land only as will make, in the whole, with what he may have received prior to that date, one hundred and sixty acres.  *Additional bounty-lands, &c*

3 March, 1855, ss. 1, 3, v. 10, p. 701.

Sec. 2426. The classes of persons embraced as beneficiaries under the preceding section, are as follows, namely:  *Classes under last section specified.*

First. Commissioned and non-commissioned officers, musicians, and privates, whether of the regulars, volunteers, rangers, or militia, who were regularly mustered into the service of the United States.

Second. Commissioned and non-commissioned officers, seamen, ordinary seamen, flotilla-men, marines, clerks, and landsmen in the Navy.

Third. Militia, volunteers, and State troops of any State or Territory, called into military service, and regularly mustered therein, and whose services have been paid by the United States.

Fourth. Wagon-masters and teamsters who have been employed under the direction of competent authority, in time of war, in the transportation of military stores and supplies.

Fifth. Officers and soldiers of the revolutionary war, and marines, seamen, and other persons in the naval service of the United States during that war.

Sixth. Chaplains who served with the Army.

Seventh. Volunteers who served with the armed forces of the United States in any of the wars mentioned, subject to military orders, whether regularly mustered into the service of the United States or not.

3 March, 1855, ss. 1, 8, 10, v. 10, p. 701.
14 May, 1856, ss. 4, 5, v. 11, p. 8.

**What classes of persons are entitled under section 2425, without regard to length of service.** SEC. 2427. The following class of persons are included as beneficiaries under section twenty-four hundred and twenty-five, without regard to the length of service rendered.

First. Any of the classes of persons mentioned in section twenty-four hundred and twenty-six who have been actually engaged in any battle in any of the wars in which this country has been engaged since seventeen hundred and ninety, and prior to March third, eighteen hundred and fifty-five.

\* \* \* \* \* \*

3 March, 1855, ss. 3, 9, 11, v. 10, p. 702.

**Widows and children of persons entitled under section 2425.** SEC. 2428. In the event of the death of any person who would be entitled to a warrant, as provided in section twenty-four hundred and twenty-five, leaving a widow, or, if no widow, a minor child, such widow or such minor child shall receive a warrant for the same quantity of land that the decedent would be entitled to receive, if living on the third day of March, eighteen hundred and fifty-five.

*Ibid.*, s. 2.

**Allowance of time of service for distance from home to place of muster or discharge.** SEC. 2433. When any company, battalion, or regiment, in an organized form, marched more than twenty miles to the place where they were mustered into the service of the United States, or were discharged more than twenty miles from the place where such company, battalion, or regiment was organized, in all such cases, in computing the length of service of the officers and soldiers of any such company, battalion, or regiment, there shall be allowed one day for every twenty miles from the place where the company, battalion, or regiment was organized to the place where the same was mustered into the service of the United States, and one day for every twenty miles from the place where such company, battalion, or regiment was discharged, to the place where it was organized, and from whence it marched to enter the service, provided that such march was in obedience to the command or direction of the President, or some general officer of the United States, commanding an army or department, or the chief executive officer of the State or Territory by which such company, battalion, or regiment was called into service.

14 May, 1856, s. 7, v. 11, p. 9.
22 March, 1852, s. 5, v. 10, p. 4.

**Deserters not entitled to bounty-land.** SEC. 2438. No person who has been in the military service of the United States shall, in any case, receive a bounty-land warrant if it appears by the muster-rolls of his regiment or corps that he deserted or was dishonorably discharged from service.

28 Sept., 1850, s. 1, v. 9, p. 520.
3 March, 1855, s. 1, v. 10, p. 701.

[A joint resolution approved August 10, 1848, vol. 9, page 340, provided that the officers, non-commissioned officers, privates and musicians of the Marine Corps, who served with the Army in the war with Mexico, should be placed, in all respects as to bounty-land and other remuneration, in addition to ordinary pay, on a footing with the officers, non-commissioned officers, privates, and musicians of the Army; this remuneration to be in lieu of prize-money and all other extra allowances.]

NOTES.—The term "allowances," when employed in a general sense, has been regarded as including bounty. Thus, see XIII, Op. 197, where it is held that the general forfeiture of pay and allowances due at the date of offense, imposed upon deserters by paragraph 1358, Army Regulations, embraced instalments of bounty due at the time of the desertion; also United States v. Landers, 2 Otto, 77, where the court goes so far as to hold that a forfeiture of "pay and allowances" *imposed by sentence*, includes bounty.—Winthrop's Digest, p. 132.

Service rendered since the 3d of March, 1855, including the late rebellion, does not entitle to bounty-lands. Only one warrant for one hundred and sixty acres can issue to a soldier for any and all service.

Where service has been rendered by a substitute, he is the person entitled to bounty land, and not his employer.

Applications for bounty-land warrants must be made to the Commissioner of Pensions; correspondence in relation to bounty in money should be addressed to the Second Auditor of the Treasury.—Pension Office Decisions, p. 86.

Officers and privates dismissed the service without trial, and remanded to the service by the President, but who, not receiving the order of the President, did not return to the service, are, notwithstanding, entitled to bounty-land.—Pension Office Decisions, p. 131.

Where any portion of the Marine Corps referred to in the act of Sept. 28, 1850, was embodied with the Army in the field and performed service as a part of the Army, it is entitled to bounty-land.—*Idem*, p. 131.

The word "service" in bounty-land acts refers to that of the soldier, not of his company.

Claim of a soldier can be valid only on one of the following conditions: 1. Must have been regularly mustered into the United States service. 2. That the services were paid for by the United States. 3. That he served with the armed forces of the United States, subject to the military orders of a United States officer.—*Idem*, p. 139.

The entire portion of the Marine Corps, whether they served on ship-board or land on the Mexican coast or in the interior, in the Mexican war, are to be considered within the true meaning of the resolution of the 10th of August, 1848, as having "served with the Army in the war with Mexico," and entitled to the bounty-land and other remuneration which that resolution provides. But in awarding it to such as received prize-money, such money should, in the account, be carried to the credit of the Government.—Op. 5, p. 155, Sept. 17, 1849, Johnson.

Under the act of March 3, 1855, and sections 2425 to 2429 R. S., members of the Marine Corps and their representatives would be entitled to bounty-land without relinquishing or returning prize-money, &c.—Pension Office Decisions, p. 131.

Not entitled to bounty-land for service in a United States ship not engaged in the Mexican war; nor for service *during* the war in a war vessel on the coast of Africa.—*Idem*, pp. 133, 141.

Pardon by the President for participation in the late rebellion does not authorize the allowance of bounty-land, the right to which is the subject of a claim against the Government and is governed by the provisions of the joint resolution of March 2, 1867.—Pension Office Decisions, p. 138.

## BOUNTY.

SEC. 4635. A bounty shall be paid by the United States for each person on board any ship or vessel of war belonging to an enemy at the commencement of an engagement, which is sunk or otherwise destroyed in such engagement by any ship or vessel belonging to the United States or which it may be necessary to destroy in consequence of injuries sustained in action, of one hundred dollars, if the enemy's vessel was of inferior force, and of two hundred dollars, if of equal or superior force, to be divided among the officers and crew in the same manner as prize-money; and when the actual number of men on board any such vessel cannot be satisfactorily ascertained, it shall be estimated according to the complement allowed to vessels of its class in the Navy of the United States; and there shall be paid as bounty to the captors of any vessel of war captured from an enemy, which they may be instructed to destroy, or which is immediately destroyed for the public interest, but not in consequence of injuries received in action, fifty dollars for every person who shall be on board at the time of such capture.

Title 54.

Bounty for persons on board vessels sunk or destroyed.

30 June, 1864, s. 11, v. 13, p. 310.

[As to bounty for the capture of vessels engaged in the slave trade with Africans on board, see under SLAVE TRADE.]

[Section 4642 provides that bounty accruing or awarded to any vessel of the Navy shall be distributed and paid to the officers and men entitled thereto, in the same manner as prize-money, under the direction of the Secretary of the Navy, and section 4643 requires every assignment of bounty money due to enlisted persons in the naval service, and all powers of attorney or other authority, to draw, receipt for, or transfer the same, to be attested by the captain or other commanding officer, and the paymaster.]

[By section 3689 of the Revised Statutes, "bounty to soldiers" is a permanent annual appropriation.]

**Title 57.**

*Colored soldiers enrolled as "slaves."*

SEC. 4723. All colored persons who enlisted in the Army during the war of the rebellion, and who are now prohibited from receiving bounty and pension on account of being borne on the rolls of their regiments as "slaves," shall be placed on the same footing, as to bounty and pension, as though they had not been slaves at the date of their enlistment.

3 March, 1873, chap. 262, v. 17, p. 601.
See Op. XV, p. 474.

[The second section of the sundry civil act, approved March 3, 1879, v. 20, p. 377, provides that all sums due upon certificates issued by the accounting officers of the Treasury in settlement of claims for pay, bounty, prize-money, or other moneys due to colored soldiers, sailors, or marines, or their legal representatives, shall be paid by the officers of the Pay Department of the Army, under the direction of the Paymaster-General, who is already charged with the payment of like dues to white soldiers.]

*Laws relating to bounty in Navy and Marine Corps.*

1 July, 1864.

That persons hereafter enlisted into the naval service or marine corps during the present war shall be entitled to receive the same bounty as if enlisted in the Army * * *. [See *post*, 4 July, 1864.]

1 July, 1864, s. 4, v. 13, p. 342.

[The foregoing act repeals the joint resolution of February 24, 1864, conferring on seamen and ordinary seamen a bounty equal to three months pay on their enlisting in the Navy.]

4 July, 1864.

*Bounty for enlisting.*

Every volunteer who is accepted and mustered into the service for a term of one year, unless sooner discharged, shall receive, and be paid by the United States, a bounty of one hundred dollars; and if for a term of two years, unless sooner discharged, a bounty of two hundred dollars; and if for a term of three years, unless sooner discharged, a bounty of three hundred dollars; one-third of which bounty shall be paid to the soldier at the time of his being mustered into the service, one-third at the expiration of one-half of his term of service, and one-third at the expiration of his term of service. And in case of his death while in service, the residue of his bounty unpaid shall be paid to his widow, if he shall have left a widow; if not, to his children, or if there be none, to his mother, if she be a widow.

\* \* \* \*

4 July, 1864, s. 1, v. 13, p. 379.

[An act, approved March 3, 1865, chap. 124, s. 5, v. 13, p. 539, provides that no person appointed or rated an officer or clerk in the Navy, shall receive any bounty while holding such appointment.]

NOTES.—April 22, 1872, chap. 114, v. 17, p. 55, authorizes $100 bounty to all volunteers who enlisted prior to July 22, 1861, for *three* years, and were mustered into service before Aug. 6, 1861, if they were honorably discharged and had not received the same for such service.

Two and three years' men who enlisted between April 12, 1861, and Dec. 24, 1863, or between April 1, 1864, and July 18, 1864, are entitled to $100 bounty under act of July 22, 1861, chap. 9, v. 12, p. 270, provided they served two years or more as enlisted men, or were honorably discharged as such on account of wounds received in line of duty before two years' service. If discharged before serving two years, and died *before* July 28, 1866, of disease contracted in the service, his heirs are entitled to the additional bounty under act of July 28, 1866, chap. 296, v. 14, p. 322. If a soldier died in the service, his heirs became entitled to any bounty to which the soldier would have been entitled under his contract.

The act of July 28, 1866, gave an additional bounty of $100 to men who enlisted and *served* for three years from April 19, 1861, and $50 to those who enlisted and *served* for two years from April 14, 1861. Not given to any one if the soldier was entitled to receive, at any time, a greater bounty than $100 under any other act or acts.

Drafted men, enrolled from March 3, 1863, to Sept. 5, 1864, for three years, or men who, from March 3, 1863, to Sept. 5, 1864, enlisted for three years as *substitutes* for drafted men, are only entitled by act of March 3, 1863, to $100 bounty, if they served two years or more, or were discharged by reason of wounds received in line of duty before two years' service. Neither they nor their heirs are entitled to additional bounty under act of July 28, 1866.

Under the act of July 4, 1864, v. 13, p. 379, if discharged "because of wounds received in the line of duty," the volunteer became entitled to the full amount of bounty therein provided; but if discharged "because of services no longer required," or by "close of war," he has no claim for balance of bounty.

All soldiers discharged by reason of wounds received in battle, or in line of duty, are entitled by acts of March 3, 1863, March 3, 1865, and joint resolution of April 12, 1866, to receive the same bounty they would have received had they served their full term of enlistment. The word *wound* is held to mean injury from *violence* received in line of duty. Bounty depends upon *being discharged by reason of the wound.*

No bounty is paid for enlistments made before April 12, 1861, nor for 100 days, or three, six, and nine months' men; nor for one year's men enlisting prior to July 18, 1864; nor to volunteers who enlisted after April 30, 1865.—From circular of Second Auditor, March 3, 1880.

The same bounties (*as to the duration of enlistment, amounts and modes of payment*) are to be PAID to "*persons*" of all grades who have, *since the 1st of July*, 1864, enlisted, or who may thereafter enlist, into the Navy or Marine Corps of the United States.

Enlisted men advanced after enlistment to any higher grade or rating, do not thereby forfeit their right to any future instalment of bounty.—Fourth Auditor, Rules 1864.

Where a soldier was enlisted in the Army as a volunteer in December, 1861, for three years, but afterward, and before the expiration of his term of enlistment, was voluntarily transferred to the naval service, in which he served out the remainder of his term: *Held*, That he is not entitled to the additional bounty provided by the act of July 28, 1866, chap. 296.—Op. XIV, 223, April 23, 1873, Williams.

Where a soldier deserted, subsequently surrendered himself, was restored to duty, and finally "honorably discharged," the fact of the mark of desertion standing against him, is no impediment to his receiving bounty.—Kelly's case, Supreme Court, 15 Wallace, p. 34.

## COAST SURVEY.

Sec.
4683. Mode of conducting surveys.
4684. Employment of officers of Army and Navy.
4685. Power to use books, &c., and to employ persons.
4686. Power to employ vessels.

Sec.
4687. Manner of employment of officers of Army and Navy.
4688. Allowances for subsistence.
4691. Disposal of charts.
——. Same.

SEC. 4683. All appropriations made for the work of surveying the coast of the United States shall be expended in accordance with the plan of reorganizing the mode of executing the survey which has been submitted to the President by a board of officers organized under the act of March three, eighteen hundred and forty-three, chapter one hundred.

Title 56.
Mode of conducting surveys.

3 March, 1843, s. 1, v. 5, p. 640.

SEC. 4684. The President shall carry into effect the plan of the board, as agreed upon by a majority of its members; and shall cause to be employed as many officers of the Army and Navy of the United States as will be compatible with the successful prosecution of the work; the officers of the Navy to be employed on the hydrographical parts, and the officers of the Army on the topographical parts of the work; and no officer of the Army or Navy shall receive any extra pay out of any appropriations for surveys.

Employment of officers of Army and Navy.

*Ibid.*

SEC. 4685. The President is authorized, in executing the provisions of this Title, to use all maps, charts, books, instruments, and apparatus belonging to the United States, and to direct where the same shall be deposited, and to employ all persons in the land or naval service of the United States, and such astronomers and other persons, as he shall deem proper.

Power to use books, &c., and to employ persons.

10 July, 1832, s. 2, v. 4, p. 571.

SEC. 4686. The President is authorized, for any of the purposes of surveying the coast of the United States, to cause to be employed such of the public vessels in actual service as he deems it expedient to employ, and to give such instructions for regulating their conduct as he deems proper, according to the tenor of this Title.

Power to employ vessels.

10 Feb., 1807, s. 3, v. 2, p. 414.
14 April, 1818, s. 1, v. 3, p. 425.

SEC. 4687. Officers of the Army and Navy shall, as far as practicable, be employed in the work of surveying the coast of the United States, whenever and in the manner required by the Department having charge thereof.

Manner of employment of officers of Army or Navy.

17 June, 1844, s. 1, v. 5, pp. 681, 691.

SEC. 4688. The Secretary of the Treasury may make such allowances to the officers and men of the Army and Navy, while employed on Coast Survey service, for subsistence, in addition to their compensation, as he may deem necessary, not exceeding the sum authorized by the Treasury regulation of the eleventh day of May, eighteen hundred and forty-four. [See note to this section Part I, p. 70.]

Allowance for subsistence.

12 June, 1858, s. 1, v. 11, pp. 319, 320.

## 216 COLLISIONS—RULES OF THE SEA.

Disposal of maps and charts.  SEC. 4691. The Secretary of the Treasury is authorized to dispose of the maps and charts of the survey of the coast of the United States at such prices and under such regulations as may from time to time be fixed by him; and a number of copies of each sheet, not to exceed three hundred, shall be distributed among foreign Governments, and Departments of our own Government, and literary and scientific associations as may be designated by the Secretary of the Treasury. [See *post*].

3 June, 1844, v. 5, p. 660.

20 June, 1878.  The charts published by the Coast Survey shall be sold at the office at Washington at the price of the printing and paper thereof, and elsewhere at the same price with the average cost of delivery added thereto; and hereafter there shall be no free distribution of such charts except to the Departments of the United States and to the several States and officers of the United States requiring them for public use in accordance with the act of June third, eighteen hundred and forty-four. [R. S., sec., 4691.]

20 June, 1878, v. 20, p. 206.

3 March, 1879.  Senators, Representatives, and Delegates to the House of Representatives shall each be entitled to not more than ten charts published by the Coast Survey, for each regular session of Congress.

3 March, 1879, v. 20, p. 377.

## COLLISIONS—RULES OF THE SEA.

Sec.
4233. Rules for preventing collisions.

Sec.
4234. Forfeiture of sailing-vessels for omission of lights.

Title 48, Chap. 5.  SEC. 4233. The following rules for preventing collisions on the water, shall be followed in the navigation of vessels of the Navy and of the mercantile marine of the United States:
Rules for preventing collisions.

### STEAM AND SAIL VESSELS.

Rule one. Every steam-vessel which is under sail, and not under steam, shall be considered a sail-vessel; and every steam-vessel which is under steam, whether under sail or not, shall be considered a steam-vessel.

### LIGHTS.

Rule two. The lights mentioned in the following rules, and no others, shall be carried in all weathers, between sunset and sunrise.

Rule three. All ocean-going steamers, and steamers carrying sail, shall, when under way, carry—

(A) At the foremast head, a bright white light, of such a character as to be visible on a dark night, with a clear atmosphere, at a distance of at least five miles, and so constructed as to show a uniform and unbroken light over an arc of the horizon of twenty points of the compass, and so fixed as to throw the light ten points on each side of the vessel, namely, from right ahead to two points abaft the beam on either side.

(B) On the starboard side, a green light, of such a character as to be visible on a dark night, with a clear atmosphere, at a distance of at least two miles, and so constructed as to show a uniform and unbroken light over an arc of the horizon of ten points of the compass, and so fixed as to throw the light from right ahead to two points abaft the beam on the starboard side.

(C) On the port side, a red light, of such a character as to be visible on a dark night, with a clear atmosphere, at a distance of at least two miles, and so constructed as to show a uniform and unbroken light over an arc of the horizon of ten points of the compass, and so fixed as to throw the light from right ahead to two points abaft the beam on the port side.

The green and red lights shall be fitted with inboard screens, projecting at least three feet forward from the lights, so as to prevent them from being seen across the bow.

Rule four. Steam-vessels, when towing other vessels, shall carry two bright white mast-head lights vertically, in addition to their side-lights, so as to distinguish them from other steam-vessels. Each of these mast-head lights shall be of the same character and construction as the masthead lights prescribed by Rule three.

Rule five. All steam-vessels, other than ocean-going steamers and steamers carrying sail, shall, when under way, carry on the starboard and ports sides lights of the same character and construction and in the same position as are prescribed for side-lights by Rule three, except in the case provided in Rule six.

Rule six. River-steamers, navigating waters flowing into the Gulf of Mexico, and their tributaries, shall carry the following lights, namely: One red light on the outboard side of the port smoke-pipe, and one green light on the outboard side of the starboard smoke-pipe. Such lights shall show both forward and abeam on their respective sides.

Rule seven. All coasting steam-vessels, and steam-vessels other than ferry-boats and vessels otherwise expressly provided for, navigating the bays, lakes, rivers, or other inland waters of the United States, except those mentioned in Rule six, shall carry the red and green lights, as prescribed for ocean-going steamers; and, in addition thereto, a central range of two white lights; the after-light being carried at an elevation of at least fifteen feet above the light at the head of the vessel. The head-light shall be so constructed as to show a good light through twenty points of the compass, namely: from right ahead to two points abaft the beam on either side of the vessel; and the after-light so as to show all around the horizon. The lights for ferry-boats shall be regulated by such rules as the board of supervising inspectors of steam-vessels shall prescribe.

Rule eight. Sail-vessels, under way or being towed, shall carry the same lights as steam-vessels under way, with the exception of the white mast-head lights, which they shall never carry.

Rule nine. Whenever, as in case of small vessels during bad weather, the green and red lights cannot be fixed, these lights shall be kept on deck, on their respective sides of the vessel, ready for instant exhibition, and shall, on the approach of or to other vessels, be exhibited on their respective sides in sufficient time to prevent collision, in such manner as to make them most visible, and so that the green light shall not be seen on the port side, nor the red light on the starboard side. To make the use of these portable lights more certain and easy, they shall each be painted outside with the color of the light they respectively contain, and shall be provided with suitable screens.

Rule ten. All vessels, whether steam-vessels or sail-vessels, when at anchor in roadsteads or fairways, shall, between sunset and sunrise, exhibit where it can best be seen, but at a height not exceeding twenty feet above the hull, a white light in a globular lantern of eight inches in diameter, and so constructed as to show a clear, uniform, and unbroken light, visible all around the horizon, and at a distance of at least one mile.

Rule eleven. Sailing pilot-vessels shall not carry the lights required for other sailing-vessels, but shall carry a white light at the mast-head, visible all around the horizon, and shall also exhibit a flare-up light every fifteen minutes.

Rule twelve. Coal-boats, trading-boats, produce-boats, canal-boats, oyster-boats, fishing-boats, rafts, or other water-craft, navigating any bay, harbor, or river, by hand-power, horse-power, sail, or by the current of the river, or which shall be anchored or moored in or near the channel or fairway of any bay, harbor, or river, shall carry one or more good white lights, which shall be placed in such manner as shall be prescribed by the board of supervising inspectors of steam-vessels.

Rule thirteen. Open boats shall not be required to carry the side-lights required for other vessels, but shall, if they do not carry such lights, carry a lantern having a green slide on one side and a red slide on the other side; and, on the approach of or to other vessels, such lantern shall be exhibited in sufficient time to prevent collision, and in such a manner that the green light shall not be seen on the port side, nor the red light on the starboard side. Open boats, when at anchor or stationary, shall exhibit a bright white light. They shall not, however, be prevented from using a flare-up, in addition, if considered expedient.

Rule fourteen. The exhibition of any light on board of a vessel of war of the United States may be suspended whenever, in the opinion of the Secretary of the Navy, the commander-in-chief of a squadron, or the commander of a vessel acting singly, the special character of the service may require it.

#### FOG-SIGNALS.

Rule fifteen. Whenever there is a fog, or thick weather, whether by day or night, fog-signals shall be used as follows:

(A) Steam-vessels under way shall sound a steam-whistle placed before the funnel, not less than eight feet from the deck, at intervals of not more than one minute.

(B) Sail-vessels under way shall sound a fog-horn at intervals of not more than five minutes.

(C) Steam-vessels and sail-vessels, when not under way, shall sound a bell at intervals of not more than five minutes.

(D) Coal-boats, trading-boats, produce-boats, canal-boats, oyster-boats, fishing-boats, rafts, or other water-craft, navigating any bay, harbor, or river, by hand-power, horse-power, sail, or by the current of the river, or anchored or moored in or near the channel or fairway of any bay, harbor, or river, and not in any port, shall sound a fog-horn, or equivalent signal, which shall make a sound equal to a steam-whistle, at intervals of not more than two minutes.

#### STEERING AND SAILING RULES.

Rule sixteen. If two sail-vessels, are meeting end on, or nearly end on, so as to involve risk of collision, the helms of both shall be put to port, so that each may pass on the port side of the other.

Rule seventeen. When two sail-vessels are crossing so as to involve risk of collision, then, if they have the wind on different sides, the vessel with the wind on the port side shall keep out of the way of the vessel with the wind on the starboard side, except in the case in which the vessel with the wind on the port side is close-hauled, and the other vessel free, in which case the latter vessel shall keep out of the way. But if they have the wind on the same side, or if one of them has the wind aft, the vessel which is to windward shall keep out of the way of the vessel which is to leeward.

Rule eighteen. If two vessels under steam are meeting end on, or nearly end on, so as to involve risk of collision, the helms of both shall be put to port, so that each may pass on the port side of the other.

Rule nineteen. If two vessels under steam are crossing so as to involve risk of collision, the vessel which has the other on her own starboard side shall keep out of the way of the other.

Rule twenty. If two vessels, one of which is a sail-vessel and the other a steam-vessel, are proceeding in such directions as to involve risk of collision, the steam-vessel shall keep out of the way of the sail-vessel.

Rule twenty-one. Every steam-vessel, when approaching another vessel, so as to involve risk of collision, shall slacken her speed, or, if necessary, stop and reverse; and every steam-vessel shall, when in a fog, go at a moderate speed.

Rule twenty-two. Every vessel overtaking any other vessel shall keep out of the way of the last-mentioned vessel.

Rule twenty-three. Where, by Rules seventeen, nineteen, twenty, and twenty-two, one of two vessels shall keep out of the way, the other shall keep her course, subject to the qualifications of Rule twenty-four.

Rule twenty-four. In construing and obeying these rules, due regard must be had to all dangers of navigation, and to any special circumstances which may exist in any particular case rendering a departure from them necessary in order to avoid immediate danger.

29 April, 1864, ch. 69, v. 13, p. 58.

NOTE.—Where the fault is wholly on one side, the party in fault must bear his own loss, and compensate the other party, if such party have sustained any damage. If neither be in fault, neither is entitled to compensation from the other. If both are in fault, the damages will be divided.—Otto, S. C., 102, p. 203. See page 100, part I, as to reports of collisions.

Forfeiture of sailing-vessels for omission of lights.

SEC. 4234. Collectors, or other chief officers of the customs, shall require all sail-vessels to be furnished with proper signal-lights, and every such vessel shall, on the approach of any steam-vessel during the night-time, show a lighted torch upon that point or quarter to which such steam-vessel shall be approaching. Every such vessel that shall be navigated without complying with the provisions of this and the preceding section, shall be liable to a penalty of two hundred dollars, one-half to go to the informer; for which sum the vessel so navigated shall be liable, and may be seized and proceeded against by way of libel, in any district court of the United States having jurisdiction of the offense.

28 Feb., 1871, c. 70, v. 16, p. 459.

# DIPLOMATIC AND CONSULAR OFFICERS.

See also MERCHANT VESSELS and SERVICE.

Sec.
1433. Navy officers temporarily exercising consular powers.
1440. Accepting appointments vacates Navy commission.
1674. Official designations, consular and diplomatic service.
1707. Protests.
1708. Lists and returns of seamen, vessels, &c.

Sec.
1709. Estates of decedents.
1710. Notification of death.
1711. Decedent's directions to be followed.
1737. False certificate of property.
1738. When consular officers may perform diplomatic functions.
1750. Depositions.
1751. Certain correspondence prohibited.

SEC. 1433. The commanding officer of any fleet, squadron, or vessel acting singly, when upon the high seas or in any foreign port where there is no resident consul of the United States, shall be authorized to exercise all the powers of a consul in relation to mariners of the United States. *Title 15, Chap. 2. Consular powers.*

20 Feb., 1845, s. 2, v. 5, p. 725.

SEC. 1440. If any officer of the Navy accepts or holds an appointment in the diplomatic or consular service of the Government, he shall be considered as having resigned his place in the Navy, and it shall be filled as a vacancy. *Accepting appointments in diplomatic service.*

30 March, 1868, s. 2, v. 15, p. 58.

SEC. 1674. The official designations employed throughout this Title shall be deemed to have the following meanings, respectively: *Title 18, Chap. 1. Definition of official designations employed in this title.*

First. "Consul-general," "consul," and "commercial agent," shall be deemed to denote full, principal, and permanent consular officers, as distinguished from subordinates and substitutes.

Second. "Deputy consul" and "consular agent" shall be deemed to denote consular officers subordinate to such principals, exercising the powers and performing the duties within the limits of their consulates or commercial agencies respectively, the former at the same ports or places, and the latter at ports or places different from those at which such principals are located respectively.

Third. "Vice-consuls," and "vice commercial agents," shall be deemed to denote consular officers, who shall be substituted, temporarily, to fill the places of consuls-general, consuls, or commercial agents, when they shall be temporarily absent or relieved from duty.

Fourth. "Consular officer" shall be deemed to include consuls-general, consuls, commercial agents, deputy consuls, vice-consuls, vice-commercial agents, and consular agents, and none others.

Fifth. "Diplomatic officer" shall be deemed to include ambassadors, envoys extraordinary, ministers plenipotentiary, ministers resident, commissioners, chargés d'affaires, agents, and secretaries of legation, and none others.

18 Aug, 1856, s. 1, v. 11, p. 64.
20 June, 1864, s. 1, v. 13, p. 138.
25 July, 1866, v. 14, p. 225.

[By section 4130 R. S. as amended, the word "minister" is understood to mean the person invested with, and exercising the principal diplomatic functions. The word "consul" is understood to mean any person invested by the United States with, and exercising the functions of Consul-General, Vice-Consul-General, Consul or Vice-Consul.]

SEC. 1707. Consuls and vice-consuls shall have the right, in the ports or places to which they are severally appointed, of receiving the protests or declarations which captains, masters, crews, passengers, or merchants, who are citizens of the United States, may respectively choose to make there; and also such as any foreigner may choose to make before them relative to the personal interest of any citizen of the United States. Copies of such acts duly authenticated by consuls or vice-consuls, under the seal of their consulates, respectively, shall be received in evidence equally with their originals in all courts in the United States. *Title 18, Chap. 2. Protests.*

14 April, 1792, s. 2, v. 1, p. 255.

SEC. 1708. Every consular officer shall keep a detailed list of all seamen and mariners shipped and discharged by him, specifying their names and the names of the vessels on which they are shipped and from *Lists and returns of seamen, vessels, &c.*

which they are discharged, and the payments, if any, made on account of each so discharged; also of the number of the vessels arrived and departed, the amounts of their registered tonnage, and the number of their seamen and mariners, and of those who are protected, and whether citizens of the United States or not, and as nearly as possible the nature and value of their cargoes, and where produced, and shall make returns of the same, with their accounts and other returns, to the Secretary of the Treasury. [See § § 4561, 4580, under MERCHANT SERVICE.]

18 Aug., 1856, s. 27, v. 11, p. 62.

**Estates of decedents.** SEC. 1709. It shall be the duty of consuls and vice-consuls, where the laws of the country permit:

First. To take possession of the personal estate left by any citizen of the United States, other than seamen belonging to any vessel, who shall die within their consulate, leaving there no legal representative, partner in trade, or trustee by him appointed to take care of his effects.

Second. To inventory the same with the assistance of two merchants of the United States, or, for want of them, of any others at their choice.

Third. To collect the debts due the deceased in the country where he died, and pay the debts due from his estate which he shall have there contracted.

Fourth. To sell at auction, after reasonable public notice, such part of the estate as shall be of a perishable nature, and such further part, if any, as shall be necessary, for the payment of his debts, and, at the expiration of one year from his decease, the residue.

Fifth. To transmit the balance of the estate to the Treasury of the United States, to be holden in trust for the legal claimant; except that if at any time before such transmission the legal representative of the deceased shall appear and demand his effects in their hands they shall deliver them up, being paid their fees, and shall cease their proceedings.

14 April, 1792, s. 2, v. 1, p. 255.

**Notification of death.** SEC. 1710. For the information of the representative of the deceased, the consul or vice-consul, in the settlement of his estate, shall immediately notify his death in one of the gazettes published in the consulate, and also to the Secretary of State, that the same may be notified in the State to which the deceased belonged; and he shall, as soon as may be, transmit to the Secretary of State an inventory of the effects of the deceased, taken as before directed.

*Idem.*

**Decedent's directions to be followed.** SEC. 1711. When any citizen of the United States, dying abroad, leaves, by any lawful testamentary disposition, special directions for the custody and management, by the consular officer of the port or place where he dies, of the personal property of which he dies possessed in such country, such officer shall, so far as the laws of the country permit, strictly observe such directions. When any such citizen so dying, appoints, by any lawful testamentary disposition, any other person than such officer to take charge of and manage such property, it shall be the duty of the officer, whenever required by the person so appointed, to give his official aid in whatever way may be necessary to facilitate the proceedings of such person in the lawful execution of his trust, and, so far as the laws of the country permit, to protect the property of the deceased from any interference of the local authorities of the country where such citizen dies; and to this end it shall be the duty of such consular officer to place his official seal upon all of the personal property or effects of the deceased, and to break and remove such seal as may be required by such person, and not otherwise.

18 Aug., 1856, s. 28, v. 11, p. 63.

**False certificate of property.** SEC. 1737. If any consul, vice-consul, commercial agent, or vice-commercial agent falsely and knowingly certifies that property belonging to foreigners is property belonging to citizens of the United States, he shall be punishable by imprisonment for not more than three years and by a fine of not more than ten thousand dollars.

28 Feb., 1803, s. 7, v. 2, p. 204.

**When consular officers may perform diplomatic functions.** SEC. 1738. No consular officer shall exercise diplomatic functions, or hold any diplomatic correspondence or relation on the part of the United States, in, with, or to the Government or country to which he is appointed, or any other country or Government, when there is in such country any officer of the United States authorized to perform diplomatic functions therein; nor in any case, unless expressly authorized by the President so to do. [See § 5335, under TREASON.]

18 Aug., 1856, s. 12, v. 11, p. 56.

SEC. 1750. Every Secretary of legation and consular officer is hereby authorized, whenever he is required or deems it necessary or proper so to do, at the post, port, place, or within the limits of his legation, consulate, or commercial agency, to administer to or take from any person an oath, affirmation, affidavit, or deposition, and to perform any notarial act which any notary public is required or authorized by law to do within the United States. Every such oath, affirmation, affidavit, deposition, and notarial act administered, sworn, affirmed, taken, had, or done, by or before any such officer, when certified under his hand and seal of office, shall be as valid, and of like force and effect within the United States, to all intents and purposes, as if administered, sworn, affirmed, taken, had, or done, by or before any other person within the United States duly authorized and competent thereto. If any person shall willfully and corruptly commit perjury, or by any means procure any person to commit perjury in any such oath, affirmation, affidavit, or deposition, within the intent and meaning of any act of Congress now or hereafter made, such offender may be charged, proceeded against, tried, convicted, and dealt with in any district of the United States, in the same manner, in all respects, as if such offense had been committed in the United States, before any officer duly authorized therein to administer or take such oath, affirmation, affidavit, or deposition, and shall be subject to the same punishment and disability therefor as are or shall be prescribed by any such act for such offense; and any document purporting to have affixed, impressed, or subscribed thereto or thereon the seal and signature of the officer administering or taking the same in testimony thereof, shall be admitted in evidence without proof of any such seal or signature being genuine or of the official character of such person; and if any person shall forge any such seal or signature, or shall tender in evidence any such document with a false or counterfeit seal or signature thereto, knowing the same to be false or counterfeit, he shall be deemed and taken to be guilty of a misdemeanor, and on conviction shall be imprisoned not exceeding three years nor less than one year, and fined in a sum not to exceed three thousand dollars, and may be charged, proceeded against, tried, convicted, and dealt with, therefor, in the district where he may be arrested or in custody. [See §§ 5392, 5393, PERJURY.]

*Title 18, Chap. 3.*
Depositions.

Penalty for perjury in such cases.

Evidence of taking the oath.

Penalty for forging certificate of oath.

18 Aug., 1856, s. 24, v. 11, p. 61.

SEC. 1751. No diplomatic or consular officer shall correspond in regard to the public affairs of any foreign Government with any private person, newspaper, or other periodical, or otherwise than with the proper officers of the United States, nor recommend any person, at home or abroad, for any employment of trust or profit under the Government of the country in which he is located; nor ask nor accept, for himself or any other person, any present, emolument, pecuniary favor, office, or title of any kind, from any such Government. [See June 17, 1874, *post.*]

Certain correspondence by officers prohibited.

*Ibid.,* s. 19, p. 59.

Nor shall any diplomatic or consular officer correspond in regard to the public affairs of any foreign Government with any private person, newspaper, or other periodical, or otherwise than with the proper officers of the United States; nor without the consent of the Secretary of State previously obtained, recommend any person at home or abroad for any employment or trust or profit under the Government of the country in which he is located; nor ask or accept for himself or any other person, any present, emolument, pecuniary favor, office, or title of any kind from any such Government.

June 17, 1874.

Certain correspondence forbidden.

Not to recommend persons for employment or accept titles or presents.

17 June, 1874, v. 18, p. 77.

# EXPATRIATION.

Sec.
1999. Right of expatriation declared.
2000. Protection of naturalized citizens in foreign countries.

Sec.
2001. Release of citizens imprisoned by foreign governments.

**Title 25.**

*Right of expatriation declared.*

SEC. 1999. Whereas the right of expatriation is a natural and inherent right of all people, indispensable to the enjoyment of the rights of life, liberty, and the pursuit of happiness; and whereas in the recognition of this principle this Government has freely received emigrants from all nations, and invested them with the rights of citizenship; and whereas it is claimed that such American citizens, with their descendants, are subjects of foreign states, owing allegiance to the governments thereof; and whereas it is necessary to the maintenance of public peace that this claim of foreign allegiance should be promptly and finally disavowed: Therefore any declaration, instruction, opinion, order, or decision of any officer of the United States which denies, restricts, impairs, or questions the right of expatriation, is declared inconsistent with the fundamental principles of the Republic.

*27 July, 1868, s. 1, v. 15, p. 223.*

*Protection to naturalized citizens in foreign states.*

SEC. 2000. All naturalized citizens of the United States, while in foreign countries, are entitled to and shall receive from this Government the same protection of persons and property which is accorded to native-born citizens.

*Ibid., s. 2, p. 224.*

*Release of citizens imprisoned by foreign governments to be demanded.*

SEC. 2001. Whenever it is made known to the President that any citizen of the United States has been unjustly deprived of his liberty by or under the authority of any foreign government, it shall be the duty of the President forthwith to demand of that government the reasons of such imprisonment; and if it appears to be wrongful and in violation of the rights of American citizenship, the President shall forthwith demand the release of such citizen, and if the release so demanded is unreasonably delayed or refused, the President shall use such means, not amounting to acts of war, as he may think necessary and proper to obtain or effectuate the release; and all the facts and proceedings relative thereto shall as soon as practicable be communicated by the President to Congress.

*Ibid., s. 3, p. 224.*

# EXTRADITION.

Sec.
5270. Fugitives from the justice of a foreign country.
5271. Evidence on the hearing.
5272. Surrender of the fugitive.
5273. Time allowed for extradition.
5274. Continuance of provisions limited.
5275. Protection of the accused.
5276. Powers of agent receiving offenders delivered by a foreign government.

Sec.
5277. Penalty for opposing agent, &c.
5278. Fugitives from justice of a State or Territory.
5279. Penalty for resisting agent, &c.
5280. Arrest of deserting seamen from foreign vessels.
5409. Allowing prisoners to escape.
5410. Application of preceding section.

**Title 66.**

*Fugitives from the justice of a foreign country.*

SEC. 5270. Whenever there is a treaty or convention for extradition between the Government of the United States and any foreign government, any justice of the Supreme Court, circuit judge, district judge, commissioner, authorized so to do by any of the courts of the United States, or judge of a court of record of general jurisdiction of any State, may, upon complaint made under oath, charging any person found within the limits of any State, district, or Territory, with having committed within the jurisdiction of any such foreign government any of the crimes provided for by such treaty or convention, issue his warrant for the apprehension of the person so charged, that he may be brought before such justice, judge, or commissioner, to the end that the evidence of criminality may be heard and considered. If, on such hearing, he deems the evidence sufficient to sustain the charge under the provisions of the proper treaty or convention, he shall certify the same, together with a copy of all the testimony taken before him, to the Secretary of State, that a warrant may issue upon the requisition of the

EXTRADITION. 223

proper authorities of such foreign government, for the surrender of such person, according to the stipulations of the treaty or convention; and he shall issue his warrant for the commitment of the person so charged to the proper jail, there to remain until such surrender shall be made.

12 Aug., 1848, s. 1, v. 9, p. 302..

SEC. 5271. In every case of complaint and of a hearing upon the return of the warrant of arrest, any depositions, warrants, or other papers offered in evidence, shall be admitted and received for the purpose of such hearing if they shall be properly and legally authenticated so as to entitle them to be received as evidence of the criminality of the person so apprehended, by the tribunals of the foreign country from which the accused party shall have escaped, and copies of any such depositions, warrants, or other papers, shall, if authenticated according to the law of such foreign country, be in like manner received as evidence; and the certificate of the principal diplomatic or consular officer of the United States resident in such foreign country shall be proof that any such deposition, warrant or other paper, or copy thereof, is authenticated in the manner required by this section. *Evidence on the hearing.*

12 Aug., 1848, s. 2, v. 9, p. 302.
22 June, 1860, v. 12, p. 84.
19 June, 1876, v. 19, p. 59.

SEC. 5272. It shall be lawful for the Secretary of State, under his hand and seal of office, to order the person so committed to be delivered to such person as shall be authorized, in the name and on behalf of such foreign government, to be tried for the crime of which such person shall be so accused, and such person shall be delivered up accordingly; and it shall be lawful for the person so authorized to hold such person in custody, and to take him to the territory of such foreign government, pursuant to such treaty. If the person so accused shall escape out of any custody to which he shall be committed, or to which he shall be delivered, it shall be lawful to retake such person in the same manner as any person accused of any crime against the laws in force in that part of the United States to which he shall so escape, may be retaken on an escape. [See §§ 5409, 5410.] *Surrender of the fugitive.*

12 Aug., 1848, s. 3, v. 9, p. 302.

SEC. 5273. Whenever any person who is committed under this title or any treaty, to remain until delivered up in pursuance of a requisition, is not so delivered up and conveyed out of the United States within two calendar months after such commitment, over and above the time actually required to convey the prisoner from the jail to which he was committed, by the readiest way, out of the United States, it shall be lawful for any judge of the United States, or of any State, upon application made to him by or on behalf of the person so committed, and upon proof made to him that reasonable notice of the intention to make such application has been given to the Secretary of State, to order the person so committed to be discharged out of custody, unless sufficient cause is shown to such judge why such discharge ought not to be ordered. *Time allowed for extradition.*

*Idem, s. 4.*

SEC. 5274. The provisions of this Title relating to the surrender of persons who have committed crimes in foreign countries shall continue in force during the existence of any treaty of extradition with any foreign Government, and no longer. *Continuance of provisions limited.*

*Idem, s. 5.*

SEC. 5275. Whenever any person is delivered by any foreign Government to an agent of the United States, for the purpose of being brought within the United States and tried for any crime of which he is duly accused, the President shall have power to take all necessary measures for the transportation and safe-keeping of such accused person, and for his security against lawless violence, until the final conclusion of his trial for the crimes or offenses specified in the warrant of extradition, and until his final discharge from custody or imprisonment for or on account of such crimes or offenses, and for a reasonable time thereafter, and may employ such portion of the land or naval forces of the United States, or of the militia thereof, as may be necessary for the safe-keeping and protection of the accused. *Protection of the accused.*

3 March, 1869, s. 1, v. 15 p. 337.

## EXTRADITION.

*Powers of agent receiving offenders delivered by a foreign Government.*

SEC. 5276. Any person duly appointed as agent to receive, in behalf of the United States, the delivery, by a foreign Government, of any person accused of crime committed within the jurisdiction of the United States, and to convey him to the place of his trial, shall have all the powers of a marshal of the United States, in the several districts through which it may be necessary for him to pass with such prisoner, so far as such power is requisite for the prisoner's safe-keeping.

*Idem*, s. 2.

*Penalty for opposing agent, &c.*

SEC. 5277. Every person who knowingly and willfully obstructs, resists, or opposes such agent in the execution of his duties, or who rescues or attempts to rescue such prisoner, whether in the custody of the agent or of any officer or person to whom his custody has lawfully been committed, shall be punishable by a fine of not more than one thousand dollars, and by imprisonment for not more than one year.

*Idem*, s. 3.

*Fugitives from justice of a State or Territory.*

SEC. 5278. Whenever the executive authority of any State or Territory demands any person as a fugitive from justice, of the executive authority of any State or Territory to which such person has fled, and produces a copy of an indictment found or an affidavit made before a magistrate of any State or Territory, charging the person demanded with having committed treason, felony, or other crime, certified as authentic by the governor or chief magistrate of the State or Territory from whence the person so charged has fled, it shall be the duty of the executive authority of the State or Territory to which such person has fled to cause him to be arrested and secured, and to cause notice of the arrest to be given to the executive authority making such demand, or to the agent of such authority appointed to receive the fugitive, and to cause the fugitive to be delivered to such agent when he shall appear. If no such agent appears within six months from the time of the arrest, the prisoner may be discharged. All costs or expenses incurred in the apprehending, securing, and transmitting such fugitive to the State or Territory making such demand, shall be paid by such State or Territory.

12 Feb., 1793, s. 1, v. 1, p. 302.

*Penalty for resisting agent, &c.*

SEC. 5279. Any agent so appointed who receives the fugitive into his custody, shall be empowered to transport him to the State or Territory from which he has fled. And every person who, by force, sets at liberty or rescues the fugitive from such agent while so transporting him, shall be fined not more than five hundred dollars or imprisoned not more than one year. [See § 5409.]

*Idem*, s. 2.

*Arrest of deserting seamen from foreign vessels.*

SEC. 5280. On application of a consul or vice-consul of any foreign government having a treaty with the United States stipulating for the restoration of seamen deserting, made in writing, stating that the person therein named has deserted from a vessel of any such government, while in any port of the United States, and on proof by the exhibition of the register of the vessel, ship's roll, or other official document, that the person named belonged, at the time of desertion, to the crew of such vessel, it shall be the duty of any court, judge, commissioner of any circuit court, justice, or other magistrate, having competent power, to issue warrants to cause such person to be arrested for examination. If, on examination, the facts stated are found to be true, the person arrested not being a citizen of the United States, shall be delivered up to the consul or vice-consul, to be sent back to the dominions of any such government, or, on the request and at the expense of the consul or vice-consul, shall be detained until the consul or vice-consul finds an opportunity to send him back to the dominions of any such government. No person so arrested shall be detained more than two months after his arrest; but at the end of that time shall be set at liberty, and shall not be again molested for the same cause. If any such deserter shall be found to have committed any crime or offense, his surrender may be delayed until the tribunal before which the case shall be depending, or may be cognizable, shall have pronounced its sentence, and such sentence shall have been carried into effect.

2 March, 1829, ch. 41, v. 4, p. 359.
24 Feb., 1855, ch. 123, v. 10, p. 614.

# FISH COMMISSIONER—FLAGS AND STANDARDS.

SEC. 5409. Whenever any marshal, deputy marshal, ministerial officer, or other person, has in his custody any prisoner by virtue of process issued under the laws of the United States by any court judge, or commissioner, and such marshal, deputy marshal, ministerial officer, or other person, voluntarily suffers such prisoner to escape, he shall be fined not more than two thousand dollars, or imprisoned for a term not more than two years, or both. — *Title 70, Chap. 4. Allowing prisoners to escape.*

21 June, 1860, v. 12, p. 69.

SEC. 5410. The preceding section shall be construed to apply not only to cases in which the prisoner who escaped was charged or found guilty of an offense against the laws of the United States, but also to cases in which a prisoner may be in custody charged with offenses against any foreign government with which the United States have treaties of extradition. — *Application of preceding section.*

Ibid.

## FISH COMMISSIONER.

Sec.
4395. Appointment of Commissioner of Fisheries.
4396. Duties of Commissioner.

Sec.
4397. Executive Department to aid investigation.
4398. Powers of Commissioner.

SEC. 4395. There shall be appointed by the President, with the advice and consent of the Senate, from among the civil officers or employés of the Government, a Commissioner of Fish and Fisheries, who shall be a person of proved scientific and practical acquaintance with the fishes of the coast, and who shall serve without additional salary. — *Title 51. Appointment of Commissioner of Fish and Fisheries.*

9 Feb., 1871, s. 1, v. 16, p. 594.

SEC. 4396. The Commissioner of Fish and Fisheries shall prosecute investigations and inquiries on the subject, with the view of ascertaining whether any and what diminution in the number of the food-fishes of the coast and the lakes of the United States has taken place; and, if so, to what causes the same is due; and also whether any and what protective, prohibitory, or precautionary measures should be adopted in the premises; and shall report upon the same to Congress. — *Duties of the Commissioner.*

Ibid., s. 2.

SEC. 4397. The heads of the several Executive Departments shall cause to be rendered all necessary and practicable aid to the Commissioner in the prosecution of his investigations and inquiries. — *Executive Departments to aid investigations.*

Ibid., s. 3.

SEC. 4398. The Commissioner may take or cause to be taken at all times, in the waters of the sea-coast of the United States, where the tide ebbs and flows, and also in the waters of the lakes, such fish or specimens thereof as may in his judgment, from time to time, be needful or proper for the conduct of his duties, any law, custom, or usage of any State to the contrary notwithstanding. — *Powers of Commissioner.*

Ibid., s. 4.

## FLAGS AND STANDARDS.

Sec.
428. Captured flags.
1554. Captured flags.
1555. Display of captured flags.

Sec.
1791. The flag to be 13 stripes and 37 stars.
1792. A star to be added for every new State.

SEC. 428. The Secretary of the Navy shall from time to time cause to be collected and transmitted to him, at the seat of Government, all flags, standards, and colors taken by the Navy from the enemies of the United States. — *Title 10. Captured flags.*

18 April, 1814, s. 1, v. 3, p. 133.

SEC. 1554. The Secretary of the Navy shall cause to be collected and transmitted to him, at the seat of Government of the United States, all such flags, standards, and colors as shall have been or may hereafter be taken by the Navy from enemies. — *Title 15, Chap. 7. Captured flags.*

18 April, 1814, s. 1, v. 3, p. 133.

11181——15

## FRAUD, FORGERY, THEFT, ETC.

Preservation of public p.

**Sec. 1555.** All flags, standards, and colors of the description mentioned in the foregoing section, which are now in the possession of the Navy Department, or may hereafter be transmitted to it, shall be delivered to the President, for the purpose of being, under his direction, preserved and displayed in such public place as he may deem proper.

*Idem.*

Title 20.

The flag to be 13 stripes and 37 stars.

**Sec. 1791.** The flag of the United States shall be thirteen horizontal stripes, alternate red and white; and the union of the flag shall be thirty-seven stars, white in a blue field.

13 Jan., 1794, v. 1, p. 314.
4 April, 1818, s. 1, v. 3, p. 415.

A star to be added for every new State.

**Sec. 1792.** On the admission of a new State into the Union one star shall be added to the union of the flag; and such addition shall take effect on the fourth day of July then next succeeding such admission.

4 April, 1818, s. 2, v. 3, p. 415.

## FRAUD, FORGERY, THEFT, &c.

Sec.
183. Clerks investigating frauds may administer oath.
5394. Stealing process, &c.
5418. Forging, &c., bid, public record, &c.
5421. Forging deed, power of attorney, &c.
5422. Having forged papers in possession.
5435. False personation.
5436. False demand on fraudulent power of attorney.

Sec.
5438. Making or presenting false claims.
5439. Embezzling arms, stores, &c.
5440. All parties to a conspiracy equally guilty.
5441. Delaying or defrauding captor or claimant, &c., of prize-property.
5456. Robbery or larceny of personal property of the United States.
5479. Counterfeiting or forging bids, bonds, &c.
— Larcenies and stolen goods.

Title 4.

Oaths, when administered by officers, &c.

**Sec. 183.** Any officer or clerk of any of the Departments lawfully detailed to investigate frauds or attempts to defraud on the Government, or any irregularity or misconduct of any officer or agent of the United States, shall have authority to administer an oath to any witness attending to testify or depose in the course of such investigation.

10 April, 1869, Res. 15, s. 2. v. 16, p. 55.
7 March, 1870, chap. 23, v. 16, p. 75.

Title 70, Chap. 4.

Stealing or altering process, procuring false bail, &c.

**Sec. 5394.** Every person who feloniously steals, takes away, alters, falsifies, or otherwise avoids any record, writ, process, or other proceeding, in any court of the United States, by means whereof any judgment is reversed, made void, or does not take effect, and every person who acknowledges, or procures to be acknowledged, in any such court, any recognizance, bail, or judgment, in the name of any other person not privy or consenting to the same, shall be fined not more than five thousand dollars or be imprisoned at hard labor not more than seven years; but this provision shall not extend to the acknowledgment of any judgment by an attorney, duly admitted for any person against whom any such judgment is had or given.

30 April, 1790, s. 15, v. 1, p. 115.
22 June, 1874, s. 10, v. 18, p. 100.

Title 70, Chap. 5.

Forging, &c., bid, public record, &c.

**Sec. 5418.** Every person who falsely makes, alters, forges, or counterfeits any bid, proposal, guarantee, official bond, public record, affidavit, or other writing, for the purpose of defrauding the United States, or utters or publishes as true any such false, forged, altered, or counterfeited bid, proposal, guarantee, official bond, public record, affidavit, or other writing, for such purpose, knowing the same to be false, forged, altered, or counterfeited, or transmits to or presents at the office of any officer of the United States any such false, forged, altered, or counterfeited bid, proposal, guarantee, official bond, public record, affidavit, or other writing, knowing the same to be false, forged, altered, or counterfeited, for such purpose, shall be imprisoned at hard labor for a period not more than ten years, or be fined not more than one thousand dollars, or be punished by both such fine and imprisonment. [See § 5479.]

5 April, 1866, s. 1, v. 14, p. 12.

Forging deed, power of attorney, &c.

**Sec. 5421.** Every person who falsely makes, alters, forges, or counterfeits; or causes or procures to be falsely made, altered, forged, or counterfeited; or willingly aids or assists in the false making, altering, forging, or counterfeiting, any deed, power of attorney, order, certificate, receipt, or other writing, for the purpose of obtaining or receiving, or of enabling any other person, either directly or indirectly, to obtain or receive from the United States, or any of their officers or agents, any sum of money; or who utters or publishes as true, or causes to be uttered or published as true, any such false, forged, altered, or counterfeited deed, power of attorney, order, certificate, receipt, or other writing, with intent to defraud the United States, knowing the same to be false, altered, forged, or counterfeited; or who transmits to, or presents at, or causes or procures to be transmitted to, or presented at, any office or officer of the Government of the United States, any deed, power of attorney, order, certificate, receipt, or other writing, in support of, or in relation to, any account or claim, with intent to defraud the United States, knowing the same to be false, altered, forged, or counterfeited, shall be imprisoned at hard labor for a period of not less than one year nor more than ten years; or shall be imprisoned not more than five years, and ned not more than one thousand dollars.

3 March, 1823, s. 1, v. 3, p. 771.

SEC. 5422. Every person who, knowingly and with intent to defraud the United States, has in his possession any false, altered, forged, or counterfeited deed, power of attorney, order, certificate, receipt, or other writing, for the purpose of enabling another to obtain from the United States, or any of their officers or agents, any sum of money, shall be fined and imprisoned at the discretion of the court. Having forged papers in possession.

Ibid., s. 2, p. 772.

SEC. 5435. Every person who falsely personates any true and lawful holder of any share or sum in the public stocks or debt of the United States, or any person entitled to any annuity, dividend, pension, prize-money, wages, or other debt due from the United States, and, under color of such false personation, transfers or endeavors to transfer such public stock or any part thereof, or receives or endeavors to receive the money of such true and lawful holder thereof, or the money of any person really entitled to receive such annuity, dividend, pension, prize-money, wages, or other debt, shall be punished by a fine of not more than five thousand dollars, and by imprisonment at hard labor not more than ten years. False personation of holder of public stocks.

3 March, 1825, s. 18, v. 4, p. 120.

SEC. 5436. Every person who knowingly or fraudulently demands or endeavors to obtain any share or sum in the public stocks of the United States, or to have any part thereof transferred, assigned, sold, or conveyed, or to have any annuity, dividend, pension, prize-money, wages, or other debt due from the United States, or any part thereof, received or paid by virtue of any false, forged, or counterfeited power of attorney, authority, or instrument, shall be punished by a fine of not more than five thousand dollars, and by imprisonment at hard labor not more than ten years. False demand on fraudulent power of attorney.

Ibid.

SEC. 5438. Every person who makes or causes to be made, or presents or causes to be presented, for payment or approval, to or by any person or officer in the civil, military, or naval service of the United States, any claim upon or against the Government of the United States, or any Department or officer thereof, knowing such claim to be false, fictitious, or fraudulent, or who, for the purpose of obtaining or aiding to obtain the payment or approval of such claim, makes, uses, or causes to be made or used, any false bill, receipt, voucher, roll, account, claim, certificate, affidavit, or deposition, knowing the same to contain any fraudulent or fictitious statement or entry, or who enters into any agreement, combination, or conspiracy to defraud the Government of the United States, or any Department or officer thereof, by obtaining or aiding to obtain the payment or allowance of any false or fraudulent claim, or who, having charge, possession, custody, or control of any money or other public property used or to be used in the military or naval service, who, with intent to defraud the United States or willfully to conceal such money or other property, delivers or causes to be delivered, to any other person having authority to receive the same, any amount of such money or other property less than that for which he received a certificate or took a receipt, and every person authorized to make or deliver any certificate, voucher, receipt, or other paper certifying the receipt of arms, ammunition, provisions, clothing, or other property so used or to be used, who makes or delivers the same to any Making or presenting false claims.

other person without a full knowledge of the truth of the facts stated therein, and with intent to defraud the United States, and every person who knowingly purchases or receives in pledge for any obligation or indebtedness from any soldier, officer, sailor, or other person called into or employed in the military or naval service any arms, equipments, ammunition, clothes, military stores, or other public property, such soldier, sailor, officer, or other person not having the lawful right to pledge or sell the same, every person so offending in any of the matters set forth in this section shall be imprisoned at hard labor for not less than one nor more than five years, or fined not less than one thousand nor more than five thousand dollars. [See §§ 3490, 3491, under CLAIMS.]

2 March, 1863, ss. 1, 3, v. 12, pp. 696, 698.

**Embezzling arms, stores, &c.** SEC. 5439. Every person who steals or embezzles, or knowingly applies to his own use, or who unlawfully sells, conveys, or disposes of, any ordnance, arms, ammunition, clothing, subsistence stores, money, or other property of the United States, furnished or to be used for the military or naval service, shall be punished as prescribed in the preceding section.

*Ibid.*

**All parties to a conspiracy equally guilty.** SEC. 5440. If two or more persons conspire either to commit any offense against the United States, or to defraud the United States in any manner or for any purpose, and one or more of such parties do any act to effect the object of the conspiracy, all the parties to such conspiracy shall be liable to a penalty of not less than one thousand dollars and not more than ten thousand dollars, and to imprisonment not more than two years.

2 March, 1867, s. 30, v. 14, p. 484.
17 May, 1879, v. 21, p. 4.

**Delaying or defrauding captor or claimant, &c., of prize-property.** SEC. 5441. Every person who willfully does any act or aids or advises in the doing of any act relating to the bringing in, custody, preservation, sale, or other disposition of any property captured as prize, or relating to any documents or papers connected with the property, or to any deposition or other document or paper connected with the proceedings, with intent to defraud, delay, or injure the United States or any captor or claimant of such property, shall be punished by a fine of not more than ten thousand dollars, or by imprisonment not more than five years, or both. [See §§ 4613–4652, PRIZE.]

30 June, 1864, s. 31, v. 13, p. 315.

**Robbery or larceny of personal property of the United States.** SEC. 5456. Every person who robs another of any kind or description of personal property belonging to the United States, or feloniously takes and carries away the same, shall be punished by a fine of not more than five thousand dollars, or by imprisonment at hard labor not less than one nor more than ten years, or by both such fine and imprisonment.

2 March, 1867, chap. 193, v. 14, p. 557.

**Counterfeiting bid, bond, &c.** SEC. 5479. If any person shall falsely make, alter, forge, or counterfeit, or cause or procure to be falsely made, altered, forged, or counterfeited, or willingly aid, or assist in the false making, altering, forging, or counterfeiting, any bond, bid, proposal, guarantee, security, official bond, public record, affidavit, or other writing for the purpose of defrauding the United States; or shall utter or publish as true, or cause to be uttered or published as true, any such false, forged, altered, or counterfeited bond, bid, proposal, guarantee, security, official bond, public record, affidavit, or other writing, for the purpose of defrauding the United States, knowing the same to be false, forged, altered, or counterfeited; or shall transmit to, or present at, or cause *to or* procure to be transmitted to, or presented at, the office of any officer of the United States, any such false, forged, altered, or counterfeited bond, bid, proposal, guarantee, security, official bond, public record, affidavit, or other writing, knowing the same to be false, forged, altered, or counterfeited, for the purpose of defrauding the United States, shall be punishable by a fine of not more than one thousand dollars, or by imprisonment at hard labor for not more than ten years, or by both such punishments. [See § 5418.]

8 June, 1872, s. 294, v. 17, p. 320.
27 Feb., 1877, chap. 69, v. 19, p. 253.

*Be it enacted by the Senate and House of Representatives of the United States of America in Congress assembled,* That any person who shall embezzle, steal, or purloin any money, property, record, voucher, or valuable thing whatever, of the moneys, goods, chattels, records, or property of the United States, shall be deemed guilty of felony, and on conviction thereof before the district or circuit court of the United States in the district wherein said offense may have been committed, or into which he shall carry or have in possession of said property so embezzled, stolen, or purloined, shall be punished therefor by imprisonment at hard labor in the penitentiary not exceeding five years, or by a fine not exceeding five thousand dollars, or both, at the discretion of the court before which he shall be convicted.

March 3, 1875.

Embezzling, stealing, &c., from United States deemed felony. penalty.

SEC. 2. That if any person shall receive, conceal, or aid in concealing, or have, or retain in his possession with intent to convert to his own use or gain, any money, property, record, voucher, or valuable thing whatever, of the moneys, goods, chattels, records, or property of the United States, which has theretofore been embezzled, stolen, or purloined from the United States by any other person, knowing the same to have been so embezzled, stolen, or purloined, such person shall, on conviction before the circuit or district court of the United States in the district wherein he may have such property, be punished by a fine not exceeding five thousand dollars, or imprisonment at hard labor in the penitentiary not exceeding five years, one or both, at the discretion of the court before which he shall be convicted; and such receiver may be tried either before or after the conviction of the principal felon, but if the party has been convicted, then the judgment against him shall be conclusive evidence in the prosecution against such receiver that the property of the United States therein described has been embezzled, stolen, or purloined.

Knowingly receiving, concealing, &c., stolen, &c., property of the United States; penalty.

May be tried before or after conviction of principal.

Approved, March 3, 1875.

## GUANO ISLANDS.

Sec.
5570. Claim of United States to islands.
5571. Notice of discovery, and proofs to be furnished.
5572. Completion of proof in case of death of discoverer.
5573. Exclusive privileges of discoverer.

Sec.
5574. Restrictions upon exportation.
5575. Regulation of guano trade.
5576. Criminal jurisdiction.
5577. Employment of land and naval forces.
5578. Right to abandon island.

SEC. 5570. Whenever any citizen of the United States discovers a deposit of guano on any island, rock, or key, not within the lawful jurisdiction of any other government, and not occupied by the citizens of any other government, and takes peaceable possession thereof, and occupies the same, such island, rock, or key may, at the discretion of the President, be considered as appertaining to the United States.

Title 72.

Claim of United States to islands.

18 Aug., 1856, s. 1, v. 11, p. 119.

SEC. 5571. The discoverer shall, as soon as practicable, give notice, verified by affidavit, to the Department of State, of such discovery, occupation, and possession, describing the island, rock, or key, and the latitude and longitude thereof, as near as may be, and showing that such possession was taken in the name of the United States; and shall furnish satisfactory evidence to the State Department that such island, rock, or key was not, at the time of the discovery thereof, or of the taking possession and occupation thereof by the claimants, in the possession or occupation of any other government or of the citizens of any other government, before the same shall be considered as appertaining to the United States.

Notice of discovery, and proofs to be furnished.

*Ibid.*

SEC. 5572. If the discoverer dies before perfecting proof of discovery or fully complying with the provisions of the preceding section, his widow, heir, executor, or administrator, shall be entitled to the benefits of such discovery, upon complying with the provisions of this Title; but nothing herein shall be held to impair any rights of discovery or any assignment by a discoverer heretofore recognized by the United States.

Completion of proof in case of death of discoverer.

2 April, 1872, s. 1, v. 17, p. 48.

230 HABEAS CORPUS.

Exclusive privileges of discoverer.
SEC. 5573. The discoverer, or his assigns, being citizens of the United States, may be allowed, at the pleasure of Congress, the exclusive right of occupying such islands, rock, or keys, for the purpose of obtaining guano, and of selling and delivering the same to citizens of the United States, to be used therein, and may be allowed to charge and receive for every ton thereof delivered alongside a vessel, in proper tubs, within reach of ship's tackle, a sum not exceeding eight dollars per ton for the best quality, or four dollars for every ton taken while in its native place of deposit.

18 Aug., 1856, s. 2, v. 11, p. 119.

Restrictions upon exportation.
SEC. 5574. No guano shall be taken from any such island, rock, or key, except for the use of the citizens of the United States, or of persons resident therein. The discoverer, or his widow, heir, executor, administrator, or assigns, shall enter into bond, in such penalty and with such sureties as may be required by the President, to deliver the guano to citizens of the United States, for the purpose of being used therein, and to none others, and at the price prescribed, and to provide all necessary facilities for that purpose within a time to be fixed in the bond; and any breach of the provisions thereof shall be deemed a forfeiture of all rights accruing under and by virtue of this Title. This section shall, however, be suspended in relation to all persons who have complied with the provisions of this Title, for five years from and after the fourteenth day of July, eighteen hundred and seventy-two.

28 July, 1866, s. 3, v. 14, p. 328.
2 April, 1872, s. 1. v. 17, p. 48.

Regulation of guano trade.
SEC. 5575. The introduction of guano from such islands, rocks, or keys, shall be regulated as in the coasting-trade between different parts of the United States, and the same laws shall govern the vessels concerned therein.

18 Aug., 1856, s. 3, v. 11, p. 120.

Criminal jurisdiction.
SEC. 5576. All acts done, and offenses or crimes committed, on any such island, rock, or key, by persons who may land thereon, or in the waters adjacent thereto, shall be deemed committed on the high seas, on board a merchant-ship or vessel belonging to the United States; and shall be punished according to the laws of the United States relating to such ships or vessels and offenses on the high seas, which laws for the purpose aforesaid are extended over such islands, rocks, and keys.

Ibid., s. 6.

Employment of land and naval forces.
SEC. 5577. The President is authorized, at his discretion, to employ the land and naval forces of the United States to protect the rights of the discoverer or of his widow, heir, executor, administrator, or assigns.

Ibid., s. 5.

Right to abandon islands.
SEC. 5578. Nothing in this Title contained shall be construed as obliging the United States to retain possession of the islands, rocks, or keys, after the guano shall have been removed from the same.

Ibid., s. 4.

## HABEAS CORPUS.

Sec.
751. Power of courts to issue writs of *habeas corpus.*
752. Power of judges to grant writs of *habeas corpus.*
753. Writs of *habeas corpus* when prisoner is in jail.
754. Application for the writ of *habeas corpus.*
755. Allowance and direction of the writ.
756. Time of return.
757. Form of return.
758. Body of the party to be produced.
759. Day for hearing.

Sec.
760. Denial of return, counter-allegations, amendments.
761. Summary hearing; disposition of party.
762. In cases involving the law of nations, notice to be served on State attorney-general.
763. Appeals in cases of *habeas corpus* to circuit court.
764. Appeal to Supreme Court.
765. Appeals, how taken.
766. Pending proceedings in certain cases, action by State authority void.

SEC. 751. The Supreme Court and the circuit and district courts shall have power to issue writs of habeas corpus.

Title 13, chap. 13

Power of courts to issue writs of *habeas corpus.*

24 Sept., 1789, s. 14, v. 1, p. 81.
10 April, 1869, s. 2, v. 16, p. 44.
2 March, 1833, s. 7, v. 4, p. 634.
5 Feb., 1867, s. 1, v. 14, p. 385.
29 Aug., 1842, s. 1, v. 5, p. 539.

HABEAS CORPUS. 231

SEC. 752. The several justices and judges of the said courts, within their respective jurisdictions, shall have power to grant writs of habeas corpus for the purpose of an inquiry into the cause of restraint of liberty.  *Power of judges to grant writs of habeas corpus.*

*Idem.*

SEC. 753. The writ of habeas corpus shall in no case extend to a prisoner in jail, unless where he is in custody under or by color of the authority of the United States, or is committed for trial before some court thereof; or is in custody for an act done or omitted in pursuance of a law of the United States, or of an order, process, or decree of a court or judge thereof; or is in custody in violation of the Constitution or of a law or treaty of the United States; or, being a subject or citizen of a foreign state, and domiciled therein, is in custody for an act done or omitted under any alleged right, title, authority, privilege, protection, or exemption claimed under the commission, or order, or sanction of any foreign state, or under color thereof, the validity and effect whereof depend upon the law of nations; or unless it is necessary to bring the prisoner into court to testify.  *Writ of habeas corpus when prisoner is in jail.*

*Idem.*

SEC. 754. Application for a writ of habeas corpus shall be made to the court or justice, or judge authorized to issue the same, by complaint in writing, signed by the person for whose relief it is intended, setting forth the facts concerning the detention of the party restrained, in whose custody he is detained, and by virtue of what claim or authority, if known. The facts set forth in the complaint shall be verified by the oath of the person making the application.  *Application for the writ of habeas corpus.*

5 Feb., 1867, s. 1, v. 14, p. 385.

SEC. 755. The court, or justice, or judge to whom such application is made shall forthwith award a writ of habeas corpus, unless it appear, from the petition itself that the party is not entitled thereto. The writ shall be directed to the person in whose custody the party is detained.  *Allowance and direction of the writ.*

*Idem.*

SEC. 756. Any person to whom such writ is directed shall make due return thereof within three days thereafter, unless the party be detained beyond the distance of twenty miles; and if beyond that distance and not beyond a distance of a hundred miles, within ten days; and if beyond the distance of a hundred miles, within twenty days.  *Time of return.*

*Idem.*

SEC. 757. The person to whom the writ is directed shall certify to the court, or justice, or judge before whom it is returnable the true cause of the detention of such party.  *Form of return.*

*Idem.*

SEC. 758. The person making the return shall at the same time bring the body of the party before the judge who granted the writ.  *Body of the party to be produced.*

*Idem.*

SEC. 759. When the writ is returned, a day shall be set for the hearing of the cause, not exceeding five days thereafter, unless the party petitioning requests a longer time.  *Day for hearing.*

*Idem.*

SEC. 760. The petitioner or the party imprisoned or restrained may deny any of the facts set forth in the return, or may allege any other facts that may be material in the case. Such denials or allegations shall be under oath. The return and all suggestions made against it may be amended, by leave of the court, or justice, or judge, before or after the same are filed, so that thereby the material facts may be ascertained.  *Denial of return, counter-allegations, amendments.*

*Idem.*

SEC. 761. The court, or justice, or judge shall proceed in a summary way to determine the facts of the case, by hearing the testimony and arguments, and thereupon to dispose of the party as law and justice require.  *Summary hearing; disposition of party.*

*Idem.*

## 232    HOMESTEADS.

**In cases involving the law of nations, notice to be served on State attorney-general.**

SEC. 762. When a writ of habeas corpus is issued in the case of any prisoner who, being a subject or citizen of a foreign state and domiciled therein, is committed, or confined, or in custody, by or under the authority or law of any one of the United States, or process founded thereon, on account of any act done or omitted under any alleged right, title, authority, privilege, protection, or exemption claimed under the commission or order or sanction of any foreign state, or under color thereof, the validity and effect whereof depend upon the law of nations, notice of the said proceeding, to be prescribed by the court, or justice, or judge at the time of granting said writ, shall be served on the attorney-general or other officer prosecuting the pleas of said State, and due proof of such service shall be made to the court, or justice, or judge before the hearing.

29 Aug., 1842, v. 5, p. 539.

**Appeals in cases of habeas corpus to circuit court.**

SEC. 763. From the final decision of any court, justice, or judge inferior to the circuit court, upon an application for a writ of habeas corpus or upon such writ when issued, an appeal may be taken to the circuit court for the district in which the cause is heard:

1. In the case of any person alleged to be restrained of his liberty in violation of the Constitution, or of any law or treaty of the United States.

2. In the case of any prisoner who, being a subject or citizen of a foreign state, and domiciled therein, is committed or confined, or in custody by or under the authority or law of the United States, or of any State, or process founded thereon, for or on account of any act done or omitted under any alleged right, title, authority, privilege, protection, or exemption, set up or claimed under the commission, order, or sanction of any foreign state or sovereignty, the validity and effect whereof depend upon the law of nations, or under color thereof.

29 Aug., 1842, v. 5, p. 539.
5 Feb., 1867, s. 1, v. 14, p. 385.
27 March, 1868, s. 2, v. 15, p. 44.

**Appeal to Supreme Court.**

SEC. 764. From the final decision of such circuit court an appeal may be taken to the Supreme Court in the cases described in the last clause of the preceding section.

29 Aug., 1842, v. 5, p. 539.

**Appeals, how taken.**

SEC. 765. The appeals allowed by the two preceding sections shall be taken on such terms, and under such regulations and orders, as well for the custody and appearance of the person alleged to be in prison or confined or restrained of his liberty, as for sending up to the appellate tribunal a transcript of the petition, writ of habeas corpus, return thereto, and other proceedings, as may be prescribed by the Supreme Court, or, in default thereof, by the court or judge hearing the cause.

29 Aug., 1842, v. 5, p. 539.
5 Feb., 1867, s. 1, v. 14, p. 385.

**Pending proceedings in certain cases, action by State authority void.**

SEC. 766. Pending the proceedings or appeal in the cases mentioned in the three preceding sections, and until final judgment therein, and after final judgment of discharge, any proceeding against the person so imprisoned or confined or restrained of his liberty, in any State court, or by or under the authority of any State, for any matter so heard and determined, or in process of being heard and determined, under such writ of habeas corpus, shall be deemed null and void.

*Idem.*

## HOMESTEADS.

| Sec. | |
|---|---|
| 2289. | Who may enter certain unappropriated public lands. |
| 2290. | Mode of procedure. |
| 2291. | Certificate and patent, when given and issued. |
| 2292. | When rights inure to the benefit of infant children. |
| 2293. | Persons in military or naval service, when and before whom to make affidavit. |
| 2296. | Homestead lands not to be subject to prior debts. |
| 2297. | When lands entered for homesteads revert to Government. |
| 2298. | Limitation of amount entered for homestead. |
| 2300. | What minors may have the privileges of this chapter. |
| 2301. | Payment before expiration of five years, rights of applicant. |
| 2304. | Soldiers' and sailors' homestead. |
| 2305. | Deduction of military and naval service from time, &c. |
| 2306. | Persons who have entered less than 160 acres, rights of. |
| 2307. | Widows and minor children of persons entitled to homestead, &c. |
| 2308. | Actual service in the Army or Navy equivalent to residence, &c. |
| 2309. | Who may enter by agent. |
| 2317. | Cultivation of trees on homestead tracts. |

# HOMESTEADS. 233

SEC. 2289. Every person who is the head of a family, or who has arrived at the age of twenty-one years, and is a citizen of the United States, or who has filed his declaration of intention to become such, as required by the naturalization laws, shall be entitled to enter one quarter-section or a less quantity of unappropriated public lands, upon which such person may have filed a pre-emption claim, or which may, at the time the application is made, be subject to pre-emption at one dollar and twenty-five cents per acre; or eighty acres or less of such unappropriated lands, at two dollars and fifty cents per acre, to be located in a body, in conformity to the legal subdivisions of the public lands, and after the same have been surveyed. And every person owning and residing on land may, under the provisions of this section, enter other land lying contiguous to his land, which shall not, with the land so already owned and occupied, exceed in the aggregate one hundred and sixty acres.

*Who may enter certain unappropriated lands.*

20 May, 1862, s. 1, v. 12, p. 392.
11 *Feb.*, 1874, chap. 25, v. 18, p. 15.

SEC. 2290. The person applying for the benefit of the preceding section shall, upon application to the register of the land-office in which he is about to make such entry, make affidavit before the register or receiver that he is the head of a family, or is twenty-one years or more of age, or has performed service in the Army or Navy of the United States, and that such application is made for his exclusive use and benefit, and that his entry is made for the purpose of actual settlement and cultivation, and not either directly or indirectly for the use or benefit of any other person; and upon filing such affidavit with the register or receiver, on payment of five dollars when the entry is of not more than eighty acres, and on payment of ten dollars when the entry is for more than eighty acres, he shall thereupon be permitted to enter the amount of land specified.

*Mode of procedure.*

20 May, 1862, s. 2, v. 12, p. 392.
21 March, 1864, s. 2, v. 13, p. 35.
21 June, 1866, s. 2, v. 14, p. 67.

SEC. 2291. No certificate, however, shall be given, or patent issued therefor, until the expiration of five years from the date of such entry; and if at the expiration of such time, or at any time within two years thereafter, the person making such entry; or if he be dead, his widow; or in case of her death, his heirs or devisee; or in case of a widow making such entry, her heirs or devisee, in case of her death, proved by two credible witnesses that he, she, or they have resided upon or cultivated the same for the term of five years immediately succeeding the time of filing the affidavit, and makes affidavit that no part of such land has been alienated, except as provided in section twenty-two hundred and eighty-eight,* and that he, she, or they will bear true allegiance to the Government of the United States; then, in such case, he, she, or they, if at that time citizens of the United States, shall be entitled to a patent, as in other cases provided by law.

*Certificate and patent, when given and issued.*

21 June, 1866, s. 2, v. 14, p. 67.
3 March, 1877, v. 19, p. 403.

[An act approved March 3, 1877, chap. 122, v. 19, p. 403, amendatory to this section, prescribes before whom oaths of proof of residence, &c., may be taken. There are also sundry acts relating to homesteads which were not considered essential in this compilation.]

SEC. 2292. In case of the death of both father and mother, leaving an infant child or children under twenty-one years of age, the right and fee shall inure to the benefit of such infant child or children; and the executor, administrator, or guardian may, at any time within two years after the death of the surviving parent, and in accordance with the law of the State in which such children, for the time being, have their domicile, sell the land for the benefit of such infants, but for no other purpose; and the purchaser shall acquire the absolute title by the purchase, and be entitled to a patent from the United States on the payment of the office-fees and sum of money above specified.

*When rights inure to the benefit of infant children.*

21 June, 1866, s. 2, v. 14, p. 67.

SEC. 2293. In case of any person desirous of availing himself of the benefits of this chapter; but who, by reason of actual service in the military or naval service of the United States, is unable to do the per-

*Persons in military or naval service, when and before whom to make affidavit.*

---

* Transferred for church, cemetery, or school purposes, or for right of way of railroads.

sonal preliminary acts at the district land-office which the preceding sections require; and whose family, or some member thereof, is residing on the land which he desires to enter, and upon which a bona-fide improvement and settlement have been made, such person may make the affidavit required by law before the officer commanding in the branch of the service in which the party is engaged, which affidavit shall be as binding in law, and with like penalties, as if taken before the register or receiver; and upon such affidavit being filed with the register by the wife or other representative of the party, the same shall become effective from the date of such filing, provided the application and affidavit are accompanied by the fee and commissions as required by law.

21 March, 1864, s. 4, v. 13, p. 35.

**Homestead lands not to be subject to prior debts.** SEC. 2296. No lands acquired under the provisions of this chapter shall in any event become liable to the satisfaction of any debt contracted prior to the issuing of the patent therefor.

20 May, 1862, s. 4, v. 12, p. 393.

**When lands entered for homestead revert to Government.** SEC. 2297. If, at any time after the filing of the affidavit, as required in section twenty-two hundred and ninety, and before the expiration of the five years mentioned in section twenty-two hundred and ninety-one, it is proved, after due notice to the settler, to the satisfaction of the register of the land-office, that the person having filed such affidavit has actually changed his residence, or abandoned the land for more than six months at any time, then and in that event the land so entered shall revert to the Government.

20 May, 1862, s. 5, v. 12, p. 393.

[An act approved 21 April, 1876, chap. 72, v. 19, p. 35, provides for the confirmation of entries of land grants prior to notice of withdrawal of lands.]

**Limitation of amount entered for homestead.** SEC. 2298. No person shall be permitted to acquire title to more than one quarter-section under the provisions of this chapter.

20 May, 1862, s. 6, v. 12, p. 393.

**What minors may have the privileges of this chapter.** SEC. 2300. No person who has served, or may hereafter serve, for a period not less than fourteen days in the Army or Navy of the United States, either regular or volunteer, under the laws thereof, during the existence of an actual war, domestic or foreign, shall be deprived of the benefits of this chapter on account of not having attained the age of twenty-one years.

*Ibid.*

**Payment before expiration of five years; rights of applicant.** SEC. 2301. Nothing in this chapter shall be so construed as to prevent any person who has availed himself of the benefits of section twenty-two hundred and eighty-nine, from paying the minimum price for the quantity of land so entered, at any time before the expiration of the five years, and obtaining a patent therefor from the Government, as in other cases directed by law, on making proof of settlement and cultivation as provided by law, granting pre-emption rights.

*Ibid.*, s. 8.

**Soldiers' and sailors' homestead.** SEC. 2304. Every private soldier and officer who has served in the Army of the United States during the recent rebellion, for ninety days, and who was honorably discharged, and has remained loyal to the Government, including the troops mustered into the service of the United States by virtue of the third section of an act approved February thirteen, eighteen hundred and sixty-two, and every seaman, marine, and officer who has served in the Navy of the United States, or in the Marine Corps, during the rebellion, for ninety days, and who was honorably discharged, and has remained loyal to the Government, shall, on compliance with the provisions of this chapter, as hereinafter modified, be entitled to enter upon and receive patents for a quantity of public lands not exceeding one hundred and sixty acres, or one quarter-section, to be taken in compact form, according to legal subdivisions, including the alternate reserved sections of public lands along the line of any railroad or other public work, not otherwise reserved or appropriated, and other lands subject to entry under the homestead laws of the United States; but such homestead settler shall be allowed six months after locating his homestead, and filing his declaratory statement, within which to make his entry and commence his settlement and improvement.

8 June, 1872, s. 1, v. 17, p. 333.

SEC. 2305. The time which the homestead settler has served in the Army, Navy, or Marine Corps shall be deducted from the time heretofore required to perfect title, or if discharged on account of wounds received or disability incurred in the line of duty, then the term of enlistment shall be deducted from the time heretofore required to perfect title, without reference to the length of time he may have served; but no patent shall issue to any homestead settler who has not resided upon, improved, and cultivated his homestead for a period of at least one year after he shall have commenced his improvements.

*Ibid.*

<small>Deduction of military and naval service from time, &c.</small>

SEC. 2306. Every person entitled, under the provisions of section twenty-three hundred and four, to enter a homestead who may have heretofore entered, under the homestead laws, a quantity of land less than one hundred and sixty acres, shall be permitted to enter so much land as, when added to the quantity previously entered, shall not exceed one hundred and sixty acres.

*Ibid.*, s. 2.

<small>Persons who have entered less than 160 acres, rights of.</small>

SEC. 2307. In case of the death of any person who would be entitled to a homestead under the provisions of section twenty-three hundred and four, his widow, if unmarried, or in case of her death or marriage, then his minor orphan children, by a guardian duly appointed and officially accredited at the Department of the Interior, shall be entitled to all the benefits enumerated in this chapter, subject to all the provisions as to settlement and improvements therein contained; but if such person died during his term of enlistment, the whole term of his enlistment shall be deducted from the time heretofore required to perfect the title.

*Ibid.*, s. 3.

<small>Widow and minor children of persons entitled to homestead, &c.</small>

SEC. 2308. Where a party at the date of his entry of a tract of land under the homestead laws, or subsequently thereto, was actually enlisted and employed in the Army or Navy of the United States, his services therein shall, in the administration of such homestead laws, be construed to be equivalent, to all intents and purposes, to a residence for the same length of time upon the tract so entered. And if his entry has been canceled by reason of his absence from such tract while in the military or naval service of the United States, and such tract has not been disposed of, his entry shall be restored; but if such tract has been disposed of, the party may enter another tract subject to entry under the homestead laws, and his right to a patent therefor may be determined by the proofs touching his residence and cultivation of the first tract and his absence therefrom in such service.

*Ibid.*, s. 4.

<small>Actual service in the Army or Navy equivalent to residence, &c.</small>

SEC. 2309. Every soldier, sailor, marine, officer, or other person coming within the provisions of section twenty-three hundred and four, may, as well by an agent as in person, enter upon such homestead by filing a declaratory statement, as in pre-emption cases; but such claimant in person shall within the time prescribed make his actual entry, commence settlements and improvements on the same, and thereafter fulfill all the requirements of law.

*Ibid.*, s. 5, p. 334.

<small>Who may enter by agent.</small>

SEC. 2317. Every person having a homestead on the public domain, under the provisions of this chapter, who, at the end of the third year of his residence thereon, shall have had under cultivation, for two years, one acre of timber, the trees thereon not being more than twelve feet apart each way, and in a good, thrifty condition, for each and every sixteen acres of such homestead, shall, upon due proof of the fact by two credible witnesses, receive his patent for such homestead.

<small>Cultivation of trees on homestead tracts.</small>

<small>3 March, 1873, s. 4, v. 17, p. 606.
3 March, 1874, ch. 55, v. 18, p. 21.
3 March, 1875, ch. 151, v. 18, p. 481.
3 March, 1875, ch. 188, v. 18, p. 516.
20 May, 1876, ch. 102, v. 19, p. 54.</small>

## IMPORTATIONS, &c.

Sec.
1624. Importing in public vessels.
2491. Prohibition upon importation of obscene articles.

Sec.
2505. Articles exempt from duty.
2791. Public vessels need not enter.

**Title 15, Chap. 10.**
*Importing in public vessels.*

SEC. 1624, Art. 12. No person connected with the Navy shall, under any pretense, import in a public vessel any article which is liable to the payment of duty. [Sec. 2760, REVENUE-CUTTER SERVICE.]

30 July, 1846, s. 10, v. 9, p. 44.

**Title 33.**
*Prohibition upon importation of obscene articles.*

SEC. 2491. All persons are prohibited from importing into the United States, from any foreign country, any obscene book, pamphlet, paper, writing, advertisement, circular, print, picture, drawing, or other representation, figure, or image on or of paper or other material, or any cast, instrument, or other article of an immoral nature, or any drug or medicine, or any article whatever, for the prevention of conception, or for causing unlawful abortion. * * *

2 March, 1857, v. 11, p. 168.
3 March, 1873, ss. 1, 3, v. 17, p. 598.

*Articles exempt from duty.*

SEC. 2503. The following articles, when imported, shall be exempt from duty: .

\* \* \* \* \* \* \*

Articles imported for the use of the United States: *Provided*, That the price of the same did not include the duty.

\* \* \* \* \* \* \*

Books, engravings, bound or unbound, etchings, maps, and charts, which shall have been printed and manufactured more than twenty years at the date of importation.

\* \* \* \* \* \* \*

Books, maps and charts imported by authority or for the use of the United States. * * * But the duty shall not have been included in the contract or price paid.

\* \* \* \* \* \* \*

Books, household effects, or libraries or parts of libraries, in use of persons or families from foreign countries, if used abroad by them not less than one year, and not intended for any other person or persons, nor for sale.

Cabinets of coins, medals, and all other collections of antiquities; coins, gold, silver, and copper; * * * coffee and tea.

\* \* \* \* \* \* \*

Diamonds, rough or uncut, philosophical and scientific apparatus, instruments and preparations, statuary, casts of marble, bronze, alabaster, plaster of Paris, paintings, drawings, and etchings, specially imported in good faith for the use of any society or institution incorporated or established for religious, philosophical, educational, scientific or literary purposes, or encouragement of the fine arts, and not intended for sale.

\* \* \* \* \* \* \*

Regalia and gems, statues, statuary, and specimens of sculpture, where specially imported, in good faith, for the use of any society incorporated or established for philosophical, literary or religious purposes, or for the encouragement of the fine arts, or for the use or by order of any college, academy, school, seminary of learning, or public library in the United States.

\* \* \* \* \* \* \*

Specimens of natural history, botany, and mineralogy, when imported for cabinets or as objects of taste or science, and not for sale.

\* \* \* \* \* \* \*

Furs, undressed; furskins of all kinds, not dressed in any manner; wearing apparel, in actual use, and other personal effects (not merchandise), professional books, implements, instruments, and tools of trade, occupation, or employment of persons arriving in the United States. But this exemption shall not be construed to include machinery or other articles imported for use in any manufacturing establishment, or for sale.

Works of art, paintings, statuary, fountains, and other works of art, the production of American artists. But the fact of such production must be verified by the certificate of a consul or minister of the United States indorsed upon the written declaration of the artist; paintings, statuary, fountains, and other works of art, imported expressly for presentation to national institutions, or to any State, or to any municipal corporation, or religious corporation or society.

3 March, 1883, chap. 121, P. E. L., p. 514.

SEC. 2791. It shall not be necessary for the master of any vessel of war, or of any vessel employed by any prince, or state, as a public packet for the conveyance of letters and dispatches, and not permitted by the laws of such prince or state to be employed in the transportation of merchandise, in the way of trade, to make report and entry.

*Title 34, Chap. 4.*

*Public vessels need not enter.*

2 March, 1799, s. 31, v. 1, p. 651.

## LIFE-SAVING SERVICE.

Establishment of life-saving stations.
Employment of crews of surfmen.
Employment of volunteer crews.
Medals of honor for saving life.
Powers and compensation of keepers.
How long stations are to be open.
General superintendent.
Assistant superintendent.
Duties of superintendent.
Revenue Marine officers as inspectors.
Investigation of shipwrecks.
Volunteer crews compensated.
Drill and exercise.
Life-saving medals.

That the Secretary of the Treasury is hereby authorized to employ crews of experienced surfmen at such of the stations herein denominated complete stations, and at such of the life-boat stations on the Pacific coast as he may deem necessary and proper, for such periods, and at such compensation, not to exceed forty dollars per month, as he may deem necessary and reasonable.

*20 June, 1874.*

*Employment of crews of surfmen.*

20 June, 1874, chap. 344, s. 5, v. 18, p. 125.

That the Secretary of the Treasury may accept the services of volunteer crews of any of the life-boat stations herein authorized, who shall be subject to the rules and regulations governing the Life-Saving service; and a list of the names of each crew shall be kept in the office of the Secretary of the Treasury. Such volunteers shall receive no compensation, except a sum of not more than ten dollars each for every occasion upon which they shall have been instrumental in saving human life, and such of the medals herein authorized as they may be entitled to under the provisions hereinafter made: *Provided*, That no payment shall be made to any person who shall not have actually participated in the efforts to save the life or lives rescued. [See June 18, 1878.]

*Volunteer crews.*

*Ibid.*, s. 6.

That the Secretary of the Treasury is hereby directed to cause to be prepared medals of honor, with suitable devices, to be distinguished as life-saving medals of the first and second class, which shall be bestowed upon any persons who shall hereafter endanger their own lives in saving, or endeavoring to save lives from perils of the sea, within the United States, or upon any American vessel: *Provided*, That the medal of the first class shall be confined to cases of extreme and heroic daring; and that the medal of the second class shall be given in cases not sufficiently distinguished to deserve the medal of the first class: *Provided, also*, That no award of either medal shall be made to any person until sufficient evidence of his deserving shall have been filed with the Secretary of the Treasury and entered upon the records of the Department. [See June 18, 1878.]

*Medals of honor—*

*Of the first class;*
*Second class.*
*Proviso.*

\* \* \* \* \* \*

*Ibid.*, s. 7.

Hereafter the compensation of the keepers of life-saving and life-boat stations and houses of refuge shall be at the rate of four hundred dollars per annum; and they shall have the powers of inspectors of customs, but shall receive no additional compensation for duties performed as such: *Provided*, That said keepers shall have authority and be required to take charge of and protect all property saved from shipwreck at which they may be present, until it is claimed by parties legally authorized to receive it, or until otherwise instructed to dispose of it by the Secretary of the Treasury; and keepers of life-saving stations shall

*June 18, 1878.*

*Keepers; powers and compensation.*

*Custodians of property saved.*

# LIFE-SAVING SERVICE.

**Residence.** be required to reside continually at or in the immediate vicinity of their respective stations.

18 June, 1878, chap. 265, s. 4, v. 20, p. 163.

**Stations to be open, how long.** That hereafter the life-saving stations upon the sea and gulf coasts at which crews are employed shall be manned and the stations opened for active service on the first day of September in each year, and so continue until the first day of May succeeding, and upon the lake coasts from the opening to the close of navigation, except such stations as, in the discretion of the Secretary of the Treasury, are not necessary to be **Residence of** manned during the full period specified; and the crews shall reside at the **crews.** stations during said periods.

*Idem*, s. 5.

**General superintendent.** That the President of the United States may, by and with the consent of the Senate, appoint a suitable person, who shall be familiar with the various means employed in the Life-Saving Service for the saving of life and property from shipwrecked vessels, as general superintendent of the Life-Saving Service, who shall, under the immediate direction of the Secretary of the Treasury, have general charge of the service and of all administrative matters connected therewith, and whose compensation shall be at the rate of four thousand dollars per annum; and **Assistant superintendent.** the Secretary of the Treasury is authorized to appoint an assistant to the general superintendent, whose compensation shall be two thousand five hundred dollars per annum.

*Idem*, s 6.

**Duties of general superintendent.** That it shall be the duty of the general superintendent to supervise the organization and government of the employés of the service; to prepare and revise regulations therefor as may be necessary; to fix the number and compensation of surfmen to be employed at the several stations within the provisions of law; to supervise the expenditure of all appropriations made for the support and maintenance of the Life-Saving Service; to examine the accounts of disbursements of the district superintendents, and to certify the same to the accounting officers of the Treasury Department; to examine the property returns of the keepers of the several stations, and see that all public property thereto belonging is properly accounted for; to acquaint himself, as far as practicable, with all means employed in foreign countries which may seem to advantageously affect the interests of the service, and to cause to be properly investigated all plans, devices, and inventions for the improvement of life-saving apparatus for use at the stations, which may appear to be meritorious and available; to exercise supervision over the selection of sites for new stations the establishment of which may be authorized by law, or for old ones the removal of which may be made necessary by the encroachment of the sea or by other causes; to prepare and submit to the Secretary of the Treasury estimates for the support of the **1874, ch. 344.** service; to collect and compile the statistics of marine disasters contem-**18 Stat., 126.** plated by the act of June twentieth, eighteen hundred and seventy-four; and to submit to the Secretary of the Treasury, for transmission to Con-**Annual report.** gress, an annual report of the expenditures of the moneys appropriated for the maintenance of the Life-Saving Service, and of the operations of said service during the year.

*Idem*, s. 7.

**Revenue Marine officers as inspectors.** That the Secretary of the Treasury may detail such officer or officers of the Revenue Marine Service as may be necessary, to act as inspector and assistant inspectors of stations, who shall perform such duties in connection with the conduct of the service as may be required of them by the general superintendent.

*Idem*, s. 8.

**Investigation of shipwrecks with loss of life.** That upon the occurrence of any shipwreck within the scope of the operations of the Life-Saving Service, attended with loss of life, the general superintendent shall cause an investigation of all the circumstances connected with said disaster and loss of life to be made, with a view of ascertaining the cause of the disaster, and whether any of the officers or employés of the service have been guilty of neglect or misconduct in the premises; and any officer or clerk in the employment of the Treasury Department who may be detailed to conduct such investigation, or to examine into any alleged incompetency or misconduct of any of the officers or employés of the Life-Saving Service, shall have

# LIFE-SAVING SERVICE. 239

authority to administer an oath to any witness attending to testify or depose in the course of such investigation. — Administering oaths.

*Idem*, s. 9.

That section six of said act of June twentieth, eighteen hundred and seventy-four, is so amended as to extend the compensation of the enrolled members of volunteer crews of life-boat stations therein named to occasions of actual and deserving service at any shipwreck, or in the relief of any vessel in distress, and that such persons as may volunteer to take the place of any absent or disabled enrolled members of a crew, and who shall be accepted by the keeper, may be paid therefor, in the discretion of the Secretary of the Treasury, a sum not to exceed eight dollars each on every such occasion: *Provided*, That all crews and volunteers employed under authority of this act who may be present at a wreck shall be required to use their utmost endeavors to save life and properly care for the bodies of such as may perish, and, when such efforts are no longer necessary, to save property and protect the same, under the direction of the senior keeper present or of the superintendent of the district, until the arrival of persons legally authorized to take charge; and for the time employed in so saving and protecting property volunteers shall be entitled to compensation not to exceed three dollars per day each, in the discretion of the Secretary of the Treasury. — Volunteer crews Compensation. 1874, ch. 344. 18 Stat., 127. Duty of crews. Volunteers. Compensation for saving property.

*Idem*, s. 10.

That the enrolled members of the crews of life-boat stations may be called out for drill and exercise in the life-boat and life-saving apparatus as often as the general superintendent may determine, not to exceed twice a month, for each day's attendance at which they shall be entitled to the sum of three dollars each. — Drill and exercise.

*Idem*, s. 11.

That the Secretary of the Treasury is hereby authorized to bestow the life-saving medal of the second class upon persons making such signal exertions in rescuing and succoring the shipwrecked, and saving persons from drowning, as, in his opinion, shall merit such recognition. — Life-saving medals.

*Idem*, s. 12.

### MEMORANDUM.

An act of Sept. 30, 1854, chap. 90, v. 9, p. 533, provided for surf and life-boats for the preservation of life and property shipwrecked. The acts of Aug. 31, 1852, chap. 112, v. 10, p. 118, and March 3, 1853, chap. 97, v. 10, p. 200, provided for life-boats and other means of rendering assistance to wrecked mariners and others on the coasts of the United States; Aug. 4, 1854, chap. 242, v. 10, p. 563, authorized the purchase of metallic surf boats, to rescue lives and property, to be located at various ports on the lakes; Dec. 14, 1854, chap. 1, v. 10, p. 597, established life-saving stations on the coasts of Long Island and New Jersey; July 20, 1868, chap. 177, v. 15, p. 113, authorized a station on Narragansett Beach; April 20, 1871, chap. 21, v. 17, p. 12, authorized the employment of experienced surfmen; June 10, 1872, chap. 415, v. 17, p. 347, established stations at Cape Cod and Block Island; March 3, 1873, chap. 307, v. 17, p. 619, authorized ton stations on the coasts of New Hampshire, Massachusetts, Virginia, North Carolina, and other places deemed necessary; June 24, 1874, chap. 344, v. 18, p. 125, provided for a number of additional stations on the lakes and on the Atlantic and Pacific coasts; June 18, 1878, chap. 265, v. 20, p. 163, reorganized the Life-Saving Service, and established additional stations, and on the 30th June, 1882, there were 190 stations in commission.

## LIGHTS AND BUOYS.

Sec.
4653. Organization of the Light-House Board.
4654. President of the Board.
4655. Chairman.
4670. Light-house districts.
4671. Light-house inspectors.

Sec.
4678. Color of buoys prescribed.
4679. Restriction on compensation of officers, &c.
4680. Officers, &c., not to be interested in contracts.
———— Jurisdiction over certain rivers.

SEC. 4653. The President shall appoint two officers of the Navy, of high rank, two officers of the Corps of Engineers of the Army, and two civilians of high scientific attainments, whose services may be at the disposal of the President, together with an officer of the Navy and an officer of engineers of the Army, as secretaries, who shall constitute the Light-House Board. — Title 55. Organization of the Light-House Board.

31 Aug., 1852, s. 8, v. 10, p. 119.

SEC. 4654. The Secretary of the Treasury shall be ex-officio president of the Light-House Board. — President of the board.

*Ibid.*, s. 9.

MERCHANT VESSELS AND SERVICE. YACHTS.

**Chairman.**
SEC. 4655. The Light-House Board shall elect, by ballot, one of their number as chairman of the board, who shall preside at their meetings, when the president is absent, and shall perform such acts as may be prescribed by the rules of the board.
*Ibid.*

**Light-house districts.**
SEC. 4670. The Light-House Board shall arrange the Atlantic, Gulf, Pacific, and Lake coasts of the United States, into light-house districts, not exceeding twelve in number. [See *post*, June 23, 1874.]
*Ibid.*, s. 12.

**Light-house inspectors.**
SEC. 4671. An officer of the Army or Navy shall be assigned to each district as a light-house inspector, subject to the orders of the Light-House Board; and shall receive for such service the same pay and emoluments that he would be entitled to by law for the performance of duty in the regular line of his profession, and no other, except the legal allowance per mile, when traveling under orders connected with his duties.
*Ibid.*

**Color of buoys prescribed.**
SEC. 4678. All buoys along the coast, or in bays, harbors, sounds, or channels, shall be colored and numbered, so that passing up the coast or sound, or entering the bay, harbor, or channel, red buoys with even numbers shall be passed on the starboard hand, black buoys with uneven numbers on the port hand, and buoys with red and black stripes on either hand. Buoys in channel-ways shall be colored with alternate white and black perpendicular stripes.
28 Sept., 1850, s. 6, v. 9, p. 504.

**Restriction upon compensation of officers &c.**
SEC. 4679. No additional salary shall be allowed to any civil, military, or naval officer on account of his being employed on the Light-House Board, or being in any manner attached to the light-house service.
31 Aug., 1852, s. 17, v. 10, p. 120.

**Officers, &c., not to be interested in contracts.**
SEC. 4680. No member of the Light-House Board, inspector, light-keeper, or other person in any manner connected with the light-house service, shall be interested, either directly or indirectly, in any contract for labor, materials, or supplies for the light-house service, or in any patent, plan, or mode of construction or illumination, or in any article of supply for the light-house service.
*Ibid.*

**June 23, 1874.**
**Jurisdiction of Light-House Board extended. 1852, ch. 112, § 8, vol. x, p. 118.**
**Additional light-house districts.**
That the jurisdiction of the Light-House Board, created by the act entitled "An act making appropriations for light-houses, light-boats, buoys, and so forth, and providing for the erection and establishment of the same, and for other purposes," approved August thirty-first, eighteen hundred and fifty-two, is hereby extended over the Mississippi, Ohio, and Missouri Rivers, for the establishment of such beacon-lights, day-beacons, and buoys as may be necessary for the use of vessels navigating those streams; and for this purpose the said board is hereby required to divide the designated rivers into one or two additional light-house districts, to be in all respects similar to the already existing light-house districts; and is hereby authorized to lease the necessary ground for all such lights and beacons as are used to point out changeable channels, and which in consequence cannot be made permanent.
23 June, 1874, v. 18, p. 204.

## MERCHANT VESSELS AND SERVICE. YACHTS.

Sec.
4511. Shipping-articles.
4512. Rules for shipping-articles.
4513. Exceptions as to shipping-articles.
4514. Penalty for shipping without agreement.
4515. Penalty for knowingly shipping seamen without articles.
4516. Lost seamen may be replaced.
4517. Shipping seamen in foreign ports.
4518. Penalty for violating preceding section.
4538. Effects of deceased seamen.
4539. Proceedings in regard to effects.
4540. Penalty for neglect in regard to seamen's effects.
4541. Duties of consular officers in regard to deceased seamen's effects.
4548. Wages payable in gold.
4559. Appointment of inspectors by consul in foreign ports.
4560. Report of inspectors.
4561. Discharge of seamen on account of unseaworthiness of vessel.

Sec.
4562. Payment of charges for inspection.
4563. Refusal to pay wages, charges, and damages; penalty.
4565. Examination of provisions.
4566. Forfeiture for false complaint.
4567. Permission to enter complaint.
4577. Return of seamen.
4578. Penalty for refusal to receive seamen.
4579. Additional allowance for transportation of destitute seamen.
4580. Extra wages on discharge.
4581. Penalty for neglect to collect extra wages.
4582. Extra wages upon discharge in case of sale.
4583. When extra wages may be remitted.
4584. Disposal of extra wages.
4585. Protest upon impressment.
4600. Reclamation and discharge of deserters.
5363. Abandonment of mariners.

## SEAMEN.

SEC. 4511. The master of every vessel bound from a port in the United States to any foreign port other than vessels engaged in trade between the United States and the British North American possessions, or the West India Islands, or the Republic of Mexico, or of any vessel of the burden of seventy-five tons or upward, bound from a port on the Atlantic to a port on the Pacific, or vice versa, shall, before he proceeds on such voyage, make an agreement, in writing or in print, with every seaman whom he carries to sea as one of the crew, in the manner hereinafter mentioned; and every such agreement shall be, as near as may be, in the form given in the table marked A, in the schedule annexed to this Title, and shall be dated at the time of the first signature thereof, and shall be signed by the master before any seaman signs the same, and shall contain the following particulars: *Title 33, Chap. 2. Shipping-articles.*

First. The nature, and, as far as practicable, the duration of the intended voyage or engagement, and the port or country at which the voyage is to terminate.

Second. The number and description of the crew, specifying their respective employments.

Third. The time at which each seaman is to be on board, to begin work.

Fourth. The capacity in which each seaman is to serve.

Fifth. The amount of wages which each seaman is to receive.

Sixth. A scale of the provisions which are to be furnished to each seaman.

Seventh. Any regulations as to conduct on board, and as to fines, short allowance of provisions, or other lawful punishments for misconduct, which may be sanctioned by Congress as proper to be adopted, and which the parties agree to adopt.

Eighth. Any stipulations in reference to advance and allotment of wages, or other matters not contrary to law.

*7 June, 1872, s. 12, v. 17, p. 264.*
*15 Jan., 1873, v. 17, p. 410.*

SEC. 4512. The following rules shall be observed with respect to agreements: *Rules for shipping-articles.*

First. Every agreement, except such as are otherwise specially provided for, shall be signed by each seaman in the presence of a shipping-commissioner.

Second. When the crew is first engaged the agreement shall be signed in duplicate, and one part shall be retained by the shipping-commissioner, and the other part shall contain a special place or form for the description and signatures of persons engaged subsequently to the first departure of the ship, and shall be delivered to the master.

Third. Every agreement entered into before a shipping-commissioner shall be acknowledged and certified under the hand and official seal of such commissioner. The certificate of acknowledgment shall be indorsed on or annexed to the agreement; and shall be in the following form:

"State of ———, County of ———:

"On this ——— day of ———, personally appeared before me, a shipping-commissioner in and for the said county, A. B., C. D., and E. F., severally known to me to be the same persons who executed the foregoing instrument, who each for himself acknowledged to me that he had read or had heard read the same; that he was by me made acquainted with the conditions thereof, and understood the same; and that, while sober and not in a state of intoxication, he signed it freely and voluntarily, for the uses and purposes therein mentioned."

*7 June, 1872, s. 13, v. 17, p. 265.*

SEC. 4513. The section forty-five hundred and eleven shall not apply to masters of vessels where the seamen are by custom or agreement entitled to participate in the profits or result of a cruise or voyage, nor to masters of coastwise nor to masters of lake-going vessels that touch at foreign ports; but seamen may, by agreement, serve on board such vessels a definite time, or, on the return of any vessel to a port in the United States, may reship and sail in the same vessel on another voyage, without the payment of additional fees to the shipping-commissioner, by either the seaman or the master. *Exception as to shipping-articles.*

*Idem, s. 12, and 27 Feb., 1877, v. 19, p. 252.*

242    MERCHANT VESSELS AND SERVICE.    YACHTS.

Penalty for shipping without agreement.

SEC. 4514. If any person shall be carried to sea, as one of the crew on board of any vessel making a voyage as hereinbefore specified, without entering into an agreement with the master of such vessel, in the form and manner, and at the place and times in such cases required, the vessel shall be held liable for each such offense to a penalty of not more than two hundred dollars. But the vessel shall not be held liable for any person carried to sea, who shall have secretly stowed away himself without the knowledge of the master, mate, or of any of the officers of the vessel, or who shall have falsely personated himself to the master, mate, or officers of the vessel, for the purpose of being carried to sea.

7 June, 1872, s. 14, v. 17, p. 265.

Penalty for knowingly shipping seamen without articles.

SEC. 4515. If any master, mate, or other officer of a vessel knowingly receives, or accepts, to be entered on board of any merchant-vessel, any seaman who has been engaged or supplied contrary to the provisions of this Title, the vessel on board of which such seaman shall be found shall, for every such seaman, be liable to a penalty of not more than two hundred dollars.

*Ibid.*    U. S. v. Steamship City of Mexico, 11 Blatch., 489.

Lost seamen may be replaced.

SEC. 4516. In case of desertion, or of casualty resulting in the loss of one or more seamen, the master may ship a number equal to the number of whose services he has been deprived by desertion or casualty, and report the same to the United States consul at the first port at which he shall arrive, without incurring the penalty prescribed by the two preceding sections.

7 June, 1872, s. 14, v. 17, p. 265.

Shipping seamen in foreign ports.

SEC. 4517. Every master of a merchant-vessel who engages any seaman at a place out of the United States, in which there is a consular officer or commercial agent, shall, before carrying such seaman to sea, procure the sanction of such officer, and shall engage seamen in his presence; and the rules governing the engagement of seamen before a shipping-commissioner in the United States, shall apply to such engagements made before a consular officer or commercial agent; and upon every such engagement the consular officer or commercial agent shall indorse upon the agreement his sanction thereof, and an attestation to the effect that the same has been signed in his presence, and otherwise duly made.

*Ibid.*, s. 15.

Penalty for violating preceding section.

SEC. 4518. Every master who engages any seaman in any place in which there is a consular officer or commercial agent, otherwise than as required by the preceding section, shall incur a penalty of not more than one hundred dollars, for which penalty the vessel shall be held liable.

*Ibid.*

Title 53, Chap. 3.

Effects of deceased seamen.

SEC. 4538. Whenever any seaman or apprentice belonging to or sent home on any merchant-vessel, whether a foreign-going or domestic vessel, employed on a voyage which is to terminate in the United States, dies during such voyage, the master shall take charge of all moneys, clothes, and effects which he leaves on board, and shall, if he thinks fit, cause all or any of such clothes and effects to be sold by auction at the mast or other public auction, and shall thereupon sign an entry in the official log-book, and cause it to be attested by the mate and one of the crew, containing the following particulars:

First. A statement of the amount of money so left by the deceased.
Second. In case of a sale, a description of each article sold, and the sum received for each.
Third. A statement of the sum due to deceased as wages, and the total amount of deductions, if any, to be made therefrom.

7 June, 1872, s. 43, v. 17, p. 271.

Proceedings in regard to effects of deceased seamen.

SEC. 4539. In cases embraced by the preceding section, the following rules shall be observed:

First. If the vessel proceeds at once to any port in the United States, the master shall, within forty-eight hours after his arrival, deliver any such effects remaining unsold, and pay any money which he has taken charge of, or received from such sale, and the balance of wages due to the deceased, to the shipping-commissioner at the port of destination in the United States.

Second. If the vessel touches and remains at some foreign port before coming to any port in the United States, the master shall report the case to the United States consular officer there, and shall give to such officer any information he requires as to the destination of the vessel and probable length of the voyage; and such officer may, if he considers it expedient so to do, require the effects, money, and wages to be delivered and paid to him, and shall, upon such delivery and payment, give to the master a receipt; and the master shall within forty-eight hours after his arrival at his port of destination in the United States produce the same to the shipping-commissioner there. Such consular officer shall, in any such case, indorse and certify upon the agreement with the crew the particulars with respect to such delivery and payment.

Third. If the consular officer does not require such payment and delivery to be made to him, the master shall take charge of the effects, money, and wages, and shall, within forty-eight hours after his arrival at his port of destination in the United States, deliver and pay the same to the shipping-commissioner there.

Fourth. The master shall, in all cases in which any seaman or apprentice dies during the voyage or engagement, give to such officer or shipping-commissioner an account, in such form as they may respectively require, of the effects, money, and wages so to be delivered and paid; and no deductions claimed in such account shall be allowed unless verified by an entry in the official log-book, if there be any; and by such other vouchers, if any, as may be reasonably required by the officer or shipping-commissioner to whom the account is rendered.

Fifth. Upon due compliance with such of the provisions of this section as relate to acts to be done at the port of destination in the United States, the shipping-commissioner shall grant to the master a certificate to that effect. No officer of customs shall clear any foreign-going vessel without the production of such certificate.

*Ibid.*, s. 44.

SEC. 4540. Whenever any master fails to take such charge of the money or other effects of a seaman or apprentice during a voyage, or to make such entries in respect thereof, or to procure such attestation to such entries, or to make such payment or delivery of any money, wages, or effects of any seaman or apprentice dying during a voyage, or to give such account in respect thereof as is above directed, he shall be accountable for the money, wages, and effects of the seaman or apprentice to the circuit court in whose jurisdiction such port of destination is situate, and shall pay and deliver the same accordingly; and he shall, in addition, for every such offense, be liable to a penalty of not more than treble the value of the money or effects, or, if such value is not ascertained, not more than two hundred dollars; and if any such money, wages, or effects are not duly paid, delivered, and accounted for by the master, the owner of the vessel shall pay, deliver, and account for the same, and such money and wages and the value of such effects shall be recoverable from him accordingly; and if he fails to account for and pay the same, he shall, in addition to his liability for the money and value, be liable to the same penalty which is incurred by the master for a like offense; and all money, wages, and effects of any seaman or apprentice dying during a voyage shall be recoverable in the courts and by the modes of proceeding by which seamen are enabled to recover wages due to them.

*Penalty for neglect in regard to seaman's effects.*

*Ibid.*, s. 45.

SEC. 4541. Whenever any such seaman or apprentice dies at any place out of the United States, leaving any money or effects not on board of his vessel, the consular officer of the United States at or nearest the place shall claim and take charge of such money and effects, and shall, if he thinks fit, sell all or any of such effects, or any effects of any deceased seaman or apprentice delivered to him under the provisions of this Title, and shall quarterly remit to the district judge for the district embracing the port from which such vessel sailed, or the port where the voyage terminates, all moneys belonging to or arising from the sale of the effects or paid as the wages of any deceased seamen or apprentices which have come to his hands; and shall render such accounts thereof as the district judge requires.*

*Duties of consular officers in regard to deceased seaman's effects.*

*Ibid.*, s. 46.

---

* Unclaimed wages and effects, after six years, go to the fund for the relief of disabled and destitute seamen. § 4545.

Wages payable in gold.

Sec. 4548. Moneys paid under the laws of the United States, by direction of consular officers or agents, at any foreign port or place, as wages, extra or otherwise, due American seamen, shall be paid in gold or its equivalent, without any deduction whatever, any contract to the contrary notwithstanding.

3 March, 1873, v. 17, p. 602.

Title 53, Chap. 5.
———————
Appointment of inspectors by consul in foreign port.

Sec. 4559. Upon a complaint in writing, signed by the first, or the second and third officers and a majority of the crew, of any vessel while in a foreign port, that such vessel is in an unsuitable condition to go to sea, because she is leaky, or insufficiently supplied with sails, rigging, anchors, or any other equipment, or that the crew is insufficient to man her, or that her provisions, stores, and supplies are not, or have not been, during the voyage, sufficient and wholesome, thereupon, in any of these or like cases, the consul or a commercial agent who may discharge any duties of a consul, shall appoint two disinterested, competent, practical men, acquainted with maritime affairs, to examine into the causes of complaint, who shall, in their report, state what defects and deficiencies, if any, they find to be well founded, as well as what, in their judgment, ought to be done to put the vessel in order for the continuance of her voyage.

20 July, 1840, v. 5, p. 396.
20 July, 1850, s. 6, v. 9, p. 441.

Report of inspectors.

Sec. 4560. The inspectors appointed by any consul or commercial agent, in pursuance of the preceding section, shall have full power to examine the vessel and whatever is aboard of her, so far as is pertinent to their inquiry, and also to hear and receive any other proofs which the ends of justice may require; and if, upon a view of the whole proceedings, the consul or other commercial agent is satisfied therewith, he may approve the whole or any part of the report, and shall certify such approval; or if he dissents, he shall certify his reasons for dissenting.

20 July, 1840, v. 5, p. 396.

Discharge of seamen on account of unseaworthiness of vessel.

Sec. 4561. The inspectors in their report shall also state whether, in their opinion, the vessel was sent to sea unsuitably provided in any important or essential particular, by neglect or design, or through mistake or accident, and in case it was by neglect or design, and the consul or other commercial agent approves of such finding, he shall discharge such of the crew as require it, each of whom shall be entitled to three months' pay in addition to his wages to the time of discharge; but if, in the opinion of the inspectors, the defects or deficiencies found to exist have been the result of mistake or accident, and could not, in the exercise of ordinary care, have been known and provided against before the sailing of the vessel, and the master shall, in a reasonable time, remove or remedy the causes of complaint, then the crew shall remain and discharge their duty; otherwise they shall, upon their request, be discharged, and receive each one month's wages in addition to their pay up to the time of discharge.

*Ibid.*

Payment of charges for inspection.

Sec. 4562. The master shall pay all such reasonable charges for inspection under such complaint as shall be officially certified to him under the hand of the consul or commercial agent; but in case the inspectors report that the complaint is without any good or sufficient cause, the master may retain from the wages of the complainants, in proportion to the pay of each, the amount of such charges, with such reasonable damages for detention on that account as the consul or commercial agent directing the inquiry may officially certify.

*Ibid.*

Refusal to pay wages and charges; damages; penalty.

Sec. 4563. Every master who refuses to pay such wages and charges shall be liable to each person injured thereby in damages, to be recovered in any court of the United States in the district where such delinquent may reside or be found, and in addition thereto be punishable by a fine of one hundred dollars for each offense.

*Ibid.*, p. 397.

Examination of provisions.

Sec. 4565. Any three or more of the crew of any merchant-vessel of the United States bound from a port in the United States to any foreign port, or being of the burden of seventy-five tons or upward, and bound from a port on the Atlantic to a port on the Pacific, or vice versa, may complain to any officer in command of any of the vessels of the United States Navy, or consular officer of the United States, or shipping-commissioner or chief officer of the customs, that the provisions or water for the use of the crew are, at any time, of bad quality, unfit for use, or deficient in quantity. Such officer shall thereupon examine the provisions or water, or cause them to be examined; and if, on examination, such provisions or water are found to be of bad quality and unfit for use, or to be deficient in quantity, the person making such examination shall certify the same in writing to the master of the ship. If such master does not thereupon provide other proper provisions or water, where the same can be had, in lieu of any so certified to be of a bad quality and unfit for use, or does not procure the requisite quantity of any so certified to be insufficient in quantity, or uses any provisions or water which have been so certified as aforesaid to be of bad quality and unfit for use, he shall, in every such case, be liable to a penalty of not more than one hundred dollars; and upon every such examination the officers making or directing the same shall enter a statement of the result of the examination in the log-book, and shall send a report thereof to the district judge for the judicial district embracing the port to which such vessel is bound; and such report shall be received in evidence in any legal proceedings.

7 June, 1872, s. 36, v. 17, p. 269.

SEC. 4566. If the officer to whom any such complaint, in regard to the provisions or the water, is made, certifies in such statement that there was no reasonable ground for such complaint, each of the parties so complaining shall be liable to forfeit to the master or owner, out of his wages, a sum not exceeding one week's wages. *Forfeiture for false complaint.*

*Ibid.*, s. 37.

SEC. 4567. If any seaman, while on board any vessel, shall state to the master that they desire to make complaint, in accordance with the two preceding sections, in regard to the provisions or the water, to a competent officer, against the master, the master shall, if the vessel is then at a place where there is any such officer, so soon as the service of the vessel will permit, and if the vessel is not then at such a place, so soon after her first arrival at such place as the service of the vessel will permit, allow such seamen, or any of them, to go ashore, or shall send them ashore, in proper custody, so that they may be enabled to make such complaint; and shall, in default, be liable to a penalty of not more than one hundred dollars. *Permission to enter complaint.*

*Ibid.*, s. 38.

SEC. 4577. It shall be the duty of the consuls, vice-consuls, commercial agents, and vice-commercial agents, from time to time, to provide for the seamen of the United States, who may be found destitute within their districts, respectively, sufficient subsistence and passages to some port of the United States, in the most reasonable manner, at the expense of the United States, subject to such instructions as the Secretary of State shall give. The seamen shall, if able, be bound to do duty on board the vessels in which they may be transported, according to their several abilities. *Return of seamen.*

28 Feb., 1803, s. 4, v. 2, p. 204.

SEC. 4578. All masters of vessels belonging to citizens of the United States, and bound to some port of the same, are required to take such destitute seamen on board of their vessels, at the request of the consuls, vice-consuls, commercial agents, or vice-commercial agents, respectively, and to transport them to the port in the United States to which such vessel may be bound, on such terms, not exceeding ten dollars for each person, as may be agreed between the master and the consul or officer. Every such master who refuses the same on the request or order of such consul or officer shall be liable to the United States in a penalty of one hundred dollars for each seaman so refused. The certificate of any such consul or officer, given under his hand and official seal, shall be presumptive evidence of such refusal, in any court of law having jurisdiction for the recovery of the penalty. No master of any vessel shall, however, be obliged to take a greater number than two men to every one hundred tons burden of the vessel, on any one voyage. *Penalty for refusal to receive seamen.*

*Ibid.*

Additional allowance for transportation of destitute seamen.

Sec. 4579. Whenever distressed seamen of the United States are transported from foreign ports where there is no consular officer of the United States, to ports of the United States, there shall be allowed to the master or owner of each vessel, in which they are transported, such reasonable compensation, in addition to the allowance now fixed by law, as shall be deemed equitable by the First Comptroller of the Treasury.

28 Feb., 1811, v. 2, p. 651.

Extra wages on discharge.

Sec. 4580. Upon the application of any seaman to a consular officer for a discharge, if it appears to such officer that he is entitled to his discharge under any act of Congress, or according to the general principles or usages of maritime law, as recognized in the United States, the officer shall discharge such seaman; and shall require from the master of the vessel from which such discharge shall be made, the payment of three months' extra wages, over and above the wages which may then be due to such seaman. When, however, after a full hearing of both parties, the cause of discharge is found to be the misconduct of the seaman, the consular officer may remit so much of the extra wages as would be, by section forty-five hundred and eighty-four, payable to the seaman. [See § 1708, Diplomatic Officers.]

18 Aug., 1856, s. 26, v. 11, p. 62.
3 March, 1873, v. 17, p. 580.

Penalty for neglect to collect extra wages.

Sec. 4581. If any consular officer, when discharging any seaman, shall neglect to require the payment of and collect the extra wages required to be paid in the case of the discharge of any seaman, he shall be accountable to the United States for the full amount of their share of such wages, and to such seaman to the full amount of his share thereof; and if any seaman shall, after his discharge, have incurred any expense for board or other necessaries at the place of his discharge, before shipping again, such expense shall be paid out of the share of three months' wages to which he shall be entitled, which shall be retained for that purpose, and the balance only paid over to him.

18 Aug., 1856, s. 26, v. 11, p. 62.

Extra wages upon discharge, in case of sale.

Sec. 4582. Whenever a vessel belonging to a citizen of the United States is sold in a foreign country, and her company discharged, or when a seaman, a citizen of the United States, is, with his own consent, discharged in a foreign country, it shall be the duty of the master to produce to the consular officer, the certified list of his ship's company, and to pay such consul or officer, for every seaman so discharged, designated on such list as a citizen of the United States, three months' pay, over and above the wages which may then be due to such seaman.

28 Feb., 1803, s. 3, v. 2, p. 203.

When extra wages may be remitted.

Sec. 4583. No payment of extra wages shall be required upon the discharge of any seaman in cases where vessels are wrecked, or stranded, or condemned as unfit for service. If any consular officer, upon the complaint of any seaman that he has fulfilled his contract, or that the voyage is continued contrary to his agreement, is satisfied that the contract has expired, or that the voyage has been protracted by circumstances beyond the control of the master, and without any design on his part to violate the articles of shipment, then he may, if he deems it just, discharge the mariner without exacting the three months' additional pay. No payment of such extra wages, or any part thereof, shall be remitted in any case, except as allowed in this section.

20 July, 1840, v. 5, p. 395.
18 Aug., 1856, s. 26, v. 11, p. 62.

Disposal of extra wages.

Sec. 4584. Whenever any consular officer upon the discharge of any seaman demands or receives extra three months' wages for such seaman, two-thirds thereof shall be paid by such officer to the seaman so discharged, upon his engagement on board of any vessel to return to the United States. The remaining third shall be retained for the purpose of creating a fund for the payment of the passages of seamen, citizens of the United States, who may be desirous of returning to the United States, and for the maintenance of American seamen who may be destitute, and may be in such foreign port; and the several sums retained for such fund shall be accounted for with the Treasury every six months by the persons receiving the same.

*Idem* and 18 Feb., 1803, s. 3, v. 2, p. 203.

SEC. 4589. The master of every vessel of the United States, any of the crew whereof shall have been impressed or detained by any foreign power, shall, at the first port at which such vessel arrives, if such impressment or detention happened on the high seas, or if the same happened within any foreign port, then in the port in which the same happened, immediately make a protest, stating the manner of such impressment or detention, by whom made, together with the name and place of residence of the person impressed or detained; distinguishing also whether he was an American citizen; and, if not, to what nation he belonged. Such master shall also transmit, by post or otherwise, every such protest made in a foreign country, to the nearest consul or agent, or to the minister of the United States resident in such country, if any such there be; preserving a duplicate of such protest, to be by him sent immediately after his arrival within the United States to the Secretary of State, together with information to whom the original protest was transmitted. In case such protest shall be made within the United States, or in any foreign country, in which no consul, agent, or minister of the United States resides, the same shall, as soon thereafter as practicable, be transmitted by such master, by post or otherwise, to the Secretary of State. *Protest upon impressment.*

28 May, 1796, s. 4, v. 1, p. 477.

SEC. 4600. It shall be the duty of consular officers to reclaim deserters and discountenance insubordination by every means within their power; and where the local authorities can be usefully employed for that purpose, to lend their aid and use their exertions to that end, in the most effectual manner. In all cases where deserters are apprehended, the consular officer shall inquire into the facts; and if he is satisfied that the desertion was caused by unusual or cruel treatment, the seaman shall be discharged, and receive, in addition to his wages to the time of the discharge, three months' pay; and the officer discharging him shall enter upon the crew-list and shipping-articles the cause of discharge, and the particulars in which the cruelty or unusual treatment consisted, and subscribe his name thereto, officially. *Title 53, Chap. 7. Reclamation and discharge of deserters by consular officers.*

7 June, 1872, s. 56, v. 17, p. 275.

SEC. 5363. Every master or commander of any vessel belonging, in whole or part, to any citizen of the United States, who, during his being abroad, maliciously and without justifiable cause forces any officer or mariner of such vessel on shore, in order to leave him behind in any foreign port or place, or refuses to bring home again all such officers and mariners of such vessel whom he carried out with him as are in a condition to return and willing to return, when he is ready to proceed on his homeward voyage, shall be punished by a fine of not more than five hundred dollars, or by imprisonment not more than six months. *Title 70, Chap. 3. Forcible abandonment of officer or mariner in foreign port.*

3 March, 1825, s. 10, v. 4, p. 117.

NOTE.—The consular and diplomatic act passed July 1, 1882, appropriates $60,000 for the relief of American seamen in foreign countries.

## VESSELS.

Sec.
4131. What are vessels of the United States. By whom may be commanded.
4132. What vessels are entitled to register.
4133. Vessels owned by non-resident citizens.
4134. Vessels owned by non-resident naturalized citizens.
4135. American vessel taking foreign flag.
4136. Wrecked vessels.
4172. Failure to report sale to foreigner.
4177. Numbers for vessels.
4178. Names of vessels to be painted on stern.
4179. Change of name of registered vessel.
4180. Penalty for fraudulent registry.
4190. Sea-letters, to what vessels issued.
4191. Making or using forged sea-letters.
4204. Conveyance of bullion, &c.
4207. Rates of consular fees.

Sec.
4238. Vessels stranded on foreign coast.
4306. Passports of United States vessels on departure to foreign country.
4307. Penalty for departing without passport.
4308. Passports of unregistered vessels.
4309. Deposit of ship's papers with consul.
4310. Penalty for failure to deposit papers with consul.
4573. } List of crew to be delivered to collected.
4574.
4575. Rules as to crew list.
5358. Plundering wrecked vessels, &c.
5364. Conspiracy to cast away vessel.
5365. Owner destroying vessel at sea.
5366. Other person destroying vessel at sea.
5367. Attempt to destroy vessel at sea.
5423. Penalty for making false passports.

SEC. 4131. Vessels registered pursuant to law, and no others, except such as shall be duly qualified, according to law, for carrying on the coasting trade and fisheries, or one of them, shall be deemed vessels of the United States, and entitled to the benefits and privileges appertain- *Title 48, Chap. 1. What are vessels of the United States.*

248    MERCHANT VESSELS AND SERVICE.    YACHTS.

By whom may be commanded.
ing to such vessels; but they shall not enjoy the same longer than they shall continue to be wholly owned by citizens and to be commanded by a citizen of the United States. And officers of vessels of the United States shall in all cases be citizens of the United States.

31 Dec., 1792. s. 1, v. 1, p. 287.

[NOTE.—An act approved April 17, 1874, chap. 107, v. 18, p. 30, provides that any alien, who in the manner provided for by law, has declared his intention of becoming a citizen of the United States, and who may have been a permanent resident of the United States for at least six months immediately previous to the granting of such license, may be licensed, as if already naturalized, as an engineer or pilot upon any steam vessel subject to inspection under the provisions of the act of Feb. 28, 1871, v. 16, p. 440.

An act approved April 18, 1874, chap. 110, v. 18, p. 31, exempts canal boats or boats employed on the internal waters or canals of any State, excepting such as are provided with sails or propelling machinery of their own adapted to lake or coastwise navigation and such as are employed in trade with the Canadas, from the provisions of the act of Feb. 18, 1793, and from the payment of all customs and other fees under any act of Congress.]

What vessels are entitled to register.
SEC. 4132. Vessels built within the United States, and belonging wholly to citizens thereof, and vessels which may be captured in war by citizens of the United States, and lawfully condemned as prize, or which may be adjudged to be forfeited for a breach of the laws of the United States, being wholly owned by citizens, and no others, may be registered as directed in this Title.

*Idem*, s. 2, p. 288.

Vessels owned by non-resident citizens.
SEC. 4133. No vessel shall be entitled to be registered, or, if registered, to the benefits of registry, if owned in whole or in part by any citizen of the United States who usually resides in a foreign country, during the continuance of such residence, unless such citizen be a consul of the United States, or an agent for and a partner in some house of trade or copartnership, consisting of citizens of the United States actually carrying on trade within the United States.

*Ibid.*

Vessels owned by non-resident naturalized citizens.
SEC. 4134. No vessel shall be entitled to be registered as a vessel of the United States, or, if registered, to the benefits of registry, if owned in whole or in part by any person naturalized in the United States, and residing for more than one year in the country from which he originated, or for more than two years in any foreign country, unless such person be a consul or other public agent of the United States. Nothing contained in this section shall be construed to prevent the registering anew of any vessel before registered, in case of a sale thereof in good faith to any citizen resident in the United States; but satisfactory proof of the citizenship of the person on whose account a vessel may be purchased shall be exhibited to the collector, before a new register shall be granted for such vessel.

27 March, 1804, s. 1, v. 2, p. 296.

American vessel taking foreign flag.
SEC. 4135. No vessel which has been recorded or registered as an American vessel of the United States, pursuant to law, and which was licensed or otherwise authorized to sail under a foreign flag, and to have the protection of any foreign government during the existence of the rebellion, shall be deemed or registered as a vessel of the United States, or shall have the rights and privileges of vessels of the United States, except under provisions of law especially authorizing such registry.

10 Feb., 1866, ch. 8, v. 14, p. 3.

Wrecked vessels.
SEC. 4136. The Secretary of the Treasury may issue a register or enrollment for any vessel built in a foreign country, whenever such vessel shall be wrecked in the United States, and shall be purchased and repaired by a citizen of the United States, if it shall be proved to the satisfaction of the Secretary that the repairs put upon such vessel are equal to three-fourths of the cost of the vessel when so repaired.

23 Dec., 1852, ch. 4, v. 10, p. 149.
23 July, 1866, ch. 213, v. 14, p. 212.

Failure to report sale to foreigners.
SEC. 4172. If any vessel registered as a vessel of the United States shall be sold or transferred, in whole or in part, by way of trust, confidence, or otherwise, to a subject or citizen of any foreign prince or state, and such sale or transfer shall not be made known, as hereinbefore directed, such vessel, together with her tackle, apparel, and furniture, shall be forfeited. If such vessel, however, be so owned in part only, and it is made to appear to the jury before whom the trial for such for-

feiture is had, that any other owner of such vessel, being a citizen of the United States, was wholly ignorant of the sale or transfer to or ownership of such foreign subject or citizen, the share or interest of such citizen of the United States shall not be subject to such forfeiture, and the residue only shall be so forfeited.

31 Dec., 1792, s. 16, v. 1, p. 295.

SEC. 4177. The Secretary of the Treasury shall have power, under such regulations as he shall prescribe, to establish and provide a system of numbering vessels so registered, enrolled, and licensed; and each vessel so numbered shall have her number deeply carved or otherwise permanently marked on her main beam; and if at any time she shall cease to be so marked, such vessel shall be no longer recognized as a vessel of the United States. *Numbers for vessels.*

28 July, 1866, s. 13, v. 14, p. 331.

SEC. 4178. The name of every registered vessel, and of the port to which she shall belong, shall be painted on her stern, on a black ground, in white letters, of not less than three inches in length.* If any vessel of the United States shall be found without having her name and the name of the port to which she belongs so painted, the owner or owners shall be liable to a penalty of fifty dollars; recoverable one-half to the person giving the information thereof; the other half to the use of the United States. *Names of vessels to be painted on stern.*

31 Dec., 1792, s. 3, v. 1, p. 288.

SEC. 4179. No master, owner, or agent of any vessel of the United States shall in any way change the name of such vessel, or by any device, advertisement, or contrivance to deceive or attempt to deceive the public, or any officer or agent of the United States, or of any State, or any corporation or agent thereof, or any person or persons, as to the true name or character of such vessel, on pain of the forfeiture of such vessel. *Change of name of registered vessel.*

5 May, 1864, s. 2, v. 13, p. 64.

SEC. 4189. Whenever any certificate of registry, enrollment, or license, or other record or document granted in lieu thereof, to any vessel, is knowingly and fraudulently obtained or used for any vessel not entitled to the benefit thereof, such vessel, with her tackle, apparel, and furniture, shall be liable to forfeiture. *Penalty for fraudulent registry.*

18 July, 1866, s. 24, v. 14, p. 184.

SEC. 4190. No sea-letter or other document certifying or proving any vessel to be the property of a citizen of the United States shall be issued, except to vessels duly registered, or enrolled and licensed as vessels of the United States, or to vessels which shall be wholly owned by citizens of the United States, and furnished with or entitled to sea-letters or other custom-house documents. *Sea-letters, to what vessels issued.*

26 March, 1810, v. 2, p. 568.

SEC. 4191. Every person who knowingly makes, utters, or publishes any false sea-letter, Mediterranean passport, or certificate of registry, or who knowingly avails himself of any such Mediterranean passport, sea-letter, or certificate of registry, shall be liable to a penalty of not more than five thousand dollars, and, if an officer of the United States, shall thenceforth be incapable of holding any office of trust or profit under the authority of the United States. *Making or using forged sea-letter, &c.*

2 March, 1803, s. 1, v. 2, p. 209.

SEC. 4204. All vessels belonging to citizens of the United States, and bound from any port in the United States to any other port therein, or to any foreign port, or from any foreign port to any port in the United States, shall, before clearance, receive on board all such bullion, coin, United States notes and bonds and other securities, as the Government of the United States or any department thereof, or any minister, consul, vice-consul, or commercial or other agent of the United States abroad, shall offer, and shall securely convey and promptly deliver the same to the proper authorities or consignees, on arriving at the port of destination; and shall receive for such service such reasonable compensation as may be allowed to other carriers in the ordinary transactions of business. *Title 48, Chap. 2. Conveyance of bullion, coin, &c., for the United States.*

4 July, 1864, s. 10, v. 13, p. 302.

---

* An act approved June 23, 1874, v. 18, p. 252, allows the name to be painted on her stern in yellow or gilt letters.

250 MERCHANT VESSELS AND SERVICE. YACHTS.

**Copy of rates of consular fees to be annexed to clearance.**

SEC. 4207. Whenever any clearance is granted to any vessel of the United States, duly registered as such, and bound on any foreign voyage, the collector of the district shall annex thereto, in every case, a copy of the rates or tariffs of fees which diplomatic and consular officers are entitled, by the regulations prescribed by the President, to receive for their services.

18 Aug., 1856, s. 16, v. 11, p. 57.

**Title 48, Chap. 5.**

**Vessels stranded on foreign coasts.**

SEC. 4238. Consuls and vice-consuls, in cases where vessels of the United States are stranded on the coasts of their consulates respectively, shall, as far as the laws of the country will permit, take proper measures, as well for the purpose of saving the vessels, their cargoes and appurtenances, as for storing and securing the effects and merchandise saved, and for taking inventories thereof; and the merchandise and effects saved, with the inventories thereof so taken, shall, after deducting therefrom the expenses, be delivered to the owners. No consul or vice-consul shall have authority to take possession of any such merchandise, or other property, when the master, owner, or consignee thereof is present or capable of taking possession of the same.

14 April, 1792, s. 3, v. 1, p. 255.

**Title 49.**

**Passports of United States vessels on departure to foreign country.**

SEC. 4306. Every vessel of the United States, going to any foreign country, shall, before she departs from the United States, at the request of the master, be furnished by the collector for the district where such vessel may be, with a passport, the form for which shall be prescribed by the Secretary of State. In order to be entitled to such passport, the master of every such vessel shall be bound, with sufficient sureties, to the Treasurer of the United States, in the penalty of two thousand dollars, conditioned that the passport shall not be applied to the use or protection of any other vessel than the one described in it; and that, in case of the loss or sale of any vessel having such passport, the same shall, within three months, be delivered up to the collector from whom it was received, if the loss or sale take place within the United States; or within six months, if the same shall happen at any place nearer than the Cape of Good Hope; and within eighteen months, if at a more distant place.

1 June, 1796, ss. 1, 2, v. 1, p. 489.
12 Feb., 1831, v. 4, p. 441.

**Penalty for departure without passport.**

SEC. 4307. If any vessel of the United States shall depart therefrom, and shall be bound to any foreign country, other than to some port in America, without such passport, the master of such vessel shall be liable to a penalty of two hundred dollars for every such offense.

1 June, 1796, s. 4, v. 1, p. 490.

**Passports of unregistered vessels.**

SEC. 4308. Every unregistered vessel owned by a citizen of the United States, and sailing with a sea-letter, going to any foreign country, shall, before she departs from the United States, at the request of the master, be furnished by the collector of the district where such vessel may be with a passport, for which the master shall be subject to the rules and conditions prescribed for vessels of the United States.

2 March, 1803, s. 1, v. 2, p. 208.

**Deposit of ship's papers with consul.**

SEC. 4309. Every master of a vessel, belonging to citizens of the United States, who shall sail from any port of the United States, shall, on his arrival at a foreign port, deposit his register, sea-letter, and Mediterranean passport with the consul, vice-consul, commercial agent, or vice-commercial agent, if any there be at such port; and it shall be the duty of such consul, vice-consul, commercial agent, or vice-commercial agent, on such master or commander producing to him a clearance from the proper officer of the port where his vessel may be, to deliver to the master all of his papers, if such master or commander has complied with the provisions of law relating to the discharge of seamen in a foreign country, and to the payment of the fees of consular officers.

28 Feb., 1803, s. 2, v. 2, p. 203.

**Penalty for failure to deposit papers with consul.**

SEC. 4310. Every master of any such vessel who refuses or neglects to deposit the papers as required by the preceding section, shall be liable to a penalty of five hundred dollars, to be recovered by such consul, vice-consul, commercial agent, or vice-commercial agent, in his own name, for the benefit of the United States, in any court of competent jurisdiction.

*Ibid.*

SEC. 4573. Before a clearance is granted to any vessel bound on a foreign voyage or engaged in the whale-fishery, the master thereof shall deliver to the collector of the customs a list containing the names, places of birth and residence, and description of the persons who compose his ship's company; to which list the oath of the captain shall be annexed, that the list contains the names of his crew, together with the places of their birth and residence, as far as he can ascertain them; and the collector shall deliver him a certified copy thereof, for which the collector shall be entitled to receive the sum of twenty-five cents.

Title 53, Chap. 5.
List of crew to be delivered to collector.

28 Feb., 1803, s. 1, v. 9, p. 203.
4 April, 1840, s. 2, v. 2, p. 370.

SEC. 4574. In all cases of private vessels of the United States sailing from a port in the United States to a foreign port, the list of the crew shall be examined by the collector for the district from which the vessel shall clear, and, if approved of by him, shall be certified accordingly. No person shall be admitted or employed on board of any such vessel unless his name shall have been entered in the list of the crew, approved and certified by the collector for the district from which the vessel shall clear. The collector, before he delivers the list of the crew, approved and certified, to the master or proper officer of the vessel to which the same belongs, shall cause the same to be recorded in a book by him for that purpose to be provided, and the record shall be open for the inspection of all persons, and a certified copy thereof shall be admitted in evidence in any court in which any question may arise under any of the provisions of this Title.

3 March, 1813, s. 3, v. 2, p. 809.

SEC. 4575. The following rules shall be observed with reference to vessels bound on any foreign voyage:

Rules as to list of crew.

First. The duplicate list of the ship's company, required to be made out by the master and delivered to the collector of the customs, under section forty-five hundred and seventy-three, shall be a fair copy in one uniform handwriting, without erasure or interlineation.

Second· It shall be the duty of the owners of every such vessel to obtain from the *collector of the customs of* the district from which the clearance is made, a true and certified copy of the shipping-articles, containing the names of the crew, which shall be written in a uniform hand, without erasures or interlineations.

Third. These documents, which shall be deemed to contain all the conditions of contract with the crew as to their service, pay, voyage, and all other things, shall be produced by the master, and laid before any consul, or other commercial agent of the United States, whenever he may deem their contents necessary to enable him to discharge the duties imposed upon him by law toward any mariner applying to him for his aid or assistance.

Fourth. All interlineations, erasures, or writing in a hand different from that in which such duplicates were originally made, shall be deemed fraudulent alterations, working no change in such papers, unless satisfactorily explained in a manner consistent with innocent purposes and the provisions of law which guard the rights of mariners.

Fifth. If any master of a vessel shall proceed on a foreign voyage without the documents herein required, or refuse to produce them when required, or to perform the duties imposed by this section, or shall violate the provisions thereof, he shall be liable to each and every individual injured thereby in damages, to be recovered in any court of the United States in the district where such delinquent may reside or be found, and in addition thereto be punishable by a fine of one hundred dollars for each offense.

Sixth. It shall be the duty of the boarding-officer to report all violations of this section to the collector of the port where any vessel may arrive, and the collector shall report the same to the Secretary of the Treasury and to the United States attorney in his district.

20 July, 1840, ch. 48, v. 5, pp. 394, 395, 397.
27 Feb., 1877, v. 19, p. 252.

| | |
|---|---|
| Title 70, Chap. 3.<br>Plundering wrecked vessels, &c. | SEC. 5358. Every person who plunders, steals, or destroys any money, goods, merchandise, or other effects, from or belonging to any vessel in distress, or wrecked, lost, stranded, or cast away, upon the sea, or upon any reef, shoal, bank, or rocks of the sea, or in any other place within the admiralty and maritime jurisdiction of the United States; and every person who willfully obstructs the escape of any person endeavoring to save his life from such vessel, or the wreck thereof; and every person who holds out or shows any false light, or extinguishes any true light, with intent to bring any vessel, sailing upon the sea, into danger, or distress, or shipwreck, shall be punished by a fine of not more than five thousand dollars, and imprisoned at hard labor not more than ten years. |

3 March, 1825, s. 9, v. 4, p. 116.

| | |
|---|---|
| Conspiracy to cast away vessel. | SEC. 5364. Every person who, on the high seas, or within the United States, willfully and corruptly conspires, combines, and confederates with any other person, such other person being either within or without the United States, to cast away or otherwise destroy any vessel, with intent to injure any person that may have underwritten or may thereafterward underwrite any policy of insurance thereon or on goods on board thereof, or with intent to injure any person that has lent or advanced, or may lend or advance, any money on such vessel on bottomry or respondentia; and every person who, within the United States, builds, or fits out, or aids in building and fitting out, any vessel with intent that the same be cast away or destroyed with the intent hereinbefore mentioned, shall be punished by a fine of not more than ten thousand dollars, and by imprisonment at hard labor not more than ten years. |

Ibid., s. 23, p. 122.

| | |
|---|---|
| Owner destroying vessel at sea. | SEC. 5365. Every person who, on the high seas, willfully and corruptly casts away or otherwise destroys any vessel of which he is owner, in whole or part, with intent to prejudice any person that may underwrite any policy of insurance thereon, or any merchant that may have goods thereon, or any other owner of such vessel, shall suffer death. [See § 5323, PIRACY.] |

26 March, 1804, s. 2, v. 2 p. 290.

| | |
|---|---|
| Other persons destroying vessel at sea, | SEC. 5366. Every person, not being an owner, who, on the high seas, willfully and corruptly casts away or otherwise destroys any vessel to which he belongs, being the property of any citizen, shall suffer death. [See § 5323, PIRACY.] |

2 March, 1804, s. 1, v. 2, p. 290.<br>3 March, 1875, v. 18, p. 479. See p. 229.

| | |
|---|---|
| Attempt to destroy vessel at sea. | SEC. 5367. Every person, not being an owner, who, on the high seas, willfully, with intent to destroy the same, sets fire to any vessel, or otherwise attempts the destruction thereof, being the property of any citizen, shall suffer imprisonment at hard labor for a term not more than ten years nor less than three years. |

29 July, 1850, s. 7, v. 9, p. 441.

| | |
|---|---|
| Title 70, Chap. 5.<br>Forging or altering ship's papers or custom-house documents. | SEC. 5423. If any person falsely makes, forges, counterfeits, or alters any instrument in imitation of, or purporting to be, an abstract or official copy, or certificate of the recording, registry, or enrollment of any vessel, in the office of any collector of the customs, or a license to any vessel, for carrying on the coasting trade, or fisheries of the United States, or a certificate of ownership, pass, passport, sea-letter, or clearance, granted for any vessel, under the authority of the United States, or a permit, debenture, or other official document granted by any collector or other officer of the customs, by virtue of his office; or passes, utters, or publishes, or attempts to pass, utter, or publish, as true, any such false, forged, counterfeited, or falsely altered instrument, abstract, official copy, certificate, license, pass, passport, sea-letter, clearance, permit, debenture, or other official document herein specified, knowing the same to be false, forged, counterfeited, or falsely altered, with an intent to defraud, he shall be punished by a fine of not more than one thousand dollars, and by imprisonment at hard labor not more than three years. [See § 4191.] |

3 March, 1825, s. 19, v. 4, p. 120.

## YACHTS.

**SEC. 4214.** The Secretary of the Treasury may cause yachts used and employed exclusively as pleasure vessels or designed as models of naval architecture, if built and owned in compliance with the provisions of sections forty-one hundred and thirty-three to forty-one hundred and thirty-five, to be licensed on terms which will authorize them to proceed from port to port of the United States, and by sea to foreign ports, without entering or clearing at the custom house, such license shall be in such form as the Secretary of the Treasury may prescribe. The owner of any such vessel, before taking out such license, shall give a bond in such form and for such amount as the Secretary of the Treasury shall prescribe, conditioned that the vessel shall not engage in any trade, nor in any way violate the revenue laws of the United States; and shall comply with the laws in all other respects. Such vessels, so enrolled and licensed, shall not be allowed to transport merchandise or carry passengers for pay. Such vessels shall have their name and port placed on some conspicuous portion of their hulls. Such vessels shall in all respects, except as above, be subject to the laws of the United States, and shall be liable to seizure and forfeiture for any violation of the provisions of this title: *Provided*, That all charges for license and inspection fees for any pleasure vessel or yacht shall not exceed five dollars, and for admeasurement shall not exceed ten cents per ton.

*Title 48, Chap. 2.* — License of yachts.

7 Aug., 1848, s. 2, v. 9, p. 274.
20 June, 1870, s. 1, v. 16, p. 171.
3 March, 1883, ch. 133, v. 22, p. 566.

**SEC. 4215.** All such licensed yachts shall use a signal of the form, size, and colors prescribed by the Secretary of the Navy; and the owners thereof, shall at all times permit the naval architects in the employ of the United States to examine and copy the models of such yachts.

Signals of yachts.

7 Aug., 1848, s. 3, v. 9, p. 274.

**SEC. 4216.** Yachts, belonging to a regularly organized yacht club of any foreign nation which shall extend like privileges to the yachts of the United States, shall have the privilege of entering or leaving any port of the United States without entering or clearing at the customhouse thereof, or paying tonnage tax.

Yachts belonging to foreign yacht-clubs.

29 June, 1870, s. 2, v. 16, p. 170.

**SEC. 4217.** For the identification of yachts and their owners, a commission to sail for pleasure in any designated yacht belonging to any regularly organized and incorporated yacht club, stating the exemptions and privileges enjoyed under it, may be issued by the Secretary of the Treasury, and shall be a token of credit to any United States official, and to the authorities of any foreign power, for privileges enjoyed under it.

Commissions to yachts.

*Ibid.*, s. 3.

**SEC. 4218.** Every yacht visiting a foreign country under the provisions of the four preceding sections shall, on her return to the United States, make due entry at the custom-house of the port at which, on such return, she shall arrive.

Entry of yachts.

*Ibid.*, s. 4, p. 171.

## MURDER, MANSLAUGHTER, MAIMING, MUTINY, &c.

Sec.
1624. Art. 6. Murder by persons on public vessels.
5325. Punishment of death by hanging.
5326. No conviction to work corruption of blood or forfeiture of estate.
5327. Whipping and the pillory abolished.
5328. Jurisdiction of State courts.
5329. Benefit of clergy.
5330. Pardoning power.
5339. Murder.
5340. Delivery of offender's body for dissection, when.
5341. Manslaughter.
5342. Attempt to commit murder or manslaughter.

Sec.
5343. Punishment of manslaughter.
5344. Officers and owners of steamboats through whose misconduct, &c., life is lost.
5345. Rape.
5346. Assault with a dangerous weapon.
5347. Maltreatment of crew by officers of vessels.
5348. Maiming, &c.
1624. Mutiny in the Navy.
5359. Inciting revolt or mutiny on shipboard.
5360. Revolt and mutiny on shipboard.
5390. Misprison of felony.
5391. Offenses committed in places ceded to the United States.

**SEC. 1624. ART. 6.** If any person belonging to any public vessel of the United States commits the crime of murder without the territorial jurisdiction thereof, he may be tried by court-martial and punished with death.

*Title 15, Chap. 10.* — Murder.

17 July, 1862, s. 1, v. 12, p. 602.

| | |
|---|---|
| Title 70, Chap. 1.<br>Punishment of death by hanging. | SEC. 5325. The manner of inflicting the punishment of death shall be by hanging. [See § 5340.]<br>30 April, 1790, s. 33, v. 1, p. 110. |
| No conviction to work corruption of blood or forfeiture of estate. | SEC. 5326. No conviction or judgment shall work corruption of blood or any forfeiture of estate.<br>*Ibid.*, s. 24, p. 117. |
| Whipping and the pillory abolished. | SEC. 5327. The punishment of whipping and of standing in the pillory shall not be inflicted.<br>28 Feb., 1839, s. 5, v. 5, p. 322. |
| Jurisdiction of State courts. | SEC. 5328. Nothing in this Title shall be held to take away or impair the jurisdiction of the courts of the several States under the laws thereof.<br>3 March, 1795, s. 26, v. 4, p. 122. |
| Benefit of clergy. | SEC. 5329. The benefit of clergy shall not be used or allowed, upon conviction of any crime for which the punishment is death.<br>30 April, 1790, s. 31, v. 1, p. 119. |
| Pardoning power. | SEC. 5330. Whenever, by the judgment of any court or judicial officer of the United States, in any criminal proceeding, any person is sentenced to two kinds of punishment, the one pecuniary and the other corporal, the President shall have full discretionary power to pardon or remit, in whole or in part, either one of the two kinds, without, in any manner, impairing the legal validity of the other kind, or of any portion of either kind, not pardoned or remitted.<br>20 Feb., 1863, s. 1, v. 12, p. 656. |
| Title 70, Chap. 3.<br>Murder. | SEC. 5339. Every person who commits murder—<br>First. Within any fort, arsenal, dock-yard, magazine, or in any other place or district of country under the exclusive jurisdiction of the United States;<br>Second. Or upon the high seas, or in any arm of the sea, or in any river, haven, creek, basin, or bay within the admiralty and maritime jurisdiction of the United States, and out of the jurisdiction of any particular State;<br>Third. Or who upon any of such waters maliciously strikes, stabs, wounds, poisons, or shoots at any other person, of which striking, stabbing, wounding, poisoning, or shooting such other person dies, either on land or at sea, within or without the United States, shall suffer death. [See § 5326.]<br>30 April, 1790, s. 3, v. 1, p. 113.<br>3 March, 1825, s. 4, v. 4, p. 115. |
| Delivery of offender's body for dissection, when. | SEC. 5340. The court before which any person is convicted of murder, may, in its discretion, add to the judgment of death, that the body of the offender be delivered to a surgeon for dissection; and the marshal who executes such judgment shall deliver the body, after execution, to such surgeon as the court may direct; and such surgeon, or some person by him appointed, shall receive and take away the body at the time of execution.<br>30 April, 1790, s. 4, v. 1, p. 113. |
| Manslaughter. | SEC. 5341. Every person who, within any of the places or upon any of the waters described in section fifty-three hundred and thirty-nine, unlawfully and wilfully, but without malice, strikes, stabs, wounds, or shoots at, or otherwise injures another, of which striking, stabbing, wounding, shooting, or other injury such other person dies, either on land or sea, within or without the United States, is guilty of the crime of manslaughter.<br>*Ibid.*, s. 7.<br>3 March, 1857, s. 1, v. 11, p. 250. |
| Attempt to commit murder or manslaughter | SEC. 5342. Every person who, within any of the places or upon any of the waters described in section fifty-three hundred and thirty-nine, attempts to commit the crime of murder or manslaughter, by any means not constituting the offense of assault with a dangerous weapon, shall be punished by imprisonment, with or without hard labor, not more than three years, and by a fine of not more than one thousand dollars.<br>3 March, 1857, s. 2, v. 11, p. 250. |

Sec. 5343. The punishment of manslaughter shall be imprisonment, not exceeding ten years and a fine not exceeding one thousand dollars, except as otherwise specially provided by law.   *Punishment of manslaughter.*

30 April, 1790, s. 7, v. 1, p. 113.
3 March, 1857, s. 3, v. 11, p. 250.
3 March, 1875, s. 1, 2, v. 18, p. 138.

Sec. 5344. Every captain, engineer, pilot, or other person employed on any steamboat or vessel, by whose misconduct, negligence, or inattention to his duties on such vessel, the life of any person is destroyed, and every owner, inspector, or other public officer, through whose fraud, connivance, misconduct, or violation of law, the life of any person is destroyed, shall be deemed guilty of manslaughter, and, upon conviction thereof before any circuit court of the United States, shall be sentenced to confinement at hard labor for a period of not more than ten years.   *Officer's and owners of steamboats through whose misconduct, &c., life is lost, guilty of manslaughter.*

28 Feb., 1871, s. 57, v. 16, p. 456.

Sec. 5345. Every person who, within any of the places or upon any of the waters specified in section fifty-three hundred and thirty-nine, commits the crime of rape shall suffer death.   *Rape.*

3 March, 1825, s. 4, v. 4, p. 115.

Sec. 5346. Every person who, upon the high seas, or in any arm of the sea, or in any river, haven, creek, basin, or bay, within the admiralty jurisdiction of the United States, and out of the jurisdiction of any particular State, on board any vessel belonging in whole or part to the United States, or any citizen thereof, with a dangerous weapon, or with intent to perpetrate any felony, commits an assault on another shall be punished by a fine of not more than three thousand dollars, and by imprisonment at hard labor not more than three years.   *Assault with a dangerous weapon.*

Ibid., s. 22, p. 121.

Sec. 5347. Every master or other officer of any American vessel on the high seas, or on any other waters within the admiralty and maritime jurisdiction of the United States, who, from malice, hatred, or revenge, and without justifiable cause, beats, wounds, or imprisons any of the crew of such vessel, or withholds from them suitable food and nourishment, or inflicts upon them any cruel or unusual punishment, shall be punished by a fine of not more than one thousand dollars, or by imprisonment not more than five years, or by both.   *Maltreatment of crew by officers of vessels.*

3 March, 1835, s. 3, v. 4, p. 776.

Sec. 5348. Every person who, within any of the places upon the land under the exclusive jurisdiction of the United States, or who, upon the high seas, in any vessel belonging to the United States, or to any citizen thereof, maliciously cuts off the ear, cuts out or disables the tongue, puts out an eye, slits the nose, cuts off the nose or lip, or cuts off or disables any limb or member of any person, with intent to maim or disfigure such person, shall be imprisoned at hard labor not more than seven years, and fined not more than one thousand dollars.

30 April, 1790, s. 13, v. 1, p. 115.

Sec. 5390. Every person who, having knowledge of the actual commission of the crime of murder or other felony upon the high seas, or within any fort, arsenal, dock-yard, magazine, or other place or district of country under the exclusive jurisdiction of the United States, conceals, and does not as soon as may be disclose and make known the same to some one of the judges or other persons in civil or military authority under the United States, is guilty of misprision of felony, and shall be imprisoned not more than three years, and fined not more than five hundred dollars.   *Title 70, Chap. 3. Misprision of felony.*

30 April, 1790, s. 6, v. 1, p. 113.

Sec. 5391. If any offense be committed in any place which has been or may hereafter be, ceded to and under the jurisdiction of the United States, which offense is not prohibited, or the punishment thereof is not specially provided for, by any law of the United States, such offense shall be liable to, and receive, the same punishment as the laws of the State in which such place is situated, now in force, provide for the like offense when committed within the jurisdiction of such State; and no   *Certain offenses committed in places ceded to United States, how punished.*

256 NATURALIZATION—CITIZENSHIP.

subsequent repeal of any such State law shall affect any prosecution for such offense in any court of the United States.

3 March, 1825, s. 3, v. 4, p. 115.
5 April, 1866, s. 2, v. 14, p. 13.

MUTINY.

**Title 15, Chap. 10.**
*Mutiny in the Navy.*

SEC. 1624. ART. 4. The punishment of death, or such other punishment as a court-martial may adjudge, may be inflicted on any person in the naval service—

First. Who makes, or attempts to make, or unites with any mutiny or mutinous assembly, or, being witness to or present at any mutiny, does not do his utmost to suppress it; or, knowing of any mutinous assembly or of any intended mutiny, does not immediately communicate his knowledge to his superior or commanding officer;

\* \* \* \* \*

17 July, 1862, s. 1, v. 12, p. 600.

**Title 70, Chap. 3.**
*Inciting revolt or mutiny on shipboard.*

SEC. 5359. If any one of the crew of any American vessel on the high seas, or other waters within the admiralty and maritime jurisdiction of the United States, endeavors to make a revolt or mutiny on board such vessel, or combines, conspires, or confederates with any other person on board to make such revolt or mutiny, or solicits, incites, or stirs up any other of the crew to disobey or resist the lawful orders of the master, or other officer of such vessel, or to refuse or neglect their proper duty on board thereof, or to betray their proper trust, or assembles with others in a tumultuous and mutinous manner, or makes a riot on board thereof, or unlawfully confines the master, or other commanding officer thereof, he shall be punished by a fine of not more than one thousand dollars, or by imprisonment not more than five years, or by both such fine and imprisonment.

3 March, 1835, s. 2, v. 4, p. 776.
30 April, 1790, s. 12, v. 1, p. 115.

*Revolt and mutiny on shipboard.*

SEC. 5360. If any one of the crew of an American vessel on the high seas, or on any other waters within the admiralty and maritime jurisdiction of the United States, unlawfully and with force, or by fraud, or intimidation, usurps the command of such vessel from the master or other lawful officer in command thereof, or deprives him of authority and command on board, or resists or prevents him in the free and lawful exercise thereof, or transfers such authority and command to another not lawfully entitled thereto, he is guilty of a revolt and mutiny, and shall be punished by a fine of not more than two thousand dollars, and by imprisonment at hard labor not more than ten years.

3 March, 1835, s. 1, v. 4, p. 775.
30 April, 1790, s. 8, v. 1, p. 113.

## NATURALIZATION—CITIZENSHIP. [See also EXPATRIATION.]

Sec.
2165. Aliens, how naturalized.
2166. Aliens honorably discharged from military service.
2167. Minor residents.
2168. Widow and children of declarants.

Sec.
2170. Residence of five years in United States.
2171. Alien enemies not admitted.
2172. Children of persons' naturalized under certain laws to be citizens.
2174. Naturalization of seamen.

NATURALIZATION.

**Title 30.**
*Aliens, how naturalized.*
*Declaration of intention.*

SEC. 2165. An alien may be admitted to become a citizen of the United States in the following manner, and not otherwise:

First. He shall declare on oath, before a circuit or district court of the United States, or a district or supreme court of the Territories, or a court of record of any of the States having common-law jurisdiction, and a seal and clerk, two years, at least, prior to his admission, that it is his bona fide intention to become a citizen of the United States, and to renounce forever all allegiance and fidelity to any foreign prince, potentate, state, or sovereignty, and, particularly, by name, to the prince, potentate, state, or sovereignty of which the alien may be at the time a citizen or subject. [See CITIZENSHIP, post, as to Chinese.]

14 April, 1802, ss. 1, 3, v. 2, pp. 153, 155.
26 May, 1824, s. 4, v. 4, p. 69.
1 Feb., 1876, chap. 5, v. 19, p. 2.

Second. He shall, at the time of his application to be admitted, declare, on oath, before some one of the courts above specified, that he will support the Constitution of the United States, and that he absolutely and entirely renounces and abjures all allegiance and fidelity to every foreign prince, potentate, state, or sovereignty; and, particularly, by name, to the prince, potentate, state, or sovereignty of which he was before a citizen or subject; which proceedings shall be recorded by the clerk of the court. *Oath to support the Constitution of the United States.*

Third. It shall be made to appear to the satisfaction of the court admitting such alien that he has resided within the United States five years at least, and within the State or Territory where such court is at the time held, one year at least; and that during that time he has behaved as a man of good moral character, attached to the principles of the Constitution of the United States, and well disposed to the good order and happiness of the same; but the oath of the applicant shall in no case be allowed to prove his residence. *Residence in United States, or States, and good moral character.*

Fourth. In case the alien applying to be admitted to citizenship has borne any hereditary title, or been of any of the orders of nobility in the kingdom or state from which he came, he shall, in addition to the above requisites, make an express renunciation of his title or order of nobility in the court to which his application is made, and his renunciation shall be recorded in the court. *Titles of nobility to be renounced.*

14 April, 1802, s. 1, v. 2, p. 153.

SEC. 2166. Any alien, of the age of twenty-one years and upward who has enlisted, or may enlist, in the armies of the United States, either the regular or the volunteer forces, and has been, or may be hereafter, honorably discharged, shall be admitted to become a citizen of the United States, upon his petition, without any previous declaration of his intention to become such; and he shall not be required to prove more than one year's residence within the United States previous to his application to become such citizen; and the court admitting such alien shall, in addition to such proof of residence and good moral character, as now provided by law, be satisfied by competent proof of such person's having been honorably discharged from the service of the United States. *Aliens honorably discharged from military service.*

17 July, 1862, s. 21, v. 12, p. 597.

SEC. 2167. Any alien, being under the age of twenty-one years, who has resided in the United States three years next preceding his arriving at that age, and who has continued to reside therein to the time he may make application to be admitted a citizen thereof, may, after he arrives at the age of twenty-one years, and after he has resided five years within the United States, including the three years of his minority, be admitted a citizen of the United States, without having made the declaration required in the first condition of section twenty-one hundred and sixty-five; but such alien shall make the declaration required therein at the time of his admission; and shall further declare, on oath, and prove to the satisfaction of the court, that, for two years next preceding, it has been his bona fide intention to become a citizen of the United States; and he shall in all other respects comply with the laws in regard to naturalization. *Minor residents.*

26 May, 1824, s. 1, v. 4, p. 69.

SEC. 2168. When any alien, who has complied with the first condition specified in section twenty-one hundred and sixty-five, dies before he is actually naturalized, the widow and the children of such alien shall be considered as citizens of the United States, and shall be entitled to all rights and privileges as such, upon taking the oaths prescribed by law. *Widow and children of declarants.*

26 March, 1804, s. 2, v. 2, p. 293.

SEC. 2170. No alien shall be admitted to become a citizen who has not for the continued term of five years next preceding his admission resided within the United States. *Residence of five years in United States.*

3 March, 1813, s. 12, v. 2, p. 811.

SEC. 2171. No alien who is a native citizen or subject, or a denizen of any country, state, or sovereignty with which the United States are at war, at the time of his application, shall be then admitted to become a citizen of the United States; * * * nor shall anything herein contained be taken or construed to interfere with or prevent the apprehen- *Alien enemies not admitted.*

sion and removal, agreeably to law, of any alien enemy at any time previous to the actual naturalization of such alien.

14 April, 1802, s. 1, v. 2, p. 153.
30 July, 1813, chap. 36, v. 3, p. 53.

**Children of persons naturalized under certain laws to be citizens.**

SEC. 2172. The children of persons who have been duly naturalized under any law of the United States, or who, previous to the passing of any law on that subject, by the Government of the United States, may have become citizens of any one of the States, under the laws thereof, being under the age of twenty-one years at the time of the naturalization of their parents, shall, if dwelling in the United States, be considered as citizens thereof; * * *

14 April, 1802, s. 4, v. 2, p. 155.

**Naturalization of seamen.**

SEC. 2174. Every seaman, being a foreigner, who declares his intention of becoming a citizen of the United States in any competent court, and shall have served three years on board of a merchant-vessel of the United States subsequent to the date of such declaration, may, on his application to any competent court, and the production of his certificate of discharge and good conduct during that time, together with the certificate of his declaration of intention to become a citizen, be admitted a citizen of the United States; and every seaman, being a foreigner, shall, after his declaration of intention to become a citizen of the United States, and after he shall have served such three years, be deemed a citizen of the United States for the purpose of manning and serving on board any merchant-vessel of the United States, anything to the contrary in any act of Congress notwithstanding; but such seaman shall, for all purposes of protection as an American citizen, be deemed such, after the filing of his declaration of intention to become such citizen.

7 June, 1872, s. 29, v. 17, p. 268.

CITIZENSHIP.

Sec.
1992. Who are citizens.
1993. Citizenship of children of citizens born abroad.
1994. Citizenship of married women.

Sec.
1996. Rights as citizens forfeited for desertion, &c.
1997. Certain soldiers and sailors not to incur the forfeitures of the last section.
— Immigration of certain classes prohibited.

**Title 25.**
**Who are citizens.**

SEC. 1992. All persons born in the United States and not subject to any foreign power, excluding Indians not taxed, are declared to be citizens of the United States.

9 April, 1866, s. 1, v. 14, p. 27.

**May 6, 1882.**
**Chinese excepted.**

Hereafter no State court or court of the United States shall admit Chinese to citizenship; and all laws in conflict with this act are hereby repealed.

6 May, 1882, s. 14, v. 22, p. 61.

**Title 25.**
**Citizenship of children of citizens born abroad.**

SEC. 1993. All children heretofore born or hereafter born out of the limits and jurisdiction of the United States, whose fathers were or may be at the time of their birth citizens thereof, are declared to be citizens of the United States; but the rights of citizenship shall not descend to children whose fathers never resided in the United States.

14 April, 1802, s. 4, v. 2, p. 155.
10 Feb., 1855, s. 1, v. 10, p. 604.

**Citizenship of married women.**

SEC. 1994. Any woman who is now or may hereafter be married to a citizen of the United States, and who might herself be lawfully naturalized, shall be deemed a citizen.

10 Feb., 1855, s. 2, v. 10, p. 604.

**Rights as citizens forfeited for desertion, &c.**

SEC. 1996. All persons who deserted the military or naval service of the United States and did not return thereto or report themselves to a provost-marshal within sixty days after the issuance of the proclamation by the President, dated the 11th day of March, 1865, are deemed to have voluntarily relinquished and forfeited their rights of citizenship as well as their right to become citizens; and such deserters shall be forever incapable of holding any office of trust or profit under the United States, or of exercising any rights of citizens thereof.

3 March, 1865, s. 21, v. 13, p. 490.

Sec. 1997. No soldier or sailor, however, who faithfully served according to his enlistment until the 19th day of April, 1865, and who, without proper authority or leave first obtained, quit his command or refused to serve after that date, shall be held to be a deserter from the Army or Navy; but this section shall be construed solely as a removal of any disability such soldier or sailor may have incurred, under the preceding section, by the loss of citizenship and of the right to hold office, in consequence of his desertion. *Certain soldiers and sailors not to incur the forfeitures of the last section.*

19 July, 1867, chap. 28, v. 15, p. 14.

It shall be unlawful for aliens of the following classes to immigrate into the United States, namely, persons who are undergoing a sentence for conviction in their own country of felonious crimes other than political or growing out of the result of such political offences, or whose sentence has been remitted on condition of their emigration, and women "imported for the purposes of prostitution." * * * *Immigration of alien convicts, &c., forbidden.*  *3 March, 1875.*

3 March, 1875, chap. 140, ss. 5, v. 18, p. 476.

[The 1st and 2d sections of the act of May 6, 1882, chap. 126, vol. 22, p. 58, suspended the immigration of Chinese laborers to the United States, after ninety days from the passage of the act, for ten years, and provided that the master of any vessel who should knowingly bring within the United States, and land or permit to be landed any Chinese laborer from any foreign port or place, should be deemed guilty of a misdemeanor and, on conviction thereof, be punished by a fine of not more than five hundred dollars for each and every such Chinese laborer so brought, and also might be imprisoned for a term not exceeding one year. The words "Chinese laborers" are to be construed to mean both skilled and unskilled laborers and Chinese employed in mining.]

NOTES.—A child born in the United States of alien parents, who have never been naturalized, is by the fact of birth a native-born citizen of the United States, entitled to all the rights and privileges of citizenship. So of children born in the United States of alien subjects who have declared their intention of becoming citizens of the United States. Children born abroad of aliens (who subsequently emigrated to the United States with their families and were naturalized here during the minority of their children) are citizens of the United States.—Op. X, pp. 328, 329, Sept. 1 and 2, 1862. Bates.

An American citizen, domiciled in a foreign country, who has taken an oath of allegiance to the foreign sovereign is not under the protection of the United States.—Murray v. The Charming Betsey 2 Cranch S. C. Brightly's Federal Digest, p. 41.

## NEUTRALITY—ALIEN ENEMIES, ETC.

Sec.
5281. Accepting a foreign commission.
5282. Enlisting in foreign service.
5283. Arming vessels against people at peace with the United States.
5284. Arming vessels to cruise against citizens of the United States.
5285. Augmenting force of foreign vessel of war.

Sec.
5286. Military expeditions against people at peace with United States.
5287. Enforcement of foregoing provisions.
5288. Compelling foreign vessels to depart.
5289. Armed vessels to give bond on clearance.
5290. Detention by collectors of customs.
5291. Construction of this Title.
—— Amending sec. 5287.

SEC. 5281. Every citizen of the United States who, within the territory or jurisdiction thereof, accepts and exercises a commission to serve a foreign prince, state, colony, district, or people, in war, by land or by sea, against any prince, state, colony, district, or people, with whom the United States are at peace, shall be deemed guilty of a high misdemeanor, and shall be fined not more than two thousand dollars, and imprisoned not more than three years. *Title 67. Accepting a foreign commission.*

20 April, 1818, s. 1, v. 3, p. 447.

SEC. 5282. Every person who, within the territory or jurisdiction of the United States, enlists or enters himself, or hires or retains another person to enlist or enter himself, or to go beyond the limits or jurisdiction of the United States with intent to be enlisted or entered in the service of any foreign prince, state, colony, district, or people, as a soldier, or as a marine or seaman, on board of any vessel of war, letter of marque, or privateer, shall be deemed guilty of high misdemeanor, and shall be fined not more than one thousand dollars, and imprisoned not more than three years. *Enlisting in foreign service.*

Idem, s. 2, p. 448.

SEC. 5283. Every person who, within the limits of the United States, fits out and arms, or attempts to fit out and arm, or procures to be fitted out and armed, or knowingly is concerned in the furnishing, fitting out, or arming, of any vessel, with intent that such vessel shall be employed in the service of any foreign prince or state, or of any colony, district, or people, to cruise or commit hostilities against the subjects, *Arming vessels against people at peace with the United States.*

citizens, or property of any foreign prince or state, or of any colony, district, or people, with whom the United States are at peace, or who issues or delivers a commission within the territory or jurisdiction of the United States, for any vessel, to the intent that she may be so employed, shall be deemed guilty of a high misdemeanor, and shall be fined not more than ten thousand dollars, and imprisoned not more than three years. And every such vessel, her tackle, apparel, and furniture, together with all materials, arms, ammunition, and stores, which may have been procured for the building and equipment thereof, shall be forfeited; one-half to the use of the informer, and the other half to the use of the United States.

*Idem, s. 3.*

**Arming vessels to cruise against citizens of the United States.** SEC. 5284. Every citizen of the United States who, without the limits thereof, fits out and arms, or attempts to fit out and arm, or procures to be fitted out and armed, or knowingly aids or is concerned in furnishing, fitting out, or arming any private vessel of war, or privateer, with intent that such vessel shall be employed to cruise, or commit hostilities, upon the citizens of the United States, or their property, or who takes the command of, or enters on board of any such vessel, for such intent, or who purchases any interest in any such vessel, with a view to share in the profits thereof, shall be deemed guilty of a high misdemeanor, and fined not more than ten thousand dollars, and imprisoned not more than ten years. And the trial for such offense, if committed without the limits of the United States, shall be in the district in which the offender shall be appprehended or first brought.

*Idem, s. 4.*

[Sec. 4090 of the Revised Statutes empowers United States ministers to issue all manner of writs to prevent citizens of the United States from enlisting in the military or naval service of a country to make war upon any foreign power with whom the United States are at peace, or in the service of one portion of the people against another portion of the same people, and to carry out this power he may resort to such force belonging to the United States as may at the time be within his reach.]

**Augmenting force of foreign vessel of war.** SEC. 5285. Every person who, within the territory or jurisdiction of the United States, increases or augments, or procures to be increased or augmented, or knowingly is concerned in increasing or augmenting, the force of any ship of war, cruiser, or other armed vessel, which, at the time of her arrival within the United States, was a ship of war, or cruiser, or armed vessel, in the service of any foreign prince or state, or of any colony, district, or people, or belonging to the subjects or citizens of any such prince or state, colony, district, or people, the same being at war with any foreign prince or state, or of any colony, district, or people, with whom the United States are at peace, by adding to the number of the guns of such vessel, or by changing those on board of her for guns of a larger caliber, or by adding thereto any equipment solely applicable to war, shall be deemed guilty of a high misdemeanor, and shall be fined not more than one thousand dollars and be imprisoned not more than one year.

20 April, 1818, s. 5, v. 3, p. 448.

**Military expeditions against people at peace with the United States.** SEC. 5286. Every person who, within the territory or jurisdiction of the United States, begins, or sets on foot, or provides or prepares the means for, any military expedition or enterprise, to be carried on from thence against the territory or dominions of any foreign prince or state, or of any colony, district, or people, with whom the United States are at peace, shall be deemed guilty of a high misdemeanor, and shall be fined not exceeding three thousand dollars, and imprisoned not more than three years.

*Idem, s. 6, p. 449.*

**Enforcement of foregoing provisions.** SEC. 5287. The district courts shall take cognizance of all complaints, by whomsoever instituted, in cases of captures made within the waters of the United States, or within a marine league of the coasts or shores thereof. In every case in which a vessel is fitted out and armed, or attempted to be fitted out and armed, or in which the force of any vessel of war, cruiser, or other armed vessel is increased or augmented, or in which any military expedition or enterprise is begun or set on foot, contrary to the provisions and prohibitions of this Title; and in every case of the capture of a vessel within the jurisdiction or protection of the United States as before defined; and in every case in which any process issuing out of any court of the United States is disobeyed or resisted by any person having the custody of any vessel of war, cruiser, or other armed vessel of any foreign prince or state, or of any colony, district, or people, or of any subjects or citizens of any foreign prince or state, or of any colony, district, or people, it shall be lawful for the President, or such other person as he shall have empowered for that purpose, to employ such part of the land or naval forces of the United States, or of the militia thereof, for the purpose of taking possession of and detaining any such vessel, with her prizes, if any, in order to the execution of the prohibitions and penalties of this Title, and to the restoring of such prizes in the cases in which restoration shall be adjudged; and also for the purpose of preventing the carrying on of any such expedition or enterprise from the territories or jurisdiction of the United States against the territories or dominions of any foreign prince or state, or of any colony, district, or people with whom the United States are at peace.

*Idem*, s. 8.
18 Feb., 1875, v. 18, p. 320.

SEC. 5288. It shall be lawful for the President, or such person as he shall empower for that purpose, to employ such part of the land or naval forces of the United States, or of the militia thereof, as shall be necessary to compel any foreign vessel to depart the United States in all cases in which, by the laws of nations or the treaties of the United States, she ought not to remain within the United States. *— Compelling foreign vessels to depart.*

20 April, 1818, s. 9, v. 3, p. 449.

SEC. 5289. The owners or consignees of every armed vessel sailing out of the ports of the United States, belonging wholly or in part to citizens thereof, shall, before clearing out the same, give bond to the United States, with sufficient sureties, in double the amount of the value of the vessel and cargo on board, including her armament, conditioned that the vessel shall not be employed by such owners to cruise or commit hostilities against the subjects, citizens, or property of any foreign prince or state, or of any colony, district, or people, with whom the United States are at peace. *— Armed vessels to give bond on clearance.*

*Idem*, s. 10.

SEC. 5290. The several collectors of the customs shall detain any vessel manifestly built for warlike purposes, and about to depart the United States, the cargo of which principally consists of arms and munitions of war, when the number of men shipped on board, or other circumstances, render it probable that such vessel is intended to be employed by the owners to cruise or commit hostilities upon the subjects, citizens, or property of any foreign prince or state, or of any colony, district, or people with whom the United States are at peace, until the decision of the President is had thereon, or until the owner gives such bond and security as is required of the owners of armed vessels by the preceding section. *— Detention by collectors of customs.*

20 April, 1818, s. 11, v. 3, p. 450.

SEC. 5291. The provisions of this Title shall not be construed to extend to any subject or citizen of any foreign prince, state, colony, district, or people who is transiently within the United States, and enlists or enters himself on board of any vessel of war, letter of marque, or privateer, which at the time of its arrival within the United States was fitted and equipped as such, or hires or retains another subject or citizen of the same foreign prince, state, colony, district, or people, who is transiently within the United States, to enlist or enter himself to serve such foreign prince, state, colony, district, or people, on board such vessel of war, letter of marque, or privateer, if the United States shall then be at peace with such foreign prince, state, colony, district, or people. Nor shall they be construed to prevent the prosecution or punishment of treason, or of any piracy defined by the laws of the United States. *— Construction of this Title.*

*Idem*, ss. 2, 13, v. 3, pp. 448, 450.
27 Feb., 1877, v. 19, p. 252.

NOTES.—An officer of the Navy has no right, without express direction from his Government, to enter the territory of a country at peace with the United States and seize property there claimed by citizens of the United States. Application for redress should be made to the judicial tribunals of the country.—Cadwalader's State Department Digest, p. 219, cites 2 Paine, 324.

A revolutionary party like a foreign belligerent party, is supreme over the country it conquers, as far and as long as its arms can carry and maintain it.—Op. IX, 140, Black, May 15, 1858.

# NEUTRALITY—ALIEN ENEMIES.

By the law of nations one Government cannot enter upon the territories of another, or claim any right whatever therein, for if this be done by force it is an usurpation, and if it be done by any underhand bargaining with individuals, who have not the explicit consent of their Government, it is mean and unfair.—Op. IX, 286, Black, March 14, 1859.

One nation cannot execute the penal laws of another, and consequently a foreign vessel engaged in the slave trade cannot lawfully be captured by an American cruiser. The African slave-trade is not contrary to the law of nations.—Cadwalader's State Department Digest, p. 217, cites 10 Wheaton, 66.

The United States cannot purchase a grant of land in, or concession of a right of way over, the territories of another nation as could an individual or private corporation, since by the law of nations one Government cannot enter upon the territory of another, or claim any right whatever therein.—Cadwalader's Digest, p. 218, cites Op. IX, 280.

The *right of search* does not exist in time of peace. A cruiser of one nation has the right to know the national character of any strange ship she may meet at sea, but the right is not a perfect one. The *right of inquiry* has well defined limitations: 1. Inquiring ship must put up his own colors, or in some way make himself fully known, before he can lawfully demand such knowledge from the other vessel. 2. If refused, may fire blank shot or cartridge. 3. If still refused, a shotted gun may be fired across bows by way of positive *summons*. 4. Any further measure must be at the peril of the inquiring vessel. If stranger is arrested, injured, or captured, and proves not a pirate, but has a lawful right to navigate the seas, the injury must be atoned for. The right of a public ship to *hail* or speak a stranger, is in all respects analogous thereto, and must be exercised within the same limits. 5. The answer by words or by hoisting flag must be taken as true. Cannot be stopped, visited, or searched. 6. The right of inquiry can be exercised only on the high seas. No naval officer has a right to go into the harbor of a nation with which his Government is at peace, to inquire into the nationality of a vessel lying there.—Op. IX, p. 456, Black, July 28, 1860. Case of the "General Miramou."

Ships of war enjoy the full rights of exterritoriality in foreign ports and territorial waters. Merchant ships are a part of the territory of their country, and are so treated on the high seas, and partially, but not wholly so, while in territorial waters of a foreign country. Crimes committed on board ship on the high seas, are triable in the country to which she belongs. In port the local authority has jurisdiction of acts committed on board of a foreign merchant ship, provided those acts affect the peace of the port, but not otherwise; and its jurisdiction does not extend to acts internal to the ship or transpiring on the high seas. The authority of the ship's country, in these cases, is not taken away by the fact that the actors are foreigners provided they be of the crew or passengers of the ship. The local authority has right to enter on board a foreign merchantman in port for the purpose of inquiry universally—but for the purpose of arrest only in matters within its ascertained jurisdiction.—Op. VIII, 73, Cushing, Sept. 5, 1856.

"Neutrals may lawfully sell at home to a belligerent purchaser, or carry themselves to the belligerent powers contraband articles subject to the right of seizure *in transitu*. The right of the neutral to transport, and of the hostile power to seize, are conflicting rights, and neither party can charge the other with criminal act." (1 Kent's Com., p. 142.) "There is nothing in our laws, or in the law of nations, that forbid our citizens from sending armed vessels as well as munitions of war to foreign ports for sale. It is a commercial venture which no nation is bound to prohibit, and which only exposes the persons engaged in it to the penalty of confiscation." (7 Wheaton, 340.) Cited in Op. XI, p. 408, Dec. 23, 1865, Speed.

## INTERNATIONAL CONVENTION—AMELIORATION OF WOUNDED, ETC.

Convention between the United States, Baden, Switzerland, Belgium, Denmark, Spain, France, Hesse, Italy, Netherlands, Portugal, Prussia, Würtemberg, Sweden, Greece, Great Britain, Mecklenberg-Schwerin, Turkey, Bavaria, Austria, Persia, Salvador, Montenegro, Servia, Bolivia, Chili, Argentine Republic, and Peru; with additional articles; for the amelioration of the wounded in armies in the field; concluded August 22, 1864; acceded by the President March 1, 1882; accession concurred in by the Senate March 16, 1882; proclaimed as to the original convention, but with reserve as to the additional articles, July 26, 1882.

**Hospitals and ambulances with sick or wounded, &c.**
ARTICLE I. Ambulances and military hospitals shall be acknowledged to be neuter, and, as such, shall be protected and respected by belligerents so long as any sick or wounded may be therein.

**Exception.**
Such neutrality shall cease if the ambulances or hospitals should be held by a military force.

**Employés, &c., respected as neutrals.**
ART. II. Persons employed in hospitals and ambulances, comprising the staff for superintendence, medical service, administration, transport of wounded, as well as chaplains, shall participate in the benefit of neutrality, whilst so employed, and so long as there remain any wounded to bring in or to succor.

**Employés, &c., protected by occupying forces.**
ART. III. The persons designated in the preceding article may, even after occupation by the enemy, continue to fulfil their duties in the hospital or ambulance which they serve, or may withdraw in order to rejoin the corps to which they belong.

Under such circumstances, when these persons shall cease from their functions, they shall be delivered by the occupying army to the outposts of the enemy.

ART. IV. As the equipment of military hospitals remains subject to the laws of war, persons attached to such hospitals cannot, in withdrawing, carry away any articles but such as are their private property. *{Employés in hospitals to take away private property, only.}*

Under the same circumstances, an ambulance shall, on the contrary, retain its equipment.

ART. V. Inhabitants of the country who may bring help to the wounded shall be respected, and shall remain free. The generals of the belligerent Powers shall make it their care to inform the inhabitants of the appeal addressed to their humanity, and of the neutrality which will be the consequence of it. *{Persons serving the wounded to remain free.}*

Any wounded man entertained and taken care of in a house shall be considered as a protection thereto. Any inhabitant who shall have entertained wounded men in his house shall be exempted from the quartering of troops, as well as from a part of the contributions of war which may be imposed. *{Houses where the wounded are cared for to be protected. Exemptions for care of wounded.}*

ART. VI. Wounded or sick soldiers shall be entertained and taken care of, to whatever nation they may belong. *{Soldiers sick or wounded to be cared for.}*

Commanders-in-chief shall have the power to deliver immediately to the outposts of the enemy soldiers who have been wounded in an engagement, when circumstances permit this to be done, and with the consent of both parties. *{Delivery of wounded, &c.}*

Those who are recognized after their wounds are healed, as incapable of serving, shall be sent back to their country. *{Soldiers incapacitated for service to be sent home.}*

The others may also be sent back, on condition of not again bearing arms during the continuance of the war. *{Conditions of return.}*

Evacuations, together with the persons under whose directions they take place, shall be protected by an absolute neutrality. *{Evacuations, &c., to have absolute neutrality.}*

ART. VII. A distinctive and uniform flag shall be adopted for hospitals, ambulances, and evacuations. It must, on every occasion, be accompanied by the national flag. An arm-badge (brassard) shall also be allowed for individuals neutralized, but the delivery thereof shall be left to military authority. *{Hospital ambulance, and evacuation flag, &c. Arm-badge.}*

The flag and the arm-badge shall bear a red cross on a white ground. *{Flag and arm-badge to bear red cross, &c.}*

ART. VIII. The details of execution of the present convention shall be regulated by the commanders-in-chief of belligerent armies, according to the instructions of their respective Governments, and in conformity with the general principles laid down in this convention. *{Execution of details of convention.}*

### ADDITIONAL ARTICLES.

ARTICLE I. The persons designated in Article II of the Convention shall, after the occupation by the enemy, continue to fulfil their duties, according to their wants, to the sick and wounded in the ambulance or the hospital which they serve. When they request to withdraw, the commander of the occupying troops shall fix the time of departure, which he shall only be allowed to delay for a short time in case of military necessity. *{Rights of employés, &c., in hospitals or ambulances.}*

ART. II. Arrangements will have to be made by the belligerent powers to insure to the neutralized person, fallen into the hands of the army of the enemy, the entire enjoyment of his salary. *{Salary of neutrals, &c., when in enemy's hands.}*

ART III. Under the conditions provided for in Articles I and IV of the Convention, the name "ambulance" applies to field hospitals and other temporary establishments, which follow the troops on the field of battle to receive the sick and wounded. *{Definition of the term "ambulance."}*

ART. IV. In conformity with the spirit of Article V of the Convention, and to the reservations contained in the protocol of 1864, it is explained that for the appointment of the charges relative to the quartering of troops, and of the contributions of war, account only shall be taken in an equitable manner of the charitable zeal displayed by the inhabitants. *{Charges for quartering of troops, and contributions, &c.}*

> Wounded to be returned to their country on condition of not again bearing arms in the war.

ART. V. In addition to Article VI of the Convention, it is stipulated that, with the reservation of officers whose detention might be important to the fate of arms and within the limits fixed by the second paragraph of that article, the wounded fallen into the hands of the enemy shall be sent back to their country, after they are cured, or sooner if possible, on condition, nevertheless, of not again bearing arms during the continuance of the war.

[*Articles concerning the Marine.*]

> Boats picking up the shipwrecked or wounded, &c.

ART. VI. The boats which, at their own risk and peril, during and after an engagement pick up the shipwrecked or wounded, or which having picked them up, convey them on board a neutral or hospital ship, shall enjoy, until the accomplishment of their mission, the character of neutrality, as far as the circumstances of the engagement and the position of the ships engaged will permit.

The appreciation of these circumstances is intrusted to the humanity of all the combatants. The wrecked and wounded thus picked and saved must not serve again during the continuance of the war.

> Religious, medical, and hospital staff of a captured vessel declared neutral.

ART. VII. The religious, medical, and hospital staff of any captured vessel are declared neutral, and, on leaving the ship, may remove the articles and surgical instruments which are their private property.

> Duties of staff officers, &c.

ART. VIII. The staff designated in the preceding article must continue to fulfill their functions in the captured ship, assisting in the removal of the wounded made by the victorious party; they will then be at liberty to return to their country, in conformity with the second paragraph of the first additional article.

> Pay and allowance of staff.

The stipulations of the second additional article are applicable to the pay and allowance of the staff.

> Captured hospital ships to remain under martial law, &c.

ART. IX. The military hospital ships remain under martial law in all that concerns their stores; they become the property of the captor, but the latter must not divert them from their special appropriation during the continuance of the war.

\*[*The vessels not equipped for fighting, which, during peace, the government shall have officially declared to be intended to serve as floating hospital ships, shall, however, enjoy during the war complete neutrality, both as regards stores, and also as regards their staff, provided their equipment is exclusively appropriated to the special service on which they are employed.*]

> Merchant vessels performing hospital duty to be treated as neutral, &c.

ART. X. Any merchantman, to whatever nation she may belong, charged exclusively with removal of sick and wounded, is protected by neutrality, but the mere fact, noted on the ship's books, of the vessel having been visited by an enemy's cruiser, renders the sick and wounded incapable of serving during the continuance of the war. The cruiser shall even have the right of putting on board an officer in order to accompany the convoy, and thus verify the good faith of the operation.

> Cargo of merchant ship protected; when; proviso.

If the merchant ship also carries a cargo, her neutrality will still protect it, provided that such cargo is not of a nature to be confiscated by the belligerents.

> Right of belligerents.

The belligerents retain the right to interdict neutralized vessels from all communication, and from any course which they may deem prejudicial to the secrecy of their operations. In urgent cases special conventions may be entered into between commanders-in-chief, in order to neutralize temporarily and in a special manner the vessels intended for the removal of the sick and wounded.

> Wounded or sick sailors and soldiers, when embarked, &c.
> Return to native country.

ART. XI. Wounded or sick sailors and soldiers, when embarked, to whatever nation they may belong, shall be protected and taken care of by their captors.

Their return to their own country is subject to the provisions of Article VI of the Convention, and of the additional Article V.

---

\* In the published English text, from which this version of the Additional Articles is taken, the paragraph thus marked in brackets appears in continuation of Article IX. It is not, however, found in the original French text adopted by the Geneva Conference, October 20, 1868.

By an instruction sent to the United States minister at Berne, January 20, 1883, the right is reserved to omit this paragraph from the English text, and to make any other necessary corrections, if at any time hereafter the Additional Articles shall be completed by the exchange of the ratifications hereof between the several signatory and adhering powers.

ART. XII. The distinctive flag to be used with the national flag, in order to indicate any vessel or boat which may claim the benefits of neutrality, in virtue of the principles of this Convention, is a white flag with a red cross. The belligerents may exercise in this respect any mode of verification which they may deem necessary. *White flag with red cross, &c., used by vessels claiming neutrality.*

Military hospital ships shall be distinguished by being painted white outside, with green strake. *Military hospitals painted white, &c.*

ART. XIII. The hospital ships which are equipped at the expense of the aid societies, recognized by the governments signing this Convention, and which are furnished with a commission emanating from the sovereign, who shall have given express authority for their being fitted out, and with a certificate from the proper naval authority that they have been placed under his control during their fitting out and on their final departure, and that they were then appropriated solely to the purpose of their mission, shall be considered neutral, as well as the whole of their staff. They shall be recognized and protected by the belligerents. *Hospital ships, &c., and staff to be treated as neutral.*

They shall make themselves known by hoisting, together with their national flag, the white flag with a red cross. The distinctive mark of their staff, while performing their duties, shall be an armlet of the same colors. The outer painting of these hospital ships shall be white with red strake. *Flag sign, &c., of neutrality.*

These ships shall bear aid and assistance to the wounded and wrecked belligerents, without distinction of nationality. *Aid and assistance to wounded and wrecked belligerents, without distinction of nationality.*

They must take care not to interfere in any way with the movements of the combatants. During and after the battle they must do their duty at their own risk and peril.

The belligerents shall have the right of controlling and visiting them; they will be at liberty to refuse their assistance, to order them to depart, and to detain them if the exigencies of the case require such a step. *Rights of belligerents to control and visit vessels, &c.*

The wounded and wrecked picked up by these ships cannot be reclaimed by either of the combatants, and they will be required not to serve during the continuance of the war. *Wounded and wrecked picked up, &c., cannot be reclaimed.*

ART. XIV. In naval wars any strong presumption that either belligerent takes advantage of the benefits of neutrality, with any other view than the interest of the sick and wounded, gives to the other belligerent, until proof to the contrary, the right of suspending the Convention, as regards such belligerent. *Right of belligerents to suspend Convention, &c.*

Should this presumption become a certainty, notice may be given to such belligerent that the Convention is suspended with regard to him during the whole continuance of the war. *Notice of suspension of Convention, &c., to be given.*

## ALIEN ENEMIES.

Sec.
4067. Removal of alien enemies.
4068. Time for removal.
4069. Jurisdiction of United States courts over alien enemies.

Sec.
4070. Duties of marshals in removing alien enemies.

SEC. 4067. Whenever there is a declared war between the United States and any foreign nation or government, or any invasion or predatory incursion is perpetrated, attempted, or threatened against the territory of the United States, by any foreign nation or government, and the President makes public proclamation of the event, all natives, citizens, denizens, or subjects of the hostile nation or government, being males of the age of fourteen years and upward, who shall be within the United States, and not actually naturalized, shall be liable to be apprehended, restrained, secured, and removed, as alien enemies. The President is authorized in any such event, by his proclamation thereof, or other public act, to direct the conduct to be observed, on the part of the United States, toward the aliens who become so liable; the manner and degree of the restraint to which they shall be subject, and in what cases, and upon what security their residence shall be permitted, and to provide for the removal of those who, not being permitted to reside within the United States, refuse or neglect to depart therefrom; and to establish any other regulations which are found necessary in the premises and for the public safety. *Title 47. Removal of alien enemies.*

6 July, 1798, s. 1, v. 1, p. 577.

**Time for removal.**

SEC. 4068. When an alien who becomes liable as an enemy, in the manner prescribed in the preceding section, is not chargeable with actual hostility, or other crime against the public safety, he shall be allowed, for the recovery, disposal, and removal of his goods and effects, and for his departure, the full time which is or shall be stipulated by any treaty then in force between the United States and the hostile nation or government of which he is a native citizen, denizen, or subject; and where no such treaty exists, or is in force, the President may ascertain and declare such reasonable time as may be consistent with the public safety, and according to the dictates of humanity and national hospitality.

*Ibid.*
6 July, 1812, chap. 130, v. 2, p. 781.

**Jurisdiction of United States courts over alien enemies.**

SEC. 4069. After any such proclamation has been made, the several courts of the United States, having criminal jurisdiction, and the several justices and judges of the courts of the United States, are authorized, and it shall be their duty, upon complaint against any alien enemy resident and at large within such jurisdiction or district, to the danger of the public peace or safety, and contrary to the tenor or intent of such proclamation, or other regulations which the President may have established, to cause such alien to be duly apprehended and conveyed before such court, judge, or justice; and after a full examination and hearing on such complaint, and sufficient cause appearing, to order such alien to be removed out of the territory of the United States, or to give sureties for his good behavior, or to be otherwise restrained, conformably to the proclamation or regulations established as aforesaid, and to imprison, or otherwise secure such alien, until the order which may be so made shall be performed.

6 July, 1798, s. 2, v. 1, p. 577.

**Duties of marshal in removing alien enemies.**

SEC. 4070. When an alien enemy is required by the President, or by order of any court, judge, or justice, to depart and to be removed, it shall be the duty of the marshal of the district in which he shall be apprehended to provide therefor, and to execute such order in person, or by his deputy, or other discreet person to be employed by him, by causing a removal of such alien out of the territory of the United States; and for such removal the marshal shall have the warrant of the President, or of the court, judge, or justice ordering the same, as the case may be.

*Ibid.*, s. 3, p. 578.

## PATENTS AND PATENTED ARTICLES.

Sec.
1537. Patent articles for marine engines.
4886. Inventions patentable.

Sec.
4887. Patents for inventions previously patented abroad.
—— Patents without fees in certain cases.

**Title 15, Chap. 6.**

**Patented articles connected with marine engines.**

SEC. 1537. No patented article connected with marine engines shall hereafter be purchased or used in connection with any steam-vessels of war until the same shall have been submitted to a competent board of naval engineers, and recommended by such board, in writing, for purchase and use.

18 July, 1861, s. 3, v. 12, p. 268.

**Title 60, Chap. 1.**

**Inventions patentable.**

SEC. 4886. Any person who has invented or discovered any new and useful art, machine, manufacture or composition of matter, or any new and useful improvement thereof, not known or used by others in this country, and not patented or described in any printed publication in this or any foreign country, before his invention or discovery thereof, and not in public use or on sale for more than two years prior to his application, unless the same is proved to have been abandoned, may, upon payment of the fees required by law, and other due proceedings had, obtain a patent therefor.

8 July, 1870, s. 24, v. 16, p. 201.

**Patents for inventions previously patented abroad.**

SEC. 4887. No person shall be debarred from receiving a patent for his invention or discovery, nor shall any patent be declared invalid, by reason of its having been first patented or caused to be patented in a foreign country, unless the same has been introduced into public use in the United States for more than two years prior to the application. But every patent granted for an invention which has been previously patented in a foreign country shall be so limited 'as to expire at the same time with the foreign patent, or, if there be more than one, at the same time with the one having the shortest term, and in no case shall it be in force more than seventeen years.

8 July, 1870, s. 25, v. 16, p. 201.

The Secretary of the Interior and the Commissioner of Patents are authorized to grant any officer of the government, except officers and employees of the Patent Office, a patent for any invention of the classes mentioned in section forty-eight hundred and eighty six of the Revised Statutes, when such invention is used or to be used in the public service, without the payment of any fee: *Provided*, That the applicant in his application shall state that the invention described therein, if patented, may be used by the government or any of its officers or employees in the prosecution of work for the government, or by any other person in the United States, without the payment to him of any royalty thereon, which stipulation shall be included in the patent.

3 Mar., 1883. Patents without fees in certain cases.

3 March, 1883, v. 22, p. 625.

NOTES.—Where proposals are invited for an article, and one of the bidders claims that he has a patent on it, the contract should not be awarded to any other unless satisfactory evidence is furnished that the other (not the patentee) has authority from the patentee to manufacture and sell it.—Op. XV, 26, July 23, 1875. Pierrepont.
An official in the military service not specially employed to make experiments may devise new and useful improvements in arms, tents, and war material, and will be entitled to the benefits of his inventions and to letters patent therefor equally with any other citizen.—C. C., VII, 219; Wallace 12, p. 236.
Where a contract between a patentee and the Government for the use of an invention provides that it may be determined by notice from the patentee, the Government can determine it only by discontinuing its use.—C. C., IV, p. 113. Affirmed by Supreme Court. See Holt's Digest, p. 88 and p. 112, for discussion of the rights of Government employés to compensation for the use of their inventions by the Government.

## PENSIONS.

Sec.
4692. Who may have pensions.
4693. Classes enumerated.
4694. Pensions for wounds received or diseases contracted only in line of duty, &c.
4695. Rates of pension for total disability.
4696. Pension according to rank.
4698½. Increase of pensions.
4699. Pension for disability not otherwise provided for.
4702. Pensions to widows, or to children under sixteen years, &c.

Sec.
4703. Increased pension to widows, &c.
4712. Provisions of pension laws extended.
4713. Commencement of pensions for prior wars.
4724. Both pension and pay not allowed, unless, &c.
4728. Navy pensions.
4729. Naval pensions to widows and children.
4756. } Service pensions.
4757. } Sea-pension funds.

SEC. 4692. Every person specified in the several classes enumerated in the following section, who has been, since the fourth day of March, eighteen hundred and sixty-one, or who is hereafter disabled under the conditions therein stated, shall, upon making due proof of the fact, according to such forms and regulations as are or may be provided in pursuance of law, be placed on the list of invalid pensioners of the United States, and be entitled to receive, for a total disability, or a permanent specific disability, such pension as is hereinafter provided in such cases; and for an inferior disability, except in cases of permanent specific disability, for which the rate of penson is expressly provided, an amount proportionate to that provided for total disability; and such pension shall commence as hereinafter provided, and continue during the existence of the disability.

Title 57. Who may have pensions.

3 March, 1873, s. 1, v. 17, p. 566.
6 June, 1874, v. 18, p. 61.
3 March, 1877, v. 19, p. 403.

SEC. 4693. The persons entitled as beneficiaries under the preceding section are as follows:
First. Any officer of the Army, including regulars, volunteers, and militia, or any officer in the Navy or Marine Corps, or any enlisted man, however employed, in the military or naval service of the United States, or in its Marine Corps, whether regularly mustered or not, disabled by reason of any wound or injury received, or disease contracted, while in the service of the United States and in the line of duty.

Classes enumerated.
Officers of Army and Navy, and enlisted men, &c.

268 . PENSIONS.

Master, &c., serving on gun-boat, &c.
Second. Any master serving on a gun-boat, or any pilot, engineer sailor, or other person not regularly mustered, serving upon any gun-boat or war-vessel of the United States, disabled by any wound or injury received, or otherwise incapacitated while in the line of duty, for procuring his subsistence by manual labor.

Volunteers, not enlisted, &c.
Third. Any person not an enlisted soldier in the Army, serving for the time being as a member of the militia of any State, under orders of an officer of the United States, or who volunteered for the time being to serve with any regularly organized military or naval force of the United States, or who otherwise volunteered and rendered service in any engagement with rebels or Indians, disabled in consequence of wounds or injury received in the line of duty in such temporary service. But no claim of a State militiaman, or non-enlisted person, on account of disability from wounds, or injury received in battle with rebels or Indians, while temporarily rendering service, shall be valid unless prosecuted to a successful issue prior to the fourth day of July, eighteen hundred and seventy-four.

Acting assistant surgeon, &c.
Fourth. Any acting assistant or contract surgeon disabled by any wound or injury received or disease contracted in the line of duty while actually performing the duties of assistant surgeon or acting assistant surgeon with any military force in the field, or in transitu, or in hospital.

Provost-marshal, &c.
Fifth. Any provost-marshal, deputy provost-marshal, or enrolling-officer disabled, by reason of any wound or injury, received in the discharge of his duty, to procure a subsistence by manual labor.

3 March, 1873, s. 1, v. 17, p. 566.
3 March, 1877, v. 19, p. 403.

Pensions for wounds received or diseases contracted only in line of duty, &c.
SEC. 4694. No person shall be entitled to a pension by reason of wounds or injury received or disease contracted in the service of the United States subsequent to the twenty-seventh day of July, eighteen hundred and sixty-eight, unless the person who was wounded, or injured, or contracted the disease was in the line of duty; and, if in the military service, was at the time actually in the field, or on the march, or at some post, fort, or garrison, or en route, by direction of competent authority, to some post, fort, or garrison; or, if in the naval service, was at the time borne on the books of some ship or other vessel of the United States, at sea or in harbor, actually in commission, or was at some naval station, or on his way, by direction of competent authority, to the United States, or to some other vessel or naval station, or hospital. [See §§ 4756, 4757, PENSION FUNDS, as to SERVICE PENSIONS.]

3 March, 1873, s. 1, v. 17, p. 567.

Rates of pension for total disability.
SEC. 4695. The pension for total disability shall be as follows, namely: For lieutenant-colonel and all officers of higher rank in the military service and in the Marine Corps, and for captain, and all officers of higher rank, commander, surgeon, paymaster, and chief engineer, respectively ranking with commander by law, lieutenant commanding and master commanding, in the naval service, thirty dollars per month; for major in the military service and in the Marine Corps, and lieutenant, surgeon, paymaster, and chief engineer, respectively ranking with lieutenant by law, and passed assistant surgeon in the naval service, twenty-five dollars per month; for captain in the military service and in the Marine Corps, chaplain in the Army, and provost-marshal, professor of mathematics, master, assistant surgeon, assistant paymaster, and chaplain in the naval service, twenty dollars per month; for first lieutenant in the military service and in the Marine Corps, acting assistant or contract surgeon, and deputy provost-marshal, seventeen dollars per month; for second lieutenant in the military service and in the Marine Corps * * * ensign, and pilot in the naval service, and enrolling officer, fifteen dollars per month; for cadet-midshipman, passed midshipman, midshipmen, clerks of admirals and paymasters and of other officers commanding vessels, * * * master's mate, and all warrant officers in the naval service, ten dollars per month; and for all other persons whose rank or office is not mentioned in this section, eight dollars per month; and the masters, pilots, engineers, sailors, and crews upon the gun-boats and war-vessels shall be entitled to receive the pension allowed herein to those of like rank in the naval service. [See § 4699.]

3 March, 1873, s. 2, v. 17, p. 567.

The pension for total disability of passed assistant engineers, assistant engineers, and cadet engineers in the naval service, respectively, shall be the same as the pensions allowed to officers of the line in the naval service with whom they have relative rank.

*March 3, 1877.*

Rate of pension to passed; assistant and cadet engineers.

3 March, 1877, v. 19, p. 403.

SEC. 4696. Every commissioned officer of the Army, Navy, or Marine Corps shall receive such and only such pension as is provided in the preceding section, for the rank he held at the time he received the injury or contracted the disease which resulted in the disability, on account of which he may be entitled to a pension; and any commission or presidential appointment, regularly issued to such person, shall be taken to determine his rank from and after the date, as given in the body of the commission or appointment conferring said rank : *Provided,* That a vacancy existed in the rank thereby conferred ; that the person commissioned was not disabled for military duty; and that he did not willfully neglect or refuse to be mustered.

Title 57.

Pension according to rank.

3 March, 1873, s. 2, v. 17, p. 567.

NOTE.—The rank of soldiers at time of disability governs rate of pension. Rank under a commission dated after the contraction of disability does not fix rate not conferred by a commission unless a vacancy existed in such rank. Pension of widow to be rated according to rank of husband at the time he received the injury which resulted in the fatal disease.—Pension Office Digest.

SEC. 4698¼. Except in cases of permanent specific disabilities, no increase of pension shall be allowed to commence prior to the date of the examining surgeon's certificate establishing the same made under the pending claim for increase; and in this, as well as all other cases, the certificate of an examining surgeon, or of a board of examining surgeons, shall be subject to the approval of the Commissioner of Pensions.

Increase of pensions.

3 March, 1873, s. 4, v. 17, p. 569.
18 *June,* 1874, ch. 298, v. 18, p. 78.

SEC. 4699. The rate of eighteen dollars per month may be proportionally divided for any degree of disability established for which section forty-six hundred and ninety-five makes no provision.

Pensions for disability not otherwise provided for.

3 March, 1873, s. 5, v. 17, p. 560.

SEC. 4702. If any person embraced within the provisions of sections forty-six hundred and ninety-two and forty-six hundred and ninety-three has died since the fourth day of March, eighteen hundred and sixty-one, or hereafter dies by reason of any wound, injury, or disease, which, under the conditions and limitations of such sections, would have entitled him to an invalid pension had he been disabled, his widow, or if there be no widow, or in case of her death, without payment to her of any part of the pension hereinafter mentioned, his child or children, under sixteen years of age, shall be entitled to receive the same pension as the husband or father would have been entitled to had he been totally disabled, to commence from the death of the husband or father, to continue to the widow during her widowhood, and to his child or children until they severally attain the age of sixteen years, and no longer; and, if the widow remarry, the child or children shall be entitled from the date of remarriage.

Pension to widows or to children under sixteen years, &c.

*Ibid.,* s. 8.

SEC. 4703. The pensions of widows shall be increased from and after the twenty-fifth day of July, eighteen hundred and sixty-six at the rate of two dollars per month for each child under the age of sixteen years, of the husband on account of whose death the claim has been, or shall be, granted. And in every case in which the deceased husband has left, or shall leave, no widow, or where his widow has died or married again, or where she has been deprived of her pension under the provisions of the pension law, the pension granted to such child or children shall be increased to the same amount per month that would be allowed under the foregoing provisions to the widow, if living and entitled to a pension: *Provided,* That the additional pension herein granted to the widow on account of the child or children of the husband by a former wife shall be paid to her only for such period of her widowhood as she has been, or shall be, charged with the maintenance of such child or children; for any period during which she has not been, or she shall not be, so charged, it shall be granted and paid to the guardian of such child or children : *Provided further,* That a widow or guardian to whom

Increased pension to widows, &c.

increase of pension has been, or shall hereafter be, granted on account of minor children, shall not be deprived thereof by reason of their being maintained in whole or in part at the expense of a State or the public in any educational institution, or in any institution organized for the care of soldier's orphans.

*Ibid.*, s. 9.

**Provisions of pension laws extended, &c.**

SEC. 4712. The provisions of this Title in respect to the rates of pension to persons whose right accrued since the fourth day of March, eighteen hundred and sixty-one, are extended to pensioners whose right to pension accrued under general acts passed since the war of the Revolution and prior to the fourth day of March, eighteen hundred and sixty-one, to take effect from and after the twenty-fifth day of July, eighteen hundred and sixty-six; and the widows of revolutionary soldiers and sailors receiving a less sum shall be paid at the rate of eight dollars per month from and after the twenty-seventh day of July, eighteen hundred and sixty-eight.

3 March, 1873, s. 18, v. 17, p. 569.

**Commencement of pensions for prior wars.**

SEC. 4713. In all cases in which the cause of disability or death originated in the service prior to the fourth day of March, eighteen hundred and sixty-one, and an application for pension shall not have been filed within three years from the discharge or death of the person on whose account the claim is made, or within three years of the termination of a pension previously granted on account of the service and death of the same person, the pension shall commence from the date of filing by the party prosecuting the claim the last paper requisite to establish the same. But no claim allowed prior to the sixth day of June, eighteen hundred and sixty-six, shall be affected by anything herein contained.

*Idem.*, s. 19, p. 573.

**Both pension and pay not allowed, unless, &c.**

SEC. 4724. No person in the Army, Navy, or Marine Corps shall draw both a pension as an invalid, and the pay of his rank or station in the service, unless the disability for which the pension was granted be such as to occasion his employment in a lower grade, or in the civil branch of the service.

30 April, 1844, v. 5, p. 657.
16 Aug, 1841, s. 2, v. 5, p. 440.

NOTE.—The object of the proviso in the act of 1844 (Sec. 4724 R. S.) was to prohibit the payment to any one serving in the Army, Navy, or Marine Corps of both pay and pension, except where the disability for which the pension is allowed is such as to have occasioned his employment in a lower grade or some civil branch of the service.—Op. XIV, p. 94, Aug. 8, 1872, Williams. See also, IV, p. 587, V, p. 51, VI, 718.

**Navy pensions.**

SEC. 4728. If any officer, warrant or petty officer, seaman, engineer, first, second, or third assistant engineer, fireman or coal-heaver of the Navy or any marine has been disabled prior to the fourth day of March eighteen hundred and sixty-one by reason of any injury received or disease contracted in the service and line of duty, he shall be entitled to receive during the continuance of his disability a pension proportionate to the degree of his disability not exceeding half the monthly pay of his rank as it existed in January eighteen hundred and thirty-five. But the pension of a chief-engineer shall be the same as that of a lieutenant of the Navy; the pension of a first assistant engineer the same as that of a lieutenant of marines; the pension of a second or third assistant engineer the same as that of a forward officer; the pension of a fireman or coal-heaver the same as that of a seaman; but an engineer, fireman or coal-heaver shall not be entitled to any pension by reason of a disability incurred prior to the thirty-first day of August eighteen hundred and forty-two.

11 Aug., 1848, ss. 2, 3, v. 9, p. 283.

**Naval pensions to widows and children.**

SEC. 4729. If any person referred to in the preceding section has died in the service, of injury received or disease contracted under the conditions therein stated, his widow shall be entitled to receive half the monthly pay to which the deceased was entitled at the date of his death; and in case of her death or marriage, the child or children under sixteen years of age shall be entitled to the pension. But the rate of pension herein allowed shall be governed by the pay of the Navy as it existed in January, eighteen hundred and thirty-five; and the pension of the widow of a chief engineer shall be the same as that of a widow of a lieutenant in the Navy; the pension of the widow of a first assistant engineer shall be the same as that of the widow of a lieutenant of marines; the pension of the widow of a second or third assistant engineer the same as that of the widow of a forward officer; the pension of the widow of a fireman or coal-heaver shall be the same as that of the widow of a seaman. But the rate of pension prescribed by this and the preceding section shall be varied from and after the twenty-fifth day of July, eighteen hundred and sixty-six, in accordance with the provisions of section four thousand seven hundred and twelve of this Title; and the widow of an engineer, fireman, or coal-heaver shall not be entitled to any pension by reason of the death of her husband if his death was prior to the thirty-first day of August, eighteen hundred and forty-two. [See March 3, 1877, following.]

11 Aug., 1848, ss. 1, 2, 3, v. 9, p. 283.

NOTE.—From and after the passage of this act, the pension for total disability of passed assistant engineers, assistant engineers, and cadet engineers in the naval service, respectively, shall be the same as the pensions allowed to officers of the line in the naval service with whom they have relative rank.—3 March, 1877, v. 19, p. 403.

### RATES FIXED BY LAW FOR TOTAL DISABILITY.

*Navy and Marine Corps.*

| | Month. |
|---|---|
| Captain and all officers of higher rank; commander; lieutenant commanding and master commanding; surgeon, paymaster and chief engineer ranking with commander by law; lieutenant colonel and all of higher rank in the Marine Corps | $30 |
| Lieutenant, passed assistant surgeon, surgeon, paymaster, and chief engineer ranking with lieutenant by law, and major in Marine Corps | 25 |
| Master, professor of mathematics, assistant surgeon, paymaster and chaplain, and captain in the Marine Corps | 20 |
| First lieutenant in the Marine Corps | 17 |
| First assistant engineer, ensign and pilot, and second lieutenant in the Marine Corps | 15 |
| Cadet midshipman, passed midshipman, midshipman, clerks of admirals, paymasters, and of officers commanding vessels, second and third sasistant engineers, masters, mates and warrant officers. | 10 |
| All enlisted men except warrant officers | 8 |

Pension Office Digest of Laws, 1881, p. 231.

| Rates and disabilities specified by law. | From July 4, 1864. | From March 3, 1865. | From June 6, 1866. | From June 4, 1872. | From June 4, 1874. | From February 28, 1877. | From June 17, 1878. | From March 3, 1879. | Act of June 16, 1880. | From March 3, 1883. |
|---|---|---|---|---|---|---|---|---|---|---|
| Loss of both hands | $25 00 | | | $31 25 | $50 00 | | $72 00 | | | |
| Loss of both feet | 20 90 | | | 31 25 | 50 00 | | 72 00 | | | |
| Loss of both eyes | 25 00 | | | 31 25 | 50 00 | | 72 00 | | | |
| Loss of an eye, the sight of the other previously lost | | | $25 00 | 31 25 | 50 00 | | 72 00 | | | |
| Loss of 1 hand and 1 foot | | $20 00 | | 24 00 | | $36 00 | | | | |
| Total disability in 1 hand and 1 foot | | | 20 00 | 24 00 | | 36 00 | | | | |
| Loss of a hand or a foot | | | 15 00 | 18 00 | | | | | | |
| **Totally or permanently disabled in same** | | | | | | | | | Extends the provisions of act of June 17, 1878. | **24 00** |
| Amputation at or above elbow or knee | | | | | | | | | | **24 00** |
| Amputation at hip-joint | | | 15 00 | 18 00 | 24 00 | | | | | **30 00** |
| Inability to perform manual labor | | | 15 00 | 18 00 | 24 00 | | $37 50 | | | |
| Ditto—equal to loss of hand or foot | | | 20 00 | 24 00 | | | | | | **24 00** |
| Regular aid and attendance | | | 25 00 | 31 25 | 50 00 | | | | | |
| Total disability in both hands | | | 25 00 | 31 25 | 50 00 | | | | | |

NOTE.—The matter in heavy-faced type has been inserted in the foregoing table to meet recent legislation.

*Rates fixed by Pension Office for certain disabilities not specified by law.*

Loss of an eye .................................................................. one-half.
Loss of a thumb ............................................................... one-half.
Loss of an index finger ...................................................... three-eighths.
Loss of a finger ................................................................ one-fourth.
Loss of a toe .................................................................... one-fourth.
Loss of a great toe ............................................................ one-half.
Inguinal hernia ................................................................. one-half.
Double inguinal hernia ...................................................... three-fourths.
Anchylosis of elbow joint ................................................... total.

Pension Office Digest of Laws, 1881, p. 232.

NOTES.—For total deafness, or deafness approaching to total, affecting one ear one-eighth of a pension may be allowed. For slight deafness in both ears, or severe or total deafness in one ear and slight deafness in the other, one-fourth of a total pension. For severe deafness of both ears, or total deafness in one ear and severe deafness in the other, one-half of a total pension; or if the deafness should exist in a degree nearly total, three-fourths of a total pension. For total deafness the pension for total disability should be allowed except in the cases for which the rate for total disability is less than $13 a month.—Pension Office Digest, p. 146.

Desertion of a soldier is a bar to widow's claim to pension. No bar if soldier returned to service and was killed in the line of duty; nor, if from a former term of service and the soldier was honorably discharged. From prior service to that for which pension is claimed in war of the rebellion no bar to pension.—Pension Office Digest, p. 150.

When an officer of the Navy dies of disease contracted while on the retired list his widow is not entitled to a pension.

*Idem*, p. 158.

"Specific" disability is such as is specified in the statutes. Injuries requiring a medical examination to ascertain and declare their nature, and as to the effect of which there is room for a difference of opinion, are not specific disabilities.—Op. Atty. Genl. Devens, May 17, 1878, P. O. Digest, p. 154.

Disability to be pensionable must be of such a character and exist to such a degree that it can be detected by the examining surgeon of the office.—P. O. Digest, p. 152.

Disability not connected with a previous disease or injury received in service is not pensionable, even if soldier's health after discharge rendered him more liable to disease. Resulting from carelessness, disregard of regulations, &c., not pensionable, nor if shown by surgeon's certificate to have existed prior to enlistment. Cause of disability must have been contracted in the line of duty as well as in the service.

*Idem*, pp. 152, 153.

Dishonorable discharge does not forfeit soldier's right to pension. Date of actual discharge is the date to which paid.

*Idem*, p. 154.

A soldier traveling under orders, in any manner, is "on the march," and in the line of duty.

*Idem*, p. 158.

When "not in line of duty:" while on furlough; while on leave to attend to private business; while violating any established Army regulation; while bathing, unless under orders to do so; suicide, unless the result of insanity; wrestling or scuffling with comrades; foraging, unless under orders, even if granted leave to do so; while confined in a military prison on charge of desertion; while undergoing sentence of court-martial.—Pension Office Decisions, pp. 157, 160.

*Arrears of Pension.*—Not due to an executor or administrator, if not applied for by a pensioner; nor to a minor if never applied for by the soldier; nor to a widow during the period the soldier was living, when he made no application therefor.—Pension Office Decisions, p. 187.

## PENSION FUNDS.

Sec.
4750. Secretary of Navy trustee of Navy pension-fund.
4751. Penalties, how to be sued for, &c.
4752. Prize-money accruing to United States to remain a fund for pensions.
4753. Naval pension-fund, how to be invested.
4754. Rate of interest on naval pension-fund.
4755. Naval pensions payable from fund.
4756. Pensions to disabled seamen and marines of twenty years' service.
4757. Pensions to disabled seamen and marines, ten years' service.

Sec.
4758. Secretary of Navy trustee of privateer pension-fund.
4759. Privateer pension-fund, how derived.
4760. To be paid into Treasury, &c.
4761. Wounded, &c., privateersmen to be placed on pension-list.
4762. Commanding officers of privateers to enter names, &c., in a journal.
4763. Transcript of journals to be transmitted to Secretary of the Navy.

Title 57.

Secretary of Navy trustee.

SEC. 4750. The Secretary of the Navy shall be trustee of the Navy pension-fund.

10 July, 1832, s. 1, v. 4, p. 572.

Penalties, how to be sued for, &c.

SEC. 4751. All penalties and forfeitures incurred under the provisions of sections twenty-four hundred and sixty-one, twenty-four hundred and sixty-two, and twenty-four hundred and sixty-three, Title "THE PUBLIC

LANDS," shall be sued for, recovered, distributed, and accounted for, under the directions of the Secretary of the Navy, and shall be paid over, one-half to the informers, if any, or captors, where seized, and the other half to the Secretary of the Navy for the use of the Navy pension-fund; and the Secretary is authorized to mitigate, in whole or in part, on such terms and conditions as he deems proper, by an order in writing, any fine, penalty, or forfeiture so incurred.

2 March, 1831, s. 3, v. 4, p. 472.

SEC. 4752. All money accruing or which has already accrued to the United States from sale of prizes shall be and remain forever a fund for the payment of pensions to the officers, seamen, and marines who may be entitled to receive the same; and if such fund be insufficient for the purpose, the public faith is pledged to make up the deficiency; but if it should be more than sufficient the surplus shall be applied to the making of further provision for the comfort of the disabled officers, seamen, and marines. [See § 4630, under PRIZE.] Prize-money accruing to the United States to remain a fund for pensions.

17 July, 1862, s. 11, v. 12, p. 607.

SEC. 4753. The Secretary of the Navy, as trustee of the naval pension-fund, is directed to cause to be invested in the registered securities of the United States, on the first day of January and the first day of July of each year, so much of such fund then in the Treasury of the United States as may not be required for the payment of naval pensions for the then current fiscal year; and upon the requisition of the Secretary, so much of the fund as may not be required for such payment of pensions accruing during the current fiscal year shall be held in the Treasury on the days above named in each year, subject to his order, for the purpose of such immediate investment; and the interest payable in coin upon the securities in which the fund may be invested, shall be so paid, when due, to the order of the Secretary of the Navy, and he is authorized and directed to exchange the amount of such interest when paid in coin, for so much of the legal currency of the United States as may be obtained therefor at the current rates of premium on gold, and to deposit the interest so converted in the Treasury to the credit of the naval pension-fund; but nothing herein contained shall be construed to interfere with the payment of naval pensions under the supervision of the Secretary of the Interior, as regulated by law. Naval pension-fund, how to be invested.

1 July, 1864, Res. 62, v. 13, p. 424.

SEC. 4754. The interest on the naval pension-fund shall hereafter be at the rate of three per centum per annum in lawful money. Rate of interest on naval pension-fund.

23 July, 1868, s. 2, v. 15, p. 170.

SEC. 4755. The Navy pensions shall be paid from the Navy pension-fund, but no payments shall be made therefrom except upon appropriations authorized by Congress. Navy pensions payable from fund.

11 July, 1870, v. 16, p. 222.
23 July, 1868, s. 2, v. 15, p. 170.
19 Jan., 1877, v. 19, p. 224.

SEC. 4756. There shall be paid out of the naval pension-fund to every person, who, from age or infirmity, is disabled from sea-service, but who has served as an enlisted person in the Navy or Marine Corps for the period of twenty years, and not been discharged for misconduct, in lieu of being provided with a home in the Naval Asylum, Philadelphia, if he so elects, a sum equal to one-half the pay of his rating at the time he was discharged, to be paid to him quarterly, under the direction of the Commissioner of Pensions; and applications for such pension shall be made to the Secretary of the Navy, who, upon being satisfied that the applicant comes within the provisions of this section, shall certify the same to the Commissioner of Pensions, and such certificate shall be his warrant for making payment as herein authorized. Half-rating to disabled enlisted persons serving twenty years in Navy or Marine Corps.

2 March, 1867, s. 6, v. 14, p. 516.

SEC. 4757. Every disabled person who has served in the Navy or Marine Corps as an enlisted man for a period not less than ten years, and not been discharged for misconduct, may apply to the Secretary of the Navy for aid from the surplus income of the naval pension-fund; and the Secretary of the Navy is authorized to convene a board of not less than three naval officers, one of whom shall be a surgeon, to examine Serving not less than ten years may receive what aid.

into the condition of the applicant, and to recommend a suitable amount for his relief, and for a specified time, and upon the approval of such recommendation by the Secretary of the Navy, and certificate thereof to the Commissioner of Pensions, the amount shall be paid in the same manner as is provided in the preceding section for the payment to persons disabled by long service in the Navy; but no allowance so made shall exceed the rate of a pension for full disability corresponding to the grade of the applicant, nor, if in addition to a pension, exceed one fourth the rate of such pension.

*Ibid.*

NOTES.—Pensions granted under sections 4756 and 4757 are wholly under control of the Secretary of the Navy, to whom applications should be made. The Pension Office also requires that claimants shall file an application, properly executed before a court of record, as an identification of the party whose claim has been adjudicated by the Navy Department.

The rule now in force regarding these pensions, is that they will be considered as commencing on the date of filing the application in the Navy Department. See Pension Office Digest, p. 191.

**Secretary of Navy trustee.** SEC. 4758. The Secretary of the Navy shall be trustee of the privateer pension-fund.

10 July, 1832, s. 1, v. 4, p. 572.

**Privateer pension-fund, how derived.** SEC. 4759. Two per centum on the net amount, after deducting all charges and expenditures, of the prize-money arising from captured vessels and cargoes, and on the net amount of the salvage of vessels and cargoes recaptured by the private armed vessels of the United States, shall be secured and paid over to the collector or other chief officer of the customs at the port or place in the United States at which such captured or recaptured vessels may arrive; or to the consul or other public agent of the United States residing at the port or place, not within the United States, at which such captured or recaptured vessels may arrive. And the moneys arising therefrom are pledged by the Government of the United States as a fund for the support and maintenance of the widows and orphans of such persons as may be slain, and for the support and maintenance of such persons as may be wounded and disabled on board of the private armed vessels of the United States, in any engagement with the enemy, to be assigned and distributed in such manner as is or may be provided by law.

26 June, 1812, s. 17, v. 2, p. 763.

**To be paid into the Treasury, &c.** SEC. 4760. The two per centum reserved in the hands of the collectors and consuls by the preceding section, shall be paid to the Treasury, under the like regulations provided for other sublic money, and shall constitute a fund for the purposes provided for by that section.

13 Feb., 1813, s. 1, v. 2, p. 709.

**Wounded, &c., privateersmen to be placed on pension-list.** SEC. 4761. The Secretary of the Interior is required to place on the pension-list, under the like regulations and restrictions as are used in relation to the Navy of the United States, any officer, seamen, or marine, who, on board of any private armed vessel bearing a commission of letter of marque, shall have been wounded or otherwise disabled in any engagement with the enemy, or in the line of their duty as officers, seamen, or marines of such private armed vessel; allowing to the captain a sum not exceeding twenty dollars per month; to lieutenants and sailing-master a sum not exceeding twelve dollars each per month; to marine carpenter, boatswain, gunner, carpenter, master's mate, and prize-masters, a sum not exceeding ten dollars each per month; to all other officers a sum not exceeding eight dollars each per month, for the highest rate of disability, and so in proportion; and to a seaman, or acting as a marine, the sum of six dollars per month, for the highest rate of disability, and so in proportion; which several pensions shall be paid from moneys appropriated for the payment of pensions.

13 Feb., 1813, s. 2, v. 2, p. 799.
2 Aug., 1813, v. 3, p. 86.

**Commanding officers of privateers to enter names, &c., in a journal.** SEC. 4762. The commanding officer of every vessel having a commission, or letters of marque and reprisal, shall enter in his journal the name and rank of any officer, and the name of any seaman, who, during his cruise, is wounded or disabled, describing the manner and extent, as far as practicable, of such wound or disability.

13 Feb., 1813, s. 3, v. 2, p. 800.

## PERJURY.

Sec. 4763. Every collector shall transmit quarterly to the Secretary of the Navy a transcript of such journals as may have been reported to him, so far as it gives a list of the officers and crew, and the description of wounds and disabilities, the better to enable the Secretary to decide on claims for pensions.

*Transcript of journals to be transmitted to Secretary of the Navy.*

*Ibid., s. 4.*

## PERJURY.

Sec.
1023. Prosecutions for perjury.
1624. To obtain claims.
5392. Punishment.

Sec.
5393. Subornation of perjury.
5396. Form of indictment for perjury.
5397. Indictment for subornation of perjury.

Sec. 1023. In prosecutions for perjury committed on examination before a naval general court-martial, or for the subornation thereof, it shall be sufficient to set forth the offense charged on the defendant, without setting forth the authority by which the court was held, or the particular matters brought before, or intended to be brought before, said court.

*Title 13, Chap. 18.*

*Prosecutions for perjury before a naval court-martial.*

17 July, 1862, s. 1, art. 13, v. 12, p. 604.

Sec. 1624. Art. 14. Fine and imprisonment, or such other punishment as a court-martial may adjudge, shall be inflicted upon any person in the naval service of the United States

\* \* \* \* \*

Who, for the purpose of obtaining, or aiding others to obtain, the approval, allowance, or payment of any claim against the United States or any officer thereof, makes, or procures or advises the making of, any oath to any fact or to any writing or other paper, knowing such oath to be false.

*Title 15, Chap. 10.*

*For the purpose of obtaining claims.*

2 March, 1863, s. 1, v. 12, p. 696.

Sec. 5392. Every person who, having taken an oath before a competent tribunal, officer, or person, in any case in which a law of the United States authorizes an oath to be administered, that he will testify, declare, depose, or certify truly, or that any written testimony, declaration, deposition, or certificate by him subscribed is true, willfully and contrary to such oath states or subscribes any material matter which he does not believe to be true, is guilty of perjury, and shall be punished by a fine of not more than two thousand dollars, and by imprisonment, at hard labor, not more than five years; and shall, moreover, thereafter be incapable of giving testimony in any court of the United States until such time as the judgment against him is reversed.

*Title 70, Chap. 4.*

*Perjury.*

30 April, 1790, s. 18, v. 1, p. 116.
3 March, 1825, s. 13, v. 4, p. 118.

Sec. 5393. Every person who procures another to commit any perjury is guilty of subornation of perjury, and punishable as in the preceding section prescribed.

*Subornation of perjury.*

33 April, 1790, s. 18, v. 1, p. 116.
3 March, 1825, s. 13, v. 4, p. 118.

Sec. 5396. In every presentment or indictment prosecuted against any person for perjury, it shall be sufficient to set forth the substance of the offense charged upon the defendant, and by what court, and before whom the oath was taken, averring such court or person to have competent authority to administer the same, together with the proper averment to falsify the matter wherein the perjury is assigned, without setting forth the bill, answer, information, indictment, declaration, or any part of any record or proceeding, either in law or equity, or any affidavit, deposition, or certificate, other than as hereinbefore stated, and without setting forth the commission or authority of the court or person before whom the perjury was committed.

*Form of indictment for perjury.*

30 April, 1790, s. 19, v. 1, p. 116.

Sec. 5397. In every presentment or indictment for subornation of perjury, it shall be sufficient to set forth the substance of the offense charged upon the defendant, without setting forth the bill, answer, information, indictment, declaration, or any part of any record or proceeding either in law or equity, or any affidavit, deposition, or certificate, and without setting forth the commission or authority of the court or person before whom the perjury was committed, or was agreed or promised to be committed.

*Indictment for subornation of perjury.*

*Ibid., s. 20.*

## PIRACY, ROBBERY.

| Sec. | Sec. |
|---|---|
| 4293. Public vessels to suppress piracy. | 5371. Robbery on shore by crew of piratical vessel. |
| 4294. Seizure of piratical vessels. | 5372. Murder, &c., upon the high seas. |
| 4295. Merchant-vessels may resist pirates. | 5373. Piracy under color of a commission from a foreign power. |
| 4296. Condemnation of piratical vessels. | 5374. Piracy by subjects or citizens of a foreign state. |
| 4297. Seizure of vessels fitted out for piracy. | |
| 4298. What vessels may be authorized to seize pirates. | 5375. Piracy in confining or detaining negroes on board vessels, &c. |
| 4299. Duty of officers of customs and marshals. | 5376. Piracy in landing, seizing, &c., negroes on any foreign shore. |
| 5323. Accessory before the fact to piracy, &c. | |
| 5324. Accessory after the fact to robbery or piracy. | 5383. Running away with or yielding up vessel or cargo. |
| 5368. Piracy under the law of nations. | 5384. Confederating, &c., with pirates. |
| 5369. Seaman laying violent hands on his commander. | 5533. Accessory after the fact of piracy; punishment. |
| 5370. Robbery upon the high seas. | |

**Title 13, Chap. 3.** SEC. 563. The district courts shall have jurisdiction of all cases arising under act for the punishment of piracy, when no circuit court is held in the district of such court.

3 March, 1823, v. 3, p. 789.
15 May, 1820, v. 3, p. 600.
30 Jan., 1823, v. 3, p. 721.

**Title 48, Chap. 8.**

*Public vessels to suppress piracy.*

SEC. 4293. The President is authorized to employ so many of the public armed vessels as in his judgment the service may require, with suitable instructions to the commanders thereof, in protecting the merchant-vessels of the United States and their crews from piratical aggressions and depredations.

3 March, 1819, s. 1, v. 3, p. 510.
30 Jan., 1823, v. 3, p. 721.

*Seizure of piratical vessels.*

SEC. 4294. The President is authorized to instruct the commanders of the public armed vessels of the United States to subdue, seize, take, and send to any port of the United States, any armed vessel or boat, or any vessel or boat, the crew whereof shall be armed, and which shall have attempted or committed any piratical aggression, search, restraint, depredation, or seizure, upon any vessel of the United States, or of the citizens thereof, or upon any other vessel; and also to retake any vessel of the United States, or its citizens, which may have been unlawfully captured upon the high seas.

3 March, 1819, s. 2, v. 3, p. 512.
30 Jan., 1823, v. 3, p. 721.

*Merchant-vessels may resist pirates.*

SEC. 4295. The commander and crew of any merchant-vessel of the United States, owned wholly, or in part, by a citizen thereof, may oppose and defend against any aggression, search, restraint, depredation, or seizure, which shall be attempted upon such vessel, or upon any other vessel so owned, by the commander or crew of any armed vessel whatsoever, not being a public armed vessel of some nation in amity with the United States, and may subdue and capture the same; and may also retake any vessel so owned which may have been captured by the commander or crew of any such armed vessel, and send the same into any port of the United States.

3 March, 1819, s. 3, v. 3, p. 513.
30 Jan., 1823, v. 3, p. 721.

*Condemnation of piratical vessels.*

SEC. 4296. Whenever any vessel, which shall have been built, purchased, fitted out in whole or in part, or held for the purpose of being employed in the commission of any piratical aggression, search, restraint, depredation, or seizure, or in the commission of any other act of piracy as defined by the law of nations, or from which any piratical aggression, search, restraint, depredation, or seizure shall have been first attempted or made, is captured and brought into or captured in any port of the United States, the same shall be adjudged and condemned to their use, and that of the captors after due process and trial in any court having admiralty jurisdiction, and which shall be holden for the district into which such captured vessel shall be brought; and the same court shall thereupon order a sale and distribution thereof accordingly, and at its discretion.

3 March, 1819, s. 4, v. 3, p. 513.
30 Jan., 1823, v. 3, p. 721.
5 Aug., 1861, s. 1, v. 12, p. 314.

PIRACY, ROBBERY. 277

SEC. 4297. Any vessel built, purchased, fitted out in whole or in part, or held for the purpose of being employed in the commission of any piratical aggression, search, restraint, depredation, or seizure, or in the commission of any other act of piracy, as defined by the law of nations, shall be liable to be captured and brought into any port of the United States if found upon the high seas, or to be seized if found in any port or place within the United States, whether the same shall have actually sailed upon any piratical expedition or not, and whether any act of piracy shall have been committed or attempted upon or from such vessel or not; and any such vessel may be adjudged and condemned, if captured by a vessel authorized as hereinafter mentioned, to the use of the United States and to that of the captors, and if seized by a collector, surveyor, or marshal, then to the use of the United States. *Seizure of vessels fitted out for piracy.*

5 Aug., 1861, s. 1, v. 12, p. 314.

SEC. 4298. The President is authorized to instruct the commanders of the public armed vessels of the United States, and to authorize the commanders of any other armed vessel sailing under the authority of any letters of marque and reprisal granted by Congress, or the commanders of any other suitable vessels, to subdue, seize, take, and, if on the high seas, to send into any port of the United States, any vessel or boat built, purchased, fitted out, or held as mentioned in the preceding section. *What vessels may be authorized to seize pirates.*

*Idem.* s. 2.

NOTES.—Piracy is defined by the law of nations to be a forcible depredation upon property on the high seas, without lawful authority, done *animo furandi;* that is, as defined, in this connection, in a spirit and intention of universal hostility. A pirate is said to be one who roves the sea in an armed vessel, without any commission from any sovereign state, on his own authority, and for the purpose of seizing by force and appropriating to himself, without discrimination, every vessel he may meet.—United States *v.* Baker, 5 Blatchford, 11, 12. Cited in Cadwalader's State Department Digest, p. 77.

To make the firing of one vessel into another a piratical aggression within the act of 1819, section 5368, R. S., it must be a first aggression unprovoked by any previous act of hostility or menace from the other side.—Cadwalader's Digest.—Op. IX, 114.

Robbery, or forcible depredation upon the high sea, *animo furandi*, is piracy by the law of nations. Cadwalader's Digest, p. 76, cites 5 Wheaton, 153. A vessel loses her national character by assuming a piratical character, and a piracy committed by a foreigner from on board such a vessel whatever, is punishable under act of 1790, section 5360, R. S.—*Idem*, p. 77, cites, 5 Wheaton, 184.

Every hostile attack, in time of peace, is not necessarily piratical. It may be by mistake, or in necessary self-defense, or to repel a supposed meditated attack by pirates. It may be justifiable, and then no blame attaches to the act; or it may be without just excuse, and then it carries responsibility in damages.—Cadwalader's Digest, p. 77, cites 11 Wheaton, 40, 41, and 2 Howard, 236.

Merchant vessels suspected of being engaged in illicit trade forbidden by the laws of Congress, may be seized and detained by public armed vessels.—Op. 3, 405.

SEC. 4299. The collectors of the several ports of entry, the surveyors of the several ports of delivery, and the marshals of the several judicial districts within the United States, shall seize any vessel or boat built, purchased, fitted out, or held as mentioned in section forty-two hundred and ninety-seven, which may be found within their respective ports or districts, and to cause the same to be proceeded against and disposed of as provided by that section. *Duties of officers of customs and marshals.*

*Idem*, s. 3.

SEC. 5323. Every person who knowingly aids, abets, causes, procures, commands, or counsels another to commit any murder, robbery, or other piracy upon the seas, is an accessory before the fact to such piracies, and every such person being thereof convicted shall suffer death. *Title 70, Chap. 1. Accessory before the fact to piracy, &c.*

30 April, 1790, s. 10, v. 1, p. 114.

SEC. 5324. Every person who receives or takes into custody any vessel, goods, or other property feloniously taken by any robber or pirate against the laws of the United States, knowing the same to have been feloniously taken, and every person who, knowing that such pirate or robber has done or committed any such piracy or robbery, on the land or at sea, receives, entertains, or conceals any such pirate or robber, is an accessory after the fact to such robbery or piracy. [See § 5533.] *Accessory after the fact to robbery or piracy.*

30 April, 1790, s. 11, v. 1, p. 114.

## PIRACY, ROBBERY.

**Title 70, Chap. 3.**
**Piracy under the law of nations.**

SEC. 5368. Every person who, on the high seas, commits the crime of piracy as defined by the law of nations, and is afterward brought into or found in the United States, shall suffer death. [See §§ 5323–5333.]

3 March, 1819, s. 5, v. 3, p. 513.
15 May, 1820, s. 2, v. 3, p. 600.
30 Jan., 1823, v. 3, p. 721.

**Seaman laying violent hands on his commander.**

SEC. 5369. Every seaman who lays violent hands upon his commander, thereby to hinder and prevent his fighting in defense of his vessel or the goods intrusted to him, is a pirate, and shall suffer death.

30 April, 1790, s. 8, v. 1, p. 113.

**Robbery upon the high seas.**

SEC. 5370. Every person who, upon the high seas, or in any open roadstead, or in any haven, basin, or bay, or in any river where the sea ebbs and flows, commits the crime of robbery, in or upon any vessel, or upon any ship's company of any vessel, or the lading thereof, is a pirate, and shall suffer death.

15 May, 1820, s. 3, v. 3, p. 600.

**Robbery on shore by crew of piratical vessel.**

SEC. 5371. Every person engaged in any piratical cruise or enterprise, or being of the crew of any piratical vessel, who lands from such vessel and on shore commits robbery, is a pirate, and shall suffer death.

*Ibid.*

**Murder, &c., upon the high seas.**

SEC. 5372. Every person who commits upon the high seas, or in any river, harbor, basin, or bay, out of the jurisdiction of any particular State, murder or robbery, or any other offense which, if committed within the body of a county, would be punishable with death by the laws of the United States, is a pirate, and shall suffer death.

30 April, 1790, s. 8, v. 1, p. 113.

**Piracy under color of a commission from a foreign power.**

SEC. 5373. Every citizen who commits any murder or robbery, or any act of hostility against the United States, or against any citizen thereof, on the high seas, under color of any commission from any foreign prince, or state or on pretense of authority from any person, is, notwithstanding the pretense of such authority, a pirate, and shall suffer death.

*Idem*, s. 9, v. 1, p. 114.

**Piracy by subjects or citizens of a foreign state.**

SEC. 5374. Every subject or citizen of any foreign state, who is found and taken on the sea making war upon the United States, or cruising against the vessels and property thereof, or of the citizens of the same, contrary to the provisions of any treaty existing between the United States and the state of which offender is a citizen or subject, when by such treaty such acts are declared to be piracy, is guilty of piracy, and shall suffer death.

3 March, 1847, v. 9, p. 175.

**Piracy in confining or detaining negroes on board vessels.**

SEC. 5375. Every person who, being of the crew or ship's company of any foreign vessel engaged in the slave-trade, or being of the crew or ship's company of any vessel owned wholly or in part, or navigated for or in behalf of any citizen, forcibly confines or detains on board such vessel any negro or mulatto, with intent to make such negro or mulatto a slave, or, on board such vessel, offers or attempts to sell, as a slave, any negro or mulatto, or on the high seas, or anywhere on tidewater, transfers or delivers to any other vessel any negro or mulatto with intent to make such negro or mulatto a slave, or lands or delivers on shore from on board such vessel any negro or mulatto with intent to make sale of, or having previously sold such negro or mulatto as a slave, is a pirate, and shall suffer death. [See §§ 5525, 5551–5560, SLAVE-TRADE.]

15 May, 1820, s. 5, v. 3, p. 601.

**Piracy in landing, seizing, &c., negroes on any foreign shore.**

SEC. 5376. Every person who, being of the crew or ship's company of any foreign vessel engaged in the slave-trade, or being of the crew or ship's company of any vessel, owned in whole or part, or navigated for, or in behalf of, any citizen, lands from such vessel, and, on any foreign shore, seizes any negro or mulatto with intent to make such negro or mulatto a slave, or decoys, or forcibly brings, or carries, or receives such negro or mulatto on board such vessel, with like intent, is a pirate, and shall suffer death.

*Idem*, s. 4, p. 600.

Sec. 5383. Every captain, other officer, or mariner, of a vessel on the high seas, or on any other waters within the admiralty and maritime jurisdiction of the United States, who piratically or feloniously runs away with such vessel, or with any goods or merchandise thereof, to the value of fifty dollars, or who yields up such vessel voluntarily to any pirate, shall be fined not more than ten thousand dollars, or imprisoned at hard labor not more than ten years, or both. *Running away with or yielding up vessel or cargo.*

8 Aug., 1846, s. 5, v. 9, p. 73.
30 April, 1790, s. 8, v. 1, p. 113.

Sec. 5384. If any person attempts or endeavors to corrupt any commander, master, officer, or mariner to yield up or to run away with any vessel, or with any goods, wares, or merchandise, or to turn pirate, or to go over to or confederate with pirates, or in any wise to trade with any pirate, knowing him to be such, or furnishes such pirate with any ammunition, stores, or provisions of any kind, or fits out any vessel knowingly and with a design to trade with, supply, or correspond with any pirate or robber upon the seas; or if any person consults, combines, confederates, or corresponds with any pirate or robber upon the seas, knowing him to be guilty of any piracy or robbery; or if any seaman confines the master of any vessel, he shall be imprisoned not more than three years, and fined not more than one thousand dollars. *Confederating, &c., with pirates.*

20 April, 1790, s. 12, v. 1, p. 115.

Sec. 5533. Every accessory after the fact to murder, robbery, or piracy, shall be imprisoned not more than three years, and fined not more than five hundred dollars. [See § 5324.] *Title 70, Chap. 8. Accessory after the fact to murder, robbery, or piracy.*

30 April, 1790, s. 11, v. 1, p. 114.

## PILOTS—PILOTAGE.

Sec.
4235. State regulation of pilots.
4236. Pilots on boundaries.

Sec.
4237. No discrimination in rates of pilotage.

Sec. 4235. Until further provision is made by Congress, all pilots in the bays, inlets, rivers, harbors, and ports of the United States shall continue to be regulated in conformity with the existing laws of the States respectively wherein such pilots may be, or with such laws as the States may respectively enact for the purpose. *Title 48, Chap. 5. State regulation of pilots.*

7 Aug., 1789, s. 4, v. 1, p. 54.

Sec. 4236. The master of any vessel coming into or going out of any port situate upon waters which are the boundary between two States, may employ any pilot duly licensed or authorized by the laws of either of the States bounded on such waters, to pilot the vessel to or from such port. *Pilots on boundaries between States.*

2 March, 1837, v. 5, p. 153.

Sec. 4237. No regulations or provisions shall be adopted by any State which shall make any discrimination in the rate of pilotage or half-pilotage between vessels sailing between the ports of one State and vessels sailing between the ports of different States, or any discrimination against vessels propelled in whole or in part by steam, or against national vessels of the United States; and all existing regulations or provisions making any such discrimination are annulled and abrogated. *No discrimination in rates of pilotage.*

13 July, 1866, v. 14, p. 93.

NOTES.—Government vessels are not required to employ and pay branch pilot upon entering the ports and harbors of the United States. The exemption extends to all public vessels whether armed or not.—Op. IV, 532, Sept. 9, 1846, Mason.

The penalties imposed by State laws for piloting vessels without due license from the State, have no application to persons employed as pilots on board public vessels of the United States, the latter vessels being within the exclusive jurisdiction of the United States.—Op. XVI, 647, Oct. 22, 1879.

The term "public vessels" does not apply to vessels of the Navy alone. Within the meaning of the inspection and navigation laws public vessels are those owned by the United States, and those used by them for public purposes. Those laws warrant no distinction between public vessels under the control of the Navy Department and public vessels under the control of any other department of the Government. Unlicensed pilots and engineers can be lawfully employed on them.—Op. XIII, p. 249, Hoar, June 1, 1870.

## POSTAGE, MAIL-MATTER, &c.

### FOREIGN POSTAGE.

Sec.
3912. Postage on foreign-mail-matter.
3913. Postage on irregular sea-letters.

Sec.
3976. Vessels carrying mails.

**Title 46, Chap. 4.**
*Postage on foreign mail-matter.*

SEC. 3912. The rate of United States postage on mail-matter sent to or received from foreign countries with which different rates have not been established by postal convention or other arrangement, when forwarded by vessels regularly employed in transporting the mail, shall be ten cents for each half ounce or fraction thereof on letters, unless reduced by order of the Postmaster-General; two cents each on newspapers; and not exceeding two cents per each two ounces, or fraction thereof, on pamphlets, periodicals, books, and other printed matter, which postage shall be prepaid on matter sent and collected on matter received; and to avoid loss to the United States in the payment of balances, the Postmaster-General may collect the unpaid postage on letters from foreign countries in coin or its equivalent.

8 June, 1872, s. 165, v. 17, p. 304.

*Postage on irregular sea-letters.*

SEC. 3913. All letters conveyed by vessels not regularly employed in carrying the mail shall, if for delivery within the United States, be charged with double postage, to cover the fee paid to the vessel.

*Ibid.*, s. 166.

**Title 46, Chap. 9.**
*United States vessels to carry mails; oath; penalty.*

SEC. 3976. The master of any vessel of the United States bound from any port therein to any foreign port, or from any foreign port to any port of the United States, shall, before clearance, receive on board and securely convey all such mails as the Post-Office Department, or any diplomatic or consular officer of the United States abroad, shall offer; and he shall promptly deliver the same, on arriving at the port of destination, to the proper officer, for which he shall receive two cents for every letter so delivered; and upon the entry of every such vessel returning from any foreign port, the master thereof shall make oath that he has promptly delivered all the mail placed on board said vessel before clearance from the United States; and if he shall fail to make such oath the vessel shall not be entitled to the privileges of a vessel of the United States. [See § 4203, MERCHANT SERVICE.]

*Ibid.*, s. 222, p. 310.

### DOMESTIC POSTAGE.

\* \* \* \* \* \* \*

*3 March, 1879.*
*Division of mail matter.*

That mailable matter shall be divided into four classes:
First, written matter;
Second, periodical publications;
Third, miscellaneous printed matter;
Fourth, merchandise.
Mailable matter of the first class shall embrace letters, postal cards, and all matters wholly or partly in writing, except as hereinafter provided.

3 March, 1879, ch. 180, s. 7, v. 20, p. 355.

*Postal cards.*

Postal cards shall be transmitted through the mails at a postage charge of one cent each, including the cost of manufacture; and drop letters shall be mailed at the rate of two cents per half ounce or fraction thereof, including delivery at letter carrier offices, and one cent for each half ounce or fraction thereof where free delivery by carrier is not established. The Postmaster-General may, however, provide, by regulation, for transmitting unpaid and duly certified letters of soldiers, sailors, and marines in the service of the United States to their destination, to be paid on delivery.

*Idem*, s. 9.

*Second class matter.*

That mailable matter of the second class shall embrace all newspapers and other periodical publications which are issued at stated intervals, and as frequently as four times a year and are within the conditions named in section twelve and fourteen.

*Idem*, s. 10.

POSTAGE, MAIL-MATTER, ETC.  281

That mail matter of the third class shall embrace books, transient newspapers, and periodicals, circulars, and other matter wholly in print (not included in section twelve) [2d class matter], proof sheets, corrected proof sheets, and manuscript copy accompanying the same, and postage shall be paid at the rate of one cent for each two ounces or fractional part thereof, and shall fully be prepaid by postage stamps affixed to said matter. Printed matter other than books received in the mails from foreign countries under the provisions of postal treaties or conventions shall be free of customs duty, and books which are admitted to the international mails exchanged under the provisions of the Universal Postal Union Convention may, when subject to customs duty, be delivered to addressees in the United States under such regulations for the collection of duties as may be agreed upon by the Secretary of the Treasury and the Postmaster-General. — *Third class matter defined.* *Rate of postage.*

*Idem*, s. 17.

That the term "circular" is defined to be a printed letter, which, according to internal evidence, is being sent in identical terms to several persons. A circular shall not lose its character as such, when the date and the name of the address and of the sender shall be written therein, nor by the correction of mere typographical errors in writing. — *"Circular" defined.*

*Idem*, s. 18.

That "printed matter" within the intendment of this act is defined to be the reproduction upon paper, by any process except that of handwriting, of any words, letters, characters, figures, or images, or of any combination thereof, not having the character of an actual and personal correspondence. — *"Printed matter" defined.*

*Idem*, s. 19.

That mailable matter of the fourth class shall embrace all matter not embraced in the first, second, or third class, which is not in its form or nature liable to destroy, deface, or otherwise damage the contents of the mail bag, or harm the person of any one engaged in the postal service, and is not above the weight provided by law, which is hereby declared to be not exceeding four pounds for each package thereof, except in the case of single books weighing in excess of that amount, and except for books and documents published or circulated by order of Congress, or official matter emanating from any of the departments of the government, or from the Smithsonian Institution, or which is not declared non-mailable* under the provision of section thirty-eight hundred and ninety-three of the Revised Statutes, as amended by the act of July twelfth, eighteen hundred and seventy-six, or matter appertaining to lotteries, gift concerts, or fraudulent schemes or devices. — *Fourth class matter.*

*Idem*, s. 20.

All mail-matter of the first class upon which one full rate of postage has been prepaid shall be forwarded to its destination, charged with the unpaid rate, to be collected on delivery. * * * — 3 March, 1879. *Deficient postage.*

3 March, 1879, s. 26, ch. 180, v. 20, p. 355.

And upon all matter of the first class * * * postage shall be charged, on and after the first day of October A. D. eighteen hundred and eighty-three at the rate of two cents for each half ounce or fraction thereof. — 3 March, 1883. *Postage on first class matter.*

3 March, 1883, s. 1, v. 22, p. 455.

### DEPARTMENTAL STAMPS.

That the Secretaries, respectively, of the Departments of State, of the Treasury, War, Navy, and of the Interior, and the Attorney-General, are authorized to make requisitions upon the Postmaster-General for the necessary amount of official postage-stamps for the use of their departments, not exceeding the amount stated in the estimates submitted to Congress; and upon presentation of proper vouchers therefor at the Treasury, the amount thereof shall be credited to the appropriation for the service of the Post-Office Department for the same fiscal year. — 3 March, 1883. *How procured.*

3 March, 1883, chap. 128, s. 2, v. 22, p. 503.

---

* Obscene books, pictures, scurrilous letters, &c.

**Inclosure to members of Congress.**

And it shall be the duty of the respective departments to inclose to Senators, Representatives, and Delegates in Congress, in all official communications requiring answers, or to be forwarded to others, penalty envelopes addressed as far as practicable, for forwarding or answering such official correspondence.

*Idem.*

NOTES.—The Department stamps can be used to prepay fees on registered letters.—Op. Asst. Att'y Gen'l, P. O. Dept., May 11, 1879.

They can also be used to pay return postage on answers to communications sent by Government officers to private individuals; the penalty envelopes cannot be so used.—*Ibid.*

Official correspondence for Canada may be sent in penalty envelopes or prepaid with Department stamps. If sent to other foreign countries embraced in the Universal Postal Union, it can be prepaid only by means of the ordinary postage stamps. It cannot be sent in the penalty envelopes.

Foreign countries to which official correspondence may be prepaid with the official postage stamps are such only as are supplied with mails from the United States by *direct* services, and not through the intermediary of Postal Union countries. The following are of that class: The Australian colonies (North, South, and West Australia, New South Wales,, Queensland, and Victoria), Tasmania, New Zealand, Chatham, Fiji, Samoan, and Norfolk Islands, *via* San Francisco; Bolivia, *via* Colon and Panama; North China destinations, *via* San Francisco, in mails to the U. S. postal agent at Shanghai.—Post-Office Department to Navy Department, 1883.

### PENALTY ENVELOPES.

**Penalty envelopes.**

That it shall be lawful to transmit through the mail, free of postage, any letters, packages, or other matters relating exclusively to the business of the Government of the United States: *Provided*, That every such letter or package to entitle it to pass free shall bear over the words

**Indorsement.**

"Official business" an indorsement showing also the name of the Department, and, if from a bureau or office, the names of the Department and bureau or office, as the case may be, whence transmitted. And if any person shall make use of any such official envelope to avoid the payment of postage on his private letter, package, or other matter in the mail, the person so offending shall be deemed guilty of a misdemeanor, and subject to a fine of three hundred dollars, to be prosecuted in any court of competent jurisdiction.

3 March, 1877, s. 5, v. 19, p. 355.

SEC. 6. That for the purpose of carrying this act into effect, it shall be the duty of each of the Executive Departments of the United States to provide for itself and its subordinate offices the necessary envelopes; and in addition to the indorsement designating the Department in which they are to be used, the penalty for the unlawful use of these envelopes shall be stated thereon.

*Idem*, s. 6.

**Use of penalty envelopes extended.**

The provisions of the above sections (act March 3, 1877) "are hereby extended to all officers of the United States Government, and made applicable to all official mail-matter transmitted between any of the officers of the United States, or between any such officer and either of the executive departments or officers of the government, the envelopes of such matter in all cases to bear appropriate indorsments containing the proper designation of the office from which the same is transmitted, with a statement of the penalty for their misuse. And the provisions of said fifth and sixth sections are hereby likewise extended and made applicable to all official mail-matter sent from the Smithsonian Institution: *Provided*, That this act shall not extend or apply to pension-agents or other officers who receive a fixed allowance as compensation for their services, including expenses for postage."

\* \* \* \* \* \*

3 March, 1879, s. 29, v. 20, p. 362.

NOTES.—This section does not impose upon the Executive Department at Washington the duty of furnishing such envelopes to the various subordinate officers throughout the United States who are under their supervision, but whose offices are not offices in those Departments, excepting, of course, cases where that duty is required by other statutory provisions than those above mentioned.—Op. XVI, p. 455, January 30, 1880, Devens.

Where the envelopes are not furnished by the Departments, they may be prepared for their own use by the officers contemplated in section 29 of said act of March 3, 1879. The statute does not require that the penalty, &c., on such envelopes should be printed rather than written.—*Ibid.*

The indorsements on the penalty envelopes may be printed, written, or impressed by stamp.—Op. Assistant Attorney-General, P. O. Department, April 21, 1879.

The penalty envelopes cannot be properly used by officers in replying to a postmaster on matters not official; for instance, when a postmaster notifies said officer of private mail matter being in the office, which will be sent to him on the return of the requisite postage, the officer cannot use the penalty stamp in making his reply.—Post-Office ruling.

Officers of the Navy, who have no "office," in the sense that term is generally used, can send official mail matter, free of postage, between themselves, or to the Executive Departments, by using envelopes bearing the indorsement "official business," with their signature and rank, and a statement of the penalty for their misuse—the indorsements to be printed, or impressed by a stamp, or written.—Op. Assistant Attorney-General, P. O. D., April 20, 1879.

The 20th section of the act of March 3, 1879 (Postal Laws and Regulations, section 251), extending to all officers of the United States Government the provisions of the sections numbered 249 and 250, Postal Laws and Regulations, for the transmission of official mail matter, requires all officers who are not departmental in their character to use envelopes which bear the appropriate indorsements, containing the name of the office from which the same are transmitted, with a statement of the penalty for their misuse; and the use of the envelopes must be absolutely restricted to official mail matter transmitted between officers of the United States, or between any such officer and either of the Executive Departments or officers of the Government. The signature of the officer and his official title is not a compliance with the law; the name of the office from which they are transmitted must also be given on the envelope.—Rule 604, Post-Office Guide, January, 1883.

Official communications may be sent by officers of the Government under cover of the penalty envelope to private individuals; but such envelopes cannot be inclosed for the purpose of eliciting a reply.—Rule 606, *Idem*.

### LETTER-SHEET ENVELOPE—DOUBLE POSTAL CARDS.

That the Postmaster-General is hereby authorized to take the necessary steps to introduce and furnish for public use a letter-sheet envelope, on which postage-stamps of the denominations now in use on ordinary envelopes shall be placed. And the Postmaster-General is also authorized to introduce and furnish for public use a double postal card, on which shall be placed two one-cent stamps, and said card to be so arranged for the address that it may be forwarded and returned, said cards to be sold for two cents apiece; and also to introduce and furnish for public use a double-letter envelope, on which stamps of the denominations now in use may be placed, and with the arrangement for the address similar to the double postal card; said letter-sheet and double postal card and double envelope to be issued under such regulations as the Postmaster-General may prescribe.

*Letter-sheet envelopes—double postal cards.*

3 March, 1879, s. 32, v. 20, p. 362.

### MONEY ORDERS.

| Sec. | Sec. |
|---|---|
| 4033. Blank applications for orders. | 4038. Changes and modification of orders. |
| 4035. Notice of orders drawn to be sent. | 4039. Repayment of orders. |
| 4036. Orders to be good for one year. | 4040. Replacing lost orders. |
| 4037. Indorsement of orders. | —— Change in fees for money-orders. |

SEC. 4033. The Postmaster-General shall supply money-order offices with blank forms of application for money-orders, which each applicant shall fill up with his name, the name and address of the party to whom the order is to be paid, the amount and the date of the application; and all such applications shall be preserved by the postmaster receiving them for such time as the Postmaster-General may prescribe.

*Title 46, Ch. 13.*
*Blank applications for orders.*

8 June, 1872, s. 107, v. 17, p. 298.

SEC. 4034. The Postmaster-General shall furnish money-order offices with printed or engraved forms for money-orders, and no order shall be valid unless it be drawn upon such form.

*Orders to be on printed blanks.*

*Ibid.*, 109.

SEC. 4035. The postmaster issuing a money order shall send a notice thereof by mail, without delay, to the postmaster on whom it is drawn.

*Notice of orders drawn to be sent.*

*Ibid.*, s. 110.

SEC. 4036. No money-order shall be valid and payable unless presented to the postmaster on whom it is drawn within one year after its date; but the Postmaster-General, on the application of the remitter or payee of any such order, may cause a new order to be issued in lieu thereof.

*Order to be good for one year.*

*Ibid.*, s. 111.

SEC. 4037. The payee of a money-order may, by his written indorsement thereon, direct it to be paid to any other person, and the postmaster on whom it is drawn shall pay the same to the person thus desig-

*Indorsement of orders.*

nated, provided he shall furnish such proof as the Postmaster-General may prescribe that the indorsement is genuine, and that he is the person empowered to receive payment; but more than one indorsement shall render an order invalid and not payable, and the holder, to obtain payment, must apply in writing to the Postmaster General for a new order in lieu thereof, returning the original order, and making such proof of the genuineness of the indorsements as the Postmaster-General may require.

*Ibid.*, s. 112.
18 Feb., 1875, v. 18, p. 320.

**Changes and modification of orders.**
SEC. 4038. After a money-order has been issued, if the purchaser desires to have it modified or changed, the postmaster who issued the order shall take it back and issue another in lieu of it, for which a new fee shall be exacted.

8 June, 1872, s. 113, v. 17, p. 298.

**Repayment of orders.**
SEC. 4039. The postmaster issuing a money-order shall repay the amount of it upon the application of the person who obtained it, and the return of the order; but the fee paid for it shall not be returned.

*Ibid.*, s. 114.

**Replacing lost orders.**
SEC. 4040. Whenever a money-order has been lost, the Postmaster-General, upon the application of the remitter or payee of such order, may cause a duplicate thereof to be issued, without charge, providing the party losing the original shall furnish a certificate from the postmaster by whom it was payable that it has not been, and will not thereafter be, paid; and a similar certificate from the postmaster by whom it was issued that it has not been, and will not thereafter be, repaid.

*Ibid.*, s. 115.

**2 March, 1883.**

**Postal notes.**
That for the transmission of small sums under five dollars through the mails the Postmaster-General may authorize postmasters at money-order offices to issue money-orders, without corresponding advices, on an engraved form to be prescribed and furnished by him; and a money-order issued on such new form shall be designated and known as a "postal note," and a fee of three cents shall be charged for the issue thereof. Every postmaster who shall issue a postal note, under the authority of the Postmaster-General, shall make the same payable to bearer, when duly receipted, at any money-order office which the remitter thereof may select, and a postal note shall in like manner be payable to bearer when presented at the office of issue; and after a postal note has once been paid, to whomsoever it has been paid, the United States shall not be liable for any further claim for the amount thereof; but a postal note shall become invalid and not payable upon the expiration of three calender months from the last day of the month during which the same was issued; and the holder, to obtain the amount of an invalid postal note, must forward it to the superintendent of the money-order system at Washington, District of Columbia, together with an application, in such manner and form as the Postmaster-General may prescribe, for a duplicate thereof, payable to such holder; and an additional fee of three cents shall be charged and exacted for the issue of the duplicate.

3 March, 1883, chap. 123, s. 1, v. 22, p. 526.

\* \* \* \* \*

**Money-order rates.**
That a money-order shall not be issued for more than one hundred dollars, and that the fees for money-orders shall be as follows, to wit:

For orders not exceeding ten dollars, eight cents.

For orders exceeding ten dollars and not exceeding fifteen dollars, ten cents.

For orders exceeding fifteen dollars and not exceeding thirty dollars, fifteen cents.

For orders exceeding thirty dollars and not exceeding forty dollars, twenty cents.

For orders exceeding forty dollars and not exceeding fifty dollars, twenty-five cents.

For orders exceeding fifty dollars and not exceeding sixty dollars, thirty cents.

For orders exceeding sixty dollars and not exceeding seventy dollars, thirty-five cents.

For orders exceeding seventy dollars and not exceeding eighty dollars forty cents.

For orders exceeding eighty dollars and not exceeding one hundred dollars, forty-five cents.

*Idem,* s. 3.

But nothing contained in this act shall be so construed as to prevent the payment, out of current money-order funds, by duplicate issued under the authority of the Postmaster-General, of any lost or invalid money-order or of any invalid postal note more than seven years old, upon the presentation of satisfactory proof to the Postmaster-General of the ownership of such money-order or upon the production of such invalid postal note in accordance with the provisions of section one of this act. * * *

Duplicate issues.

*Idem,* s. 5.

## PRIZE.

| Sec. | | Sec. | |
|---|---|---|---|
| 4613. | Application of provisions of Title. | 4630. | Share of captors. |
| 4614. | What are "vessels of the Navy." | 4631. | Distribution of proceeds to captors. |
| 4615. | Duties of commanding officer upon making captures. | 4632. | What vessels are entitled to share. |
| | | 4633. | What officers are entitled to share. |
| 4616. | Statement of claim to share in prize. | 4634. | Determination of shares. |
| 4617. | Duties of prize-master. | 4635. | Bounty for persons on board vessels sunk or destroyed. |
| 4621. | Appointment of prize-commissioners. | | |
| 4622. | Duties of prize-commissioners. | 4639. | Costs and expenses. |
| 4624. | Appraisal, &c., of property taken for Government. | 4640. | Payment of expenses from prize-fund. |
| | | 4641. | Payment of prize-money. |
| 4625. | Proceedings for adjudication where property is not sent in. | 4642. | Distribution of bounty, salvage, &c. |
| | | 4643. | Assignments, &c., of prize-money and bounty. |
| 4626. | Delivery of property on stipulation. | 4652. | Recaptures. |
| 4627. | When property may be sold. | 5310. | Property taken on inland waters. |
| 4628. | Mode of making sale. | 5441. | Delaying or defrauding captor or claimant. |

SEC. 4613. The provisions of this Title shall apply to all captures made as prize by authority of the United States, or adopted and ratified by the President of the United States.

Title 54.

Application of provisions of Title.

30 June, s. 33, v. 13, p. 315.

SEC. 4614. The term "vessels of the Navy," as used in this Title, shall include all armed vessels officered and manned by the United States, and under the control of the Department of the Navy.

What are vessels of the Navy.

*Ibid.,* s. 32.

SEC. 4615. The commanding officer of any vessel making a capture shall secure the documents of the ship and cargo, including the log-book, with all other documents, letters, and other papers found on board, and make an inventory of the same, and seal them up, and send them, with the inventory, to the court in which proceedings are to be had, with a written statement that they are all the papers found, and are in the condition in which they were found; or explaining the absence of any documents or papers, or any change in their condition. He shall also send to such court, as witnesses, the master, one or more of the other officers, the supercargo, purser, or agent of the prize, and any person found on board whom he may suppose to be interested in, or to have knowledge respecting, the title, national character, or destination of the prize. He shall send the prize, with the documents, papers, and witnesses, under charge of a competent prize-master and prize-crew, into port for adjudication, explaining the absence of any usual witnesses; and in the absence of instructions from superior authority as to the port to which it shall be sent, he shall select such port as he shall deem most convenient, in view of the interests of probable claimants, as well as of the captors. If the captured vessel, or any part of the captured property, is not in condition to be sent in for adjudication, a survey shall be had thereon and an appraisement made by persons as competent and impartial as can be obtained, and their reports shall be sent to the court in which proceedings are to be had; and such property, unless appropriated for the use of the Government, shall be sold by the authority of the commanding officer present, and the proceeds deposited with the assistant treasurer of the United States most accessible to such court, and subject to its order in the cause. [See § 1624, Art. 15, page 12.]

Duties of commanding officer upon making capture.

*Ibid.,* s. 1, p. 306.

SEC. 4616. If any vessel of the United States shall claim to share in a prize, either as having made the capture, or as having been within signal distance of the vessel or vessels making the capture, the commanding

Statement of claim to share in prize.

286　　　　　　　　　　　　　　　PRIZE.

officer of such vessel shall make out a written statement of his claim, with the grounds on which it is founded, the principal facts tending to show what vessels made the capture, and what vessels were within signal distance of those making the capture, with reasonable particularity as to times, distances, localities, and signals made, seen, or answered; and such statement of claim shall be signed by him and sent to the court in which proceedings shall be had, and shall be filed in the cause.

*Ibid.*, s. 2, p. 307.

**Duties of prize-master.** SEC. 4617. The prize-master shall make his way diligently to the selected port, and there immediately deliver to a prize-commissioner the documents and papers, and the inventory thereof, and make affidavit that they are the same, and are in the same condition as delivered to him, or explaining any absence or change of condition therein, and that the prize-property is in the same condition as delivered to him, or explaining any loss or damage thereto; and he shall further report to the district attorney and give to him all the information in his possession respecting the prize and her capture; and he shall deliver over the persons sent as witnesses to the custody of the marshal, and shall retain the prize in his custody until it shall be taken therefrom by process from the prize-court. [See § 5441.]

*Ibid.*, s. 3.

[Secs. 4618–19–20 relates to libels, duties of district attorneys, &c.]

**Appointment of prize-commissioners.** SEC. 4621. Any district court may appoint prize-commissioners, not exceeding three in number; of whom one shall be a retired naval officer, approved by the Secretary of the Navy, who shall receive no other compensation than his pay in the Navy, and who shall protect the interests of the captors and of the Department of the Navy in the prize-property; and at least one of the others shall be a member of the bar of the court, of not less than three years' standing, and acquainted with the taking of depositions.

30 June, 1864, s. 5, v. 13, p. 307.

**Duties of prize-commissioners.** SEC. 4622. The prize-commissioners, or one of them, shall receive from the prize-master the documents and papers, and inventory thereof, and shall take the affidavit of the prize-master required by section forty-six hundred and seventeen, and shall forthwith take the testimony of the witnesses sent in, separate from each other, on interrogatories prescribed by the court, in the manner usual in prize-courts; and the witnesses shall not be permitted to see the interrogatories, documents, or papers, or to consult with counsel, or with any persons interested, without special authority from the court; and witnesses who have the rights of neutrals shall be discharged as soon as practicable. The prize-commissioners shall also take depositions de bene esse of the prize-crew and others, at the request of the district attorney, on interrogatories prescribed by the court. They shall also, as soon as any prize-property comes within the district for adjudication, examine the same, and make an inventory thereof, founded on an actual examination, and report to the court whether any part of it is in a condition requiring immediate sale for the interests of all parties, and notify the district attorney thereof; and if it be necessary to the examination or making of the inventory that the cargo be unladen, they shall apply to the court for an order to the marshal to unlade the same, and shall, from time to time, report to the court anything relating to the condition of the property, or its custody or disposal, which may require any action by the court, but the custody of the property shall be in the marshal only. They shall also seasonably return into court, sealed and secured from inspection, the documents and papers which shall come to their hands, duly scheduled and numbered, and the other preparatory evidence, and the evidence taken de bene esse, and their own inventory of the prize-property; and if the captured vessel, or any of its cargo or stores, are such as in their judgment may be useful to the United States in war, they shall report the same to the Secretary of the Navy. [See § 5441.]

*Ibid.*, s. 6, p. 308.

[Sec. 4623 defines the duty of the marshal.]

**Appraisal, &c., of property taken for Government.** SEC. 4624. Whenever any captured vessel, arms, munitions, or other material are taken for the use of the United States before it comes into the custody of the prize court, it shall be surveyed, appraised, and inventoried, by persons as competent and impartial as can be obtained, and the survey, appraisement, and inventory shall be sent to the court in which proceedings are to be had; and if taken afterward, sufficient notice shall first be given to enable the court to have the property appraised for the protection of the rights of the claimants and captors. In all cases of prize-property taken for or appropriated to the use of the Government, the Department for whose use it is taken or appropriated shall deposit the value thereof with the assistant treasurer of the United States nearest to the place of the session of the court, subject to the order of the court in the cause.

*Ibid.,* s. 27, p. 314.

SEC. 4625. If by reason of the condition of the captured property, or if because the whole has been appropriated to the use of the United States, no part of it has been or can be sent in for adjudication, or if the property has been entirely lost or destroyed, proceedings for adjudication may be commenced in any district the Secretary of the Navy may designate; and in any such case the proceeds of anything sold, or the value of anything taken or appropriated for the use of the United States, shall be deposited with the assistant treasurer in or nearest to that district, subject to the order of the court in the cause. If, when no property can be sent in for adjudication, the Secretary of the Navy shall not, within three months after any capture, designate a district for the institution of proceedings, the captors may institute proceedings for adjudication in any district. And if in any case of capture no proceedings for adjudication are commenced within a reasonable time, any parties claiming the captured property may, in any district court as a court of prize, move for a monition to show cause why such proceedings shall not be commenced, or institute an original suit in such court for restitution, and the monition issued in either case shall be served on the attorney of the United States for the district, and on the Secretary of the Navy, as well as on such other persons as the court shall order to be notified. Proceedings for adjudication where property is not sent in.

*Ibid.,* s. 28.

SEC. 4626. No prize-property shall be delivered to the claimants on stipulation, deposit, or other security, except where there has been a decree of restitution and the captors have appealed therefrom, or where the court, after a full hearing on the preparatory proofs, has refused to condemn the property on those proofs, and has given the captors leave to take further proofs, or where the claimant of any property shall satisfy the court that the same has a peculiar and intrinsic value to him, independent of its market-value. In any of these cases, the court may deliver the property on stipulation or deposit of its value, if satisfied that the rights and interests of the United States and captors, or of other claimants, will not be prejudiced thereby; but a satisfactory appraisement shall be first made, and an opportunity given to the district attorney and naval prize-commissioner to be heard as to the appointment of appraisers. Any money deposited in lieu of stipulation, and all money collected on a stipulation, not being costs, shall be deposited with the assistant treasurer, in the same manner as proceeds of a sale. Delivery of property on stipulation.

*Ibid.,* s. 26, p. 313.

SEC. 4627. Whenever any prize-property is condemned, or at any stage of the proceedings is found by the court to be perishing, perishable, or liable to deteriorate or depreciate, or whenever the costs of keeping the same are disproportionate to its value, the court shall order a sale of such property; and whenever, after the return-day on the libel, all the parties in the interest who have appeared in the cause agree thereto, the court may make such order; and no appeal shall operate to prevent the making or execution of such order. When property may be sold.

*Ibid.,* s. 8, p. 308.

SEC. 4628. Upon a sale of any prize-property by order of the court, the Secretary of the Navy shall employ an auctioneer of known skill in the branch of business to which any sale pertains, to make the sale, but the sale shall be conducted under the supervision of the marshal, and the collecting and depositing of the gross proceeds shall be by the auctioneer or his agent. Before any sale the marshal shall cause full catalogues and schedules to be prepared and circulated, and a copy of each shall be returned by the marshal to the court in each cause. The Mode of making sale.

marshal shall cause all sales to be advertised fully and conspicuously in newspapers ordered by the court, and by posters, and he shall, at least five days before the sale, serve notice thereof upon the naval prize commissioner, and the goods shall be open to inspection at least three days before the sale.

*Ibid.*

[SEC. 4629 authorizes transfer of property to another district for sale.]

**Share of captors.** SEC. 4630. The net proceeds of all property condemned as prize, shall, when the prize was of superior or equal force to the vessel or vessels making the capture, be decreed to the captors; and when of inferior force, one-half shall be decreed to the United States and the other half to the captors, except that in case of privateers and letters of marque, the whole shall be decreed to the captors, unless it shall be otherwise provided in the commissions issued to such vessels. [See §§ 4752, 4759, PENSIONS.]

*Ibid.*, s. 10, p. 309.

**Distribution of proceeds to captors.** SEC. 4631. All prize-money adjudged to the captors shall be distributed in the following proportions:

First. To the commanding officer of a fleet or squadron, one-twentieth part of all prize-money awarded to any vessel or vessels under his immediate command.

Second. To the commanding officer of a division of a fleet or squadron, on duty under the orders of the commander-in-chief of such fleet or squadron, a sum equal to one-fiftieth part of any prize-money awarded to a vessel of such division for a capture made while under his command, such fiftieth part to be deducted from the moiety due to the United States, if there be such moiety, otherwise from the amount awarded to the captors; but such fiftieth part shall not be in addition to any share which may be due to the commander of the division, and which he may elect to receive, as commander of a single ship making or assisting in the capture.\*

Third. To the fleet captain, one-hundredth part of all prize-money awarded to any vessel or vessels of the fleet or squadron in which he is serving, except in a case where the capture is made by the vessel on board of which he is serving at the time of such capture; and in such case he shall share, in proportion to his pay, with the other officers and men on board such vessel.\*

Fourth. To the commander of a single vessel, one-tenth part of all the prize-money awarded to the vessel under his command, if such vessel at the time of the capture was under the command of the commanding officer of a fleet or squadron, or a division, and three-twentieths if his vessel was acting independently of such superior officer.

Fifth. After the foregoing deductions, the residue shall be distributed and proportioned among all others doing duty on board, including the fleet-captain, and borne upon the books of the ship, in proportion to their respective rates of pay in the service.

*Ibid.*, s. 10, p. 309.
8 June, 1874, chap. 256, v. 18, p. 63.

NOTES.—The rate of pay which the officer was in receipt of *at the time the capture was made* is the measure of his allowance out of the proceeds; not the increased pay resulting from his promotion afterwards. Immaterial if his promotion gave him a title to the increased pay from and including the date of capture. A commander of a single ship is limited to one-tenth, although the amount would exceed that if paid according to his rank. It is the same if he was entitled to three-twentieths.—Op. XV, 64, Dec. 10, 1875, Pierrepont. *Albemarle* case. But see Op. XIV, 365, *post.*

Prize is distributed according to the law existing at the date or time of the capture. The law regulating the distribution of prize-money is a conditional grant by Congress; as soon as the conditions are fulfilled the grant becomes absolute.—Op. XI, 102, Sept. 30, 1864, Bates.

An officer commissioned to a higher grade, prior to a capture, although from delay or other causes the promotion had not reached him at the time, and he was on the prize-list in the lower capacity, is entitled to share in the higher grade if in the performance of the duties thereof. If he was entitled to pay in the higher grade, he was entitled to share accordingly in the prize.—Op. XIV, 365, Feb. 6, 1874, Williams. See also XIII, 413.

---

\*An act of June 8, 1874, chap. 256, v. 18, p. 63, provided that paragraphs 2 and 3 should apply to officers serving as commanders of divisions and fleet captains from April, 1861, and that their shares should be paid in the same manner as provided for division commanders in said paragraphs—the payments to be made out of the Naval Pension Fund.

An officer who usurps command of a vessel cannot claim a share in prizes captured. "Commanding officer means an officer legally in command." In the construction of the prize act in England, the court held that the words "on board" meant only such persons as belonged to the vessel, and that being corporeally on board was not sufficient.—Op. XI, p. 147, Jan. 19, 1865, Speed.

An officer absent from his command, for the purpose of attending to his private affairs, is not entitled to share in prizes captured during his absence. Although he may have attended to a certain piece of business while absent, or by the orders of a superior of the command, not having been detailed for that business and it not appearing that the detail of an officer from the fleet to attend to it was necessary, he is not entitled to share.—Op. XI, p. 327, Aug. 24, 1865, Speed. Temple's case.

SEC. 4632. All vessels of the Navy within signal-distance of the vessel or vessels making the capture, under such circumstances and in such condition as to be able to render effective aid, if required, shall share in the prize; and in case of vessels not of the Navy, none shall be entitled to share except the vessel or vessels making the capture; in which term shall be included vessels present at and rendering actual assistance in the capture. *What vessels are entitled to share.*

30 June, 1864, s. 10, v. 13, p. 309.

SEC. 4633. No commanding officer of a fleet or squadron shall be entitled to receive any share of prizes captured by any vessel or vessels not under his command, nor of such prizes as may have been captured by any vessels intended to be placed under his command, before they have acted under his orders. Nor shall the commanding officer of a fleet or squadron, leaving the station where he had command, have any share in the prizes taken by ships left on such station after he has gone out of the limits of his command, nor after he has transferred his command to his successor. No officer or other person who shall have been temporarily absent on duty from a vessel on the books of which he continued to be borne, while so absent, shall be deprived, in consequence of such absence, of any prize money to which he would otherwise be entitled. And he shall continue to share in the captures of the vessels to which he is attached, until regularly discharged therefrom. *What officers are entitled to share.*

*Ibid.*

NOTES.—A commander of a squadron is not entitled to share in prizes taken by a vessel thereof, after he had transferred the command to his successor, although the captures were made in pursuance of instructions issued by him before the transfer.—Op. X, p. 9, March 4, 1864, Bates. Wilkes's claim.

A flag officer of a squadron is not entitled to the share of prize-money accruing to the captain of his flag-ship from captures made by that ship while her captain was detached on account of illness, and the flag officer was *de facto* in command of her. The usage of the naval service gave the command of the ship to the officer next in rank to the detached commander. If there was a commander of the capturing vessel in law or fact, within the terms of the statute of distribution, at the time the capture was made, he is entitled to the commander's share; if there was no such, then that share is part of the common fund, in which all concerned have a proportional right.—*Idem.*

A vessel which arrives within the limits of a command to which it is to be attached, and the commander thereof reports by letter to the commander-in-chief for further instructions, which are given but not received until after certain captures have been made, was within the "immediate command" of the commanding officer of the fleet, who is entitled to share.—Op. XI, p. 94, Sept. 12, 1864. claim of Admiral Lee.

SEC. 4634. Whenever a decree of condemnation is rendered, the court shall consider the claims of all vessels to participate in the proceeds, and for that purpose shall, at as early a stage of the cause as possible, order testimony to be taken tending to show what part should be awarded to the captors, and what vessels are entitled to share; and such testimony may be sworn to before any judge or commissioner of the courts of the United States, consul or commercial agent of the United States, or notary public, or any officer of the Navy highest in rank, reasonably accessible to the deponent. The court shall make a decree of distribution, determining what vessels are entitled to share in the prize, and whether the prize was of superior, equal, or inferior force to the vessel or vessels making the capture. The decree shall recite the amount of the gross proceeds of the prize subject to the order of the court, and the amount deducted therefrom for costs and expenses, and the amount remaining for distribution, and whether the whole of such residue is to go to the captors, or one-half to the captors and one-half to the United States. *Determination of shares.*

*Ibid.*, s. 9.

11181——19

290 PRIZE.

**Bounty for persons on board vessels sunk or destroyed.**  SEC. 4635. A bounty shall be paid by the United States for each person on board any ship or vessel of war belonging to an enemy at the commencement of an engagement, which is sunk or otherwise destroyed in such engagement by any ship or vessel belonging to the United States or which it may be necessary to destroy in consequence of injuries sustained in action, of one hundred dollars, if the enemy's vessel was of inferior force, and of two hundred dollars, if of equal or superior force, to be divided among the officers and crew in the same manner as prize-money; and when the actual number of men on board any such vessel cannot be satisfactorily ascertained, it shall be estimated according to the complement allowed to vessels of its class in the Navy of the United States; and there shall be paid as bounty to the captors of any vessel of war captured from an enemy, which they may be instructed to destroy, or which is immediately destroyed for the public interest, but not in consequence of injuries received in action, fifty dollars for every person who shall be on board at the time of such capture.

*Ibid.*, s. 11 p. 310.

**Costs and expenses.**  SEC. 4639. All costs and all expenses incident to the bringing in, custody, preservation, insurance, sale, or other disposal of prize-property, when allowed by the court, shall be charged upon such property, and shall be paid from the proceeds thereof, unless the court shall decree restitution free from such charge.

*Ibid.*, s. 14.

**Payment of expenses from prize-fund.**  SEC. 4640. No payment shall be made for any prize-fund, except upon the order of the court. All charges for work and labor, materials furnished, or money paid, shall be supported by affidavit or vouchers. The court may, at any time, order the payment, from the deposit made with the assistant treasurer in the cause, of any costs or charges accrued and allowed. When the cause is finally disposed of, the court shall make its order or orders on the assistant treasurer to pay the costs and charges allowed and unpaid; and in case the final decree shall be for restitution, or in case there shall be no money subject to the order of the court in the cause, any cost or charges allowed by the court, and not paid by the claimants, shall be a charge upon, and be paid out of, the fund for defraying the expenses of suits in which the United States is a party or interested.

*Ibid.*

**Payment of prize-money.**  SEC. 4641. The net amount decreed for distribution to the United States, or to vessels of the Navy, shall be ordered by the court to be paid into the Treasury of the United States, to be distributed according to the decree of the court. The Treasury Department shall credit the Navy Department with each amount received to be distributed to vessels of the Navy; and the persons entitled to share therein shall be severally credited in their accounts with the Navy Department with the amounts to which they are respectively entitled. In case of vessels not of the Navy, and not controlled by any Department of the Government, the distribution shall be made by the court to the several parties entitled thereto, and the amounts decreed to them shall be divided between the owners and the ship's company, according to any written agreement between them, and in the absence of such agreement, one-half to the owners and one-half to the ship's company, according to their respective rates of pay on board; and the court may appoint a commissioner to make such distribution, subject to the control of the court, who shall make due return of his doings, with proof of actual payments by him, and who shall receive no other compensation, directly or indirectly, than such as shall be allowed him by the court. In case of vessels not of the Navy, but controlled by either Executive Department, the whole amount decreed to the captors shall be divided among the ship's company.

*Ibid.*, s. 15.

**Distribution of bounty, salvage, &c.**  SEC. 4642. All ransom-money, salvage, bounty, or proceeds of condemned property, accruing or awarded to any vessel of the Navy, shall be distributed and paid to the officers and men entitled thereto in the same manner as prize-money, under the direction of the Secretary of the Navy. [See § 3689, APPROPRIATIONS.]

*Ibid.*, s. 11, p. 310.

SEC. 4652. When any vessel or other property shall have been captured by any force hostile to the United States, and shall be recaptured, and it shall appear to the court that the same had not been condemned as prize before its recapture, by any competent authority, the court shall award a meet and competent sum as salvage, according to the circumstances of each case. If the captured property belonged to the United States, it shall be restored to the United States, and there shall be paid from the Treasury of the United States the salvage, costs, and expenses ordered by the court. If the recaptured property belonged to persons residing within or under the protection of the United States, the court shall adjudge the property to be restored to its owners, upon their claim, on the payment of such sum as the court may award as salvage, costs, and expenses. If the recaptured property belonged to any person permanently resident within the territory and under the protection of any foreign prince, government, or state in amity with the United States, and by the law or usage of such prince, government, or state, the property of a citizen of the United States would be restored under like circumstances of recapture, it shall be adjudged to be restored to such owner, upon his claim, upon such terms as by the law or usage of such prince, government, or state would be required of a citizen of the United States under like circumstances of recapture; or when no such law or usage shall be known, it shall be adjudged to be restored upon the payment of such salvage, costs, and expenses as the court shall order. The whole amount awarded as salvage shall be decreed to the captors, and no part to the United States, and shall be distributed as in the case of proceeds of property condemned as prize. Nothing in this Title shall be construed to contravene any treaty of the United States.

*Ibid.*, s. 29, p. 314.

Recaptures.

NOTES.—Salvage is the compensation allowed to persons by whose voluntary assistance a ship at sea or her cargo or both have been saved in whole or in part from impending sea-peril, or in recovering such property from actual peril or loss, as in cases of shipwreck, derelict, or recapture. Three elements are necessary to a valid salvage claim: 1. A marine peril; 2. Service voluntarily rendered when not required as an existing duty or from a special contract. 3. Success in whole or in part, or that the service rendered contributed to such success. Proof of success, to some extent, is as essential as proof of service; for if the property is not saved, or if it perishes, or in case of capture, if it is not retaken, no compensation will be allowed. Compensation as salvage is not viewed by the admiralty courts merely as pay on the principle of *quantum meruit*, or as a remuneration *pro opere et labore*, but as a reward given for perilous services voluntarily rendered, and as an inducement to mariners to embark in such dangerous enterprises to save life and property. (Voluntary sailors, if not successful, are entitled to nothing. When engaged to go out to the assistance of a vessel in distress they are to be paid according to their efforts, even though the labor and service may not prove beneficial to the vessel or cargo. The Undaunted, 1 Lush. 90).—Otto, S. C., 101, p. 384, case of the Sabine.

To constitute a *maritime derelict* the property at sea must not only be abandoned, but the abandonment must be without hope of recovery. (2 Kent's Com., 357, and cases cited.) And when such derelicts are found they are to be held, by the general rule of civilized countries, perquisites or *droits* of the admiralty, subject to be reclaimed by the owner, but without any other claim on the part of the finder than to his reasonable salvage remuneration cases cited.) What constitutes a reasonable salvage remuneration is, of course, a question for judicial determination in each case.—Op. XI, p. 2, Nov. 20, 1863, Bates.

Officers and crews of public ships of the United States are not entitled to salvage, civil or military, as of complete legal right. It is against public policy. Wirt (Op. July 22, 1824) said, "it was not demandable in the case of preservation of property of the United States, because the officers and crew have done no more than their duty." Attorney-General Johnson advised that it was allowable in a case of portable foreign property (Op., 20 June, 1849). The Supreme Court allowed it in the case of the Amistad (XV Peters, 518). The Secretary has the power to forbid the demand of it by any public ship under his orders.—Op. VII, p. 756, Cushing, July 8, 1856.

Where a vessel at sea is in imminent danger, and a part of either vessel or cargo is voluntarily sacrificed to save the rest, and the sacrifice is successful, the portion saved must contribute *pro rata* to make the loss good. The direct and immediate consequences of involuntary stranding not subjects of general average; *after* stranding, to avert peril surrounding vessel and cargo, owners of cargo to contribute by way of general average proportion of expenses voluntarily incurred and sacrifices voluntarily made. Injury to vessel in act of stranding not a subject of general average.—Op. IX, p. 447, July 19, 1860, Black.

Where a vessel put into a harbor "in a furious storm," leaking, was run ashore and wrecked through no fault or misconduct on the part of the master and crew, the owners are under no legal obligation to remove the wreck, although it may be a serious obstruction to navigation.—Op. XV, p. 71. See also p. 285, as to the authority of the Government as to the removal of wrecks which are obstructions.

The word "wrecked" as used in section 4136 Revised Statutes (concerning the registering of vessels) is applicable to a vessel which is disabled and rendered unfit for navigation, whether by the wind, waves, stranding, fire, explosion of boilers, or other casualty.—Op. XV, p. 402, Dec. 5, 1877.

The officers and crew of a vessel in the naval marine of the United States are entitled to salvage for saving a French ship, the objection that Government vessels are not thus entitled being invalid. The rule is universal in the United States, that salvage rendered by the naval marine is to be compensated in like manner as that rendered by the private marine.—Op. V, p. 116, June 20, 1849, Johnson. See also Op. XII, p. 289, on the subject.

It is well settled that' where a vessel is voluntarily run ashore to prevent a total loss of vessel and cargo, but is afterwards recovered so as to be able to perform her voyage, the loss resulting from the stranding is to made good by general average contribution. The contribution applies to the Government as well as to individuals.—C. C. XV, p. 392.

|Title 69.

Property taken on inland waters.

SEC. 5310. No property seized or taken upon any of the inland waters of the United States by the naval forces thereof shall be regarded as maritime prize; but all property so seized or taken shall be promptly delivered to the proper officers of the courts.

2 July, 1864, s. 7, v. 13, p. 377.

Title 70, Chap. 5.

Delaying or defrauding captor or claimant, &c., of prize-property.

SEC. 5441. Every person who willfully does any act or aids or advises in the doing of any act relating to the bringing in, custody, preservation, sale, or other disposition of any property captured as prize, or relating to any documents or papers connected with the property, or to any deposition or other document or paper connected with the proceedings, with intent to defraud, delay, or injure the United States or any captor or claimant of such property, shall be punished by a fine of not more than ten thousand dollars, or by imprisonment not more than five years, or both. [See §§ 4613–4652.]

30 June, 1864, s. 31, v. 13, p. 315.

## QUARANTINE AND NATIONAL BOARD OF HEALTH.

Sec.
4792. State health-laws to be observed by United States officers.
— Refrigerating vessels.
— Vessels for quarantine.
— Contagious diseases from infected ports.
— Medical inspectors at consulates.

Sec.
— Distribution of regulations.
— Health officer's certificates.
— Detail of officers on Board of Health.
— Limitation of act.
— Further appropriations.

Title 58.

State health laws to be observed by United States officers, &c.

SEC. 4792. The quarantine and other restraints established by the health-laws of any State, respecting any vessels arriving in, or bound to, any port or district thereof, shall be duly observed by the officers of the customs revenue of the United States, by the masters and crews of the several revenue-cutters, and by the military officers commanding in any fort or station upon the sea-coast; and all such officers of the United States shall faithfully aid in the execution of such quarantines and health-laws, according to their respective powers and within their respective precincts, and as they shall be directed, from time to time, by the Secretary of the Treasury. But nothing in this Title shall enable any State to collect a duty of tonnage or impost without the consent of Congress.

23 Feb., 1799, s. 1, v. 1, p. 619.

18 April, 1879.

Refrigerating ship.

Appropriation.

That the Secretary of the Treasury be, and hereby is, authorized to contract for the purchase or construction of such steam vessel, and refrigerating machinery, or to arrange with the Navy Department for the use of such vessel as may be recommended by the National Board of Health to disinfect vessels and cargoes from ports suspected of infection with yellow fever or other contagious disease; the construction of the same, if such construction shall be recommended by said Board of Health, to be under the inspection of an officer of the Bureau of Steam Engineering of the Navy, who may, at the request of the Secretary of the Treasury, be detailed by the Secretary of the Navy for that purpose; and for the purpose of such purchase or construction, the sum of two hundred thousand dollars or so much thereof as may be necessary, to be immediately available, is hereby appropriated out of any moneys in the Treasury not otherwise appropriated.

18 April, 1879, v. 21, p. 1.

14 June, 1879.

Vessels for quarantine.

That the Secretary of the Navy be, and he is hereby, authorized, in his discretion, at the request of the National Board of Health, to place gratuitously, at the disposal of the commissioners of quarantine, or the proper authorities at any of the ports of the United States, to be used by them temporarily for quarantine purposes, such vessels or hulks belonging to the United States as are not required for other uses of the national Government, subject to such restrictions and regulations as the said Secretary may deem necessary to impose for the preservation thereof.

14 June, 1879, joint resolution, v. 21, p. 50.

That it shall be unlawful for any merchant ship or vessel from any foreign port where any contagious or infectious disease exists, to enter any port of the United States except in accordance with the provisions of this act, and all rules and regulations of State boards of health and all rules and regulations made in pursuance of this act; and any such vessel which shall enter, or attempt to enter, a port of the United State, in violation thereof, shall forfeit to the United States a sum, to be awarded in the discretion of the court, not exceeding one thousand dollars, which shall be a lien upon said vessel, to be recovered by proceedings in the proper district court of the United States. And in all such proceedings the United States district attorney for such district shall appear on behalf of the United States, and all such proceedings shall be conducted in accordance with the rules and laws governing cases of seizure of vessels for violation of the revenue laws of the United States. <sub>*(marginalia: 2 June, 1879. Contagious diseases. Vessels from infected ports. Penalty. Proceedings.)*</sub>

SEC. 2. All such vessels shall be required to obtain from the consul, vice-consul, or other consular officer of the United States at the port of departure, or from the medical officer, where such officer has been detailed by the President for that purpose, a certificate in duplicate setting forth the sanitary history of said vessel, and that it has in all respects complied with the rules and regulations in such cases prescribed for securing the best sanitary condition of the said vessel, its cargo, passengers, and crew; and said consular or medical officer is required, before granting such certificate, to be satisfied the matters and things therein stated are true; and for his services in that behalf he shall be entitled to demand and receive such fees as shall by lawful regulation be allowed, to be accounted for as is required in other cases. <sub>*(marginalia: Bill of health. Fees.)*</sub>

That upon the request of the National Board of Health the President is authorized to detail a medical officer to serve in the office of the consul at any foreign port for the purpose of making the inspection and giving the certificates hereinbefore mentioned: *Provided,* That the number of officers so detailed shall not exceed at any one time six: <sub>*(marginalia: Medical inspectors at consulates.)*</sub>

\* \* \* \* \* \* \*

SEC. 5. That the National Board of Health shall from time to time issue to the consular officers of the United States and to the medical officers serving at any foreign port, and otherwise make publicly known, the rules and regulations made by it and approved by the President, to be used and complied with by vessels in foreign ports for securing the best sanitary condition of such vessels, their cargoes, passengers, and crews, before their departure for any port in the United States, and in the course of the voyage; and all such other rules and regulations as shall be observed in the inspection of the same on the arrival thereof at any quarantine station at the port of destination, and for the disinfection and isolation of the same, and the treatment of cargo and persons on board, so as to prevent the introduction of cholera, yellow fever, or other contagious or infectious diseases; and it shall not be lawful for any vessel to enter said port to discharge its cargo or land its passengers except upon a certificate of the health officer at such quarantine station, certifying that said rules and regulations have in all respects been observed and complied with, as well on his part as on the part of the said vessel and its master, in respect to the same and to its cargo, passengers and crew; and the master of every such vessel shall produce and deliver to the collector of customs at said port of entry, together with the other papers of the vessel, the said certificates required to be obtained at the port of departure, and the certificate herein required to be obtained from the health officer at the port of entry. <sub>*(marginalia: Distribution of Regulations. Health officer's certificates.)*</sub>

\* \* \* \* \* \* \*

SEC. 7. That the President is authorized, when requested by the National Board of Health, and when the same can be done without prejudice to the public service, to detail officers from the several Departments of the Government, for temporary duty, to act under the direction of said board, to carry out the provisions of this act; and such <sub>*(marginalia: Detail of officers.)*</sub>

officers shall receive no additional compensation except for actual and necessary expenses incurred in the performance of such duties.

\* \* \* \* \* \* \*

SEC. 10. This act shall not continue in force for a longer period than four years from the date of its approval. [See March 3, 1883, *post.*]

2 June, 1879, v. 21, p. 5.

**3 Mar., 1883.**
**Appropriation for Board, &c.**

For the National Board of Health. For compensation and personal expenses of members of the board ten thousand dollars. The President of the United States is hereby authorized, in case of a threatened or actual epidemic, to use a sum, not exceeding one hundred thousand dollars, out of any money in the Treasury not otherwise appropriated, in aid of State and local boards or otherwise, in his discretion, in preventing and suppressing the spread of the same and maintaining quarantine at points of danger.

3 March, 1883, v. 22, p. 613. Sundry civil act.

## RAILROADS AND TELEGRAPHS.

### RAILROADS.

| Sec. | Sec. |
|---|---|
| 5258. Inter-State communication. | 5261. Roads may bring suit. |
| 5260. Payments to be withheld from certain roads. | —— Sundry provisions. |

**Title 64.**
**Inter-State communication.**

SEC. 5258. Every railroad company in the United States, whose road is operated by steam, its successors and assigns, is hereby authorized to carry upon and over its road, boats, bridges, and ferries, all passengers, troops, government supplies, mails, freight, and property on their way from any State to another State, and to receive compensation therefor, and to connect with roads of other States so as to form continuous lines for the transportation of the same to the place of destination. But this section shall not affect any stipulation between the Government of the United States and any railroad company for transportation or fares without compensation, nor impair or change the conditions imposed by the terms of any act granting lands to any such company to aid in the construction of its road, nor shall it be construed to authorize any railroad company to build any new road or connection with any other road without authority from the State in which such railroad or connection may be proposed. And Congress may at any time alter, amend, or repeal this section.

15 June, 1866, ss. 1, 2, v. 14, p. 66.

**Secretary of the Treasury to withhold payment to certain railroads.**

SEC. 5260. The Secretary of the Treasury is directed to withhold all payments to any railroad company and its assigns, on account of freights or transportation over their respective roads of any kind, to the amount of payments made by the United States for interest upon bonds of the United States issued to any such company, and which shall not have been re-imbursed, together with the five per centum of net earnings due and unapplied, as provided by law.

3 March, 1873, s. 2, v. 17, p. 508.
22 *June*, 1874, v. 18, p. 200.

**Companies may sue in Court of Claims.**

SEC. 5261. Any such company may bring suit in the Court of Claims to recover the price of such freight and transportation, and in such suit the right of such company to recover the same upon the law and the facts of the case shall be determined, and also the rights of the United States upon the merits of all the points presented by it in answer thereto by them; and either party to such suit may appeal to the Supreme Court; and both said courts shall give such cause or causes precedence of all other business.

3 March, 1873, s. 2, v. 17, p. 508.

NOTES.—An act approved July 12, 1876, chap. 179, v. 19, p. 78, regulates compensation for carrying mails over land-grant roads.
An act approved March 3, 1879, chap. 183, v. 20, p. 410, provides for the adjustment of accounts for transportation of the Army, &c., by certain railroads, subject to the provisions of this section.
An act approved June 19, 1878, chap. 316, v. 20, p. 109, established the office of Auditor of Railroads and contains sundry provisions relative to his duties, &c.
The second section of the act of May 7, 1878, chap. 96, v. 20, p. 56, provides that the whole amount of compensation due to certain railroads therein mentioned, for services rendered to the Government, shall be retained by the United States, one-half thereof to be applied to the liquidation of the interest paid and

to be paid by the United States upon the bonds so issued by it to each of the corporations, and the other half to be turned into the sinking fund provided for in said act.

An act approved June 22, 1874, chap. 414, vol. 8, p. 200, directed the Secretary of the Treasury to require payment of the railroad companies of all sums of money due, or to become due, the United States for the five per centum of the net earnings provided for by the act of July 1, 1862, chap. 120, v. 12, p. 489, or by any other acts, for the construction of a railroad and telegraph line from the Missouri River to the Pacific Ocean, and in case of their refusal to pay, to certify the fact to the Attorney-General for suit.

## TELEGRAPHS.

Sec.
5266. Government to have priority in transmission of messages.
5267. Government entitled to purchase lines.
5268. Acceptance of obligation to be filed.

Sec.
5269. Penalty for refusal to transmit dispatches.
—— Departmental telegraph.
—— Destroying telegraph lines.

SEC. 5266. Telegrams between the several Departments of the Government and their officers and agents, in their transmission over the lines of any telegraph company to which has been given the right of way, timber, or station lands from the public domain shall have priority over all other business, at such rates as the Postmaster-General shall annually fix. And no part of any appropriation for the several Departments of the Government shall be paid to any company which neglects or refuses to transmit such telegrams in accordance with the provisions of this section.

*Title 65.*
*Government to have priority in transmission of messages.*

24 July, 1866, s. 2, v. 14, p. 221.
8 June, 1872, s. 17, v. 17, p. 287.
10 June, 1872, s. 1, v. 17, p. 366.

NOTE.—The Postmaster-General in his circular fixing rates for the fiscal year ending June 30, 1883, says: "All officers of the United States Government should indorse upon official messages transmitted by them the words 'official business,' and should report to the Postmaster-General any charges in excess of the rates."—See Op. XIV, 63, 123, 173, 313; XVI, 353; XV, 554, 579, regarding the transmission of messages over lines.

SEC. 5267. The United States may, for postal, military, or other purposes, purchase all the telegraph lines, property, and effects of any or all companies acting under the provisions of the act of July twenty-fourth, eighteen hundred and sixty-six, entitled "An act to aid in the construction of telegraph lines, and to secure to the Government the use of the same for postal, military, and other purposes," or under this Title, at an appraised value, to be ascertained by five competent, disinterested persons, two of whom shall be selected by the Postmaster-General of the United States, two by the company interested, and one by the four so previously selected.

*Government entitled to purchase lines.*

24 July, 1866, s. 3, v. 14, p. 221.

SEC. 5268. Before any telegraph company shall exercise any of the powers or privileges conferred by law such company shall file their written acceptance with the Postmaster-General of the restrictions and obligations required by law.

*Acceptance of obligation to be filed.*

*Ibid.,* s. 4.

SEC. 5269. Whenever any telegraph company, after having filed its written acceptance with the Postmaster-General of the restrictions and obligations required by the act approved July twenty-fourth, eighteen hundred and sixty-six, entitled "An act to aid in the construction of telegraph lines, and to secure to the Government the use of the same for postal, military, and other purposes," or by this Title, shall, by its agents or employés, refuse or neglect to transmit any such telegraphic communications as are provided for by the aforesaid act, or by this Title, or by the provisions of section two hundred and twenty-one, Title "THE DEPARTMENT OF WAR," authorizing the Secretary of War to provide for taking meteorological observations at the military stations and other points of the interior of the continent, and for giving notice on the northern lakes and sea-board of the approach and force of storms, such telegraph company shall be liable to a penalty of not less than one hundred dollars and not more than one thousand dollars for each such refusal or neglect, to be recovered by an action or actions at law in any district court of the United States.

*Penalty for refusal to transmit dispatches.*

10 June, 1872, s. 1, v. 17, p. 366.
20 Feb., 1877, chap. 63, v. 19, p. 232.
27 Feb., 1877, chap. 69, v. 19, p. 252.

**23 June, 1874.**

*Wilfully and maliciously destroying works or property of national telegraph lines.*

That any person or persons who shall wilfully or maliciously injure or destroy any of the works or property or material of any telegraphic line constructed and owned, or in process of construction, by the United States, or that may be hereafter constructed and owned or occupied and controlled by the United States, or who shall wilfully or maliciously interfere in any way with the working or use of any such telegraphic line, or who shall wilfully or maliciously obstruct, hinder, or delay the transmission of any communication over any such telegraphic line, shall be deemed guilty of a misdemeanor, and, on conviction thereof in any district court of the United States having jurisdiction of the same, shall be punished by a fine of not less than one hundred nor more than one thousand dollars, or with imprisonment for a term not exceeding three years, or with both, in the discretion of the court.

23 June, 1874, v. 18, p. 250.

NOTE.—Section 223 of the Revised Statutes authorizes the Secretary of War to establish signal stations at light-houses and at such of the life-saving stations as may be suitably located for the purpose, and to connect the same with such points as may be necessary for the proper discharge of the signal service by means of a suitable telegraph line in cases where no lines are in operation, to be constructed, maintained and worked under the direction of the chief signal officer of the Army or the Secretary of War and the Secretary of the Treasury. Subsequent acts provide for the construction, under the Secretary of War, of military telegraph lines, and that private dispatches of lawful nature may be transmitted over them, whenever the same are not needed for public use, at reasonable rates, not to exceed the usual rates charged by private telegraph companies—the proceeds thereof to be accounted for and paid into the Treasury of the United States.—See v. 18, p. 51, and v. 20, p. 206.

**4 Feb., 1874.**

*Capitol and departmental telegraph.*

That the lines of telegraph, connecting the Capitol with the various Departments in Washington, constructed under and by virtue of the act of Congress approved March third, eighteen hundred and seventy-three, entitled "An act making appropriations for sundry civil expenses of the Government for the fiscal year ending June thirtieth, eighteen hundred and seventy-four, and for other purposes," be, and the same are hereby, placed under the supervision of the officer in charge of the public buildings and grounds; and that the said officer be authorized and empowered to make rules and regulations for the working of said lines. And the Secretary or Head of each Executive Department, and the Congressional Printer, are hereby authorized to detail one person from their present force of employees to operate the instruments in said Departments and printing office, and each House of Congress may provide for the employment of an operator in their respective wings of the Capitol, at a compensation not exceeding one hundred dollars per month, during the sessions of Congress.

4 Feb., 1874, v. 18, p. 14.

**7 Mar., 1874.**

*Provided*, That said lines of telegraph shall be for the use only of Senators, Members of Congress, Judges of the United States courts, and officers of Congress and of the Executive Departments, and solely on public business.

7 March, 1874, v. 18, p. 20.

NOTE.—An appropriation is made annually and expended under direction of the War Department, for care of the telegraph connecting the capitol with the Departments and Government Printing Office. See v. 22, chap. 143, p. 615, March 3, 1883.

## RESERVED TIMBER AND LANDS.

| Sec. | Sec. |
|---|---|
| 2458. Live-oak and red-cedar lands. | 2463. Clearance of vessels laden with live-oak, prosecution of depredators. |
| 2459. Selection of live-oak and red-cedar tracts. | 4205. Duties of collectors of customs. |
| 2460. Protection of live-oak and red-cedar timber. | 5388. Depredations on timber-lands. |
| 2461. Cutting or destruction of live-oak or red-cedar, penalty. | —— Protection of shade-trees, fences, &c. |
| 2462. Vessels employed in carrying away live-oak and red-cedar, forfeiture of. | |

**Title 32, Chap. 11.**

*Live-oak and red-cedar lands.*

SEC. 2458. The Secretary of the Navy is authorized, under the direction of the President, to cause such vacant and unappropriated lands of the United States as produce the live-oak and red-cedar timbers to be explored, and selection to be made of such tracts or portions thereof, where the principal growth is of either of such timbers, as in his judgment may be necessary to furnish for the Navy a sufficient supply of the same.

1 March, 1817, s. 1, v. 3, p. 347.
15 May, 1820, v. 3, p. 607.
3 March, 1827, s. 3, v. 4, p. 242.

SEC. 2459. The President is authorized to appoint surveyors of public lands, who shall perform the duties prescribed in the preceding section, and report to him the tracts by them selected, with the boundaries ascertained and accurately designated by actual survey of water-courses; and the tracts of land thus selected with the approbation of the President shall be reserved, unless otherwise directed by law, from any future sale of the public lands, and be appropriated to the sole purpose of supplying timber for the Navy of the United States; but nothing in this section contained shall be construed to prejudice the prior rights of any person claiming lands, which may be reserved in the manner herein provided.  *Selection of live-oak and red-cedar tracts.*

1 March, 1817, s. 1, v. 3, p. 347.

SEC. 2460. The President is authorized to employ so much of the land and naval forces of the United States as may be necessary effectually to prevent the felling, cutting down, or other destruction of the timber of the United States in Florida, and to prevent the transportation or carrying away any such timber as may be already felled or cut down; and to take such other and further measures as may be deemed advisable for the preservation of the timber of the United States in Florida.  *Protection of live-oak and red-cedar timber.*

23 Feb., 1822, v. 3, p. 651.

SEC. 2461. If any person shall cut, or cause or procure to be cut, or aid, assist, or be employed in cutting, or shall wantonly destroy, or cause or procure to be wantonly destroyed, or aid, assist, or be employed in wantonly destroying any live-oak or red-cedar trees, or other timber standing, growing, or being on any lands of the United States, which, in pursuance of any law passed, or hereafter to be passed, have been reserved or purchased for the use of the United States, for supplying or furnishing therefrom timber for the Navy of the United States; or if any person shall remove, or cause or procure to be removed, or aid, or assist, or be employed in removing from any such lands which have been reserved or purchased, any live-oak or red cedar trees, or other timber, unless duly authorized so to do, by order, in writing, of a competent officer, and for the use of the Navy of the United States; or if any person shall cut, or cause or procure to be cut, or aid, or assist, or be employed in cutting any live-oak or red-cedar trees, or other timber on, or shall remove, or cause or procure to be removed, or aid, or assist, or be employed in removing any live-oak or red-cedar trees or other timber, from any other lands of the United States, acquired, or hereafter to be acquired, with intent to export, dispose of, use, or employ the same in any manner whatsoever, other than for the use of the Navy of the United States; every such person shall pay a fine not less than triple the value of the trees or timber so cut, destroyed, or removed, and shall be imprisoned not exceeding twelve months. [See § 4751, PENSION FUND.]  *Cutting or destruction of live-oak or red-cedar, penalty.*

2 March, 1831, s. 1, v. 4, p. 472.

SEC. 2462. If the master, owner, or consignee of any vessel shall knowingly take on board any timber cut on lands which have been reserved or purchased as in the preceding section prescribed, without proper authority, and for the use of the Navy of the United States; or shall take on board any live-oak or red-cedar timber cut on any other lands of the United States, with intent to transport the same to any port or place within the United States, or to export the same to any foreign country, the vessel on board of which the same shall be taken, transported, or seized, shall, with her tackle, apparel, and furniture, be wholly forfeited to the United States, and the captain or master of such vessel wherein the same was exported to any foreign country against the provisions of this section shall forfeit and pay to the United States a sum not exceeding one thousand dollars. [See § 4751, PENSION FUND, NAVY.]  *Vessels employed in carrying away live-oak and red-cedar, forfeiture of.*

*Idem, s. 2.*

SEC. 2463. It shall be the duty of all collectors of the customs within the States of Alabama, Mississippi, Louisiana, and Florida, before allowing a clearance to any vessel laden in whole or in part with live-oak timber, to ascertain satisfactorily that such timber was cut from private lands, or, if from public ones, by consent of the Navy Department. And it is also made the duty of all officers of the customs, and of the land officers within those States, to cause prosecutions to be seasonably instituted against all persons known to be guilty of depredations on, or injuries to, the live-oak growing on the public lands. [See § 4751, PENSION FUND, NAVY.]  *Clearance of vessels laden with live-oak; prosecution of depredators.*

2 March, 1833, s. 3, v. 4, p. 647.

# 298  RESERVED TIMBER AND LANDS.

**Title 48, Chap. 2.**
Clearance of vessel laden with live-oak.

SEC. 4205. Collectors of the collection-districts within the States of Florida, Alabama, Mississippi, and Louisiana, before allowing a clearance to any vessel laden in whole or in part with live-oak timber, shall ascertain satisfactorily that such timber was cut from private lands, or, if from public lands, by consent of the Department of the Navy.

3 March, 1833, s. 3, v. 4, p. 647.

**Title 70, Chap. 3.**
Depredations on timber lands.

SEC. 5388. Every person who unlawfully cuts, or aids or is employed in unlawfully cutting, or wantonly destroys, or procures to be wantonly destroyed, any timber standing upon lands of the United States, which, in pursuance of law, may be reserved or purchased for military or other purposes, shall pay a fine of not more than five hundred dollars, and be imprisoned not more than twelve months.

3 March, 1859, v. 11, p. 408.

**3 Mar., 1875.**
Cutting or injuring trees on lands of U. S. reserved or purchased for public use.

Punishment.

SEC. 1. That if any person or persons shall knowingly and unlawfully cut, or shall knowingly aid, assist, or be employed in unlawfully cutting, or shall wantonly destroy or injure, or procure to be wantonly destroyed or injured, any timber-tree or any shade or ornamental tree, or any other kind of tree, standing, growing, or being upon any lands of the United States, which, in pursuance of law, have been reserved, or which have been purchased by the United States for any public use, every such person or persons so offending, on conviction thereof before any circuit or district court of the United States, shall, for every such offense, pay a fine not exceeding five hundred dollars, or shall be imprisoned not exceeding twelve months.

Breaking fences, &c., inclosing lands of U. S. reserved or purchased for public use.

Punishment.

SEC. 2. That if any person or persons shall knowingly and unlawfully break or destroy any fence, wall, hedge, or gate inclosing any lands of the United States, which have, in pursuance of any law, been reserved or purchased by the United States for any public use, every such person so offending, on conviction, shall, for every such offense, pay a fine not exceeding two hundred dollars, or be imprisoned not exceeding six months.

Breaking fences &c., and driving cattle, &c., on to lands of U. S. reserved for public use.

Permitting cattle, &c., to enter through inclosures of such lands.

Punishment.

Proviso.

SEC. 3. That if any person or persons shall knowingly and unlawfully break, open, or destroy any gate, fence, hedge, or wall inclosing any lands of the United States, reserved or purchased as aforesaid, and shall drive any cattle, horses, or hogs upon the lands aforesaid for the purpose of destroying the grass or trees on the said grounds, or where they may destroy the said grass or trees, or if any such person or persons shall knowingly permit his or their cattle, horses, or hogs to enter through any of said inclosures upon the lands of the United States aforesaid, where the said cattle, horses, or hogs may or can destroy the grass or trees or other property of the United States on the said land, every such person or persons so offending, on conviction, shall pay a fine not exceeding five hundred dollars, or be imprisoned not exceeding twelve months: *Provided,* That nothing in this act shall be construed to apply to unsurveyed public lands and to public lands subject to pre-emption and homestead laws, or to public lands subject to an act to promote the development of the mining resources of the United States, approved May tenth, eighteen hundred and seventy-two.

3 March, 1875, v. 18, p. 481.

**April 30, 1878.**
Deposit of collections for depredations.

Seizure of timber exported.

All moneys heretofore, and that shall hereafter be, collected for depredation upon the public lands shall be covered into the Treasury of the United States, as other moneys received from the sale of public lands. * * *

If any timber cut on the public lands shall be exported from the Territories of the United States, it shall be liable to seizure by United States authority wherever found. * * *

30 April, 1878, ch. 76, s. 2, v. 20, p. 46.

NOTES.—Under section 4751, the Secretary of the Navy has power to mitigate any fine, penalty, or forfeiture incurred under the provisions of the sections designated therein; and this power may be exercised by him as well where the proceedings, civil or criminal, have not been instituted with his knowledge and by his direction as where they have been thus instituted.—Op. XV, 436, Devens, Jan. 23, 1878.

Live-oak timber cut, in violation of law, for the purposes of transportation, is not subject to forfeiture, so as to give informers a right to a distributive portion of it, such timber being all the while, in law, the property of the United States. The act of March 2, 1831, makes no provision for the forfeiture of timber.—Op. IV, 247, Nelson, Sept. 2, 1843.

The moneys referred to in the act of April 30, 1878, chap. 76, are that part of the penalty which is payable to the Secretary of the Navy, under sec. 4751, PENSION FUNDS.—Op. July 19, 1883. Phillips.

## REVENUE-CUTTER SERVICE.

Sec.
1492. Rank with the Navy.
2749. Number of officers and men.
2750. Grades of engineers.
2751. Appointment of commissioned officers.
2752. Qualifications of captains and lieutenants.
2753. Compensation of officer of revenue-cutter service.
2754. Wages of petty officers and crews.
2755. Officers on duty entitled to one Navy ration per day.

Sec.
2756. Contracts for rations authorized.
2757. Revenue officers to co-operate with the Navy.
2760. Powers and duties of officers of revenue-cutters.
—— Appointment of cadets.
—— Detail for life-saving service.

SEC. 1492. The officers of the revenue-cutter service when serving, in accordance with law, as a part of the Navy, shall be entitled to relative rank, as follows: Captains, with and next after lieutenants commanding in the Navy; first lieutenants, with and next after lieutenants in the Navy; second lieutenants, with and next after masters in line in the Navy; third lieutenants, with and next after ensigns in the Navy.   *Title 15, Chap. 4. Revenue-cutter officers serving as part of the Navy.*

4 July, 1863, s. 4, v. 12, p. 640.
2 March, 1799, s. 98, v. 1, p. 699.
16 July, 1862, ss. 1, 11, v. 12, pp. 583, 585.

SEC. 2749. The officers for each revenue-vessel shall be one captain, and one first, one second, and one third lieutenant, and for each steam-vessel, in addition, one engineer and one assistant engineer; but the Secretary of the Treasury may assign to any vessel a greater number of officers whenever in his opinion the nature of the service which she is directed to perform requires it. And vessels of both descriptions shall have such number of petty officers and men as in the opinion of the Secretary are required to make them efficient for their service.   *Title 34, Chap. 3. Number of officers and men.*

25 July, 1861, s. 2, v. 12, p. 275.
31 July, 1876, v. 19, p. 107.

SEC. 2750. The grades of engineers shall be chief engineer, and first and second assistant engineer, with the pay and relative rank of first, second, and third lieutenant, respectively.   *Grades of engineers.*

4 Feb., 1863, s. 2, v. 12, p. 639.

SEC. 2751. The commissioned officers of the revenue-cutter service shall be appointed by the President, by and with the advice and consent of the Senate.   *Appointment of commissioned officers.*

*Idem*, s. 1.

SEC. 2752. No person shall be appointed to the office of captain, first, second, or third lieutenant, of any revenue-cutter, who does not adduce competent proof of proficiency and skill in navigation and seamanship.   *Qualifications of captains and lieutenants.*

2 March, 1855, s. 2, v. 10, p. 630.

SEC. 2753. The compensation of the officers of the revenue-cutter service shall be at the following rates while on duty:   *Compensation of officers of revenue-cutter service.*

Captains, twenty-five hundred dollars a year each.
First lieutenants and chief engineers, eighteen hundred dollars a year each.
Second lieutenants and first assistant engineers, fifteen hundred dollars a year each.
Third lieutenants and second assistant engineers, twelve hundred dollars a year each.
And at the following rates while on leave of absence or while waiting orders:
Captains, eighteen hundred dollars a year each.
First lieutenants and chief engineers, fifteen hundred dollars a year each.
Second lieutenants andr fist assistant engineers, twelve hundred dollars a year each.
Third lieutenants and second assistant engineers, nine hundred dollars a year each.

28 Feb., 1867, s. 1, v. 14, p. 416.

SEC. 2754. The wages of petty officers and seamen of the revenue-cutter service shall not exceed the average wages paid for like services on the Atlantic or Pacific coast, respectively, in the merchant service.   *Wages of petty officers and crews.*

4 Feb., 1863, s. 3, v. 12, p. 640.

# REVENUE-CUTTER SERVICE.

**Rations.**

SEC. 2755. Each officer of the revenue-cutter service, while on duty, shall be entitled to one Navy ration per day.

28 Feb., 1867, s. 2, v. 14, p. 416.

**Contracts for rations.**

SEC. 2756. The Secretary of the Treasury may cause contracts to be made for the supply of rations for the officers and men of the revenue-cutters.

2 March, 1799, s. 98, v. 1, p. 699.

NOTE.—Officers of the revenue-cutter service belong to the civil service, as contradistinguished from the naval and military—are subject to removal by the President, with the concurrence of the Senate in confirming the nomination of a successor.—Op. XV, p. 396, Nov. 13, 1877, Devens.

**Revenue officers to co-operate with the Navy.**

SEC. 2757. The revenue-cutters shall, whenever the President so directs, co-operate with the Navy, during which time they shall be under the direction of the Secretary of the Navy, and the expenses thereof shall be defrayed by the Navy Department. [See §§ 5557, 5558 SLAVE-TRADE.]

*Idem.*

**Powers and duties of officers of revenue-cutters.**

SEC. 2760. The officers of the revenue cutters shall respectively be deemed officers of the customs, and shall be subject to the direction of such collectors of the revenue, or other officers thereof, as from time to time shall be designated for that purpose. They shall go on board all vessels which arrive within the United States or within four leagues of the coast thereof, if bound for the United States, and search and examine the same, and every part thereof, and shall demand, receive, and certify the manifests required to be on board certain vessels, shall affix and put proper fastenings on the hatches and other communications with the hold of any vessel, and shall remain on board such vessels until they arrive at the port or place of their destination.

*Idem,* s. 99, p. 700.

**31 July, 1876.**

**Appointment of cadets.**

Hereafter upon the occurring of a vacancy in the grade of third lieutenant in the Revenue Marine Service, the Secretary of the Treasury may appoint a cadet, not less than eighteen nor more than twenty-five years of age, with rank next below that of third lieutenant, whose pay shall be three-fourths that of a third lieutenant, and who shall not be appointed to a higher grade until he shall have served a satisfactory probationary term of two years, and passed the examination required by the regulations of said service; and upon the promotion of such cadet another may be appointed in his stead; but the whole number of third lieutenants and cadets shall at no time exceed the number of third lieutenants now authorized by law.

31 July, 1876, v. 19, p. 102.

[The 8th section of the act approved June 18, 1878, chap. 265, v. 20, p. 163, provides that the Secretary of the Treasury may detail such officer or officers of the Revenue Marine Service as may be necessary to act as inspectors and assistant inspectors of life-saving stations, who shall perform such duties in connection with the conduct of the service as may be required of them by the general superintendent.]

## SLAVE-TRADE, KIDNAPPING, COOLY-TRADE.

Sec.
2158. Cooly-trade prohibited.
2159. Vessels employed in cooly-trade shall be forfeited.
2160. Building vessels to engage in cooly-trade, how punished.
2161. Punishment for violation of section 2158.
2162. This Title not to interfere with voluntary emigration.
2163. Examination of vessels.
—— Transporting from Oriental countries subjects without consent.
5378. Equipping vessels for slave-trade.
5379. Transporting persons to be held as slaves.
5381. Serving in vessels transporting slaves.
5382. Same.
5524. Receiving or carrying away any person to be sold or held as a slave.
5525. Kidnapping.
5551. Equipping, &c., vessel for slave-trade; forfeiture of vessel.
5552. Penalty on persons building, equipping, &c.
5553. Forfeiture of vessel transporting slaves.
5554. Penalty for receiving persons on board to be sold as slaves.

Sec.
5557. Seizure of vessels engaged in the slave-trade.
5558. Proceeds of condemned vessels, how distributed.
5559. Disposal of persons found on board seized vessels.
5560. Apprehension of officers and crew.
5561. Removal of persons delivered from seized vessels.
5562. Bounty.
5563. To what port captured vessels sent.
5564. When owners of foreign vessels shall give bond.
5565. Distribution of penalties.
5566. Contracts for reception in Africa of persons delivered from seized vessels.
5567. Instructions to commanders of armed vessels.
5568. Contracts for reception, &c., in West Indies of persons delivered from seized vessels.
5569. Instructions to commanders of armed vessels.

### COOLY TRADE.

SEC. 2158. No citizen of the United States, or foreigner coming into or residing within the same, shall, for himself or for any other person, either as master, factor, owner, or otherwise, build, equip, load, or otherwise prepare, any vessel, registered, enrolled, or licensed, in the United States, for the purpose of procuring from any port or place the subjects of China, Japan, or of any other oriental country, known as "coolies," to be transported to any foreign port, or place, to be disposed of, or sold, or transferred, for any time, as servants or apprentices, or to be held to service or labor.

*Title 29.*
*Cooly-trade prohibited.*

19 Feb., 1862, s. 1, v. 12, p. 340.
9 Feb., 1869, v. 15, p. 269.

SEC. 2159. If any vessel, belonging in whole or in part to a citizen of the United States, and registered, enrolled, or otherwise licensed therein, be employed in the "cooly-trade," so called, contrary to the provisions of the preceding section, such vessel, her tackle, apparel, furniture, and other appurtenances, shall be forfeited to the United States, and shall be liable to be seized, prosecuted, and condemned in any of the circuit courts or district courts of the United States for the district where the vessel may be found, seized, or carried.

*Vessels employed in cooly-trade shall be forfeited.*

*Ibid.*

SEC. 2160. Every person who so builds, fits out, equips, loads, or otherwise prepares, or who sends to sea, or navigates, as owner, master, factor, agent, or otherwise, any vessel, belonging in whole or in part to a citizen of the United States, or registered, enrolled, or licensed within the same, knowing or intending that such vessel is to be or may be employed in that trade, contrary to the provisions of section twenty-one hundred and fifty-eight, shall be liable to a fine not exceeding two thousand dollars, and be imprisoned not exceeding one year.

*Building vessels to engage in cooly-trade, how punished.*

19 Feb., 1862, s. 2, v. 12, p. 340.

SEC. 2161. Every citizen of the United States who, contrary to the provisions of section twenty-one hundred and fifty-eight, takes on board of any vessel, or receives or transports any such subjects as are described in that section, for the purpose of disposing of them in any way as therein prohibited, shall be liable to a fine not exceeding two thousand dollars and be imprisoned not exceeding one year.

*Punishment for violation of section 2158.*

*Ibid.*, s. 3.

SEC. 2162. Nothing herein contained shall be deemed to apply to any voluntary emigration of the subjects specified in section twenty-one hundred and fifty-eight, or to any vessel carrying such person as passenger on board the same, but a certificate shall be prepared and signed by the consul or consular agent of the United States residing at the port

*This Title not to interfere with voluntary emigration.*

from which such vessel may take her departure, containing the name of such person, and setting forth the fact of his voluntary emigration from such port, which certificate shall be given to the master of such vessel; and the same shall not be given until such consul or consular agent is first personally satisfied by evidence of the truth of the facts therein contained. [See 3 March, 1875, *post*.]

*Ibid.*, s. 4.

**Examination of vessel.**

SEC. 2163. The President is empowered, in such way and at such time as he may judge proper, to direct the vessels of the United States, and the masters and commanders thereof, to examine all vessels navigated or owned in whole or in part by citizens of the United States, and registered, enrolled, or licensed under the laws thereof, whenever, in the judgment of such master or commanding officer, reasonable cause exists to believe that such vessel has on board any subjects of China, Japan, or other Oriental country, known as "coolies"; and, upon sufficient proof that such vessel is employed in violation of the preceding provisions, to cause her to be carried, with her officers and crew, into any port or district within the United States, and delivered to the marshal of such district, to be held and disposed of according to law.

**No charge upon particular persons immigrating, &c.**

*Ibid.*, s. 6, p. 341.

**3 Mar., 1875.**

**Citizen of United States transporting subject of China or Japan without free consent.**

**Penalty.**

**Contract for service void.**

That if any citizen of the United States, or other person amenable to the laws of the United States, shall take, or cause to be taken or transported, to or from the United States any subject of China, Japan, or any Oriental country, without their free and voluntary consent, for the purpose of holding them to a term of service, such citizen or other person shall be liable to be indicted therefor, and, on conviction of such offense, shall be punished by a fine not exceeding two thousand dollars and be imprisoned not exceeding one year; and all contracts and agreements for a term of service of such persons in the United States, whether made in advance or in pursuance of such illegal importation, and whether such importation shall have been in American or other vessels, are hereby declared void.

3 March, 1875, s. 2, v. 18, p. 477.

### KIDNAPPING AND SLAVE TRADE.

**Title 70, Chap. 3.**

**Equipping vessels for slave-trade.**

SEC. 5378. Every person who builds, fits out, equips, loads, or otherwise prepares, or sends away, either as master, factor, or owner, any vessel, in any port or place within the jurisdiction of the United States, or causes such vessel to sail from any port or place whatsoever, within such jurisdiction, for the purpose of procuring any negro, mulatto, or person of color from any foreign kingdom or country, to be transported to any port or place whatsoever, to be held, sold, or otherwise disposed of as a slave, or held to service or labor, shall be punished by a fine of not less than one thousand dollars, nor more than five thousand dollars, one-half to the use of the United States and the other half to the use of the person prosecuting the indictment to effect, and shall, moreover, be imprisoned at hard labor for a term not more than seven years, nor less than three years. [See § 5551.]

20 April, 1818, s. 3, v. 3, p. 451.

**Transporting persons to be held as slaves.**

SEC. 5379. Every citizen or other person resident within the jurisdiction of the United States, who takes on board, receives, or transports from any foreign kingdom or country, or from sea, any negro, mulatto, or person of color, in any vessel, for the purpose of holding, selling, or otherwise disposing of such person as a slave, or to be held to service or labor, shall be punished as prescribed in the preceding section.

*Ibid.*, s. 4.

**Serving in American vessels transporting slaves.**

SEC. 5381. Every citizen of the United States, or other person residing therein, who voluntarily serves on board of any American vessel employed or made use of in the transportation of slaves from any foreign country or place to another, shall be punished by a fine of not more than two thousand dollars, and by imprisonment not more than two years.

10 May, 1800, s. 2, v. 2, p. 70.

**Serving in foreign vessels employed in the slave-trade.**

SEC. 5382. Every citizen of the United States who voluntarily serves on board of any foreign vessel employed in the slave-trade, shall be punished as prescribed in the preceding section.

*Ibid.*, s. 3, p. 71.

SLAVE-TRADE, KIDNAPPING, COOLY-TRADE.

Sec. 5524. Every master or owner or person having charge of any vessel who receives on board any other person, with the knowledge or intent that such person is to be carried from any State, Territory, or district of the United States to a foreign country, state, or place, to be held or sold as a slave, or carries away from any State, Territory, or district of the United States any such person, with the intent that he may be so held or sold as a slave, shall be punished by a fine of not more than five thousand nor less than five hundred dollars, or by imprisonment not more than five years, or by both. [See § 5379.]

21 May, 1866, s. 2, v. 14, p. 50.

*Title 70, Chap. 7.*
Receiving on board a vessel, or carrying away any person to be sold or held as a slave.

Sec. 5525. Every person who kidnaps or carries away any other person, with the intent that such other person be sold into involuntary servitude, or held as a slave; or who entices, persuades, or induces any other person to go on board any vessel or to any other place with the intent that he may be made or held as a slave, or sent out of the country to be so made or held; or who in any way knowingly aids in causing any other person to be held, sold, or carried away to be held or sold as a slave, shall be punished by a fine of not less than five hundred nor more than five thousand dollars, or by imprisonment not more than five years or by both. [See § 5375, PIRACY.]

*Ibid.*, s. 1.

Kidnapping.

That whoever shall knowingly and wilfully bring into the United States, or the Territories thereof, any person inveigled or forcibly kidnapped in any other country, with intent to hold such person so inveigled or kidnapped in confinement or to any involuntary service, and whoever shall knowingly and wilfully sell, or cause to be sold, into any condition of involuntar*il*y servitude, any other person for any term whatever, and every person who shall knowingly and wilfully hold to involuntary service any person so sold and bought, shall be deemed guilty of a felony, and, on conviction thereof, be imprisoned for a term not exceeding five years, and pay a fine not exceeding five thousand dollars.

Sec. 2. That every person who shall be accessory to any of the felonies herein declared, either before or after the fact, shall be deemed guilty of a felony, and, on conviction thereof be imprisoned for a term not exceeding five years and pay a fine not exceeding one thousand dollars.

23 June, 1874, chap. 464, v. 18, p. 251.

23 June, 1874.

Bringing into the United States kidnapped persons.

Penalty.

Sec. 5551. No person shall, for himself, or for another, as master, factor, or owner, build, fit, equip, load, or otherwise prepare any vessel, in any port or place within the jurisdiction of the United States, or cause any vessel to sail from any port or place within the jurisdiction of the same, for the purpose of procuring any negro, mulatto, or person of color, from any foreign kingdom, place, or country, to be transported to any port or place whatsoever, to be held, sold, or otherwise disposed of, as a slave, or to be held to service or labor; and every vessel so built, fitted out, equipped, laden, or otherwise prepared, with her tackle, apparel, furniture, and lading, shall be forfeited, one moiety to the use of the United States, and the other to the use of the person who sues for the forfeiture, and prosecutes the same to effect. [See § 5375, PIRACY.]

20 April, 1818, s. 2, v. 3, p. 451.
22 March, 1794, s. 1, v. 1, p. 347.

Title 71.

Equipping, &c., vessel for slave-trade; forfeiture of vessel.

Sec. 5552. Every person so building, fitting out, equipping, loading, or otherwise preparing or sending away any vessel, knowing or intending that the same shall be employed in such trade or business, contrary to the provisions of the preceding section, or any ways aiding or abetting therein, shall, besides the forfeiture of the vessel, pay the sum of two thousand dollars; one moiety thereof to the use of the United States, and the other moiety thereof to the use of the person who sues for and prosecutes the same to effect. [See § 5378.]

22 March, 1794, s. 2, v. 1, p. 349.

Penalty on persons building, equipping, &c.

Sec. 5553. Every vessel employed in carrying on the slave-trade, or on which is received or transported any negro, mulatto, or person of color, from any foreign kingdom or country, or from sea, for the purpose of holding, selling, or otherwise disposing of such person as a slave, or of holding such person to service or labor, shall, together with her tackle, apparel, furniture, and the goods and effects which may be found on board, or which may have been imported thereon in the same voy-

Forfeiture of vessel transporting slaves.

age, be forfeited; one moiety to the United States, and the other to the use of the person who sues for and prosecutes the forfeiture to effect. [See §§ 5378, 5379.]

20 April, 1818, s. 4, v. 3, p. 451.
10 May, 1800, s. 4, v. 2, p. 71.

*Penalty for receiving persons on board to be sold as slaves.*

SEC. 5554. If any citizen of the United States takes on board, receives, or transports any negro, mulatto, or person of color, for the purpose of selling such person as a slave, he shall, in addition to the forfeiture of the vessel, pay for each person, so received on board or transported, the sum of two hundred dollars, to be recovered in any court of the United States; the one moiety thereof to the use of the United States, and the other moiety to the use of the person who sues for and prosecutes the same to effect.

22 March, 1794, s. 4, v. 1, p. 349.

*Seizure of vessels engaged in the slave-trade.*

SEC. 5557. The President is authorized, when he deems it expedient, to man and employ any of the armed vessels of the United States to cruise wherever he may judge attempts are making to carry on the slave-trade, by citizens or residents of the United States, in contravention of laws prohibitory of the same; and, in such case, he shall instruct the commanders of such armed vessels to seize, take, and bring into any port of the United States, to be proceeded against according to law, all American vessels, wheresoever found, which may have on board or which may be intended for the purpose of taking on board, or of transporting, or may have transported any negro, mulatto, or person of color, in violation of the provisions of any act of Congress prohibiting the traffic in slaves.

10 May, 1800, s. 4, v. 2, p. 71.
2 March, 1807, s. 7, v. 2, p. 428.
3 March, 1819, s. 1, v. 3, p. 532.

*Proceeds of condemned vessels, how distributed.*

SEC. 5558. The proceeds of all vessels, their tackle, apparel, and furniture, and the goods and effects on board of them, which are so seized, prosecuted, and condemned, shall be divided equally between the United States and the officers and men who seize, take, or bring the same into port for condemnation, whether such seizure be made by an armed vessel of the United States or revenue cutter thereof; and the same shall be distributed as is provided by law for the distribution of prizes taken from an enemy.

*Ibid.*

*Disposal of persons found on board seized vessels.*

SEC. 5559. The officers and men, to be entitled to one-half of the proceeds mentioned in the last section, shall safely keep every negro, mulatto, or person of color, found on board of any vessel so seized, taken, or brought into port, for condemnation, and shall deliver every such negro, mulatto, or person of color, to the marshal of the district into which he may be brought, if into a port of the United States, or if elsewhere, to such person as may be lawfully appointed by the President, in the manner directed by law; transmitting to the President, as soon as may be after such delivery, a descriptive list of such negroes, mulattoes, or persons of color, in order that he may give directions for the disposal of them.

3 March, 1819, s. 1, v. 3, p. 532.

*Apprehension of officers and crew.*

SEC. 5560. The commanders of such commissioned vessels shall cause to be apprehended, and taken into custody, every person found on board of such offending vessel, so seized and taken, being of the officers or crew thereof, and him convey, as soon as conveniently may be, to the civil authority of the United States, to be proceeded against in due course of law.

*Ibid*, and 10 May, 1800, s. 4, v. 2, p. 71.

*Removal of persons delivered from seized vessels.*

SEC. 5561. The President is authorized to make such regulations and arrangements as he may deem expedient for the safe-keeping, support, and removal beyond the limits of the United States, of all such negroes mulattoes, or persons of color, as may be delivered and brought within their jurisdiction; and to appoint a proper person residing upon the coast of Africa as agent, for receiving the negroes, mulattoes, or persons of color delivered from on board vessels seized in the prosecution of the slave-trade, by commanders of United States armed vessels.

3 March, 1819, s. 2, v. 3, p. 533.

SEC. 5562. A bounty of twenty-five dollars shall be paid to the officers and crews of the commissioned vessels of the United States, or revenue-cutters, for each negro, mulatto, or person of color, who may be, as hereinbefore provided, delivered to the marshal or agent duly appointed to receive such person; and the Secretary of the Treasury is required to pay, or cause to be paid, to such officers and crews, or their agent, such bounty for each person so delivered.

*Ibid.,* s. 3.

*Bounty.*

SEC. 5563. It shall be the duty of the commander of any armed vessel of the United States, whenever he makes any capture under the preceding provisions, to bring the vessel and her cargo, for adjudication, into some of the ports of the State or Territory to which such vessel so captured may belong, if he can ascertain the same; if not, then to be sent into any convenient port of the United States.

*Ibid.,* s. 5.

*To what port captured vessels sent.*

SEC. 5564. Every owner, master, or factor of any foreign vessel, clearing out for any of the coasts or kingdoms of Africa, or suspected to be intended for the slave-trade, and the suspicion being declared to the officer of the customs by any citizen, on oath, and such information being to the satisfaction of the officer, shall first give bond, with sufficient sureties, to the Treasurer of the United States, that none of the natives of Africa, or any other foreign country or place, shall be taken on board such vessel, to be transported or sold as slaves, in any other foreign port or place whatever, within nine months thereafter.

22 March, 1794, s. 3, v. 1, p. 349.

*When owners of foreign vessels shall give bond.*

SEC. 5565. The forfeitures which may hereafter be incurred under any of the preceding provisions, and which are not otherwise expressly disposed of, shall accrue and be one moiety thereof to the use of the informer, and the other moiety to the use of the United States, except where the prosecution is first instituted on behalf of the United States, in which case the whole shall be to their use.

10 May, 1800, s. 7, v. 2, p. 71.

*Distribution of penalties.*

SEC. 5566. It may be lawful for the President to enter into contract with any person, society, or body-corporate, for a term not exceeding five years, to receive from the United States, through their duly constituted agent upon the coast of Africa, all negroes, mulattoes, or persons of color, delivered from on board vessels seized in the prosecution of the slave-trade, by commanders of the United States armed vessels, and to provide such negroes, mulattoes, and persons of color with comfortable clothing, shelter, and provisions, for a period not exceeding one year from the date of their being landed on the coast of Africa, at a price in no case to exceed one hundred dollars for each person so clothed, sheltered, and provided with food; and any contract so made may be renewed by the President from time to time as found necessary, for periods not to exceed five years on each renewal.

16 June, 1860, s. 1, v. 12, p. 40.

*Contracts for reception in Africa of persons delivered from seized vessels.*

SEC. 5567. The President is authorized to issue instructions to the commanders of the armed vessels of the United States, directing them, whenever it is practicable, and under such rules and regulations as he may prescribe, to proceed directly to the coast of Africa, and there hand over to the agent of the United States all negroes, mulattoes, and persons of color delivered from on board vessels seized in the prosecution of the slave-trade; and they shall afterward bring the captured vessels and persons engaged in prosecuting such trade to the United States for trial and adjudication.

*Ibid.,* s. 2, p. 41.

*Instructions to commanders of armed vessels.*

SEC. 5568. It may be lawful for the President to enter into arrangement, by contract or otherwise, with one or more foreign governments having possessions in the West Indies or other tropical regions, or with their duly constituted agent, to receive from the United States, for a term not exceeding five years, at such place as may be agreed upon, all negroes, mulattoes, or persons of color, delivered from on board vessels seized in the prosecution of the slave-trade, by commanders of United States armed vessels, and to provide them with suitable instruction, and with comfortable clothing and shelter, and to employ them, at wages, under such regulations as may be agreed upon, for a period not exceeding five years from the date of their being landed at the place agreed upon. But

*Contracts for reception, &c., in West Indies, of persons delivered from seized vessels.*

11181——20

306 TREASON, REBELLION, CONSPIRACY, AND INSURRECTION.

the United States shall incur no expenses on account of such negroes, mulattoes, or persons of color, after having landed them at the place agreed upon. And any arrangement so made may be renewed by the President from time to time, as may be found necessary, for periods not exceeding five years on each renewal.

17 July, 1862, s. 1, v. 12, p. 592.

*Instructions to commanders of armed vessels.*

SEC. 5569. The President is authorized to issue instructions to the commanders of the armed vessels of the United States, directing them, whenever it is practicable, and under such regulations as he may prescribe, to proceed directly to such place as shall have been agreed upon with any foreign government, or its duly constituted agent, under the provisions of the preceding section, and there deliver to the duly constituted authorities or agents of such foreign government all negroes, mulattoes, or persons of color, taken from on board vessels seized in the prosecution of the slave trade; and they shall afterward bring the vessel and persons engaged in prosecuting such trade to the United States for trial and adjudication. [See §§ 2158.]

*Ibid.*, s. 2.

## TREASON, REBELLION, CONSPIRACY, AND INSURRECTION.

Sec.
1042. Militia to be called out.
1043. Apportioned among States.
1044. Subject to rules of war.
——. Arms to be furnished.
1033. Copy of indictment, &c., to be furnished.
1034. Entitled to counsel.
2111. Sending seditious messages; penalty.
2112. Carrying seditious messages; penalty.
2113. Correspondence with foreign nations to excite Indians to war; penalty.
5297. Insurrection against a State government.
5298. Insurrection against the Government of the United States.
5299. Power to suppress insurrection in violation of civil rights.
5300. Proclamation to insurgents to disperse.
5331. Treason.
5332. Punishment of treason.

Sec.
5333. Misprision of treason.
5334. Inciting or engaging in rebellion or insurrection.
5335. Criminal correspondence with foreign governments.
5336. Seditious conspiracy.
5337. Recruiting soldiers or sailors to serve against the United States.
5338. Enlistment to serve against the United States.
5406. Conspiring to intimidate witnesses, &c.
5407. Conspiracy to defeat the enforcement of the laws.
5440. All parties to a conspiracy equally guilty.
5518. Conspiracy to prevent holding office.
5519. Conspiracy to deprive any person of equal protection of the laws.

*Title 16.*

*Orders of President in case of invasion.*

SEC. 1642. Whenever the United States are invaded, or are in imminent danger of invasion from any foreign nation or Indian tribe, or of rebellion against the authority of the Government of the United States, it shall be lawful for the President to call forth such number of the militia of the State or States, most convenient to the place of danger, or scene of action, as he may deem necessary to repel such invasion, or to suppress such rebellion, and to issue his orders for that purpose to such officers of the militia as he may think proper.

28 Feb., 1795, s. 1, v. 1, p. 424.

*Militia, how apportioned.*

SEC. 1643. When the militia of more than one State is called into the actual service of the United States by the President, he shall apportion them among such States according to representative population.

17 July, 1862, s. 1, v. 12, p. 597.

*Subject to rules of war.*

SEC. 1644. The militia, when called into the actual service of the United States for the suppression of rebellion against and resistance to the laws of the United States, shall be subject to the same rules and articles of war as the regular troops of the United States.

28 Feb., 1795, s. 4, v. 1, p. 424.
29 July, 1861, s. 3, v. 12, p. 282.

*March 3, 1879.*

*Arms to be furnished for protection of public property.*

That upon the request of the head of any Department, the Secretary of War be, and he hereby is, authorized and directed to issue arms and ammunition whenever they may be required for the protection of the public money and property, and they may be delivered to any officer of the Department designated by the head of such Department, to be accounted for to the Secretary of War, and to be returned when the necessity for their use has expired.

3 March, 1879, chap 183, v. 20, p. 410.

NOTE.—The President's proclamation, Aug. 20, 1866, 14 Stat., 817, was an authoritative declaration that the rebellion was suppressed, and it is to be so regarded on and after that date. The recognition and adoption of the time so designated in the act of March 2, 1867, 14 Stat., 428, gives to it the force and sanction of positive law, and makes it binding and conclusive on the courts.— C. C., IV, p. 1. See Wallace, 12, p. 700.

TREASON, REBELLION, CONSPIRACY, AND INSURRECTION. 307

SEC. 1033. When any person is indicted of treason, a copy of the indictment and a list of the jury, and of the witnesses to be produced on the trial for proving the indictment, stating the place of abode of each juror and witness, shall be delivered to him at least three entire days before he is tried for the same. When any person is indicted of any other capital offense, such copy of the indictment and list of the jurors and witnesses shall be delivered to him at least two entire days before the trial. *Title 13, Chap. 18.* Copy of indictment and list of jurors and witnesses.

30 April, 1790, s. 29, v. 1, p. 118.

SEC. 1034. Every person who is indicted of treason, or other capital crime, shall be allowed to make his full defense by counsel learned in the law; and the court before which he is tried, or some judge thereof, shall immediately, upon his request, assign to him such counsel, not exceeding two, as he may desire, and they shall have free access to him at all seasonable hours. He shall be allowed, in his defense, to make any proof that he can produce by lawful witnesses, and shall have the like process of the court to compel his witnesses to appear at his trial, as is usually granted to compel witnesses to appear on behalf of the prosecution. Persons indicted for capital crimes entitled to counsel and to compel witnesses.

*Idem.*

SEC. 2111. Every person who sends any talk, speech, message, or letter to any Indian nation, tribe, chief, or individual, with an intent to produce a contravention or infraction of any treaty or law of the United States, or to disturb the peace and tranquility of the United States, is liable to a penalty of two thousand dollars. *Title 28, Chap. 3.* Sending seditious messages; penalty.

30 June, 1834, s. 13, v. 4, p. 731.

SEC. 2112. Every person who carries or delivers any talk, message, speech, or letter, intended to produce a contravention or infraction of any treaty or law of the United States, or to disturb the peace or tranquility of the United States, knowing the contents thereof, to or from any Indian nation, tribe, chief, or individual, from or to any person or persons whatever, residing within the United States, or from or to any subject, citizen, or agent of any foreign power or state, is liable to a penalty of one thousand dollars. Carrying seditious messages; penalty.

*Idem.*, s. 14.

SEC. 2113. Every person who carries on a correspondence, by letter or otherwise, with any foreign nation or power, with an intent to induce such foreign nation or power to excite any Indian nation, tribe, chief, or individual, to war against the United States, or to the violation of any existing treaty; or who alienates, or attempts to alienate, the confidence of any Indian or Indians from the Government of the United States, is liable to a penalty of one thousand dollars. [See § 5335] Correspondence with foreign nations, to excite Indians to war; penalty.

*Idem*, s. 15.

SEC. 5297. In case of an insurrection in any State against the government thereof, it shall be lawful for the President, on application of the legislature of such State, or of the executive, when the legislature cannot be convened, to call forth such number of the militia of any other State or States, which may be applied for, as he deems sufficient to suppress such insurrection; or, on like application, to employ, for the same purposes, such part of the land or naval forces of the United States as he deems necessary. *Title 69.* Insurrection against a State government.

28 Feb., 1795, s. 1, v. 1, p. 421.
3 March, 1807, v. 2, p. 443.

SEC. 5298. Whenever, by reason of unlawful obstructions, combinations, or assemblages of persons, or rebellion against the authority of the Government of the United States, it shall become impracticable, in the judgment of the President, to enforce, by the ordinary course of judicial proceedings, the laws of the United States within any State or Territory, it shall be lawful for the President to call forth the militia of any or all the States, and to employ such parts of the land and naval forces of the United States as he may deem necessary to enforce the faithful execution of the laws of the United States, or to suppress such rebellion, in whatever State or Territory thereof the laws of the United States may be forcibly opposed, or the execution thereof forcibly obstructed. Insurrection against the Government of the United States.

29 July 1861, s. 1, v. 12, p. 281.

308　TREASON, REBELLION, CONSPIRACY, AND INSURRECTION.

Power to suppress insurrection in violation of civil rights.
SEC. 5299. Whenever insurrection, domestic violence, unlawful combinations, or conspiracies in any State so obstructs or hinders the execution of the laws thereof, and of the United States, as to deprive any portion or class of the people of such State of any of the rights, privileges, or immunities, or protection, named in the Constitution and secured by the laws for the protection of such rights, privileges, or immunities, and the constituted authorities of such State are unable to protect, or, from any cause, fail in or refuse protection of the people in such rights, such facts shall be deemed a denial by such State of the equal protection of the laws to which they are entitled under the Constitution of the United States; and in all such cases, or whenever any such insurrection, violence, unlawful combination, or conspiracy, opposes or obstructs the laws of the United States, or the due execution thereof, or impedes or obstructs the due course of justice under the same, it shall be lawful for the President, and it shall be his duty, to take such measures, by the employment of the militia or the land and naval forces of the United States, or of either, or by other means, as he may deem necessary, for the suppression of such insurrection, domestic violence, or combinations.

20 April, 1871, s. 3, v. 17, p. 14.

Proclamation to insurgents to disperse.
SEC. 5300. Whenever, in the judgment of the President, it becomes necessary to use the military forces under this Title, the President shall forthwith, by proclamation, command the insurgents to disperse and retire peaceably to their respective abodes, within a limited time.

29 July, 1861, s. 2, v. 12, p. 282.

Title 70, Chap. 2.
Treason.
SEC. 5331. Every person owing allegiance to the United States who levies war against them, or adheres to their enemies, giving them aid and comfort within the United States or elsewhere, is guilty of treason.

30 April, 1790, s. 1, v. 1., p. 112.

Punishment of treason.
SEC. 5332. Every person guilty of treason shall suffer death; or, at the discretion of the court, shall be imprisoned at hard labor for not less than five years, and fined not less than ten thousand dollars, to be levied on and collected out of any or all of his property, real and personal, of which he was the owner at the time of committing such treason, any sale or conveyance to the contrary notwithstanding; and every person so convicted of treason shall, moreover, be incapable of holding any office under the United States.

17 July, 1862, ss. 1, 3, v. 12, p. 589.

Misprision of treason.
SEC. 5333. Every person, owing allegiance to the United States and having knowledge of the commission of any treason against them, who conceals, and does not, as soon as may be, disclose and make known the same to the President or to some judge of the United States, or to the governor, or to some judge or justice of a particular State, is guilty of misprision of treason, and shall be imprisoned not more than seven years, and fined not more than one thousand dollars.

30 April, 1790, s. 2, v. 1, p. 112.

Inciting or engaging in rebellion or insurrection.
SEC. 5334. Every person who incites, sets on foot, assists, or engages in any rebellion or insurrection against the authority of the United States, or the laws thereof, or gives aid or comfort thereto, shall be punished by imprisonment not more than ten years, or by a fine of not more than ten thousand dollars, or by both of such punishments; and shall, moreover, be incapable of holding any office under the United States. [See §§ 5297.]

17 July, 1862, s. 2, v. 12, p. 590.

Criminal correspondence with foreign governments.
SEC. 5335. Every citizen of the United States, whether actually resident or abiding within the same, or in any foreign country, who, without the permission or authority of the Government, directly or indirectly, commences or carries on any verbal or written correspondence or intercourse with any foreign government, or any officer or agent thereof, with an intent to influence the measures or conduct of any foreign government, or of any officer or agent thereof, in relation to any disputes or controversies with the United States, or to defeat the measures of the Government of the United States; and every person, being a citizen of, or resident within, the United States, and not duly authorized, who counsels, advises, or assists in any such correspondence, with such intent, shall be punished by a fine of not more than five thousand

dollars, and by imprisonment during a term not less than six months, nor more than three years; but nothing in this section shall be construed to abridge the right of a citizen to apply, himself or his agent, to any foreign government or the agent thereof for redress of any injury which he may have sustained from such government, or any of its agents or subjects. [See § 1738, DIPLOMATIC OFFICERS, and § 2113.]

30 Jan., 1799, ch. 1, v. 1, p. 613.

SEC. 5336. If two or more persons in any State or Territory conspire to overthrow, put down, or to destroy by force the Government of the United States, or to levy war against them, or to oppose by force the authority thereof; or by force to prevent, hinder, or delay the execution of any law of the United States; or by force to seize, take, or possess any property of the United States contrary to the authority thereof; each of them shall be punished by a fine of not less than five hundred dollars and not more than five thousand dollars; or by imprisonment, with or without hard labor, for a period not less than six months, nor more than six years, or by both such fine and imprisonment. Seditious conspiracy.

31 July, 1861, ch. 23, v. 12, p. 284.
20 April, 1871, s. 2, v. 17, p. 13.

SEC. 5337. Every person who recruits soldiers or sailors within the United States to engage in armed hostility against the same, or who opens within the United States a recruiting station for the enlistment of such soldiers or sailors, to serve in any manner in armed hostility against the United States, shall be fined not less than two hundred dollars, nor more than one thousand dollars, and imprisoned not less than one year, nor more than five years. Recruiting soldiers or sailors to serve against the United States.

6 Aug., 1861, s. 1, v. 13, p. 317.

SEC. 5338. Every soldier or sailor enlisted or engaged within the United States, with intent to serve in armed hostility against the same, shall be punished by a fine of one hundred dollars, and by imprisonment not less than one year, nor more than three years. Enlistment to serve against the United States.

Ibid, s. 2.

SEC. 5406. If two or more persons in any State or Territory conspire to deter, by force, intimidation, or threat, any party or witness in any court of the United States from attending such court, or from testifying to any matter pending therein, freely, fully, and truthfully, or to injure such party or witness in his person or property on account of his having so attended or testified, or to influence the verdict, presentment, or indictment of any grand or petit juror in any such court, or to injure such juror in his person or property on account of any verdict, presentment, or indictment lawfully assented to by him, or of his being or having been such juror, each of such persons shall be punished by a fine of not less than five hundred nor more than five thousand dollars, or by imprisonment, with or without hard labor, not less than six months nor more than six years, or by both such fine and imprisonment. Title 70, Chap. 4.<br>Conspiring to intimidate party, witness, or juror.

20 April, 1871, s. 2, v. 17, p. 13.

SEC. 5407. If two or more persons in any State or Territory conspire for the purpose of impeding, hindering, obstructing, or defeating, in any manner, the due course of justice in any State or Territory, with intent to deny to any citizen the equal protection of the laws, or to injure him or his property for lawfully enforcing, or attempting to enforce, the right of any person, or class of persons, to the equal protection of the laws, each of such persons shall be punished by a fine of not less than five hundred nor more than five thousand dollars, or by imprisonment, with or without hard labor, not less than six months nor more than six years, or by both such fine and imprisonment. Conspiracy to defeat enforcement of the laws.

Ibid.

SEC. 5440. If two or more persons conspire either to commit any offense against the United States, or defraud the United States in any manner or for any purpose, and one or more of such parties do any act to effect the object of the conspiracy, all the parties to such conspiracy shall be liable to a penalty of not more than ten thousand dollars or to imprisonment for not more than two years, or to both fine and imprisonment, in the discretion of the court. Title 70, Chap. 5.<br>All parties to a conspiracy equally guilty.

2 March, 1867, s. 30, v. 14, p. 484.
17 May, 1879, v. 21, p. 4.

**Title 70, Chap. 7.**

*Conspiracy to prevent accepting or holding office under United States.*

SEC. 5518. If two or more persons in any State or Territory conspire to prevent, by force, intimidation, or threat, any person from accepting or holding any office, trust, or place of confidence under the United States, or from discharging any duties thereof; or to induce by like means any officer of the United States to leave any State, district, or place, where his duties as an officer are required to be performed, or to injure him in his person or property on account of his lawful discharge of the duties of his office, or while engaged in the lawful discharge thereof, or to injure his property so as to molest, interrupt, hinder, or impede him in the discharge of his official duties; each of such persons shall be punished by a fine of not less than five hundred nor more than five thousand dollars, or by imprisonment, with or without hard labor, not less than six months nor more than six years, or by both such fine and imprisonment. [See § 5407.]

31 July, 1861, ch. 33, v. 12, p. 284.
20 April, 1871, s. 2, v. 17, p. 13.

*Conspiracy to deprive any person of the equal protection of the laws.*

SEC. 5519. If two or more persons in any State or Territory conspire, or go in disguise on the highway or on the premises of another, for the purpose of depriving, either directly or indirectly, any person or class of persons of the equal protection of the laws, or of equal privileges and immunities under the laws; or for the purpose of preventing or hindering the constituted authorities of any State or Territory from giving or securing to all persons within such State or Territory the equal protection of the laws; each of such persons shall be punished by a fine of not less than five hundred nor more than five thousand dollars, or by imprisonment, with or without hard labor, not less than six months nor more than six years, or by both such fine and imprisonment. [See § 5336.]

20 April, 1871, s. 2, v. 17, p. 13.

# SUPPLEMENT.

Pensions.
Reserved timber lands.
Public printing.
Assistant surgeons not in line of promotion.
Disbursing agents.
Coaling stations, Isthmus of Panama.
Wrecked and derelict property.
Prize-money to the Wyoming.
Extra pay, Mexican war.
Opinions—Court of Claims—
    Longevity pay.
    Grades in the Navy.
    Retirement of warrant officers.

Opinions—Court of Claims—Continued.
    Rations to marine officers.
    Mileage to officers, Navy.
    Government property—alienation.
    Decisions of Auditors.
    Retirement of officers.
    Retired officers not to act as counsel.
    Contracts to be in writing.
    Government liabilities.
    Assignment of prize-money, &c.
    Disbursing officers.
    Ordnance and gunpowder.
    Decimal system.

## PENSIONS.

*The following amendment should be added to section 4702, page 269.*

**Amendment, sec. 4702.** Except when such widow has continued to draw the pension money after her remarriage, in contravention of law, and such child or children have resided with and been supported by her, their pension will commence at the date to which the widow was last paid.

7 Aug., 1882, ch. 438, v. 22, p. 345.

**Commencement of pensions. 25 January, 1879.** That all pensions which have been granted under the general laws regulating pensions, or may hereafter be granted, in consequence of death from a cause which originated in the United States service during the continuance of the late war of the rebellion, or in consequence of wounds, injuries, or disease received or contracted in said service during said war of the rebellion, shall commence from the date of the death or discharge from said service of the person on whose account the claim has been or shall hereafter be granted, or from the termination of the right of the party having prior title to such pension: *Provided*, The rate of pension for the intervening time for which arrears of pension are hereby granted shall be the same per month for which the pension was originally granted.

25 Jan., 1879, ch. 23, s. 1, v. 20, p. 265.

**Arrears of pensions. 3 March, 1879.** That the rate at which the arrears of invalid pensions shall be allowed and computed in the cases which have been or shall hereafter be allowed shall be graded according to the degree of the pensioner's disability from time to time and the provisions of the pension laws in force over the period for which the arrears shall be computed.

That section one of the act of January twenty-fifth, eighteen hundred and seventy-nine, granting arrears of pensions shall be construed to extend to and include pensions on account of soldiers who were enlisted or drafted for the service in the war of the rebellion, but died or incurred disability from a cause originating after the cessation of hostilities; and before being mustered out: *Provided*, That in no case shall arrears of pensions be allowed and paid from a time prior to the date of actual disability.

3 March, 1879, ch. 187, s. 1, v. 20, p. 469.

All pensions which have been, or which may hereafter be, granted in consequence of death occurring from a cause which originated in the service since the fourth day of March, eighteen hundred and sixty-one, or in consequence of wounds or injuries received or disease contracted since that date shall commence from the death or discharge of the person on whose account the claim has been or is hereafter granted if the disability occurred prior to discharge, and if such disability occurred after the discharge then from the date of actual disability or from the termination of the right of party having prior title to such pension: *Provided*, The application for such pension has been or is hereafter filed with the Commissioner of Pensions prior to the first day of July eighteen hundred and eighty, otherwise the pension shall com-

**Pensions, war of 1812.**

mence from the date of filing the application; but the limitation herein prescribed shall not apply to claims by or in behalf of insane persons and children under sixteen years of age.

*Ibid.*, s. 2.

An act approved March 9, 1878, chap. 28, vol. 20, p. 97, authorizes the names of the surviving officers and men, including militia and volunteers, who served fourteen days in the war with Great Britain of 1812, or who were in any engagement and were honorably discharged, and the surviving widows of such, to be placed on the pension rolls. It also restores pensions to such of them as had been stricken from the rolls for engaging in the rebellion or encouraging it; no arrearages to be paid.

**Pensions under special and general acts.**

The fifth section of the act approved July 25, 1882, chap. 349, v. 22, p. 176, provides "that no person who is now receiving or shall hereafter receive a pension under a special act shall be entitled to receive in addition thereto a pension under the general law, unless the special act expressly states that the pension granted thereby is in addition to the pension which said person is entitled to receive under the general law.

**Pension for loss of sight of both eyes.**

An act approved March 3, 1879, chap. 200, v. 20, p. 484, provides that the act of June 17, 1878, increasing the pensions of soldiers and sailors who have lost both their hands, or both their feet, or the sight of both eyes in the service of the country, shall be so construed as to include all soldiers and sailors who have become totally blind from causes occurring in the service of the United States.

## RESERVED TIMBER LANDS.

**3 March, 1878.**

**Examination of timber lands in Florida.**

That the Secretary of the Navy be, and he is hereby, authorized to cause an examination to be made of the condition of all lands in the State of Florida which have been set apart or reserved for naval purposes, excepting the reservation upon which the navy-yard at Pensacola is located, and to ascertain whether or not such reserved lands are or will be of any value to the Government of the United States for naval purposes.

SEC. 2. That all of said lands which, in the judgment of the Secretary of the Navy, are no longer required for naval purposes shall, as soon as practicable, be certified by him to the Secretary of the Interior, and be subject to entry and sale in the same manner and under the same conditions as other public lands of the United States: *Provided*, That all persons who have in good faith made improvements on said reserved lands so certified at the time of the passage of this act, and who occupy the same, shall be entitled to purchase the part or parts so occupied and improved by them, not to exceed one hundred and sixty acres to any one person at one dollar and twenty-five cents per acre within such reasonable time as may be fixed by the Secretary of the Interior.

SEC. 3. That the sum of three thousand dollars, or much thereof as may be necessary, is hereby appropriated, out of any money in the Treasury not otherwise appropriated, to enable the Secretary of the Navy to carry out the provisions of this act.

3 March, 1879, ch. 189, v. 20, p. 470.

## PUBLIC PRINTING.

**Allotments.**

The act of March 3, 1883, v. 22, p. 629, which appropriates for printing and binding for the Executive Departments, provides that no more than an allotment of one-half of the sum appropriated shall be expended in the two first quarters of the fiscal year, and no more than one-fourth thereof in either of the two last quarters, except that in addition thereto in either of the said last quarters the unexpended balances of allotments for preceding quarters may be expended.

## ASSISTANT SURGEONS (NOT IN LINE OF PROMOTION).

**3 March, 1883.**

**Pay.**

Pay of two assistant surgeons, not in the line of promotion, who shall hereafter, after fifteen years' service, be entitled to receive, as annual pay, when at sea two thousand one hundred dollars, when on shore duty one thousand eight hundred dollars, and when on leave or waiting orders, one thousand six hundred dollars.

3 March, 1883, s. 1, v. 22, p. 472.

## DISBURSING AGENTS OF PUBLIC BUILDINGS.

An act approved August 7, 1882, chap. 433, vol. 22, p. 306, provides that "any disbursing agent who has been or may be appointed to disburse any appropriation for any United States court-house and post-office, or other building or grounds, not located within the city of Washington, shall be entitled to the compensation allowed by law to collectors of customs for such amounts as have been or may be disbursed. *Compensation.*

## COALING STATIONS AT ISTHMUS OF PANAMA.

To enable the Secretary of the Navy to establish at the Isthmus of Panama naval stations and depots of coal for the supply of steamships of war, two hundred thousand dollars, to be available for expenditure as soon as suitable arrangements can be made to the proposed end.

3 March, 1881. Sundry civil act, v. 21, p. 448.

## WRECKED AND DERELICT PROPERTY.

Sec. 3755 of the Revised Statutes (resolution of 21 June, 1870, v. 16, p. 380) authorizes the Secretary of the Treasury to make such contracts and provisions as he may deem for the interest of the Government for the preservation, sale, or collection of any property, or the proceeds thereof, which may have been wrecked, abandoned, or become derelict, being within the jurisdiction of the United States, and which ought to come to the United States, * * * [But see following.] *Duty of Secretary of the Treasury.*

An act approved June 14, 1880, sec. 4, chap. 211, v. 21, p. 197, provides that "whenever hereafter the navigation of any river, lake, harbor, bay, or other navigable water of the United States, shall be obstructed or endangered by any sunken vessel or water-craft, it shall be the duty of the Secretary of War, upon satisfactory information thereof, to cause reasonable notice of not less than thirty days to be given, personally or by publication at least once a week in the newspaper published nearest the locality of such sunken vessel or craft, to all persons interested in such vessel or craft, or in the cargo thereof, of the purpose of said Secretary, unless such vessel or craft shall be removed as soon thereafter as practicable by the parties interested therein, to cause the same to be removed." If not removed the Secretary treats the same as abandoned and derelict, and proceeds to remove it, sells it to the highest bidder for cash, after due notice, and deposits in the Treasury to the credit of a fund for the removal of such obstructions to navigation. The provisions of this act apply to all such wrecks whether removed under this or any other act of Congress. *Duty of the Secret'ry of War.*

An act of August 2, 1882, chap. 375, v. 22, p. 208, enlarges the power given the Secretary of War by the act of June 14, 1880, so that he may, in his discretion, sell and dispose of any such vessel, or cargo, or property therein, before the raising or removal thereof.

## PRIZE-MONEY TO WYOMING AND TAKIANG.

An act approved February 22, 1883, chap. 51, vol. 22, p. 421, provides for payment by the Secretary of the Treasury of $140,000 to the officers and crew, or their legal representatives, of the Wyoming and Takiang (latter manned from the Jamestown) for destruction of hostile vessels in the straits of Simonoseki, &c., in 1863, to be distributed in the same manner as prize-money. *Prize-money to Wyoming, &c.*

## EXTRA PAY, MEXICAN WAR.

An act approved February 19, 1879, chap. 90, v. 20, p. 316, provides for three months' extra pay (removing limitations contained in the act of July 19, 1848) to those who served in the Army, Navy, Marine Corps, and Revenue Marine in the war with Mexico. *Extra pay Mexican war.*

## OPINIONS OF THE COURT OF CLAIMS, VOL. 18.

Longevity pay for officers of the Navy was first established by law in 1835. It was then allowed only to surgeons. Officers of the Navy on the retired list are not entitled to increase of pay by reason of lon- *Longevity pay.*

gevity while on that list. The periods of five years' service mentioned in Rev. Stat., sec. 1556, for increase of pay, are "grades" within the meaning of Revised Statutes, sec. 1588.

C. C., v. 18, p. 111, 1883. Thornley's case.
Also, p. 537, Brown's case.

*Grades in the Navy.* The word "grade" in sec. 1588, R. S., refers to the divisions of officers into five years' periods of service. An officer retired in the third period of five years' service is entitled to 75 per cent. of the sea-pay of that pay grade, and not to the highest pay of a chief engineer who has served over twenty years. [Use of words "grade" and "rank" in the several statutes relative to the Navy is discussed in this opinion.]

C. C., v. 18, p. 339. Rutherford's case.

*Grades in the Navy.* In the Navy there are grades for duty, for honor, and for pay, some by name and others by description. A lieutenant has a grade *of* his class and also a grade *in* his class upon which his pay is fixed, depending upon length of service. A lieutenant retired in the first five years of service because not recommended for promotion, is entitled to one-half of his sea-pay at the time of retirement, and no more.

C. C., v. 18, p. 347. McClure's case.

*Retirement of warrant officers.* The act of August 3, 1861, chap. 42, s. 23 (12, Stat. L., 291,, now R. S., secs. 1448, 1455), applies to warrant officers, and they may be retired the same as commissioned officers. The President's act in retiring a boatswain in 1872 was legal and valid.

C. C., v. 18, p. 537. Brown's case.

*Rations to marine officers.* An officer in the Marine Corps, attached to a sea-going vessel, is not entitled to the ration allowed by R. S., sec. 1578, to a naval officer so attached; he is, by R. S., sec. 1612, subjected to the provisions of R. S., sec. 1269. [The various statutes prior to the Revised Statutes regulating allowances of rations to officers of the Army, Navy, and Marine Corps are considered and examined in this opinion.]

C. C., v. 18, p. 625. Reid's case.

*Mileage to officers.* The act of 1835 (4 Stat. L., 755), which provided that ten cents a mile should be allowed to naval officers for traveling expenses while traveling under orders, made no distinction between traveling in or out of the country. That provision was not repealed by the act of April 17, 1866 (14 Stat. L., 38), nor by the act of July 15 1870 (16 Stat. L., 332), and was in force during the period of the claimant's traveling in 1872. So settled in Temple's case (14 C. C., 377 and 105, U. S. R., 97.)

C. C., v. 18, p. 83. Graham's case.

*Government property.* No public officer, without express authority of Congress, has a right to contract for the alienation of any property of the Government for any purpose.

C. C., v. 18, p. 352. Flores's case.

*Decisions of Auditors.* It is no part of the duties of the Auditors (except the Sixth Auditor) to make decisions binding in any way upon anybody, and their opinions and decisions upon controverted questions, if they choose to give them, have no official determining force. They are only to examine accounts, certify balances, and transmit them to the proper Comptroller for his decision thereon. (R. S., secs. 276–300.)

C. C., v. 18, p. 707. Ridgeway's case.

*Retirement of officers.* Congress may retire an officer from active service and place him on the retired list with a rank different from that which attaches to his office by general laws, and may change the mere rank of an officer on the active or retired list at pleasure, without coming in conflict with the Constitution. (Decisions of the C. C., XV, p. 151) affirmed by Supreme Court.

C. C., Woods' case, v. 18, p. 761.

*Retired officers not to act as counsel.* A retired officer of the Army is an "officer of the United States" within the meaning of R. S., sec. 5498, which prohibits, under penalty of fine or imprisonment, or both, every such officer from acting as an agent or attorney for prosecuting any claim against the United States, &c. To appear and argue a case for a claimant would be to support a claim against the United States, and would subject the officer to the penalty prescribed by statute.

C. C., v. 18, p. 25. Tyler's case.

Negotiations, correspondence, proposals, and acceptances, although conducted in writing, but signed only in part by one party and in part by the other, are not sufficient compliance with R. S., sec. 3744, to constitute a valid contract by the Secretaries of War, Navy, and Interior, which requires such contracts to be "reduced to writing and signed by the contracting parties with their names at the end thereof." *Contracts in writing.*

C. C., v. 18, p. 165. Case of South Boston Iron Co.

The liability of the Government does not generally depend upon the amount of money appropriated. The United States can no more discharge its contracts by part performance than can an individual person do so. Congress may fail to appropriate the money due to a public creditor, in whole or in part, and then leave the public officers without authority to pay him, but the liability remains. *Liabilities of the Government.*

C. C., v. 18, p. 281. Mitchell et. al.

## ASSIGNMENTS OF PRIZE-MONEY AND BOUNTY.

SEC. 4643. Every assignment of prize or bounty money due to persons enlisted in the naval service, and all powers of attorney or other authority to draw, receipt for, or transfer the same, shall be void unless the same be attested by the captain, or other commanding officer, and the paymaster. [See sec. 1430, p. 92.] *Assignments, &c., of prize-money and bounty.*

30 June, 1864, s. 12, v. 12, p. 310.

## DISBURSING OFFICERS.

SEC. 3643. All persons charged by law with the safe-keeping, transfer and disbursement of the public moneys, other than those connected with the Post-Office Department, are required to keep an accurate entry of each sum received and of each payment or transfer. *Entry of receipts and payments.*

6 Aug., 1846, s. 16, v. 9, p. 63.

## ORDNANCE AND GUNPOWDER.

The words "ordnance" and "gunpowder" in section thirty-seven hundred and twenty-one of the Revised Statutes shall be construed to mean offensive and defensive arms, ammunition and explosives, the apparatus for their military use, and the materials for producing the whole, and also transportation, necessary information concerning them, and whatever is requisite in military experiments with them. *5 Aug., 1882. Meaning of words "ordnance" and "gunpowder."*

5 Aug., 1882, chap. 391, v. 22, p. 288.

## DECIMAL SYSTEM.

SEC. 3563. The money of account of the United States shall be expressed in dollars or units, dimes or tenths, cents, or hundredths, and mills or thousands, a dime being the tenth part of a dollar, a cent the hundredth part of a dollar, a mill the thousandth part of a dollar; and all accounts in the public offices and all proceedings in the courts shall be kept and had in conformity to this regulation. *Decimal system established.*

2 April 1792, s. 20, v. 1, p. 250.

## EXPLANATION.

The act of June 8, 1880, establishing the office of Judge Advocate-General of the Navy should have appeared on page 181, under NAVY DEPARTMENT, instead of on page 109, where it will be found.

The references P. E. L. are to the Pamphlet edition of the Statutes at Large, which are now embraced in vol. 22 of the Statutes. The paging corresponds with the volume.

# INDEX.

[The heavy-faced figures in the section column indicate the articles for the government of the Navy, section 1624.]

### A.

|  | Sec. | Page. |
|---|---|---|
| ABANDONED PROPERTY— | | |
| collection and sale of (supplement) | | 313 |
| ABSENCE— | | |
| from duty or station without leave | **8** | 10 |
| after leave has expired | **8** | 10 |
| from command without leave, reduction to ordinary seamen | **9** | 10 |
| of members of general courts-martial | **45–47** | 17 |
| granting leave of, discrimination in favor of faithful and obedient | 1431 | 92 |
| of marine officers on account of sickness or wounds | 1265 | 116 |
| to employés in the Executive Departments | | 145 |
| of heads of Departments and Bureaus | 177–179 | 146 |
| ABUSE— | | |
| of inhabitants on shore, or subject to orders | **8** | 10 |
| of persons on vessels under convoy | **8** | 10 |
| of persons taken on prizes | **17** | 12 |
| ACCESSORIES— | | |
| to piracy, robbery, &c | 5323, 5324 | 277 |
| ACCIDENTS— | | |
| to vessels, report to be made to collectors of customs | | 100 |
| ACCOUNTS— | | |
| of men transferred to accompany them | 20 | 13 |
| balances stated by accounting officers, conclusive upon Executive branch | 191 | 125 |
| but subject to revision by Congress or proper courts | 191 | 125 |
| head of Department may submit facts affecting correctness | 191 | 125 |
| in which the United States are concerned to be settled in the Treasury Department | 236 | 125 |
| in matters of, fiscal year to commence July 1 | 237 | 126 |
| to be settled within each fiscal year | 250 | 126 |
| except where distances make extension necessary | 250 | 126 |
| for which President may fix period for settlement | 250 | 126 |
| reports to Congress from Auditors charged with examination of | 260 | 126 |
| settled by Auditors to be examined by Comptrollers | 273 | 126 |
| form of keeping and settling, to be determined by Comptroller | 273 | 126 |
| preservation of, to be superintended by Comptroller | 273 | 126 |
| accruing in Navy Department to be received and examined by Fourth Auditor | 277 | 127 |
| who will certify and transmit to Second Comptroller for decision | 277 | 127 |
| of receipts and expenditures of public money to be kept by Auditor | 283 | 127 |

| | Sec. | Page. |
|---|---|---|
| ACCOUNTS—Continued. | | |
| finally adjusted by Comptroller to be received and preserved by Auditors | 283 | 127 |
| adjustment of, under general account of advances | | 135 |
| in examination of, Auditor may administer oaths | 297 | 127 |
| of lost or captured vessels, credits to paymaster | 284 | 128 |
| accounting officers to fix day of loss | 286 | 128 |
| last quarterly returns basis of computation of credits | 287 | 128 |
| compensation to seamen for loss of effects | 288 | 128 |
| to be paid to widow, &c., in case of death | 289 | 128 |
| compensation to officers for loss of effects | 290 | 129 |
| schedule and certificate required | 290 | 129 |
| arrears of, Second Comptroller to prescribe rules for payment | 274 | 126 |
| of disbursements, by order of commanding officer, to be allowed | 285 | 167 |
| commanding officer to be accountable | 285 | 167 |
| balances due on, suit on refusal to pay over | 957 | 167 |
| stay of proceedings and injunctions | 957 | 167 |
| of officers in arrears, salary not to be paid | 1766 | 168 |
| defendant may ask for suit, &c | 1766 | 168 |
| of money not authorized as salary, to be rendered monthly | 3622 | 169 |
| to be sent to proper bureau within 10 days after expiration, and passed to proper accounting officer | 3622 | 169 |
| of disbursing officers to be sent direct to accounting officer | 3622 | 169 |
| failure to do so to be explained | 3622 | 169 |
| time for rendering, may be extended by Secretary of the Treasury | 3622 | 169 |
| of disbursements to be rendered according to appropriations | 3623 | 169 |
| suit to be instituted on failure to payover balance due on | 3624 | 169 |
| commission of officer forfeited in case of judgment against him | 3624 | 170 |
| and liable to interest on balance until paid | 3624 | 170 |
| failure to render, according to law, embezzlement | 5491 | 171 |
| punishable by fine and imprisonment | 5491 | 171 |
| in suits, transcript of books evidence | 5494 | 171 |
| presenting false receipts and vouchers to be allowed in conversion | 5496 | 171 |
| ACCOUNTING OFFICERS (see also ACCOUNTS)— | | |
| to allow disbursements made by order of commanding officer | 285 | 167 |
| to hold commanding officer accountable | 285 | 167 |
| to withhold salary of persons in arrears | 1766 | 168 |
| if defendant applies, to report balance to Solicitor for suit | 1766 | 168 |
| certain accounts to be passed by Bureaus to the | 3622 | 169 |
| accounts of disbursing officers to be rendered to | 3622 | 169 |
| penalty for failing to do so | 5491 | 171 |
| to state account of delinquents for suit | 3625–3633 | 165, 6 |
| payment by, of lost or stolen checks | 300, 3647 | 172, 3 |
| decisions of Auditors not binding | | 314 |
| ACCOUTERMENTS— | | |
| for naval detachments co-operating with the Army | 1135 | 107 |
| soldiers forbidden to sell, furnished them | 3748 | 194 |
| embezzling, misappropriating, &c | 5439 | 195 |
| ACKNOWLEDGMENTS— | | |
| before whom they may be taken | 1778 | 144 |

INDEX. 319

|  | Sec. | Page. |
|---|---|---|
| ACTS OF CONGRESS— | | |
| enacting clause prescribed  | | 199 |
| construction of, editing, publishing, &c  | | 202–3 |
| ACTION— | | |
| neglecting to prepare for, punishment  | 4 | 9 |
| ACTING OFFICERS. (*See* VOLUNTEER SERVICE.) | | |
| ADMIRAL.— | | |
| grade to cease on becoming vacant  | 1362 | 45 |
| one allowed  | 1363 | 46 |
| allowed a secretary  | 1367 | 46 |
| with rank and allowances of a lieutenant  | 1367 | 46 |
| no appointment from civil life when on sea service, May 4, 1878 | | 46 |
| assignment of line officer as secretary May 4, 1878 | | 46 |
| pay of, thirteen thousand dollars  | 1556 | 65 |
| ADMIRAL (Vice)— | | |
| grade to cease on becoming vacant  | 1362 | 45 |
| one allowed  | 1363 | 46 |
| allowed a secretary  | 1367 | 46 |
| with rank and allowances of a lieutenant  | 1367 | 46 |
| no appointment from civil life when on sea service  | | 46 |
| assignment of line officer as, May 4, 1878 | | 46 |
| ADMIRAL (Rear)— | | |
| one allowed on active list  | 1363 | 46 |
| selection of, during war  | 1364 | 46 |
| during peace  | 1366 | 46 |
| assignment of line officers as secretaries and clerks to  | | 46 |
| ADVANCES— | | |
| of money, pay officers not to make  | 1389 | 63 |
| nor of articles or commodities  | 1389 | 63 |
| to persons in the naval service  | 3648 | 170 |
| to disbursing officers and on contracts  | 3648 | 170 |
| "general account of," provisions concerning  | | 135 |
| to persons on distant stations  | 1563 | 168 |
| ADVANCEMENT (for heroism) (*see also* PROMOTION)— | | |
| limiting number of officers not to preclude  | 1364 | 46 |
| of marine officers for distinguished conduct  | 1605 | 109 |
| and on receiving vote of thanks  | 1607 | 110 |
| limit in numbers not to preclude  | 1597, 1606 | 108–9 |
| ADVERTISEMENTS— | | |
| when they may be omitted (notes)  | | 24 |
| written authority required for publishing  | 3828 | 129 |
| to be presented with bill before payment  | 3828 | 129 |
| what may be published in District of Columbia, July 31, 1878 | | 129 |
| price for, not to exceed commercial rates, June 20, 1878 | | 129 |
| to be sworn to by publisher, June 20, 1878 | | 129 |
| Departments may provide special rates for, June 20, 1878 | | 129 |
| to appear in six papers in District of Columbia, January 21, 1881 | | 129 |
| price not to exceed commercial rates, January 21, 1881 | | 129 |
| to be published in accordance with section 3828, January 21, 1881 | | 129 |
| to appear for all purchases and contracts  | 3709 | 130 |
| except for personal services  | 3709 | 130 |
| unless exigencies require immediate delivery  | 3709 | 130 |

|  | Sec. | Page. |
|---|---|---|
| ADVERTISEMENTS—Continued. | | |
| to appear in one or more papers where supplies are to be furnished. | 3718 | 130 |
| for a sufficient time previously | 3709 | 130 |
| for transportation to be for not less than five days | 3718 | 130 |
| for provisions, &c., for at least four weeks | 3718 | 130 |
| estimates for, to be given in detail | 3666 | 131 |
| expenditures to be accounted for by each Bureau | 3666 | 131 |
| AFFIDAVITS— | | |
| making false, to procure claims | 5438 | 227 |
| AFFIRMATION— | | |
| meets requirement of an oath under the statutes | | 199 |
| AGENTS— | | |
| of the United States abroad, to disburse money, appointment of | 1550 | 138 |
| to give bond | 3614 | 138 |
| special, to disburse money, to give bond | 3614 | 138 |
| of a firm, not to be employed to do business with it | 1783 | 138 |
| penalty for so acting | 1783 | 138 |
| for Executive Departments not to be employed beyond provision of law, August 15, 1876 | | 140 |
| public officers not to act as, for claims | 5498 | 155 |
| ex-employés forbidden to act as, for claims | 190 | 152 |
| for claims, to take oath of allegiance | 3478 | 154 |
| retired officers cannot act as | | 314 |
| AID OR EXECUTIVE— | | |
| detail of line officers to act as | 1469 | 47 |
| authority and orders of | 1469 | 47 |
| ALIENS— | | |
| punishment for depriving, of rights | 5510 | 20 |
| how they may become citizens | 2165 | 256 |
| honorably discharged from the service of the United States may become citizens | 2166 | 257 |
| minor residents, how made citizens | 2167 | 257 |
| when widows and children of, are citizens | 2168 | 257 |
| must reside within U. S. five years before admitted to citizenship | 2170 | 257 |
| subjects of other countries at war with United States not to become citizens | 2171 | 257 |
| enemies, removal of, not to be interfered with | 2171 | 257 |
| enemies, removal of, in time of war | 4067 | 265 |
| time allowed for departure | 4068 | 266 |
| apprehension of, when dangerous to the public peace | 4069 | 266 |
| removal of, to be done by marshal | 4070 | 266 |
| ALLOWANCES. (See PAY.) | | |
| AMBULANCES— | | |
| immunity of, in operations of war | | 262 |
| AMERICAN EPHEMERIS. (See NAUTICAL ALMANAC.) | | |
| AMERICAN GROWTH AND MANUFACTURE— | | |
| hemp and its preparations to be of | 3725 | 27 |
| preference to, in purchases | 3728 | 27 |
| bunting, contracts for, in open market | 3729 | 27 |
| AMMUNITION— | | |
| wasting or permitting waste of | 8 | 10 |
| misappropriating, wrongfully selling, etc | 14 | 11 |
| purchasing or receiving from those not authorized to sell | 14 | 11 |
| unlawful disposition of, by persons in military or naval service | 5438, 5439 | 195 |

# INDEX.

|  | Sec. | Page. |
|---|---|---|
| AMPUTATIONS— | | |
| rates of pension in cases of | | 271 |
| APPOINTMENTS— | | |
| pay from acceptance of | 1560 | 68 |
| except when bond is required | 1560 | 68 |
| opinions and decisions relating to, notes | | 104–148 |
| to fill vacancies during recess of Senate | 1761 | 147 |
| accepting, contrary to law | 1771 | 149 |
| making, contrary to law | 1772 | 149 |
| Secretary of Treasury to be notified of, &c | 1774 | 149 |
| APPRENTICES— | | |
| seven hundred and fifty may be enlisted annually | 1417 | 90 |
| to serve during minority | 1417 | 90 |
| preference to honorably discharged, in promoting | 1417 | 90 |
| to be between 14 and 18 years, when enlisted | 1418 | 91 |
| and to have consent of parents and guardians | 1419 | 91 |
| minors under 14 years not to be enlisted | 1420 | 91 |
| APPROPRIATIONS— | | |
| purchases, &c., not to be made without adequate | 3732 | 28 |
| except for clothing, fuel, forage, &c | 3732 | 28 |
| estimates for, for Navy Department, to be furnished Secretary by bureaus | 430 | 130 |
| in communicating estimates of, calculations on which based to be stated | 3660 | 130 |
| for printing and binding, to be submitted | 3661 | 130 |
| estimates for, for compensation, to be founded on law | 3662 | 131 |
| estimates for, for new buildings, to be accompanied by plans | 3663 | 131 |
| subsequent estimates, to state sums expended, &c | 3663 | 131 |
| if in excess of original, reasons to be stated | 3663 | 131 |
| estimates for, if unusual, to be explained | 3664 | 131 |
| as well as variations of previous ones, and new items | 3664 | 131 |
| in estimating for, amount of, outstanding to be stated, &c | 3665 | 131 |
| objects, under Navy Department, for which estimates must be given in detail | 3666 | 131 |
| expenditures to be accounted for | 3666 | 131 |
| under pay of Navy, estimates to be classified, February 28, 1881 | | 132 |
| for demands and claims on pension fund | 3667 | 132 |
| annual estimates for, to be submitted through Secretary of the Treasury | 3669 | 132 |
| to be included in the book of estimates | 3669 | 132 |
| appropriations by former acts to be added | 3670 | 132 |
| estimates for, to be furnished by 1st of October annually, March 3, 1875 | | 132 |
| extracts from report to be published with, March 3, 1875 | | 132 |
| to be drawn from Treasury by warrants, upon requisition | 3673 | 132 |
| countersigned by Comptroller and registered by Auditor | 3673 | 132 |
| warrants to specify particular appropriation to which chargeable | 3675 | 133 |
| to which money will be charged on the orders | 3675 | 133 |
| for Navy Department, to be under control of the Secretary of the Navy | 3676 | 133 |
| for bureaus, to be kept separate in the Treasury | 3676 | 133 |
| to be applied solely to these objects | 3678 | 133 |

| | Sec. | Page. |
|---|---|---|
| APPROPRIATIONS—Continued. | | |
| not to be exceeded in any one year | 3679 | 133 |
| so as to involve Government for future payment | 3679 | 133 |
| for commissions, to be made before accounts are passed | 3681 | 133 |
| for contingent, not to be paid for official compensation | 3682 | 133 |
| special, not to be available for more than two years | 3685 | 133 |
| without further provision of law | 3685 | 133 |
| for publishing foreign hydrographic surveys, when to be applied | 3686 | 134 |
| board to be ordered to report on data | 3686 | 134 |
| of a permanent annual character, indicated | 3689 | 134 |
| balances of annual, applicable to expenses of the year only | 3690 | 134 |
| except to fulfill contracts | 3690 | 134 |
| or in case of permanent or indefinite appropriations | 3690 | 134 |
| remainder to be carried to surplus fund | 3690 | 134 |
| balances not drawn against for two years to go to surplus fund | 3691 | 134 |
| if not required in settlement of accounts | 3691 | 134 |
| appropriations for public debt excepted | 3691 | 134 |
| not to apply to permanent specific appropriations, June 20, 1874 | | 135 |
| nor to appropriations for harbors, public buildings, &c., June 20, 1874 | | 135 |
| nor to pay of Navy and Marine Corps, June 20, 1874 | | 135 |
| nor prevent the fulfillment of contracts, June 20, 1874 | | 135 |
| moneys from sale of condemned clothing to revert to original | 3692 | 135 |
| or from sale of materials, &c., exploring expeditions | 3692 | 135 |
| general account of advances to be kept, June 12, 1878 | | 135 |
| provisions concerning the same, June 12, 1878 | | 135 |
| expended for naval service to be reported to Congress by Secretary of Treasury, June 19, 1878 | | 135 |
| balances in hand of disbursing agents to be appended, June 19, 1878 | | 135 |
| for construction of buildings, to be expended within limits | | 196 |
| style and title of acts, making | | 200 |
| ARMS— | | |
| misappropriating, applying to own use, &c | 14 | 11 |
| purchasing or receiving, from those not authorized to sell | 14 | 11 |
| soldiers forbidden to sell, furnished them | 3748 | 194 |
| pledging or selling, by persons in Army or Navy | 5438 | 195 |
| issue of, by Secretary of War for protection of public property, March 1, 1879 | | 306 |
| ARMY— | | |
| transportation, &c., for naval detachments co-operating with | 1135 | 107 |
| also with rations | 1143 | 107 |
| ARREST— | | |
| by order of commanding officer | 24 | 14 |
| to be tried, officer, to deliver up sword | 44 | 17 |
| to confine himself to limits | 44 | 17 |
| marines exempt from personal, for debt or contract | 1610 | 110 |
| ARREARS— | | |
| the Second Comptroller to prescribe rules for payment of | 274 | 126 |
| of pensions, payment of (supplement) | | 311 |
| ARSON— | | |
| of buildings in navy-yards, &c | 5385, 5386 | 59 |
| of vessels, timber, lumber, &c | 5386, 5387 | 59 |

|   |   | Sec. | Page. |
|---|---|---|---|
| **ARSENALS—** | | | |
| murder within, punishment of death | | 5339 | 254 |
| wilfully striking, stabbing, &c., within, guilty of manslaughter | | 5341 | 254 |
| attempting murder or manslaughter within, fine and imprisonment | | 5342 | 254 |
| committing rape within, punishment of death | | 5345 | 255 |
| maiming, &c., within, fine and imprisonment | | 5348 | 255 |
| other offenses within, not described, how punished | | 5391 | 255 |
| **ARTIFICIAL LIMBS—** | | | |
| conditions on which furnished | | 4787 | 42 |
| classes of persons entitled to | | 4787 | 43 |
| commutation in money for | | 4788–4790 | 43 |
| to be paid by Commissioner of Pensions | | 4789 | 43 |
| transportation to persons entitled to | | 4791 | 43 |
| **ARTICLES—** | | | |
| governing the Navy | | 1624 | 7 |
| to be hung up and read | | 20 | 13 |
| punishment for offenses not enumerated in | | 22 | 13 |
| **ASSAULTING—** | | | |
| superior officer, how punishable | | 4 | 8 |
| or striking persons in the Navy | | 8 | 10 |
| persons within forts, arsenals, yards, &c | | 5339, 5341, 5346 | 254, 5 |
| **ASSESSMENTS—** | | | |
| for political purposes forbidden, August 15, 1876; January 16, 1883, page 209 | | 1546 | 207 |
| **ASSIGNMENT—** | | | |
| of wages by enlisted men | | 1576 | 70 |
| void unless attested by commander and paymaster | | 1576 | 70 |
| commanding officer to discourage | | 1430 | 92 |
| of pay of persons in Marine Corps not valid prior to discharge | | 1291 | 120 |
| of claims void under certain circumstances | | 3477 | 153 |
| of prize-money and bounty (supplement) | | | 315 |
| of contracts | | 3737 | 28 |
| **ASIA—** | | | |
| citizens of the United States not to engage in the coolie trade | | 2158 | 301 |
| **ASSIMILATED RANK—** | | | |
| to warrant officers, President may give | | 1491 | 102 |
| **ASSISTANT PAYMASTERS.** (*See* PAYMASTERS, ASSISTANT.) | | | |
| **ASSISTANT ENGINEERS.** (*See* ENGINEERS, ASSISTANT.) | | | |
| **ASSISTANT NAVAL CONSTRUCTORS.** (*See* NAVAL CONSTRUCTORS.) | | | |
| **ASSISTANT SURGEONS.** (*See* SURGEONS, ASSISTANT,) | | | |
| **ASYLUMS.** (*See* HOSPITALS.) | | | |
| **ATTORNEY-GENERAL—** | | | |
| to report on validity of title of land purchased | | 355 | 57 |
| district attorneys and Departments to assent | | 355 | 57 |
| expenses payable from contingent | | 355 | 57 |
| to give advice when required by President | | 354 | 136 |
| or by the heads of Departments | | 356 | 136 |
| questions of law to be sent to, by Secretary of Navy | | 357 | 136 |
| and referred to proper officer in Department of Justice | | 357 | 136 |
| opinions of subordinates to, approved, same as of Attorney-General | | 358 | 136 |
| conducting and arguing of suits in the interest of the United States | | 359 | 136 |

|  | Sec. | Page. |
|---|---|---|
| ATTORNEY-GENERAL—Continued. | | |
| may require any solicitor of Department to perform duty | 360 | 137 |
| legal services by officers of Department of Justice without fee | 361 | 137 |
| may employ and retain counsellors to assist district attorneys | 363 | 137 |
| shall provide services of counsel for Departments | 364 | 137 |
| to be paid on his certificate | 365 | 137 |
| to receive a commission from head of Department | 366 | 137 |
| and take oath taken by district attorneys | 366 | 137 |
| may send officers of Department of Justice to any State | 367 | 137 |
| who shall receive actual and necessary expenses | 370 | 138 |
| account of which to be vouched by affidavit | 370 | 138 |
| to cause to be edited and printed opinions of the law offices | 383 | 138 |
| ATTORNEYS (powers of). (*See* POWERS OF ATTORNEY.) | | |
| ATTORNEYS— | | |
| for the Government to be provided by the Attorney-General | 187 | 138 |
| heads of Departments not to employ | 189 | 138 |
| but call on Department of Justice | 189 | 138 |
| employed by Department of Justice, when extra compensation is allowed, June 20, 1874 | | 72 |
| for claims to take oath of allegiance | 3478 | 154 |
| who may administer same | 3479 | 154 |
| public officers forbidden to act as | 5498 | 155 |
| ex-employés in Departments not to act as, &c | 190 | 152 |
| AUDITORS. (*See* ACCOUNTS.) | | |
| AWNINGS— | | |
| estimates for, to be in detail | 3662 | 132 |

## B.

|  | Sec. | Page. |
|---|---|---|
| BAD CONDUCT DISCHARGE— | | |
| by sentence of a court-martial | 30 | 14 |
| BAGGAGE— | | |
| allowance for transportation of | 1566 | 72 |
| BAND (Marine)— | | |
| pay of, performing at Capitol, &c | 1613 | 114 |
| leader and members | | 117 |
| BANKERS— | | |
| receiving unauthorized deposits of public funds, guilty of embezzlement | 5497 | 172 |
| BATTLE— | | |
| treacherously yielding in, punishment for | 4 | 8 |
| cowardice or negligence in, punishment for | 4 | 8 |
| deserting duty or station, punishment for | 4 | 8 |
| not properly obeying orders in time of, punishment for | 4 | 9 |
| not joining in, punishment for | 4 | 9 |
| BEANS— | | |
| allowance in Navy ration | 1580 | 83 |
| BENEFIT OF CLERGY— | | |
| when not allowed | 5329 | 254 |
| BETRAYING TRUST— | | |
| corrupting any person to | 5 | 9 |
| in time of war, punishment for | 4 | 8 |
| BIDS. (*See* CONTRACTS.) | | |

INDEX. 325

| | Sec. | Page. |
|---|---|---|
| BIENNIAL REGISTER— | | |
| preparation and printing | 510 | 188 |
| BILLS OF HEALTH— | | |
| estimate for, to be in detail | 3666 | 132 |
| BINDING. (*See* PUBLIC PRINTING.) | | |
| BISCUIT— | | |
| allowance in Navy ration | 1580 | 83 |
| flour for, and baking of | 3727 | 84 |
| BLUE BOOK (Biennial Register)— | | |
| preparation and printing of | 510 | 188 |
| BOARD OF HEALTH. (*See* QUARANTINE.) | | |
| BOARDS OF INVESTIGATION— | | |
| powers of, &c., note | | 19 |
| BOARD OF VISITORS— | | |
| appointment of, to Naval Academy | | 54 |
| BOATSWAINS. (*See* WARRANT OFFICERS.) | | |
| BOILER MATERIALS— | | |
| may be purchased at lowest market price, June 14, 1878 | | 31 |
| to be subject to tests, June 14, 1878 | | 31 |
| BONDS— | | |
| to be furnished by contractors | 3719 | 26 |
| to be given by pay officers of the Navy | 1383 | 62 |
| to be renewed when Secretary requires | 1384 | 62 |
| to be given by special agents, disbursing money | 3614 | 138 |
| new appointments not to affect | 1385 | 62 |
| disbursing clerks to give | 176 | 146 |
| civilian storekeepers on foreign stations to give | 1415 | 56 |
| officers, storekeepers, on foreign stations to give | 1439 | 57 |
| commencement of pay of officers, giving | 1560 | 68 |
| BOOKS— | | |
| Estimates for, to be given in detail | 3666 | 131 |
| expenditure to be accounted for by each bureau | 3666 | 131 |
| BOUNTY LANDS— | | |
| classes of persons entitled to, in certain wars | 2418, 2419 | 210, 11 |
| may receive Treasury scrip, instead | 2418, 2419 | 210, 11 |
| militia and volunteers in war of 1812, entitled to | 2420 | 211 |
| military land bounty received under prior acts, a bar to receiving | 2421 | 211 |
| period of captivity, to be estimated in account of service | 2422 | 211 |
| warrants to be received from Department of the Interior | 2423 | 211 |
| widows of soldiers, etc., entitled to | 2424 | 211 |
| additional for services in certain wars | 2425 | 211 |
| beneficiaries under this section, named | 2426, 2427 | 211, 12 |
| in case of death, who entitled | 2428 | 212 |
| service allowed for distance traveled | 2433 | 212 |
| desertion or dishonorable discharge forfeits claim to | 2438 | 212 |
| to Marine Corps, who served with Army | | 212 |
| opinions and decisions, concerning | | 213 |
| BOUNTY (money)— | | |
| on enlistment, to be fixed by President | 1569 | 92 |
| to captors, for each person on vessel of enemy | 4635 | 213 |
| to colored persons enlisted in the Army during the rebellion | 4723 | 214 |
| to persons in the naval service during the rebellion, 1st and 4th of July, 1864 | | 214 |

|  |  | Sec. | Page. |
|---|---|---|---|
| BOUNTY (money)—Continued. | | | |
| | opinions and decisions relative to (notes) | | 214 |
| | for re-enlisting under honorable discharge | 1573 | 69 |
| | assignment of, to be attested | 4643 | 315 |
| BOXING MASTER— | | | |
| | of Naval Academy, pay of | | 54 |
| BRANDING— | | | |
| | punishment by, not to be inflicted | 49 | 17 |
| BREAD— | | | |
| | baking of, by special contract | 3727 | 27 |
| | allowance of, in Navy ration | 1581 | 83 |
| | flour for and baking of | 3727 | 84 |
| BREVETS— | | | |
| | conditions on which conferred on officers of the Marine Corps | 1209–1604 | 109 |
| | to date from particular action | 1210 | 109 |
| | not to entitle to increased pay | 1264 | 109 |
| | assignment of officers according to brevet rank | 1211 | 109 |
| | only when engaged in actual hostilities, March 3, 1883 | | 109 |
| | entitled to precedence of command | 1211 | 109 |
| | entitled to wear uniform of actual rank only | 1212 | 109 |
| | and to be addressed in same way | 1212 | 109 |
| BRIBERY— | | | |
| | of United States officers and Members of Congress | 5450, 5451–5500 | 208 |
| | Members of Congress accepting bribes, punishment for | 5501 | 209 |
| | disqualification for office | 5502 | 209 |
| BULLION— | | | |
| | merchant vessels to transport, for the United States | 4204 | 249 |
| | to receive reasonable compensation therefor | 4204 | 249 |
| BUNTING— | | | |
| | not required to be purchased from lowest bidder | 3721 | 26 |
| | American, may be procured by contract in open market | 3729 | 27 |
| BUOYS— | | | |
| | along coasts, in harbors, &c., to be placed by Light-House Board | 4678 | 240 |
| BUREAUS (*see also* NAVY DEPARTMENT)— | | | |
| | chiefs of, entitled to highest sea pay | 1565 | 69 |
| | selection of chiefs of, in Navy Department | 420–426 | 181 |
| BUTTER— | | | |
| | allowance of, in Navy ration | 1580 | 83 |
| | procurement of | 3721–3726 | 84 |

## C.

|  |  | Sec. | Page. |
|---|---|---|---|
| CADET ENGINEERS (*see also* NAVAL ACADEMY)— | | | |
| | no more appointments to be made | 1512 | 51 |
| | pay of | 1556 | 53 |
| CADET MIDSHIPMEN (*see also* NAVAL ACADEMY)— | | | |
| | no more to be appointed; naval cadets substituted | 1512 | 51 |
| | pay of, on active list | 1556 | 53 |
| CAMP EQUIPAGE— | | | |
| | to be furnished naval detachments co-operating with the Army | 1135 | 107 |
| CANDLES— | | | |
| | for yards, estimates for, to be in detail | 3666 | 131 |

INDEX. 327

|  | Sec. | Page. |
|---|---|---|
| CAPITAL OFFENSES— | | |
| in the Navy, what constitutes | 4 | 8 |
| sentences, how determined | 50 | 17 |
| to be confirmed by President | 50 | 17 |
| counsel to be provided for persons indicted for | 1034 | 307 |
| CAPTAINS— | | |
| forty-five allowed on active list | 1363 | 46 |
| pay of, on the active list | 1556 | 65 |
| on the retired list | 1588 | 70 |
| to command vessels of second rate | 1529 | 94 |
| CAPTIVITY— | | |
| period of, counted in service for bounty lands | 2422 | 211 |
| CAPTURED— | | |
| continuation of pay to, crews of vessels | 1575 | 69 |
| CAPTURES— | | |
| punishment for failing to make | 4 | 8 |
| CARPENTERS. (See WARRANT OFFICERS.) | | |
| CARTS— | | |
| estimates for, to be in detail | 3666 | 131 |
| CEDAR TIMBER. (See RESERVED LANDS.) | | |
| CEMETERIES (national)— | | |
| monuments, headstones, and registers | 4877 | 43 |
| who may be buried in | 4878 | 44 |
| CERTIFICATES OF MERIT— | | |
| additional pay for, in the Army | 1285 | 118 |
| CHALLENGE— | | |
| sending or accepting, to fight duel | 8 | 10 |
| CHAPLAINS— | | |
| not to exceed twenty-four on active list | 1395 | 22 |
| to be appointed by President and Senate | 1395 | 22 |
| not to be under twenty-one or over thirty-five when appointed | 1396 | 22 |
| to conduct worship according to forms of their church | 1397 | 22 |
| to report services performed annually | 1398 | 22 |
| relative rank of, on active list | 1479 | 22 |
| rank of, when retired from age or lenghth of service | 1481 | 22 |
| pay of, on the active list | 1556 | 22 |
| CHARWOMEN— | | |
| number and pay of, in Navy Department building | | 184 |
| CHARTS— | | |
| preparation of, by Hydrographic Office | 432 | 44 |
| disposition of, to navigators | 432 | 44 |
| at cost of paper and printing, February 14, 1879 | | 45 |
| money to be paid into Treasury | 433 | 44 |
| of foreign surveys, restriction on publishing | 3686 | 44 |
| of coast surveys, disposition of | 4691 | 216 |
| CHARGES— | | |
| persons ordered to trial to be furnished with copies of | 43 | 16 |
| when other, may be preferred | 43 | 16 |
| CHECKS AND DRAFTS— | | |
| lost, drawn by officers no longer in service, how paid | 300, 3647 | 172–3 |
| issue of duplicates after six months | 3646 | 173 |
| or within three years from date of original | 3646 | 173 |
| upon giving bonds with security | 3646 | 173 |

|  | Sec. | Page. |
|---|---|---|
| CHECKS AND DRAFTS—Continued. | | |
| lost, issue not to apply to checks exceeding $3,000 | 3646 | 173 |
| furnished for disbursement to be collected, &c | 3651 | 174 |
| exchange for gold and silver at par allowable | 3651 | 174 |
| premium from sale of, to be accounted for | 3652 | 174 |
| outstanding three years or more to be covered into Treasury | 306 | 172 |
| to credit of party entitled to receive pay therefor | 306 | 172 |
| and to appropriation of "outstanding liabilities" | 306 | 172 |
| issue of warrant in favor of payee or bona fide holder | 307, 308 | 172–3 |
| disbursing officers to make return of | 310 | 173 |
| amounts not drawn against for three years to be covered into Treasury | 309 | 173 |
| to be credited to the officer in whose name they stand | 309 | 173 |
| speedy presentation of, to be enforced by Secretary of the Treasury | 3645 | 173 |
| circulation as a medium to be guarded against | 3645 | 173 |
| CHIEF CONSTRUCTOR— | | |
| Chief of Bureau of Construction to have title of | 1471 | 55 |
| and the relative rank of Commodore | 1471 | 65 |
| and the highest sea pay of his grade | 1565 | 69 |
| CHIEF CLERKS (of Departments and Bureaus)— | | |
| to supervise duties of other clerks | 173 | 145 |
| and see that they are faithfully performed | 173 | 145 |
| and that they are distributed with equality | 174 | 145 |
| to revise distribution from time to time | 174 | 145 |
| to report monthly to his superior any defects | 174 | 145 |
| which report the head of Department shall examine, &c. | 175 | 145 |
| CHINA— | | |
| immigration of laborers from, suspended, May 6, 1882 | | 259 |
| involuntary transportation of subjects of | 2158, 2163 | 301 |
| CITIZENSHIP— | | |
| forfeited by deserters not returning after proclamation | 1996 | 33 |
| disability removed if serving to April 19, 1865 | 4749 | 34 |
| laws relative to naturalization | 2165–2174 | 256–8 |
| persons born in United States, not subject to foreign power, declared citizens | 1992 | 258 |
| exclusive of Indians not taxed | 1992 | 258 |
| and Chinese, May 6, 1882 | | 258 |
| of children born abroad | 1993 | 258 |
| of married women | 1994 | 258 |
| forfeited by deserters under certain conditions | 1996 | 258 |
| not applicable to those who served until April 19, 1865 | 1997 | 259 |
| CIVIL EMPLOYÉS (*see also* CIVIL SERVICE and CLERKS)— | | |
| of Naval Academy, number and pay of | | 54 |
| CIVIL ENGINEERS— | | |
| one allowed in Bureau of Yards and Docks | 416 | 23 |
| one allowed each yard where required | 1413 | 23 |
| to be appointed by the President and Senate | 1413 | 23 |
| relative rank of, General Orders No. 263 | 1478 | 23 |
| pay of, on the active list | 1556 | 23 |
| CIVIL RIGHTS (*see also* CONSPIRACY)— | | |
| punishment for depriving citizens of | 5510 | 20 |

INDEX. 329

| | Sec. | Page. |
|---|---|---|
| CIVIL SERVICE (*see also* CLERKS)— | | |
|   President to prescribe regulations for admission to the | 1753 | 141 |
|     and to appoint Civil-Service Commissioners, January 16, 1883. | | 141 |
|   Civil-Service Commission, salaries, duties, &c | | 141 |
|   rules to carry out civil-service act | | 141 |
|     1. Open competitive examinations to test fitness | | 141 |
|       to be practical in their character | | 141 |
|       and to relate to duties to be performed | | 141 |
|     2. Selections to be made from those highest graded | | 141 |
|     3. Appointments in Departments at Washington to be apportioned among States, &c | | 141 |
|       applicants to make oath as to residence | | 141 |
|     4. Probationary period before absolute appointment | | 141 |
|     5. Persons in, not under obligation to contribute to political fund | | 141 |
|       nor to render any political service | | 141 |
|       failure to do either not to work removal or prejudice | | 141 |
|     6. Civil employés not to use authority to coerce political action | | 142 |
|     7. Non-competitive examinations, when competent persons fail to compete | | 142 |
|     8. Duties of appointing power, to the Commissioners | | 142 |
|       to notify Commission of resignations, removals, &c | | 142 |
|   commissioners to make regulations for examinations | | 142 |
|     subject to the rules made by the President | | 142 |
|     to make investigations touching enforcement of rules | | 142 |
|     to make annual report to President | | 142 |
|   places of meeting of board of examiners, section 3 | | 142 |
|   penalty for corruptly defeating objects of Commission, section 5 | | 142 |
|   heads of Departments may revise existing classifications, section 6 | | 143 |
|     for the purpose of examinations | | 143 |
|   no employment or promotion without examination under the rules, section 7 | | 143 |
|   preference to the honorably discharged from Army and Navy, unaffected by the act | | 143 |
|     nor is the President's authority under section 1753 | | 143 |
|   habitual use of intoxicating liquors a bar to appointment, section 8 | | 143 |
|   not more than two members of same family eligible, section 9 | | 143 |
|   recommendations of Congressmen not to be considered, section 10 | | 143 |
|     except as to character or residence of applicant, section 10 | | 143 |
|   preference to the honorably discharged from wounds or disability | 1754 | 143 |
|     if possessing capacity and qualifications | 1754 | 143 |
|     also in making reductions of force, August 15, 1876 | | 143 |
| CLAIMS— | | |
|   presentation of false or fraudulent | 14 | 11 |
|   conspiracy to procure allowance of false | 14 | 11 |
|   procuring or advising the making of false papers, to secure | 14 | 11 |
|   making false oath, to secure | 14 | 11 |
|   subpœna of witnesses in cases of, against the United States | 184 | 151 |
|     compensation to witnesses | 185 | 152 |
|     failing to testify, punishment | 186 | 152 |
|   Attorney-General, to furnish professional service in cases of | 187 | 152 |

|  | Sec. | Page. |
|---|---|---|
| CLAIMS—Continued. | | |
|    ex-employés not to prosecute certain, within two years, &c | 190 | 152 |
|       nor to aid in their prosecution | 190 | 152 |
|    by or against United States to be adjusted in Treasury Department | 236 | 152 |
|    compromise of, on report of district attorney | 3469 | 153 |
|    transfer and assignment of, void, except, &c | 3477 | 153 |
|    agents prosecuting, to take oath of allegiance | 3478 | 153 |
|    existing prior to April 30, 1861, not to be paid to disloyal parties | 3480 | 153 |
|       pardon, not to authorize payments | 3480 | 153 |
|       exception as to claims founded on contracts, &c | 3480 | 153 |
|    unlawfully taking or using public papers in prosecuting | 5454 | 153 |
|       punishment by fine and imprisonment | 5454 | 154 |
|    officers of the United States forbidden to act as agents for | 5498 | 155 |
|       subject to fine and imprisonment | 5498 | 155 |
|       not to receive compensation in matters of ...! | 1782 | 207 |
|    judgments to be withheld from claimant debtors to the United States | | 155 |
|       proceedings when claimant denies indebtedness | | 155 |
|       claimant entitled to interest if action judgment is against United States | | 155 |
|    wilfully made for more than is due not to be allowed | | 155 |
|    set-off against, when claimant owes the United States, March 3, 1875 | | 155 |
|    presenting or causing to be presented false | 5438 | 227 |
| CLERKS (Navy)— | | |
|    to commanders of squadrons and vessels | | 46 |
|       not to be appointed from civil life | | 46 |
|    at Naval Academy, pay of | | 54 |
|    to pay officers, when and where allowed | 1386–1388 | 63 |
|    to commandants of yards and stations, pay of | 1556 | 67 |
|       paymasters, pay of | 1556 | 68 |
|    to storekeepers and agents, estimates for, to be in detail | 3666 | 132 |
| CLERKS (in the Executive Departments) (*see also* CIVIL SERVICE)— | | |
|    arranged into first, second, third, and fourth classes | 163 | 139 |
|       with salaries of $1,200, $1,400, $1,600, and $1,800 respectively | 167 | 139 |
|    women may be appointed to clerkships | 165 | 139 |
|       employed in subordinate clerical capacity to receive $900 | 167 | 139 |
|       and as copyists and counters, the same | 167 | 139 |
|    temporarily employed, to receive same salaries as regulars | 168 | 140 |
|    number regulated by the appropriations | 169 | 140 |
|       and only at such rate of pay, August 5, 1882 | | 140 |
|    not to receive extra pay unless expressly authorized | 170 | 140 |
|    not to be paid from contingent appropriations, August 5, 1882 | | 140 |
|    not to be detailed from outside the District for duty therein, August 5, 1882 | | 140 |
|       except temporary details for duty, August 5, 1882 | | 140 |
|    lapsed salaries to be covered into the Treasury, August 5, 1882 | | 141 |
|    head of Department may alter distribution of, among bureaus | 166 | 139 |
|    not to be employed beyond provision of law, August 15, 1876 | | 140 |
|    preference to honorably discharged soldiers and sailors, in retention | | 143 |
|    revision of classification under civil-service rules | | 143 |
|    head of Department may prescribe regulations to govern | 161 | 145 |
|       and for care and preservation of records | 161 | 145 |

INDEX. 331

| | Sec. | Page. |
|---|---|---|
| CLERKS (in the Executive Departments) (*see also* CIVIL SERVICE)—Continued. | | |
| not less than seven hours' labor required of | | 145 |
| except Sundays and holidays | | 145 |
| hours may be extended or limited by special order | | 145 |
| when extended, no additional compensation allowed | | 145 |
| absence of, not to exceed thirty days in any one year | | 145 |
| except in case of sickness | | 145 |
| or without pay | | 145 |
| CLOTHING— | | |
| misappropriating, wrongfully selling, &c. | 14 | 11 |
| purchasing or receiving, from those not authorized to sell | 14 | 11 |
| to be procured after advertisement | 3718 | 25 |
| sales from condemned, disposition of proceeds | 3618 | 198 |
| may be procured without adequate appropriation | 3732 | 28 |
| not to exceed necessities of the current year | 3732 | 28 |
| for cadets, to be procured by storekeeper at Academy | 1527 | 64 |
| CLOTHES— | | |
| soldiers selling, furnished them, punishment for | 3748 | 194 |
| pledging, &c., by persons in Army or Navy | 5438 | 195 |
| COAL— | | |
| for use by Government in District of Columbia, how procured | 3711 | 32 |
| depots of, for steamships of war | 1552 | 97 |
| at Isthmus of Panama (supplement) | | 313 |
| COALING DOCK— | | |
| at Port Royal, erection of | | 60 |
| COAL-HEAVERS— | | |
| additional pay to seamen, &c., performing duty as | 1570 | 69 |
| pay and bounty, to be fixed by the President | 1569 | 69 |
| granting of honorable discharges to | 1426 | 92 |
| bounty pay for re-enlisting | 1573 | 69 |
| COASTERS' HARBOR ISLAND— | | |
| erection of wharf and boat-houses | | 60 |
| cession by State accepted | | 60 |
| COAST SURVEY— | | |
| provisions of law relative to the | 4683–4691 | 215 |
| disposition of maps and charts | | 216 |
| COCOA— | | |
| allowance of, in Navy rations | 1580 | 83 |
| COINS— | | |
| gold, standard weight and denomination of | 3511 | 175 |
| silver, denomination and weight of | 3513 | 175 |
| standard of both gold and silver | 3514 | 175 |
| minor, denomination and alloy of | 3515 | 175 |
| inscriptions | 3517 | 175 |
| adjustment of weights of gold | 3535 | 176 |
| of silver | 3536 | 176 |
| of minor | 3537 | 176 |
| gold, legal tender at nominal value | 3585 | 176 |
| of standard silver, one dollar, legal tender, at nominal value (note) | | 176 |
| trade dollar, not a legal tender (note) | | 176 |
| exchange of minor silver, June 3, 1879 | | 176 |
| minor silver, a tender not exceeding $10, June 3, 1879 | | 176 |
| value of foreign, to be proclaimed annually | 3564 | 176 |

|  | Sec. | Page. |
|---|---|---|
| COINS—Continued. | | |
| estimate of, January 1, 1883 (table) | | 177 |
| foreign, received for dues, to be recoined | 3566 | 177 |
| not a legal tender in payment of debts | 3584 | 177 |
| sovereign or pound sterling, valuation of | 3565 | 177 |
| of Spain and Mexico, rates of valuation | 3567 | 177 |
| COIN— | | |
| merchant vessels to transport, for the United States | 4204 | 249 |
| to receive reasonable compensation therefor | 4204 | 249 |
| COLLEGES— | | |
| detail of engineers as professors of | | 39 |
| COLLISIONS— | | |
| rules of the sea to avoid | 4233 | 216 |
| ferfeiture for omission of lights | 4234 | 218 |
| reports of loss of property or lives by | | 100 |
| COLOR— | | |
| persons not to be deprived of rights on account of | 5510 | 20 |
| COLORS. (See FLAGS.) | | |
| COMBINATIONS— | | |
| joining in unlawful | 8 | 10 |
| COMMANDANTS— | | |
| of yards, to be selected by the President | 1542 | 58 |
| COMMANDING OFFICERS— | | |
| to show good example of virtue, &c | 1 | 8 |
| to guard against immoral practices | 1 | 8 |
| to inspect conduct of those under them | 1 | 8 |
| neglecting to overtake and capture enemy | 4 | 9 |
| neglecting to afford relief to United States vessels or their allies | 4 | 9 |
| neglecting to prepare for action | 4 | 9 |
| not joining in battle | 4 | 9 |
| failing to encourage officers and men | 4 | 9 |
| unlawful combinations against | 8 | 10 |
| to transmit complete prize-lists | 15 | 12 |
| to have entry on books of all men received | 20 | 12 |
| to send muster-rolls of crew to Department | 20 | 13 |
| to send list of officers and passengers to Department | 20 | 13 |
| to note on ships' books desertions and deaths | 20 | 13 |
| to see that paymaster secures property of persons dying | 20 | 13 |
| not to receive men without their accounts | 20 | 13 |
| to send accounts with men transferred | 20 | 13 |
| to make frequent inspections of the provisions | 20 | 13 |
| to consult with surgeon as to sanitary condition of crew | 20 | 13 |
| to use all means to preserve health of crew | 20 | 13 |
| to set apart convenient place for the sick | 20 | 13 |
| to attend, or appoint some one to attend, final paying off of crew | 20 | 13 |
| to cause articles Navy to be hung up and read | 20 | 13 |
| authority of, over crews of lost vessels | 21 | 13 |
| punishment they may inflict | 24 | 14 |
| to be entered on the ship's log | 24 | 14 |
| when to exercise consular powers | 1433 | 19 |
| accountable for disbursements upon their order | 285 | 167 |
| duties in connection with prizes, as to vessels engaged in the cooly trade | 2163 | 302 |

INDEX. 333

| | Sec. | Page. |
|---|---|---|
| COMMANDING OFFICERS—Continued. | | |
|     to discourage sale by crew of wages, prize-money, &c | 1430 | 92 |
|     to attest assignment of prize-money and bounty | 4643 | 313 |
| COMMANDERS— | | |
|     eighty-five allowed on the active list | 1363 | 46 |
|     pay of, on the active list | 1556 | 65 |
|         on the retired list | 1588 | 70 |
|     to command vessels of third rate | 1529 | 94 |
|     may be ordered to command yards | 1542 | 58 |
| COMMISSIONS— | | |
|     dates of, not to changed by benefit of continuous service, March 3, 1883 | | 21 |
|     not to be changed without authority of law | 1506 | 82 |
|     opinions and decisions concerning | | 104 |
|     new boards not to affect existing | 1385 | 62 |
| COMMISSIONS OF INQUIRY— | | |
|     expense not to be allowed without appropriation | 3681 | 133 |
| COMMODORES— | | |
|     ten allowed on the active list | 1363 | 46 |
|     pay of, on the active list | 1556 | 65 |
|         on the retired list | 1588 | 70 |
|     to command vessels of first rate | 1529 | 94 |
| COMMUTE— | | |
|     officers ordering summary courts no power to, sentences | 33 | 15 |
|         general courts-martial no power to, sentences | 54 | 18 |
| COMMUTATION— | | |
|     officers entitled to, for rations | 1578 | 83 |
|     price of rations, thirty cents | 1585 | 83 |
| COMPTROLLER (see ACCOUNTS and ACCOUNTING OFFICERS)— | | |
|     original contracts to be filed in office of | 3743 | 29 |
| COMPROMISE— | | |
|     of claims, on report of district or special attorneys | 3469 | 153 |
| CONFINEMENT— | | |
|     by order of commanding officer | 24 | 14 |
|     by a sentence of summary court | 30 | 15 |
|     forfeiture of pay during (note) | | 18 |
|     no other punishment than, in absence of commanding officer | 25 | 14 |
| CONGRESS— | | |
|     officers of Government not to contract with members of | 3742 | 29 |
|     members of, not to be interested in contracts | 3739 | 29 |
|         exceptions in certain cases | 3740 | 29 |
|     members of not to receive money, &c., for procuring place or contract | 1781 | 207 |
|         nor compensation for service in matters before the Department | 1782 | 207 |
|         accepting bribes, &c., punishment for | 5500, 5501 | 208–9 |
|             disqualified for holding office | 5502 | 209 |
| CONGRESSIONAL DIRECTORY— | | |
|     printing and distribution of | 77, 3801 | 188 |
| CONSPIRACY— | | |
|     to overthrow the Government | 5336 | 309 |
|         or delay the execution of the laws | 5336, 5407 | 309 |
|     to intimidate persons before the courts | 5406 | 309 |

|  | Sec. | Page. |
|---|---|---|
| CONSPIRACY—Continued. | | |
| to defraud the Government, all parties equally guilty | 5440 | 309 |
| to prevent acceptance of or holding office | 5518 | 310 |
| to deprive any one of equal protection of the laws | 5519 | 310 |
| to defraud the United States, punishment for | 5440 | 228 |
| CONSTANT LABOR— | | |
| extra pay to marines employed in | 1287 | 119 |
| CONSULAR OFFICERS— | | |
| commanding officers authorized to exercise powers of | 1433 | 19 |
| Navy officers accepting appointment as, vacate commissions | 1440 | 19 |
| ships' papers to be deposited with | 4309 | 250 |
| to obtain clearance for vessels | 4309 | 250 |
| vessels to have tariff of fees annex, to which consuls are entitled | 4207 | 250 |
| discharge of seamen on application to | 4580 | 246 |
| collection of extra wages due | 4581 | 246 |
| to be paid by master of vessel | 4582 | 246 |
| may discharge seamen without extra wages, &c | 4583 | 246 |
| disposition of extra wages of seamen by | 4584 | 246 |
| duties as to seamen impressed | 4589 | 247 |
| deserters to be reclaimed by | 4600 | 247 |
| meaning of the words, defined | 1674 | 219 |
| right to receive protests and declarations of citizens of the United States | 1707 | 219 |
| to keep list of mariners shipped and discharged | 1708 | 219 |
| also of number of vessels arriving and departing | 1708 | 219 |
| and nature and value of cargoes | 1708 | 219 |
| duties as to deceased citizens of the United States | 1709–1711 | 220 |
| making false certificate of property | 1737 | 220 |
| when they may perform diplomatic functions | 1738 | 220 |
| depositions may be taken by | 1750 | 221 |
| not to correspond in regard to affairs of any foreign Government, June 17, 1874 | 1751 | 221 |
| to take charge of effects of deceased merchant seamen | 4541 | 243 |
| to be present at shipment of merchant seamen abroad | 4517 | 242 |
| money paid by, to American seamen, to be in gold or its equivalent | 4548 | 244 |
| may order inspection of vessels as to seaworthiness | 4559 | 244 |
| to provide for destitute seamen | 4577 | 245 |
| CONSTRUCTION AND REPAIR— | | |
| qualifications for appointment as chief of | 425 | 54 |
| to have rank of commodore, title of chief constructor | 1471 | 55 |
| CONTEMPT— | | |
| treating superior officer with | 8 | 10 |
| CONTEMPT OF COURT— | | |
| punishment for | 42 | 16 |
| courts of inquiry may punish for | 57 | 18 |
| CONTINGENT— | | |
| appropriations, not to be used in paying Department employés, August 5, 1882 | | 140 |
| allowance of, for newspapers, &c | 192–1779 | 161–2 |
| papers to be preserved and filed | 192 | 161 |
| expenditure of, to be reported to Congress in detail, June 20, 1874, | 193 | 161–2 |
| disbursing officer to return precise statements and receipts | 193 | 161 |

## INDEX. 335

| | Sec. | Page. |
|---|---|---|
| CONTINGENT—Continued. | | |
| estimate for, to be furnished Secretary by Bureaus | 430 | 162 |
| failing to make reports of, punishment for | 1780 | 162 |
| appropriations for, to be under control of the Secretary of the Navy | 3676 | 162 |
| not to be paid for official or clerical compensation, August 7, 1874 | 3682 | 162 |
| nor for personal services in District of Columbia, August 5, 1882 | | 162 |
| nor for purchase of articles not necessary for the public service | 3683 | 162 |
| expenditures to be by written order of the Secretary | 3683 | 162 |
| CONTRABAND OF WAR— | | |
| contracts for, without advertising | 3721 | 26 |
| CONTRACTS— | | |
| to be advertised for, except for personal services, &c | 3709 | 24 |
| and other articles specified | 3718 | 25 |
| articles of American growth and manufacture preferred in making. | 3728 | 27 |
| relinquishment of reservations, on | 3730 | 27 |
| for buildings and improvements, not to exceed appropriations | 3733 | 28 |
| not to be made without authority of law | 3732 | 28 |
| except for clothing, subsistence, &c | 3732 | 28 |
| for stationery, for one year only | 3735 | 28 |
| for other supplies, for one year only | 3735 | 28 |
| not to be transferred | 3737 | 28 |
| members of Congress not to be interested in | 3739 | 29 |
| exceptions in certain cases | 3740 | 29 |
| contracts to contain such provision | 3741 | 29 |
| officers of the Government making, with Government | 3742 | 29 |
| to be deposited with the Second Comptroller, &c | 3743 | 29 |
| to be reduced to writing | 3744 | 29 |
| and signed by contracting parties | 3744 | 29 |
| copy to be filed in Returns' Office | 3744 | 29 |
| oath as to making, &c | 3745 | 30 |
| failure to make return, a misdemeanor | 3746 | 30 |
| printed instructions to be furnished to officers making | 3747 | 30 |
| copies of, may be furnished by Returns' Office | 515 | 30 |
| for erection or repair of buildings without authority, forbidden | 5503 | 31 |
| for rent of buildings without appropriation, forbidden, March 3, 1877 | | 31 |
| for tobacco, how to be made, March 3, 1880 | | 31 |
| for fuel, for use in the District of Columbia | 3711–3713 | 32 |
| appropriations available for fulfillment of, after two years | | 135 |
| for site of buildings, not to be in excess of appropriation | | 196 |
| in which members of Congress are interested, void | 1781 | 207–8 |
| members of Congress not to receive compensation for services in procuring | 1782–5500 | 207–8 |
| giving money to secure, forbidden | 5451 | 208 |
| members of the Light-House Board, not to be interested in | 4680 | 240 |
| for removing wrecked property | | 310 |
| to be in writing, and signed by parties (decision C. C.) | | 315 |
| failure to fulfill, &c., opinions, &c. (notes) | | 24, 27 |
| assignment and transfer of (notes) | | 28 |
| when executive officers may have interest in | | 29 |

|  | Sec. | Page. |
|---|---|---|
| CONVOY— | | |
| failing to perform duty when acting as | 8 | 10 |
| maltreating officers and crews of vessels under | 8 | 10 |
| receiving compensation for services as | 8 | 10 |
| CO-OPERATION— | | |
| of Navy or Marine Corps with the Army | 1135–1143 | 107 |
| of Revenue Marine with the Navy | 1492 | 299 |
| COOLY TRADE— | | |
| provisions of law relative to the | 2158–2163 | 301–3 |
| COPIES. (*See* PUBLIC RECORDS.) | | |
| COPYISTS (in the Departments)— | | |
| women employed as, to receive $900 per annum | 167 | 139 |
| number and pay regulated by appropriations, August 5, 1882 | | 140 |
| not to be paid from contingent appropriations, August 5, 1882 | | 140 |
| nor employed beyond provision of law, August 15, 1876 | | 140 |
| CORDAGE (cotton)— | | |
| authority to introduce it into the Navy, June 10, 1880 | | 31 |
| CORPORATIONS— | | |
| members of, not to be employed as agents to do business with such | 1783 | 138 |
| contracts with | 3740 | 29 |
| CORPORAL PUNISHMENT— | | |
| when adjudged with pecuniary, may be remitted | 5330 | 254 |
| CORRESPONDENCE— | | |
| by consular and diplomatic officers on matters of foreign Governments forbidden | 1751 | 221 |
| to disturb the peace, with Indians, penalty | 2111, 2112 | 307 |
| with foreign nations, to incite Indians to war | 2113 | 307 |
| criminal, with foreign Governments | 5335 | 308 |
| CORRUPTION OF BLOOD— | | |
| no conviction or judgment to work | 5326 | 254 |
| COTTON CORDAGE— | | |
| authority to introduce it into the Navy, June 10, 1880 | | 31 |
| COUNSEL— | | |
| to be assigned to persons charged with capital crimes | 1034 | 307 |
| employment of, by Department of Justice | 363, 364 | 137 |
| retired officers cannot act as, against United States | | 314 |
| COUNTERFEITING— | | |
| signatures, &c., to secure payment of claims | 14 | 11 |
| in various ways, punishment for | | 227–9 |
| COURT OF CLAIMS— | | |
| in suits before, Attorney-General to furnish Departments with copy of petition | 188 | 156 |
| Departments to furnish Attorney-General with statement of facts, &c. | 188 | 156 |
| stating cause, &c., if claim was rejected | 188 | 156 |
| in cases of same class, statement of one to suffice | 188 | 156 |
| matters over which it has jurisdiction | 1059 | 156–7 |
| transmission of claims from Congress | 1060 | 157 |
| judgments for set-offs or counter-claims | 1061 | 157 |
| losses by paymasters, &c., decrees to be paid | 1062 | 157 |
| claims involving disputed facts, to be referred by Departments | 1063 | 157 |
| or where decision will affect a class of cases | 1063 | 158 |
| or where authority, right, &c., is denied under Constitution | 1063 | 158 |

INDEX. 337

| | Sec. | Page. |
|---|---|---|
| COURT OF CLAIMS—Continued. | | |
|     and where courts can take jurisdiction on voluntary action of claimants | 1063 | 158 |
|     cases transmitted on certificate of Auditor or Comptroller | 1064 | 158 |
|     payment of final judgment on decrees | 1065 | 158 |
|     claims pending in other courts, not to be presented | 1067 | 158 |
|     limitation for presentation of claims | 1069 | 158 |
|         exceptions specified | 1069 | 158 |
|     what the petition shall set forth | 1072 | 159 |
|     disloyal claimants, dismissal of petition | 1073 | 159 |
|         burden of proof as to loyalty | 1074 | 159 |
|     power to call on the Departments for information | 1076 | 159 |
|     fraud in proof, &c., to forfeit claim | 1086 | 159 |
|     new trial, on motion of claimant | 1087 | 159 |
|         on motion of the United States | 1088 | 159 |
|     payment of final judgments on appeal to Supreme Court | 1089 | 160 |
|         when interest shall be allowed | 1090 | 160 |
|     interest not allowed, on judgment of Court of Claims | 1091 | 160 |
|         unless upon express contracts | 1091 | 160 |
|     payment of judgment, a full discharge | 1092 | 160 |
|     cost of printing record, to be taxed against losing party | | 160 |
|     fraudulently claiming more than is due, claim not to be allowed | | 160 |
|     matters or claims before Congress, may be referred, March 3, 1883 | | 160 |
|         also those before the Departments, March 3, 1883 | | 160 |
|     jurisdiction does not extend to claims for destruction of property during the rebellion | | 161 |
|         nor for occupation and use of real estate at seat of war | | 161 |
|         nor to claims barred by provisions of law | | 161 |
|         nor to disloyal claimants | | 161 |
|     defense of the United States, to be conducted by Attorney-General and assistants | | 161 |
|     parties in interest may testify | | 161 |
|     continuation of reports until final action | | 161 |
| COURTS OF INQUIRY— | | |
|     by whom they may be ordered | 55 | 18 |
|     of whom they shall consist | 56 | 18 |
|     may summon witnesses, administer oaths, and punish contempts | 57 | 18 |
|     shall only state facts | 57 | 18 |
|     not to give opinion unless required | 57 | 18 |
|     oath to be administered to members by judge-advocate | 58 | 18 |
|         to be administered to judge-advocate | 58 | 18 |
|     rights of party whose conduct is inquired into | 59 | 18 |
|     proceedings, in what manner authenticated | 60 | 19 |
|         to be evidence before courts-martial in cases not capital | 60 | 19 |
|         to be transmitted to Judge-Advocate-General of the Navy (foot-note) | | 16 |
|     nature and character of (note) | | 19 |
|     parties not entitled to record of, as a right (note) | | 19 |
|     character, scope, &c. (notes) | | 19 |
| COURTS-MARTIAL, GENERAL— | | |
|     by whom convened | 38 | 16 |
|     commander in waters of United States not to convene, except by express authority of President | 38 | 16 |

# 338 INDEX.

|  | Sec. | Page. |
|---|---|---|

**COURTS-MARTIAL, GENERAL,—**Continued.
    of whom they shall consist............................................. 39   16
    not more than one-half members to be junior to officer tried ...... 39   16
    senior officer to preside, members to rank by seniority ............ 39   16
    oath to be administered by president to judge-advocate ............ 40   16
    oath to be administered to members by judge-advocate .............. 40   16
    oath to be administered to witnesses by the president............... 41   16
    refusing to testify, or prevaricating before, punishable ............ 42   16
    accused to be furnished with copy of charges........................ 43   16
        none other to be preferred, except, &c........................... 43   16
    new charges, reasonable time for defense ........................... 43   17
    accused, at own request, a competent witness....................... 43   17
        failure to request, not presumptive evidence against him .... 43   17
    officer arrested for trial by, to deliver up sword .................... 44   17
        to confine himself to limits assigned ........................... 44   17
    proceedings of, when commenced, not to be suspended or delayed........................................................... 45   17
    court to sit daily, except Sundays, unless adjourned by proper authority...................................................... 45   17
    members of, not to absent themselves, except in case of sickness... 46   17
        or are ordered to go on duty ................................... 46   17
    members absent, witnesses to be recalled when they resume...... 47   17
        testimony to be read over....................................... 47   17
        witness to acknowledge the same, &c........................... 47   17
    in sentence of suspension, pay and emoluments may be included. 48   17
    not to inflict punishment by branding, marking, flogging, or tattooing.......................................................... 49   17
    death sentence to be concurred in by two-thirds of the members. 50   17
        to be inflicted only in cases provided for in the Articles ...... 50   17
    sentences, except death, to be determined by a majority of members........................................................... 50   17
    to adjudge punishment adequate to offense ......................... 50   17
    may recommend person convicted to clemency ...................... 51   17
        reasons to be stated on record .................................. 51   17
    judgment to be authenticated by signatures of president, members, and judge-advocate............................................ 52   17
    sentence to loss of life to be confirmed by President of the United States.......................................................... 53   17
    sentence of dismissal of commissioned or warrant officer to be confirmed by President of the United States ................. 53   17
    other sentences may be executed on confirmation of officer ordering court...................................................... 53   17
    officer authorized to convene, may reverse, remit, or mitigate .... 54   18
        but is not to commute............................................ 54   18
    proceedings to be sent to Judge-Advocate-General (foot note) ....     16
    opinions and decisions regarding (notes) ............................     18
    persons concerned entitled to copy of proceedings (note)..........     18
    officers of Marine Corps may associate with Army officers on...... 1342   107
    perjury committed before, in prosecutions, offense set forth sufficient............................................................. 1023   275

**COURTS-MARTIAL, SUMMARY—**
    by whom ordered ..................................................... 26   14
    of whom to consist ................................................... 27   14

|  | Sec. | Page. |
|---|---|---|
| COURTS-MARTIAL, SUMMARY—Continued. | | |
| oath of members and recorder | 28 | 14 |
| testimony before, to be given orally | 29 | 14 |
| punishments, they may inflict | 30 | 14 |
| may disrate for incompetency | 31 | 15 |
| execution of sentence of | 32 | 15 |
| sentence of, involving loss of pay | 32 | 15 |
| remission of sentence of, by officer ordering | 33 | 15 |
| submission of case to another court | 33 | 15 |
| sentence of, producing serious injury | 33 | 15 |
| proceedings of, to be conducted with conciseness | 34 | 15 |
| to be transmitted to Judge-Advocate-General (note) | | 16 |
| punishments of, may be inflicted by a general court-martial | 35 | 15 |
| COWARDICE— | | |
| in time of battle, punishment for | 4 | 8 |
| CREW— | | |
| muster rolls of, to be sent to Department | 20 | 13 |
| sanitary condition of, to be preserved | 20 | 13 |
| place to be set apart for sick and disabled | 20 | 13 |
| attendance at final paying off of | 20 | 13 |
| of vessels lost, authority of officers over | 21 | 13 |
| CRUISE— | | |
| meaning of the word (note) | | 97 |
| CRUELTY— | | |
| to persons subject to orders | 8 | 10 |

## D.

|  | Sec. | Page. |
|---|---|---|
| DEATH— | | |
| punishment of, by sentence of courts-martial | 4 | 8– |
| sentence of, to require concurrence of two-thirds of members of court | 50 | 17 |
| and in cases only as provided in the Articles | 50 | 17 |
| to be confirmed by the President of the United States | 53 | 17 |
| punishment by, to be by hanging | 5225 | 254 |
| benefit of clergy not allowed | 5329 | 254 |
| body may be delivered for dissection | 5340 | 254 |
| crimes for which it may be inflicted | 1624, 5339, 5345 | 253–4–6 |
| DEATHS— | | |
| to be monthly noted on ship's books | 20 | 13 |
| property to be taken care of by paymaster | 20 | 13 |
| DEBT— | | |
| marines exempt from personal arrest for | 1610 | 110 |
| DEBTS (due the United States)— | | |
| priority given to the United States in insolvent cases | 3466 | 163 |
| or when estate is insufficient to pay all claims | 3466 | 163 |
| executors failing to satisfy debts due United States liable | 3467 | 163 |
| sureties on bond satisfying the United States to have priority against estate | 3468 | 163 |
| may bring suit upon the bond to recover | 3468 | 163 |
| compromise of, on report of district attorneys or special agents | 3469 | 163 |
| not applicable to claims under postal laws | 3469 | 163 |
| at sales on executions, the United States may be purchaser | 3470 | 163 |
| but not at greater sum than the judgment | 3470 | 163 |

|  | Sec. | Page. |
|---|---|---|
| DEBTS (due the United States)—Continued. | | |
| poor debtors, proceedings in case of | 3471 | 163 |
| imprisoned debtors, discharge of, by the President | 3472 | 164 |
| due by claimants, to be set off in adjustment, March 3, 1875 | | 164 |
| refusing to the set-off, Government to withhold amount | | 164 |
| and institute suit for recovery | | 164 |
| judgment against United States, balance with interest to be paid over | | 164 |
| DECIMAL SYSTEM— | | |
| money accounts to be expressed in (supplement) | 3563 | 315 |
| DECORATIONS (by foreign Governments)— | | |
| not to be publicly shown or exposed, January 31, 1881 | | 21 |
| to be presented through Department of State, January 31, 1881 | | 21 |
| not to be delivered without authority of Congress, January 31, 1881 | | 21 |
| DEFAULTERS. (See DISBURSING OFFICERS.) | | |
| DEFLECTIVE TURRET— | | |
| appropriation for testing Clark's | | 99 |
| DENTIST— | | |
| of Naval Academy, pay of | | 54 |
| DEPARTMENT OF THE NAVY. (See NAVY DEPARTMENT.) | | |
| DEPARTMENT OF JUSTICE (see also ATTORNEY-GENERAL)— | | |
| attorneys employed by, may be allowed extra compensation | | 72 |
| DEPARTMENTS (see also CLERKS and CIVIL SERVICE)— | | |
| regulations may be prescribed by the heads of, for their government | 161 | 145 |
| temporary vacancies in. (See under VACANCIES.) | | |
| report of employés in, to be made annually to Congress | 194 | 146 |
| officers acting without authority in, not to be paid | 1760 | 147 |
| unless office is subsequently sanctioned by Congress | 1760 | 147 |
| employés not to solicit contributions for making presents, &c | 1784 | 208 |
| political contributions in the, forbidden | | 209 |
| (See TENURE OF OFFICE and VACANCIES.) | | |
| DERELICT— | | |
| what constitutes a maritime (note) | | 291 |
| care and disposition of property (supplement) | | 313 |
| DESICCATED— | | |
| vegetables, how they may be procured | 3726 | 27 |
| potatoes, a part of the Navy ration | 1580 | 83 |
| tomatoes, substitute for potatoes | | 84 |
| DESCRIPTIVE LIST— | | |
| of persons received on ship board | 20 | 12 |
| of men transferred | 20 | 13 |
| DESERTER— | | |
| officer quitting post before resignation is accepted, declared a | 10 | 10 |
| not returning, after proclamation, forfeit citizenship | 1996 | 33 |
| and to be incapable of holding office | 1996 | 34 |
| certain soldiers and sailors excepted | 1997 | 34 |
| DESERTERS— | | |
| punishment for receiving and entertaining | 8 | 10 |
| failing to give notice as to | 8 | 10 |
| enlistment of, forbidden | 19 | 12 |
| from naval or military service not to be enlisted | 1420 | 33 |

|  | Sec. | Page. |
|---|---|---|
| DESERTERS—Continued. | | |
|   sailors and soldiers faithfully serving to April 19, 1865, not deemed_ | 4749 | 34 |
|     but forfeiture of pension not remitted_ | 4749 | 34 |
|     construed solely as a removal of disability from loss of citizenship_ | 4749 | 34 |
|   fine and imprisonment for harboring_ | 5455 | 34 |
|   effect of pardon in cases of (notes)_ | | 34 |
|   apprehending of, estimates for, to be in detail_ | 3666 | 132 |
| DESERTING— | | |
|   duty or station, in battle, punishment for_ | 4 | 9 |
| DESERTION— | | |
|   or enticing desertion in time of war, punishment for_ | 4 | 8 |
|   or enticing desertion in time of peace, how punished_ | 8 | 10 |
|   penalty for enticing_ | 1553 | 33 |
|   to be entered on ship's books_ | 20 | 13 |
|   pardons by the President in cases of (notes)_ | | 34 |
|   fine and imprisonment for enticing or procuring_ | 5455 | 34 |
|   effect of pardon and forfeiture, in cases of (notes)_ | | 34 |
|   forfeits claim to bounty land_ | 2438 | 212 |
|   of merchant seamen in foreign ports_ | 5280 | 224 |
| DESTITUTE SEAMEN. (See MERCHANT SERVICE.) | | |
| DETENTION— | | |
|   additional pay to enlisted men for period of_ | 1572 | 69 |
| DIES— | | |
|   of a national character, execution of at the mints_ | 3551 | 180 |
| DIPLOMATIC SERVICE (see also CONSULAR OFFICERS)— | | |
|   officers of Navy accepting appointment in, regarded as resigning_ | 1440 | 19 |
| DISABILITY. (See PENSIONS.) | | |
| DISAFFECTION— | | |
|   in time of battle, punishment for_ | 4 | 8 |
| DISBURSING CLERKS— | | |
|   to be appointed from fourth class_ | 176 | 146 |
|     to give bond_ | 176 | 156 |
|       which may be increased and renewed_ | 176 | 146 |
|     to receive additional compensation_ | 176 | 146 |
|     to superintend building, when directed_ | 176 | 146 |
| DISBURSING OFFICERS (see also DISTRESS WARRANTS and EMBEZZLEMENT)— | | |
|   balance on hand, statement to be submitted to Congress by Secretary Treasury_ | | 135 |
|   losing Government funds, &c., recourse to Court of Claims_ | 1059 | 156 |
|     payment of decrees by accounting officers_ | 1062 | 157 |
|   to make precise statements of expenditure of contingent funds_ | 193 | 161 |
|   distress warrants may issue against delinquent_ | 3625–3638 | 165–7 |
|   disbursements by, on order of commanding officer, to be allowed_ | 285 | 167 |
|     on satisfactory evidence of the order and disbursement_ | 285 | 167 |
|     commanding officer to be held responsible_ | 285 | 167 |
|   delinquent, court to grant judgment at return term_ | 957 | 167 |
|     unless defendant claims credits under oath_ | 957 | 167 |
|       when continuance may be granted to next term_ | 957 | 167 |
|       continuance when defendant pleads *non est factum*, &c _ | 957 | 167 |
|   not to advance or loan money, public or private_ | 1389, 3639, 5488 | 167–70 |
|   advances to, by order of the President_ | 1563, 3648 | 168–70 |

## 342　INDEX.

| | Sec. | Page. |
|---|---|---|
| DISBURSING OFFICERS—Continued. | | |
| 　abroad, to be appointed by President and Senate | 1550 | 168 |
| 　　special to give bond | 3614 | 168 |
| 　in arrears, not to be paid compensation | 1766 | 168 |
| 　　when withheld, may ask for suit | 1766 | 168 |
| 　　which Solicitor of Treasury will commence | 1766 | 168 |
| 　forbidden to carry on trade with Government funds | 1788 | 168 |
| 　　the offense a misdemeanor, punishable by fine | 1788 | 168 |
| 　　and incapacity for holding office | 1788 | 168 |
| 　to deposit public money with Treasurer or Assistant Treasurer | 2620 | 168 |
| 　　and to draw only as required in favor of party entitled | 3620 | 169 |
| 　may deposit in any public depository under written authority | 3620 | 169 |
| 　　or keep it in any other manner on written order of Secretary of Treasury | 3620 | 169 |
| 　transfers to, by Treasurer, to be by draft or warrant | 3620 | 169 |
| 　having money not authorized to retain, to pay same to Treasurer or other depositary | 3621 | 169 |
| 　　and take duplicate receipts therefore | 3621 | 169 |
| 　　and render accounts monthly to proper Bureau | 3622 | 169 |
| 　　　within ten days after expiration | 3622 | 169 |
| 　　to be passed to proper accounting officer | 3622 | 169 |
| 　accounts and vouchers to be sent direct to proper accounting officer | 3622 | 169 |
| 　　when in default to furnish satisfactory explanation | 3622 | 169 |
| 　　time for rendering may be extended by Secretary of Treasury. | 3622 | 169 |
| 　other returns and reports from, may be required by head of Department | 3622 | 169 |
| 　to render accounts of application of moneys according to appropriation | 3623 | 169 |
| 　refusing to pay over balance, suit may be instituted | 3624 | 169 |
| 　　commission forfeited, in case judgment is obtained | 3624 | 170 |
| 　　and 6 per cent. interest until money is repaid | 3624 | 170 |
| 　　and to be deemed guilty of embezzlement | 5492 | 171 |
| 　not to exchange public money for other funds without orders | 3639 | 170 |
| 　　or use, loan, or deposit same in banks | 3639 | 170 |
| 　　but to make transfers and payments as directed | 3639, 5488 | 170 |
| 　may be advanced money to perform their duties | 3648 | 170 |
| 　guilty of extortion, subject to fine or imprisonment | 5481–5496 | 170–1 |
| 　requiring receipt or voucher for more than paid, guilty of embezzlement | 5483 | 170 |
| 　　and fine in double the sum and imprisonment | 5483 | 170 |
| 　bankers, &c., receiving unauthorized deposits from, punishable | 5497 | 172 |
| 　refusing to pay drafts drawn by proper accounting officers, embezzlement | 5495 | 171 |
| 　presenting receipts without having made payment, how punished | 5496 | 171 |
| 　deceased or out of service, payment of lost checks of | 300, 3647 | 172, 173 |
| 　exchange of funds by, what allowable | 3651 | 174 |
| 　to make payments in moneys furnished them | 3651 | 174 |
| 　　if in drafts, to collect and pay from proceeds | 3651 | 174 |
| 　　　unless an exchange can be made for gold or silver at par. | 3651 | 174 |
| 　　to be suspended for violating these provisions | 3651 | 174 |
| 　　and reported to the President with facts | 3651 | 174 |
| 　　who will restore or remove from office as he may deem proper | 3651 | 174 |

|  | Sec. | Page. |
|---|---|---|
| DISBURSING OFFICERS—Continued. | | |
| to make return of premiums from sale of drafts | 3652 | 174 |
| and credit same to the United States in their accounts | 3652 | 174 |
| under penalty of dismissal for failure to do so | 3652 | 174 |
| to make return of outstanding checks | 310 | 173 |
| accounts of unchanged for three years, to be covered in | 309 | 173 |
| to keep accurate entry of sums received and paid out | 3643 | 315 |
| disbursing appropriations for public buildings, extra compensation | | 313 |
| DISCHARGED PERSONS— | | |
| liable to arrest and trial for fraud | 14 | 12 |
| DISCHARGE— | | |
| of men who enlisted in foreign ports | 1422 | 91 |
| of men whose terms are up | 1422 | 91 |
| of machinists in the Navy | | 93 |
| of officers of the volunteer service | | 101 |
| travel pay to officers of Marine Corps, after | 1289 | 119 |
| marines after | 1290 | 119 |
| dishonorable, forfeits claim to bounty land | 2438 | 212 |
| honorable from military service entitles aliens to naturalization | 2166 | 257 |
| DISHONORABLE DISCHARGE— | | |
| forfeits claim to bounty land | 2438 | 212 |
| DISLOYAL— | | |
| claims of persons, not to be paid | 3480 | 154 |
| DISMISSED— | | |
| officers liable to trial for fraud | 14 | 12 |
| DISMISSAL— | | |
| officer liable to, for refusing to deliver up sword when arrested for trial | 44 | 17 |
| or for going beyond limits prescribed | 44 | 17 |
| of commissioned or warrant officers, sentence to be confirmed by President of United States | 53 | 17 |
| in time of peace, by sentence of court-martial only | 1229 | 35 |
| officers resigning to escape, not again to become officers of the Navy | 1441 | 35 |
| except in case of pardon (note) | | 35 |
| by order of President or sentence of general court-martial only | 1624 | 35 |
| by order of President, officer may demand trial | 1624 | 35 |
| order of dismissal void, under certain conditions | 1624 | 35 |
| pay on restoration (June 22, 1874) | | 35 |
| opinions and decisions regarding | | 36 |
| in case of suit and judgment, for illegally retaining public moneys | 3024 | 169 |
| DISOBEDIENCE— | | |
| of lawful orders, punishment for | 4–8 | 8–10 |
| DISRATING— | | |
| of rated persons for incompetency | 31 | 15 |
| DISRESPECT— | | |
| treating superior officer with | 8 | 10 |
| DISTRESS WARRANTS— | | |
| issue of, against delinquent disbursing officers, &c | 3625 | 165 |
| amount of delinquency, &c., to be stated | 3626 | 165 |
| sale of goods and chattels by marshal | 3627 | 165 |
| seizure and imprisonment of delinquents | 3627 | 165 |
| absconding delinquents, sale of chattels of | 3628 | 165 |
| amount due a lien on property of delinquent and sureties | 3629 | 165 |

|  | Sec. | Page. |
|---|---|---|
| DISTRESS WARRANTS—Continued. | | |
| to remain from date of levy until discharged | 3629 | 165 |
| sale of lands, &c., when chattels are insufficient | 3630 | 165 |
| conveyance of marshal to be valid title | 3631 | 166 |
| surplus to be returned to delinquent | 3632 | 166 |
| against disbursing officers failing to render accounts, &c | 3633 | 166 |
| Comptroller to certify account to Solicitor of Treasury | 3633 | 166 |
| may issue against any officer charged with disbursement of public money | 3634 | 166 |
| postponement, with approval of Secretary of the Treasury | 3635 | 166 |
| may be stayed altogether on bill of complaint | 3636 | 166 |
| or an injunction granted on sufficient surety | 3636 | 166 |
| which is not to impair lien | 3636 | 166 |
| interest added where injunction was asked merely for delay | 3636 | 166 |
| by whom injunction may be granted or dissolved | 3636 | 166 |
| appeal to circuit judge by aggrieved party | 3637 | 166 |
| who may permit it or grant injunction | 3637 | 167 |
| proceedings in such cases | 3637 | 167 |
| legal right of United States to recover taxes, &c., not impaired | 3638 | 167 |
| DISTRICT OF COLUMBIA— | | |
| inspection and purchase of fuel for use in | 3711–3713 | 32 |
| one naval cadet allowed at Academy from | 1513 | 51 |
| advertisements not to be published in papers in. July 31, 1876 | | 129 |
| unless supplies or labor are for use in. July 31, 1876 | | 129 |
| six newspapers authorized to publish advertisements in. January 21, 1881 | | 129 |
| charges not to exceed commercial rates. January 21, 1881 | | 129 |
| to be published in accordance with section 3828. January 21, 1881 | | 129 |
| holidays declared in | | 145 |
| detail of clerks from outside, restricted | | 140 |
| contingent Navy, not to be used for paying for personal services in | | 162 |
| DISTILLED SPIRITS— | | |
| how admitted on board vessels | 13 | 11 |
| DIVINE SERVICE— | | |
| performance and attendance on | 2 | 8 |
| irreverent behavior at, to be punished | 3 | 8 |
| chaplains to conduct, according to forms of church | 1397 | 22 |
| to report annually, performance of | 1398 | 22 |
| DOCKAGE— | | |
| estimates for, to be in detail | 3666 | 131 |
| DOCUMENTS. (See PUBLIC DOCUMENTS.) | | |
| DOUBLE-TURRETED MONITORS— | | |
| appropriation for launching | | 100 |
| amount due contractors for keeping, to be reported to Congress | | 100 |
| completion of engines and machinery | | 100 |
| DRAFTS. (See CHECKS.) | | |
| DRAUGHTSMEN (in the Departments)— | | |
| not to be employed beyond provision of law. August 15, 1876 | | 140 |
| nor to be paid from contingent appropriations. August 5, 1882 | | 140 |
| numbers and rates of pay governed by appropriations. August 5, 1882 | | 140 |
| allowed in Navy Department | 416 | 182–3 |
| in Hydrographic Office | | 45 |

INDEX. 345

|  | Sec. | Page. |
|---|---|---|
| DRAWING— |  |  |
| professor of, at Naval Academy | 1528 | 74 |
| assistant professor of |  | 54 |
| DRAWINGS— |  |  |
| estimates for, to be given in detail | 3666 | 131 |
| expenditures to be accounted for | 3666 | 131 |
| DRIED APPLES— |  |  |
| allowance of, in Navy ration | 1580 | 83 |
| DRIVING TEAMS— |  |  |
| estimates for, to be in detail | 3666 | 131 |
| DRUNKENNESS— |  |  |
| punishment for | 8 | 9 |
| a bar to promotion in the Navy |  | 76 |
| a bar to appointment under civil-service rules |  | 143 |
| DUEL— |  |  |
| sending or accepting challenge to fight | 8 | 10 |
| acting as second in | 8 | 10 |
| DUTY— |  |  |
| culpable inefficiency in the performance of | 8 | 10 |
| DYING— |  |  |
| seamen on merchant vessels dying abroad, care of effects | 4538 | 242 |
| penalty for violating requirements of law | 4540 | 243 |
| abroad, with personal effects on shore, care of | 4541 | 243 |

### E.

|  | Sec. | Page. |
|---|---|---|
| EFFECTS. (*See* PERSONAL EFFECTS.) |  |  |
| EIGHT HOURS— |  |  |
| a day's work for laborers, &c., in Government employ | 3738 | 29 |
| EIGHT-HOUR LAW— |  |  |
| appropriation for payment of claims under | 3689 | 134 |
| ELECTIONS— |  |  |
| troops not to be brought to places of | 2002, 5510 | 20 |
| except to repel armed enemies of the United States | 2002, 5510 | 20 |
| officers of Navy not to interfere in | 2003 | 20 |
| punishment for intimidating voters at | 5529 | 21 |
| and for prescribing qualifications of voters at | 5530 | 21 |
| punishment for interfering with officers of | 5531 | 21 |
| disqualification for holding office, by interfering in | 5532 | 21 |
| increase of force at yards, prior to |  | 59 |
| EMBEZZLEMENT— |  |  |
| of ordnance, arms, and other equipments | 14 | 11 |
| exacting receipt for greater sum than paid | 5483 | 170 |
| person offending subject to fine and imprisonment | 5483 | 170 |
| depositing public money in unauthorized place | 5488 | 170 |
| or loaning or converting it to own use | 5488 | 170 |
| Treasurer, or other depositary, failing to keep, guilty of | 5489 | 170 |
| officers guilty of extortion, under color of office, guilty of | 5481 | 170 |
| custodian of public money, failing to keep, &c., guilty of | 5490 | 171 |
| failing to render accounts, as required by law, guilty of | 5491 | 171 |
| or to make deposit when required | 5492 | 171 |
| upon trial for, transcript from books of Treasury sufficient evidence | 5494 | 171 |
| refusal to pay drafts or orders of accounting officers, declared | 5495 | 171 |

346　　　　　　　　　　　　　　　INDEX.

|  | Sec. | Page. |
|---|---|---|
| EMBEZZLEMENT—Continued. | | |
|     transmitting false receipts, to be allowed in accounts, declared | 5496 | 171 |
|     bankers, &c., knowingly receiving unauthorized deposits of public money, guilty of | 5497 | 172 |
|     of Government money, property, &c., March 3, 1875 | | 229 |
| EMIGRATION— | | |
|     from Oriental countries | | 302 |
|     of Chinese laborers forbidden | | 259 |
|     of alien convicts not allowed | | 259 |
| EMOLUMENTS— | | |
|     may be included in sentence of suspension | 48 | 17 |
|     to continue to crews of wrecked vessels | 1574 | 93 |
|         officers and crews of captured vessels | 1575 | 93 |
|     definition of the term (notes) | | 61 |
| ENEMY— | | |
|     destroying public property not in possession of, punishment for | 4 | 8 |
|     striking flag to, without authority, punishment for | 4 | 8 |
|     intercourse with, how punishable | 4 | 8 |
|     receiving letters or messages from | 4 | 8 |
|     bounty for each person captured on vessel of an | 4635 | 213 |
|     giving aid and comfort to, guilty of treason | 5531 | 308 |
| ENGINEER CORPS— | | |
|     grades and number of officers in | 1390 | 37 |
|     restriction on filling vacancies in, March 3, 1883 | | 37 |
|     rank of officers, on active list | 1476 | 38 |
|     rank, retired from age or length of service | 1481 | 38 |
|     rank of graduates, from Naval Academy | 1484 | 38 |
|     relative rank, no authority for military command | 1488 | 38 |
|     pay of officers of, on active list | 1556 | 38 |
|     detail of officers of, for colleges, February 26, 1879 | | 39 |
|     appointment of graduated cadets to | 1512 | 51 |
|     cadet-engineers abolished | 1512 | 51 |
| ENGINEER-IN-CHIEF— | | |
|     Chief of Bureau of Steam Engineering to have title of | 1471 | 38 |
|         and the relative rank of Commodore | 1471 | 38 |
|     to be appointed from the Chief Engineers | 424 | 36 |
|         and to be a skillful engineer | 424 | 36 |
|     to have highest sea-pay of his grade | 1565 | 69 |
| ENGINEERS (Chief)— | | |
|     number and rank | 1390 | 37 |
|     to be appointed with advice of Senate | 1391 | 37 |
|     designation of, as fleet engineer | 1393 | 37 |
|     filling of vacancies, March 3, 1883 | | 37 |
|     pay of, on active list | 1556 | 38 |
| ENGINEERS (Passed Assistant)— | | |
|     number and rank of | 1390, 1476 | 37–38 |
|     to be appointed with advice of Senate | 1391 | 37 |
|     filling of vacancies, March 3, 1883 | | 37 |
|     pay of, on active list | 1556 | 38 |
| ENGINEERS (Assistant)— | | |
|     number and rank of | 1390, 1476 | 37–38 |
|     to be appointed with advice of Senate | 1391 | 37 |
|     limits of age and qualifications for appointment | 1392 | 37 |

INDEX. 347

| | Sec. | Page. |
|---|---|---|
| ENGINEERS (Assistant)—Continued. | | |
| to be appointed from graduates of the Academy | 1512 | 51 |
| pay of, on active list | 1556 | 38 |
| ENGINEERS (in the Departments)— | | |
| not to be employed beyond provision of law, August 15, 1876 | | 140 |
| number and pay of, in Navy Department building | | 184 |
| ENGLISH STUDIES— | | |
| professor of, at Naval Academy | 1528 | 74 |
| assistant professors of | | 54 |
| ENGRAVING— | | |
| Bureau of, may print impressions from vignettes | | 188 |
| for public documents. (See PUBLIC PRINTING.) | | |
| ENLISTMENT— | | |
| of minors between 14 and 18, not to be made without consent of parents | 19 | 12 |
| of deserters forbidden | 19 | 12 |
| of intoxicated persons forbidden | 19 | 12 |
| in the Navy, number authorized | 1417 | 90 |
| in Marine Corps, to be for a term not less than five years | 1608 | 110 |
| of minors in the naval service | 1418, 1419, 1420 | 91 |
| of persons in the United States to serve against the same | 5337, 5338 | 309 |
| ENSIGNS— | | |
| number allowed on active list | 1363 | 46 |
| assignment of, as clerks to commanding officers. May 4, 1878 | . | 46 |
| to be steerage officers, except, &c. | 1490 | 47 |
| pay of, on the active list | 1556 | 65 |
| on the retired list | 1588 | 70 |
| ENVELOPES (penalty). (See POSTAGE.) | | |
| EQUIPMENTS— | | |
| misappropriating, wrongfully selling, &c. | 14 | 11 |
| purchasing or receiving from those not authorized to sell | 14 | 11 |
| ESTATE— | | |
| no conviction or judgment to work forfeiture of | 5326 | 254 |
| ESCAPE— | | |
| suffering prisoners to | 8 | 10 |
| ESTIMATES. (See under APPROPRIATIONS.) | | |
| ETHICS— | | |
| professor of, at Academy a professor of mathematics | 1528 | 74 |
| EVIDENCE (see also PUBLIC RECORD)— | | |
| Little & Brown's edition of laws to be taken as | 908 | 190 |
| oaths and acknowledgments before justices, &c. | 1778 | 191 |
| copies from the returns-office valid as | 896 | 190 |
| EXAMINATION FOR PROMOTION. (See PROMOTION.) | | |
| EXAMINATION— | | |
| pay and rank of officers absent, when entitled to | 1562 | 68 |
| EXCHANGE— | | |
| of funds for gold or silver only, allowable | 3651 | 174 |
| premiums received on, to be accounted for | 3652 | 174 |
| EXECUTIVE OR AID— | | |
| detail of officer to act as | 1469 | 47 |
| authority defined | 1469 | 47 |
| staff officer, senior, right of communication | 1470 | 47 |
| EXPATRIATION— | | |
| right of, declared | 1999 | 222 |

|  | Sec. | Page. |
|---|---|---|
| EXPENDITURES (*see also* ACCOUNTS)— | | |
| to be published each fiscal year | 237 | 126 |
| accounts of, to be settled in each year | 250 | 126 |
| for naval service, Secretary of Treasury to submit annual report to Congress, June 19, 1878 | 260 | 135 |
| with statement of balances in hand of disbursing agents | | 135 |
| EXPLORING EXPEDITIONS— | | |
| sale of stores, &c., money to revert to appropriation | 3692 | 44 |
| sale of articles used in, use of proceeds | 3618 | 198 |
| EXTORTION— | | |
| punishment of officers guilty of | 5481 | 170 |
| EXTRADITION— | | |
| provisions of law relating to | 5270–5410 | 222–5 |
| EXTRA DUTIES— | | |
| as a punishment | **24–30** | 14, 15 |
| EXTRA PAY (*see also* PAY, EXTRA)— | | |
| not allowed to officers on Light-House Board | 4679 | 240 |

## F.

|  | Sec. | Page. |
|---|---|---|
| FALSE CLAIMS— | | |
| papers, receipts, perjury, and forgery | **14** | 11 |
| FALSEHOOD— | | |
| punishment for, in the Navy | **8** | 9 |
| FALSE OATHS— | | |
| knowingly making, punishment for | **14** | 11 |
| FALSE MUSTER— | | |
| making or signing of any | **8** | 10 |
| FELONY— | | |
| misprision of, punishment for | 5390 | 255 |
| FINES— | | |
| on persons in Navy and Marine Corps, to go to hospitals | 4809 | 39 |
| for unlawfully cutting timber, to go to pension fund | 4751 | 272 |
| FIRE ENGINES— | | |
| estimates for, to be given in detail | 3666 | 131 |
| expenditure to be accounted for | 3666 | 131 |
| FIREMEN— | | |
| additional pay to seamen, &c., performing duty as | 1570 | 69 |
| enlistment of, in the Navy | 1417 | 90 |
| pay and bounty, fixed by Board | 1569 | 92 |
| number and pay of, in Navy Department building | | 184 |
| FIRMS— | | |
| copartners not to be received as sureties on contracts | 3722 | 26 |
| members of, not to be appointed agents to do business with such | 3614 | 138 |
| FISCAL YEAR— | | |
| in matters of accounts to commence July 1 | 237 | 126 |
| expenditure of public money to be settled within the | 250 | 126 |
| FISH COMMISSIONER— | | |
| duties and powers of the | 4395–4396, 4398 | 225 |
| Executive Department to render aid to | 4397 | 225 |
| FLAG OFFICER— | | |
| selection of, to command squadrons | 1434 | 46 |
| assignment of retired officers as | 1464 | 87 |

INDEX. 349

| | Sec. | Page. |
|---|---|---|
| FLAG (of the United States)— | | |
| to be of stripes and stars, &c | 1791 | 226 |
| additional star for each State admitted to the Union | 1792 | 226 |
| FLAGS— | | |
| estimates for, to be in detail | 3666 | 132 |
| captured, to be sent to seat of Government | 428–1554 | 225 |
| to be delivered to the President and preserved | 1555 | 226 |
| FLEET SURGEON— | | |
| appointment of, and duties | 1373, 1374 | 48 |
| pay of | 1556 | 49 |
| FLOGGING— | | |
| punishment by, not to be inflicted | 49 | 17 |
| FLORIDA— | | |
| examination of timber lands in | | 312 |
| FLOUR— | | |
| may be procured as most advantageous | 3727 | 27 |
| allowance in Navy ration | 1580 | 83 |
| FORAGE (Marine Corps)— | | |
| may be procured without adequate appropriation | 3732 | 28 |
| in kind, allowance of, and to whom, June 14, 1878 | 1270, 1271 | 120 |
| allowance for horses, owned and in actual use, June 14, 1878 | 1272 | 120 |
| and when on duty in field or at posts, June 14, 1878 | | 120 |
| no discrimination against officers east of the Mississippi, May 4, 1880 | | 120 |
| provided they are mounted, May 4, 1880 | | 120 |
| and actually keep and own their animals, May 4, 1880 | | 120 |
| commutation for, not allowed, March 3, 1883 | | 120 |
| FOREIGN COINS. (*See* COINS.) | | |
| FOREIGN SUPPLIES— | | |
| not required to be purchased from lowest bidder | 3721 | 26 |
| FORFEITURE— | | |
| of pay and emoluments by sentence of court (note) | | 18 |
| of estate, conviction or judgment not to work | 5326 | 254 |
| FORFEITURES— | | |
| repealing acts not to extinguish | 13 | 200 |
| limit to maintenance of suit for | 1047 | 200 |
| provided person can be found in the United States | 1047 | 200 |
| not affected by repeals in Revised Statutes | 5598 | 201 |
| FORGERY— | | |
| committing, to secure payment of claims | 14 | 11 |
| of various kinds, punishment for | | 227–9 |
| of ship's papers, or altering them, penalty for | 5423 | 252 |
| FOUNDRY— | | |
| for heavy ordnance, selection of location | | 60 |
| FOURTH AUDITOR (*see also* ACCOUNTS)— | | |
| to adjust liabilities, with "general account of advances" | | 135 |
| FRAUD— | | |
| punishment for | 8 | 9 |
| executing, attempting, or countenancing any | 14 | 12 |
| discharged persons liable to trial for | 14 | 12 |
| dismissed officers liable to trial for | 14 | 12 |
| clerks investigating, authorized to administer oaths | 183 | 226 |
| punishment for, of various kinds | | 227–9 |

|  | Sec. | Page. |
|---|---|---|
| FREIGHT— | | |
| receiving, on public vessels without authority | 8 | 10 |
| estimates for, to be given in detail | 3666 | 131 |
| expenditure under each bureau to be accounted for | 3666 | 13 |
| FRESH MEAT— | | |
| substitute for salt meat in Navy ration | 1580 | 83 |
| FUEL— | | |
| may be purchased for the Navy in manner most advantageous | 3728 | 27 |
| may be procured without adequate appropriation | 3732 | 28 |
| not to exceed the necessities of current year | 3732 | 28 |
| for use in District of Columbia, contracts for | 3711 | 32 |
| inspector and weigher to be appointed | 3711 | 32 |
| fees to which entitled from vendor | 3711 | 32 |
| no payment without his certificate | 3713 | 32 |
| accounting officers to be furnished with copy of appointment | 3712 | 32 |
| for Marine Corps may be furnished in kind according to law and regulations | 1270 | 120 |
| regulation prices | | 121 |
| for yards, estimates for, to be in detail | 3666 | 131 |
| FUGITIVES— | | |
| from service not to be returned | 18 | 12 |
| FUNERAL EXPENSES— | | |
| of officers dying in the United States not allowed | 1587 | 20 |
| one month's sea-pay for those dying abroad | 1587 | 20 |
| estimates for, to be in detail | 3666 | 131 |
| FURLOUGH— | | |
| pay of officers on, on active list | 1557 | 68 |
| on retired list | 1593 | 70 |
| transfer to retired pay list | 1594 | 71 |
| authority of Secretary of Navy to place officers on | 1442 | 19 |
| general definition of (note) | | 19 |

## G.

|  | Sec. | Page. |
|---|---|---|
| GAMBLING— | | |
| punishment for | 8 | 9 |
| GENERAL ACCOUNT OF ADVANCES— | | |
| provisions concerning opening of | | 135 |
| GENERAL AVERAGE— | | |
| rule as to contribution in cases of (notes) | | 291-2 |
| GENERAL COURTS-MARTIAL. (See COURTS-MARTIAL, GENERAL.) | | |
| GENERAL ORDERS— | | |
| refusal of obedience to any lawful | 8 | 10 |
| issued by Secretary of Navy, recognized as regulations | 1547 | 19 |
| to be furnished officers of the Navy | 1548 | 20 |
| GESTURES AND MENACES— | | |
| using, towards others | 8 | 10 |
| GIFTS (see also DECORATIONS and BRIBES)— | | |
| from subordinates to official superiors, forbidden | 1784 | 208 |
| GOLD— | | |
| reception of, as freight | 8 | 10 |
| transportation of, in merchant vessels | 4204 | 249 |
| no exchange of Government funds except for, or silver | 3651 | 174 |
| wgaes to merchant seamen to be paid in, by consuls | 4548 | 244 |

|  | Sec. | Page. |
|---|---|---|
| GOLD AND SILVER COINS. (*See* COINS.) | | |
| GOOD EXAMPLE— | | |
|     commanding officers to show | 1 | 8 |
| GOVERNMENT FOUNDRY— | | |
|     selection of site for | | 60 |
| GOVERNMENT HOSPITAL FOR INSANE. (*See* INSANE.) | | |
| GRADES— | | |
|     of officers of the Navy defined (decisions) | | 80, 311 |
| GRATUITY— | | |
|     to machinists discharged from Navy | | 93 |
|     to seamen, promoted for heroism, &c | 1407 | 90 |
| GREENWICH— | | |
|     meridian for nautical purposes | 435 | 56 |
| GUARANTEE— | | |
|     required from bidders | 3719, 3722 | 26 |
|     penalty for making false | 5418, 5479 | 226–8 |
| GUANO ISLANDS— | | |
|     provisions of law relative to | 5570–5578 | 229–30 |
| GUNNERS. (*See* WARRANT OFFICERS.) | | |
| GUNPOWDER— | | |
|     not required to be purchased of lowest bidder | 3721 | 26 |
| GYMNAST— | | |
|     of Naval Academy, salary of | | 54 |

## H.

|  | Sec. | Page. |
|---|---|---|
| HABEAS CORPUS— | | |
|     provisions of law relative to the | 752–766 | 230–2 |
|         decisions regarding (note) | | 91 |
| HAZING— | | |
|     at the Naval Academy forbidden, June 23, 1874 | | 53 |
|     cadets engaged in, to be tried by court-martial | | 53 |
|     on conviction to be dismissed | | 53 |
|         and thereafter ineligible to readmission | | 53 |
| HEALTH OF CREW— | | |
|     to be looked after and preserved | 20 | 13 |
| HEMP— | | |
|     for Navy to be of American growth | 3725 | 27 |
|         where as good and cheap as foreign | 3725 | 27 |
|     advertisement for | 3718 | 25 |
| HEROISM— | | |
|     advancement for, not precluded by law limiting grade | 1364 | 46 |
|     advancement for, in battle | 1506 | 77 |
|     advancement of marine officers for | 1605–1606 | 109 |
| HOLIDAYS— | | |
|     in the District of Columbia, days declared, June 28, 1870 | | 145 |
| HOME MANUFACTORIES— | | |
|     preference to, in purchases for the Navy | 3728 | 27 |
|         provided price and quality being equal | 3728 | 27 |
| HOMESTEADS— | | |
|     provisions of law relative to | | 232–5 |
| HONORABLE DISCHARGE— | | |
|     of naval cadets | 1512 | 51 |
|     three months' pay for reinlisting under | 1573 | 69 |

352    INDEX.

|  | Sec. | Page. |
|---|---|---|
| HONORABLE DISCHARGE—Continued. | | |
| of aliens from the military service, admission to naturalization | 2166 | 257 |
| decisions regarding (notes) | | 35 |
| HORSES— | | |
| for which forage is allowed in Marine Corps, June 18, 1878 | | 120 |
| to be owned and actually kept by officers, June 18, 1878 | | 120 |
| for yards, estimates to be in detail | 3666 | 131 |
| HOSPITALS (Navy)— | | |
| deduction from pay of officers and men for | 1614, 4808 | 39 |
| Secretary of Navy, general charge of | 4807 | 39 |
| fines of officers and men, to go to maintenance of | 4809 | 39 |
| sites to be procured for | 4810 | 39 |
| permanent, for disabled officers and seamen | 4810 | 39 |
| rations of persons admitted, to go to | 4812 | 39 |
| pensions to be deducted | 4813 | 40 |
| erection of, at Hot Springs, Ark | | 40 |
| authority to close | | 40 |
| immunity of, in operations of war | | 262 |
| HOT SPRINGS, ARK.— | | |
| erection of hospital at | | 40 |
| HULLS AND SPARS— | | |
| of vessels, condition on which repaired | 1538 | 95 |
| HYDROGRAPHIC OFFICE— | | |
| attached to Bureau of Navigation | 431 | 44 |
| objects of | 431 | 44 |
| maps, charts, &c., furnished to navigators | 432 | 44 |
| at cost price of paper and printing | | 45 |
| moneys to be paid into Treasury for further publications | 433 | 44 |
| foreign surveys, provision as to publishing | 3686 | 44 |
| civil employés allowed in | | 44 |

### I.

|  | Sec. | Page. |
|---|---|---|
| IMMIGRATION— | | |
| from Oriental countries, involuntary, prohibited | 2158 | 301 |
| IMPORTATIONS— | | |
| not allowed in public vessels, of articles subject to duty | 1624 | 236 |
| which may be made free of duty | 2503 | 236 |
| obscene books, pamphlets, &c., not to be imported | 2491 | 236 |
| vessels not engaged in, not subject to entry | 2791 | 237 |
| IMPRISONMENT— | | |
| for life, in place of sentence of death | 7 | 9 |
| in the Navy, by sentence of court | 14 | 11 |
| for debt, discharge of prisoners by the President | 3472 | 164 |
| of delinquent debtors | 3627 | 165 |
| INCOMPETENCY— | | |
| discharge of rated persons for | 31 | 15 |
| INDEMNITY— | | |
| for lost clothing, appropriation for | 3689 | 134 |
| for loss of personal effects | 287–290 | 128, 9 |
| INDIANS— | | |
| inciting them to war, by messages, &c | 2111, 2112 | 307 |
| correspondence with foreign powers for same purpose | 2113 | 307 |
| not taxed, not entitled to citizenship | 1992 | 258 |

# INDEX. 353

| | Sec. | Page. |
|---|---|---|
| **INFERIOR OFFICERS—** | | |
| meaning of the words in the Constitution (note) | | 104 |
| **INJUNCTIONS—** | | |
| in cases of distress warrants | 3636, 3637 | 166 |
| **INSANE (of the Navy and Marine Corps)—** | | |
| may be cared for in other than Government asylum | 1551 | 40 |
| allowance per annum | 1551 | 40 |
| Government hospital for, in District of Columbia | 4843 | 40 |
| persons entitled to admission | 4843 | 40 |
| limitation on admission | | 41 |
| transfer of convicts to | | 41 |
| inmates of National Home, admitted to | | 41 |
| other persons that may be admitted (notes) | | 41 |
| resigning while (notes) | | 36 |
| **INSOLVENT—** | | |
| proceedings, in cases of debtors to the United States | 3466 | 163 |
| **INSPECTION—** | | |
| of provisions, by commanding officer | 20 | 13 |
| of vessels of the Navy | | 95 |
| of merchant vessels, and outfits | 4559–4577 | 244–45 |
| of vessels for War Department | 1437 | 94 |
| **INSPECTOR OF FUEL—** | | |
| for use by Government in District of Columbia, appointment and duties | 3711 | 32 |
| **INSPECTOR OF TIMBER—** | | |
| of yards, may be discontinued | 1416 | 57 |
| **INSURGENTS—** | | |
| to be commanded to disperse | 5300 | 308 |
| **INSURRECTION—** | | |
| against the State government, militia may be called forth | 5297 | 307 |
| against United States Government, militia and land and naval forces may be employed, to suppress | 5298 | 307 |
| to deprive classes of civil rights, militia, military, and naval forces may be called out | 5299 | 308 |
| insurgents to be commanded to disperse | 5300 | 308 |
| **INTERCOURSE—** | | |
| with enemy or rebel without leave, punishment for | 4 | 8 |
| **INTOXICATING BEVERAGES—** | | |
| habitual use of, a bar to civil appointments | | 143 |
| **INTOXICATED PERSONS—** | | |
| enlistment of, forbidden | 19 | 12 |
| **INVENTORY—** | | |
| of public property, to be kept by Departments | 197 | 193 |
| additions to, and sales to be noted | 197 | 193 |
| of stores in the yards to be taken | | 197 |
| **INVESTIGATION—** | | |
| boards of, limited as to powers (note) | | 19 |
| **ISTHMUS OF PANAMA—** | | |
| appropriation for coaling stations at | | 313 |

## J.

| | | |
|---|---|---|
| **JAPAN—** | | |
| involuntary transportation of subjects of | 2158, 2163 | 301–2 |

11181——23

|  |  | Sec. | Page. |
|---|---|---|---|
| JEWELS— | | | |
| | reception of, as freight | 8 | 10 |
| JUDGE-ADVOCATE-GENERAL— | | | |
| | appointment of, authorized | | 109 |
| |     rank and pay | | 109 |
| |     office to be in Navy Department | | 109 |
| |     duties prescribed | | 109 |
| | employés in office of | | 184 |
| | proceedings of courts and boards to be sent to (foot-note) | | 16 |
| |     also communications pertaining to same (foot-note) | | 16 |
| JUDGE-ADVOCATE— | | | |
| | of general courts-martial, oath to be taken by | 40 | 16 |
| |     to administer oath to members | 40 | 16 |
| JUDGMENT— | | | |
| | of courts-martial, how authenticated | 52 | 17 |
| JURISDICTION (*see also* PUBLIC GROUNDS)— | | | |
| | of State courts not impaired in matter of certain punishment | 5328 | 254 |
| | crimes committed within the, of the United States ......5339–5342, 5391 | | 254–5 |
| | over sites for public works | 355 | 192 |
| | of naval courts-martial, as to crimes committed within State limits (note) | | 13 |

## K.

|  |  | Sec. | Page. |
|---|---|---|---|
| KIDNAPPING— | | | |
| | provisions of law in relation to, June 23, 1874 | 5525 | 303 |

## L.

|  |  | Sec. | Page. |
|---|---|---|---|
| LABOR— | | | |
| | incidental, estimates for, to be in detail | 3666 | 131 |
| LABORERS— | | | |
| | eight hours a day's work for all engaged by the Government | 3738 | 29 |
| | at yards, to be employed for skill and efficiency | 1544 | 58 |
| |     pay only for time employed | 1545 | 58 |
| |     not required to contribute for political purposes | 1546 | 58 |
| |     not to be removed for political opinions | 1546 | 58 |
| |     wages, how regulated, July 16, 1862 | | 58 |
| LABORERS (in the Departments)— | | | |
| | to receive $660 per annum, unless otherwise appropriated for | 167 | 139 |
| | number to be governed by appropriations, August 5, 1882 | 169 | 140 |
| |     as also their rates of pay, August 5, 1882 | 169 | 140 |
| | not to be employed beyond appropriations, August 15, 1876 | | 140 |
| |     nor to be paid from contingent appropriations, August 5, 1882 | | 140 |
| LAND (*see also* PUBLIC PROPERTY)— | | | |
| | not to be purchased without authority of law | 5736 | 28 |
| LANDSMEN (*see also* SEAMEN)— | | | |
| | marines may be substituted for | 1618 | 110 |
| LAND-WARRANTS. (*See* BOUNTY LAND.) | | | |
| LEAVING STATION— | | | |
| | before relieved, punishment for | 4 | 8 |
| LEGAL REPRESENTATIVES— | | | |
| | definition of (notes) | | 129 |
| LENGTH OF SERVICE— | | | |
| | staff corps to rank according to | 1485 | 81 |
| | estimates of, in conferring rank | 1486 | 81 |

INDEX. 355

| | Sec. | Page. |
|---|---|---|
| LENGTH OF SERVICE—Continued. | | |
| credit to officers for, while enlisted men, March 3, 1883 | | 101 |
| volunteer officers, to be credited with | 1412 | 101 |
| rates of pay to marines, according to | 1283 | 118 |
| additional pay for | 1281, 1282, 1284 | 118 |
| LIBERTY— | | |
| deprivation of, on shore | 24, 30 | 14–15 |
| citizens deprived of, in foreign countries, proceedings authorized | 2001 | 222 |
| preference, to the faithful and obedient | 1431 | 92 |
| LIBRARIAN (Assistant)— | | |
| of Naval Academy, pay of | | 54 |
| LICENSE— | | |
| required of Navy officers to command in merchant service (note) | | 22 |
| LIEUTENANT COMMANDERS— | | |
| number of, on active list | 1363 | 46 |
| assignment of, at naval stations | 1435 | 47 |
| and as navigators and watch officers | 1435 | 47 |
| and as first lieutenants of vessels | 1435 | 47 |
| pay of, on the active list | 1556 | 65 |
| on the retired list | 1588 | 70 |
| to command vessels of fourth rate | 1529 | 94 |
| not to be retired except for physical disability | 1445 | 85 |
| LIEUTENANTS— | | |
| number allowed on active list | 1363 | 47 |
| detail of, as secretaries, May 4, 1878 | | 47 |
| pay of, on the active list | 1556 | 65 |
| on the retired list | 1588 | 70 |
| not to be retired, unless for physical disability | 1445 | 85 |
| LIEUTENANTS (senior)— | | |
| number allowed on the active list | 1363 | 46 |
| pay of, on the active list | 1556 | 65 |
| on the retired list | 1588 | 70 |
| LIEUTENANTS (junior)— | | |
| number allowed on the active list | 1363 | 46 |
| pay of, on the active list | 1556 | 65 |
| on the retired list | 1588 | 70 |
| title of master changed to | | 45 |
| LIFE-SAVING DRESS— | | |
| authority to introduce it into the Navy | | 32 |
| LIFE-SAVING SERVICE— | | |
| Statutes relating to the | | 237–9 |
| LIGHT-HOUSE BOARD— | | |
| organization of the | 4653 | 239 |
| Secretary of the Treasury *ex-officio* president | 4654 | 239 |
| election of chairman | 4655 | 240 |
| arrangement of the coasts into light-house districts | 4670 | 240 |
| detail of Navy officers as inspectors | 4671 | 240 |
| to survey the channels, &c | 4678 | 240 |
| officers on, not allowed additional salaries | 4679 | 240 |
| nor to be interested in contracts, &c | 4680 | 240 |
| jurisdiction of, extended, June 23, 1874 | | 240 |
| LIGHTS— | | |
| to be used on vessels | 4233 | 216 |
| showing false, to wreck vessels, penalty for | 5358 | 252 |

|  | Sec. | Page. |
|---|---|---|
| LINE OFFICERS (*see also under each grade*)— | | |
| grades and number of, authorized | 1362 | 45 |
| promotion of, regulated, August 5, 1882 | | 46 |
| number allowed on active list | 1363 | 46 |
| existing commissions not to be vacated | 1364 | 46 |
| assignment of, as secretaries and clerks, May 4, 1878 | | 46 |
| to rank according to dates of commissions | 1467 | 47 |
| commanding, to take precedence | 1468 | 47 |
| as chiefs of Bureaus, relative rank of commodore | 1472 | 47 |
| assignments of, as flag officers | 1434 | 46 |
| change in title of certain grades of. 3 March, 1883 | | 45 |
| "line of duty," definition (note) | | 272 |
| LITHOGRAPHING. (*See* PUBLIC PRINTING.) | | |
| LIVE-OAK TIMBER. (*See* RESERVED LANDS.) | | |
| LOANS— | | |
| of public moneys by disbursing officers forbidden | 1389, 1788, 3639, 5488, 5490, 5497 | 167–72 |
| pay officers not to make, of money or commodities | 1389 | 63 |
| LOST CLOTHING— | | |
| indemnity for, a permanent annual appropriation | 3689 | 134 |
| allowances and payments for | 284, 286, 288 | 128 |
| LOST VESSELS (*see also* VESSELS)— | | |
| authority of officers over crew of | 21 | 13 |

## M.

|  | Sec. | Page. |
|---|---|---|
| MACHINISTS— | | |
| discharge of, from the Navy. June 16, 1880 | | 93 |
| entitled to gratuity | | 93 |
| MACHINERY— | | |
| estimates for, to be given in detail | 3666 | 131 |
| expenditures to be accounted for | 3666 | 131 |
| repairs to, on vessels limited | | 96 |
| of steam vessels, patented articles, use of | 1537 | 266 |
| MAGAZINE— | | |
| keeper of, at yards may be discontinued | 1416 | 57 |
| and duties performed by gunners | 1416 | 57 |
| MAIL MATTER. (*See* POSTAGE.) | | |
| MAIMING— | | |
| persons, within forts, arsenals, on vessels at sea, &c | 5348 | 255 |
| MALTREATMENT— | | |
| of officers and crews of vessels under convoy | 8 | 10 |
| of persons in the Navy subject to orders | 8 | 10 |
| of inhabitants on shore | 8 | 10 |
| of crews of prize-vessels forbidden | 17 | 12 |
| of crews of merchant vessels | 5347 | 55 |
| MANSLAUGHTER— | | |
| committed within forts, arsenals, &c | 5339 | 254 |
| or attempt to commit | 5342 | 254 |
| or upon the high seas, in bays, &c | 5339–5342 | 254 |
| punishment for | 5343 | 255 |
| officers by whose misconduct vessels are lost, guilty of | 5344 | 255 |
| MANUFACTURES— | | |
| of the United States, preference in purchase of supplies | 3728 | 27 |
| contractors for supplies to be manufacturers | 3722 | 26 |

INDEX. 357

|  | Sec. | Page. |
|---|---|---|
| MAPS— | | |
| estimates for, to be given in detail | 3666 | 131 |
| expenditures to be accounted for | 3666 | 131 |
| to accompany public documents, engraving of | 3778, 3779 | 186 |
| MARINES (*see also* MARINE CORPS)— | | |
| deduction from pay, for hospitals | 1614, 4808 | 39 |
| rations deducted, when admitted to hospital | 4812 | 39 |
| pensions also | 4813 | 40 |
| admission to insane asylums | 1551, 4843 | 40 |
| entitled to artificial limbs, &c | 1176 | 42 |
| MARINE BAND— | | |
| extra pay to | 1613 | 114 |
| pay of the musicians of | | 117 |
| MARINE-HOSPITAL SERVICE— | | |
| admission of insane of, to Government asylum | | 41 |
| MARINE CORPS— | | |
| co-operating with Army, to be furnished with supplies, &c | 1135 | 107 |
| to be furnished with rations | 1143 | 107 |
| may be associated with officers of Army, on court-martial duty | 1342 | 107 |
| orders of senior to be obeyed | 1342 | 107 |
| precedence, when on marches | 1342 | 107 |
| transfer to, from the Army, of enlisted men | 1421 | 107 |
| not to release from indebtedness | 1421 | 107 |
| officers, number and grades authorized | 1596 | 108 |
| non-commissioned officers and privates | 1596 | 108 |
| limit in number, not to preclude advancement for distinguished conduct | 1597 | 108 |
| staff, to be separate from the line | 1598 | 108 |
| appointments from graduated naval cadets | 1599 | 108 |
| credit for volunteer service to be given officers | 1600 | 108 |
| colonel commandant, to have rank and pay of a colonel | 1601 | 108 |
| to be appointed from officers of the Corps | 1601 | 108 |
| rank of staff officers | 1602 | 108 |
| rank of officers, same as similar grades in the Army | 1603 | 109 |
| Judge-Advocate-General of Navy may be appointed from officers of | | 109 |
| with rank and pay of a colonel | | 109 |
| brevet commissions, conferred on same conditions as in the Army | 1604 | 109 |
| in time of war for distinguished conduct | 1209 | 109 |
| by President and Senate | 1209 | 109 |
| to bear date from particular action | 1210 | 109 |
| assignment to duty according to brevet rank | 1211 | 109 |
| only when engaged in active hostilities. 3 March, 1883 | | 109 |
| not to entitle to precedence except when so assigned | 1211 | 109 |
| entitles to uniform of actual rank only | 1212 | 109 |
| and to be addressed by title of actual rank | 1212 | 109 |
| not to entitle to increase of pay | 1264 | 109 |
| advancement of officers for distinguished conduct | 1605 | 109 |
| limit in number not to prevent | 1606 | 109 |
| advancement one grade, on receiving vote of thanks | 1607 | 110 |
| enlistments, to be for a period of not less than five years | 1608 | 110 |
| oaths, of officers and men, same as for the Army | 1609 | 110 |
| form for enlisted men | 1342 | 110 |
| enlisted men exempt from personal arrest for debt or contract | 1610 | 110 |

|  | Sec. | Page. |
|---|---|---|
| MARINE CORPS—Continued. | | |
| formation of corps into companies and detachments | 1611 | 110 |
| may be detached for service on vessels, as President may direct | 1616 | 110 |
| officers not to exercise command over navy-yards or vessels | 1617 | 110 |
| marines may be substituted for landsmen | 1618 | 110 |
| liable to duty in forts or garrisons | 1619 | 111 |
| or to any other duty on shore | 1619 | 111 |
| military regulations for, as President may prescribe | 1620 | 111 |
| subject to laws and regulations for government of the Navy | 1621 | 111 |
| except when on detached service with the Army | 1621 | 111 |
| then to the Rules and Articles of War | 1621 | 111 |
| post-traders for, appointment of. 24 July, 1876 | | 111 |
| officers of, leaving posts before acceptance of resignation, deserters | 1624 | 111 |
| officers and men entitled to same pay and bounty as infantry in the Army | 1612 | 114 |
| pay of the musicians known as the Marine Band | 1613 | 114 |
| monthly deduction from pay, for hospitals | 1614 | 114 |
| officers and men, entitled to one Navy ration daily | 1615 | 114 |
| officers of, attached to sea-going vessels not allowed rations (decision) | | 314 |
| pay table of officers—and laws applying | | 115 |
| additional pay for each five years' service | 1262 | 115 |
| limitation thereto | 1263 | 115 |
| pay table of enlisted men | | 117 |
| longevity pay, for volunteer service. June 18, 1878 | | 115 |
| how computed. June 30, 1882 | | 116 |
| pay of officers, absent from duty | 1265 | 116 |
| extension, without deduction | | 116 |
| pay of colonel, not to exceed $4,500 | 1267 | 116 |
| lieutenant-colonel, not to exceed $4,000 | 1267 | 116 |
| payments to be made monthly | 1268 | 116 |
| no allowance, except as especially provided | 1269 | 116 |
| who served with Army, on same footing as to bounty land | | 212 |
| MARINE CORPS—RETIREMENT. (*See* RETIREMENT, MARINE CORPS.) | | |
| MARINE SCHOOLS— | | |
| loan of public vessels for purposes of | | 97 |
| MARKED— | | |
| supplies under contract to be marked | 3731 | 28 |
| otherwise, not to be received | 3731 | 28 |
| MARKING— | | |
| punishment by, not to be inflicted | 49 | 17 |
| MASTER AT ARMS— | | |
| refusing to receive prisoners | 8 | 10 |
| suffering prisoners to escape | 8 | 10 |
| dismissing prisoners without orders | 8 | 10 |
| MASTER— | | |
| title of, changed to junior lieutenant | | 45 |
| MASTERS— | | |
| pay of, on the active list | 1556 | 65 |
| on the retired list | 1538 | 70 |
| MASTER MECHANICS— | | |
| at yards, from what classes to be appointed, &c | 1543 | 58 |
| MATERIALS (old). (*See* SALES.) | | |

# INDEX. 359

| | Sec. | Page. |
|---|---|---|
| MATES— | | |
|     may be rated under authority of the Secretary | 1408 | 47 |
|         not to discharge, from enlistment | 1409 | 47 |
|     pay of | 1556 | 47 |
| MATHEMATICS. (*See* PROFESSORS OF—) | | |
| MEASURERS OF TIMBER— | | |
|     at yards may be discontinued | 1416 | 57 |
| MEAT (fresh and preserved)— | | |
|     allowance of, in Navy ration | 1581 | 83 |
| MECHANICS (*see also* NAVY-YARDS)— | | |
|     eight hours a day's work for all, in Government employ | 3738 | 29 |
| MECHANICS (in the Departments)— | | |
|     not to be employed beyond provision of law, August 15, 1876 | | 140 |
|     number and pay governed by appropriation, August 5, 1882 | | 140 |
|     not to be paid from contingent appropriations | | 140 |
| MEDALS OF HONOR— | | |
|     to seamen promoted for gallantry | 1407 | 90 |
|     for saving life, bestowed by the Secretary of the Treasury | | 237–39 |
| MEDICINES AND MEDICAL ATTENDANCE—. | | |
|     when expenses for, may be allowed officers | 1586 | 20 |
|     not required to be purchased from lowest bidder | 3721 | 26 |
| MEDICAL CORPS— | | |
|     number of, allowed on active list | 1368 | 48 |
|     appointments to be made by President and Senate | 1369 | 48 |
|     relative rank of officers of | 1474 | 48 |
|     relative rank when retired from age or length of service | 1481 | 49 |
| MEDICAL DIRECTORS— | | |
|     fifteen allowed on the active list | 1368 | 48 |
|         with relative rank of captain | 1474 | 49 |
|     pay of | 1556 | 49 |
| MEDICAL INSPECTORS— | | |
|     fifteen allowed on the active list | 1368 | 48 |
|         with relative rank of commander | 1474 | 49 |
|     pay of on the active list | 1556 | 49 |
| MEDICAL PURPOSES— | | |
|     admission on board ship of distilled spirits for | 13 | 11 |
| MEDICINE AND SURGERY (Bureau of)— | | |
|     chief to be appointed from list of surgeons | 426 | 48 |
|         to have relative rank of commodore | 1471 | 49 |
|         and title of Surgeon-General | 1471 | 49 |
|         rank of commodore when retired, &c | 1473 | 49 |
|     detail of assistant, to chief of | 1375 | 49 |
| MEMBERS OF CONGRESS. (*See* CONGRESS.) | | |
| MENACES— | | |
|     punishment for using, in the Navy | 8 | 10 |
| MERCHANDISE— | | |
|     receiving, as freight without authority | 8 | 10 |
|     receiving, for traffic | 8 | 10 |
|     subject to duty, not to be imported in public vessels | 12 | 11 |
| MERCHANT SERVICE— | | |
|     license required of Navy officers to command in (note) | | 22 |
| MERCHANT SERVICE (seamen)— | | |
|     dying abroad, duties of consular officers | 1709–1711 | 220 |
|     deserting in foreign ports, recovery of | 5280 | 223 |

|  | Sec. | Page. |
|---|---|---|
| MERCHANT SERVICE (seamen)—Continued. | | |
| shipping articles, what they shall show | 4511 | 241 |
| rules with regard to agreements with seamen | 4512 | 241 |
| cases in which they shall not apply | 4513 | 241 |
| shipping without agreement, penalty therefor | 4514 | 242 |
| shipping knowingly, contrary to law | 4515 | 242 |
| lost seamen may be replaced | 4516 | 242 |
| shipment of seamen in foreign ports | 4517 | 242 |
| to be done in presence of consul | 4517 | 242 |
| penalty for violating this provision | 4518 | 242 |
| deceased seamen on vessels, master to take charge of effects | 4538-9-40 | 242-3 |
| effects on shore, consul to take charge of | 4541 | 243 |
| seamen, to be paid by consul in gold or equivalent | 4548 | 244 |
| may make complaint of seaworthiness of vessel | 4559 | 244 |
| or of her provisions and stores | 4559 | 244 |
| when inspection will be ordered | 4559 | 244 |
| duties and powers of inspectors | 4560-4561 | 244 |
| master to pay charges of inspection | 4562 | 244 |
| complaints, groundless, deduction from seamen's wages | 4562 | 244 |
| refusal of master to pay charges, penalty | 4563 | 244 |
| seamen may make complaint of provisions before sailing | 4565 | 244 |
| duties of customs officers in such cases | 4565 | 244 |
| forfeiture on false complaint | 4566 | 244 |
| permission to go on shore to enter complaint | 4567 | 245 |
| destitute seamen to be provided for by consuls | 4577 | 245 |
| and sent to the United States | 4577 | 245 |
| penalty when masters of vessels refuse to take them | 4578 | 245 |
| allowance for passage | 4579 | 246 |
| discharge of seamen, by authority of consuls | 4580 | 246 |
| payment of extra wages or remission of | 4580 | 246 |
| duties of consul in this respect | 4581 | 246 |
| extra wages to seamen when vessel is sold abroad | 4582 | 246 |
| when they may be remitted | 4583 | 246 |
| disposition of such wages | 4584 | 246 |
| seamen impressed in foreign port, proceedings | 4589 | 247 |
| seamen deserters, reclamation of, by consuls | 4600 | 247 |
| seamen forced ashore or left behind in foreign ports | 5363 | 247 |
| MERCHANT VESSELS. (See VESSELS, MERCHANT.) | | |
| MESSAGES— | | |
| bringing seducing, from an enemy | 5 | 9 |
| sending or delivering seditious | 2111-2112 | 307 |
| MESSENGERS, ASSISTANT (in the Departments)— | | |
| to receive $720 per annum | 167 | 139 |
| laws relating to messengers applicable [see below] | | |
| MESSENGERS (in the Departments)— | | |
| to receive $840 per annum | 167 | 139 |
| number to be governed by appropriations, August 5, 1882 | 169 | 140 |
| as also their rates of pay, August 5, 1882 | 169 | 140 |
| not to be paid from contingent appropriations, August 5, 1882 | | 140 |
| nor to be employed beyond provision of law, August 15, 1876 | | 140 |
| METRIC SYSTEM— | | |
| of weights and measures, legalized | 3569 | 178 |
| tables of measures and weights | 3570 | 179 |

INDEX.      361

|  | Sec. | Page. |
|---|---|---|
| MEXICAN WAR— | | |
| additional pay for service, on certificate of merit, in, to noncommissioned officers of Marine Corps | 1285 | 118 |
| extra pay for services in the, to Navy and Marine Corps | | 313 |
| MIANTONOMOH— | | |
| building and fitting of turret and pilot-house | | 100 |
| MIDSHIPMAN— | | |
| title of, changed to junior ensign | | 45 |
| pay of, after graduation | 1556 | 65 |
| on the retired list | 1588 | 70 |
| MILEAGE (*see also* TRAVEL)— | | |
| to officers of the Navy traveling abroad, decision | | 314 |
| MILITARY COMMAND— | | |
| staff officers not to exercise | 1488 | 81 |
| MILITARY OUTFITS— | | |
| soldiers forbidden to sell, furnished them | 3748, 5438 | 194–5 |
| MILITIA— | | |
| called into service to repel invasion, &c | 1642 | 306 |
| subject to Articles of War, &c | 1644 | 306 |
| to be apportioned among the States | 1643 | 306 |
| may be called out to suppress insurrection | 5297 | 307 |
| MILK— | | |
| use of, in Navy ration | 1581 | 83 |
| MINORS— | | |
| between 14 and 18 years may be enlisted | 1418 | 91 |
| but not without consent of parents or guardians | 1419, 1420 | 91 |
| MINT— | | |
| dies of a national character may be executed at the | 3551 | 180 |
| MISAPPROPRIATING— | | |
| ordnance, arms, equipments, &c | 14 | 194 |
| MISCELLANEOUS RECEIPTS— | | |
| proceeds of sale of old materials to be turned into Treasury as | 3618 | 198 |
| MISCONDUCT— | | |
| officers not to be retired for | 1456 | 86 |
| but to be brought to trial | 1456 | 86 |
| may be dropped with not more than one year's pay. 5 August, 1882 | | 85 |
| MISPRISION— | | |
| of felony, punishment for | 5390 | 255 |
| MITIGATION— | | |
| of sentences of general courts-martial | 33, 54 | 15, 18 |
| decisions and opinions concerning (notes) | | 18 |
| MODELS— | | |
| estimates for, to be given in detail | 3666 | 131 |
| expenditures to be accounted for | 3666 | 131 |
| of yachts, may be copied by United States naval architects | 4215 | 253 |
| MOLASSES— | | |
| allowance of, in Navy ration | 1580 | 83 |
| MONEY— | | |
| delivering less than named in receipt | 14 | 11 |
| false certificate as to receipt of | 14 | 11 |
| stealing, embezzling, misappropriating, &c | 14 | 11 |
| MONEY ORDERS. (*See* POSTAGE.) | | |

862                                    INDEX.

|  | Sec. | Page. |
|---|---|---|
| MONITORS— | | |
| double turreted, appropriations for engines of | | 100 |
| approaching for launching | | 100 |
| may be removed to navy-yards | | 100 |
| MURDER— | | |
| commission of, by persons in the Navy | 6 | 9 |
| indictment for offense, not limited | 1043 | 200 |
| on public vessels, without territorial jurisdiction of the United States | 1624 | 253 |
| within forts, dock-yards, arsenals, &c | 5339 | 254 |
| on the high seas, in bays, &c | 5339 | 254 |
| body of convict may be delivered for dissection | 5340 | 254 |
| attempting to commit, within forts, on the seas, &c | 5342 | 254 |
| MUSTER ROLLS— | | |
| of ships' crews to be sent to Secretary Navy | 20 | 13 |
| casualties to be accounted for | 20 | 13 |
| MUTINY— | | |
| punishment for, in the naval service | 4 | 8 |
| on merchant vessels on the high seas | 5359 | 256 |
| MUTINOUS WORDS— | | |
| utterance of, punishment for | 8 | 10 |

## N.

|  | Sec. | Page. |
|---|---|---|
| NAMES— | | |
| of registered vessels to be painted on stern | 4178 | 249 |
| not to be changed for purposes of deceit | 4179 | 249 |
| of vessels of the Navy, how determined | 1531 | 94 |
| no two to bear the same name | 1532 | 94 |
| of purchased may be changed | 1533 | 94 |
| NATIONAL BOARD OF HEALTH (*see also* QUARANTINE)— | | |
| construction of refrigerating ship on recommendation of | | 292 |
| hulks to be placed gratuitously at disposition of | | 292 |
| duties connected with infected vessels, contagious diseases, &c | | 293 |
| detail of medical officers for service at foreign ports | | 293 |
| detail of officers of Department for service under | | 293 |
| appropriations for | | 294 |
| NATIONAL CEMETERIES— | | |
| inclosures, headstones, and registers | 4877 | 43 |
| who may be buried in | 4878 | 44 |
| NATIONAL FOUNDRY— | | |
| selection of site for | | 60 |
| NATIONAL HOME— | | |
| admission of insane inmates of, to Government Insane Asylum | | 41 |
| what persons entitled to admission | 4832 | 41 |
| disposition of their pensions | | 42 |
| NATURALIZATION— | | |
| of aliens, requirements to be fulfilled | 2165–2174 | 256–8 |
| of persons who have served in the merchant service | 2174 | 258 |
| NATURALIZED— | | |
| citizens of the United States, protection to, in foreign countries | 2000, 2001 | 222 |
| NAUTICAL ALMANAC— | | |
| Superintendent and pay of | 436 | 50 |
| printing and distribution of | | 50 |

INDEX. 363

| | Sec. | Page. |
|---|---|---|
| NAUTICAL ALMANAC—Continued. | | |
|     money from sale of, to go to printing appropriation | | 50 |
|     civil employés, allowed in office of | | 50 |
| NAUTICAL BOOKS— | | |
|     publication of, by Hydrographic Office | 432 | 44 |
|     sale, and disposition of proceeds | 433 | 44 |
| NAVAL ACADEMY— | | |
|     graduates of, to rank according to proficiency | 1483, 1521 | 51 |
|     to be established at Annapolis | 1511 | 51 |
|     appointment of naval cadets | 1512 | 51 |
|     disposition of the graduates | 1512 | 51 |
|     number of cadets allowed | 1513 | 51 |
|     notification to members of vacancies | 1514 | 51 |
|     examination of candidates for admission | 1515 | 51 |
|     candidates failing mentally or physically | 1516 | 52 |
|     age for admission | 1517 | 52 |
|     candidates to be actual residents of districts | 1517 | 52 |
|     traveling expenses, when admitted | | 52 |
|     cadets not appointed in accordance with law not to be paid | 1518 | 52 |
|     cadets deficient at examination not to be continued at | 1519 | 52 |
|     academic course to be six years | 1520 | 52 |
|     education of naval constructors and steam engineers | 1522 | 52 |
|     special course of study and training for cadets | | 53 |
|     studies at, not to be pursued on Sunday | 1526 | 53 |
|     detail of paymaster as storekeeper | 1527 | 53 |
|     assignment of professors of mathematics on duty at | 1528 | 53 |
|     pay of naval cadets | | 53 |
|     cadets entitled to rations or commutation therefor | 1577 | 53 |
|     hazing at, law relating to | | 53 |
|     Board of Visitors, appointment of | | 54 |
|     pay of civil employés at | | 54 |
| NAVAL ADVISORY BOARD— | | |
|     organization and duties of | | 98 |
| NAVAL ASYLUM— | | |
|     establishment of | 4810 | 39 |
|     regulations for government, prescribed by Secretary of Navy | 4811 | 39 |
| NAVAL CADETS. (*See* NAVAL ACADEMY.) | | |
| NAVAL CONSTRUCTORS— | | |
|     appointed by President, with advice of Senate | 1402 | 54 |
|     may perform duty at yards and stations | 1404 | 54 |
|     relative rank of | 1477 | 55 |
|     rank of, on retirement from age or length of service | 1481 | 55 |
|     education of, at Naval Academy | 1522 | 55 |
|     pay on active list | 1556 | 55 |
|     retired list | 1588 | 70 |
| NAVAL CONSTRUCTORS (Assistant)— | | |
|     appointment of naval cadets as | 1403 | 55 |
|     relative rank of lieutenant or master | 1477 | 55 |
|     pay on the active list | 1556 | 55 |
|     retired list | 1588 | 70 |
| NAVAL OBSERVATORY— | | |
|     officer superintending, entitled to duty pay | 434 | 56 |
|     adopted as the American meridian | 435 | 56 |

| | Sec. | Page. |
|---|---|---|
| NAVAL OBSERVATORY—Continued. | | |
| professors of mathematics assignable to duty at | 1401 | 56 |
| pay of civil employés authorized | | 56 |
| purchase of new site for | | 56 |
| NAVIGATION (Bureau)— | | |
| established in the Navy Department | 419 | 181 |
| appointment of chief of | 422 | 181 |
| with relative rank of commodore, if of less rank | 1472 | 182 |
| pay of | 1565 | 182 |
| civil employés in, authorized | | 182 |
| NAVY DEPARTMENT (*see also under each Bureau*)— | | |
| to be known as the Department of the Navy | 415 | 180 |
| Secretary of the Navy to be its head | 415 | 180 |
| pay of | | 183 |
| general duties prescribed | 417 | 180 |
| custody of books and property | 418 | 180 |
| bureaus established and distribution of business among them | 419 | 181 |
| to retain charge and custody of their books | 420 | 181 |
| duties to be performed under authority of the Secretary | 420 | 181 |
| orders of, to have full force as from the Secretary | 420 | 181 |
| appointment of chiefs of | 421–426 | 181 |
| pay of chiefs of | 1565 | 182 |
| staff officers serving full term as chiefs, exempt from sea service | 1436 | 182 |
| except in time of war | 1436 | 182 |
| chiefs of, rank and title | 1471 | 182 |
| rank on retirement | 1473 | 182 |
| line officer, chief of, rank of commodore | 1472 | 182 |
| Secretary to make reports to Congress on subjects named | 429 | 181 |
| allowance and salaries of civil employés | 416 | 182–3 |
| office of Judge-Advocate-General of the Navy established | | 109 |
| NAVY DEPARTMENT BUILDING— | | |
| appointment of superintendent of, March 3, 1883 | | 184 |
| employés authorized, and their pay | | 184 |
| NAVY HOSPITAL FUND. (*See* HOSPITAL FUND.) | | |
| NAVY PENSION FUND. (*See* PENSION FUND.) | | |
| NAVY REGULATIONS— | | |
| force and effect of (notes) | | 19 |
| orders, regulations, &c., to be considered | 1547 | 19 |
| punishment for violating | 8 | 10 |
| officers to be furnished with | 1548 | 20 |
| NAVAL STOREKEEPERS— | | |
| appointed by President, with advice of Senate | 1413 | 56 |
| at yards, where necessary | 1413 | 56 |
| appointment of citizens as, on foreign stations | 1414 | 56 |
| when Navy officers cannot be ordered | 1414 | 56 |
| required to give bond | 1415 | 56 |
| pay | 1568 | 57 |
| commissioned or warrant officers ordered as, on foreign stations | 1438 | 56 |
| required to give bond | 1439 | 57 |
| pay of, when so acting | 1567 | 57 |
| of Naval Academy to be a paymaster | 1527 | 57 |
| to procure stores and other necessaries | 1527 | 57 |
| may be discontinued at yards | 1416 | 57 |

|  | Sec. | Page. |
|---|---|---|
| NAVAL SUPPLIES. (*See* CONTRACTS.) | | |
| NAVY-YARD COMMISSION— | | |
| appointment and duties of | | 59 |
| NAVY-YARDS— | | |
| validity of title for lands purchased for, to be determined | 355 | 57 |
| district attorneys and Departments to furnish information | 355 | 57 |
| expense to be paid from contingencies | 355 | 57 |
| civil engineer and storekeeper may be appointed at | 1413 | 57 |
| civil officers may be discontinued at | 1416 | 57 |
| selection of commandants, not below commander | 1542 | 58 |
| mechanical departments, selection of heads for | 1543 | 58 |
| laborers to be employed for skill and efficiency | 1544 | 58 |
| salaries only to employés estimated for | 1545 | 58 |
| per diem employés to be paid for actual time | 1545 | 58 |
| workingmen exempt from political contributions | 1546 | 58 |
| not to be discharged for political opinions | 1546 | 58 |
| assent of State may be procured to erect buildings | 1838 | 58 |
| fuel for, how purchased | 3728 | 58 |
| appropriation before purchase of land for | 3736 | 58 |
| eight hours to constitute a day's work | 3738 | 58 |
| wages of workmen, how fixed | | 58 |
| arson of buildings, punishment prescribed | 5385–5386 | 59 |
| of vessels, timber, &c | 5386–5387 | 59 |
| increase of force prior to elections, procedure | | 59 |
| wet-dock for Norfolk yard | | 59 |
| commission to report on discontinuance of | | 59 |
| coaling-dock at Port Royal | | 60 |
| Government foundry, commission to select | | 60 |
| Coasters' Harbor Island, wharf to be erected | | 60 |
| closing of yards, authority given | | 60 |
| yard at Washington excepted | | 60 |
| marine officers, not to exercise command over | 1617 | 110 |
| inventory of stores in, to be taken | | 197 |
| appraisal and sale of | | 197 |
| soliciting and receiving contributions in, for political purposes, forbidden | | 209 |
| punishment for certain crimes and offenses committed in, | 5339, 5341, 5342, 5345, 5348, 5391 | 254–6 |
| NEGLECT— | | |
| of duty, punishment for | 8 | 10 |
| of orders, punishment for | 8 | 10 |
| NEUTRALITY— | | |
| arming vessels to cruise against United States vessels | 5284 | 260 |
| augmenting force of foreign vessels of war | 5285 | 260 |
| military expeditions against people at peace with the United States | 5286 | 260 |
| district courts to take cognizance of complaints | 5287 | 260 |
| compelling foreign vessels to depart | 5288 | 261 |
| military and naval force may be used for the purpose | 5288 | 261 |
| armed vessels before sailing to give bond | 5289 | 261 |
| may be detained by collectors of customs | 5290 | 261 |
| until decision of President or bond is given | 5290 | 261 |
| foreign subjects may enlist on armed vessels under certain conditions | 5291 | 261 |

# 366 INDEX.

|  | Sec. | Page. |
|---|---|---|
| NEUTRALITY—Continued. | | |
|     if their country be at peace with the United States | 5291 | 261 |
|     decisions and opinions concerning (notes) | | 261–2 |
|     amelioration of the wounded, international convention | | 262–5 |
|         hospital service, non-combatants, neutral persons, &c. | | 262–5 |
|     alien enemies, removal, arrest, &c. | 4067–4070 | 265–6 |
| NEWSPAPERS— | | |
|     annual allowance from contingent fund, for | 192, 193, 1779 | 161–2 |
|     in the District of Columbia, in which to advertise | | 129 |
| NOBILITY— | | |
|     title of, renouncement to become citizens of the United States | 2165 | 267 |

## O.

|  | Sec. | Page. |
|---|---|---|
| OATH— | | |
|     to be administered in summary courts | 28 | 14 |
|         in general courts-martial | 40, 41 | 16 |
|         in courts of inquiry | 58 | 18 |
|     of public officers making return of contracts | 3745 | 30 |
|     to be taken by officers and men of the Marine Corps | 1609 | 110 |
|         form for enlisted men | 1342 | 110 |
|     to be taken by persons appointed to office | 1756–57 | 144 |
|         before whom it may be taken | 1758 | 144 |
|         to be preserved and filed | 1759 | 144 |
|     requirement of, deemed complied with by an affirmation | | 199 |
|     may be administered by auditor, in settling accounts | 297 | 127 |
|     under laws of the United States, before whom may be taken | 1778 | 144 |
|     to be taken by claim agents | 3478–9 | 154 |
|     to be taken by aliens to become citizens | 2165 | 256 |
| OBSERVATORY. (See NAVAL OBSERVATORY.) | | |
| OFFENDERS— | | |
|     failing to detect and bring to punishment | 8 | 10 |
| OFFENSES ON SHORE— | | |
|     punishment for committing | 23 | 14 |
|     jurisdiction in matter of trial (note) | | 13 |
| OFFICE (see also CIVIL SERVICE)— | | |
|     persons in the Navy not to hold, in Territories | 1860 | 20 |
|     disqualification for, by interfering in elections, &c. | 5532 | 21 |
|     deserters incapable of holding | 1996, 1997, 1998 | 33–4 |
|     conspiracy to prevent persons accepting or holding | 5518 | 310 |
|     disqualified for, by engaging in rebellion | 5334 | 308 |
|         by committing treason | 5332 | 308 |
|     decisions, &c., as to appointment to (notes) | | 100 |
|     as to suspension, tenure of office act (notes) | | 148 |
| OFFICERS— | | |
|     list of, on vessels to be sent to Secretary of the Navy | 20 | 13 |
|         through whose negligence life is lost, guilty of manslaughter | 5344 | 255 |
|     of vessels, to be citizens of the United States | 1428, 4131 | 94, 247 |
| OIL— | | |
|     for yards, estimates for, to be in detail | 3666 | 131 |
| OLD MATERIAL. (See SALES.) | | |
| OPINIONS (see ATTORNEY-GENERAL)— | | |
|     of Attorney-General, editing and printing of | 383 | 138 |
|         distribution from time to time | 383 | 138 |

INDEX. 367

| | Sec. | Page. |
|---|---|---|
| OPPRESSION— | | |
| of persons subject to orders............................. | 8 | 10 |
| ORDERS (*see* GENERAL ORDERS)— | | |
| disobedience of lawful, how punishable.................... | 4 | 8 |
| not properly observing in battle, punishment for............ | 4 | 9 |
| negligence or carelessness in obeying..................... | 8 | 10 |
| issued by Secretary prior to July 14, 1862, recognized as regulations of the Navy ....................................... | 1547 | 19 |
| ORDNANCE (Bureau)— | | |
| establishment of, in the Navy Department.................. | 419 | 181 |
| appointment of Chief.................................. | 422 | 181 |
| with relative rank of Commodore, &c ................ | 1472 | 182 |
| pay of .............................................. | 1565 | 182 |
| civil employés allowed in................................. | | 182 |
| ORDNANCE— | | |
| condemned, sale of, and use of proceeds. March 3, 1875...... | | 198 |
| not required to be purchased from lowest bidder ............ | 3721 | 26 |
| misappropriating, stealing, &c............................ | 14 | 11 |
| purchasing or receiving from those not authorized to sell ...... | 14 | 11 |
| Government foundry for heavy ............................ | | 60 |
| meaning of the word in section 3721 ...................... | | 315 |
| ORIENTAL COUNTRIES— | | |
| immigration from ...................................... | | 259, 302 |
| OUTSTANDING LIABILITIES— | | |
| amount of unpaid checks, to be deposited as ................ | 306, 307, 308 | 172 |
| OXEN— | | |
| used in yards, estimates for, to be in detail................. | 3666 | 131 |

### P.

| | Sec. | Page. |
|---|---|---|
| PACKING-BOXES— | | |
| estimates for, to be in detail ............................ | 3666 | 132 |
| PANAMA— | | |
| Isthmus of, appropriation for coaling stations at ............ | | 313 |
| PARDON— | | |
| in case of both pecuniary and corporal punishment .......... | 5330 | 254 |
| decisions and rulings, in reference to (notes) .............. | | 151 |
| of cadets for hazing, not recommended (notes) ............. | | 54 |
| not to authorize payment of disloyal claimant .............. | 3480 | 154 |
| PAROLE— | | |
| pay of prisoners to cease after ........................... | 1288 | 119 |
| traveling expenses allowed............................... | 1288 | 116 |
| PASSED ASSISTANT SURGEONS. (*See* SURGEONS, PASSED ASSISTANT.) | | |
| PASSED ASSISTANT PAYMASTERS. (*See* PAYMASTERS, PASSED ASSISTANT.) | | |
| PASSED ASSISTANT ENGINEERS. (*See* ENGINEERS, PASSED ASSISTANT.) | | |
| PASSENGERS— | | |
| lists of, on vessels, to be sent to Secretary of the Navy........ | 20 | 13 |
| PASSPORT— | | |
| for vessels to be furnished by collector ..................... | 4306 | 250 |
| penalty for departing without............................ | 4307 | 250 |
| for unregistered vessels ................................. | 4308 | 250 |

# 368 INDEX.

|  | Sec. | Page. |
|---|---|---|
| PATENTED— | | |
| articles connected with steam-engines, conditions of use or purchase | 1537 | 266 |
| inventions not previously known may be | 4886 | 266 |
| also those previously patented abroad | 4887 | 266 |
| inventions may be, by officers, without fees, on certain conditions. | | 267 |
| PAY OF THE NAVY— | | |
| estimates for, to be in detailed classifications | | 132 |
| to be used only for its legitimate purposes. June 19, 1878 | | 135 |
| not to be carried to the surplus fund. June 20, 1874 | | 135 |
| payments to officers and men not to exceed the appropriation | 1569 | 69 |
| PAY— | | |
| may be included in sentence of suspension | 48 | 17 |
| forfeiture of, during confinement or suspension (note) | | 18 |
| no additional, for service in volunteer army or navy, March 3, 1883 | | 21 |
| of Superintendent of the Observatory | 434 | 56 |
| civil employés allowed at the Observatory | | 56 |
| of civilian store-keepers, foreign stations | 1568 | 57 |
| officers, store-keepers on foreign stations | 1567 | 57 |
| does not include rations or subsistence (notes) | | 61 |
| pay account not commercial paper (notes) | | 61 |
| and emoluments include quarters | | 61 |
| of officers, on the active list | 1556 | 65–67 |
| on furlough, half of leave pay | 1557 | 68 |
| prescribed in sections 1556 and 155 to be total compensation | 1558 | 68 |
| of volunteer service, same as Regular Navy | 1559 | 68 |
| of officers commences on acceptance | 1560 | 68 |
| except where bond is required | 1560 | 68 |
| when promoted. June 22, 1874 | 1561 | 68 |
| absent, when subject to examination | 1562 | 68 |
| performing duties of acting paymaster | 1564 | 69 |
| of chiefs of bureaus | 1565 | 69 |
| of officers in charge of stores, foreign squadrons | 1567 | 69 |
| of rated men, to be fixed by the President | 1569 | 69 |
| additional when serving as firemen and coal-heavers | 1570 | 69 |
| detained beyond time of enlistment | 1572 | 69 |
| three months' additional, re-enlisting under honorable discharge | 1573 | 69 |
| of crew of wrecked vessels, to continue, &c | 1574 | 69 |
| of officers and men of vessels taken by the enemy | 1575 | 69 |
| assignment of, by enlisted persons, how attested | 1576 | 70 |
| of officers on the retired list | 1588 | 70 |
| certain rear-admirals, promoted after retirement | 1589 | 70 |
| retired, third assistant engineers | 1590 | 70 |
| of retired officers on active duty | 1592 | 70 |
| on furlough | 1593 | 70 |
| no increase of, after retirement | 1591 | 70–88 |
| of officers on coast survey, subsistence in addition to | 4688 | 70 |
| pro rata, for part of year | 2687 | 72 |
| per diem, of persons attending courts-martial, &c., estimates for, in detail | 3666 | 132 |
| of assistant surgeons not in line of promotion | | 312 |
| longevity, to officers of the Navy (decision) | | 313 |

|  |  | Sec. | Page. |
|---|---|---|---|
| PAY, EXTRA (*see also* under PAY)— | | | |
| not allowed to clerks with annual salary | | 170 | 71 |
| nor for performing duties of another office, except, &c | | 1763, 1764 | 71 |
| not allowed for disbursement of money | | 1765 | 71 |
| nor for other duty not authorized by law | | 1765 | 71 |
| unless appropriations are made therefor | | 1765 | 71 |
| for disbursing appropriations for construction of public buildings. | | 3654 | 72, 313 |
| no civil officer to receive, beyond salary. June 20, 1874 | | | 72 |
| not to apply to payment of attorneys by Department of Justice | | | 72 |
| for service in the Mexican war | | | 313 |
| to Marine band | | 1613 | 114 |
| PAY (Marine Corps)— | | | |
| same as to the infantry of the Army | | 1612 | 114 |
| of the Marine band | | 1613 | 114 |
| deductions for Navy hospital fund | | 1614 | 114 |
| pay-table, and laws on which based | | 1261 | 115 |
| additional, for each five years' service | | 1262 | 115 |
| total not to exceed 40 per centum of yearly pay | | 1263 | 115 |
| longevity pay for volunteer service, June 18, 1878 | | | 115 |
| manner of computing, June 30, 1882 | | | 116 |
| brevets confer no title to additional | | 1264 | 116 |
| when absent, on leave or sick | | 1265 | 116 |
| of colonel not to exceed $4,500 | | 1267 | 116 |
| lieutenant-colonel not to exceed $4,000 | | 1267 | 116 |
| to be made monthly by paymaster | | 1268 | 116 |
| pay-table of enlisted men | | | 117 |
| statutes on which based | | 1280–1285 | 118 |
| additional on re-enlistment | | 1281–1283 | 118 |
| retention of, on re-enlistment | | 1282 | 118 |
| forfeiture of retained | | 1282 | 118 |
| additional, on re-enlisting under honorable discharge | | 1284 | 118 |
| past continuous service to be considered | | 1284 | 118 |
| additional, upon certificate of merit, Army | | 1285 | 118 |
| rated according to length of service | | 1283 | 118 |
| for service in Mexican war | | 1283 | 119, 313 |
| continuation of, during captivity | | 1288 | 119 |
| not to continue after parole | | 1288 | 119 |
| artificers and laborers, increased pay when detailed as | | 1287 | 119 |
| for travel, to officers discharged | | 1289 | 119 |
| to soldiers discharged | | 1290 | 119 |
| assignment of, previous to discharge not valid | | 1291 | 120 |
| no allowances in addition to, except, &c | | 1269 | 120 |
| when mounted, to receive pay, emoluments, &c., of cavalry | | 1270 | 120 |
| not to be carried to surplus fund | | | 135 |
| PAY CORPS (*see also* DISBURSING OFFICERS)— | | | |
| grades and number allowed | | 1376 | 61 |
| restriction on promotions in | | | 61 |
| appointments to, by President, with the advice of the Senate | | 1378 | 62 |
| examination before appointment | | 1379 | 62 |
| limits as to age, not under 21 nor over 26 | | 1379 | 62 |
| acting appointments in ships at sea, &c | | 1381 | 62 |
| appointment of "Fleet Paymaster" | | 1382 | 63 |

|  | Sec. | Page. |
|---|---|---|
| PAY CORPS—Continued. | | |
| pay to which entitled | 1564 | 63 |
| bonds to be given by officers of | 1383 | 62 |
| new bonds when required | 1384 | 62 |
| not affected by new commission | 1385 | 62 |
| preparation of (memorandum) | | 63 |
| clerks allowed | 1386–1387–1388 | 63 |
| advances and loans not to be made by officers of | 1389 | 63 |
| duties of, not required to be performed by commanding officers | 1432 | 63 |
| relative rank of officers of | 1475 | 63 |
| retirement of officers from age or length of service | 1481 | 63 |
| storekeeper at Academy to be an officer of | 1527 | 64 |
| pay of officers of, on active list | 1556 | 64 |
| PAYMASTER-GENERAL— | | |
| Chief of Bureau of Provisions and Clothing to have title of | 1471 | 63 |
| with relative rank of commodore | 1471 | 63 |
| PAYING OFF— | | |
| of crew, officer to attend | 20 | 13 |
| PAY DIRECTORS— | | |
| thirteen authorized on active list | 1376 | 61 |
| with relative rank of captain | 1475 | 63 |
| pay of, on the active list | 1556 | 64 |
| on retired list | 1588 | 70 |
| PAY INSPECTORS— | | |
| thirteen allowed on active list | 1376 | 61 |
| with relative rank of commander | 1475 | 63 |
| pay of, on active list | 1556 | 64 |
| on retired list | 1588 | 70 |
| PAYMASTERS OF THE FLEET— | | |
| designation of, by the President | 1382 | 62 |
| clerks to which entitled | 1386 | 63 |
| pay of | 1556 | 64 |
| PAYMASTERS— | | |
| to take care of property of persons dying on board ship | 20 | 13 |
| forty, allowed on the active list | 1376 | 61 |
| to be promoted from passed assistants | 1380 | 62 |
| office becoming vacant at sea, how filled | 1381 | 62 |
| pay to which entitled | 1381–1564 | 62–64 |
| to give bond in the sum of $25,000 | 1383 | 62 |
| new bonds when required | 1384 | 62 |
| bond not affected by new commission | 1385 | 62 |
| "of the fleet," designation by President | 1382 | 63 |
| when allowed clerks | 1386–1388 | 63 |
| not to loan or advance money | 1389 | 63 |
| commanding officers not required to act as | 1432 | 63 |
| relative rank of | 1475 | 63 |
| retirement from age or length of service | 1481 | 63 |
| detail of, as storekeeper at the Naval Academy | 1527 | 64 |
| pay of, on the active list | 1556 | 64 |
| on the retired list | 1588 | 70 |
| settlement of accounts of, on lost vessels | 284 | 128 |
| PAYMASTERS (Passed Assistant)— | | |
| twenty allowed on the active list | 425 | 61 |
| with relative rank of lieutenant or master | 1475 | 63 |

INDEX. 371

|  | Sec. | Page. |
|---|---|---|
| PAYMASTERS (Passed Assistant)—Continued. | | |
|    appointed by President, with the advice of the Senate | 1378 | 62 |
|    to be promoted from assistants | 1380 | 62 |
|    office becoming vacant at sea, how filled | 1381 | 62 |
|       pay to which entitled | 1564 | 64 |
|    to give bond for $15,000 | 1383 | 62 |
|       new ones when required | 1384 | 62 |
|    when allowed clerks | 1386–1388 | 63 |
|    not to advance or loan money | 1389 | 63 |
|    commanding officers not required to perform duties of | 1432 | 63 |
|    pay of, on active list | 1556 | 64 |
|       on the retired list | 1588 | 70 |
| PAYMASTERS (Assistant)— | | |
|    ten allowed on the active list | 425 | 61 |
|       with relative rank of master or ensign | 1475 | 63 |
|    appointed by President, with the advice of the Senate | 1378 | 62 |
|       if not over 26 or under 21 years of age | 1379 | 62 |
|          after examination | 1379 | 62 |
|    office becoming vacant at sea, how filled | 1381 | 62 |
|    acting, to receive pay of grade | 1564 | 64 |
|    to give bond for $10,000 | 1383 | 62 |
|       and new one when required | 1384 | 62 |
|    new commission not to affect bond | 1385 | 62 |
|    when allowed clerks | 1386–1388 | 63 |
|    not to advance or loan money | 1389 | 63 |
|    commanding officers not to perform duties of | 1432 | 63 |
|    pay of, on the active list | 1556 | 64 |
|       on the retired list | 1588 | 70 |
| PEASE— | | |
|    allowance in Navy ration | 1580 | 83 |
| PECUNIARY— | | |
|    punishment with corporal, pardon or remission of either | 5330 | 254 |
| PENALTY ENVELOPES. (*See* POSTAGE.) | | |
| PENALTIES (*see also* FINES)— | | |
|    incurred, not affected by repealing acts | | 200 |
|    limit as to suits for | 1047 | 200 |
|    incurred, not affected by previous statute | 5598 | 201 |
| PENITENTIARY— | | |
|    punishment by imprisonment in | 7 | 9 |
| PENSIONS— | | |
|    deduction of, from persons admitted to hospitals | 4813 | 40 |
|    of persons admitted to national homes, disposition of | | 42 |
|    amendment of section 4702 (supplement) | | 311 |
|    commencement of, under general laws | | 311 |
|    arrears of, payment | | 312 |
|    for survivors of the war of 1812 | | 312 |
|    under both special and general laws, prohibition | | 312 |
|    for loss of sight of both eyes | | 312 |
|    invalid, to persons disabled since March 4, 1861 | 4692 | 267 |
|       to continue during disability | 4692 | 267 |
|    classes, in military and naval service, entitled to invalid | 4693 | 267 |
|    for wounds, or sickness contracted since July 27, 1868 | 4694 | 268 |
|       wounds, &c., must have been received in line of duty | 4694 | 268 |

|  | Sec. | Page. |
|---|---|---|
| PENSIONS—Continued. | | |
| line of duty defined, in Army and Navy (notes p. 272) | 4694 | 268 |
| rate of, for total disability in Navy and Marine Corps | 4695 | 268 |
| extended to masters, pilots, &c., on gun-boats | 4695 | 268 |
| to engineers in the naval service. March 3, 1877 | | 269 |
| according to rank, when disability originated | 4696 | 269 |
| rank to be determined by date of commission, &c | 4696 | 269 |
| provided a vacancy existed in the rank | 4696 | 269 |
| that the person was not disabled | 4696 | 269 |
| nor did not refuse to muster | 4696 | 269 |
| increase of, except for permanent specific disability, not to commence prior to surgeon's certificate | 4698½ | 269 |
| certificate of surgeon of examining board to be approved by Commissioner of Pensions | 4698½ | 269 |
| disability not otherwise provided for, amount allowed | 4699 | 269 |
| to widow and children, since March 4, 1861 | 4702 | 269 |
| to commence from death of husband or father | 4702 | 269 |
| if widow remarries, children alone entitled, except, &c | 4702 | 269–311 |
| increase to widow, after July 25, 1866, for each child | 4703 | 269 |
| to continue during widowhood or maintenance | 4703 | 269 |
| of persons whose rights accrued prior to March 4, 1861 | 4712 | 270 |
| commencement in such cases | 4713 | 270 |
| and pay not to be drawn at same time | 4724 | 270 |
| unless employed in lower grade, or civil branch of the service | 4724 | 270 |
| to persons in naval service disabled prior to March 4, 1861 | 4728 | 270 |
| rate of, to engineers, firemen, and coal-heavers in the Navy | 4728 | 270 |
| but not for disability prior to August 31, 1842 | 4728 | 270 |
| to their widows and children in case of death | 4729 | 270 |
| rates governed by pay as it existed January, 1835 | 4729 | 290 |
| but varied after 25th July, 1866 | 4729 | 270 |
| table of rates for total disability of officers | | 271 |
| for specific disabilities | | 271 |
| for disabilities not specified by law | | 272 |
| for twenty years' service in Navy or Marine Corps | 4756 | 273 |
| in lieu of home in the Naval Asylum | 4756 | 273 |
| equal to one-half of pay of rating when discharged | 4756 | 273 |
| for ten years' service in Navy or Marine Corps | 4757 | 273 |
| not to exceed rate for full disability | 4757 | 273 |
| to be paid from the naval pension fund | 4752 | 273 |
| PENSION FUND (Navy)— | | |
| Secretary of the Navy to be the trustee of | 4750 | 272 |
| fines and penalties for cutting timber to go to credit of | 4751 | 272 |
| power of the Secretary to mitigate fines | 4751 | 272 |
| to be invested in registered securities semi-annually | 4753 | 273 |
| interest payable semi-annually in coin to the Secretary of the Navy | 4753 | 273 |
| which may be exchanged for currency | 4753 | 273 |
| to be at the rate of 3 per cent. per annum, lawful money | 4754 | 273 |
| pensions to be paid from, upon appropriations by Congress | 4755 | 273 |
| to be used for paying service pensions | 4756, 4757 | 273 |
| moneys accruing to the United States from prizes to be placed to credit of | 4752 | 273 |
| for the payment of pensions | 4752 | 273 |

INDEX. 373

|  | Sec. | Page. |
|---|---|---|
| PENSION FUND (privateer)— | | |
| Secretary of the Navy to be trustee of | 4758 | 274 |
| provisions of law concerning | 4759–5763 | 274 |
| PERIODICALS— | | |
| restriction on purchase of | 1779 | 162 |
| PERJURY— | | |
| committing, to secure payment of claims | 14 | 11 |
| committed before naval general courts-martial | 1023 | 275 |
| for the purpose of obtaining allowances, claims, &c | 1624 | 275 |
| by statements under oath, knowing them to be untrue | 5392 | 275 |
| penalty, imprisonment, fine, and incapacity for office | 5392 | 275 |
| procuring others to commit, guilty of subornation of perjury | 5393 | 275 |
| and punishable in same manner as perjury | 5393 | 275 |
| forms of indictment, sufficiency and manner of presenting | 5396 | 275 |
| presentments or indictments for subornation of | 5397 | 275 |
| PERMANENT APPROPRIATIONS— | | |
| what to be considered | 3689 | 134 |
| PERSONAL EFFECTS— | | |
| compensation to crews for loss of | 288 | 128 |
| to officers for loss of | 289 | 128 |
| of seamen on board of merchant vessels, deceased | 4538, 4539 | 242 |
| penalty for violating law of requirements | 4540 | 243 |
| of seamen dying in foreign ports, consul to take care of | 4541 | 243 |
| PERSONAL SERVICES— | | |
| advertisement for contracts for, not required | 3709 | 130 |
| PETTY OFFICERS. (See SEAMEN.) | | |
| PHYSICS— | | |
| assistant professor of, at the Naval Academy | | 54 |
| PICKLES— | | |
| allowance of, in Navy ration | 1580 | 83 |
| how procured | 3726 | 84 |
| PILLORY— | | |
| standing in, as a punishment not to be inflicted | 5327 | 254 |
| jurisdiction of State courts not impaired | 5328 | 254 |
| PILOTAGE— | | |
| estimates for, to be in detail | 3666 | 132 |
| to be regulated by State laws | 4235 | 279 |
| employment of pilots on State boundaries | 4236 | 279 |
| discrimination not to be made in vessels between different States | 4237 | 279 |
| nor against vessels propelled in whole or in part by steam | 4237 | 279 |
| nor against national vessels | 4237 | 279 |
| Government vessels not bound to take pilots (notes) | | 279 |
| PIRACY— | | |
| what courts have jurisdiction of offenses | 563 | 276 |
| acts of, defined, and penalty prescribed | 4293–4296 | 276 |
| | 5323, 5324 | 277 |
| | 5368–5384 | 277–9 |
| accessories after the fact, how punished | 5533 | 279 |
| public vessels may be authorized to seize persons engaged in | 4298 | 277 |
| custom-house officers, &c., to proceed against vessels fitted for | 4299 | 277 |
| definition of, opinions, &c., (notes) | | 277 |
| PLANS— | | |
| of buildings, &c., expense of changing, not to be paid without authority of Congress | | 196 |

|   | Sec. | Page. |
|---|---|---|
| PLANS—Continued. | | |
| to accompany estimates for buildings | 3663 | 131 |
| to be approved by the Secretary of the Treasury, &c | 3734 | 192 |
| of yachts may be copied by naval architects | 4215 | 253 |
| PLEDGE— | | |
| by soldiers of clothing, accouterments, &c., forbidden | 3748 | 194 |
| of public property by persons in custody thereof | 5438 | 195 |
| by persons in naval or military service of supplies, &c | 5438 | 195 |
| PLUNDERING— | | |
| and abusing inhabitants on shore | 8 | 10 |
| POLICE DUTIES— | | |
| extra, as punishment | 30 | 15 |
| POISONING— | | |
| of persons within the jurisdiction of the United States | 5339 | 254 |
| POLITICAL PURPOSES— | | |
| contributions for, prohibited in the Government service. August 15, 1876 | | 209 |
| promotion or degradation for, not allowed. January 16, 1883 | | 209 |
| POLITICAL FUND— | | |
| persons in civil service not required to contribute to. January 16, 1883 | | 141 |
| nor to render any political service | | 141 |
| failing to do either not to work removal or prejudice | | 141 |
| POLLS— | | |
| troops not to be brought to the | 2002, 5528 | 20-1 |
| except to repel enemies of the United States | 2002, 5528 | 20-1 |
| PORK (salt)— | | |
| allowance of, in Navy rations | 1580 | 83 |
| PORTRAITS— | | |
| impressions from, may be furnished by Bureau of Engraving | | 188 |
| PORT ROYAL HARBOR— | | |
| erection of coaling dock and warehouse | | 60 |
| POST TRADERS— | | |
| appointment of, in the Marine Corps. July 24, 1876 | | 111 |
| POSTAL CARDS. (*See* POSTAGE.) | | |
| POSTAGE (Navy)— | | |
| estimates for, to be in detail | 3666 | 131 |
| POSTAGE (mail matter)— | | |
| rates of foreign, not embraced in postal convention | 3912 | 280 |
| in vessels not regularly employed to carry mail | 3913 | 280 |
| vessels in merchant service to receive mails | 3976 | 280 |
| rates of postage allowed | 3976 | 280 |
| domestic, division into classes. March 3, 1879 | | 280 |
| postal cards, transmission of, through the mail | | 280 |
| issue of double, authorized | | 283 |
| letters of soldiers and sailors, provision for transmitting | | 280 |
| mailable matter of second class defined | | 280 |
| of third and fourth classes defined | | 281 |
| "circular" and "printed matter" defined | | 281 |
| on matter of first class, two cents half an ounce | | 281 |
| one full rate paid, matter to be forwarded | | 281 |
| Department stamps, how to be procured | | 281 |
| for what purposes they can be used (notes) | | 282 |
| penalty envelopes to bear certain indorsements | | 282 |

|  | Sec. | Page. |
|---|---|---|
| POSTAGE (mail matter)—Continued. | | |
|     for what purposes they can be used | | 282 |
|     letter-sheet envelopes, issue of, authorized | | 283 |
|     money orders, laws relative to | 4033–4040 | 283–4 |
|         in what sums issued, and fees | | 284 |
|     postal notes, regulations as to issue and use | | 284 |
| POTATOES (desiccated)— | | |
|     allowance in Navy ration | 1580 | 83 |
|     substitution of desiccated tomatoes for | | 84 |
| POUND STERLING— | | |
|     value of, in payments | 3565 | 177 |
| POWERS OF ATTORNEY— | | |
|     for assignment of wages, prize money, &c., attestation of | 1430–1576–4643 | 92, 93, 315 |
|         assigning claims, &c., how made and attested | 3477 | 153 |
|         falsely making, altering, &c | 5421–22 | 226 |
|         using, to secure wages, &c | 5436 | 227 |
| PRECEDENCE— | | |
|     of commanding officers | 1468 | 79 |
|     of aid or executive to commanding officer | 1469 | 79 |
|     of officers in processions, on courts, &c | 1489 | 81 |
|     between officers of Army and Marine Corps co-operating | 1342 | 107 |
| PREMIUMS— | | |
|     from sale of drafts or checks to be accounted for | 3652 | 174 |
|     for recruiting, estimates for, to be in detail | 3666 | 132 |
| PRESENTS (from foreign governments)— | | |
|     to be tendered through Department of State. January 21, 1881 | | 21 |
|     not to be accepted without authority of Congress. January 21, 1881 | | 21 |
|         nor publicly shown or exposed upon the person receiving them | | 21 |
| PRESENTS— | | |
|     to superiors, contributions for, not to be solicited | 1784 | 208 |
|     superiors not to receive, from subordinates | 1784 | 208 |
| PRESERVED MEATS— | | |
|     allowance of, in Navy rations | 1580 | 83 |
|     how they may be procured | 3726 | 84 |
| PRISONERS— | | |
|     master-at-arms neglecting duty as to, or allowing escape of | 8 | 10 |
|     pay of marines, to continue during captivity | 1288 | 119 |
|         to cease when paroled | 1288 | 119 |
|     allowing, in custody under law to escape | 5409 | 225 |
| PRIVATEER PENSION FUND. (*See* PENSION FUND.) | | |
| PRIZE— | | |
|     attempts to defraud in matters of | 5441 | 228 |
|     vessels condemned as, entitled to register | 4132 | 248 |
|     money accrued to United States from proceeds of, to go to pension fund | 4752 | 273 |
|     provisions of law relative to | 4613–5441 | 285–92 |
| PRIZE-MONEY— | | |
|     commanding officers to discourage sale of, by men | 1430 | 92 |
|         when to attest powers of attorney | 1430 | 92 |
|     assignments of, by men, to be attested by commanding officer | 4643 | 315 |
|     attempting to obtain, by false papers | 5436 | 227 |
|     appropriation for payment of, to captors | 3689 | 134 |

|  | Sec. | Page. |
|---|---|---|
| PRIZE LISTS— | | |
| commanding officers to transmit | 15 | 12 |
| PRIZE VESSELS (*see also* PRIZE)— | | |
| property not to be removed from, until adjudged as prize | 16 | 12 |
| crews of, not to be pillaged nor maltreated | 17 | 12 |
| PROCEEDINGS— | | |
| of courts and boards to be sent to the Judge-Advocate-General (foot-note) | | 16 |
| of summary courts, how conducted | 34 | 15 |
| of general courts-martial, suspension of | 45 | 17 |
| authentication of | 52 | 17 |
| revision of | 54 | 18 |
| party interested entitled to copy of (note) | | 18 |
| of courts of inquiry, authentication of | 60 | 19 |
| parties not entitled to copy of, as a right (note) | | 19 |
| opinions and decisions on (notes) | | 19 |
| PROFANE SWEARING— | | |
| punishment for | 8 | 9 |
| PROFESSORS (civil)— | | |
| at Naval Academy, pay of | | 54 |
| PROFESSORS OF MATHEMATICS— | | |
| superintendency of Nautical Almanac may be placed under | 436 | 73 |
| to receive shore-duty pay of grade | 436 | 73 |
| number not to exceed twelve | 1399 | 73 |
| appointed by the President, with the advice of the Senate | 1400 | 73 |
| after examination. January 20, 1881 | | 74 |
| to perform such duties as Secretary may assign | 1401 | 73 |
| relative rank of, on the active list | 1480 | 73 |
| when retired from age or length of service | 1481 | 73 |
| pay of, on the active list | 1556 | 74 |
| on the retired list | 1588 | 70 |
| assignment of, as professors at the Naval Academy | 1528 | 74 |
| PROMOTION— | | |
| pay of officers on, commencement of increase | 1561 | 68 |
| of seamen for heroism | 1407 | 74 |
| medal and gratuity allowed | 1407 | 74 |
| officers not recommended for, to be retired | 1447 | 74 |
| unless for immoral conduct, &c., then to be dismissed. August 5, 1882 | | 76 |
| of officer next in rank, in case of vacancy from retirement | 1458 | 74 |
| to only one-half of vacancies in line, until number is reduced. August 5, 1882 | | 74 |
| same in staff corps. March 3, 1883 | | 75 |
| physical examination and qualification before | 1493 | 75 |
| exception in case of wounded officers | 1494 | 75 |
| to grade limited in number, when entitled to increased pay | 1495 | 75 |
| mental, moral, and professional examination before | 1496 | 75 |
| of commodores to rear-admirals, in time of peace | 1497 | 75 |
| examining board to be senior in rank to officer examined | 1498 | 75 |
| power to take testimony | 1499 | 75 |
| and to swear witnesses | 1499 | 75 |
| facts prior to last examination not to be inquired into | | 75 |
| unless continuing fact shows unfitness | | 75 |

INDEX. 377

| | Sec. | Page. |
|---|---|---|
| PROMOTION—Continued. | | |
|     re-examination in cases where this provision is violated | | 76 |
|     right of officer examined to be present | 1500 | 76 |
|         his statement, testimony of witnesses, and examination to be recorded | 1501 | 76 |
|     record and finding of board to be presented to President | 1502 | 76 |
|         with matter from the files on which judgment is based | 1502 | 76 |
|     no rejection for, until after public examination | 1503 | 76 |
|         unless on failure of candidate to appear | 1503 | 76 |
|     form of report or recommendation of board | 1504 | 76 |
|     suspension for one year of officers, below grade of commander, not professionally qualified | 1505 | 76 |
|         with corresponding loss of date | 1505 | 76 |
|         dropped on failing on re-examination | 1505 | 76 |
|     rejected, on account of drunkenness or misconduct, to be dropped. August 5, 1882 | | 76 |
|         with not more than one year's pay. August 5, 1882 | | 76 |
|     advancement for conspicuous conduct in battle authorized | 1506 | 77 |
|         although grade may be full | 1507 | 77 |
|     advancement on receiving vote of thanks | 1508 | 77 |
|         vacancy from retirement or death of such, not to be filled | 1509 | 77 |
|         to affect such officer only | 1509 | 77 |
|         retention on active list not to interfere with promotion of others | 1509 | 77 |
|     commencement of pay of officers promoted in regular order | 1561 | 77 |
|         or absent when entitled to examination | 1562 | 78 |
|         rank to which entitled | 1372 | 78 |
|     of marine officers for gallantry | 1605 | 109 |
|         or on receiving vote of thanks | 1607 | 109 |
| PROPERTY (*see also* DERELICT)— | | |
|     wrecked and derelict, disposition of | | 313 |
|     on shore, plundering or injuring | 8 | 10 |
| PROPOSALS. (*See* CONTRACTS.) | | |
| PROTECTION— | | |
|     of American citizens in foreign countries | 2001 | 222 |
| PROVISIONS— | | |
|     wasting or permitting waste of | 8 | 10 |
|     inspection of, to made by commanding officer | 20 | 13 |
|     precautions for preservation of, to be taken | 20 | 13 |
|     for the Navy, how procured | 3718 | 25 |
|     to be furnished naval detachments co-operating with Army | 1135 | 107 |
| PROVISIONS AND CLOTHING (Bureau)— | | |
|     chief to be a paymaster of not less than ten years' standing | 425 | 61 |
|         to have rank of commodore and title of Paymaster-General | 1471 | 63 |
|         pay of | 1565 | 182 |
|         rank when retired | 1473 | 182 |
|         serving full term, exempt from sea duty except during war | 1436 | 182 |
|     civil employés allowed in | | 183 |
| PROVOKING WORDS— | | |
|     use of, in the Navy | 8 | 10 |
| PUBLIC BUILDINGS (*see also* PUBLIC PROPERTY, BUILDINGS, &c.)— | | |
|     not to be commenced without full plans and estimates | 3734 | 28 |
|         cost not to exceed estimates | 3734 | 28 |

378  INDEX.

|  | Sec. | Page. |
|---|---|---|
| BUBLIC BUILDINGS—Continued. | | |
|     not to be erected or repaired, &c., at greater cost than appropriation | 5503 | 31 |
|     rent of, in the District of Columbia | | 31 |
|     extra compensation for disbursing appropriations for | 3654 | 72 |
| PUBLIC DOCUMENTS (*see also* PUBLIC PRINTING)— | | |
|     annual reports to be furnished Public Printer by 1st November | 196 | 185 |
|     Opinions of Attorney-General to be edited and printed | 383 | 185 |
|         distribution of same | | 185 |
|     Secretary of the Interior charged with custody of | 497 | 185 |
|         distribution of, by him | 500, 505 | 185 |
|     Congressional Directory, to be printed | 77, 3801 | 188 |
|     Biennial Register, preparing and printing of | 510 | 188 |
|     extra copies of, may be furnished by Public Printer | 3809 | 187 |
|     may be bound, at cost, by Public Printer, for Congressmen | | 187 |
| PUBLIC PRINTING AND BINDING— | | |
|     Public Printer to purchase all materials, &c., necessary for | 3760 | 185 |
|         to take charge of all matter, &c | 3760 | 185 |
|         may purchase in open market, under special authority | 3778 | 186 |
|             amount restricted. February 1, 1878 | | 186 |
|         to procure the engraving and lithographing for charts, maps, &c | 3779 | 186 |
|             after advertisement and contract, if over $1,200 | 3780 | 186 |
|         may make immediate contracts, in exigencies, &c | 3780 | 186 |
|     not otherwise provided for by law, to be done by Government Printer | 3786 | 186 |
|     bureaus or offices restricted in printing their reports | 3788 | 186 |
|     to be executed only on written requisitions | 3789 | 186 |
|     form and style, to be determined by Public Printer | 3790 | 186 |
|     Public Printer to keep an account of all | 3802 | 186 |
|         not to print in excess of the appropriation | 3802 | 187 |
|     style of binding specifically indicated, June 20, 1878 | | 187 |
|     estimates for, to be furnished by Public Printer. June 20, 1878 | | 187 |
|     cost of printing to be placed to debit of Department. June 20, 1878 | | 187 |
|     certificate of head of Department, as to necessity of, June 20, 1878 | | 187 |
|     Public Printer to do binding at cost, on application of Congressmen, December 10, 1877 | | 187 |
|         may furnish extra documents at cost and 10 per cent. added | 3809 | 187 |
|     annual reports to be furnished to Congress at first meeting | 3810 | 187 |
|     accounts of, to be rendered to Secretary of Treasury quarterly | 3815 | 187 |
|     condition of, to be reported to Congress at opening | 3821 | 187 |
|     impressions from vignettes and portraits by Bureau Engraving | | 188 |
|     sale of Nautical Almanac, proceeds to go to appropriation for | | 50 |
| PUBLIC PROPERTY— | | |
|     unlawfully destroying, punishment for | 4 | 8 |
|     not preventing unlawful destruction of | 8 | 10 |
|     wasting or permitting waste of | 8 | 10 |
|     delivering less than named in receipt | 14 | 11 |
|     false certificate as to receipt of | 14 | 11 |
|     misappropriating or wrongfully selling | 14 | 11 |
|     purchasing, from parties not authorized to sell | 14 | 11 |
|     cannot be alienated by officers (decision) | | 314 |

INDEX. 379

| | Sec. | Page. |
|---|---|---|
| PUBLIC PROPERTY, BUILDINGS, AND GROUNDS— | | |
|     no expenditures for, until validity of title is established | 355 | 192 |
|         nor until consent of legislature is obtained | 355 | 192 |
|         district attorneys to assist in examining titles | 355 | 192 |
|         heads of Departments to furnish evidence of titles | 355 | 192 |
|             expenses of procuring, payable from contingent | 355 | 192 |
|     assent of legislature to purchase of lands to be procured | 1838 | 192 |
|     contracts for buildings, &c., not to exceed appropriations | 3733, 5503 | 192 |
|         penalty for violation of this provision | 5503 | 192 |
|     land not to be purchased without authority of law | 736 | 192 |
|     decisions, &c., on purchase of lands (notes) | | 192–3 |
|     inventory of public property to be kept | 197 | 193 |
|         additions to, and sales, &c., to be noted | 197 | 193 |
|         of stores in the navy-yards to be taken | | 197 |
|     willfully stranding vessels, injuring equipment, &c. Article 4 | 1624 | 193 |
|     unlawfully destroying public property. Article 4 | 1624 | 194 |
|     stealing, embezzling, &c., public property, March 3, 1875 | | 194 |
|     purchasing, &c., from persons unauthorized to sell, March 3, 1875 | | 194 |
|     selling, by soldiers, of clothing, &c., furnished them | 3748 | 194 |
|         or receiving or having possession of same | 3748 | 194 |
|     arson of dwellings within forts, &c | 5385 | 195 |
|         armories, arsenals, &c | 5386 | 195 |
|         of vessels of Navy, equipments, &c | 5387 | 195 |
|     concealing, selling, and pledging public property | 5438 | 195 |
|     exacting receipts for more than delivered, &c | 5438 | 195 |
|     embezzling arms, stoves, ammunition, &c | 5439 | 195 |
|     robbery of personal property belonging to the United States | 5456 | 195 |
|     water in public buildings, not to be wasted | | 196 |
|     drawings and specifications required, before commencing buildings | | 196 |
|         appropriations to be within the limits of the law | | 196 |
|         expenses in change of plan, not allowed without authority of Congress | | 196 |
|     vessels, sale of, by direction of the President | 1540 | 197 |
|         by the Secretary of the Navy | 1541 | 197 |
|         stricken from register, after appraisement | | 197 |
|     old material, sale of, disposition of proceeds | 1541, 3617, 3618 | 197–8 |
|         detailed statement to be in book of estimates | 3672 | 198 |
|         report of, to be made in annual report. August 5, 1882 | | 197 |
|     ordnance condemned, sale of, &c. March 3, 1878 | | 198 |
|     issue of arms by Secretary of War, to protect. March 1, 1879 | | 306 |
| PUBLIC OR DEPARTMENT RECORDS— | | |
|     fees for copying, in Department of State | 213 | 189 |
|     copies from, under seal, admitted as evidence | 882 | 189 |
|     in office of Solicitor of Treasury, evidence | 883 | 190 |
|     transcripts from, in Treasury Department in case of suits, under seal, evidence | 886 | 190 |
|         when originals may be required | 886 | 190 |
|     trial for embezzlement, transcript from books of Treasury sufficient | 887 | 190 |
|     copies of returns in Returns office, admitted as evidence | 888 | 190 |
|     copies of consular records, under seal, evidence | 896 | 190 |

# 380 INDEX.

|  | Sec. | Page. |
|---|---|---|
| PUBLIC OR DEPARTMENT RECORDS—Continued. | | |
|     willfully destroying, punishable by fine and imprisonment | 5403 | 191 |
|         or taking or carry away unlawfully, punishable by fine and imprisonment | 5403 | 191 |
|     custodians of, willfully destroying, &c., punishment prescribed | 5408 | 191 |
|     decisions and opinions regarding (notes) | | 189 |
| PUBLIC WORSHIP— | | |
|     conducted by chaplain according to form of church of which a member | 1397 | 22 |
| PUNISHMENT— | | |
|     by order of commanding officer | 24 | 14 |
|     for offenses not specified | 22 | 13 |
|     for offenses committed on shore | 23 | 14 |
|     by officer temporarily commanding | 25 | 14 |
|     by general courts-martial | 35 | 15 |
|     by summary courts-martial | 30 | 14 |
|     corporal and pecuniary, adjudged, remission or pardon of either | 5330 | 254 |

## Q.

|  | Sec. | Page. |
|---|---|---|
| QUARANTINE— | | |
|     estimates for expenses of, to be in detail, by the Secretary of the Navy | 3666 | 132 |
|     expenses of vessels of the Navy in foreign ports, estimates to be in detail | 3666 | 132 |
|         expenditures to be accounted for | 3666 | 132 |
|     restraints established by State laws to be observed | 4792 | 292 |
|     refrigerating or disinfecting ship for purposes of. April 18, 1879 | | 292 |
|     hulks for, to be furnished by Secretary of the Navy. June 14, 1879 | | 292 |
|     contagious diseases and vessels from infected ports. June 2, 1879 | | 293 |
|     detail of medical officers for service at foreign ports | | 293 |
|         officers from the Departments for National Board of Health | | 292 |
|         no extra compensation allowed | | 293 |
| QUARRELING— | | |
|     with persons in the Navy, punishment for | 8 | 10 |
|     or fomenting quarrels between persons | 8 | 10 |
| QUARTERS— | | |
|     pusillanimously crying for, in battle, how punished | 4 | 8 |
| QUARTERS (of Marine Corps)— | | |
|     allowance to officers | 1270 | 120 |
|     may be procured without adequate appropriation | 3732 | 28 |
|     the terms pay and emoluments include (notes) | | 61 |

## R.

|  | Sec. | Page. |
|---|---|---|
| RACE— | | |
|     persons not to be deprived of rights, on account of | 5510 | 20 |
| RAILROADS— | | |
|     inter-State communication by | 5258 | 294 |
|     withholding of payments from land-grant | 5260 | 294 |
|         companies may bring suit | 5261 | 294 |
| RANK— | | |
|     members of general courts-martial to take place according to | 39 | 16 |
|     of officers not to be changed by benefit of continuous service, March 3, 1883 | | 21 |
|     nor except under authority of law | 1506 | 82 |

INDEX. 381

|  | Sec. | Page. |
|---|---|---|
| RANK—Continued. | | |
| of chief engineers | 1390–1476 | 37–8 |
| of passed assistant engineers | 1390–1476 | 37–8 |
| assistant engineers | 1390–1476 | 37–8 |
| of chief of Bureau of Steam Engineering | 1471 | 38 |
| of engineers retired from age or length of service | 1481 | 38 |
| of assistant surgeons, absent when entitled to examination | 1372 | 48 |
| of line officers, in grades | 1362 | 45 |
| of junior lieutenants and junior ensigns. March 3, 1883 | | 46 |
| of secretary to admiral and vice-admiral | 1367 | 46 |
| relative, between officers of the Army and Navy | 1466 | 78 |
| of line officers according to date of commission | 1467 | 79 |
| commanding officers to take precedence in | 1468 | 79 |
| of aid or executive | 1469 | 79 |
| rights of staff officers, senior | 1470 | 79 |
| relative, of chiefs of bureaus | 1471 | 79 |
| of line officer, chief of bureau, below grade of commodore | 1472 | 79 |
| of officers retired from staff bureaus, from age, &c | 1473 | 79 |
| of staff corps on the active list | 1476–1480 | 79–80 |
| serving faithfully forty-five years, when retired | 1481 | 80 |
| or when retired at age of sixty-two years after forty-five years' service | 1481 | 80 |
| retired from causes incident to the service | 1482 | 81 |
| of graduates at Academy | 1483, 1484, 1521 | 81–82 |
| relative, of staff corps, according to length of service | 1485 | 81 |
| in what manner estimated | 1486 | 81 |
| of staff officers gives no additional right to quarters | 1487 | 81 |
| nor to exercise military command | 1488 | 81 |
| precedence according to, in processions on shore, courts, &c | 1489 | 81 |
| assimilated, President may give to warrant officers | 1491 | 81 |
| of officers of revenue-cutter service co-operating with Navy | 1492 | 81 |
| of commandant of the Marine Corps | 1601 | 82 |
| adjutant, paymaster, and quartermaster | 1602 | 82 |
| of officers of Marine Corps same as similar grades in the Army | 1603 | 82 |
| of Judge-Advocate-General of the Navy | | 82 |
| RANSOM— | | |
| money distributable in same manner as prize | 4642 | 290 |
| RAPE— | | |
| within forts, arsenals, &c., punishable by death | 5345 | 255 |
| RATES— | | |
| of vessels of the Navy for commands | 1529 | 94 |
| RATING— | | |
| of all persons on board ship to be entered on books | 20 | 12 |
| reduction of, by commanding officer | 24 | 14 |
| by summary court | 30 | 15 |
| of seamen as mates, not to discharge from enlistment | 1409 | 102 |
| RATIONS— | | |
| to Navy and Marine Corps co-operating with Army | 1143 | 82 |
| midshipmen and naval cadets entitled to | 1577 | 82 |
| officers at sea, or attached to sea-going vessels, entitled to | 1578 | 83 |
| not so attached, and doing duty, not allowed | 1579 | 83 |
| except ensigns of junior grade and cadets | 1579 | 83 |
| and petty officers, seamen, &c | 1579 | 83 |

|  | Sec. | Page. |
|---|---|---|
| RATIONS—Continued. | | |
| constituents of the Navy ration | 1580 | 83 |
| substitution for component parts when necessary | 1581 | 83 |
| of extract of coffee, for coffee and sugar, | 1581 | 83 |
| if acceptable to the men | 1581 | 83 |
| of desiccated tomatoes for desiccated potatoes | | 84 |
| diminution of daily allowance, when necessary | 1582 | 83 |
| written orders to be given therefor, and report made | 1582 | 83 |
| stopped for the sick to be accounted for by paymaster | 1583 | 83 |
| additional, of tea or coffee and sugar, at first "turning out" | 1584 | 83 |
| thirty cents commutation price of | 1585 | 83 |
| not allowed to retired officers | 1595 | 83 |
| personnel of Marine Corps entitled to | 1615 | 83 |
| duration of contracts for certain articles for, extended | 3721 | 84 |
| preserved meats, pickles, butter, and desiccated vegetables for, procurement of | 3726 | 84 |
| purchase of flour and baking of bread for | 3727 | 84 |
| deduction of, for naval hospitals from patients therein | 4812 | 84 |
| marine officers attached to sea-going vessels not entitled to (decision) | | 314 |
| to officers of the Revenue Marine | 2755–6 | 300 |
| REAR-ADMIRALS (see ADMIRALS, Rear)— | | |
| pay of, on the active list | 1556 | 65 |
| retired as captains and subsequently promoted | 1589 | 70 |
| on the retired list | 1588 | 70 |
| REBELS— | | |
| intercourse with, how punishable | 4 | 8 |
| receiving letters or messages from | 4 | 8 |
| REBELLION— | | |
| certain persons who engaged in, ineligible to office | 1786 | 150 |
| Congress may remove disability (note) | | 150 |
| claims of persons who engaged in, not to be allowed | 3480 | 154 |
| time for serving process not included in time engaged in | 1048 | 201 |
| American vessels taking foreign flag during, not entitled to register | 4135 | 248 |
| provisions of law in relation to | 1642–5519 | 306–10 |
| RECAPTURED— | | |
| property of the United States (notes) | 4652 | 291 |
| RECEIPTS— | | |
| giving false or fraudulent | 14 | 11 |
| false receipts and papers to defraud the United States | 5418–5479 | 227–8 |
| RECEIPTS AND EXPENDITURES— | | |
| for naval service, Secretary of Treasury to submit annual report to Congress | | 135 |
| with statement of balances in hands of disbursing officers | | 135 |
| RECORDER— | | |
| of summary courts, any officer may be ordered to act as | 27 | 14 |
| RECORDS. (See PUBLIC RECORDS AND EVIDENCE.) | | |
| RECORD OF COURT MARTIAL— | | |
| persons interested entitled to copy (note) | | 18 |
| of court of inquiry, party not entitled to, as a right (note) | | 19 |
| RECRUITING— | | |
| premium for and expenses of, estimates to be in detail | 3666 | 132 |
| expenditures to be accounted for by Bureau | 3666 | 132 |

|  | Sec. | Page. |
|---|---|---|
| REDUCTION— | | |
| to rating of ordinary seaman, of officers absent from command without leave | 9 | 10 |
| RE-ENLISTMENT— | | |
| pay on, under honorable discharge | 1573 | 69 |
| pay of marines upon | 1281 | 118 |
| one dollar per month retained | 1282 | 118 |
| forfeited, unless serving faithfully until discharged | 1282 | 118 |
| REINSTATEMENT— | | |
| opinions and decisions relating to (notes) | | 104 |
| RELIEF— | | |
| failing to afford, in battle | 4 | 9 |
| of destitute seamen | 4577–8 | 245 |
| REGULATIONS— | | |
| refusing obedience to any lawful | 8 | 10 |
| orders, instructions, &c., recognized as | 1547 | 19 |
| definition and force of (notes) | | 19 |
| copy to be furnished each officer entering the service | 1548 | 20 |
| (of a Department) definition and force of (notes) | | 19 |
| President may prescribe military, for Marine Corps | 1620 | 111 |
| for the Executive Departments | | 145 |
| REMISSION— | | |
| of sentence of summary court-martial | 33 | 15 |
| of general court-martial | 54 | 18 |
| decisions concerning (notes) | | 18 |
| of either corporal or pecuniary punishment, where both are adjudged | 5330 | 254 |
| RENT— | | |
| of buildings in District of Columbia, by Government | | 31 |
| estimates for, to be in detail | 3666 | 131 |
| REPORTS— | | |
| penalty for failing to make, to Congress, as required | 1780 | 162 |
| REPRIMAND— | | |
| punishment by, not to be entered on ship's log | 24 | 14 |
| REPROACHFUL WORDS— | | |
| punishment for using, in the Navy | 8 | 10 |
| RESERVATIONS— | | |
| relinquishment of, on contracts | 3730 | 27 |
| RESERVED TIMBER-LANDS— | | |
| examination of, in Florida | | 312 |
| for live oak and cedar timber for the Navy | 2458 | 296 |
| appointment of surveyors, to select | 2459 | 297 |
| selections, reserved from public sale | 2459 | 297 |
| employment of naval force to prevent depredations upon | 2460 | 297 |
| penalty for cutting, destroying, and removing timber from | 2461 | 297 |
| forfeiture of vessel unlawfully engaged in transporting timber from | 2462 | 297 |
| before clearing vessels, collectors to ascertain character of timber | 2463, 4205 | 297–8 |
| and to cause prosecutions to be instituted | 2463 | 297 |
| land officers to cause prosecutions | 2463 | 297 |
| fines and penalties, to go to pension fund | 4751 | 273 |
| unlawfully cutting timber on any land of the United States | 5388 | 298 |
| or wantonly destroying or injuring same | | 298 |
| if exported, liable to seizure wherever found | | 298 |

|  | Sec. | Page. |
|---|---|---|
| RESERVED TIMBER-LANDS—Continued. | | |
|  moneys for depredations to be covered into the Treasury (see note) | | 298 |
| RESIGNATION— | | |
|  quitting post before acceptance of, desertion | 10 | 10 |
|  officer accepting appointment in diplomatic or consular service considered a | 1440 | 19 |
|  to escape dismissal by sentence of court-martial, a bar to restoration | 1441 | 35 |
|  opinions and decisions concerning (notes) | | 36 |
| RESOLUTIONS— | | |
|  of Congress, enacting clause prescribed | | 199 |
| RETIRED— | | |
|  officers cannot act as agents or counsel for claims against the Government (decision) | | 314 |
| RETURNS OFFICE— | | |
|  copies of contracts to be filed in | 3744 | 29 |
|  preservation of same | 512–514 | 30 |
|  copies may be furnished on payment therefor | 515 | 30 |
| RETIREMENT— | | |
|  after forty years' service, on own application | 1443 | 84 |
|  after sixty-two years of age, if below grade of vice-admiral | 1444 | 84 |
|   not applicable to certain junior grades | 1445 | 85 |
|    who are to be retired for physical or mental disability only | 1445 | 85 |
|  after fifty-five years' service, on receiving a vote of thanks | 1446 | 85 |
|   and if not below the grade of commander | 1446 | 85 |
|  when not recommended for promotion by both Boards | 1447 | 85 |
|  not authorized for misconduct and drunkenness. August 5, 1882 | 1456 | 85–6 |
|   but to be discharged with not more than a year's pay | | 85 |
|  inability to comply with orders, officer to go before Board for | 1448 | 85 |
|   or if incapacitated in judgment of the President | 1448 | 85 |
|  composition of the Retiring Board | 1448 | 85 |
|   its powers and duties | 1449 | 85 |
|   oath of members | 1450 | 85 |
|   to report cause of incapacity | 1451 | 85 |
|   record and decision to be laid before the President | 1452 | 85 |
|  incapacity, result of incident to the service, retired pay allowed | 1453 | 86 |
|   when not an incident, furlough pay | 1454 | 86 |
|    or wholly retired with one year's pay | 1454 | 86 |
|  officer to have a full and fair hearing before | 1455 | 86 |
|   unless retired at own request | 1455 | 86 |
|    or from length of service | 1455 | 86 |
|    or from failing in examination | 1455 | 86 |
|  after, to be placed on retired list of grade to which belonging | 1457 | 86 |
|   to be continued on the Register | 1457 | 86 |
|   to be entitled to wear the uniform | 1457 | 86 |
|   to be subject to regulations, &c | 1457 | 86 |
|   to be withdrawn from command, except in case of war | 1459 | 86 |
|   not to be employed on active duty except in time of war | 1462 | 86 |
|   in time of war, may be assigned commands | 1463 | 86 |
|    with rank and title of flag officer | 1464 | 87 |
|    and receive obedience from older commissions | 1464 | 87 |
|    and may be restored to active list, on vote of thanks | 1465 | 87 |
|   not entitled to rations | 1595 | 88 |

INDEX. 385

| | Sec. | Page. |
|---|---|---|
| RETIREMENT—Continued. | | |
| no promotion nor increased pay after August 5, 1882 | | 88 |
| wholly retired to be omitted from Register | 1457 | 86 |
| filling vacancies caused by | 1458 | 86 |
| rank of chiefs of staff bureaus on retirement | 1473 | 87 |
| of staff corps retired from age or length of service | 1481 | 87 |
| retired from causes incident to the service | 1482 | 87 |
| pay of officers when retired | 1588 | 87 |
| rear-admirals retired as captains | 1589 | 87 |
| officers retired as third assistant engineers | 1590 | 87 |
| retired officers on active duty | 1592 | 88 |
| retired on furlough | 1593 | 88 |
| transfer from furlough to retired pay-list | 1594 | 88 |
| of warrant officers (decision) | | 314 |
| RETIREMENT (Marine Corps)— | | |
| to be in like cases and conditions as the Army | 1622 | 111 |
| except in formation of the Board | 1622 | 111 |
| selection and composition of the Board | 1623 | 111 |
| after forty years' consecutive service as a commissioned officer, on application | 1243 | 112 |
| thirty years in the service, on own application | 1243 | 112 |
| after forty years' service as officer or soldier, or both, on own application. June 30, 1882 | | 112 |
| after sixty-four years of age, compulsory. June 30, 1882 | | 112 |
| explanatory of the above. March 3, 1883 | | 112 |
| from active service, when incapacitated for duty | 1245 | 112 |
| or wholly retired, as President may direct | 1245 | 112 |
| powers and duties of Board for | 1247–1252 | 112–3 |
| officer to have a full and fair hearing | 1253 | 113 |
| to be retired on actual rank | 1254 | 113 |
| exceptions made. March 3, 1875 | | 113 |
| to be withdrawn from command and promotion after | 1255 | 113 |
| to be entitled to wear uniform of rank | 1256 | 113 |
| to be continued on the Register | 1256 | 113 |
| to be subject to articles of war and to trial | 1256 | 113 |
| vacancies caused by, to be filled by next officer in rank | 1257 | 113 |
| pay of retired officers | 1274 | 113 |
| of officers wholly retired | 1275 | 113 |
| rank and pay under certain conditions of. March 3, 1875 | | 113 |
| opinions and decisions | | 114, 314 |
| REVENUE-CUTTER SERVICE— | | |
| rank of officers of, co-operating with the Navy | 1492 | 299 |
| provisions of law relating to the | 2749–2755 | 299 |
| co-operating with Navy, to be under direction of Secretary of the Navy | 2757 | 300 |
| expenses to be defrayed by Navy Department | 2757 | 300 |
| officers of, to go on board vessels arriving in United States | 2760 | 300 |
| shall be deemed officers of the customs for that purpose | 2760 | 300 |
| filling of vacancies in grade of third lieutenant. July 31, 1876 | | 300 |
| detail of officers of, for Life-Saving Service (note) | | 300 |
| REVISED STATUTES AND STATUTES AT LARGE— | | |
| definition of certain words used in | 1–6 | 199 |
| form of enacting clause in acts and resolutions | 7–10 | 199 |

11181——25

|                                                                                  | Sec. | Page. |
|---|---|---|
| REVISED STATUTES AND STATUTES AT LARGE—Continued. | | |
| style and title of appropriation acts | 11 | 200 |
| repeal not to revive former acts | 12 | 200 |
| not to affect liabilities, penalties, &c | 13 | 200 |
| to be preserved by officers and delivered to successors | 1777 | 200 |
| treason and other capital offenses, limitation to indictment | 1043 | 200 |
| except in the case of murder | 1043 | 200 |
| or of persons fleeing from justice | 1045 | 200 |
| offenses not capital, limit to prosecution | 1044 | 200 |
| except as to persons fleeing from justice | 1045 | 200 |
| crimes under revenue laws, limitation to prosecution | 1046 | 200 |
| limit as to maintenance of suits under the laws | 1047 | 200 |
| time beyond reach of legal process not to be taken | 1048 | 201 |
| effect of Revised Statutes on acts passed prior to December 1, 1873 | 5596 | 201 |
| not to affect acts done, rights accrued, &c | 5597 | 201 |
| nor right to office, or change the tenure thereof | 5597 | 201 |
| prosecutions and punishments not affected by repeals in Revised Statutes | 5598 | 201 |
| acts of limitation not affected by repeals in Revised Statutes | 5599 | 201 |
| arrangement of Revised Statutes no presumption of legislative construction | 5600 | 201 |
| Revised Statutes [1st edition] not to affect acts passed subsequent to December 1, 1873 | 5601 | 201 |
| acts and resolutions to be preserved by Secretary of State | 204 | 202 |
| Revised Statutes, publication and distribution of. June 20, 1874 | | 202 |
| to be stereotyped and substantially bound | | 202 |
| editing, printing, and sale of the United States Statutes | | 202–3 |
| opinions and decisions on force, &c., of statutes (notes) | | 203 |
| RICE— | | |
| allowance of, in Navy ration | 1580 | 83 |
| ROBBERY— | | |
| of personal property belonging to the United States | 5456 | 195 |
| on the high seas, in bays, on vessels, &c | 5323, 5324, 5370, 5371, 5373, 5383, 5384 | 277–9 |
| accessories after the fact, how punished | 5533 | 279 |
| ROPE-WALK— | | |
| superintendent of, to be appointed from civil life | 1543 | 58 |
| RULES OF THE SEA— | | |
| to prevent collisions | 4233 | 216 |

## S.

| | | |
|---|---|---|
| SAILMAKERS. (See WARRANT OFFICERS.) | | |
| SAILING DIRECTIONS— | | |
| publication of, for the Navy and commerce | 431 | 44 |
| SAILS AND RIGGING— | | |
| of vessels, conditions on which repaired | 1530 | 95 |
| SALARIES (see also EXTRA PAY AND CIVIL SERVICE)— | | |
| lapsed, to be covered into the Treasury. August 5, 1882 | | 140 |
| SALES— | | |
| of military or naval supplies, unlawfully, by persons in the service | 5438 | 195 |
| of public vessels by order of the President | 1540 | 95 |
| by the Secretary of the Navy | 1541 | 95 |
| of vessels stricken from the Register. March 3, 1883 | | 96 |

INDEX. 387

| | Sec. | Page. |
|---|---|---|
| **SALES**—Continued. | | |
| of materials that cannot be advantageously used | 1541 | 95 |
| of stores, &c., of surveying expeditions | 3692 | 44 |
| proceeds from, to be paid into the Treasury | 3617 | 198 |
| exceptions authorized | 3618 | 198 |
| removal from office for violating these provisions | 3619 | 198 |
| report of proceeds, to be included in Book of Estimates | 3672 | 198 |
| of stores unfit for further use. August 5, 1882 | | 197 |
| of condemned ordnance, disposition of proceeds. March 3, 1875 | | 198 |
| **SALT PORK**— | | |
| allowance of, in Navy ration | 1580 | 83 |
| **SALVAGE**— | | |
| distribution of, in same manner as prize | 4642, 4652 | 290–1 |
| defined, and decisions and opinions concerning (notes) | | 291 |
| **SANITARY**— | | |
| condition of crew to be inquired into | 20 | 13 |
| **SCANDALOUS CONDUCT**— | | |
| punishment for, in the Navy | 8 | 9 |
| **SCIENTIFIC SCHOOLS**— | | |
| detail of engineers as professors of | | 39 |
| **SCRUBBERS**— | | |
| number and pay of, in Navy Department building | | 184 |
| **SEAL**— | | |
| impressed on paper valid in law | 6 | 199 |
| on copies of records | 882–3 | 189–90 |
| **SEA LETTERS**— | | |
| vessels owned by United States citizens only, entitled to | 4190 | 249 |
| issuing or using false, punishment for | 4191 | 249 |
| **SEAMEN** (merchant). (*See* MERCHANT SERVICE). | | |
| **SEAMEN** (navy)— | | |
| promotion for extraordinary heroism, &c | 1407 | 90 |
| with gratuity and medal of honor | 1407 | 90 |
| enlisted for not less than two years, may be rated as mates | 1408 | 90 |
| not discharged from enlistment thereby | 1409 | 90 |
| number authorized to be enlisted | 1417 | 90 |
| transfer from Army to serve as | 1421 | 91 |
| not to release from indebtedness or penalty | 1421 | 91 |
| to be sent home on expiration of enlistment | 1422 | 91 |
| to Atlantic or Pacific coast, according to enlistment | 1422 | 91 |
| if longer detention not essential | 1422 | 91 |
| subject to the laws and regulations during detention | 1423 | 91 |
| discharge of, on expiration of term in foreign ports if enlisted abroad | 1422 | 91 |
| detention if necessary beyond term | 1422 | 91 |
| to be subject to regulations and laws | 1423 | 91 |
| detention of, not to exceed thirty days after vessel arrives in United States | 1422 | 92 |
| one-fourth additional pay for detention beyond term | 1422, 1572 | 92–3 |
| voluntary re-enlisting when detained, one-fourth more pay | 1422, 1572 | 92–3 |
| shipping articles to contain substance of certain sections | 1422–1425 | 92 |
| to be granted honorable discharges according to form | 1426–7 | 92 |
| names of entitled, to be sent to the Secretary of the Navy | 1429 | 92 |
| to be discouraged from selling prize-money, wages, &c | 1430–4643 | 92–3 |
| commanding officers to attest powers of attorney only, &c | 1430–4643 | 92 |

|  | Sec. | Page. |
|---|---|---|
| SEAMEN (navy)—Continued. | | |
| when assignment is to commence | 1576 | 93 |
| faithful and obedient, discrimination in behalf of, as to liberty | 1431 | 92 |
| pay of, to be fixed by the President | 1569 | 92 |
| whole, not to exceed appropriation for the year | 1569 | 92 |
| performing duty of firemen and coal-heavers, additional pay to | 1570 | 93 |
| of wrecked vessels, who did their duty, pay to continue | 1574 | 93 |
| of captured vessels, who did their duty, pay to continue | 1574 | 93 |
| dying in service, or in destitute condition, burial in national cemeteries | 4878 | 93 |
| machinists, discharge of. June 16, 1880 | | 93 |
| SEA SERVICE— | | |
| what service shall be regarded as | 1571 | 20 |
| definition and benefits of (note) | | 20 |
| SECRETARY— | | |
| of Naval Academy, pay of | 1556 | 67 |
| to Admiral and Vice-Admiral on shore, rank and pay of | 1367-1556 | 46-67 |
| when on sea duty not to be appointed from civil life. May 4, 1878 | | 46 |
| to rear-admirals, to be an officer not below the grade of lieutenant. May 4, 1878 | | 46 |
| SEDITIOUS— | | |
| utterance of words, punishment prescribed | 8 | 10 |
| conspiracy to overthrow the Government | 5336 | 309 |
| correspondence with Indians | 2111, 2112 | 307 |
| SELLING (see also SALES)— | | |
| wrongfully, public stores and property | 14 | 11 |
| SENTENCES— | | |
| of summary courts-martial, execution of | 32 | 15 |
| of general courts-martial, determination and execution of | 50, 53 | 17 |
| effect of disapproval (note) | | 18 |
| power of review after approval (note) | | 18 |
| SERVICE— | | |
| credit for volunteer or regular, Army and Navy. March 3, 1883 | | 21 |
| no additional pay therefor | | 21 |
| SHIPPING ARTICLES— | | |
| of the Navy, to contain substance of sections 1422-1424 | 1425 | 93 |
| for the merchant service | 4511-12-13 | 241 |
| SHIPWRECKED (see also WRECKED VESSELS and VESSELS)— | | |
| continuation of pay to crews of vessels | 1574 | 69 |
| SHORE— | | |
| offenses committed on, by persons in the Navy | 23 | 14 |
| SHORE DUTY— | | |
| necessity and period of employment on, to be stated in order. March 3, 1883 | | 22 |
| SICK— | | |
| care and attendance on members of crew | 20 | 13 |
| SILVER— | | |
| reception of, as freight on naval vessels | 8 | 10 |
| transportation of, by merchant vessels | 4204 | 249 |
| SITES— | | |
| for public buildings, examination of title of land purchased | 355 | 192 |
| contract for, not to exceed appropriation | | 196 |

# INDEX. 389

| | Sec. | Page. |
|---|---|---|
| SLAVE TRADE— | | |
| provisions of law in relation to | 5378–5569 | 302–6 |
| SLEEPING ON WATCH— | | |
| punishment for | 4 | 8 |
| SMALL-STORES FUND— | | |
| value of issues of stores to be credited to. February 14, 1879 | | 32 |
| resources to be applied to purchase of small stores. February 14, 1879 | | 32 |
| SOLITARY CONFINEMENT— | | |
| on bread and water, by order of commanding officer | 24 | 14 |
| in irons, single or double | 24 | 14 |
| by sentence of summary court, in irons, &c | 30 | 15 |
| SOVEREIGN— | | |
| English, value of, in payments by or to the Treasury | 3565 | 177 |
| SPANISH— | | |
| professor of, at the Naval Academy | 1528 | 53 |
| assistant professor | | 54 |
| SPIES— | | |
| punishment of | 5 | 9 |
| SPIRITS— | | |
| distilled, admission of, on vessels for medical purposes only | 13 | 11 |
| STAFF OFFICERS (*see also* under each head)— | | |
| senior to executive, right of communication | 1470 | 47 |
| relative rank of, gives no additional right to quarters | 1487 | 81 |
| nor right to exercise command | 1487 | 81 |
| precedence of, in own corps and with the line | 1486 | 81 |
| on boards, &c., according to rank | 1489 | 81 |
| STAFF— | | |
| of Marine Corps, separated from the line | 1598 | 108 |
| STAMPS, DEPARTMENTAL. (*See* POSTAGE.) | | |
| STANDARDS. (*See* FLAGS.) | | |
| STATE, WAR, AND NAVY BUILDING. (*See* NAVY DEPARTMENT BUILDING.) | | |
| STATIONERY— | | |
| to be contracted for for one year only | 3735 | 28 |
| STATION OR DUTY— | | |
| absence from, without leave | 8 | 10 |
| before being regularly relieved | 4 | 8 |
| deserting in time of battle, punishment for | 4 | 9 |
| STATUTES. (*See* REVISED STATUTES.) | | |
| STEALING (*see also* PUBLIC PROPERTY)— | | |
| public property, money, &c | 14 | 11 |
| STEAM ENGINEERING (Bureau)— | | |
| establishment of, in the Navy Department | 419 | 181 |
| chief to be appointed from the chief engineers | 424 | 181 |
| and to be a skillful engineer | 424 | 181 |
| with relative rank of commodore | 1471 | 182 |
| and title of engineer-in-chief | 1471 | 182 |
| exempt from sea service after a full term, &c | 1436 | 182 |
| with rank of commodore when retired | 1472 | 182 |
| pay, the highest of his grade | 1565 | 182 |
| civil employés authorized for Bureau | | 183 |
| STEAM ENGINES— | | |
| estimates for, in yards, to be given in detail | 3666 | 131 |

|  | Sec. | Page. |
|---|---|---|
| STEAM ENGINES—Continued. | | |
| expenditures to be accounted for | 3666 | 131 |
| conditions of use and purchase of patented articles for | 1537 | 266 |
| STEEL CRUISERS— | | |
| construction of, authorized | | 98–99 |
| STEERAGE OFFICERS— | | |
| ensigns to be, unless assigned to duty as watch or division officers | 1490 | 47 |
| STORES (*see also* CONTRACTS and PUBLIC PROPERTY)— | | |
| not to be disposed of by persons in the Navy on private account | 11 | 11 |
| of exploring and surveying expeditions, sale of | 3692 | 44 |
| STRANDED (*see also* WRECKED)— | | |
| vessels on foreign coasts, duty of consuls as to | 4238 | 250 |
| foreign, purchased by citizens of the United States, entitled to register | 4136 | 248 |
| STRANDING— | | |
| vessel willfully, punishment for | 4 | 8 |
| of vessel, through negligence | 8 | 10 |
| STRIKING FLAG— | | |
| without authority, punishment for | 4 | 8 |
| STRIKING SUPERIOR OFFICER— | | |
| how punishable | 4 | 8 |
| STRIKING OR ASSAULTING— | | |
| superior officer | 4 | 8 |
| persons in the Navy, punishment for | 8 | 10 |
| STUDIES— | | |
| naval cadets deficient in | 1519 | 52 |
| at Academy, not to be pursued on Sunday | 1526 | 53 |
| special course of, for cadets. August 5, 1882 | | 53 |
| SUBSISTENCE— | | |
| may be procured without adequate appropriation | 3732 | 28 |
| to persons honorably discharged from Marine Corps until reaching home | 1289, 1290 | 119 |
| SUBSISTENCE STORES— | | |
| misappropriating, wrongfully selling, &c | 14 | 11 |
| purchasing or receiving from those not authorized to sell | 14 | 11 |
| SUFFRAGE— | | |
| residence required to exercise, in Territories | 2002 | 20 |
| officers of the Navy not to interfere in right of | 2003 | 20 |
| punishment for intimidating persons from exercising | 5529 | 21 |
| or for prescribing qualifications of | 5530 | 21 |
| disqualification for office for interfering with the right of | 5532 | 21 |
| SUGAR— | | |
| allowance of, in Navy ration | 1580–1 | 83 |
| SUITS. (*See* DISTRESS WARRANT and DISBURSING OFFICERS.) | | |
| SUNDAY— | | |
| studies at the Academy not to be pursued on | 1526 | 53 |
| SUPERINTENDENT— | | |
| of the Naval Academy. (*See* Naval Academy.) | | |
| of the Naval Observatory to receive shore-pay of his grade | 434 | 56 |
| of the Nautical Almanac, who may be assigned as | 436 | 50 |
| of the rope-walks at navy-yards | 1543 | 58 |
| of the mechanical departments of navy-yards | 1543 | 58 |
| of the Navy Department building, appointment of | | 184 |
| number and pay of employés in office of | | 184 |

| | Sec. | Page. |
|---|---|---|
| SUPPLIES (see also CONTRACTS)— | | |
| not to be disposed of on private account by persons in the Navy | 11 | 11 |
| President to make regulations for procuring, &c | 1549 | 24 |
| no payments in advance for | 3648 | 24 |
| to be procured after advertising | 3709–3718–3721 | 24–5 |
| except when public exigencies require immediate delivery | 3709 | 24 |
| purchase of, for Navy, to be made under direction of the Secretary | 3714 | 25 |
| agents and contractors for, to render accounts for settlement | 3714 | 25 |
| to be furnished by contract with lowest bidder | 3718 | 25 |
| articles excepted from this requirement | 3718 | 25 |
| surety not to exceed twice the contract price | 3718 | 25 |
| proposals for, to be opened in presence of bidders | 3710, 3718, 3723 | 25–6 |
| and to be preserved and reported to Congress | 3720 | 26 |
| report to contain schedule by classes, &c | 3720 | 26 |
| guarantee to enter into contract, with security, to accompany proposal | 3719 | 26 |
| bids not to be considered without | 3719 | 26 |
| bidder failing to bond, contract to be made with some other party | 3719 | 26 |
| difference to be charged up and recovered | 3719 | 26 |
| contractors failing, damages to be sued for | 3720 | 26 |
| defaulting contractors and sureties not eligible as bidders | 3722 | ·26 |
| copartners of firms not to be received as sureties for firm or each other | 3722 | 26 |
| contractors, same Bureau, not to be received as sureties for each other | 3722 | 26 |
| fictitious bids not to be entertained | 3722 | 26 |
| more than one bid not to be received from same party | 3722 | 26 |
| in his own or name of others | 3722 | 26 |
| manufacturers or regular dealers only to receive contracts | 3722 | 26 |
| in foreign countries, how to be contracted for | 3723 | 26 |
| to be awarded to lowest bidder | 3723 | 27 |
| paymasters to furnish official certificates of purchases | 3723 | 27 |
| excessive prices, in proposals for classes, bid may be rejected | 3724 | 27 |
| hemp, and preparations of, to be American | 3725 | 27 |
| preserved meats, pickles, butter, desiccated vegetables, how procured | 3726 | 27 |
| flour, to be purchased as may be most advantageous | 3727 | 27 |
| and bread baked therefrom | 3727 | 27 |
| home manufacture, and growth, preference to | 3728 | 27 |
| fuel for the Navy, to be procured in the manner most advantageous | 3728 | 27 |
| for use in District of Columbia | 3711–32 | 32 |
| bunting, American, may be contracted for in open market | 3729 | 27 |
| to be marked with name of contractors | 3731 | 28 |
| otherwise not to be received | 3731 | 28 |
| stationery or other supplies to be contracted for for one year | 3735 | 28 |
| contracts for, not to be made without law and appropriation | 3732 | 28 |
| certain articles excepted | 3732 | 28 |
| sales of old, proceeds to be deposited in the Treasury | 3618 | 198 |
| SURETIES— | | |
| required of contractors in twice the amount | 3718, 3719 | 25, 26 |
| to be sued, in case of default | 3719 | 26 |
| defaulting, not to be received on other contracts | 3722 | 26 |
| to bonds of pay officers | 1383 | 62 |

|  | Sec. | Page. |
|---|---|---|
| SURGEONS— | | |
| chief of Bureau of Medicine and Surgery to be appointed from | 426 | 181 |
| fifty allowed on the active list | 1368 | 48 |
| qualifications for appointment | 1369, 1370 | 48 |
| detail of, as "surgeon of fleet" | 1373 | 48 |
| and duties as such | 1374 | 48 |
| detail of, as assistant to Bureau | 1375 | 49 |
| relative rank of | 1474 | 49 |
| pay of, on the active list | 1556 | 49 |
| on the retired list | 1588 | 70 |
| rank of, retired from age or length of service | 1481 | 49 |
| SURGEONS (Passed Assistant)— | | |
| number allowed on active list | 1368 | 48 |
| detail of, as assistants to Bureau | 1375 | 49 |
| relative rank of | 1474 | 49 |
| pay of, on the active list | 1556 | 49 |
| on the retired list | 1588 | 70 |
| SURGEONS (Assistant)— | | |
| not in line of promotion, pay of | | 312 |
| age, qualification, and manner of appointment | 1370 | 48 |
| absent, when entitled to examination | 1372 | 48 |
| may be detailed as assistant to Bureau | 1375 | 49 |
| temporary acting, in time of war | 1411 | 49 |
| relative rank of | 1481 | 49 |
| pay of, on the active list | 1556 | 50 |
| on the retired list | 1588 | 70 |
| SURGICAL APPLIANCES— | | |
| appropriation for, for disabled persons | | 43 |
| SURPLUS FUND— | | |
| balances of appropriations not needed to be carried to | 3690 | 134 |
| not drawn against for two years to be carried to | 3691 | 134 |
| if not required in settling accounts | 3691 | 134 |
| or for existing contracts | 3691 | 134 |
| not to apply to permanent specific appropriation, &c. June 20, 1874 | | 135 |
| nor to pay of the Navy or Marine Corps | | 135 |
| SURVEYING EXPEDITIONS— | | |
| sale of stores and supplies, money to revert to appropriation | 3692 | 44 |
| sale of articles used in, use of proceeds | 3618 | 198 |
| SUMMARY COURTS-MARTIAL. (*See* COURTS-MARTIALS, SUMMARY.) | | |
| SUSPENSION— | | |
| from duty, by order of commanding officer | 24 | 14 |
| sentence of, may include pay and emoluments | 48 | 17 |
| opinions and decisions concerning (notes) | | 18 |
| of officers failing professionally on examination | 1505 | 76 |
| of civil officers (*see* tenure-of-office) | | 147 |
| SWORD— | | |
| officer arrested for trial to deliver up | 44 | 17 |
| on pain of dismissal | 44 | 17 |

**T.**

| TATTOOING— | | |
|---|---|---|
| punishment by, not to be inflicted | 49 | 17 |

## INDEX. 393

| | Sec. | Page. |
|---|---|---|
| **TEA—** | | |
| allowance of, in Navy ration | 1580 | 83 |
| imported, not subject to duty | 2503 | 236 |
| **TELEGRAPHS—** | | |
| Government to have priority in transmitting despatches | 5266 | 295 |
| at rates established by Postmaster-General | 5266 | 295 |
| entitled to purchase lines | 5267 | 295 |
| companies to file written acceptances of obligations | 5268 | 295 |
| refusal to transmit dispatches, penalty prescribed | 5269 | 295 |
| injuring maliciously telegraph lines, punishment for | | 296 |
| Capitol and Departmental lines | | 296 |
| **TENURE-OF-OFFICE—** | | |
| money not to be paid as salary for unauthorized offices | 1760 | 147 |
| unless subsequently sanctioned by law | 1760 | 147 |
| money not to be paid to persons holding or exercising office contrary to sections 1767 to 1779 | 1762 | 147 |
| nor shall any claim be paid or allowed to such | 1762 | 148 |
| penalty for violation of these provisions | 1762 | 148 |
| to be during term for which appointed | 1767 | 148 |
| unless removed with advice and consent of Senate | 1767 | 148 |
| authority of the President to suspend civil officers | 1768 | 148 |
| until next session of the Senate | 1768 | 148 |
| except judges of courts of the United States | 1768 | 148 |
| and to designate another to perform duties | 1768 | 148 |
| who will take oath, give bond, and receive the pay of the office | 1768 | 148 |
| nomination in place of suspended officer to be made to Senate | 1768 | 148 |
| on refusal to confirm, another to be made | 1768 | 148 |
| nominations to fill all vacancies to be made to Senate within thirty days after commencement of session | 1768 | 148 |
| authority to fill vacancies happening during recess of Senate | 1769 | 149 |
| commissions to expire at end of ensuing session | 1769 | 149 |
| if not confirmed, office to remain in abeyance | 1769 | 149 |
| without salary, fees, or emoluments | 1769 | 149 |
| until filled by advice of Senate | 1769 | 149 |
| duties in mean time to be performed by other officer authorized by law | 1769 | 149 |
| duration of offices limited by law not to be extended, &c | 1770 | 149 |
| accepting or holding office contrary to tenure-of-office act a high misdemeanor | 1771 | 149 |
| punishable by fine and imprisonment | 1771 | 149 |
| same as to removal, appointment, and employment | 1772 | 149 |
| commissions to be delivered after adjournment of Senate | 1773 | 149 |
| President to notify Secretary of Treasury of appointments without advice of Senate | 1774 | 149 |
| Secretary of Treasury to notify accounting and disbursing officers | 1774 | 149 |
| list of persons nominated and rejected to be furnished officers of Treasury by Secretary of Senate | 1775 | 149 |
| also of nominations made and not confirmed | 1775 | 149 |
| certain persons ineligible to office | 1786 | 150 |
| except as members of Congress or State legislatures | 1786 | 150 |
| may be prosecuted to removal | 1786 | 150 |

|  |  | Sec. | Page. |
|---|---:|---:|---:|
| TENURE-OF-OFFICE—Continued. | | | |
| holding office to which ineligible, a misdemeanor | | 1787 | 150 |
| opinions and decisions as to power of the President and the Executive Departments | | | 150 |
| TERRITORIES— | | | |
| term of residence for officers and men to vote in | | 1860 | 20 |
| persons in Navy not to hold office in | | 1860 | 20 |
| punishment for depriving persons of rights in | | 5510 | 20 |
| punishment for officers of the Navy prescribing qualifications of voters in | | 5530 | 21 |
| interfering with officers of elections in | | 5531 | 21 |
| TESTIMONY— | | | |
| before summary courts, to be given orally | | 29 | 14 |
| punishment for refusing to give, before courts-martial | | 42 | 16 |
| THANKSGIVING DAY— | | | |
| public holiday in the District of Columbia | | | 145 |
| THANKS OF CONGRESS. (*See* VOTE OF THANKS.) | | | |
| THEFT— | | | |
| punishment for, in the Navy | | 8 | 9 |
| of money, property, &c., belonging to the United States. March 3, 1875 | | | 194 |
| TIMBER LANDS. (*See* RESERVED LANDS.) | | | |
| TIMBER INSPECTORS— | | | |
| of yards may be discontinued | | 1416 | 57 |
| TIMBER WHEELS— | | | |
| estimates for, to be in detail | | 3666 | 131 |
| TITLES. (*See* PUBLIC PROPERTY.) | | | |
| TOBACCO— | | | |
| advertising for proposals. March 3, 1881 | | | 31 |
| bids to be accompanied by samples | | | 31 |
| lowest, for Navy standard, to be accepted | | | 31 |
| TOMATOES (desiccated)— | | | |
| substitute for desiccated potatoes in Navy ration | | | 84 |
| TOOLS— | | | |
| estimates for purchase and repair, to be in detail | | 3666 | 131 |
| TORPEDOES— | | | |
| appropriation for purchase of | | | 32 |
| condition, as to its expenditure | | | 32 |
| TOWAGE— | | | |
| estimates for, to be in detail | | 3666 | 132 |
| TRADE AND TRAFFIC— | | | |
| officers carrying on, with public funds, guilty of a misdemeanor | | 1788 | 168 |
| punishable by fine, removal from, and incapacity for, office | | 1788 | 168 |
| in stores, &c., on vessels and at yards forbidden | | 8-11 | 10-11 |
| TRANSFER— | | | |
| of contracts forbidden | | 3737 | 28 |
| of accounts of enlisted men | | 20 | 13 |
| from furlough to retired pay list | | 1594 | 88 |
| of soldiers, to serve in the Navy or Marine Corps | | 1421 | 91 |
| not to release from indebtedness or penalty | | 1421 | 91 |
| of prize-money, wages, &c., by seamen | 1430, 1576, 4643 | 92, 93, | 315 |
| from volunteer to the regular Navy. March 3, 1883 | | 1412 | 101 |
| of claims void under certain circumstances | | 3477 | 153 |

INDEX. 395

| | Sec. | Page. |
|---|---|---|
| TRANSFERRED— | | |
| account of men, to accompany them | 20 | 13 |
| descriptive list of men, to accompany them | 20 | 13 |
| TRANSPORTS— | | |
| examination of, for War Department | 1437 | 94 |
| TRANSPORTATION— | | |
| may be procured without adequate appropriation | 3732 | 28 |
| to be furnished officers, seamen, and marines, co-operating with Army | 1135 | 107 |
| also for baggage, provisions, and cannon | 1135 | 107 |
| to officers of Marine Corps to homes after honorable discharge | 1289 | 119 |
| marines to homes after honorable discharge | 1290 | 119 |
| advertisement for, of articles, to appear not less than five days | 3718 | 130 |
| estimates for, to be given in detail | 3666 | 131 |
| expenditures for, under each Bureau to be accounted for | 3666 | 131 |
| TRAVEL— | | |
| eight cents a mile allowed officers for, in the United States. June 20, 1876 | | 72 |
| and only when actually performed at own expense | 1566 | 72 |
| and under order or approval of Secretary Navy. January 18, 1875 | | 73 |
| abroad, actual expenses only, in lieu of mileage. August 3, 1882 | | 73 |
| by the most direct route | | 73 |
| necessity for, to be certified by officer giving order | | 73 |
| allowance for transportation of baggage | 1566 | 72 |
| allowance for Government employés sent away as witnesses | 850 | 73 |
| items of expense to be sworn to | 850 | 73 |
| no other compensation authorized | 850 | 73 |
| for cadets admitted to Academy | | 73 |
| eight cents a mile to marine officers | 1273 | 117 |
| by shortest usually traveled route | 1273 | 117 |
| necessity for, to be stated in the order, March 3, 1883 | | 117 |
| allowed to prisoners after parole | 1288 | 119 |
| allowance to marine officers honorably discharged | 1289 | 119 |
| marines honorably discharged | 1290 | 119 |
| how computed | 1290 | 119 |
| expenses for, estimates to be in detail | 3666 | 131 |
| TREASON— | | |
| indictment to be found within three years | 1043 | 200 |
| time when absent in rebellion not embraced | 1048 | 201 |
| provisions of law in relation to | 1033–1034 | 307 |
| TRUSSES— | | |
| to whom furnished | 1176 | 42 |
| examination of applicants for | 1177 | 42 |
| to be purchased by Surgeon-General of the Army | 1178 | 42 |
| TRUST— | | |
| betrayal of, in time of war, punishment for | 4 | 8 |
| corrupting any person to betray | 5 | 9 |

### V.

| | Sec. | Page. |
|---|---|---|
| VACANCIES— | | |
| in the head of Department, first or sole assistant to perform duties | 177 | 146 |

|  | Sec. | Page. |
|---|---|---|
| VACANCIES—Continued. | | |
| unless the President otherwise directs | 177 | 146 |
| or the head of any other Department | 179 | 147 |
| or any other commissioned officer in either Department | 179 | 147 |
| if the President so directs | 179 | 147 |
| temporary appointment not to exceed ten days, in case of death or resignation | 180 | 147 |
| temporary appointments under section 177 and 178 to be made as therein provided, except during recess of the Senate | 181 | 147 |
| officer performing duties of another, not entitled to any other compensation than that of his proper office | 182 | 147 |
| in the head of a Bureau, assistant or deputy to perform duties | 178 | 146 |
| if there be none, then the chief clerk | 178 | 146 |
| unless the President otherwise directs, as in section 179 | 178 | 146 |
| VEGETABLES— | | |
| allowance of, in Navy ration | 1580–81 | 83 |
| desiccated, how procured | 3726 | 84 |
| VESSELS (NAVY)— | | |
| willfully stranding or injuring, punishment for | 4 | 8 |
| standing of, through negligence | 9 | 10 |
| condemned, cannot be exchanged for others (note) | | 95 |
| the term "vessel," used in the statutes, indicates every description of water-craft | 3 | 199 |
| definition of, as used in Title "Prize" | 4614 | 285 |
| name of enlisted men on, to be entered on ship's books | 20 | 12 |
| date, place, and term of enlistment to be given | 20 | 12 |
| list of officers and passengers on, to be sent to Secretary Navy | 20 | 12 |
| muster roll of crew to be forwarded to Department | 20 | 13 |
| lost, authority of officers over crew of | 21 | 13 |
| officers or men acting contrary to discipline of the Navy | 21 | 13 |
| shipwrecked, continuation of pay to crew | 1574 | 69 |
| captured, continuation of pay to officers and crew | 1575 | 69 |
| officers of, to be citizens of United States | 1428 | 94 |
| division into four classes for commands | 1529 | 94 |
| classification by guns | 1530 | 94 |
| how to be named | 1531 | 94 |
| not more than one to bear same name | 1532 | 94 |
| names of purchased, may be changed | 1533 | 94 |
| to be kept in actual service, as President may direct | 1534 | 94 |
| residue to be laid up in ordinary | 1534 | 94 |
| to be officered and manned as President may direct | 1535 | 94 |
| to cruise in aid of distressed navigators | 1536 | 95 |
| and be fully prepared to render assistance | 1536 | 95 |
| when patented articles may be used on steam vessels | 1537 | 95 |
| repairs to hull and spars, not over $3,000 to be expended | 1538 | 95 |
| until necessity and probable cost is determined by Board | 1538 | 95 |
| of whom Board shall consist | 1538 | 95 |
| repairs to sails and rigging, not over $1,000 to be expended | 1539 | 95 |
| until necessity and probable cost is determined by Board | 1539 | 95 |
| of whom Board shall consist | 1539 | 95 |
| repairs to wooden ships not to exceed 20 per cent. of cost of new ones. March 3, 1883 | | 96 |
| engines and machinery not to exceed 20 per cent. of cost of new ones. March 3, 1883 | | 96 |

INDEX. 397

| | Sec. | Page. |
|---|---|---|
| VESSELS (Navy)—Continued. | | |
| out of repair, President may direct sale of | 1540 | 95 |
| Secretary of the Navy may order sale of | 1541 | 95 |
| report to be made to Congress | 1541 | 95 |
| Board for the examination of all. August 5, 1882 | | 95 |
| to report those unfit for further service | | 95 |
| whose names will be stricken from the Register. March 3, 1883 | | 96 |
| examination, as often as once in three years | | 95 |
| stricken from the Register, to be advertised and sold | | 96 |
| not for less than appraised value | | 96 |
| in course of construction, removal of | | 96 |
| establishment of coal depots for | Supplement and 1552 | 97–313 |
| employment against piratical aggressions | 4293 | 97 |
| on surveying coast | 4686 | 97 |
| definition of "public vessels" (note) | | 97 |
| to be furnished for marine schools. June 20, 1874 | | 97 |
| hulks, to be placed at disposal of quarantine authorities. June 14, 1879 | | 97 |
| "steam cruisers," appropriations for, &c | | 98–9 |
| double-turreted monitors, launching of. August 5, 1882 | | 100 |
| completion of engines and boilers. March 3, 1883 | | 100 |
| sustaining accident, report to be made. June 20, 1874 | | 100 |
| marine officers not to exercise command over | 1617 | 110 |
| lost, credits to paymasters of | 284 | 128 |
| date of loss, to be fixed by accounting officers | 286 | 128 |
| compensation to crew for personal effects | 287 | 128 |
| payment to widow in case of death | 289 | 128 |
| compensation to officers for personal effects | 290 | 129 |
| schedule and certificate required | 290 | 129 |
| continuation of pay to crews of | 1574–5 | 93 |
| in distress, estimates for, to be in detail | 3666 | 132 |
| sunk or destroyed, appropriation for clothing, &c | 3689 | 133 |
| not employed in transportation of merchandise, not subject to entry | 2791 | 237 |
| wrecked within waters of the United States, disposition of | | 313 |
| VESSELS (merchant)— | | |
| wrecked or condemned, extra wages not to be paid to seamen | 4583 | 246 |
| of the United States, what are deemed | 4131 | 247 |
| not entitled to privileges unless wholly owned by citizens | 4131 | 247 |
| and commanded by them | 4131 | 247 |
| officers of, to be citizens of the United States | 4131 | 247 |
| entitled to register, those built within the United States | 4132 | 248 |
| and belonging to citizens thereof | 4132 | 248 |
| also vessels condemned as prize and forfeited under law, if owned by citizens | 4132 | 248 |
| not entitled to register by citizens residing in a foreign country | 4133 | 248 |
| unless a consul of the United States | 4133 | 248 |
| or concerned in a house, composed of citizens of the United States carrying on trade themselves | 4133 | 248 |
| nor if owned by naturalized citizens residing abroad a fixed time | 4134 | 248 |
| unless by a consul or public agent of the United States | 4134 | 248 |

| | Sec. | Page. |
|---|---|---|
| VESSELS (merchant)—Continued. | | |
| may be registered anew, if sold in good faith to citizen of the United States | 4134 | 248 |
| proof of citizenship to be exhibited | 4134 | 248 |
| American vessels taking foreign flag during rebellion not entitled to register | 4135 | 248 |
| wrecked and purchased by citizens of the United States may be registered | 4136 | 248 |
| provided repairs equal three-fourths of cost | 4136 | 248 |
| registered in the United States, transferred to foreign subjects | 4172 | 248 |
| forfeited under certain conditions | 4172 | 248 |
| to have number carved or marked on main beam | 4177 | 249 |
| not so marked, no longer recognized as an American vessel | 4177 | 249 |
| names and port of registry to be painted on stern | 4178 | 249 |
| if not, liable to penalty | 4178 | 249 |
| names of, not to be changed for purposes of fraud | 4179 | 249 |
| on pain of forfeiture of vessel | 4179 | 249 |
| obtaining fraudulent register, liable to forfeiture | 4189 | 249 |
| of citizens of the United States, only, entitled to sea-letters, &c. | 4190 | 249 |
| punishment for issuing or using false sea-letters | 4191 | 249 |
| to receive on board gold, bullion, &c., of the United States for transportation | 4204 | 249 |
| to receive reasonable compensation therefor | 4204 | 249 |
| tariffs or fees consuls are entitled to from | 4207 | 250 |
| stranded on foreign coasts, duties of consuls | 4238 | 250 |
| passports to be furnished by collectors | 4306 | 250 |
| requirements to obtain same | 4306 | 250 |
| penalty for departing without | 4307 | 250 |
| for unregistered vessels | 4308 | 250 |
| to deposit papers with consular officer | 4309 | 250 |
| penalty for failure to do so | 4310 | 250 |
| consul to obtain clearance for vessel | 4309 | 250 |
| list of crew to be delivered to collector of customs before clearance | 4573 | 251 |
| to be examined by him and certified | 4574 | 251 |
| bound on foreign voyage, rules as to crew list, &c | 4575 | 251 |
| wrecked, penalty for plundering | 5358 | 252 |
| showing false lights that vessels may be | 5358 | 252 |
| conspiracy to cast away | 5364 | 252 |
| willfully casting away | 5365–5367 | 252 |
| settlement of accounts of crew of lost | 287 | 128 |
| forging or altering ship's papers, penalty for | 5423 | 252 |
| yachts, legal requirements relative to | 4214–4218 | 253 |
| lost by misconduct, negligence, &c., officers, guilty of manslaughter | 5344 | 255 |
| mutiny on board, how punished | 5359 | 256 |
| revolt, and usurping command, punishment for | 5360 | 256 |
| VICE-ADMIRAL (see also ADMIRAL, VICE)— | | |
| pay of | 1556 | 65 |
| grade to cease on becoming vacant | 1362 | 45 |
| VIGNETTES— | | |
| impressions from, may be furnished by Bureau of Engraving | | 188 |
| VISITORS— | | |
| Board of, at Academy, appointment | | 54 |

|  | Sec. | Page. |
|---|---|---|
| VOLUNTEERS— | | |
| national homes for disabled | 4832 | 41 |
| insane, admission to Government Asylum | | 41 |
| in the rebellion, acts relative to bounty to | | 214–15 |
| officers and men of Marine Corps to receive credit for | 1600 | 108 |
| longevity pay, computation of, &c | | 115–16 |
| appointment of acting assistant surgeons in time of war | 1411 | 101 |
| transfer from, to regular Navy, credit for service | 1412 | 101 |
| credit to marine officers for | 1600 | 101 |
| discharge and transfer of officers of | | 101 |
| credit in regular Navy for, March 3, 1883 | | 101 |
| no additional pay for, March 3, 1883 | | 101 |
| admission to national homes of volunteer soldiers and sailors | | 41–42 |
| VOTERS— | | |
| punishment for officers of Navy intimidating | 5529 | 21 |
| and for prescribing qualifications of | 5530 | 21 |
| VOTE OF THANKS— | | |
| advancement of officers receiving | 1508 | 77 |
| such officers only affected | 1509 | 77 |
| retention on active list | 1509 | 77 |
| not to interfere with promotion of others | 1509 | 77 |
| vacancy from retirement or death not to be filled | 1510 | 77 |
| restoration of officers to active list on receiving | 1465 | 87 |
| advancement of marine officers on receiving | 1607 | 110 |
| VOTING— | | |
| term of residence required by persons in the Navy in Territories for | 1860 | 20 |
| VOUCHERS— | | |
| penalty for using false | 14 | 11 |

## W.

|  | Sec. | Page. |
|---|---|---|
| WAGES— | | |
| assignment of, by enlisted men | 1576 | 93 |
| to be attested by commander and paymaster | 1576 | 93 |
| sale of, to be discouraged | 1430 | 92 |
| attempting to obtain, by false papers | 5435, 5436 | 227 |
| of workmen at navy-yards, how fixed | | 58 |
| WARRANT OFFICERS— | | |
| retirement of, opinion Court of Claims | | 314 |
| as many as actually necessary may be appointed | 1405 | 102 |
| boatswains, gunners, carpenters, and sailmakers, denominated | 1406 | 102 |
| promotion of seamen to, for heroic conduct | 1407 | 102 |
| with gratuity and medal of honor | 1407 | 102 |
| not to discharge from enlistment | 1409 | 102 |
| assignment of gunners, as keepers of magazines | 1416 | 102 |
| in appointment of, preference to honorably discharged men | 1417 | 102 |
| may be ordered in charge of stores on foreign stations | 1438 | 102 |
| bond required in such cases | 1439 | 102 |
| assimilated rank may be given to, by the President | 1491 | 102 |
| pay of, on the active list | 1556 | 103 |
| on the retired list | 1588 | 70 |

|  | Sec. | Page. |
|---|---|---|
| WARRANTS— | | |
| drawn on Treasury by Secretary Navy to be countersigned by Second Comptroller | 273 | 126 |
| and registered by Fourth Auditor | 3675 | 127 |
| money to be drawn from Treasury by | 3673, 3675 | 127 |
| to state appropriations to which chargeable | 3675 | 127 |
| to be countersigned by Comptroller and Auditor | 3673 | 127 |
| WASTING— | | |
| ammunition and other public property | 8 | 10 |
| WATCHMEN (Navy)— | | |
| estimates for, to be in detail | 3666 | 131 |
| WATCHMEN (in the Departments)— | | |
| to receive $720 per annum | 167 | 139 |
| not to be employed beyond appropriations, August 15, 1876 | | 140 |
| number and pay regulated by appropriations, August 5, 1882 | | 140 |
| not to be paid from contingent appropriations, August 5, 1882 | | 140 |
| number and pay of, in Navy Department Building | | 184 |
| WATER— | | |
| in public buildings to be shut off | | 196 |
| WEIGHTS AND MEASURES— | | |
| employment of metric system legalized | 3569 | 178 |
| tables of measure and weight | 3570 | 179 |
| WET DOCK— | | |
| at Norfolk, land for | | 59 |
| WHARFAGE— | | |
| estimates for, to be in detail | 3666 | 131 |
| WHIPPING— | | |
| punishment of, not to be inflicted | 5327 | 254 |
| jurisdiction of State courts not impaired | 5328 | 254 |
| WITNESSES— | | |
| before courts-martial, oath of | 41 | 16 |
| punishment for refusing to testify, &c | 42 | 16 |
| persons on trial may be, at own requests | 43 | 16 |
| sent from place of business, traveling expenses allowed | 850 | 73 |
| subpœna of, in cases of claims against the United States | 184 | 151 |
| compensation allowed | 185 | 152 |
| punishment for refusing to testify | 186 | 152 |
| conspiring to intimidate before the courts | 5406 | 309 |
| WOMEN— | | |
| may be appointed to similar clerkships as men | 165 | 139 |
| with the same compensation | 165 | 139 |
| employed in subordinate clerical duties to receive $900 | 167 | 139 |
| as copyists and counters the same | 167 | 139 |
| and when temporarily employed as clerks | 167 | 139 |
| WOOD— | | |
| for use by Government in District of Columbia, how procured | 3711 | 32 |
| allowance of, in Marine Corps | | 124 |
| WORKINGMEN— | | |
| not to be required to contribute for political purposes | 1546 | 207 |
| not to be removed for political opinions | 1546 | 207 |
| WORKMEN— | | |
| eight hours a day's work for all, employed by Government | 3738 | 29 |
| WOUNDED— | | |
| amelioration of, international convention | | 262 |

INDEX. 401

|  | Sec. | Page. |

WRECKED (*see also* VESSELS)—
  vessels, disposition of, by Secretary of War and Treasury (Supplement) .................................................................... 313
  vessels of foreign country, purchased by citizens without register. 4136 248
      on foreign coasts, duty of consuls .......................... 4238 250
  vessels, penalty for plundering .................................. 5358 252
  showing false lights, that vessels may be........................ 5358 252
  definition of the word as used in section 4136 (note) ............ 291
WYOMING—
  prize-money to officers and crew of............................. 313

## Y.

YACHTS—
  for pleasure, may be licensed by the Secretary of the Treasury... 4214 253
    owner to give bond not to engage in trade .................. 4214 253
      nor violate the revenue laws............................ 4214 253
    not to transport merchandise or passengers for pay........... 4214 253
    name to be on hulls ...................................... 4214 253
    subject to the laws and liable to seizure.................. 4214 253
    charges for license and inspection......................... 4214 253
  signals to be prescribed by Secretary of the Navy................ 4215 253
  naval architects permitted to examine and copy models .......... 4215 253
  foreign, privileges allowed to................................... 4216 253
  commissions to, as a token of credit abroad...................... 4217 253
  returning from abroad to make entry at custom-house ............. 4218 253
YARDS AND DOCKS (Bureau)—
  established in the Navy Department .............................. 419 181
  selection of chief of............................................ 421, 422 181
    rank...................................................... 1472 182
    pay....................................................... 1565 182
  civil employés authorized in .................................... 183

11181——26

www.ingramcontent.com/pod-product-compliance
Lightning Source LLC
Chambersburg PA
CBHW030423300426
44112CB00009B/832